Transactions of the Royal Historical Society

SIXTH SERIES

X

CAMBRIDGE
UNIVERSITY PRESS

Published by the Press Syndicate of the University of Cambridge
The Edinburgh Building, Cambridge CB2 2RU, United Kingdom
40 West 20th Street, New York, NY 10011–4211, USA
10 Stamford Road, Oakleigh, Melbourne 3166, Australia
Ruiz de Alarcón 13, 28014 Madrid, Spain

First published 2000

A catalogue record for this book is available from the British Library

ISBN 0 521 79352 1 hardback

SUBSCRIPTIONS. The serial publications of the Royal Historical Society, *Royal Historical Society Transactions* (ISSN 0080–4401) and Camden Fifth Series (ISSN 0960–1163) volumes may be purchased together on annual subscription. The 2000 subscription price (which includes postage but not VAT) is £60 (US$99 in the USA, Canada and Mexico) and includes Camden Fifth Series, volumes 15 and 16 (published in July and December) and Transactions Sixth Series, volume 10 (published in December). Japanese prices are available from Kinokuniya Company Ltd, P.O. Box 55, Chitose, Tokyo 156, Japan. EU subscribers (outside the UK) who are not registered for VAT should add VAT at their country's rate. VAT registered subscribers should provide their VAT registration number.

Subscription orders, which must be accompanied by payment, may be sent to a bookseller, subscription agent or direct to the publisher: Cambridge Univeristy Press. The Edinburgh Building, Shaftesbury Road, Cambridge CB2 2RU, UK; or in the USA, Canada and Mexico: Cambridge University Press, Journals Fulfillment Department, 110 Midland Avenue, Port Chester, NY 10573–4930, USA. Prices include delivery by air.

SINGLE VOLUMES AND BACK VOLUMES. A list of Royal Historical Society volumes available from Cambridge University Press may be obtained from the Humanities Marketing Department at the address above.

Printed and bound in the United Kingdom by Butler & Tanner, Frome and London

CONTENTS

TRANSACTIONS OF THE
ROYAL HISTORICAL SOCIETY

PRESIDENTIAL ADDRESS

By P.J. Marshall

BRITAIN AND THE WORLD IN THE EIGHTEENTH CENTURY: III, BRITAIN AND INDIA

READ ON 26 NOVEMBER 1999

THESE addresses have been trying to explore the obvious paradox in eighteenth-century Britain's fortunes overseas: a North American empire, as I suggested last year, deeply rooted in the rich soil of a close-knit transatlantic community, was to come crashing down in the gale unleashed by the new imperial anxieties and ambitions of Britain's rulers. A British empire was, however, to be successfully planted in the unpromising terrain of alien Asian peoples. It is to the creation of this new Indian empire that I wish now to turn.

To contemporaries at the time and to nearly all historians since, the imperial ventures in west and east seemed to be fundamentally different. They might or might not be included in the fold of Britishness, but Americans were without question part of the same European and specifically British world. They had shared in the great developments, scientific rationality, economic productivity, constitutional liberty and, British people reluctantly and lately conceded, military capacity that were believed to have transformed Britain itself. Even those who insisted most strictly on the exercise of an overriding imperial authority recognised that such people could only be governed with their co-operation. Any explanation of the failure of empire must therefore explain why that co-operation had been withheld.

By contrast India seemed to eighteenth-century opinion to be part of a quite different world, largely untouched by the recent experiences of Europe. Indian Muslims were assumed to be sharing in the atrophy that was believed to have sapped all Islamic societies from the Ottoman empire eastwards, while Hindus were universally supposed to be committed by immovable religious prescription to ancient custom to a degree that made them immune to all outside influences. For the historian Robert Orme, 'Nothing seems to have been wanting to the happiness' of Hindus 'but that others should have looked on them with the same indifference with which they regard the rest of the world. . . . They have always been immensely rich, and always remained incapable of defending their wealth.'[1] Even for Edmund Burke, the most sympathetic public interpreter of India, there was a glaring contrast between 'the improved state of Europe, with the improved state of arts and the improved state of laws, and (what is more material) the improved state of military discipline' and 'the general fall of Asia, and the relaxation and dissolution of its governments, with the fall of its warlike spirit and the total disuse almost of all parts of military discipline'.[2] The military backwardness and lack of political capacity of Indian people were thought to leave them ripe for foreign conquest. The story of the rise of empire in India was thus focused on the imposition of rule on a docile people after the successful application of force at Plassey, Buxar and on many subsequent occasions.

Explanations for India's subordination to Britain, broadly in terms of the stagnation induced by its long isolation that left it incapable of resisting the power of European arms, were generally to hold the field throughout the colonial period. They are now, however, increasingly challenged. Stereotypes of an unchanging India living largely in isolation from the rest of the world until British conquests set off processes of modernisation are generally discredited. Interesting attempts are indeed being made to find common trends affecting early modern Eurasia that make it possible to suggest that Europe and Asia had connected rather than separate histories.[3]

The contrast between west and east, empire based on co-operation and empire based on force, now looks less stark than it did. There were of course fundamental differences between an Asian world directly touched by Europeans only at its peripheries and an Atlantic world shaped by a long process of European settlement. Even so, the creation of a British empire in India now seems to many historians less an

[1] 'Dissertation on the Establishments made by the Mahomedan Conquerors in Indostan' in *A History of the Military Transactions of the British Nation in Indostan* (2 vols., 1763–78), I, 7–8.

[2] *The Writings and Speeches of Edmund Burke*, vol. VI, *India: The Launching of the Hastings Impeachment 1786–88*, ed. P.J. Marshall (Oxford, 1991), 283.

[3] See the essays in *Modern Asian Studies*, 31 (1997), especially 463–546, Victor Lieberman, 'Transcending East–West Dichotomies: State and Culture Formation in Six Ostensibly Disparate Areas', and 735–62, Sanjay Subrahmanyam. 'Connected Histories: Notes Towards the Reconfiguration of Early Modern Eurasia'.

exercise of untrammelled power and more the exertion of power in ways which were profoundly influenced by important elements of Indian society. Both in America and in India the people shaped the imperial system that ruled over them.

Pre-colonial India was much less closely integrated into the British economy than were the West Indian and North American colonies. In the first half of the eighteenth century imports from all Asia to Britain were generally worth less than half the value of those from the Americas and exports from Britain to Asia were only worth about a quarter of those crossing the Atlantic.[4] While a great many individual ships from ports all over the British Isles passed to and from America with multitudes of emigrants as well as with goods, a relatively small number of large ships belonging to the East India Company made the passage round the Cape of Good Hope, and the British subjects resident in Asia could be counted only in hundreds. A convincing case can, however, be made that India was already entering into what has been called an 'international division of labour' linking west and east.[5] The East India Company's trade was one of the main conduits through which India received American silver in the quantities that enabled silver rupees to become the standard currency throughout the Mughal empire. In return India exported the cotton textiles that clothed western Europe and the European and slave populations of the Americas and that were a major item for the West African trade. By one calculation the production of textiles for export through the East India companies increased employment in Bengal, the most important area of production for Europe, by about a tenth.[6] By contrast, the implications of massive Indian textile imports for European employment were stark and produced popular disorder and protective legislation in Britain and France.[7]

India's role in international trade in the early modern period was built on what many historians describe as an indigenous commercial capitalism which had evolved on its own momentum, but had similarities

[4] See tables in Jacob M. Price, 'The Imperial Economy, 1700–1776', in *The Oxford History of the British Empire*, ed. P.J. Marshall, vol. II, *The Eighteenth Century* (Oxford University Press, 1998), 101.

[5] Frank Perlin's phrase, 'Proto-industrialisation and Pre-colonial South Asia', *Past and Present*, 98 (1983), 60.

[6] Om Prakash, *The New Cambridge History of India*, II, 5, *European Commercial Enterprise in pre-Colonial India* (Cambridge University Press, 1998), 317. For criticism of this estimate, see Sushil Chaudhury, 'European Trading Companies and the Bengal Textile Industry in the First Half of the Eighteenth Century: The Pitfalls of Applying Quantitative Methods', *Modern Asian Studies*, 27 (1993), 321–40.

[7] Michel Morineau, 'The Indian Challenge, Seventeenth and Eighteenth Centuries' in *Merchants, Companies and Trade: Europe and Asia in the Early Modern Era*, ed. Sushil Chaudhury and M. Morineau (Cambridge University Press, 1999), 243–75.

to that of pre-industrial Europe.[8] In most parts of India cultivators sold surplus crops for cash which they used to pay their taxes. There was a very large internal trade in agricultural produce, many commodities also being exported by sea. The textiles shipped to Europe were only a small part of a huge output for markets within India and for other parts of Asia. These trades depended to a large extent on credit extended by merchants who operated both at the level of local village markets and in great trading ports, where they owned ships that carried Indian goods throughout maritime Asia from the Persian Gulf to southern China. Banking businesses remitted money by bills of exchange across India.

There seems also to have been a degree of political as well as of economic convergence between the trajectories of early modern India and early modern Europe. Commercial expansion in India had made it possible for Europeans to become participants in its coastal economies during the seventeenth century; political changes in the eighteenth century were to enable Europeans to exert military and ultimately state power inland.

An overarching Mughal imperial system for most of India gave way in the eighteenth century to a series of what amounted to regional states, often based on a degree of distinct ethnic and cultural identity. To contemporary British observers and to subsequent historians these changes were a story of decline and fall. To quote Burke again, 'Viceroys grew into independence, partly by the dreadful calamities and concussions of that Empire. ... Then the Princes became independent, but their independence led to their ruin.'[9] This was the tone of nearly all nineteenth-and most twentieth-century historiography. The replacement of the Mughals by a fragmenting of authority is now, however, not necessarily seen as evidence of political failure or of a slide into disorder, but rather as a process of evolution towards what has even been called a 'more "modern"' order in India.[10] The successor states, it is argued, had existed in embryo within a Mughal system that had never exerted a tightly centralised control.[11] In a process of decentralisation new states emerged that were more capable than the Mughals had been of effectively tapping the wealth being generated by

[8] Perlin, 'Proto-industrialisation', 33; David Washbrook, 'South Asia, the World System and World Capitalism' in *South Asia and World Capitalism*, ed. Sugata Bose (Delhi, 1990), 60; K. N. Chaudhuri, *Trade and Civilisation in the Indian Ocean: An Economic History from the Rise of Islam to 1750* (Cambridge University Press, 1985), 208–14.

[9] *Writings and Speeches*, VI, 311.

[10] D.A. Washbrook, 'Progress and Problems: South Asian Economic and Social History *c.* 1720–1860', *Modern Asian Studies*, 22 (1988), 68.

[11] For a recent statement of this view, see Muzaffar Alam and Sanjay Subrahmanyam, 'L'état Moghol et sa fiscalité, xvie–xviiie siècles', *Annales: histoire, sciences sociales*, 49 (1994), 189–217.

increased agricultural output and a greater volume of trade. Tax yields were enhanced by more rigorous local administration and by involving moneyed men in bidding to collect them. Trade was more closely regulated by the state and taxed more heavily. Most of the new rulers also borrowed from bankers in advance of their tax revenues. Higher tax yields and ready money advanced by bankers enabled states to spend more heavily on professional armies. There is thus some resemblance at least between regimes in India and Europe that were maximising the yield of their tax resources and using the capacity of the state to borrow to the full in order to enhance their military power. Historians of India are willing to apply the concept of a 'military-fiscal state' to some of the new entities of the eighteenth century.[12]

Europeans were able first to gain influence within some of these new states and later to adapt them to their own purposes as they assumed authority over them. Many recent interpretations of the eighteenth century stress the strong continuities between the indigenous regimes succeeding the Mughals and the early rule of the British East India Company. It too was built on taxes rigorously collected and used to maintain large armies. These interpretations also stress the role of Indian agency, however unwittingly, in the rise of the British to dominance and in shaping the new colonial order. Power was won by forming alliances with Indian groups and was at first largely exercised through Indian intermediaries.

A number of distinguished scholars are not at all persuaded by such interpretations of the eighteenth century in India. They still see a qualitative difference for the worse between the great empire that collapsed and the mostly transitory regional states that succeeded it. These states were too weak to stand against what was in their view a violent foreign conquest that established an entirely new predatory colonial order.[13]

That coercion was a major element in European dealings with Indians throughout the eighteenth century cannot be denied. Even early in the century, Europeans periodically resorted to violence at sea to enforce their commercial objectives. In mid-century rulers in Bengal were elevated or deposed at the point of British bayonets. At the end of the century massive deployments of British troops destroyed the

[12] Notably Burton Stein, 'State Formation and Economy Reconsidered', *Modern Asian Studies*, 19 (1985), 387–413.

[13] M. Athar Ali, 'Recent Theories of Eighteenth-century India', *Indian Historical Review*, 8 (1987), 102–10; Z. U. Malik, 'The Core and the Periphery: A Contribution to the Debate on the Eighteenth Century', *Proceedings of the Indian History Congress, 51st Session* (Calcutta, 1990), 169–99; Irfan Habib, 'The Eighteenth Century in Indian Economic History', in *On the Eighteenth Century as a Category of Asian History: Van Leur in Retrospect*, ed. Leonard Blussé and Femme Gaastra (Aldershot, 1998), 217–36.

Mysore state and were threatening the Marathas. Yet at every stage accommodations between British and Indian interests were also crucial to the rise of British ascendancy. Accommodations were based on the self-interest of both sides. To achieve any objective, be it commercial, military or political, Indian assistance was indispensable to Europeans who were able to offer valuable services to certain groups in Indian society in return for this assistance.

The pattern of accommodation had been set in seaborne trade in the seventeenth century. Europeans depended on the toleration of Indian rulers to establish themselves at first with the customary immunities of other mercantile communities. In some cases these immunities were gradually extended until they were turned into enclaves under European authority. Recognition that Europeans brought in bullion and certain valued commodities as well as generating wealth and employment seem to have disposed rulers to put up with such intrusions. The British resident in India of necessity maintained very close relations with Indian commercial communities. The Company obtained its goods through networks of merchants and brokers. Private British merchants traded by sea in ships built in India, largely sailed by Indian crews, often financed by money borrowed from Indians and carrying a high proportion of freight for Indian clients. Europeans in return were important customers of Indian merchants, offering them valuable services as shippers of goods and skills as ships' commanders, navigators and gunners.

British–Indian commercial collaboration in the pursuit of advantages for both sides continued for some years after the first conquests. In exploiting the immediate opportunities opened to them by political power, such as diverting state revenues into private pockets or imposing control over certain trades for their own advantage, Europeans were at first largely dependent on the finance and expertise of Indian businessmen, who acted as their agents; these were the banians of Bengal or dubashes of Madras. Such people profited greatly, often becoming richer than their nominal masters. As the Company's armies began to wage war all over India, they depended on the great Indian banking businesses, especially on those based at Benares, for remitting the funds for the regular payments on which the loyalty of the troops depended.[14]

From the sixteenth century at least, Indian rulers had begun to value European skills in land warfare as well as at sea. Numerous Europeans were employed as artillery men and in the armouries of Mughal armies. During the eighteenth century European and Indian military systems

[14] Lakshmi Subramanian, *Indigenous Capital and Imperial Expansion: Bombay, Surat and the West Coast* (Delhi, 1996).

began to converge closely. Some of the successor states to the Mughals developed armies along European lines, deploying massed infantry drilled and armed in the European manner. The demand for European officers and artificers increased. As the British and French began to fight one another on a scale that approximated to contemporary European warfare, they had of necessity to enter what has been called 'the Indian military labour market' to recruit the sepoys that provided the major part of their infantry.[15] At first sepoys served under Indian officers, like the remarkable Yusuf Khan, appointed by the British as 'commander of all the sepoys rais'd and employ'd ... on the Coast of Coromandel' in the 1750s and entrusted with important administrative responsibilities as well.[16] By the end of the century Indian officers had been systematically demoted to make way for the now ubiquitous British ones. Yet the Company armies were still distinctly British–Indian ones. The sepoys served on their own terms. The soldiers of the Bengal army in particular developed a privileged status, defining themselves as a high-caste force to which only what they deemed to be appropriate recruits were acceptable and whose traditions of diet, festivals and other conditions of service had to be observed by the Company.[17]

Merchants had a strictly subordinate place in the ideal order of Mughal governance. Yet in southern India from the sixteenth century, and in the eighteenth century in some of the states that emerged from Mughal rule elsewhere, sharp distinctions between trade and finance, on the one hand, and politics and administration, on the other, were being eroded. Aristocrats augmented their wealth through trade and merchants sought profits from farming state revenues. Mir Jumla, a person of Persian origin, who traded extensively by sea, managed a large proportion of the revenue of the kingdom of Golconda and ended his life as a general of the emperor Aurangzeb, is a conspicuous early example.[18] Later ones are the great merchants such as the brothers 'Omichand' (Amirchand) and Deepchand or Khwaja Wajeed, who served the nawabs of Bengal as managers of the saltpetre and salt trades of Bihar and sought political interest at the nawabs' court to protect their investments.[19] Individual Europeans aspired to play similar

[15] Dirk Kolff, *Naukar, Rajput and Sepoy: The Ethnohistory of the Military Labour Market in Hindustan 1450–1850* (Cambridge University Press, 1990), 176–81.

[16] H.H. Dodwell, *Sepoy Recruitment in the Old Madras Army* (Calcutta, 1922), 7. See also Susan Bayly, *Saints, Goddesses and Kings: Muslims and Christians in South Indian Society* (Cambridge University Press, 1989), 194–9.

[17] Seema Alavi, *The Sepoys and the Company: Tradition and Transition in Northern India 1770–1830* (Delhi, 1995), chap. 2.

[18] Sanjay Subrahmanyam, *The Political Economy of Commerce: Southern India 1500–1650* (Cambridge University Press, 1990), 322–7.

[19] Kumkum Chatterjee, *Merchants, Politics and Society in Early Modern India: Bihar 1733–1820* (Leiden, 1996), 71–100.

roles and to diversify their trading interests by profiting from the resources of Indian states. In the later seventeenth century Englishmen collected revenue from small grants of coastal land in southern India.[20] In the eighteenth century individual Frenchmen were doing the same.[21] Dupleix and Bussy received huge grants of territory in the 1750s, allocated to them personally, from the revenue of which they were to maintain forces for the service of those who were trying to establish themselves as the *subahdars* of the Deccan.[22]

Their involvement in Indian states gave Europeans the opportunities to intervene decisively in the 1750s, both in the south and in Bengal, backing claimants to thrones or conspiracies to depose rulers. Intervention quickly led to the subordination of the Carnatic and to the effective incorporation of Bengal into the British empire. Europeans at once began to refer to these changes as a 'revolution'. For a considerable time, however, many Indians appear to have believed that what in retrospect seems so palpably to have been leading to an entirely new order might in fact be a continuation of the late-Mughal one into which the British could be absorbed and made to serve Indian purposes.

Some Indian rulers were indeed able to manipulate British power to their own purposes. In the Carnatic, Muhammad Ali Khan, Nawab of Arcot, usually assumed to be a hapless puppet at the mercy of the imperious commands issued to him from Madras or of the intrigues of Europeans at his court, was able to use the shield of British protection to extend his territory and to develop, in the words of a recent scholar, 'a tradition of kingship which was authentically Islamic'.[23] The Wazirs of Awadh also used British force to win and consolidate a great extension of territory in Rohilkhand. They worked out mechanisms for limiting the effect of British demands and they too developed an Islamic monarchy, if of a rather different kind, in their new capital at Lucknow.[24]

In Bengal within a few years of Plassey and in other provinces by the end of the century, Indian authority had patently given way to foreign rule. Yet the foreigners seem to have had little difficulty in inducing the kind of men who had served the Mughal regimes to apply their skills and impart their knowledge. For some, notably in the early stages of conquest in Bengal, great wealth could be accumulated under

[20] Elizabeth Saxe, 'Fortune's Tangled Web: Trading Networks of English Entrepreneurs in Eastern India, 1657–1717' (Ph. D. thesis Yale University, 1978), 42, 69–70.

[21] Catherine Manning, *Fortunes à faire: The French in Asian Trade, 1719–48* (Aldershot, 1996), 211.

[22] Alfred Martineau, *Bussy et l'Inde française* (Paris, 1935), 140–8; H.H. Dodwell, *Dupleix and Clive: The Beginning of Empire* (London, 1920), 86.

[23] S. Bayly, *Saints, Goddesses and Kings*, 171.

[24] Richard B. Barnett, *North India Between Empires: Awadh, the Mughals and the British, 1720–1801* (Berkeley, 1980); Michael H. Fisher, *A Clash of Cultures: Awadh, the British and the Mughals* (New Delhi, 1988).

the aegis of ignorant foreigners. Ganga Govind Singh administered the revenues of Bengal under Warren Hastings, and in the process built up a fortune that some Europeans estimated in millions of pounds sterling.[25] But material reward seems not to have been the only motive for serving the Company. There are indications that the British were not at first seen as foreigners who were qualitatively different from others, more or less alien, who held power in India. The loyalty of Indian administrators, especially if they were Muslims, was first and foremost to an ideal of governance, which was that of the Mughal empire, and it was their duty to try to make those actually vested with power conform to these ideals, to which even the British nominally paid homage. They had after all received the *diwani* of Bengal as the emperor's 'faithful servants' in consideration of their 'attachment and services' to him.[26] Of Muhammad Reza Khan, the minister who ran Bengal for the British in the 1760s, it has been written that 'his constant aim ... was to persuade his English masters to accept Mughal ideas as their own'.[27] 'Room had been found in the past for all nationalities in the imperial service; there was no reason why the English should not be found a place.'[28] They were granted Mughal titles. Some Company servants were not oblivious of the obligations that went with their titles. Among Warren Hastings's titles was *Aman al-Daula*, 'security of the state'. He never performed the duties implied by this title to the Mughal emperor in person (indeed he did him a major disservice by cancelling his stipend from Bengal), but he did encounter the emperor's eldest son when he fled to Lucknow in 1784. Hastings then rode behind the prince's elephant on his entry into the city and was later depicted sitting apparently deferentially at his feet in a coloured sketch by Zoffany, who was in Lucknow at the time. Hastings was strongly tempted, he confessed, to try to restore the prince to Delhi by British military force, 'an Act which would have reflected a lasting Honor on my reputation in India'.[29]

Hopes that men such as Hastings might be absorbed into an Indian

[25] 'Indian Officials under the East India Company in eighteenth-century Bengal' in P.J. Marshall, *Trade and Conquest: Studies on the Rise of British Dominance in India* (Aldershot, 1993).

[26] C.U. Aitchison, *A Collection of Treaties, Engagements and Sunnuds Relating to India and Neighbouring Countries* (6 vols., Calcutta, 1862–4), I, 60.

[27] Abdul Majed Khan, *The Transition in Bengal, 1756–1775: A Study of Muhammad Reza Khan* (Cambridge University Press, 1969), 16.

[28] Ibid., p. 12. A similar point is made in C.A. Bayly, *Empire and Information: Intelligence Gathering and Social Communication in India, 1780–1870* (Cambridge University Press, 1996), 86. For reactions to the British as aliens, see Kumkum Chatterjee, 'History as Self-Representation: The Recasting of a Political Tradition in Late Eighteenth-Century Eastern India', *Modern Asian Studies*, 32 (1998), 913–48.

[29] Sydney C. Grier, *The Letters of Warren Hastings to his Wife* (Edinburgh, 1905), 302. Hastings recorded his various meetings with the prince at Lucknow from May to August 1784 in his diary, B[ritish] L[ibrary], Add MS. 39879.

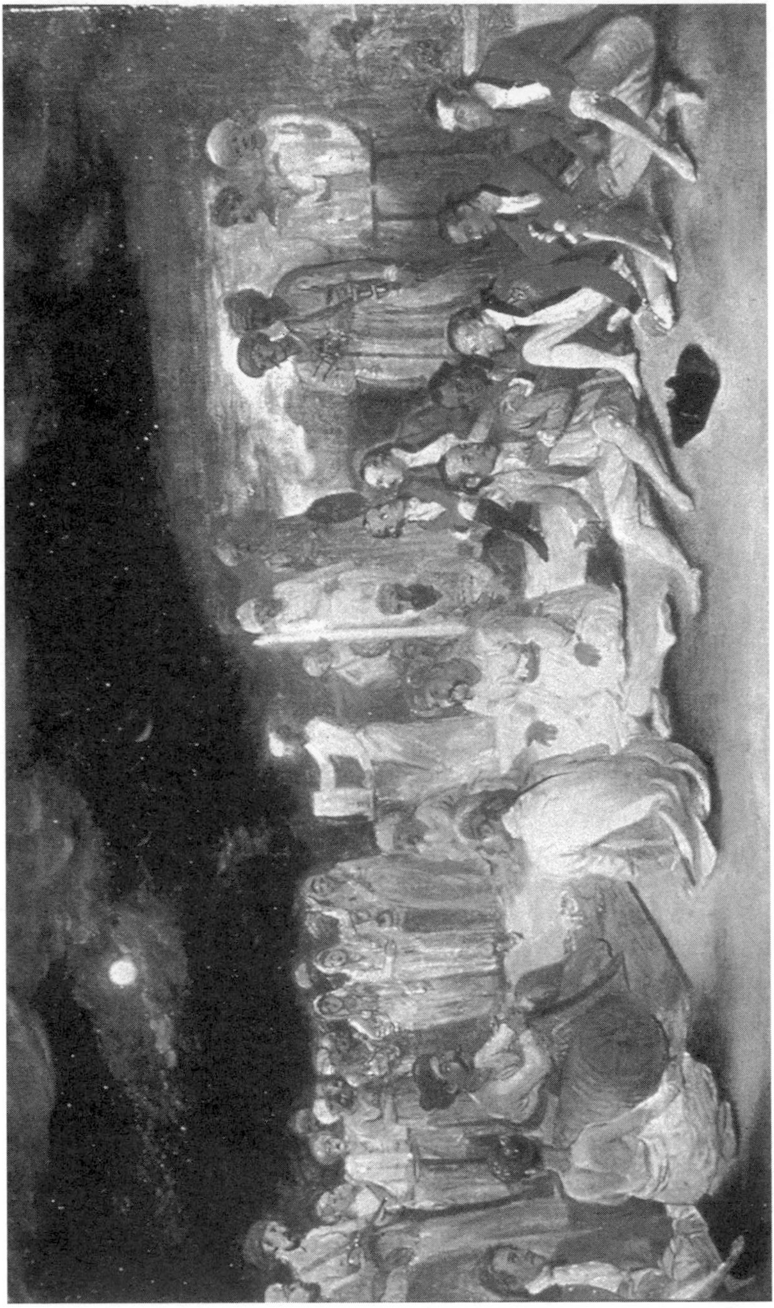

Prince Jawan Bakht and Warren Hastings at Lucknow, 1784

polity and be made to serve Indian purposes were not quite as futile as they seem in retrospect. Europeans had been absorbed into Indian systems in the past and were to continue to be so absorbed well into the nineteenth century. Numerous Portuguese 'renegades' or mercenaries had sought service with Indian rulers.[30] Bussy was for a time effectively minister of the Nizam of Hyderabad.[31] At the end of the eighteenth century the Piedmontese de Boigne and the Frenchman Perron commanded the troops of the Maratha Mahadaji Sindhia and held huge estates from him in northern India. Various Europeans and Americans held high military commands under Ranjit Singh of the Panjab in the early nineteenth century. Even if it was hardly conceivable that they would formally renounce their allegiance to the Company, senior British Company servants in the mid-eighteenth century were under only tenuous control from home and their support could often be bought by Indian grandees who were prepared to pay generously enough. Was it therefore unreasonable for Mir Jafar to expect great future services after Plassey for the nawabs of Bengal from the lavishly rewarded Robert Clive, for whom he had a paternal regard and who was after his death to tell his Begam that 'I consider myself and all the English Gentleman to be your highness's children and that we regard you as our mother'?[32]

Clive, however, was one of those men in crucial positions who would ensure that the British East India Company would remain an alien force in India pursuing ultimately alien objectives. For such people the making of money was of course a preoccupation of the highest importance, but money was not an end in itself; it was to enable them to take appropriate positions in British society. Clive and Hastings were typical in their strong sense of locality and their ambition to restore or recover ancestral property, Styche in Shropshire for Clive and Daylesford in the Cotswolds for Hastings. Both men, however, wanted rather more than honourable retirement in local society. They and others like them who had risen high in the service were conscious that they were serving the nation and not just a trading company. In the wars of the 1750s they had successfully defended important British commercial interests against the French and against Indian enemies. 'There is no part of the world in which British arms have, of late years, acquired more honour' than in India, wrote Robert Orme, the Company servants' own historian.[33] Clive's success at Plassey was indeed

[30] Sanjay Subrahmanyam, *The Portuguese Empire in Asia 1500–1700: A Political and Economic History* (1993), 249–61.

[31] Martineau, *Bussy*, 140.

[32] Brajenranath Banerji, 'The Mother of the Company', *Bengal Past and Present*, 32 (1926), 46.

[33] *Military Transactions in Indostan*, I, 34.

to be commemorated as a national triumph together with three other huge pictures – pantheons of admirals and generals and a depiction of the surrender of Montreal – by Francis Hayman for the Rotunda in Vauxhall Gardens.[34] With the gains made by the wars and the grant of the Bengal *diwani*, the Company's governors were well aware that they were administering a huge national asset that could confer great advantages on Britain but whose loss could cripple British commerce and credit.

Public recognition and rewards should follow great services. Victory at Plassey turned Clive's hopes to 'getting into Parliament' and to 'being taken some Notice of by his Majesty'.[35] There is 'no other interest in this kingdom but what arises from great possessions', he was later to write.[36] Hastings wrote early in his government that he had 'catched the desire of applause in public life' and that he wished to be esteemed 'in the general opinion of mankind'.[37] He confessed to 'a more than ordinary degree of ambition to act in an elevated sphere under my sovereign and to recommend myself more and more to his favour'.[38]

It was impossible for those who sought wealth, reputation and advancement in India not to see themselves as acting on a global stage of British interests. Although there is little to suggest that Clive and the others who intervened so forcefully in the affairs of Indian states in the 1750s did so with any sense of incorporating the gains that they made into a world-wide British empire, as the consequences of their intervention became apparent it was an outcome that they quickly accepted. As early as 1759 in his well-known letter to Pitt, Clive raised the possibility of 'the nation's assistance' being required 'to maintain so wide a dominion' in India.[39] The nature of this dominion was to be defined by men in India rather than at home.[40]

What the East India Company had acquired in India was a series of rights, conditional on rendering service and with other rights parallel to them or overlapping them. The Company held land around Madras as a *jagir*, technically a grant of revenue for the maintenance of troops. The so-called Northern Circars were at first an *inam* or gift from the

[34] Brian Allen, *Francis Hayman* (New Haven, 1987), 68–9.

[35] G.W. Forrest, *The Life of Robert, Lord Clive* (2 vols., 1918), II, 37.

[36] Cited in Philip Lawson and Bruce Lenman, 'Robert Clive, "the Black Jagir" and British Politics', *Historical Journal*, 26 (1983), 813.

[37] G.R. Gleig, *Memoirs of the Life of the Right Honourable Warren Hastings* (3 vols., 1841), I, 375.

[38] Ibid., I, 472.

[39] Forrest, *Clive*, II, 176.

[40] The uncertainties of opinion at home are brought out in Huw V. Bowen, 'A Question of Sovereignty? The Bengal Land Revenue Issue, 1765–67', *Journal of Imperial and Commonwealth History*, 16 (1988), 155–76.

Mughal emperor and then held by treaty with the Nizam of Hyderabad, which required the Company to maintain troops for his support and to pay him a subsidy when troops were not required.[41] In Bengal the Company had at first acquired *zamindari* rights to collect revenue in and around Calcutta. After 1765 they acted as the emperor's *diwan*. Formally their duties as *diwan* were separate from the duties of the *nazim*, vested in the nawabs of Bengal, and they were subject to checks by officials directly responsible to the emperor.

Leading Company servants had little patience with these ambiguous complexities.[42] They seem to have believed that they had won for Britain dominions comparable to those in other parts of the world. Like those who planned reforms in America, they thought in terms of sovereignty backed by effective military power. The Mughals had, in their view, been sovereigns over their empire. During the eighteenth century that sovereignty had been usurped and, as Clive put it, 'absolute' sovereignty had passed to the provincial governors or nawabs. Plassey had given the British 'absolute power' over Bengal.[43] He wrote in 1759 of 'so large a sovereignty' in Bengal in the hands of the Company.[44] On the way back to India in 1764 he reflected on the possibility of 'making such strides to power and dominion as must I think end in parliamentary inquiry and a national dominion'.[45] The grant of the *diwani* eliminated any doubts about the matter in his mind. 'All must belong either to the Company or to the Nabob' and now it clearly belonged to the Company. 'The power is lodged where it can only be lodged with safety to us'.[46] Hastings used almost identical language in his evidence to the House of Commons in 1767. The nawabs of Bengal had the 'powers of [a] Sovereign independant of [the] Mogul', but now 'The Company is Master of the power and may be Master of the Government and it is out of the Nabobs power to controul them.'[47] As Governor after 1772 he was in no doubt that 'the sovereignty of this country [is] wholly and absolutely vested in the Company',[48] a view that he upheld uncompromisingly thereafter.

Sovereignty must be asserted by military power, the first priority of

[41] Aitchison, *Collection*, V, 12–18.

[42] See the discussion in C.A. Bayly, 'The British Military-Fiscal State and Indigenous Resistance: India 1750–1820' in *Origins of Nationality in South Asia: Patriotism and Ethical Government in the Making of Modern India* (Delhi, 1998), 241–51.

[43] *A Letter to the Proprietors of East India Stock from Lord Clive* (1764), 36, 46.

[44] Forrest, *Clive*, II, 176.

[45] Letter to George Grenville, 14 Oct. 1764, Huntington Library, MS HM 31637.

[46] *Fort William–India House Correspondence*, 14, *1752–81*, ed. Ambar Prasad (Delhi, 1985), 174.

[47] BL, Add MS, 18469, fos. 26–7.

[48] Gleig, *Hastings*, I, 393.

the raj from 1757 until 1947. Now it was 'in your power to be as great as you please in the kingdom of Bengal', Clive told the Directors immediately after Plassey. 'The sinews of war are in your own possession, and there wants nothing but supplies of men and military stores to keep up your priviledges and acquisitions.'[49] The acceptance of the *diwani* was accompanied by plans for an enlarged army which quickly came into being. In the south the Madras Council reflected that the Company's objectives were 'formerly wholly Commercial' now had 'become partly Commercial and partly Military'. Therefore 'that Reputation which the Company's Arms have justly acquired' must be maintained by using their army to overawe any power within the Carnatic that might presume to 'hopes of Independence'.[50]

Military force enabled the Company servants to subordinate all competing claims to authority within what they regarded as their territory. The Company's army was to be the only military force in Bengal. The troops of the nawabs were quickly disbanded. The armed men kept up by the Bengal *zamindars* to sustain their standing as local potentates were dispersed. British troops enabled the Nawab of Arcot to extend his authority over the *poligars* and 'little kingdoms' of the south at the price of dismantling of most of his own forces and his total reliance on the British as his protectors.[51] The army of the Wazir of Awadh was considerably reduced and the main task of defending his territory or coercing his subjects passed to British garrisons.

The ambitions of the new Company regimes that were claiming and enforcing an absolute authority were at first largely confined to securing commercial advantages and to maximising revenues, above all to pay for their large military establishments. The consequences of closer control over the textiles being produced for export or of the distribution of commodities like salt and opium and of an enhanced revenue demand, where it could be realised, were no doubt immediate and severe for considerable sections of the population now under British rule. Yet neither the personnel involved in government, except at the highest levels, nor the manner in which it operated changed significantly in the early years. These were still recognisably Indian regimes dependent on Indian expertise. Continuity with the past was real enough, even if the potential for change in the future was equally apparent.

One of the scholars who is sceptical of the current tendency to interpret

[49] *Fort William–India House Correspondence*, II, *1757–59*, ed. H.N. Sinha (Delhi, 1957), 250.

[50] To Directors, 3 Sept. 1763, BL, Oriental and India Office Collections E/4/300, fo. 211.

[51] Jim Phillips, 'A Successor to the Moguls: the Nawab of the Carnatic and the East India Company, 1763–1785', *International History Review*, 7 (1985), 364–89.

the rise of British dominance in India in the eighteenth century in evolutionary terms has written that 'colonialism had blue-blooded European ancestry' and that the new British regimes were 'essentially different' in their 'nature and objectives' from anything that had gone before.[52] If 'colonialism' is interpreted in strictly eighteenth-century terms, there is much to be said for this point of view. The Company's regime was acting on the same assumptions and pursuing the same objectives as British colonial governments elsewhere. The British in India in the age of Clive and Hastings were on the way to achieving much of what British governments were failing to achieve in America. In India the flow of trade between metropole and overseas territory was now safeguarded by strong military forces at the disposal of a local executive claiming to act with a sovereign authority that could override autonomies and privileges in the territory under its control. These were the objectives of a British parliamentary state, not of rulers who adhered to Mughal traditions.

Other parts of the argument for the imposition of an essentially alien colonial regime in the mid-eighteenth century are less convincing. The objectives of the new regime once in power may indeed have been distinctively British but the means by which power was won and was at first exercised were still Indian. Denials that the British had owed much to 'compromises and collaboration with certain indigenous groups and classes' invest them with a capacity to determine events which they manifestly did not possess.[53] Eighteenth-century India was not the inert victim of overwhelming force from a more 'advanced' civilisation. It was not differences but increasing similarities between Indian and European conditions that the British could exploit. But to do so they had to render services that were acceptable, in the short run, to important elements in Indian society. Even when a military apparatus was created capable of subduing opposition within the Company's territories and more uncertainly, as early wars with the Marathas and Mysore showed, of trying to impose its will outside them, it was still built on Indian taxation, Indian finance, Indian administrative expertise and Indian soldiers.

British ambitions spanned the world in the later eighteenth century. Their objectives, commercial advantage, military security and clearly recognised authority, were essentially the same in America and in India. In America it is beyond question that these objectives could only be achieved with the active co-operation of large sections of the colonial population. In India too such objectives could only be realised if local allies could be found. As I suggested in my first address, the story of

[52] M. Athar Ali, 'Recent Theories of Eighteenth-Century India', 109.
[53] Ibid., 108.

Britain's rise to global supremacy needs to be more than an analysis of Britain's undoubted strengths. Whether these strengths could be used effectively or not ultimately depended on the dispositions of the peoples whom the British encountered in a world that was changing in both west and east in ways that were largely beyond the comprehension of contemporaries and, it must be said, are little clearer to us. We can perhaps, though, be reasonably sure that easy explanations, such as an immobile and vulnerable Asia or the irresistible march of the European world economy armed with a superior technology, will tell us relatively little.

ENLIGHTENMENT AND REVOLUTION: NAPLES 1799

By John Robertson

READ 22 JANUARY 1999

TWO hundred years ago today, on 22 January 1799, French troops forced their way into the city of Naples. In doing so, they confirmed the authority of the Neapolitan Republic which had been proclaimed, one and indivisible, the day before by a group of patriots who had taken control of the Castel Sant'Elmo, the fortress on the hill immediately above the centre of the city. Thus began the last of the revolutions which can be regarded as the offspring of the great French Revolution of 1789. There is no denying that the Neapolitan Revolution, like its predecessors in northern Italy and elsewhere, depended on French military intervention. The patriots were not in control of the city before 22 January, and needed the French to quell the popular violence and disorder which had swept the city for the previous week. And when, after three months, the French withdrew their forces, the republicans' hold on the city was too precarious to last more than a few weeks.

But the Neapolitan Republic of 1799 was not simply the puppet of French military occupation. There was a revolution in Naples. It was a revolution precipitated, not by the French, but by the actions, at once rash and feeble, of the Bourbon King of Naples, Ferdinando IV. Although the Directory had sanctioned military support for the revolution in Rome in 1798, it was most reluctant to commit the over-extended French forces still further south to attempt the conquest of the kingdom of Naples. Egged on by the British envoy Sir William Hamilton, however, the king had joined the alliance of Austria and Britain in May 1798, and in November had sent his troops into Roman territory, entering the city himself on 29 November. It quickly became clear that the Neapolitan advance was unsustainable; and on 23 December, as his forces retreated, Ferdinando, his queen Maria Carolina, and assorted ministers, along with Hamilton and his wife, Emma, all took flight on Nelson's warships for Palermo, carrying with them the gold held by the Neapolitan banks. The king had appointed the marchese Francesco Pignatelli as Vicar to exercise royal authority; it was he who distributed arms to the people, but also, on 12 January 1799, negotiated terms with General Championnet, agreeing to an indemnity of two-and-a-half million ducats. Four days later he too fled to Palermo. The crown thus left 'the people' in arms but under no legitimate authority; it virtually obliged the French to occupy the city; and it burdened whatever regime succeeded it with a heavy financial obligation.

The Neapolitan patriots were fortunate in the French commander, who was more republican than his masters in the Directory. Championnet had befriended Neapolitan exiles in Rome, and several were attached to his army. Once in control of the city he endorsed the immediate establishment of a 'Provisional Government' and facilitated its actions; the difference he made was underlined by the obstructiveness of his successor, General MacDonald. But the institution of the republic and the content of its programme were the work of the Neapolitan patriots themselves. The speed and vigour of their initiatives was remarkable. By the end of January the Provisional Government had reconstituted the administration of the city, issued 'General instructions' for a new structure of government in the provinces, and decreed the first specific reforms, including the abolition of primogeniture and *fedecommissa* (a form of entail). Further reforms to the judical system, including the introduction of public trials and the abolition of the magistracies regulating commerce, followed in mid-February. Reform of the feudal system, probably the single most important objective of the revolution, was slower to be agreed, in part because MacDonald made difficulties; proposals were ready by 7 March, but a decree was not issued until 25 April, with provisions which had become more aggressively anti-baronial. A final group of reforms, including the abolition of torture, was announced early in May.[1]

The republicans worked fast; they well knew that they did so under adverse pressures. On 2 April a small squadron of English warships appeared in the Bay of Naples, encouraging an abortive anti-republican conspiracy within the city, and capturing the islands of Capri, Ischia and Procida. But the greatest threat was on land. In late February Cardinal Ruffo crossed from Sicily to Calabria to raise the banner of the *Santa Fede* on the Bourbons' behalf. By the end of March he was in control of Calabria, and in April conflicts broke out across the kingdom, from Basilicata to the Abruzzo. When the French left Naples at the end of April (apart from a small garrison in Sant'Elmo), the Provisional Government took the initiative in organising its own defence. But once the army of the *Santa Fede* reached the city, on 13 June,

[1] An authoritative acount of the revolution is one by Anna Maria Rao, in Part I of Anna Maria Rao and Pasquale Villani, *Napoli 1799–1815. Dalla Repubblica alla monarchia amministrativa* (Naples, [1995]); on the feudal law, see also Giuseppe Gallasso, 'La legge feudale napoletana del 1799' in idem., *La filosofia in soccorso de' governi. La cultura napoletana del settecento* (Naples, 1989), 633–60.

resistance could be sustained for no more than two days, before the republicans retired to Sant'Elmo. By 21 June they had agreed with Ruffo the terms of their capitulation.

It is not difficult for those of liberal inclinations to take a positive view of the Neapolitan revolution. It has several points in its favour. The quality of its leadership was high. At its head were the intellectual elite of the kingdom: among them the chemist and President of the Provisional Government Carlo Lauberg, the philosopher and active member of the legislative commission Francesco Mario Pagano, the botanist Domenico Cirillo, and the agronomist and historian Melchiorre Delfico. These were joined by the brightest of the younger generation, including Annibale Giordano, Vincenzio Russo and Franceso Saverio Salfi. The ablest bishops, Andrea Serrao and Domenico Forges Davanzati, identified with the Republic; and so did many younger members of the great noble families: Caracciolo, Serra di Cassano, Carafa, Pignatelli. Most appealing of all has been the Portugese-descended Eleonora di Fonseca Pimentel, subsequently portrayed as the heroine of a stream of novels and dramas. The revolutionaries' intentions, moreover, may be thought of as genuinely reformist: though certainly radical in relation to the burdens of feudalism, their measures were based on a commitment to the rule of law from which they did not depart. Even when the revolution was radicalised in April and May, there was no deliberate terror. But what is most in their favour is the contrast between their behaviour and the revenge wreaked upon them once the Bourbons were restored. Within a week the capitulation was dishonoured, Nelson setting a wretched example by summarily hanging the republican admiral Caracciolo from the fore yard-arm.[2] Ruffo's conciliatory policy was abandoned, and patriots were rounded up. By September 8,000 trials were in process in the kingdom. More than a thousand were exiled; and several thousand more imprisoned. But it was the executions, some 120 in Naples, which made the revolution's reputation. The nobles, like Serra di Cassano, were beheaded; but the others, including Cirillo, Pagano and Fonseca Pimentel, were hung in the great, bleak Piazza del Mercato, pushed from ladders while little urchins, the *tirapiedi*, clung to their feet.

With so many admirable qualities, the Neapolitan revolution is easily portrayed as a heroic tragedy. The classic account of its significance was that fashioned on its centenary in 1889 by a group of young Neapolitan liberals, headed by Benedetto Croce. For Croce 1799 was

[2] Nelson's role in these events has recently been reassessed by Carlo Knight, 'Sir William Hamilton e il mancato rispetto, da parte di Lord Nelson, della "Capitolazione" del 1799', *Atti della Accademia Pontaniana*, new series, XLVII (1999), 373–97, where it is suggested that it was Hamilton, rather than Nelson, who deceived the patriots into thinking that the capitulation would be honoured.

the moment when the southern reformers vindicated their claim to the moral and political leadership not only of Naples, but of Italy as a whole. The suppression of the republic had meant the loss of the reformers' best opportunity, and condemned the south anew to backwardness.[3] This view of the revolution was to take a firm hold of the Italian liberal imagination, and was quickly picked up by foreign sympathisers, including several English women historians in the early twentieth century.[4] Not surprisingly, modern historical scholarship, much of it by Neapolitans, has questioned and qualified this judgement. I do not want simply to repeat this re-assessment. Instead, I shall focus on a question which is at least implicit in the liberal view of 1799, and which has a more general historical resonance: the question of the relation between Enlightenment and Revolution.

The historiography of this question is marked by its origins in the accusation laid against the French Revolution by its contemporary opponents, notably the abbé Barruel, that it was the direct outcome of an anti-Christian conspiracy by the *philosophes*.[5] Polemic was subsequently transformed into serious historical analysis by Tocqueville, who found that while there had been no *philosophe* conspiracy, it was the case that the *gens de lettres*, finding themselves excluded from the practical politics of reform, had devoted their energies to abstractions. As a result, 'liberty' had come to mean very different things to the men of letters and to those who still thought in the terms of the *ancien régime*.[6] Tocqueville's argument was confined to France, but since 1945 there have been at least two major accounts of the relation between Enlightenment and Revolution which have advanced a comparable thesis, applied to Europe more generally. To Reinhard Koselleck, the Enlightenment was the creation of thinkers excluded from the absolutist state,

[3] The centenary publication, edited by Benedetto Croce, Giuseppe Ceci, Michelangelo D'Ayala and Salvatore Di Giacomo, was entitled *La Rivoluzione Napoletana del 1799 illustrata con ritratti, vedute, autografi ed altri documento figurativi e grafici del tempo* or, more briefly, *Albo illustrativo della rivoluzione napoletano del 1799* (Naples 1899, facsimile reprint 1998); on the initiative behind it: Thomas Willette, '1799/1899: heroic memory in the centennial of the *Repubblica Napoletana*', *Journal of Modern Italian Studies*, 4, 3 (1999), 369–79. Croce's own writings on the revolution were published in Benedetto Croce, *La rivoluzione napoletana del 1799* (first edition, 1887, revised editions, 1896, 1911, 1926, 1948, reprinted from the last in Naples, 1998).

[4] Constance H.D. Giglioli (née Stocker), *Naples in 1799. An Account of the Revolution of 1799 and of the Rise and Fall of the Parthenopean Republic* (London, 1903) (who suggests the detail of the *tirapiedi* on pages 350–1); and Lacy Collison-Morley, *Naples through the Centuries* (London, 1925), 141–52 – the author acknowledging her debts to Croce in the Preface, vii.

[5] On the early historiography of the Enlightenment, see Vincenzo Ferrone and Daniel Roche (eds), *L'Illuminismo. Dizionario Storico* (Rome and Bari, 1997), 'Postfazione', 521–31.

[6] Alexis de Tocqueville, *L'ancien régime et la révolution*, (1856, Paris, 1964), esp. part II ch. xi and part III.

who took refuge in masonic lodges and cultivated a utopian politics which left them fatally ill-equipped to direct a revolution.[7] Less disenchanted, Franco Venturi suggested that utopianism partnered reform throughout the Enlightenment, though he prefered to talk of its contribution to 'the crisis of the ancien régime' rather than to revolution.[8]

Framed in this way, nevertheless, the question of the relation of Enlightenment to revolution has all too easily been identified with that of the 'intellectual' or 'cultural' origins of the (French) Revolution.[9] The critical question has become that of whether, as Darnton has put it, books do cause revolutions; and study of the Enlightenment is liable to be reduced to investigation of the diffusion of ideas.[10] As even social and cultural historians of the Enlightenment have begun to realise, this does no justice to their subject. There was more to the Enlightenment, both within and beyond France, than a small group of men of letters preoccupied with abstractions about reason and liberty. Two tendencies within recent Enlightenment scholarship suggest that the question of its relation to revolution needs to be reconsidered. One is the new interest in the Enlightenment's understanding and practice of sociability: the ways in which it responded to the forms of association offered by the towns and cities of the eighteenth century: academies, salons, debating societies, masonic lodges, libraries and *musées*.[11] There is also a fresh interest in the later 1770s and 1780s as forming a distinct 'late' phase of the Enlightenment, in which the intellectual agenda was set by Rousseau and by the new themes of sensibility and naturalism.[12] If the question of the relation between Enlightenment and Revolution is

[7] Reinhard Koselleck, *Critique and Crisis. Enlightenment and the Pathogenesis of Modern Society* (Oxford, 1988; originally published in German in 1959).

[8] Franco Venturi, *Utopia and Reform in the Enlightenment* (Cambridge University Press, 1971).

[9] The classic discussions are Daniel Mornet, *Les origines intellectuelles de la révolution française 1715–1787* (Paris, 1933) and Roger Chartier, *The Cultural Origins of the French Revolution* (Durham and London, 1991).

[10] Robert Darnton, *The Forbidden Bestsellers of Pre-Revolutionary France* (New York and London, 1995), Part III; See also his earlier 'The high Enlightenment and the low life of literature', *Past and Present*, 51 (1971), 81–115. To the surprise of some of his readers, Darnton still adheres to a very traditional understanding of what he termed the 'high Enlightenment': 'George Washington's false teeth', *New York Review of Books*, XLIV, 5 (27 March 1997), 34–8.

[11] Exemplary of this approach: Dena Goodman, *The Republic of Letters. A Cultural History of the French Enlightenment* (Ithaca and London, 1994).

[12] See especially Vincenzo Ferrone, *I profeti dell'illuminismo. Le metamorfosi della ragione nel tardo settecento italiano* (Rome and Bari, 1989); though already preoccupied with the imminence of revolution, an early and fundamental contribution to the study of this 'late' period of the Enlightenment was Robert Darnton, *Mesmerism and the End of the Enlightenment in France* (Cambridge, Mass., 1968).

worth studying, it is the implication of such work that the complex character of the Enlightenment itself must first be appreciated. It is not a question reducible to the formula: 'do books cause revolutions?'

The question tends not to be asked so directly of Naples. This is probably because there exists a Neapolitan alternative to the Barruel or Tocqueville thesis, to which modern historians have felt obliged to respond along different lines. The author of the equivalent Neapolitan thesis was Vincenzo Cuoco, whose *Saggio storico sulla rivoluzione napoletana del 1799* was written in disillusioned exile immediately after the events, and first published in 1801.[13] The revolution had failed, Cuoco believed, because it was a 'passive revolution', in which a small band of republicans had tried to impose abstract French ideas on a people ignorant of their meaning and unprepared to receive them. This dependence on foreign models was already, as Cuoco began by pointing out, a feature of the Bourbon court of Ferdinando and Maria Carolina; their culpability for the events of 1799 was beyond extenuation. But the republicans' infatuation with the French Revolution, with its grand ideas and conspiratorial 'clubs', meant that they neglected to involve *il popolo*, 'the people', in their programme, and thus failed to make the revolution 'active'.[14] The end of the revolution was certainly a tragedy,[15] but it was also a catastrophe, as damaging in the long term as any natural disaster. The weakness of the kingdom was confirmed and increased, while all prospect of reform seemed to have been lost, probably for many years.[16]

Modern historians have mounted a powerful, if not unqualified, defence of the Neapolitan revolutionaries from Cuoco's strictures. The southern Italian 'Jacobins', it is pointed out, were by no means simply clones of the French. In exile in France and northern Italy in the later 1790s, following the first Bourbon crackdown of 1794–95, they had formulated a new, 'Italian' democratic republicanism. They were also well aware that if revolution was to be extended to the entire peninsula, it would have to be 'active', engaging the support of the people.[17] A

[13] Vincenzo Cuoco, *Saggio storico sulla rivoluzione di Napoli* (first published Milan, 1801, and revised by the author for a second edition, also published in Milan, in 1806). I have used the second edition, reprinted with an introduction by Pasquale Villani (Naples 1999). In his introduction, and again in the Preface to the second edition, Cuoco disavowed the intention to write the history of the revolution: the events, he admitted, were still too recent. But he hoped to anticipate and influence the judgement which posterity would pass on those (including Cuoco himself) who participated in it.

[14] Cuoco, *Saggio storico*, esp. chs xvi–xxi.

[15] Cuoco's enumeration of the martyred patriots was the starting-point for subsequent liberal mythology: *Saggio storico*, ch l: 'Taluni patrioti'.

[16] Cuoco, *Saggio storico*, Introduzione, Conclusione.

[17] Giuseppe Galasso, 'I giacobini meridionali', in his *La filosofia in soccorso de' governi*, 509–48; Galasso points out that 'Italy' meant, literally, the peninsula, and excluded the islands.

commitment to 'active' revolution was evident in Naples in 1799, in practice as well as in theory, as the patriots anticipated Cuoco's criticism in their efforts to overcome popular passivity.[18] While the terminology of the republic's constitution, and of the proposals for provincial administration, was derived from north Italian and ultimately French models, a conscious attempt was made to adapt it to Neapolitan circumstances. From the outset, considerable effort was also put into winning popular support. The assistance of religion was not disdained: the blood of San Gennaro was duly observed to liquefy, while liberty trees were planted with a priestly or episcopal benediction. The newspaper of the republic, the *Monitore Napolitano*, edited by Fonseca Pimentel, made a point of printing material in the dialect. The extent to which the revolution was made 'active' in the provinces was more variable, but even there republicans made more effort than Cuoco gave them credit for.[19] Most misleading of all, however, was his depiction of 'the people' as a single homogenous bloc, counterposed to the revolutionaries. Study of the counter-revolutionary *Sanfedisti* suggests that far from being a movement of pure reaction, the counter-revolutionries' coherence was dependent on Ruffo's ability to mediate the acute divisions within provincial society, divisions which had been aggravated by the actions of the monarchy itself earlier in the 1790s. Ruffo's achievement in containing peasant hostility to feudal exactions, while not alienating the local elites on whom stability depended, was ill-appreciated by the king and queen. But it ensured that the conflicts which erupted throughout the south as the *Sanfedisti* advanced were in the nature of a civil war, and did not escalate into all-out social war.[20]

Acquitting the revolutionaries of the charge of imposing abstract French ideas on the populace may have helped to clear away some of the obstacles to study of the question I have in mind, the relation

---

The fundamental study of the revolutionaries' experience of exile is Anna Maria Rao, *Esuli. L'emigrazione politica italiana in Francia 1792–1802* (Naples 1992).

[18] Maria Antonietta Visceglia, 'Genesi e fortuna di una interpretazione storiografica: la rivoluzione napoletana del 1799 come "rivoluzione passiva"', *Annali della Facoltà di Magistero, Universita di Lecce*, I (1970–71), 172–88.

[19] Rao and Villani, *Napoli 1799–1815*, Part I chs. iv–v. For recent critical reflections in English on the supposed 'passivity' of the revolution, see John A. Davis, 'The Neapolitan Revolution 1799–1999: between History and Myth', and Anna Maria Rao, 'Popular Societies in the Neapolitan Republic of 1799', both in *Journal of Modern Italian Studies*, 4, 3 (1999), 350–69.

[20] Rao and Villani, *Napoli 1799–1815*, Part I, ch vi; and John A. Davis, 'The *Santafede* and the crisis of the ancien regime in southern Italy', in *Society and Politics in the Age of the Risorgimento. Essays in Honour of Denis Mack Smith*, ed. John A. Davis and Paul Ginsborg, (Cambridge University Press, 1991), 1–25, an analysis which Davis has since developed further in 'Rivolte popolari e controrivoluzione nel mezzogiorno continentale', *Studi storici*, 39 (1998), 603–22.

between Enlightenment and revolution in Naples; but it has not encouraged attention to the question itself. There remain good reasons why the question should nevertheless be asked. Above all there is the prominent part taken in the revolution by men of letters who had previously been distinguished exponents of the Enlightenment – men such as Cirillo, Delfico and, most notably, Pagano. At the same time, there are the apparent continuities between the reforms introduced by the republic and those advocated earlier, by the same men and others, under the monarchy. On the face of it, these connections in personnel and reforming objectives are evidence that some relation between Enlightenment, reform and revolution is likely to have existed. There is at least a potential opportunity, therefore, to assess the extent to which the revolution was consistent with the aspirations of the Enlightenment, and even, perhaps, to gauge the 'success' or 'failure' of its prescriptions for the betterment of Neapolitan society.

In the remainder of this paper, I outline an analysis of the relation between Enlightenment and reform and revolution in Naples from the restoration of the monarchy in 1734 to the revolution of 1799. At this stage it is no more than an outline, or framework, of an analysis, several of whose themes I hope to develop elsewhere. But I intend to argue, against the reductionist tendency of so much social or 'cultural' history of ideas, that if the relation is to be better understood it will be on the basis of acknowledging the structural differences between the Enlightenment as an intellectual movement and the political processes of reform and revolution. We need to respect the distances separating thought, politics and social development before we seek to connect them.

In eighteenth-century Naples reform had become an issue before the advent of the Enlightenment. A strong expectation of reform accompanied the restoration of the kingdom's independence in 1734, when Carlo Borbone, son of Philip V of Spain and his second wife Elizabeth Farnese, led an army into Naples and ejected the Austrian viceroy. Even if the Neapolitans themselves were passive observers of the change, the opportunity was one for which the Neapolitan elite had been mentally preparing for almost fifty years. Under the Spanish monarchy before 1707 (and, by implication, under the Austrian monarchy since), they had come to believe, Naples had been *un regno governato in provincia* – a kingdom governed as a province. In that condition it had been in the interest of the Spanish to divide and rule, and in particular to appease the Neapolitan baronage by repeated extensions of their feudal authority in the provinces. Elaborated in a tract of 1710 by Paolo Mattia Doria, 'Massime del governo spagnolo', which circulated in manuscript, this critique was given a much broader base by the publication in 1723 of Pietro Giannone's *Storia civile del regno di Napoli.* With commanding intellectual authority, Giannone set out the historical foundations for the kingdom's independence, demonstrating the cumulative coherence of its laws and, above all, the invalidity of the papacy's pretensions to exercise civil and ecclesiastical authority over it. By 1734, there was thus a powerful sense that independence was the kingdom's due, and that it would, almost automatically, make possible the solution to the social division, economic isolation and political weakness it had long suffered as a 'province'.[21]

It is important to recognise, even so, that reform was not the natural priority of the new monarchy. Carlo Borbone owed his throne to the dynastic ambition and diplomatic intelligence of his mother, exploiting the temporary weakness of the Emperor; and to keep it he had to fulfil his dynastic and diplomatic obligations to Spain, to France and to Britain. An Austrian attempt to regain the kingdom had to be defeated in 1744, war being followed in due course by diplomatic *rapprochement*, sealed by the marriage of Carlo's son, Ferdinando, to the Austrian Maria Carolina. At the same time, the new dynasty needed to re-create a court, refurbishing the old palaces in Naples and building modern ones, as at Caserta, and embellishing them with the great Farnese art collection. Such 'dynastic' priorities were a necessary consequence of the manner in which Carlo Borbone acquired the kingdom, and need to be respected by historians: 'reform' would be pursued on terms compatible with them.

In the event, the new monarchy responded promptly to the expectations of its subjects. Headed by the purposeful Joachim de Montealegre, Marchese de Salas, who had previous experience of Philip V's French-inspired reform programme in Spain, and guided by the wily Tuscan jurist Bernardo Tanucci, the government of Carlo VII took initiatives on several fronts. Easiest to contemplate, because they reinforced the political priorities of the monarchy, were measures against the Church. The refusal to accept papal demands for the investiture of the new king was followed by an attempt to restrict clerical immunity and assert (at least in principle) the royal right to tax clerical goods. Here the legacy of Giannone was a useful resource; for although Giannone

[21] Paolo Mattia Doria, *Massime del governo spagnolo a Napoli* (1709–10), edited by G. Galasso and V. Conti (Naples, 1973). Pietro Giannone, *Storia civile del Regno di Napoli*, four vols. (Naples, 1723). For comment on the 'provincial' theme, Giuseppe Giarrizzo, 'Un "regno governato in provincia": Napoli tra Austria e Spagna 1690–1740', in *P.M. Doria fra rinnovamento e tradizione*, ed. G. Papuli (Galatina, 1985), 311–25; and on Neapolitan political culture under the Austrian Habsburgs, Giuseppe Ricuperati, 'Napoli e i viceré austriaci 1707–1734', in AA.VV., *Storia di Napoli*, vol. VII (Cava de' Tirreni, 1972), 347–457. But for the sense of expectation which greeted the new monarchy, see above all Franco Venturi, *Settecento riformatore, I: Da Muratori a Beccaria, 1730–1764* (Turin, 1969), 28–46.

himself had been in exile since 1723, and was by now in prison in Savoy, his friends and disciples actively promoted these and subsequent anti-curial initiatives. Other reforms were directed at the organisation of the law courts and the codification of the laws of the kingdom; these would have begun to curb the independent jurisdictions of the nobility as well as the privileges of the lawyers. Institutionally and technically, however, such reforms represented an enormous challenge, and Tanucci shrank from following them through.[22]

Perhaps the greatest hopes were attached to the third of the new monarchy's initiatives, the promotion of commerce. Advised by Doria and others, the government created a new tribunal specifically for the purpose in 1739, the Supremo Magistrato del Commercio. In proposing the new magistracy to a meeting of nobles and ministers in June, Montealegre held out the prospect that the natural advantages of the kingdom would at last be harnessed by protection of native products such as silk, while commerce would be encouraged by the introduction of a standard system of regulation in the ports.[23]

Alas, the proceedings of the Supremo Magistrato del Commercio did not match these expectations. It first convened on 5 November 1739, with a membership of nobles, 'togati' or ministers of the robe, and 'ministri negozianti' or merchant counsellors. It was immediately agreed to meet twice a week in the early evening, 'from 23 hours until 2 at night in winter, with the possibility of bringing forward the hours in summer, if appropriate'. Priority was to be given to the establishment of consuls in the ports, and to the determination of their jurisdictions.[24] It quickly became clear that this would not be straightforward. The noble members objected that the consuls would usurp the jurisdiction of the barons. The *togati* responded that a new set of laws would be needed, since consuls from a merchant background would not have the requisite knowledge of the existing laws. By 20 November, the

[22] On the reform initiatives of the 1730s, Elvira Chiosi, 'Il Regno dal 1734 al 1799', in *Storia del mezzogiorno*, vol. IV, part ii, *Il Regno dagli Angioini ai Borboni* (Naples, 1986), 384–96; and Raffaele Ajello, 'Legislazione e crisi del diritto commune nel Regno di Napoli. Il tentativo di codificazione Carlino', in *Studi e ricerche sul settecento*, ed. E. Sestan (Naples, Istituto italiano per gli studi storici, 1968), 172–223.

[23] Archivio di Stato di Napoli (hereafter ASN), manuscripts of the Tribunali antichi, Fasc. 1728: 'Supremo Magistrato del Commercio', ff. 3–12: 'Registro delle deliberazioni prese nelle conferenze, ordinate da S[ua] M[ajesta] tenersi nella Secr[eter]ia di Stato, Guerra e Marina, circa il commercio, 10 Giugno 1739'.

[24] ASN, Tribunali antichi 1728, (new foliation) ff. 1–2: 'Relazione succinto di quanto è stato agitato, deliberato, ed oprato nella prima sessione del supremo magistrato del commercio tenuta il 5 di Novembre 1739.' The decision on the hours of meeting is on f. 1v: the hours of the day were calculated, in Naples as in much of Italy, as beginning at or just before sunset. See Roberto Colzi, 'Che ora era? Raffronto tra le ore all'italiana e alla francese a Roma', *Studi Romani*, XLIII (1995), 93–102.

magistrates were clearly divided into three interests.[25] On 23 November they became embroiled in a new argument, when two nobles disputed precedence, and the *togati* claimed that they alone should vote to resolve the dispute, since it was a matter of law; it was late in the evening before this meeting ended.[26] Summoned to a conference by Montealegre on 25 November, the magistrates humbly agreed to try again. A compromise was reached over the consuls, and discussion began on measures to encourage silk manufacture.[27] But even before the end of 1739 it had become clear that no radical change in the regulatory framework of Neapolitan commerce would be achieved. For all the hopes attached to it, the new magistracy was still locked into modes of procedure inherited from the sixteenth century, and hostage to the entrenched rivalry of nobility and *togati*.[28] Its minutes are striking evidence of the obstacles to reform within the structure of government which the new monarchy had taken over.

The advent of the Enlightenment in Naples can be dated almost as precisely as the restoration on the monarchy, to 1753–4. It was effectively the initiative of one man, the abbé and university professor Antonio Genovesi. His *Discorso sopra il vero fine delle lettere e delle scienze* (1753) was its manifesto, and his chair in 'Commerce and mechanics', created for him in 1754 by Bartolomeo Intieri, was its platform.[29] For Intieri, a Tuscan agronomist who had come to Naples more than twenty years earlier, the chair was the culmination of a series of initiatives he had taken to encourage interest in Newtonian science and in the study of commerce; he had been an early and enthusiastic reader of Jean-François Melon's *Essai politique sur le commerce* (1734).[30] For Genovesi, the chair represented the opportunity for a new beginning, in both his own and the kingdom's intellectual life. He himself had previously taught

[25] ASN, Tribunali antichi 1728 (new foliation), ff. 41–2, 39–40, 37–8, 35–6, 33–4: 9, 13, 16, 17, 20 9bre [Novembre] 1739.

[26] ASN, Tribunal antichi 1728 ff. 31–2: 23 9bre 1739: emphasising the 'indecency' (*indecenza*) of such discord, the president finally persuaded the *togati* to desist, and since it was 'più delle tre ore di notte', to agree to postpone a decision on the issue.

[27] ASN, Tribunali antichi 1728 ff. 25–30: 'Conferenza coll'intervento del Magistrato Supremo di Commercio a 25 9bre 1739'; ff. 23, 21–2, 17–18, 19–20, 15–16, 13–14: 26 9bre 1739, primo Decembre, 3 Xbre, 7 Xbre, 10 Xbre, and 14 Xbre 1739.

[28] On the sixteenth century, Raffaele Ajello, 'Alle origini del problema meridionale nell'età moderna', the introduction to his *Una società anomala. Il programma e la sconfitta della nobiltà napoletana in due memoriali cinquecenteschi* (Naples, 1996), 9–260.

[29] On the creation of the chair 'di commercio e di meccanica': Venturi, *Da Muratori a Beccaria*, 562–5; it was effectively the first university chair in political economy in Europe.

[30] Franco Venturi, 'Alle origini dell'Illuminismo napoletano: dal carteggio di Bartolomeo Intieri', *Rivista Storica Italiana*, LXXI (1959), 416–56; and *Da Muratori a Beccaria*, pp. 552–62. Vincenzo Ferrone, *Scienza, natura, religione: mondo newtoniano e cultura Italiana nel primo settecento* (Naples, 1982), 546–60.

philosophy, and had aspired to be a professor of theology. His transformation into a professor of commerce, however, was far more than a personal conversion. Genovesi believed that his countrymen had fallen behind the leading nations of Europe in their thinking, and specifically in their thinking about the material and moral welfare of society in the age of commerce. It was a sensitivity shared by other Italian observers: what was once the richest and intellectually most advanced country in Europe was now well behind the northern European nations in both respects, and apparently in danger of falling still further back. But Genovesi's apprehension of the point was unusully sharp, and it led him to seek – with a puposefulness matched only by Beccaria and Verri in Milan – the participation of Naples in the European movement of the Enlightenment. Genovesi's initiative, in other words, was not simply a response to the frustration of the restored monarchy's first efforts at reform; and it should not be thought of as marking another phase of reform. His objectives were intellectual and educational, not immediately political.

To fulfil them, he began a programme of translation and commentary on French and British economic writing. The most substantial undertaking was the *Storia del commercio della Gran Bretagna* (1757–8), an Italian version of John Cary's 1695 *Essay on the State of England*, which Genovesi and his brother translated from the more recent, expanded, French edition by Vincent de Gournay and Georges-Marie Butel-Dumont, and to which he added extensive notes. Genovesi shared Intieri's admiration for Melon, praising his demonstration that commerce could be studied as a science; but he was also quick to read and engage with the work of Melon's critic, David Hume (in a French edition of the *Discours politiques*). He likewise responded promptly to Montesquieu's *Esprit des Lois*, the first Italian translation of which was published in Naples in 1751. In commenting on these and other works Genovesi was keen to apply their lessons to the circumstances of the kingdom; but he also sought to engage with their arguments in general terms, treating political economy as a science the understanding of whose principles must precede their application. His own synthetic economic writing, the *Lezioni di Commercio o sia d'economia civile* (1765–7), was a critical response to a Europe-wide discussion, written on the assumption that political economy was a common Enlightenment discourse.[31]

A second dimension to Genovesi's activity was equally characteristic

[31] Antonio Genovesi, *Storia del commercio della Gran Bretagna* etc., in *Scritti economici*, ed. M.L. Perna, 2 vols. (Naples, 1984); *Delle lezioni di commercio o sia d'economia civile* (Naples, 1765, 1767, with a second edition in 1768 and 1770); the first edition was reprinted in the series *Scrittori classici italiani di economia politica*, ed. P. Custodi, vols. VII–X, (Milan 1803–4).

of the Enlightenment. At the heart of the *Discorso delle lettere e delle scienze* was an appeal to the *studiosa gioventù* of the kingdom to take up the study of letters and sciences, to enlighten the nation and to animate its industry. Genovesi called for an Academy of the Learned to be instituted in the capital, to which all the learned, and especially *gli illuminati giovani* (the enlightened youth) in the provinces could communicate their discoveries to the improvement of agriculture, commerce and the manufacturing arts. Though he also appealed to 'the great' and to the clergy to encourage these interests, it was to the young, the third or middle rank, that Genovesi looked for the leadership now required to harness the natural advantages of the kingdom and restore its greatness.[32] In effect, the *Discorso* was a call to educate a new elite which would be free of the stifling prejudices of the nobility and *togati*, and committed to the *bene commune* of the country.

Genovesi would later underline the importance of education in the chapter of the *Lezioni* devoted specifically to 'the condition and natural strengths of the kingdom in respect to arts and commerce'. Believing that command of the people's 'opinions' was the key to government, he advocated both the encouragement and the public inspection of schools and the university. Teaching in these should be from published books, not private manuscripts; the secretive methods of the freemasons, Genovesi agreed, were contrary to good laws. There was no serious danger of a people being over-educated, as Mandeville and others had suggested; on the contrary, the education of both peasants and women would be positively beneficial. For without a much more extensive education, there was no prospect of remedying the kingdom's backwardness in the sciences and the arts: the arts of agriculture as much as those of luxury.[33]

The clarity of Genovesi's strategy for public education is as striking as his persistence in advocating it. His was no longer the traditional humanist ideal of the good counsellor, who advised ministers directly by means of manuscript memoranda. Instead Genovesi had chosen to appeal to men of good will outside the ranks of government, using his lectures and his programme of publications to create, for the first time in Naples, a genuinely informed, independent body of public opinion. In the terms of recent Enlightenment scholarship, he sought to establish a 'public sphere', separate and at a distance from the 'private sphere'

[32] Antonio Genovesi, *Discorso sopra il vero fine delle lettere e delle scienze* (Naples, 1753), in *Scritti economici*, 9–57, esp. 47–50.

[33] Genovesi, *Lezioni di commercio*, Parte Prima, cap. XXII 'Dello stato e delle naturali forze del Regno di Napoli per rispetto all'arti e al commercio', ss. iv (& note), ix-xxi. Revisions which Genovesi made to these passages in the second edition of the work are noted by Franco Venturi, *Illuministi italiani V Riformatori napoletani*, (Milan & Naples, 1962), 224–35.

of the court and the royal administration.[34] Only if there emerged a public with the knowledge to form and the freedom to express its opinions, his initiatives implied, would the kingdom's intellectual life be opened to the great issues of human welfare now being discussed elsewhere in Europe, and its rulers be enabled to benefit from the new ideas.

The strategy of pursuing Enlightenment before reform was also well suited to its time, the last two decades of Tanucci's long ministry. The old jurist distrusted the new man of letters, and particularly the political economist. The gulf between the two was acutely evident in 1764, when famine struck several parts of Italy, Tuscany and Naples hardest of all.[35] Genovesi responded by publishing the works of an earlier Tuscan agronomist and a member of the Gournay circle in favour of freeing the grain trade from controls, adding his own forceful commentaries on the urgency of doing so in the present straits of the kingdom.[36] Tanucci preferred to intensify controls, attempting to force the declaration of stocks of grain and compel its sale at a fixed price; once the immediate crisis was over he strengthened the monopoly of the *Annona* which procured the capital's grain supply on terms weighted against the provincial producers.[37]

Tanucci was much more willing to take on the Church, and was happy to call upon Genovesi's assistance for this purpose. In 1767 he committed the monarchy, in alliance with the other Bourbon powers, to the expulsion of the Jesuits and the expropriation of their property; as an affirmation of intellectual allegiance, Tanucci subsequently sanctioned the publication of a new edition of Giannone's *Storia civile* (1770). But this was consistent with the anti-clerical traditions of the Neapolitan jurists: though Genovesi willingly devoted his final years (and failing health) to the cause, the campaign against the Church did not mark the minister's conversion to the Enlightenment. Not until Tanucci was finally removed from power at the instigation of Maria Carolina, in 1776, was the monarchy willing to respond to the climate of Enlight-

[34] On this point, Maria Luisa Perna, 'L'universo communicativo di Antonio Genovesi', in *Editoria e cultura a Napoli nel XVIII secolo*, ed. Anna Maria Rao (Naples, 1998), 391–404; and on Genovesi's educational objectives, Elvira Chiosi, *Lo spirito del secolo. Politica e religione a Napoli nell'età dell'illuminismo* (Naples, 1992), ch. 3: 'Intellettuali e plebe', 79–85.

[35] On the impact of the famines, Franco Venturi, *Settecento riformatore, V.i: L'Italia dei lumi 1764–1790* (Turin, 1987), 221–423.

[36] *L'agricoltore sperimentato di Cosimo Trinci con alcune giunte dell'abate Genovesi* (Naples, 1764; originally published in Lucca, 1726); and *Riflessioni sull'economia generale dei grani, tradotte dal Francese, con un discorso preliminare del Signor Abbate Genovesi* (Naples, 1765), a translation of Claude Herbert, *Essai sur la police générale des grains* (1754), both reprinted in *Scritti economici*, II, 869–1130, 1131–235.

[37] Paolo Macry, *Mercato e società nel Regno di Napoli. Commercio del grano e politica economica del '700* (Naples, 1974), 413–37.

enment opinion which Genovesi (who died in 1769) had worked so hard to create.

By the later 1770s a new generation of men of letters had emerged to succeed Genovesi: Giuseppe Maria Galanti, Francesco Longano, Gaetano Filangieri, Francesco Mario Pagano, Giuseppe Palmieri, the brothers Domenico and Francescantonio Grimaldi, Domenico Cirillo and Melchiorre Delfico. Directly or indirectly they were all Genovesi's pupils; and they were confident that they lived in an age, in Filangieri's phrase, in which 'la filosofia è venuta in soccorso de' governi' – philosophy has come to the aid of rulers. Moreover the government's willingness to accept philosophy's offer of assistance meant that from the late 1770s until the early 1790s Enlightenment and reform did intersect: expectations were as high as in the 1730s, and this time the achievements were by no means negligible.

As before, but with a new confidence, the crown made its priority the limiting of the independence of the Church. First in 1776, and again, definitively, in the later 1780s, it challenged Rome's entitlement to the *Chinea*, the ceremonial presentation of a white horse to the Pope as a symbol of feudal homage. Disputes with more substantial implications occurred over the crown's rights of appointment, culminating in the contested nomination of Andrea Serrao as Bishop of Potenza in 1782, and over the decision to appropriate and sell monastic property in Calabria after the disastrous earthquake of 1784.[38] Again the legacy of Giannone was invoked: Giuseppe Cestari was encouraged to prepare another edition of the *Storia civile* (1792–3), and Eleonora Fonseca Pimentel translated a treatise of 1707 by Niccolo Caravita denying the Papacy any right over the kingdom.[39] But the monarchy was now also willing to pursue reform in the sphere to which Genovesi had sought to redirect attention: the economy, and the feudal system which was regarded as such an obstacle to its development.

In 1782 the government created a new Supremo Consiglio delle Finanze, and gave it a status and authority significantly greater than those of the old Supremo Magistrato del Commercio. The new Council was not a tribunal, but was given powers over the several magistracies with economic responsibilities, and was expected to send visitors into the provinces to gather information on the state of agriculture and commerce.[40] Advice was sought from those with

[38] Elvira Chiosi, *Andrea Serrao* (Naples, 1981).

[39] Elvira Chiosi, 'La tradizione giannoniana nella seconda metà del settecento', in Raffaele Ajello (ed.), *Pietro Giannone e il suo tempo*, 2 vols. (Naples, 1980), 763–823. The tract translated by Fonseca Pimentel was the *Nullum Ius* of Niccolo Caravita; the Italian title was *Niun diritto compete al Sommo Pontefice sul Regno di Napoli* (Naples, 1790).

[40] Chiosi, 'Il Regno dal 1734 al 1799', *Storia del Mezzogiorno*, IV.ii, 437–8.

economic expertise. Ferdinando Galiani was appointed one of its secretaries, contributing memoranda on opportunities for external trade and in particular a commercial treaty with Russia.[41] Giuseppe Maria Galanti was encouraged to extend his initial investigation of economic conditions in the Molise into a comprehensive 'geographical and political description' of the entire kingdom.[42] Reform was still frustrated by privilege, especially in manufacturing. But internal trade was gradually liberalised: tolls were abolished in 1792, and the various *annona* which controlled the marketing of grain and other foods were dismantled. A particularly sharp critique of the operation of these in the fish trade was contributed by Pagano in 1789: the future republican unhesitatingly looked to the king, as 'the Titus of our times', to remove the abuse.[43] Least tractable was the issue of feudal property, and the practices of primogeniture and entails which supported it. Neverthless, Filangieri's eloquent denunciation of 'la gran macchina de' feudi' as the greatest obstacle to the kingdom's development, reinforced by Galanti's detailed investigations of the conditions of life in the provinces, created a climate of opinion which encouraged the Supremo Consiglio delle Finanze to decide in 1791 to sell as allodial land fiefs which had 'devolved' to the crown. Although the attempt to implement the decision ran into fierce opposition, the monarchy was widely perceived to have begun, at long last, to dismantle a system which symbolised as well as entrenched the kingdom's backwardness.[44]

Even in this later period, however, the apparent vindication of Filangieri's belief that philosophy was coming to the aid of governments should not lead to a simple assimilation of the Enlightenment in Naples with the cause of reform. For the Enlightenment was at the same time also strengthening its independent social base and extending its intellectual range. The standard-bearer of Genovesi's legacy was Giuseppe Maria Galanti, who proclaimed his discipleship in a precocious *Elogio* of the master in 1772. A more substantial homage was the

[41] Furio Diaz, 'L'Abbate Galiani consigliere di commercio estero', *Rivista Storica Italiana*, LXXX (1968), 854–92.

[42] Giuseppe Maria Galanti, *Descrizione del Molise* (1781); *Nuova descrizione storica e geografica delle Sicilie* (1786–90, 2nd ed. 1793–4). Others involved with the the work of the Council were Domenico Grimaldi and Giuseppe Palmieri; Gaetano Filangieri was belatedly and briefly a member from 1787 until his death in 1788.

[43] Francesco Mario Pagano, *Ragionamento sulla libertà del commercio del pesce in Napoli, diretto al Regio Tribunale dell'Ammiragliato e Consolato di Mare* (Naples, 1789), reprinted by Venturi in *Illuministi Italiani V: Riformatori Napoletani*, 842–53.

[44] Pasquale Villani, 'Il dibattito sulla feudalità nel Regno di Napoli dal Genovesi al Canosa', in *Saggi e ricerche sul settecento*, ed. Sestan, 252–331; Anna Maria Rao, *L''amaro della feudalità'. La devoluzione di Arnone e la questione feudale a Napoli alla fine del '700* (Naples, 1984).

remarkable series of publishing initiatives by which Galanti attempted to extend the intellectual horizons of the Neapolitan public. In common with other branches of the capital's commercial life, Neapolitan publishing was a world of privileges and defensive monopolies, in which even those willing to take on new works struggled to secure a return.[45] Galanti tackled these difficulties head on. In 1777 he established the *Società letteraria di Napoli*, later the *Società letteraria e tipografica*, and entered into commercial correspondence with the celebrated *Société typographique de Neuchâtel* and other Swiss publishing houses. Among the publications of the Neapolitan Society was the 'Collection of philosophic and political histories of ancient and modern nations', in which series Galanti included his own works on the ancient inhabitants of Italy and on the Molise, a translation of the multi-volume 'general history' of the Abbé Millot, and an anthology of writings by contemporary French and Scottish historians, including Condillac, Chastellux, Hume, Adam Ferguson and William Robertson. When the *Società Letteraria* finally went into administration in 1782, Galanti established the *Gabinetto letterario*, through which he brought out his long-projected translation of the whole of Robertson's *History of Charles V* (1787–9). (His former partners, meanwhile, brought out a translation of the Scot's *History of America* in 1789.) Galanti's commercial acumen may not have matched his intellectual enthusiasm, for which he was mocked by Galiani; but his efforts were unrivalled as an individual contribution, of time as well as money, to the practical enlargement of the 'public sphere' in the kingdom of Naples.[46]

But perhaps the most striking social aspect of the late Enlightenment in Naples was its association with Freemasonry. With the eclipse of Tanucci, a constant enemy of the movement, the number of lodges grew rapidly, both in the capital and in the provinces. Every rite was represented, along with several individual hybrids. Nobles and men of letters both provided enthusiastic recruits, creating an unprecedented forum for social interaction. A group of men of letters in the capital, including Longano, Cirillo, Francescantonio Grimaldi, Pagano and Filangieri, were particularly associated with the 'Harmony' Lodge, following the English rite; and the same group and others also met at the villa of the brothers Di Gennaro, the dukes of Belforte and Cantalupo, between Mergellina and Posillipo. (Among the men of letters, Galanti was the one major figure to keep his distance from

[45] For an overview of Neapolitan publishing in the century, Anna Maria Rao, ed., 'Introduzione' to *Editoria e cultura a Napoli nel XVIII secolo*, 3–55.

[46] Maria Luisa Perna, 'Giuseppe Maria Galanti editore', in *Miscellanea Walter Maturi* (Turin, 1966), 221–58, an excellent account, which Rachele Via, *Il libro e la storia delle idee. Le Società Tipografiche di Napoli e Neuchâtel alla fine del '700* (Soveria Mannelli, 1995), supplements.

Freemasonry.) Lodges were also constituted in several provincial cities, on the mainland and in Sicily.[47]

The enthusiasm displayed by the men of letters for the secretive, 'private' world of masonry is not, on the face of it, easily reconciled with an Enlightenment emphasis on the public. As Ferrone has argued, however, the appeal of the lodges seems to have lain in the opportunity they offered for independent voluntary association, for which there were otherwise few legitimate openings in the kingdom, least of all in the provinces.[48] Given Maria Carolina's interest in Freemasonry, which had frustrated Tanucci's last attempts to suppress it, there was also a potential connection with the court. But if the connection existed, its only substantial result appears to have been the *Reale Accademia di Scienze e Belle Lettere*, founded in 1779 with (in part) a masonic inspiration. In the event the Academy was too closely regulated by the court to satisfy the men of letters, and soon became inactive.[49] Later, in the early 1790s, the lodges do seem to have provided a framework for clandestine 'Jacobin' activity;[50] but there is little to suggest that they had such a political character in the 1780s. The popularity of Freemasonry in Naples may well attest to the difficulty of establishing a genuinely 'public' sphere in the kingdom, but the lodges at least offered men of letters a form of institutional sociability which was largely independent of the court, the royal administration and the church.

For all their optimism over the prospects for reform, most of those active in this phase of the Enlightenment in Naples continued to keep their distance from government. Their approach remained that of Genovesi: the cultivation of an educated and informed public opinion, through which philosophers might indirectly guide the reforming activity of government.[51] By far the most eloquent and developed statement of this strategy was offered by Gaetano Filangieri, the acknowledged leader of the new generation of Enlightenment philosophers.

Filangieri's *La scienza della legislazione*, most of which he wrote before

[47] Ferrone, *I profeti dell'illuminismo*, 207–18, 246–50; Giuseppe Giarrizzo, *Massoneria e illuminismo nell'Europa del Settecento* (Venice, 1994), 176–9.

[48] Ferrone, *I profeti dell'illuminismo*, 247–8.

[49] On the Neapolitan Academy, Elvira Chiosi, '*Lumen accessit*', ch. 4 of her *Lo spirito del secolo*, 107–42; by comparison, it has been argued that its Torinese counterpart did provide a public forum for the collaboration of court and lodge: Vincenzo Ferrone, 'The Accademia Reale delle Scienze: cultural sociability and men of letters in Turin of the Enlightenment under Vittorio Amadeo III', *Journal of Modern History*, 70 (1998), 519–60.

[50] Giarrizzo, *Massoneria e illuminismo*, 390–6.

[51] The most notable exception to this pattern was the economist Ferdinando Galiani. Mortified by his recall from Paris in 1769, after a diplomatic indiscretion made it impossible for Tanucci to continue his posting as Secretary to the Neapolitan embassy, Galiani apparently welcomed the opportunity to serve as Secretary to the *Supremo Consiglio delle Finanze* from 1782.

he was thirty, was published in successive pairs of volumes in 1780, 1783 and 1785. His ambition was no less than to be the new Montesquieu; but where Montesquieu had sought only to explain the variety of laws as they were, Filangieri would establish the 'rules' of legislation as it ought to be.[52] By adopting these rules, Filangieri argued, the rulers of Europe would be able to reform their archaic law codes, to the improvement of their economies, the better administration of justice and punishment and the provision of public education.[53] Education was especially important to Filangieri (as to Genovesi), because it was the key to the formation of *l'opinione pubblica*: where the people were properly educated, public opinion would be 'wise and virtuous'. To reinforce the effect of education, Filangieri also advocated liberty of the press, on condition that every publication should bear the name of its author, to ensure that the freedom should not be abused.[54]

But Filangieri did not merely restate Genovesi's plea for public education and free discussion. Underlying his argument was a new and radical conception of public opinion as the expression of the ultimate sovereignty of the people. A legitimate government, according to Filangieri, was one which was able to represent the wills of the individual members of the society.[55] Filangieri did not envisage that the people would normally exercise supreme power themselves: a perfect democracy was possible only in the smallest states. But laws should only be made or reformed after consulting *la volontà de' popoli*, the will of the people, and with the support of the majority of the votes of public opinion. The legitimacy of a monarchy was thus as dependent on public opinion as that of a republic.[56] In consequence, the role of philosophers too had been transformed. When Filangieri proclaimed that in the past fifty years 'philosophy has come to the aid of rulers', he was not thinking in terms of their traditional role as the counsellors of kings. Philosophy now had a far greater responsibility, as the guide and voice of a public opinion which had the authority of the people's

[52] Gaetano Filangieri, *La scienza della legislazione*, first published in Naples, vols. I–II, 1780, III–IV, 1783, V–VI, 1785, with a further two volumes published posthumously in 1791 (Filangieri having died in 1788). I have used the edition entitled *La Scienza della legislazione, con giunta degli opuscoli scelti*, published in six volumes by the Società Tipografica de' Classici Italiani (Milan, 1822). For Filangieri's statements of intent, see the 'Introduzione' and 'Piano ragionato dell'opera' in vol. I, 3–14, 17–19.

[53] Population, agriculture and commerce were treated in Book II of the *Scienza della legislazione*, the administration of justice and punishment in Book III, and education in Book IV.

[54] Filangieri, *Scienza della legislazione*, Book IV 'Delle legge che riguardano l'educazione, i costumi e l'istruzione pubblica', esp. parts i, ch 2 and iii, ch 43.

[55] ibid, Book I 'Delle regole generali della scienza legislativa', ch I, esp p. 54.

[56] ibid, Bk I, chs 7, 10, pp. 86–7, 100–5.

will.[57] In this perspective, the willingness of Filangieri and his friends to encourage the reforming initiatives of the Bourbon monarchy represented far more than the simple identification of Enlightenment with reform; in principle, at least, the role of the philosophers was to facilitate the subordination of the monarchy to the will of the people. Well might Filangieri believe that a 'pacifica rivoluzione' was now in preparation, in the kingdom of Naples and throughout Europe.[58]

Filangieri's radicalisation of Genovesi's concept of public opinion was accompanied by a change in the intellectual interests of the new generation. Genovesi's interest in political economy was not forgotten: one of the earliest products of the second phase of the Enlightenment in Naples was an Italian version of Melon's *Essai politique sur le commerce*, published with notes and an introductory discourse by Longano in 1778.[59] As we have seen, Filangieri devoted the second book of the *Scienza della legislazione* to economic issues; and investigation of the specific economic and social conditions of the kingdom was a primary concern of Palmieri, Longano and, above all, Galanti. Even so, there are signs that the Neapolitans were disregarding more recent developments in economic thinking in favour of another interest of the late Enlightenment: the philosophy of history. This was the real subject of Longano's introduction to Melon.[60] It also underpinned Filangieri's treatment of legislation, informing in particular his conviction of the exceptional longevity of feudalism in the kingdom of Naples; and it inspired Galanti not only to translate and publish the best contemporary European historians, but to write the history of southern Italy before its conquest by the Romans.[61] There is one treatment of the subject, however, which deserves particular attention, both for its intellectual quality and because of its author's involvement in the Revolution of 1799 – Francesco Mario Pagano's *Saggi politici*.

Pagano published two versions of the *Saggi politici*, the first in two parts in 1783 and 1785, the second, corrected and enlarged (but also without sections present in the first), in 1791–2. The full title of the first edition gives the best indication of its contents: *Del civile corso delle nazioni*,

[57] ibid, Bk IV, part iii, ch 43, p. 39: 'philosophers rule by directing opinion, and kings philosophise in order to obtain the votes of that opinion'.

[58] ibid, Introduzione, 11.

[59] [J-F. Melon], *Saggio politico sul commercio, tradotto dal francese colle annotazioni dell' Ab. Longano*, 2 vols. (Naples, 1778).

[60] [Melon], *Saggio politico*, 'Discorso del notatore, su l'origine, progressi, vicende ed influenza del commercio degli Europei', i-xxxi; on which Ferrone, *I profeti dell'illuminismo*, 273–4; more fully, 'La fondazione panteistica dell'eguaglianza. Contributo al pensiero politico di Franceso Longano', *Rassegna Iberistica*, 56 (1996), 193–202.

[61] Melissa Calaresu, 'Images of ancient Rome in late eighteenth-century Neapolitan historiography', *Journal of the History of Ideas*, 58, 4 (1997), 641–61; on Galanti in particular, 649–56.

o sia de' principi, progressi, e decadenza delle società. (The short title 'Political Essays', he explained, was an indication that his treatment of the subject did not claim to be comprehensive.) In scope and subject-matter the work might be compared with the Scottish philosopher Adam Ferguson's *Essay on the History of Civil Society*, published some twenty years earlier in 1767 (and from which Galanti had published an extract in 1781).[62] Like Ferguson, Pagano traced the progress of society through the savage and barbarian states to the cultivated and polite, elaborating the attributes of each before finally explaining why polite societies were liable to grow corrupt and fall into decline. But beside these similarities, the differences between the two works are also marked, and reveal the extent to which Pagano was responding to specific preoccupations of the later Enlightenment.

There was certainly no equivalent in Ferguson for the first of Pagano's 'Essays', 'The period of human affairs, and the analysis of the human spirit as it was after the first physical catastrophes on earth.' Here Pagano outlined the natural history of man, depicting the earliest stage of human life as the struggle for survival in the face of the great natural catastrophes which had periodically struck the earth. These catastrophes included the great floods recorded in the traditions of the eastern nations and in the myth of Atlantis, as well as major earthquakes and volcanic eruptions. Their human and animal survivors, Pagano argued, would have had to take refuge on mountain tops and in caves, while the shock of such disasters would have reduced men's spirits to a state of extreme terror and self-pity. Out of their terror came the first gentile religions: unable to understand natural causes, men supposed that the gods were punishing them for a failure of worship. In due course these beliefs became the myths recorded by Hesiod, Homer and the ancient poets, which with the traditions of the eastern nations now offered the only access to the age of catastrophes.[63]

In developing this account of the beginnings of history Pagano frequently refered to his Neapolitan predecessor in the philosophy of history, Giambattista Vico. Homage to 'il nostro Vico' for his interpretation of ancient poetry and his theory of the cyclical *corso* of history was offset, however, by an insistence on their differences. Pagano emphasised that natural history and human history must be joined, not

[62] The comparison was drawn by an Italian reviewer of the first edition of the *Saggi politici*: see Franco Venturi, 'Scottish echoes in eighteenth-century Italy', in Istvan Hont and Michael Ignatieff (eds), *Wealth and Virtue. The shaping of political economy in the Scottish Enlightenment* (Cambridge University Press, 1983), 361–2.

[63] Francesco Mario Pagano, *Saggi politici. De' principii, progressi e decadenza delle società*, Edizione seconda, corretta ed accresciuta, (1791–2), edited by Luigi Firpo and Laura Salvetti Firpo (Naples, 1993), Saggio 1, 'Del periodo di tutte l'umane cose e dell'analisi dello spirito umano qual fu dopo le fisiche catastrofi della Terra'.

separated; and he reversed Vico's dismissal of ancient eastern, and particularly Egyptian wisdom, asserting that this was indeed our oldest source of knowledge of the world.[64] The emphasis on the inter-relation of natural and human history was a feature of late Enlightenment thought generally, and reflected the impact of the works of Buffon and Boulanger. But the recreation of the earliest natural and human history on the basis of ancient Egyptian wisdom reflected something more: the strong interest in the hermetic tradition which several Neapolitans, Longano, Cirillo and Francescantonio Grimaldi, as well as Pagano, appear to have derived from Freemasonry. The inspiration has been suggestively discussed by Ferrone and Giarrizzo; but it was advertised by Pagano himself, in the remarkable encomium upon the society of the lodges which he included in the dedication to the first edition of the *Saggi*.[65]

Even when Pagano moves on to savage and barbarian societies, the originality of his treatment is striking. Where Ferguson emphasised the role of conflict in forming societies, Pagano focussed simply on physical force: of men over women, wives being taken by abduction and rape, and of men over men, the stronger taking the weaker as their 'clients'. The family remained the only unit in this state, justice being conducted by vendetta.[66] It was in barbarian societies that the first public assemblies occurred; but the heads of families had responded by coming together to form an 'aristocrazia feudale', keeping the plebs as their clients or vassals. Such had been the condition of Rome in the early republic, and again of Europe after the barbarian invasions. Only very gradually did such societies learn to regulate the vendetta with the duel, to respect property, and to engage in agriculture and trade.[67]

By contrast, polite and cultivated societies were distinguished by the rule of written law and moderate government. The equality of citizens before the laws secured 'civil liberty'; but since men were unequal in strength and skill, 'political liberty' for all was unattainable. Pagano

[64] Pagano, *Saggi politici*, 13: 'Introduzione', where Pagano described Vico as opening a new path in the study of the moral and political sciences, breaking free of the long Italian preoccupation with the 'morals of states'; also p. 50: Saggio I, cap. i, where Vico is hailed as 'il primo a tentare ... tal nuovo e sconosciuto sentiero di ridurre a filosofia la storia', but where Pagano also makes it clear that human affairs are to be studied in conjunction with the phenomena of nature, and are subject to laws as constant as those governing nature; and pp. 64–70, 73: cap. viii–xi, for repeated criticism of Vico for his dismissal of the ancient wisdom of the Egyptians and Chaldeans. And pp. 117–18n, cap. xxx, on Vico's insight into mythology as the history of social progress.

[65] Francesco Mario Pagano, *De saggi politici. Volume I, Del civile corso delle Nazioni o sia de' principi, progressi, e decadenza delle società* (Naples, 1783), 'A coloro che legeranno', xix–xx. Ferrone, *I profeti dell'illuminismo*, chs. V–VI; Giarrizzo, *Massoneria e illuminismo*, 350–8.

[66] Pagano, *Saggi politici*, II, 'Del selvaggio stato degli uomini e dell'origine delle famiglie'.

[67] ibid, III, 'Dell'origine e stabilmento delle prime società'; IV, 'Del progresso delle barbare società. Del terzo ed ultimo loro periodo'.

expected rather that extremes of wealth would be mitigated by the emergence of a 'middle order', and he suggested that a division of powers could be maintained by a separate tribunal of independent magistrates. Such societies generally prefered commerce to war; and they honoured and educated women, recovering society's 'lost half'.[68] Their flaw was their vulnerability to corruption: luxury and a refined sensibility would encourage men to put their self-interest before that of the public, and eventually to surrender their liberty to despotism. Since men will not voluntarily return to a simpler state, the likeliest outcome of decline is conquest and a renewal of barbarism. Only if there were to be a fresh natural catastrophe would the cycle of human history begin all over again.[69]

Pagano had ended the first edition of the *Saggi* with two chapters in which he outlined the history of the kingdom of Naples in these terms, explaining its reduction to 'a feudal and dependent kingdom', but suggesting that the reforms begun by 'il gran Carlo' and continued by 'l'immortale Ferdinando', now offered a real prospect of restoring its ancient splendour.[70] Since the second edition dispensed with these chapters, it was suggested by Venturi that it be taken to mark the beginning of Pagano's disillusionment with the monarchy.[71] Less political in his judgements, Ferrone nevertheless believes that the *Saggi politici* reflect a deep disenchantment over the prospects of the kingdom.[72] But if we look at the Introduction which Pagano added to the second edition, a rather different interpretation of its significance is possible. Pagano used this introduction to outline the genesis of philosophical history – and to distinguish his version of it from the theories of his contemporaries. Among these were Rousseau, attacked by Pagano on several grounds, Ferguson, and the natural historians Buffon and Bailly.[73] The implication is that Pagano was now confident that his work belonged in a wider European setting, a confidence which would have been reinforced by its translation into French and (prospectively) German.[74] Such a contribution to the Enlightenment debate on the

[68] ibid, v, 'Delle società colte e polite'.

[69] ibid, vi, 'Della decadenza delle nazioni'.

[70] Pagano, *De saggi politici*, vol. ii (1785), vii, chs viii 'Generale prospetto della storia del Regno', x [i.e. ix], 'Continuazione, e conchiusione dell'opra'.

[71] Franco Venturi, *Illuministi Italiani V: riformatori napoletani* (Milan and Naples, 1962), 'Nota introduttiva' to the selection of Pagano's works, 823–5.

[72] Ferrone, *I profeti dell'illuminismo*, 298–300.

[73] Pagano, *Saggi politici*, 'Introduzione a' saggi politici', 9–44.

[74] A French translation of the first edition of the *Saggi politici* was begun by the Secretary to the French Legation in Naples, Aumary Duval, working under Pagano's eye; but it was still unfinished by 1799, when he gave it up. By contrast a German translation (likewise of the first edition) by Johann Gottfried Müller was published in 1796 in Leipzig, in two volumes, entitled *Versuche über den bürgerlichen Lauf der Nationen, oder über den Ursprung,*

progress and decline of societies in general had less need to display its specifically Neapolitan origins by praising the Bourbon kings and alluding to the lodges. By the beginning of the 1790s, therefore, Pagano's intellectual interests were taking him beyond his Neapolitan context, underlining the difference between the Enlightenment and the politics of reform within the monarchy. It would seem to be as mistaken to assume a necessary connection between them in the early 1790s as in the early 1750s.

If Enlightenment cannot simply be identified with reform, a direct connection between Enlightenment and revolution is even less likely. Nevertheless, adjustment to revolutionary circumstances was precisely what was required of Pagano and the surviving philosophers of his generation in the mid- and later 1790s. Although reform was still on the monarchy's agenda in the early 1790s, the execution of the French king and queen in 1793 provoked an abrupt reversal of the outlook in Naples: henceforth Maria Carolina and her husband would equate reform with revolution, and make it almost impossible to support one without engaging in the other. Pagano himself does not seem to have participated in the first Jacobin–masonic conspiracies in Naples in 1794; but he acted as counsel for the defence of those accused of doing so. Under suspicion, he was eventually denounced and imprisoned in 1796. Released in 1798, he went into exile in Rome, under its revolutionary republic. There he delivered and published a short address 'on the relation between agriculture, the arts and commerce' to the newly formed Society of that name, which provides some indication of the extent to which he was able to adapt his thinking to revolutionary circumstances.

The address was a rhetorical setpiece, in which a radicalisation of Pagano's language is clearly evident. He had no inhibitions about addressing the circumstances of a 'democratic' government, or in acknowledging that it required not only the 'formula' of democracy, but a 'revolutionising' of public spirit. But Pagano also continued to affirm that political change could not occur like a natural catastrophe, and that laws could never oblige men to return to an earlier state, any more than a butterfly could turn back into a caterpillar. He thus repudiated any recourse to an agrarian law as a solution to centuries of neglect of the land around Rome by great proprietors. Equally he rejected the view that democracy required the renunciation of commerce and the arts of luxury, because luxury was incompatible with

Fortgang und Verfall der bürgerlichen Gesellschaften; the Prefaces were dated 1790 and 1791, but it does not seem to be known whether and when Pagano came to hear of the translation.

patriotism. Commerce, he pointed out, was essential for countries which were sterile, or which needed a navy to defend their liberty. There were reforms, however, which would not overturn property right or disable commerce. Such measures could include a prohibition on wills or testamentary devices which divided an inheritance unequally (which Pagano believed contrary to natural equity); the 'progressive' taxation of large holdings; the encouragement of emphyteusis leases (leases for a period of years); and a programme of practical education by Agricultural Societies. In other words, radical legislative measures were just and desirable, if they went with the grain of historical development and the operation of a commercial economy. The opportunity to curb excessive riches for the benefit of public utility should be taken; but an attempt simply to reverse the outcome of history would be both ineffective and ruinous.[75]

Within four months Pagano had returned to Naples to play a leading role in the newly declared Republic. Appointed to the Committee responsible for drafting legislation for the Provisional Government, he actively contributed to framing all its major reforming measures.[76] The abolition of primogeniture and entails, which Pagano had already supported in Rome, was only the first of these. He next took a leading part in discussions over the law to abolish feudal right: here he sought to avoid the total alienation of the nobility by offering them some economic incentive to participate in the subsequent improvement of agriculture. Equally significant was his contribution to the drafting of the republic's constitution; and when this was published, on 1 April 1799, it was with an accompanying address by Pagano explaining its principles.

The purpose of the address was to explain the respects in which the proposed constitution differed from that of the French republic.[77] The declaration of the rights of man, Pagano accepted, was the 'solid and immutable base' of a modern constitution. But it was a mistake of the original (French) declaration to represent equality as itself a 'right' of man; rather, all rights derived from the single right of men in nature

[75] Francesco Mario Pagano, *Sulla relazione dell'agricoltura, delle arti e del commercio*, delivered to the Società di agricoltura, arti e commercio in Rome on 20 September 1798, and published in Rome in that year, reprinted in Delio Cantimori and Renzo de Felice (eds), *Giacobini italiani*, vol. II, (Bari 1964), 365–76.

[76] Venturi, 'Nota introduttiva', *Illuministi Italiani V: Riformatori Napoletani*, 828–32; but the fullest account and assessment of Pagano's role during the republic is that by Melissa Calaresu, 'Political culture in late eighteenth-century Naples: the writings of Francesco Mario Pagano' (Ph.D. thesis, University of Cambridge, 1994), ch. 7: 'Towards Revolution?: the late Neapolitan Enlightenment and the Parthenopean Republic of 1799'.

[77] Francesco Mario Pagano, address accompanying the *Progetto di costituzione della Repubblica Napolitana presentato al Governo Provvisorio dal Comitato di Legislazione*, reprinted by Venturi, *Illuministi Italiani V: Riformatori Napoletani*, 908–19.

to self-preservation and improvement.[78] From this came the right to liberty of thought, as well as the rights to property and to resistance in the face of despotism. In clarifying this last, political, right, however, Pagano sounded a note of caution: it was impossible to be precise about the identity of the 'people' who were to exercise it, since the people should not be understood to include either the ignorant and degraded plebs, or the 'gangrenous' aristocracy. The implications of this caution became evident when Pagano explained specific provisions of the new constitution. Instead of an assembly to propose legislation, this was entrusted to a restricted senate, charged with ensuring that the laws were properly framed. A college of censors, composed of men of wisdom who were more than fifty years old, was added in order to take responsibility for public education, moral as well as intellectual, and thus for preserving the republic from corruption. Finally, and directly in line with a suggestion in the *Saggi politici*, there was to be a tribunal of ephors (whose minimum age would be 45), with the responsibility of ensuring a balance between the legislative and executive powers, and hence of preventing the republic from becoming despotic.[79]

Pagano's writings of 1798–9 are too few and too brief to be the basis of definitive general conclusions about the relation between Enlightenment and revolution in the Neapolitan case. Nevertheless, some points seem clear. Pagano evidently had few inhibitions about active participation in the very public forum of a revolutionary republic. Faithful to the radical intuitions of his friend Filangieri, Pagano lived the Enlightenment commitment to public discussion as the means to form opinion and influence legislation. His masonic allegiance proved to be no bar to such public, political sociability – though equally it does not seem to have led him to involvement in the conspiracies of 1794, perhaps the closest documentable connection between the lodges and revolutionary activity.

Nevertheless, Pagano also remained true to Filangieri's conviction that it was for philosophers to direct public opinion: the provisions for a legislative senate, a college of censors and a tribunal of ephors were open expressions of his belief that the wise and experienced should exercise moral and political leadership over the people. Pagano may have had the example of the new American constitution in mind; but the proposals also suggest his general unease with the implications of democracy.[80] Even if he almost certainly experienced the events of the

[78] Pagano had mentioned the existence of this original right in the 'Introduzione' to the second edition of the *Saggi politici* (p. 17), but had not then presented it as the source of 'the rights of man'.

[79] Cf. Pagano, *Saggi politici*, Saggio v, ch xxii, pp. 356–7.

[80] On the character of Pagano's republicanism: Anthony Pagden, 'Francesco Mario Pagano's "Republic of Virtue": Naples 1799', in Biancamaria Fontana (ed), *The invention*

mid-1790s as a sharp break in his life, cutting him off from the world he had known hitherto, and demanding that he make radical intellectual and political adjustments,[81] he was still attached to his Enlightenment past. As far as possible he sought to remain consistent to the principles of his earlier work, and to his conception of the philosopher's role in the public sphere; and he did not hide his disagreements with the younger Jacobins over their indiscriminate hostility to luxury and radical conception of democracy. Pagano was clearly aware that some distance separated his thinking from that of the new generation of revolutionaries.

At a deeper intellectual level, the distance was perhaps even greater. Pagano was an exceptionally compelling exponent of the late eighteenth-century sense of the potential of natural catastrophes to plunge society back to its primitive beginnings; but he did not believe that human will and law could achieve anything so radical. Change in human society was a slower, longer-term, process: while reform was possible, revolution, in the sense of the abrupt transformation of the social order, was not. Even if Pagano acted in 1799 as if he was convinced that the replacement of the monarchy by a republic represented an excellent opportunity for reform, the pace of events was too fast for the fulfillment of his hopes. It was not simply that the Neapolitan republic was so short-lived; but the working out of social change required, on Pagano's own historical philosophy, a time-scale far longer than that needed to enact measures of legislation.

In this respect, I suggest, Pagano's part in the events of 1799 makes a point for the Neapolitan Enlightenment as a whole. The outcome of the Enlightenment in Naples should not be identified simply with the defeat of the revolution of 1799. If the Enlightenment of Genovesi, of Filangieri and of Pagano is to be judged, it should be in the longer perspective advocated by its own historical and social philosophy. As it happened, Cuoco's fear that as a result of the failings of the republic of 1799 an opportunity had been lost for the forseeable future was not borne out: 1799 was not the end of all reform. The advent of direct French rule in 1806, lasting until 1815, allowed many of the measures proposed by the republic to be carried through, and what was achieved was not afterwards reversed by the restored Bourbons. Most crucially, feudal rights and common lands were privatised, permitting the development of individual landownership. Whether the economic and social consequences of this long-sought change, in the form of a new regime

---

of the modern republic (Cambridge, 1994), 139–53. But the evidence that his was a 'modern republicanism' seems to me to be exiguous.

[81] A point convincingly emphasised by Galasso, 'I giacobini meridionali', *La filosofia in soccorso de' governi*, 513–15.

of latifundist landownership, answered the expectations of the reformers is open to question.[82] But the eventual occurrence of the change tends to confirm that the success or failure of the Enlightenment is not to be assessed exclusively in relation to the revolution of 1799; the true test of the Enlightenment in Naples lies in the longer term, in the actual progress of the society of the Italian south over the next half century and beyond.

[82] On latifundism in the Italian south in the nineteenth century: Marta Petrusewicz, *Latifundium. Moral economy and material life in a European periphery* (Ann Arbor, Michigan, 1996).

KWAME NKRUMAH AND THE CHIEFS: THE FATE OF 'NATURAL RULERS' UNDER NATIONALIST GOVERNMENTS

By Richard Rathbone

READ 5 MARCH 1999

THERE is a popular and reasonably accurate view of pre-colonial government in Africa which believes that Africans were governed by rulers who are usually referred to as chiefs.[1] While there were some societies in Africa where authority was exercised in a less obviously hierarchical fashion,[2] most African polities were dominated by individual rulers whose legitimacy depended, as in so many other parts of the world, upon descent and by their near monopoly of material or spiritual means of coercion. Historians of Africa have obviously been interested in the fate of these institutions over time and have broadly concluded that by the twentieth century these monarchies were dying institutions. There are several studies of very varied cases which range from the virtual extinction of chieftaincy at the hands of colonial powers[3] to others in which colonialism deprived traditional rulers of absolute sovereignty and did so by shielding them from the simultaneous corrosion and vitalisation of modernisation.[4] Like most generalisations, this is caricature. But it is fair to say that modern historiography has regarded chiefs and chieftaincy as the peripheral tags of a pre-modern order; where chieftaincy survived into the second half of the twentieth century, it was because of the un-natural, instrumental preservation of these archaic forms of government and value allocation, by colonialism. Chiefs are widely viewed as conservative. They have been described as being the unwitting or knowing dupes of the reactionary agendas of, first, colonial policy-makers and, later, tribalist politicians; one of

[1] Much of the West African nineteenth-century travel literature and that of the early colonial administrators refers to these rulers as kings. The twentieth century use of the title 'chief' was clearly an intentional demotion connoting domination. It was also, I believe, an attempt after 1901 to escape the confusion in official papers between the British King and subject monarchs.

[2] Such societies are frequently if not always accurately referred to as 'acephalous'.

[3] See for example Jean Suret-Canale's *Essays on African History; from the slave trade to neocolonialism* (translated by Christopher Hurst). (London, 1984).

[4] A position adopted by many of the authors in Michael Crowder and Obaro Ikime (eds), *West African Chiefs; their changing status under colonial rule and independence* (New York, 1970).

the reviewers of Dennis Austin's *Politics in Ghana* described chiefs' 'reactionary ideas and their dedication to tribalistic and ritualistic oligarchy'.[5] Without these manipulative agencies, the argument goes, Africa would have shared in the universal history which has seen the demise of *anciens régimes* from Paris to Peking. What passes for chieftaincy today, or forty years ago, bears scant resemblance to Africa's ancient forms of government. Deprived of the props provided by colonialism, chieftaincy lost its relevance; and, in a rapidly modernising world, it withered and died. In some cases its corpse was then preserved rather like that of Lenin, something to be looked at rather than listened to.[6]

None of these arguments is entirely without merit; much is persuasive. However, when one moves from the general to the particular, the argument begins to creak. In this paper I try to make some sense out of the modern history of chieftaincy in southern Ghana, and to rescue chieftaincy from the harsh and frequently silly judgements to which it has been subjected. Secondly, I argue that in some areas chieftaincy was sufficiently powerful to compete with the nationalist movement for control of the countryside; and, once in government, nationalists used all their powers to undermine the authority of chieftaincy. Implicitly I suggest that Ghanaian chieftaincy in the second half of the twentieth century was transformed by political processes and not by the operation of some arcane, organic historical laws of motion. I begin by looking at the historiography and then at the political history of chieftaincy in the 1950s.

The millennium threatens us with the inevitable broadsheet inventories of the twentieth century's 'hinges of history'. The processes which have been rather portentously called the 'End of Empire' will figure in these checklists. Historians have documented and analysed the epics of decolonisation.[7] And we are gradually beginning to be reflective enough to see that these processes transformed metropolitan lives as well as those of the citizens of British colonies. Those of us who are interested in the modern histories of those colonies have, however, paid rather less attention to the significance of the local political processes which unfolded during the period of decolonisation. This owes something to the nature of the sources; the Public Record Office's value as a collection of sources for the political history of those states on the brink of independence declines as measures of devolution ensure that more and

[5] (London, 1964). The review appears in *African Affairs*, vol. 64. No. 255, January 1965.

[6] This has been most recently elaborated in Mahmood Mamdani's *Citizen and subject; contemporary Africa and the legacy of colonialism*. Princeton, 1996.

[7] For Ghana specifically see Richard Rathbone (ed.), *Ghana* (British documents on the end of Empire series) (London, 1992).

more decision-making is located in local legislatures.[8] And in the ex-colonies, access to late and especially post-colonial records in National Archives has been inhibited for a number of reasons.[9] But the neglect of domestic political history in the period immediately before and after the attaining of independence also owes something to the drift of the historiography. The modern historiography of Africa has tended to be enraptured, utterly understandably, by the stirring epics of the 'nationalist struggle'. It is almost as if Independence Day constituted the End of History. Published modern West African history is, in many respects, the history of nationalism and successful nationalists.[10] That view of history lingers on in Ghana; it continues, for example, to order the calendar of public holidays and the naming of streets. But there it is a contested history.

So far as the history of Ghana in the 1950s and 1960s is concerned, the domination of this skein of nationalist history and the silencing of other narratives raises problems. Those problems are first encountered in the realm of peoples' memories and then in the local archives. Many Ghanaians remember a different, less triumphal history; they remember instead a history of brutal political competition in the countryside. And while the Public Record Office provides us with a detailed account of the process of the transfer of power, the archival sources in Ghana tell a rather different story about the 1950s. That story is more concerned with local struggles for power. Those struggles were partly about the resolution of the old question of 'who governs'? But they were also complex struggles about the nature of the post-colonial state. Those who worry about the contemporary relevance of historical research can be reassured; an analysis of those struggles provides us with a better historical guide to the modern topography of Ghanaian politics than recitals of the heroic struggle between a nationalist movement and the British.

Ghana's successful nationalist party, the Convention Peoples' Party, whose leader Kwame Nkrumah became the cynosure of the world's

[8] This issue is explored more fully in Richard Rathbone, 'Transferring power in Ghana: some thoughts on what the archives might be telling us', in *Ghana Studies*, vol. 1, no. 1, 1999, pp. 1–11.

[9] Although the backlog is currently being addressed, the bulk of the post-independence government record in Ghana remained unsorted and uncatalogued within the Ministries. Until very recently the National Archives of Ghana was in reality the National Archives of the colonial Gold Coast.

[10] With the notable exception of Jean Allman's study of the National Liberation Movement, *The Quills of the Porcupine* (Wisconsin, 1994), there is, for example, very little analysis of opposition parties in late colonial Ghana.

gaze in the 1950s,[11] dominates the historiography. So far as domestic politics are concerned, it was the country's government for the fifteen years between 1951 and 1966, when it was ousted by the country's first military coup. It is said to have been a mass party and its wide support is attested to by pre-independence electoral victories in 1951, 1954 and 1956 even if it never secured more than 25 per cent of the votes of the enfranchised electorate in those contests. Its triumph in the Presidential election in 1960, when it secured more than 90 per cent of the vote, was less obviously a fair result.[12] It was a vigorous, even dashing, modern party dedicated to the liberation of the new nation from not only colonialism but also from the scourges of poverty, conservative social practice, illiteracy and ill-health. Colonial rule was widely unpopular by the 1940s; tired, unimaginative and apparently incapable of adapting to rapid social change, it had lost its way. Most Ghanaians, as well as most of the pioneer scholars who studied Ghana in the 1950s, acknowledged the necessity of the kind of programme to which the CPP was committed.[13] If that is so, then why did the Party as government have such a major struggle to assert its control over the countryside where more than 90 per cent of the population lived and where the bulk of the nation's wealth was created on farms or in mines?

The answer to that question is to be found in the somewhat ignored history of chieftaincy in the 1950s. To begin with it is entirely reasonable to ask what a chief was. There is no single form of chieftaincy in Ghana; the colonial state which took shape most especially from 1874 to 1896 encompassed several forms of chieftaincy. Some pre-colonial chiefs were mighty monarchs commanding large populations and significant resources. Others were minor figures with no significant *prise*. In the cultural melange that came to comprise the Gold Coast, chieftaincy had varied meanings; and those meanings changed over time. Some chiefs were largely ritual figures; others combined spiritual roles with extensive temporal powers. What matters is that the British decided at an early stage of their over-rule that they would govern through these traditional figures. Local revenues proved to be low and this ruled out more direct and hence costly forms of administration. Thus local government and local justice were placed firmly on the

[11] Few other leaders of geo-politically unimportant countries the physical size of Britain and with a population of about 7 million made the cover of *Time Magazine*. Nkrumah's international reputation was, and remains, extraordinary.

[12] The elections are covered in great detail in Dennis Austin's masterpiece *Politics in Ghana, 1945–1960* (London, 1964).

[13] That is implicit in Denis Austin's *Politics in Ghana* and in David Apter, *The Gold Coast in Transition* (Princeton, 1955).

shoulders of traditional rulers. The everyday life of Ghanaians was regulated and judged by chiefs. In time this essentially pragmatic response to the quotidian problems of governance became sacralised within the extremely leaky philosophy of Indirect Rule.[14]

As suggested earlier, some of the historiography has argued, ignorantly in my view, that this role was tantamount to chiefly collaboration with the colonial regime.[15] This charge can only be made by those who have convinced themselves that nationalism and modernisation were synonyms and assume that these *anciens régimes* were capable of survival only when colonial regimes propped them up. As the close relationship between chieftaincy and the business of the colonial state disadvantaged the modern coastal elites whose political aspirations were more obviously democratic if also self-serving, it has also been read as yet more evidence of a colonial policy of divide and rule. Writing off chiefs as mere collaborators is, however, a charge that can only be made by those who have also failed to look closer at Ghana's history in the inter-war period.[16] Here it is clear that the most prominent chiefs, including some quite spectacularly clever men, recognised how dependent colonial rulers were upon their services. Professor Kwame Arhin argues that 'colonial government took away the power of traditional rulers and gave them authority in local government'[17] and the evidence suggests that they used that authority to ensure that they wielded considerable power in rural areas. This leverage was used by chiefs to aggregate more and more powers in the realms of both administration and the justice system. They created room for manœuvre by their genuine control of material and human resources, most obviously in the form of access to land and labour. They provided an ideological justification of their power by an astute reification of 'custom' and especially 'customary law'. These they successfully presented as the only legitimate, 'natural' systems which governed the control of land, of marriage, succession and the 'constitutions' under which chiefs ruled.[18] These ideas and these local laws began to define a *chasse gardée* where a succession of weak administrations feared to tread. The inter-war period especially was a time when, as John Dunn memorably puts it, 'the administration's moral sensitivity to traditional legitimacy was in a

[14] The particular history of Ghana's 'Native Administration' is outlined in the first chapter of Richard Rathbone, *Nkrumah and the chiefs* (Oxford).

[15] This was for example the burden of Robert Fitch and Mary Oppenheimer, *Ghana; the end of the illusion* (New York, 1968).

[16] Published material on this period is sadly rare. David Kimble's magisterial *Political History of Ghana* (Oxford, 1964) ends in 1928.

[17] See Kwame Arhin, *Traditional rule in Ghana; past and present* (Accra, 1985) p. 108.

[18] These processes are brought out in Robert Addo-Fening, *Akyem Abuakwa, 1700–1943 from Ofori Panin to Sir Ofori Atta* (Trondheim, 1997) and Richard Rathbone, *Murder and politics in colonial Ghana* (New Haven, 1993).

particularly inflamed condition'.[19] Under-recognised in the scholarly literature, this too was an anti-colonial struggle in which the wider and deeper extension of colonial rule and western ideology was often successfully resisted; and over time more and more local governmental and judicial functions were taken over by African rulers. This remarkable process receives slight attention in the literature because the British were not the only victims of this process; it was also a struggle in which the predecessors of the modern nationalist parties which dominate the political narrative from the end of the Second World War were outflanked and marginalised. If the historiography tends to be nationalist, chiefs are un-surprisingly cast in an unflattering light.

Chieftaincy was, accordingly, transformed by colonial rule; but it also transformed itself into a significant political force. In that process chieftaincy 'neither behaved simply as an instrument in the hands of the colonial rulers nor ... drew its political power solely from its capacity to elicit the support of the colonial regime'.[20] What it had become was unwelcome not merely to the largely urban, modern, elite but, increasingly, to the colonial regime. Chieftaincy had become less easy to control and to regulate. It had struggled for and had achieved a degree of control over the lives of large numbers of men and women. By the 1930s, chieftaincy was a powerful institution which had skilfully harnessed new opportunities. And it had done so by ring-fencing its activities with a culturally and hence politically sensitive ideology. The politics of each chieftaincy were ordered by chiefly readings of 'custom'; the outcomes of succession disputes, wrangles over jurisdiction and legal processes were increasingly if grudgingly accepted by the colonial administration. Colonial resistance to the policies and actions of major chiefs could all too easily lead on to major disputes with powerful elements of this key agency of local government and local justice which delivered, and delivered cheaply, both law and order. The colonial authorities were as thoroughly aware of the deficiencies of this utterly undemocratic system as were the nationalists. But they never quite got round to reforming it, a matter which was roundly condemned as cowardly by Lord Hailey and other influential colonial critics.[21]

Reform became a matter of urgency in the course of the Second World War. The supply crisis demanded enhanced production of much which was produced in Ghana. Its exports – gold, bauxite, industrial diamonds as well as cocoa and vegetable fats – satisfied not only the

[19] In John Dunn and A.F. Robertson, *Dependence and opportunity; political change in Ahafo* (Cambridge, 1973), p. 170.

[20] John Dunn in Dunn and Robertson, *Dependence and opportunity*, p. 93.

[21] Most notably in Hailey, *Native Administration in the British African territories* (London, 1951). Colonial Office reactions can be seen in PRO CO 96/810/6.

Ministry of Food's demands but also earned dollars in a period of sterling crisis. But because chieftaincy had its own preoccupations, it was soon recognised that it was a notably poor agency for mobilising effort when it came to 'development', the new concern of colonial rule in West Africa.[22] After 1945 this recognition folded rather neatly into the new Labour Government's developing colonial policy which resolved to democratise from the bottom up and thus to displace chieftaincy in favour of forms of Local Government modelled on those of the British Isles.[23] But even if the arguments for reform were marshalled, the colonial regime lacked the will and by 1948 also lacked the legitimacy to reform without the huge risk of extensive disorder.

Politics had overtaken policy and the Gold Coast was caught up in rioting at the end of February and the beginning of March, 1948. The Commission of Enquiry[24] appointed to look into the causes of the disturbances had harsh things to say about chieftaincy. The evidence suggests that this was in part ventriloquised by those from whom they took evidence. In a brief three-week visit, the three Commissioners, with no prior experience of West Africa, spoke mostly with those Africans who had been marginalised by the chiefly political offensive in the inter-war period, the nationalist intelligentsia. The Commissioners denounced chiefs as undemocratic, heads of doomed *ancien régimes* whose time had come. These were harsh judgements and Andrew Cohen (then Assistant Under-Secretary of State in the Colonial Office's Africa Division) minuted on the Commission Report that 'The whole of the analysis suffers from the prejudice felt by the Commission against Chiefs.'[25] But their recommendations were rapidly engrossed in policy and practice. In short order an all-African Committee was appointed to draft a new constitution and to make recommendations for an entirely new system of Local Government.[26] More sympathetic to or troubled about chieftaincy than the British Commissioners, they nonetheless produced, in 1949, a framework which, once enacted, would mark the end of the extended experiment with Indirect Rule.

The Gold Coast's first general elections were held in 1951 and were won, handsomely, by Nkrumah and his Convention Peoples' Party.

[22] This argument was made first and most persuasively by Richard Crook in 'Decolonization, the colonial state and chieftaincy in Ghana' in *African Affairs*, vol. 85, no. 338 (January, 1986), pp. 75–107.

[23] See Ronald Hyam, *The Labour Government and the end of Empire* (British Documents on the End of Empire series) (London, 1992), vol. 1.

[24] The Commission of Enquiry into disturbances in the Gold Coast was chaired by Aiken Watson, KC, and its Report was published as Col. 231 in 1948.

[25] PRO CO 96/796/5, 29 June 1948. There is some justice in the comment.

[26] The Committee on Constitutional Reform was chaired by Mr Justice Henley Coussey and its Report was published as Col. 248 in 1949.

The Party's earlier relationship with chieftaincy is of considerable importance for what follows. The Party, formally launched in June 1949, had split from the older nationalist party, the United Gold Coast Convention, which had brought Nkrumah back from Britain in November 1947 and whose General Secretary he remained until he resigned or they dismissed him, depending upon which version of the events one entertains. But it had been a there in embryonic form from the middle of 1948. Its roots, ideology and leadership were fundamentally urban. That leadership was quick to realise that it was imperative to capture support in the countryside if it was to command national authority and, in the fullness of time, votes. As we have virtually no records for the Party, we cannot know whether its unfolding rural strategy was the result of intention or reaction. We can say, however, that the party's distinctive personality in the countryside was intimately shaped by its complex relationships with chieftaincy, most especially in the southern half of the country.

To understand that we need a brief, generalised excursion into political anthropology. In what became the political cockpit of southern Ghana, chieftaincy appears to have had one consistent attribute in the first half of the twentieth century. It generated abrasive factionalism. Some Ghanaian authorities claim, for instrumental if very sympathetic reasons, that chiefs are elected and emerge through democratic processes;[27] that normative view conflicts with the considerable evidence of turmoil which accompanied a large proportion of successions that fill innumerable files in the National Archives of Ghana.[28] However succession is viewed, it is almost always the case that a successful claimant will thereafter be opposed by the parties or factions of unsuccessful claimants. These conflicts are referred to as 'stool disputes'. They could result in frequent depositions of chiefs; there were at least 160 such 'destoolments' between 1900 and 1939 in the southern third of the country alone. This has been read by some scholars as evidence of something close to rural revolution; commoners, it is claimed, excited by democratic ideas, were in increasing numbers identifying themselves with the anti-chiefly aspect of nationalist ideology.[29] This is a flawed analysis.

[27] See for example Kofi Busia, *The position of the chief in the modern political system of Ashanti* (London, 1951).

[28] A matter which persists to this day. At the time of writing the succession to the late Asantehene, who died in March 1999, was being hotly contested in Ghana's law courts. It was an unusual situation only inasmuch as the struggle was also taking place on the Internet.

[29] This is essentially the argument of several of the authors in Paul Jenkins (ed) *Akyem Abuakwa and the politics of the inter-war period in Ghana* (Basle, 1975).

Chieftaincy was, *inter alia*, an elaborate system of patronage. Successful factions enjoyed the distribution of favours; in the colonial period that meant licences to build, to trade, to be public letter-writers and to establish shrines; it also gave access to scholarships and jobs around the palace. Factions supporting unsuccessful claimants were excluded from even these limited pork barrels. As chiefs can be deposed, thwarted factions live in active hope of future success. Chieftaincy politics are accordingly fraught. But the aspirations of excluded factions were not the extirpation of chieftaincy but rather the eventual accession of their patron. Rural volatility, and the Ghanaian countryside was very volatile,[30] had very little to do with a more generalised hostility towards chieftaincy of the sort expressed by the Convention Peoples' Party. It presents instead as a complex patchwork of individual competitions for power.

The Convention Peoples' Party had, as already suggested, set out its opposition to chieftaincy at an early stage. While there is little illumination to be gained by theoretical discussions about what is and is not 'revolutionary' and while it never quite brought off a revolution, it was a revolutionary party; it was committed not only to the expulsion of the British but also to the radical re-ordering of Ghanaian society, and this included the complete ending of chiefly authority. It inveighed against chiefs as imperialist stooges, and raged about the arbitrary quality of a rural order dominated by those qualified to rule by birth rather than by achievement. This was, they said often enough, the dawning of the 'age of the Common Man'.

This very public hostility to chieftaincy was partly a matter of ideology and partly the opening shots in a protracted struggle for rural control. The particular reception of this ideology in the countryside matters greatly. The extensive evidence suggests that this frequently stated anti-aristocratic principle was read as an invitation to those who opposed specific chiefs in rural areas; it was an invitation which was very widely accepted. And it really was expressed as an invitation. The Party's newspaper was no stranger to incitement. In a memorable series of pieces it expressed sympathy with those who faced 'the temptation of marching into the homes of the chiefs and bring [*sic*] them to account, as what happened in the French Revolution when the women of France marched from Paris to Marseilles [*sic*] to bring the King back to Paris to give account for his behaviour'. In similar vein it suggested that 'once it can be proved that the chiefs are false to their oaths, the people are exempted ... from their

[30] The shock expressed by the British at the outbreak of rioting in February and March 1948 was partly because it was urban unrest. The colonial administration was far more used to the regularity of rural riots.

allegiance'.[31] Local opponents of this or that chief came out in support of the CPP. In many cases rural Party branches were actually founded by members of embittered, losing factions. Local grievances could now be re-written as elements of a national campaign. Aggrieved factions now used the relatively sophisticated resources of local Party branches to harass their opponents. Individual chiefs were denounced in the Party's newspaper, *The Accra Evening News* and at Party rallies as discontented factions attached themselves to the CPP. In case after case it seems that the formation of rural branches of the CPP almost always coincided with a long-standing rural struggle for a chieftaincy. The CPP's flags flew in towns and villages which were hostile to incumbent chiefs; party flags had a particular place in the politics of the 1940s and 1950s demarcating the terrain of this or that party.[32] In turn beleaguered chiefs drew what support they could from national political organisations which opposed the CPP. The polarisation of many 'stool disputes' in southern Ghana along national lines is a notable feature of the Ghanaian political landscape from 1949.[33] It is worth repeating that the evidence suggests strongly that rural support for the CPP usually represented antipathy to individual chiefs rather than a more comprehensive, widespread disaffection with chieftaincy.

Although the 1951 elections ushered in an experiment with diarchy, the CPP's success at the polls and their large majority allowed it to exercise something very close to full self-government in matters of local government. The primary material in both Accra and Kew exudes a sense of the relief of British administrators who could now happily leave the wretchedly complicated task of unravelling and controlling rural areas to Africans. There is little doubt that the CPP's Central Committee had every intention to scrap chieftaincy as soon as possible. Several prominent members of the Party were widely reported as having made just that commitment before the first general election of 1951.

The Party was, however, bound to carry through the detailed reforms of Local Government which had been painstakingly drafted in the previous two years. Those who had drafted the new constitution, the all-African Coussey Committee, had found a transitional place for

[31] *The Accra Evening News*, 7 September 1950.

[32] The origins of this probably lie in the Fante tradition of the coastal towns where the ancient militias, the *asafo* companies, each boasted distinctive flags which were prominent on festival days and during the frequent bouts of inter-company fighting.

[33] There are several accounts of just this process. The struggles in Wenchi and Manya Krobo are to be found in David Apter, *Gold Coast in transition*, pp. 257–72 and that in Ofinso is dealt with in great detail in Richard Crook's excellent but sadly unpublished thesis 'Local elites and national politics in Ghana; a case study of political centralization and local politics in Offinso (Ashanti) 1945–66', London, 1978. There are other cases discussed in Richard Rathbone's *Nkrumah and the chiefs*.

chieftaincy in their framework, but now the overwhelming need, CPP Ministers insisted, was to make 'the popular will effective'.[34] While the new Local Government structure, which was ushered in from the end of 1951, was to be dominated by elected Local Councils, the nominees of Chiefs' councils were to enjoy 30 per cent of the seats on those councils. Importantly, chiefs were to lose direct access to their old sources of revenue – rents, concession royalties and local imposts. Local Councils were now charged with the collection of these rents and taxes and were required to make allocation for Chiefs and Chiefs' Councils by agreement. Plans were also drawn up to reform the old Native Jurisdiction.

Nothing contained in the reform was to prove simple to achieve. First, the newly elected councils were in most cases dominated by CPP members who, in rural areas, were frequently extremely hostile to incumbent chiefs. The smooth running of local councils and especially fiscal supersession required agreements between chiefs' councils and the local councils; agreements between warring parties are always hard to come by and so it proved in Ghana in the 1950s. Local revenue was either not collected or so poorly collected that central government was required to subsidise local expenditure from central funds in increasing amounts. As the Chief Regional Officer was to report to his Minister 'Local Councils have had the effect of arousing every parochial jealousy and tribal antipathy and it is certain that much dissatisfaction will be expressed ... by non-co-operation ... the Minister's attention should be called to the need ... to "soften up" the opposition to direct taxation and all existing institutions.'[35] Inefficient and corrupt as the old Native Authority system under Indirect Rule might have been, it had been a functioning system; its replacement proved to be almost certainly as corrupt and inefficient, and definitely more costly than sincere reformers had hoped. In many Local Council areas it was reported that 'local government administration ... has completely broken down'.[36]

The same problems haunted the long overdue reform of the local justice system. The question was repeatedly examined by Select Committees by successive CPP governments; all of them concluded that the Native Courts were inefficient and frequently corrupt and that the entire system should be scrapped and replaced by a mixture of

[34] Executive Council memorandum by Edward Asafu Adjaye, Minister for Local Government, 28 July 1951. National Archives of Ghana (NAG) ADM 13/2/1.

[35] A.J. Loveridge to Minister of Local Government, 11 December 1951. NAG ADM 13/2/2.

[36] This quotation is drawn from a Cabinet memorandum on the situation in Agona for 7 January 1954, NAG ADM 13/2/15, but there are many other examples of such conclusions by the Minister of Local Government.

stipendiary and lay magistrates' courts. The caseload of such courts was considerable. In the Colony, the southern third of the country, and the Ashanti Region, the country's 'middle belt', more than 93,000 cases were heard in 1949–50.[37] The cost implications of reform as well as the somewhat surprising shortage of lawyers to man this jurisdiction inhibited reform and the system was to remain in place well beyond 1957, the date of Independence; despite the mythology of an over-abundance of West African lawyers, there was a shortage of legally trained people in the Gold Coast. In 1946, of the 136 Gold Coast students in Britain, only 12 were reading law. In 1948 only 29 out of a cohort of 253 were law students.[38] The only significant change brought about in the judicial system was the replacement of chiefs and royals on judicial panels by large numbers of local CPP clients. This change was engineered by using the Minister's power to make Native Court Variation Orders which were taken through Cabinet and then announced in the *Government Gazette*. There appear to be very few of these courts whose membership was not so altered from July 1952, the first case encountered,[39] right through to independence itself in March 1957. The substitution of dependable Party supporters for large numbers of discarded court panel members who were demonstrably royal or clients of chiefs is consistent throughout this long trail of evidence. A judicial system once dominated by frequently *parti pris* chiefs was now to be dominated by no less *parti pris* political activists. Ordinary rural Ghanaians, long habituated to a less than fair local justice system dominated by royals, were now exposed to the same flawed system but one which was now ordered by the Party rather than by chiefly patronage.

If there were practical problems in replacing chieftaincy and the systems inherent in the old structure of Indirect Rule, the government also faced political problems with reform. Chieftaincy had been stripped of much of the formal power it had fought for and then enjoyed in the inter-war period. Some of its most prominent figures, men with national reputations, with access to the press and with significant local support struggled against these processes and in many cases made resolution of the problems of supersession virtually impossible. Frustration ensured that local branches of the Party, dominant in most Local Councils, became even more active in campaigns to depose obdurate local rulers. Innumerable destoolment cases flooded into the offices of the new Ministry of Local Government which, like its colonial predecessor,

[37] See *Report of the Commission on Native Courts* (Accra, 1951).

[38] It was 1958 before the University College of Ghana was to enjoy a Law Faculty of its own.

[39] See Cabinet *Minutes* for 11 July 1952, NAG ADM 13/2/6.

found it hard to steer a neat course between vehemently argued but impossibly complex cases based upon differing readings of customary law. And a government with a strong commitment to development was faced by increasing turbulence in the very areas which produced the bulk of national wealth.

The bitter relationship between incumbent chiefs and the governing party was a complex matter. In each chiefdom a particular history informed the precise nature of local political topography. In some areas chiefs presciently came out in support of the government, recognising that local development would depend upon its largesse. Others remained profoundly hostile to a reforming government which was committed to terminating chiefly influence in local government. And at the end of 1954, shortly after the elections which had granted something very close to formal internal self-government, these complex stand-offs became even more highly politicised. The CPP's election manifesto had argued for the removal of the last vestiges of chiefly membership of Local Councils. This was necessary, it was explained, in order to end 'the continual friction ... it is not the intention of the CPP to destroy chieftaincy but rather to adapt it to its democratic practices ... A spirit of liberty, of national consciousness pervades the country and THE COMMON PEOPLE have come to feel that they are as good as the so-called aristocrats who have ignored and despised them ...'[40] This was inflammatory language and the fire was soon ablaze.

By the turn of the year, the disaffection of some in Ghana's central Ashanti Region had resulted in the formation of a political party, the National Liberation Movement.[41] It proclaimed a conservative nationalism which it opposed to the CPP's socialism. And it sought to curb what was perceived as the excessive accretion of power in Accra by the CPP by demanding an independence constitution which would be federal in nature; this they believed would counter the CPP's centralising tendencies. The CPP Central Committee was later to angrily dismiss this charge: 'the NLM ... have ... mischievously misconstrued the term "democratic centralism" [the guiding principle of the Convention Peoples' Party], the Central Committee is anxious to explain ... that the term is synonymous with "Parliamentary Democracy"'.[42]

The NLM's lack of a significant parliamentary presence – the CPP had won 72 of the 104 seats in the 1954 elections – led to a violent,

[40] *The Evening News*, 4 May 1954.

[41] The most comprehensive account of the history of the NLM is Jean Allman, *The quills of the porcupine*, Madison, Wisconsin, 1993.

[42] *The Daily Graphic*, 2 March 1956.

extra-parliamentary struggle in the countryside. The NLM sought to gather support from beyond its ethnic heartland, the great historical state of Asante; and it was reasonably successful in forging alliances with parties reflecting other instances of regional disaffection with what was undoubtedly a southern-based governing party directing much of the flow of development funding to the south. These parties included urban Moslems, the irredentist party of the Ewe-speaking people of South Eastern Ghana and the party which spoke for the much-neglected Northern Territories.[43]

However, the NLM was, at heart, an Asante party. It made a patriotic case and underlined it by making common cause with the beleaguered Asante chiefs. Because of their proximate bruising experience of CPP government, many of the most significant non-Asante chiefs also proclaimed their support for the NLM. In almost every case chieftaincy then, as now, served as an embodiment of place, a matrix of past and present and a symbolic representation of treasured particularity. Given that the NLM's rationale was perceived or real regional deprivation, it is not surprising that chieftaincy came to stand as something close to an embodiment not only of place but also of resistance to perceived affronts. The CPP argued that what was being resisted was the introduction of a progressive modern state in which archaic ideas like ethnicity and chieftaincy had no place. According to the Minister of Local Government 'the Gold Coast was being developed in a socialist way ...'.[44] The government's opponents argued that socialism was a western importation which conspired to destroy chieftaincy and chieftaincy was in turn the very essence of locality and identity.

The CPP government was in a cleft stick when it came to combating the NLM. It had a huge parliamentary majority but still lacked full control over its security forces, something it acquired only on Independence Day. It also felt constrained by the fact that the Conservative government of the United Kingdom, who still held the keys to the door of independence, was suspicious of a party which many on the Tory benches in both Lords and Commons regarded as extremist and even communist. Lashing out at the NLM would have served its opponents well by confirming the accusations of critics who regarded the CPP as Stalinist; the major opposition newspaper, *The Ashanti Pioneer*, ran a weekly strip-cartoon version of *Animal Farm* to underline just this point. There is no doubt that Napoleon the pig was supposed to represent the Prime Minister, Kwame Nkrumah.

[43] The Moslem Association Party, the Togoland Congress and the Northern Peoples' Party respectively.

[44] Speaking at Kwahu on 11 July 1954 and reported in *The Evening News*, 12 July 1954.

Consequently the government attempted to be emollient by the usual parliamentary avenues of Select Committees and Round Table discussions;[45] none of these olive branches bore fruit, not least because the opposition boycotted these efforts. It was a dialogue of the deliberately unhearing. The modernising CPP argued, as we might argue, that a party that had been popularly elected, and there was no doubt about that, had the legal right to carry through its manifesto pledges. Those who argued that chieftaincy was the embodiment of the subnational particularities of Ghana stressed that a parliamentary majority was no mandate to ignore history and local dignity. The resulting stand-off led almost ineluctably to a further, unscheduled election in 1956, intended to be a tie-breaker, which again returned the CPP to office with a huge majority.

Below the level of this well-known national political struggle, the CPP was in a serious quandary. Its control over the Ashanti Region and some of the major southern chieftaincies was diminishing, not least because of the NLM's successful use of intimidation. Many Local Councils could not function and their work was being conducted by small Committees of Administration appointed by the Minister of Local Government (and directly answerable to him) by Cabinet Order, the legislative relict of the Order-in-Council. They were not discussed by the Legislative Assembly. Such cases were so numerous that Cabinet discussed them in batches.[46] The collection of local taxes was failing and the required financial contribution from central government was increasing considerably precisely at the same moment as the world cocoa price, upon which government revenue depended, was set to fall for the first time in twelve years. Local services declined. The best source on these issues is the *Report of the Commissioner for Local Government Enquiries*.[47] It amounts to a devastating summary of the almost entirely malign consequences of the introduction of modern local government. An extended survey by the distinguished journalist Bankole Timothy came to similar conclusions. 'Politics,' he wrote, 'is destroying the future of Local Government and impeding progress.'[48] Local government was, the Minister admitted, wracked by 'nepotism, party-political manoeuverings or petty local squabbles' and progressive local government was being undermine 'by arbitrary dismissals and unwarranted

[45] The details of this sequence of events are to be found in Richard Rathbone (ed), *Ghana* (British Documents on the end of Empire series), vol. 2, London, 1992.

[46] For example, the Local Councils of Asokore, Nkoranza and Tongu were all suspended at a single Cabinet meeting on 19 April 1955. See NAG ADM 13/2/22. Compared with the flood of such decisions in the post-independence era, however, this amounted to a trickle.

[47] Published in Accra, 1957. The Commissioner was Arthur Greenwood.

[48] See *The Daily Graphic* (Accra) for 11, 27 and 28 1956.

promotions or appointments'.[49] This was no slight admission given that the vast majority of these councils were dominated by members of the Minister's own governing party. In many areas the local court system floundered as contending political party branches, the perpetrators of many of the cases of violence and criminal damage heard by those courts, intimidated court members. Wherever the NLM enjoyed significant support, the government's authority was being challenged.

Although the documentary evidence is slight, it is clear that this turmoil prompted a profound change in government tactics when it came to the increasingly vexed issue of chieftaincy. It was to be a quite remarkable *volte face* for a government wedded to the elimination of chieftaincy and committed to a unitary state in which local loyalties would give way to a radical commitment to Ghanaian citizenship. Government had believed that the increasing denial to chiefs of formal administrative and judicial roles would reduce their local significance; attrition and the palpable attractions of modernisation would work together to see off the chiefs. After all, what was most wanted in rural areas – decent water supplies, electrification, road-, school- and clinic-building – required central government expenditure and this was controlled by the government party. This entirely rational plan was not working and the NLM had simply provided unco-operative chiefs with more oxygen. The initial ambition of removing chiefs in all but their ceremonial roles had to be abandoned. In its place a policy emerged which now actively courted the support of sitting chiefs by inducements or coercion; most of these concerned either promises to provide the comforts of pipe-borne water or electrification or, more alarmingly, threats to deny obdurate chieftaincies development funds. Krobo Edusei, the CPP's most prominent figure in the Ashanti Region and, by then, Minister of the Interior, was reported to have made a speech during a bye-election campaign in Aflao in which he said 'You think I am a fool to give you water to drink and vote against me? After the election if you vote CPP, I will give you water to drink ...'[50] Where threats failed, government went out of its way to encourage the support of rival chiefly claimants by adding the weight of local party organisation to their causes. It abandoned its generalised hostility and now became openly involved in local chieftaincy politics. This significant shift in policy can only be accounted for by a recognition that Chiefs had proved to be a considerable impediment whose significance as

[49] Cabinet memorandum by the Minister of Local Government, 14 August, 1956. NAG ADM 13/2/31.

[50] *The Ashanti Pioneer*, 14 October 1958. The electors of Aflao returned an independent candidate and accordingly did not get piped water.

rallying-points had become even more uncomfortably apparent in a period of national conflict. To take further extensive action against them would have provoked more unrest and might have provided the British government with the excuse to delay independence. The policy shifted towards the incorporation of chiefs by a variety of tactics.

As independence grew closer the government, once committed to the destruction of chieftaincy, now threw its support behind chiefs of dissident states which were enraged by their historical subjection to particular Paramount chiefs; but it did so only when those Paramounts were opponents of the government. Perversely perhaps, a party which had inveighed against the divisiveness of ethnic ties now took sides in essentially ethnic disputes where there was a chance of weakening the power of chiefly enemies. The most notable case was that of the creation in 1958 of a new, ethnically based region, Brong Ahafo, which had the effect of dividing the Ashanti Region in half; this greatly damaged the power of the most prominent chiefly opponent of the government, the Asantehene.

Even more strikingly, after independence in 1957, the government of a Party with a long record of opposition to chieftaincy was beginning to stress that it regarded chiefs as 'an arm of government'.[51] It could now make that comment with more confidence because it had abandoned the destruction of chieftaincy. By taking legal powers which required the government's formal recognition of a chief, it could now withdraw recognition and thus depose chiefs. Such legal controls were to find their final form in the Chiefs (Recognition) Act in March 1959. These powers were felt by previous colonial governments to have been far too risky to contemplate even if in some cases they wished that they had enjoyed them. As the veteran nationalist, Dr J.B. Danquah, a sworn enemy of the CPP, said, 'No chief in Ghana was made chief by the Queen ... Everything about Chieftaincy existed by customary law and that alone.'[52] Although this exaggeration ignores the restructuring by the British of hierarchies in Asante after 1900, it did point to a significant contrast between the colonial and post-colonial position of chieftaincy. Chiefs could in effect now be legally removed by government.[53] But these 'gatekeeping' powers also allowed government to contemplate the creation of new chiefs. Now, as the Minister of Local Government reminded an audience of chiefs 'what the Chiefs forget is the fact that a Chief is a Chief partly because the Government

[51] The Minister of Local Government speaking to the Joint Provincial Council of Chiefs reported in *The Daily Graphic*, 12 August 1957.

[52] In the Divisional Court in Accra on 27 January 1959.

[53] The most dramatic case was the dismissal of the old NLM stalwart, Ofori Atta II of Akyem Abuakwa, who was removed from office, not without a fight, in 1958.

recognises him as such'.[54] It was now elevating party clients who were sub-chiefs to Paramount status, thus undermining the 'many Paramount Chiefs whose actions indicate that they deliberately intend to impede the Government ... and prevent minor chiefs from securing justice';[55] and in doing this it even created, if it is not oxymoronic, new 'traditional states'. Government now intervened and did so heavy handedly in that 'traditional' world where the British had so feared to tread. Using its huge parliamentary majority, government now took the legal powers which allowed it to make and unmake chiefs and to sweep aside tradition and history in the process; older understandings about traditional protocol, tables of precedence and hierarchy were ignored. Chiefs sympathetic to the CPP were recognised by government and those who in the face of significant coercion retained their hostility to the government were 'de-recognised' and thus removed. The lists of 'destooled' and then de-recognised chiefs, and government-preferred and thus recognised substitutes for the latter part of 1957 and 1958, quite literally involve hundreds of people. Amongst its agencies, government used their newly created Regional Commissioners,[56] intendants or Commissars in all but name, who, the evidence suggests, were to circumvent the chaos of local government by controlling the business of Local Councils and controlling the new breed of chiefs with a rod of iron. This amounted to the politicisation of regional administration. The Commissioners were Members of the Legislative Assembly, enjoyed Cabinet rank and reported directly to Cabinet. By a clever finesse, the limited amount of regional devolution promised in the Independence Constitution was abandoned; and the sole national role allotted by the constitution to Chiefs, the consultative Regional Houses of Chiefs, was ignored. By the time of the creation of the First Republic in 1960, chieftaincy and more importantly individual chiefs depended upon government for their very existence. Rather than crushing chieftaincy, the CPP had instead domesticated it. Addressing the Eastern Regional House of Chiefs in 1959, the Minister of Local Government said, 'It is a plain fact that the chiefs are the same as the Government.'[57] The government now controlled the countryside. And it did so with the nervous support of its chiefly clients. To return to the opening propositions it is clear that chieftaincy's decline was not ordained by organic change, by natural processes, but was, rather, the outcome of the documentable political processes of ten turbulent years.

Matters were not to rest here. After its fall in 1966, the new military

[54] Reported in the *Daily Graphic*, 12 August 1957.

[55] Cabinet memorandum by the Minister of Local Government on the withdrawal of recognition of the Okyenhene of Akyem Abuakwa, 15 October 1957. NAG ADM 13/2/41.

[56] They were first appointed in October 1957.

[57] Eastern Regional House of Chiefs *Minutes*, 30 March 1960.

government dismissed all of those chiefs installed or promoted by the CPP government – a very large number – and it re-installed the deposed. But it and successor governments were never to return to chiefs the access to resources which had allowed them to exercise such authority in the later colonial period; these were now definitively nationalised. Remarkably, however battered, distorted, constructed and deconstructed chieftaincy might be, it now enjoys considerable popular esteem. Highly qualified people jostle for chieftaincies and stool disputes continue to take up page after page of the Ghanaian press. Certainly the retreat of the state and the resulting enhanced significance of locality in Ghanaian identities has given chieftaincy a new lease of life. In this, the extensive Ghanaian diaspora, organised in Hamburg, Miami, Toronto and London in home-town associations, have played a significant but as yet unstudied part. Beyond that lies the largely unprovable contention that chieftaincy continues to act, as it always has acted, as a comforting, necessary matrix of past and present, an affirmation of local values. Chiefs are 'ours' in ways that much-mistrusted politicians cease to be 'ours' once they are elected. Lastly, their long history, however convolute that might be, suggests that chiefs might represent a more dependable set of values than those of the discredited discourse of modernisation which has provided ordinary Ghanaians with so very few tangible rewards.

BARTOLUS OF SASSOFERRATO AND FREE CITIES*

The Alexander Prize Lecture

By Magnus Ryan

READ 23 APRIL 1999

'Well are ye called the Free People.' – *Bagheera*

BARTOLUS of Sassoferrato (1314–1357)[1] is as famous to legal historians and specialists in the history of political ideas as he is unkown outside those areas of research. His obscurity is owed not to his mind but to his genre: the commentary on Justinian's *Corpus Iuris Civilis*, and the occasional monograph of more systematic yet still legalistic lineaments. Of the thousands of lawyers who studied, taught and applied Roman law from its rediscovery in the late eleventh century to the end of the middle ages, there are perhaps three or four who command universal respect, some of whom we shall encounter in what follows. Only Bartolus radiates the nimbus of genius. In the realm of political ideas, he has – perversely, perhaps – best been served by Anglophone historiography, beginning with the classic study published in 1913 by C.N.S. Woolf, continuing by way of Walter Ullmann's numerous articles and most recently subjected to a full-scale analysis by Joseph Canning in his study of the ideas of Bartolus' most famous pupil, Baldus de Ubaldis (*d.* 1400). From the very organisation of Woolf's book, it is as

*An early version of this essay was read to Dr L.A. Siedentop's seminar at Keble College, Oxford, in 1996. The kernel of the argument was presented in 1997 at Corpus Christi College, Oxford, where the remarks of Rees Davies and Maurice Keen were particularly helpful, at Kalamazoo in 1998 under the chairmanship of Stephen Lahey, and at St Peter's College, Oxford. I owe profound thanks to George Garnett of St Hugh's College, Oxford, whose tireless energy in discussion and illegible handwriting in numerous margins have greatly improved this essay at every stage of its evolution over the years, and to Hugo Tucker of Reading University, whose vigilance and sensitivity over many evenings of absorbing and often hilarious debate have greatly enhanced my understanding of the texts at issue. For much help of a more general nature over many years concerning the fourteenth century, I wish to thank Peter Linehan of St John's College, Cambridge, and Patrick Zutshi of Corpus Christi College, Cambridge. Joseph Canning of the University of Wales, Bangor, kindly read this paper after its delivery. As humble thanks for years of support, enthusiasm, and encouragement, this essay is respectfully dedicated to my former supervisor, Peter Stein.

[1] For the date of Bartolus' death, see most recently O. Condorelli, '*Homo parve stature et coloris turgide et gibbosus* ... Bartolo da Sasoferrato nell'anonima descrizione del ms. Napoli, Biblioteca nazionale, VII. D. 77', *Rivista Internazionale di Diritto Comune* 6 (1995), 357–64.

if three centuries had waited for Bartolus to resolve what Woolf called *The Problem of the Empire*, which is the title of the longest section of the book, 180 pages in which Bartolus' name appears but sporadically. It is as if the crisis unleashed by Pope Gregory VII at Canossa would only be laid to theoretical rest in the lecture-rooms of Perugia, where Bartolus spent most of his all-too-short professional life teaching. For Ullmann, Bartolus was the first medieval lawyer to make the ancient texts of Justinian's *Corpus Iuris Civilis* respond to medieval reality.[2] The upshot, and at the same time the theme of this lecture, is best expressed by Jo Canning, who identifies with Bartolus' jurisprudence the first 'juristic justification for the legal sovereignty of the independent Italian cities as it actually existed'.[3]

Bartolus' fame derives from two related ideas. The first is more in the nature of a methodological principle than a specifically juristic argument. It is that since city-states in northern and central Italy have, as a matter of demonstrable fact, been exercising independently the powers of government since time out of mind, their right to do so should be acknowledged. The second idea is that these cities which recognise no superior should be regarded as being their own superiors. In the absence or actually in defiance of the Roman emperor, the real *princeps*, to whose jurisdiction it belongs in theory, any such city should be treated as a prince unto itself: *civitas sibi princeps*. The notion of *civitas sibi princeps* was, I shall argue, indeed a piece of brilliance.[4] My contention will be that we have failed to explain why, and consequently failed to isolate its most important shortcoming.

Let us begin where scholarship on Bartolus has always begun since Woolf: with the empire.[5] Roman law left jurists little room for manoeuvre when they sought to justify civic autonomy against the claims of the empire. According to D. 1.4.1, 'What has pleased the prince has the force of law.' In itself this does not amount to much, for there could be other sources of law apart from what has pleased the prince. But the passage continues, 'since by the *Lex regia* passed concerning his command, the people confers all its command and power to him and on him'. Elsewhere, Justinian repeats the point: '... by an ancient law which was called the *Lex regia* all right and all power of the Roman

[2] W. Ullmann, '*De Bartoli Sententia*: *Concilium repraesentat mentem populi*', *Bartolo da Sassoferrato. Studi e Documenti per il VI Centenaro* (2 vols., Milan, 1962), vol. 2, 707–33.

[3] J. Canning, *The Political Thought of Baldus de Ubaldis* (Cambridge University Press, 1987), 97.

[4] It will be clear, therefore, that I follow Canning's assessment of the idea as a juristic masterstroke (ibid., 96–7).

[5] The following introduction to the problem of the empire is not intended as an exhaustive study, still less to replace those of Woolf, F. Ercole ('Studi sulla dottrina politica e sul diritto pubblico di Bartolo', in *Da Bartolo all'Althusio. Saggi sulla storia del pensiero pubblicistico del Rinascimento italiano*, Florence, 1932, 54–156) and Canning, *Baldus*.

people have been transferred to the imperial power . . .'[6] Direct grant by the Roman people is not the only source of imperial power. Novel 6 does not mention the people, only God: 'The greatest gifts of God to mankind by the heavenly mercy are the priesthood and the empire, the one ministering to divine matters, the other presiding over and attending with diligence to human matters.' That made the question asked at C. 1.14.2 purely rhetorical: 'For what is greater, what more sacrosanct than the imperial majesty?' It justified the triumphant declaration of D. 14.2.9: 'I am the Lord of the lands of the earth.'

Other passages in Roman law gave weight to custom, that is to say, the daily habits of the people, and made it not merely an alternative but actually a competitor to imperial law. D. 1.3.32 states that in some situations no written law is used, so custom is applied, and continues:

> Immemorial custom is observed as a law, not without good reason; and this is what is called law established by usage. Indeed, in as much as statutes themselves are binding for no other reason than that they are accepted by the judgement of the people, therefore anything whatever which the people show their approval of, even when there is no written rule, ought properly to be binding on all.

That seems to contradict the passages cited already, which make the will of the prince the uncontested source of law, and a certain amount of the medieval jurisprudence about to be reviewed is concerned with this passage. Justinian had, however, set strict limits to the application of custom as an expression of the people's will: 'The authority of custom and long-established usage is not negligible, but it is not valid to the point at which it overcomes reason or law.'[7]

The other jaw of the theoretical vice was the lawyers' conviction that the entire Christian people was subject to the empire and therefore to the Roman law. The passage already quoted from Novel 6 naming the empire and the church as the two gifts of God to mankind implies no limitation to 'human matters' within the purview of the empire. It is also implicit in the epithet *dominus mundi* (D. 14.2.9) that there could be no pockets of autonomy within this universal empire, set from on high as the consort of the universal church. Against the backdrop of these and similar assertions of universality, even quite innocent passages took on political overtones, such as the statement at D. 1.5.17 that all inhabitants of imperial territory are now Roman citizens 'and cannot be deprived of their city'. If the empire was the consort of the church,

[6] *Constitutio Deo Auctore* (tit. *De conceptione Digestorum*): '. . . cum enim lege antiqua, quae regia nuncupabatur, omne ius omnisque potestas populi Romani in inperatoriam translata sunt potestatem . . .' All citations of the Roman law follow *Corpus Iuris Civilis*, ed. P. Krueger, T. Mommsen, and R. Scholl (3 vols., Berlin, 1886–1895).

[7] Code (hereafter C.) 8.52.2.

it had to survive as long as the church, that is, until the crack of doom. Stated compactly, the lesson was: once in, never out, and all are in.

The concrete result: at the Diet of Roncaglia in 1158 Barbarossa established that 'All jurisdiction and all administrative circumscriptions are in the hand of the *princeps*, and all judges should receive their administration from the *princeps* and give an oath as has been defined by law.' There could be no more forceful an application of the Justinianic principle that it pertains to the care of the *princeps*, not the goodwill of the people, to create magistrates.[8] Four of the standard-setting lawyers of mid-twelfth-century Bologna (Bulgarus, Iacobus, Martinus and Ugo, the so-called Four Doctors) witnessed this and other declarations at Roncaglia. They were probably responsible for writing them.[9] Theory and practice were not far apart for such men, and it is therefore not surprising that the glossators attempted from the outset of legal science at Bologna to resolve the theoretical conundrum created by Justinian concerning the relationship between law and custom, the emperor's will and the people's will. Irnerius attempted to resolve the tension by interpreting D. 1.3.32 as referring to an epoch in which the Roman people still had the power to create law:

> This applied in the times in which the people still had the power of laying down the law and so by the tacit consent of the people laws were abrogated. But nowadays, since this power has been transferred to the emperor, the disuse of a particular law by the people has no effect.[10]

Custom and law were the only categories the glossators had with which to makes sense of reality. If the local norms of, say, Milan or Piacenza were not laws in any acceptable sense then they could only be customs. Whatever was done, therefore, with this question would set the limits of political independence not only of the North Italian cities but also of other areas formerly subject to the empire. By insisting on a once-and-for-all interpretation of the *Lex regia* Irnerius set his face against the force of any local statute running counter to Roman law.

Irnerius' attitude pervades much of thirteenth-century jurisprudence, the most apposite example being Odofredus de Denariis' commentary

[8] Digest (hereafter D.) 48.14.1. For the Roncaglian text, see V. Colorni, 'Die drei verschollenen Gesetze des Reichstages bei Roncaglia', trans. G. Dolezalek, *Untersuchungen zur Deutschen Staats-und Rechtsgeschichte*, new series, 12 (1969).

[9] Ibid.

[10] A. Gouron, 'Coutume contre loi chez les premiers glossateurs', *Renaissance du Pouvoir Législatif et Genèse de l'État* (*Publications de la Société D'Histoire du Droit et des Institutions des Anciens Pays de Droit Écrit*, IV, Montpellier, 1988), 117–30.

on the Peace of Constance.[11] In the treaty, Barbarossa had recognised that some cities held certain rights of criminal jurisdiction, for the administration of which elected civic officials had to swear fealty either to him or his representatives. The document itself was frequently included in the text of Roman law at the universities and was therefore fair game for a jurist, but what Odofredus says relegates the treaty to virtual irrelevance. First, it is an imperial concession to some cities only. In the strict terminology of legal theory, it was a privilege, of which the distinguishing expression was 'Concedimus'. It was in perfect keeping with the legal status of the Peace that Frederick II revoked it in July1226.[12] This more than counteracted the force of Barbarossa's injunction that the dispositions of the Peace were to last *in perpetuum*. All lawyers knew what an elastic concept perpetuity was, particularly in relation to imperial grants.[13] Crucially, he maintains that modern *podestà* are but municipal magistrates, who had no jurisdiction in criminal matters before the Peace of Constance, and who, by definition, do not enjoy the power of pure command or *merum imperium* necessary to make law.[14] Finally, the Peacc of Constance actually reserves to the emperor precisely those powers which the cities most wanted to detach from him: he approves the election of the magistrates and takes an oath of fealty from them.[15]

Only the prince can establish general laws and equity, only the prince or his delegate can pronounce judgements of blood. Odofredus founds this rationale on the *Lex regia*: pure command (*merum imperium*) is the power to decide the law, jurisdiction. Jurisdiction was what the Roman people handed over to the emperor and it can never take it

[11] G. Dolezalek, 'I commentari di Odofredo e Baldo alla Pace di Costanza', *La Pace di Costanza 1183* (*Studi e Testi di Storia Medioevale*, 8, Bologna, 1984), ed. A. Boscolo and G. Rondini, 35–59. For the text, see ms. Vienna, Österreichische Nationalbibliothek 294 (hereafter Vienna ONB 294), fo. 24va–26vb. For the Peace of Constance itself, see *MGH Dip.* x.iv (Hanover, 1990), 68–77.

[12] *MGH Const.* ii, n. 107, section 3. Odofredus does not mention this.

[13] Odofredus spends some time on the various senses of the expression, and explicitly states towards the end of his discussion (Vienna ÖNB 294 fo. 24vb, ad verba *In perpetuum*) 'Item si posita fuerit civitas in banno imperatoris quasi patiatur capitis diminutionem [...] vel in banno domini pape posita fuerit. his autem casibus potest dici privilegia cessare ...' Note that for Odofredus the treaty is self-evidently a privilege.

[14] Vienna ÖNB 294, fo. 25ra, ad verba *in criminalibus*: 'Sed certe ego puto potestates qui hodie eliguntur esse municipales magistratus ut C. de munici. magi. l. una [C. 1.56.1], vel defensores civitatum ut in aut. de defens. nos igitur [Nov. 15, = Auth. 3.2.pr.], qui non habent merum imperium ut C. de defen. ci. l. defensores ita [C. 1.55.8] et l. defensores civitatum oblatos [C. 1.55.7] et in aut. iusiurand. quod prestatur ab hiis qui administrationem suscipiunt, et equius [Nov. 8, = Auth. 2.3], et sic non habebant ante hanc pacem iurisdictionem in criminalibus, sed hec conceditur eis...'

[15] See in particular section 8 of the Peace: 'Consules, qui in civitatibus constituentur, tales sint, qui fidelitatem nobis fecerint vel faciant, antequam consulatum recipiant.'

back.[16] In the framework laid down by Justinian the care of the *status rei Romanae* pertained exclusively to the emperor, and this conception of the public law included the control and appointment of magistrates.[17] There was no sense in arguing on behalf of a given city that it had never been part of the empire because all the relevant ones had, and were known to have been.

Azo (*d.* 1220/1229),[18] the teacher of the great Accursius, offered a solution not by questioning the dogma that only the emperor could enact law – that would have been impossible – but by refining it. Only the emperor *alone* can make law. This is true; no other single person can do so. But if the single and private individuals are considered as members of a corporation, as *universi* rather than as *singuli*, then different results follow.[19] What had been given could be taken back. On this reasoning, although the empire as an institution had been established by God in heaven, as far as earth was concerned it had been established by people, specifically the people of Rome. By God's authority, but by the people's ministry, as Accursius would sum it up.[20] The prince truly was set over all men, he was in reality *maior singulis*. But he was not set above the totality of all men, he was *minor universis*.

One particular application of the repeatable *Lex regia* deserves attention because it reveals the critical flaw in the theory. During Alfonso

[16] On the relationship between *imperium* and *iurisdictio*, see now J. Vallejo, *Ruda Equidad, Ley Consumada. Concepcion de la Potestad normativa 1250–1350* (Madrid, 1992), 329–393.

[17] D. 1.1.2.

[18] The date of Azo's death is now uncertain, thanks to E. Conte, 'Un *sermo pro petendis insigniis* al tempo di Azzone e di Bagaratto', in *Rivista di Storia del Diritto Italiano* LX (1987), 71–86.

[19] An excellent analysis in Q. Skinner, 'Political Philosophy', *The Cambridge History of Renaissance Philosophy*, ed. Q. Skinner, E. Kessler, J. Kraye (Cambridge, 1988), 391–4. For the argument itself, see *Azonis Lectura super Codicem* (*Corpus Glossatorum Juris Civilis* III, Turin, 1966), p. 44 at C. 1.14.12, ad verba *soli imperatori.* The final and most accessible statement of the case was that of Accursius in the *Glossa ordinaria* to D. 1.3.9 ('Non ambigitur senatum ius facere posse'): 'Sed an hodie hoc opus possit facere senatus? Respon. secundum Io. non sic hodie, nisi princeps permiserit, ut C. eod. l. fi. [C. 1.14.12] quae est contra: ubi dicit, quod solus princeps facit legem. item facit ad idem, quia populus omne suum imperium in eum transtulit: ut C. de ve. iur. enu. l. i. § sed et hoc studiosum [C. 1.17.1.7]. Alii dicunt, quod hodie potest populus Romanus et senatus eius facere legem: ut hic. nec ob. d. l. fi. quia solus Imperator potest, id est, ipse solus, et nullus alius solus: et revocare potest populus Romanus quod concessit, sicut et iudex qui delegat, cum sibi proprietas remanserit: ut infra, de officio eius cui man. est iur. l. i. § fi. [D. 1.21.1].' See *Pandectarum Iuris Civilis Tomus Primus* [...], Lyon 1585, col. 30. The 'Io.' referred to here is Iohannes Bassianus, teacher of Azo, who disappears from the sources in 1193. For the sake of accuracy, it should be noted that both Accursius and Odofredus associate fundamental aspects of this theory with Hugolinus de Presbyteriis, who died in 1233. He, too, was taught by Bassianus.

[20] Accursius, gl. *De coelo*, in *Volumen*, Lyon 1585, col. 249: 'De coelo: imo populus de terra [...] sed Deus constituit permittendo, et populus Dei dispositione. Vel dic Deus constituit auctoritate, populus ministerio.'

X's bid for the title of emperor, the Pisans carried out an imperial election on behalf of the entire Roman people in the capacity of *negotiorum gestores*. The institution of *negotiorum gestio* belongs to the Roman law of quasi-contractual obligation. Under specific circumstances it allowed the performance of legally binding acts on behalf of someone else without that person's knowledge. Under the present circumstances, Alfonso could not get to Rome; had he done so the Roman people would not have elected him, nor would the pope have crowned him. The device of *negotiorum gestio* was used by the Pisans as a means of making concrete this 'little' *Lex regia*. Bartolus was to point out the problems inherent in Azo's theory of the *Lex regia* with particular reference to this event. He emphasised the licence it seemed to give every other city to elect its own emperor. Since this was precisely what the Pisans had already done we should take that criticism as more than just a purist's reaction. Put simply, Azo's theory was useless unless there was agreement over who constituted the Roman people.

The main features of the theoretical landscape in which Bartolus is supposed to have moved are therefore as follows. A universal empire claimed the allegiance of cities in Italy which refused to obey. The single historical act by which a medieval emperor had apparently recognised the claims of the cities to rule themselves was the Peace of Constance, which turned out upon closer inspection to be a useless theoretical weapon.[21] No twelfth- or thirteenth-century attempt to resolve the issue had succeeded, not even the most sophisticated idea, which came from Azo, according the people a separate, elevated status as a corporation, as whose delegate the emperor ruled over each person individually.

Bartolus begins his analysis by asking whether all peoples are subject to the empire. The emperor does rule over all *de iure*: he is *dominus universalis*, which is not such an obstinate denial of contemporary reality as it appears, since Bartolus means something very specific:

> I say that the emperor is the lord of the entire world in a true sense. Nor does it conflict with this that others are lords in a particular sense, for the world is a sort of *universitas*. Hence someone can possess the said *universitas* without owning the particular things within it.[22]

Further, he is *dominus universalis* because he has jurisdiction over every-

[21] For later medieval developments in Milan concerning the Peace of Constance, see J.W. Black, 'The Limits of Ducal Authority: a Fifteenth-Century Treatise on the Visconti and their Subject Cities', in *Florence and Italy. Renaissance Studies in Honour of Nicolai Rubinstein*, ed. P. Denley and C. Elam (London, 1988), 149–60.

[22] Bartolus at D. 6.1.1. from *Bartolus super prima parte Digesti Veteris* (Lyon, 1505), hereafter cited as Bartolus, *Digestum Vetus* (Lyon 1505), fo. 172rb.

thing: *dominus quoad jurisdictionem*, as Bartolus puts it.[23] At this juncture we encounter a problem in the shape of the papacy, which claimed to rule a sizeable portion of central Italy directly, and the two Sicilies as feudal overlord of the Aragonese and Angevin dynasties.

To appreciate the extent of this difficulty, both in practice and in theory, we need only recall that *cause célèbre* in the history of papal–imperial relations from 1314, an episode which turned on precisely this point of jurisdiction over the Papal Patrimony and the kingdom of Sicily, the controversy between the emperor Henry VII and Pope Clement V. The upshot was the issue of the papal bull *Pastoralis cura*, which by Bartolus' time was part of the canon law and taught at the universities.[24] *Pastoralis cura* comes to the defence of King Robert of Sicily, the leader of Guelph opposition to the empire, who had been summoned by Henry VII to answer charges of treason at Pisa, had stayed away and consequently been convicted *in absentia*. The relevant section explains that

> The emperor could not summon the king who at that time was known to all as staying outside the *districtus imperii*, in the kingdom of Sicily.

In other words, the emperor was not the ordinary judge of Robert for all the time the latter was outside his jurisdiction. As long as he stayed in Sicily, he was under the jurisdiction of the pope. The bull provides pointed evidence that the work of Bartolus and his fellow commentators was not solely a matter of making the ancient laws of Rome fit modern, medieval facts: this law made it possible to be outside the emperor's jurisdiction and it stood in a collection of decretals – the Clementines – published in 1317, when Bartolus was already a child.

Why does Bartolus not simply recognise that the Roman law had been superseded by canon law? His conception of the empire will not allow him to concede that it is obsolete and should be forgotten. What matters in the present context is that if it is an aspect of the emperor's office to have jurisdiction over everyone and everything, the sort of legal order described in *Pastoralis cura* is challenging the disposition of God.

It is axiomatic that the inhabitants of the papal patrimony belong to the Roman people.[25] All peoples are within the empire either because they are ruled directly by it (the Germans, or some of them), or because they have prescribed rights formerly but no longer exercised by the

[23] Bartolus at *Constitutio Omnem*, from Bartolus, *Digestum Vetus* (Lyon 1505), fo. 3ra–b.

[24] E. Friedberg, *Corpus Iuris Canonici* (2 vols. Leipzig 1879, repr. Graz 1959), vol. 2, cols. 1151–1153, = *Constitutiones Clementinae* 2.11.2.

[25] For what follows see Bartolus at D. 49.15.24 (cited from *Bartolus super secunda parte Digesti Novi*, Lyon 1504), fo. 229va–230ra.

emperor (as we shall see, the cities), or because they rule themselves by imperial grant (some of the Lombard cities thanks to the Peace of Constance) or by custom, defined by contrast to Roman law, or finally by outright rejection of the emperor's authority. In all cases they are defined by Roman law, or by the gaps left by the retreat of imperial power to Germany. As the emperor ceases to exercise those powers others step in, but the powers themselves are again evidence of the membership of that particular people in the *populus Romanus*, for how else could they be exercising them?[26] If Bartolus was brilliant, we will hope that this argument is not the reason.[27]

When Bartolus discusses the capacity of a superior to summon individuals to his court he says:[28]

> Some territorial units are distinct, but are nevertheless all under the same lord, just as the Roman empire is divided into provinces [*praesidatus*].

This is, so to speak, as far as Henry VII and his lawyers had taken the issue when they summoned King Robert to Pisa.[29] For them the empire was exhaustive of Christendom, and wherever Robert may have been when the summons was issued, he was certainly somewhere in Christendom. But Bartolus has a second category of territorial unit:

> Some are distinct and separate and not under the same lord, as is the case with the lands of the empire and the lands of the pope, and then no summons runs between one territory and the other.[30]

The crucial question is: how has the papacy come to enjoy this exceptional status as a temporal lord within the empire? The justification is very hard to find. To be precise, it is hard to find one because Bartolus offers two, which are incompatible.

The first is the predictable one of grant. The inhabitants of the Patrimony are still part of the *populus Romanus* because lordship over them has been donated by Constantine to Pope Sylvester in the

[26] A sensitive explanation by Canning, *Baldus*, 47 (referring to Bartolus' comments at D. 49.15.24): 'This division of jurisdiction means that a single form, and therefore kind of authority is being exercised by two different people.'

[27] A judgement of Woolf's (*Bartolus*, 28): 'The line of argument, we may repeat, is weak perhaps: but the conclusion is clear and very important.'

[28] Bartolus at C. 1.3.31, cited here from *Bartolus super prima parte Codicis* (hereafter: Bartolus, *Codex*), Lyon 1505, fo. 25vb: 'Quedam territoria sunt distincta sub uno tantum domino sunt omnia, ut imperium romanum est divisum per presidatus. tunc unus preses potest citare in provinciam alterius, que tamen est sub eodem domino [...]'.

[29] See *Volumen*, Lyon 1585, cols. 824–853.

[30] Bartolus at C. 1.3.31 immediately following the passage quoted two notes above: 'quedam sunt territoria que sunt separata, nec tamen sub eodem domino, ut territorium imperii et pape, et tunc non potest fieri citatio de uno territorio ad aliud ...'.

notorious Donation of Constantine. This would bring the lands of the church under one of Bartolus' general arguments for the identity of empire and Christendom. It would be the argument that some peoples have their autonomy by grant and therefore are subject to the emperor indirectly. But this is not enough because in that case the kingdom of Sicily and Pisa would be under the same ultimate jurisdiction and Robert should not have been shielded by the pope in *Pastoralis cura.* However, the sense in which the Donation of Constantine is a grant is a rather strange one, and requires a brief explanation.

The Donation of Constantine is not helpfully named. It was used in the thirteenth and fourteenth centuries to exemplify the pope's powers to give the emperor his empire. According to the Donation, Constantine renounced his symbols of rule to Sylvester in gratitude for his conversion and miraculous recovery from leprosy. The pope then allowed him to rule over the Eastern Empire and re-granted such powers as were necessary to do this, eschewing direct exercise of these powers on his own account. At Christmas, 800 AD, he transferred the Empire to Charlemagne, thereby founding the notion of *translatio imperii.* As far as the papal position was concerned, it was as much the Donation of Sylvester as that of Constantine. This, then, is the grant which Bartolus uses to explain the existence of the lands of the church as a separate territorial entity with appurtenant jurisdiction.

Romanists found the Donation a challenging explanation because it so clearly broke the only rule to which even the most extreme imperialists subjected the emperor, who was otherwise deemed to be released from the laws (*legibus solutus*), since it was by the emperor's decree that the laws were laws at all.[31] He was thought to be called Augustus from *augeo* [to augment].[32] He was not meant to diminish the empire and such a vast alienation of *imperium* as the Donation of Constantine would constitute precisely that. Moreover, no emperor could bind his successor: who was to stop an emperor from revoking the Donation?

> This donation was in respect of jurisdiction, so that the pope could have jurisdiction temporally and spiritually. But the law says elsewhere that even if he wanted to try a thousand times he could not abdicate that *imperium* from himself, but would have to renounce into the hands of a superior.[33]

[31] D. 1.3.31.

[32] See Accursius at *Constitutio Omnem*, cited here from *Digestum Vetus seu Pandectarum Iuris Civilis tomus primus* (Lyon 1585), fo. 2ra, gloss *Augustus*: 'Quia eius debet esse propositi, ut augeat imperium . . .'.

[33] Bartolus at *Constitutio Omnem*, from Bartolus, *Digestum Vetus* (Lyon 1505), fo. 3rb: '. . . Illa donatio fuit respectu iurisdictionis ut haberet temporaliter et spiritualiter

We should expect, on the evidence of what we have seen already of Bartolus' main theory, that no such superior could be found, but on this occasion he does find one:

> The emperor and the church proceed from God as from their efficient cause [...] Therefore by making a gift to the church he abdicates and hands it over to a superior, for God is such a superior. The pope is the vicar of God so he seems to hand over jurisdiction to God himself.[34]

This is Bartolus' first explanation of the existence of the Patrimony and not even he believes it. It is completely out of step with Roman law, and Bartolus rather ruefully concludes this part of the argument with the candid observation that he is teaching in Perugia, which is a papal city, therefore it seems only prudent to uphold the Donation of Constantine.[35]

His second explanation of how the papacy has come to occupy this unique position in central Italy leans heavily on canon law, and is a variation of *translatio imperii*. The first empire was that of Babylon, then came the Persians, then the Greeks who were in turn supplanted by the Romans. Whereas all previous transfers had left one people completely bereft of the empire, so that the Romans took all, leaving the Greeks nothing, what happens under the Romans is rather different. Bartolus explains this change in principle as follows:

> Finally, with the advent of Christ this Roman empire became His, and so His vicar possesses both swords, the spiritual and the temporal.[36]

This forces Bartolus to add a final refinement to the statement that the

iurisdictionem. Sed lex alibi dicit quod imperium istud si millies vellet a se abdicare non posset nisi superiori daret: ut l. legatum, infra de offi. presi. [=D. 1.18.20].'

[34] *Ibid.*: '... Respondeo quod imperator et ecclesia processerunt a deo tanquam a causa efficienti [...] Ergo donando ecclesie abdicat a se et dat in manibus superioirs sicut est ipse deus. papa est vicarius eius et sic quasi ipsi deo donare videtur ...'.

[35] A useful summary at Canning, *Baldus*, 48. See for the classic exegesis D. Maffei, *La Donazione di Costantino nei Giuristi Medievali* (Milan, 1964), 185–90. For the passage itself, see Bartolus, *Digestum Vetus* (Lyon 1505), fo. 3ra: 'Videte, nos sumus in terris amicis ecclesiae: et ideo dico quod illa donatio valeat. Sed si quis vellet tenere opinionem quod non valuerit, posset respondere ad contraria et probare opinionem suam per casum dictae legis Digna vox [=C. 1.14.4].'

[36] Bartolus at *Constitutio Ad reprimendum* (*Volumen*, Lyon 1585, col. 824): 'Vel tertio inherendo opinioni sanctae ecclesiae primo fuit imperium Babylonis, secundo fuit imperium Persarum et Medorum. Tertio fuit imperium Graecorum. Quarto fuit imperium Romanoru. Ultimo adveniente Christo istud Romanum imperium coepit esse Christi imperium: et ideo apud Christi vicarium est uterque gladius, scilicet spiritualis et temporalis.'

emperor is universal lord. Before Christ the entire empire depended on him alone and he was for that reason *dominus mundi*. With Christ's advent, the empire came to Him and descended to His vicar, who then transferred it to the secular prince. It is still the empire of the Romans, but only in the religious sense in which all Christians are of the *populus Romanus*. As he made that transfer, the pope reserved to himself the principle aspects of sovereignty. This is all in clear contradiction with Bartolus' original Donation thesis, for according to that the lands of the church were an isolated block of papal jurisdiction within the wider empire. According to this, however, the empire is but the exception to the universal Christly *dominium* exercised by the Pope.[37]

In this vein Bartolus points out that the emperor's exclusively temporal power stops at the papal border, whereas the pope's spiritual power extends to all Christians whether they reside in the lands of the Church or not. This is what the two-swords analogy would demand, but Bartolus goes further by building upon the notion that the empire comes from God via the pope. If the pope has reserved ultimate jurisdiction, it would follow that he is a greater judge than the emperor, a judge who can issue summons to laymen outside the papal patrimony in temporal matters too, for 'He is vicar of the one whose is the earth and the fullness thereof.' If Christ owned the world then it followed that His vicar did in his place, and no distinction between *dominium* as ownership and *dominium quoad iurisdictionem* or *quoad protectionem* could alter that.[38] Bartolus requires the pope to be vicar of Christ in this far-reaching sense, because otherwise the Donation is not renunciation into the hands of a superior *dominus*, the only situation in which such an alienation of jurisdiction by the emperor would be legal.

So much for the Patrimony and the bull *Pastoralis cura*, concerning which Bartolus' theory is plainly a mess. What about autonomous city-states? Bartolus' position is well known and can be set out briefly. Sovereignty cannot be alienated by the emperor. It can only be delegated. According to Bartolus the Italian cities have not, generally, the right of sovereignty but have usurped it. This means that if a city wishes to defend itself as an autonomous entity it must either prove concession from the prince – a concession which can never be final but remains a delegated jurisdiction – or, if there be no such delegation, the city must prove ancient exercise, such that none can remember a time when the city did not have these powers. This is prescription, although it is not clear how such a city could plead the continual good

[37] Woolf, *Bartolus*, 97–98: 'The only admirable thing in such a discussion is the honest avowal of so dishonest a method of arriving at a conclusion.' For further discussion, see Canning, *Baldus*, 48ff.

[38] See Bartolus' comments at D. 6.1.1 (Bartolus, *Digestum Vetus*, Lyon 1505, fo. 200ra).

faith throughout its exercise of these powers which was one of the preconditions of successful prescription. Bartolus' final claim is the most important: 'However, if the city can prove that it has exercised *merum imperium*, then the claim is valid.'[39] In other words the city will cease to rank as a usurper once it has been demonstrated by the passage of years to have been a usurper. Once custom has been proven, the city can keep its *imperium*. Thanks to this, the city can expedite its own litigation by judges appointed from within. If there is an appeal from the highest tribunal in the city, it will necessarily go to the city's superior. But supposing, as seems to be the case, that this city accepts and recognises no superior? Then it must be its own superior, and here is the *civitas sibi princeps*.[40]

I have traced the exact genesis of this idea in Bartolus' writings for a good reason, which is that it allows us to back-track up the argument. Let us start with the conclusion, which is that cities enjoy the right to govern themselves because they have been doing so for a long time already, thanks to an original act of usurpation. Why stop at cities? What is to prevent the emperor, now the delegate of the pope (thanks to the Donation of Constantine and Christ's full ownership of the world), employing the same argumentative stratagem against the papacy as the cities have employed against him? Why should he not claim that, since he has exercised sovereignty over large areas of the papal patrimony, he does so *de facto*, just as the cities exclude him from their government *de facto*? For there is now no difference between *de facto* exercise of power arising from usurpation and *de iure* exercise of power. In that case, the pope has no answer to Henry VII when he demands the handover of Robert of Naples, and *Pastoralis cura* therefore becomes a dead letter. This is the technical expression of what is at heart a very simple problem with Bartolus' theory. The entire structure of debate had been set by Roman law. To suspend the operation of Roman law in one case, so as to allow *de facto* autonomy to cities, is to undermine not just the emperor's right to rule, but also the pope's right.

[39] Bartolus at C. 2.3.28 (Bartolus, *Codex*, Lyon 1505, fo. 49va): 'Scitis quod civitates communiter italie non habent merum imperium, sed usurpaverunt. Dico tamen si civitas vellet se defendere et merum imperium exercere quod habet necesse allegare concessionem principis. Item longissimum tempus quo dicta civitas merum imperium exercuit, isto casu posito quod non probaretur de concessione principis, tamen si probaret se exercuisse merum imperium valet . . .'.

[40] Bartolus at D. 49.1.1 (*Bartolus super secunda parte Digesti Novi*, Lyon 1504, fo. 208rb): 'Pone quod est civitas, que non recognoscit superiorem, et que eligit ipsa sibi rectorem, nec habet alium officialem: quis erit iudex appellationis? Respondeo: ipse populus, seu ordo qui ipsum officialem facit, quia solus reperitur superior ipsi populo, et sibi princeps est . . .' We will see shortly that the immediate context of this phrase – appeals from the city's courts – is not coincidental in so far as it presupposes internal challenges to civic jurisdiction.

With that once established, we might wish to explore another anomaly of Bartolus' theory. There is no legislation from the fourteenth-century emperors concerning Italian cities. There is, however, a mass of papal legislation, witness the entire law code promulgated by Cardinal Gil Albornoz, attentive, it is true, to the liberty of the cities, yet nonetheless asserting a claim to much more than just a vacuous papal overlordship.[41] Here, we might say, with the fainéant emperors of the fourteenth century as a comparison, is a *real* universal authority, which legislates, controls within the limits of the possible the appointment of civic magistrates, sends armies. Few historical *bons mots* have been so annihilatingly refuted by the event as Pierre Flote's taunt to Boniface VIII in the last years before the papacy's escape to Avignon: 'vestra potestas verbalis ...' Witnesses of Bertrand du Poujet's legation in the 1320s might rather have dwelt on the practical aspects of the affair: the submission of the proud Bologna to papal officials, and, most instructively in the present context, the disbanding of republican organs of consultative government there.[42] Can Bartolus' theory of the *civitas sibi princeps*, which we have just presented in the manner normal amongst historians, take account of this? The answer is quite clearly not. If the theory of the *civitas sibi princeps* belongs so securely in the context we have just given it, then something very important is missing. It might, on a charitable and not particularly legalistic reading of that most legalistic construct of prescription, provide a counterweight to the empire;[43] it provides absolutely no defence against papal claims, claims which were made in the most concrete of terms. The emperor, to make the point clear, was a far less serious problem than the pope, yet the pope is barely mentioned by Bartolus.

These considerations prompt a review of the place of the *civitas sibi princeps* in Bartolus' thought, and consequently a review of the place of Bartolus' thought in the tradition of Roman law theory since Irnerius and the early days of Bologna. As a contribution to the debate about Italian cities within the empire, the theory is a shambles. Secondly, is it not strange that Bartolus opts for such a technical and abstruse formulation: the city is prince unto itself? Why not simply say that the government is the *podestà*, scrutinised by the council or a number of councils, which in turn derive their legitimacy from their majoritarian

[41] A. Wolf, 'Die Gesetzgebung der entstehenden Territorialstaaten,' *Handbuch der Quellen und Literatur der neueren europäischen Privatrechtsgeschichte*, vol. 1, *Mittelalter*, ed. H. Coing (Munich, 1973), 517–800 at 714ff; P. Colliva, *Il Cardinale Albornoz, Lo Stato della Chiesa, Le 'Constitutiones Aegidianae' (1353–1357)*, *Studia Albornotiana* XXXII (Bologna, 1977), 101–66 in general, and 135 in particular.

[42] P. Partner, *The Lands of St. Peter* (London, 1972), 317–18.

[43] For the risks of building a theory of civic autonomy on prescription, see Bartolus' own comments at D. 39.3.1 and C. 3.34.1.

representation of the citizens, all according to another of Bartolus' more celebrated ideas: *concilium representat mentem populi*?[44] This would not only cover republican constitutions. It would also be relevant to the signorial constitutions of those cities which had elected a lord to govern them, unfettered by the cumbersome apparatus of consultation and division of powers which vitiated republican government. In both cases, an original act of election could account for the existence of government and its right to function as a coercive authority. Why does Bartolus need the double abstraction not merely of a city, but of a city which is governed by its own disembodied *princeps*?

The answer to this is at the same time the explanation of the weakness in Bartolus' theory of papacy and empire in relation to the cities. The *civitas sibi princeps* is aimed first and foremost at those who denied the right of their fellows to govern them within the city itself. It addresses what modern parlance terms problems of internal sovereignty, not those of external sovereignty. The vast majority of Bartolus' writings, in common with those of his colleagues, address the legal disputes arising from the practice of republican and signorial government. Politics was an unforgiving business in fourteenth-century Italy: if the Guelphs got in, the Ghibellines were expelled; either that or subjected to penal constraints in fiscal and electoral law which effectively removed them from the body of citizens. It is a pardonable exaggeration to say that governments did not represent anyone in Italian cities in the fourteenth century, because outside government there was so often only exile, dispossession or a strictly limited right of domicile. This had immediate and long-lasting effects on political vocabulary, the very language, in fact, of legitimacy and so of legal theory, all the more so since it had been a fact of life for so long. The signs are everywhere in the surviving documentation, and they appear early. We might be in Mantua, witnessing the treaty of 1208 between Cremona, Verona, Azo of Este and the Counts of Sanbonifacio, in which reference is made to the obligations of Verona to 'the knights of Brescia, who have retired [i.e. been expelled] from Brescia *and whom we take to be the commune of Brescia*:'[45] proof, this, both of the normative sense of the word 'commune' and its wilful application according to interest and party. Alternatively, we might be with the knights of Brescia themselves, who twelve years later sent a spokesman to an imperial legate in Borgo San Donino in order to exonerate themselves of the charge of having expelled the *podestà* Maffeo da Correggio and denying

[44] Woolf, *Bartolus*, 181ff; W. Ullmann, '*De Bartoli Sententia*' *passim*; Canning, *Baldus*, 95ff.

[45] J. Ficker, *Forschungen zur Reichs-und Rechtsgeschichte Italiens* IV (Innsbruck 1868–74, repr. Aalen 1961), 266–68: '... et militum Brixie, qui exierunt Brixie, quos intelligimus esse commune Brixie.'

him his agreed salary. Neither the knights, *nor the commune* are liable; the *popolares* should pay, for it was they who had resisted the new *podestà* at the very moment of his installation.[46] Here, in sharp contrast to the explicit statement of the Mantuan text, the commune is no longer the exiled knights, nor indeed any concrete group, but something outside them all.

It is not surprising, yet it is rarely mentioned in connection with Bartolus, that lawyers had frequently been employed by those left out in the cold – literally, in many cases – by the vicissitudes of zero-sum politics. A considerable, if chaotic, body of ideas had long been in circulation at the universities concerning exactly these themes. Some time after 1270, Fredericus de Schalis was commissioned to write a consultation on how membership of the Bolognese Lambertazzi faction should be defined. In this particular instance, one member of a favoured group, the Lambertazzi di Granata, found himself on the blacklist as well as the list of the politically reliable. He had attended council meetings, and was consequently accused of contravening the statute passed by the victorious faction of the Geremei, forbidding the Lambertazzi all access to the organs of government.[47] Now, it should not have over-stretched a lawyer's ingenuity to prove that not all Lambertazzi were Lambertazzi, yet the argument which follows is curiously troubled and complex. Fredericus' predominant concern in his consultation is to prove that local statute does have sufficient force to exclude the Lambertazzi in general, aside from the particular difficulties of the case, caused by a bureaucratic anomaly:[48]

[46] Ibid, 314–16: 'Sed dixit [the speaker is Uberto de Gambara, the emissary of the knights of Brescia] quod communi displicuit et parti militum, quod ipse [Maffeo] recessit de civitate, et de violentia ei facta; et quod parata fuit pars militum ipsum tenere in potestaria et ei iurare; quare dicebat, quod pars ipsa, que fecerat dictam violentiam, ipsum salarium solvere debebat et non commune, nec pars militum.'

[47] I have been unable to trace the precise statute and amendment referred to by Fredericus. Statutes passed by the Geremei discriminating against the Lambertazzi by forbidding them access to governmental office are, however, legion in *Statuti di Bologna dell'anno 1288*, ed. G. Fasoli and P. Sella (*Studi e Testi* 73, Vatican 1937). See, for example, II. 8 ('De Lambertaciis qui non possunt habere offitium nec esse consiliarii'), V. 47, V. 73, V. 104, V. 152 (mentioning registers of proscribed persons amongst the Lambertazzi and a list of those exempt from such proscription who have sworn the Geremei oath). See also *Memoriale Historicum Rerum Bononiensium ab anno MCIX usque ad MCCCCXXVIII, auctore Matthaeo de Griffonibus* (*Rerum Italicarum Scriptores* 18), col. 122 for a reference to what appears to be the precise measure ('... quod non possent ire in rure, nec ascendere palatium ...').

[48] Ms. Vatican, Biblioteca Apostolica Vaticana, Archivio San Pietro A. 29, hereafter Vatican A.S.P. A. 29, fo. 187rb: 'Item certum est quod ascendere palacium alicui lambertacio in casu isto est delictum, et hoc potuit facere statutum quod appellatur ius civile vel municipale civitatis. et hoc est quod statuta civitatum dicimus [...] et casus sunt speciales in corpore iuris ubi cavetur quod iura municipalia non valent contra iura communia [...] Alias regulariter dicimus quod iura municipalia et consuetudines locorum

> Furthermore, it is certain that to enter the palazzo in this case is a crime for any of the Lambertazzi, and civic statute which is called the civil law or municipal law of the city can establish this [...] And there are special cases described in the [Roman] law where municipal laws have no validity against the common law [...]. But otherwise, we say generally that municipal law and the customs of specific places derogate from the Roman law and are obeyed in those cases for which they have been specifically passed...

The Lambertazzi response would surely be that this law has indeed and all too obviously been passed for a specific set of circumstances: its sole intent is to keep them out of government. What sense does it make, then, to call this the law of the city? It is rather the law of the Geremei, who are now in control of the city.

It speaks volumes that the glossators were frequently incapable even of defining a city.[49] In the same manuscript of legal consultations and school-room discussions as the last text by Fredericus, an anonymous author asks what exactly is meant when a king concedes a privilege to the cities and citizens of his realm.[50] 'A city is a multitude of people gathered together to live by law.' This commonplace of Ciceronian extraction is of but limited use in the present context since the law is being used effectively to remove people from the city. Then again, 'a city is an honest collection of many people living together in closely neighbouring buildings'. Who is to define honesty here? Other intellectual traditions of some power in this period were therefore negated by these practical and legal considerations. Cicero had defined a *res publica* as preeminently a *res populi*, a thing belonging to or relating in some essential way to the people, and had then gone on to define a people as a multitude brought together by, amongst other common goals and aspirations, the common perception of what was right, of

derogantur iuri civili et servantur in ea causa ubi facta sunt...' On this manuscript see F. Migliorino, '*Dominus meus in legibus*: The search for a Liber Quaestionum of Martinus Syllimani', *The Two Laws. Studies in Medieval legal History Dedicated to Stephan Kuttner*, ed. L. Mayali and S. Tibbetts (Washington, 1990), 121–51.

49 A general remark in this sense in U. Meier, *Mensch und Bürger. Die Stadt im Denken spätmittelalterlicher Theologen, Philosophen und Juristen* (Munich, 1994), 132, which is to be preferred to the comments of G. Tabacco, *The Struggle for Power in Medieval Italy. Structures of Political Rule* (Cambridge, 1989), 190, where the focus on the lawyers is nevertheless welcome.

50 Vatican A.S.P. A. 29, fo. 224vb, incipit: 'Rex concessit privilegium sive beneficium civitatibus vel civibus regni sui. Queritur [primo] civitatum vel civium appellacione [que] terre et persone [contineantur].' The corrections in brackets are supplied from Vatican, Biblioteca Apostolica Vaticana, Chigi. E.VIII.245, hereafter Vatican Chigi E.VIII. 245, fo. 85vb, where the text is attributed to Iacobus de Belvisio, author of the most influential commentary on the *Libri Feudorum*, and luminary of the university of Naples.

what should be law (*consensus iuris*).[51] To see how far one could get with that, we have only to consider the obvious fact that many of these cities had different laws for different sections of the population, 'legislating' for themselves in their own protection.

Cinus of Pistoia, the man who more than any other shaped Bartolus' own ideas, had to address precisely this issue in one of his consultations.

> Although by the common law, the term 'people' includes nobles and magnates, by the customary law of virtually all Italy, it embraces only the plebs. Whence it is that we talk about the commune and the popolo. The word commune signifies both the magnates and the common people, but the councils of the cities and the decrees of the magnates are distinct. For the council of the commune and the decrees of the commune are one thing, the council and the decrees of the popolo another.

Cinus' dizzying swings from popolo to magnates, councils and communes (all within the same city) are not the result of legalistic brio.[52] Taken together with the foregoing examples of how helpless lawyers were when it came to identifying the collectivities which ordered expulsions, or functioned as the recipients of privileges, they surely provide some stimulus to approach Bartolus' *civitas sibi princeps* from within rather than from without, in relation to its worst and most immediate enemies, which were its own citizens, however simplistic that word has now been shown to be.[53]

Neither the government (or, rather, to follow Cinus, governments) nor the citizen body will serve as source and focus of political obligation, first because for practical purposes they are frequently one and the same; secondly, because as such they are elements in the volatile reaction. They do not and cannot stand above it. Everything depends on how we define our collectivity, the composite entity which constitutes the city and/or its *populus*. Yet it seems that no concrete identification

[51] Cicero, *De republica*, 2.42, known in the Middle Ages via Augustine, *De civitate dei* 2.21.

[52] Vatican Chigi E.VIII. 245, fo. 137ra: 'Licet de iure communi appellatio populi etiam magnates [supply: et] nobiles complectantur, de iure tamen consuetudinario quasi totius ytalie appellatio populi non continet nisi plebeios. Et hinc venit quod dicimus commune et populus, quod appellatio communis significat etiam magnates et populi plebeios, tamen distincta sunt consilia civitatum et ordines [et?] decreta decurionum. nam aliud consilium et decretum communis et aliud consilium et decretum populi.' Note that Cinus adds yet another interpretation of a commune to the two we have just encountered from Brescia.

[53] The standard treatment of citizenship in Bartolus is by Canning, *Baldus*, 171–79, to which I have nothing to add. It is, however, relevant to my present argument that citizenship could take so many different qualified and limited forms short of full political participation, such that the question of who constituted the citizen body raises an extremely complex set of issues.

between the *populus* and particular groups of political players would do, for they changed too frequently and too radically. With the city taken as an abstraction, however, which is its own superior, the problem can be clarified. If a faction attempts to gain power, their crime is not committed against those currently in power. Those in power are in most cases no different in kind from their would-be supplanters. One faction is as good as another, one might say, and it is at best capricious to grace the most powerful faction with the title *civitas*, *populus*, or *commune*. Even if one has a favourite (as Bartolus of course does in the shape of his beloved Perugian constitutional arrangements), one would be hard-put to justify that choice against the excluded. Moreover, as we have seen, these separate words can under some circumstances apply to separate organs of government with discrete powers within the same city. None of them describes the whole collective, not even *commune*. Before whom or what can this insurrection be said to be an offence, then? If there were only a superior, perhaps the emperor or the pope, this would not be a difficulty, although we shall soon note an irony in precisely this context.[54] The whole point is, in any case, that this is a free city, recognising no superior. This superior cannot be the fleshly government of the *podestà* or the council (or one of them!) because these people and councils are but the figureheads of factions, as such no different and certainly no better than the insurgents themselves. But call the city its own superior, reify public powers to form an abstraction on behalf of which government takes place, and you have something which can function as a subject of rights, as the bearer of sovereignty.

The desirability of such an abstraction is clear enough from the statement in his treatise *De guelphis et gebellinis*: 'those who hold the *res publica* by tyranny detain it by force from the *res publica* itself or its superior lord, not from any private person'.[55] The same thought is expressed in Bartolus' *De regimine civitatis*, where judges who rule alone in a given territory are not the same as kings, who of course also rule alone, 'For they (scil. the judges) have to judge according to the laws, nor do they have royal status but one appropriate to ministers, nor do regalian rights pertain to them but rather to the cities which they rule

[54] See the uncontroversial dismissal of the matter at *De tyranno*, lines 555ff, where the reference to the *Lex Iulia maiestatis* makes it clear that Bartolus envisages a city with a superior when he asks, 'Sed in quam legem incidunt tyranni et per quam legem veniunt deponendi?' All citations of *De tyranno*, *De guelphis et gebellinis* and *De regimine civitatis* are by line numbers, and follow the edition of D. Quaglioni, *Politica e Diritto nel Trecento Italiano (Il Pensiero Politico* 11, Florence, 1983).

[55] *De guelphis et gebellinis*, 149–51: '. . . quia illi qui occupatam per tyrannidem tenent rem publicam, vi eam possident ab ipsa re publica vel domino superiori, non ab aliquo privato.'

or another superior, or the fisc ...'[56] The first passage proves that in Bartolus' mind it was essential for there to be a superior of some sort if insurrection and consequent tyranny were to constitute a crime.[57] The somewhat clumsy formulation he chooses in this instance is that the *res publica* is being withheld from the *res publica*. The meaning of the second *res publica* in this sentence is revealed by the quotation from *De regimine civitatis*, where the word used is *civitas*, a *civitas* which is at the same time a superior.

No medieval jurist before Bartolus had even come close to resolving the issue, although the texts cited above from the works of some of his forerunners show plainly enough that many had tried. Entrenched in discussions of the *populus Romanus* and its putative powers to discipline the *princeps*, Azo argued past the point: there *was* no *princeps*, and if the 'people' were not the *populus Romanus*, no other abstraction of people would help. Contrary to what is occasionally implied in more general studies, there was no readily available theory of human corporations in Roman law. Roman law, in fact, is obstinately unresponsive to the attractions of treating groups of people as corporate individuals. The expression *universitas* more often denotes a collectivity of things, rights, and obligations in Roman law, than people. Canon law had a sophisticated apparatus of corporations, but insisted that no corporation could found itself: it needed a superior to recognise it and appoint its visible, flesh-and-blood spokesman.[58] If that were possible for the Italian cities, they would not be free cities recognising no superior, so the problem would not arise.

The tensions in Bartolus' ideas about the interaction between free cities and wider sovereign bodies such as the empire are real and important, but they are only so crassly obvious because these matters were not Bartolus' primary concern. It was more urgent to decide what happened within a city once the jurisdiction of the emperor had been denied. If he did not have disciplinary powers, who did? Every example of the kind of *quaestiones* and *consilia* discussed above is proof that answers were sought to these questions by the people most nearly touched by the reality of government. Every *tractatus de bannitis* indicates the same. The emperor was largely an irrelevance in such matters. A further advantage of looking at the *civitas sibi princeps* in this way is that

[56] *De regimine civitatis*, 181–4: 'Isti enim habent iudicare secundum leges, nec tenent statum regium sed competentem ministris, nec ad eos competunt regalia sed ad civitates quas regunt, vel ad alium superiorem, vel fiscum ...'.

[57] An analogous, more detailed, statement of the same position at *De tyranno*, 144ff, where there can be no tyranny in a locality in which no jurisdiction is exercised in the first place, either *de facto* or *de iure*.

[58] B. Tierney, *Foundations of the Conciliar Theory. The Contribution of the Medieval Canonists from Gratian to the Great Schism* (Cambridge, 1955), 106–53.

Bartolus' silence about the papacy's possible claims to rule the free cities ceases to be a problem. If the papacy governs, where it governs, there is no need for a city prince unto itself, just as there is no need for it in cities still acknowledging the emperor. Where no such recognition is given, the problem is not so much to justify that independence against a universal power, but rather to justify a claim by anyone to govern in that city as it stands, and therefore to find a rationale for condemning those who seek to subvert that government.

A survey of the *consilia* the fourteenth-century lawyers wrote for ruling families would corroborate much of this. These texts are the other political advice books of the Italian middle ages, but like the majority of their more congenially written prose counterparts, they consistently refrain from advocating concrete legal retribution for the wrongs inflicted by governments recognising no superior.[59] One is frequently exasperated by this failing, and driven to ask why the lawyers did not lend their knowledge of detail to the abstract generalisations of, say, John of Salisbury or Thomas Aquinas, both of whom had sanctioned tyrannicide in works well known to the Italian jurists of the fourteenth century and much prized by them. The answer is simple. Strong government was not the problem such lawyers had to face, let alone over-mighty government. Wearying succession of weak governments was the chief difficulty, exacerbated by the lack of a cogent justification of local government good against those whose obedience it needed, those who at the same time were most likely to challenge it. If Bartolus' *civitas sibi princeps* is taken as one of the most sophisticated attempts to achieve this, its failure as an argument against imperial pretensions should surely be forgiven.

Bartolus still, however, leaves us with a riddle. If the argument advanced above be accepted, we should not expect much of an engagement on Bartolus' part with the problem of civic autonomy against the interests of the empire. We should, however, expect him to insist on the difference between legitimate government and tyranny, on the difference between a politically empowered collective and a mere faction. Specifically, this is the question with which he begins the third section of *De Guelphis et Gebellinis*, the first sustained attempt by a medieval jurist to establish the legality or otherwise of the quotidian

[59] Baldus' démarche in his *consilium* for the Visconti known as *Rex Romanorum* is the most famous example. See Canning, *Baldus*, 221–27, and for an alternative interpretation to that advanced by Canning and by myself, the important discussion of K. Pennington, *The Prince and the Law 1200–1600. Sovereignty and Rights in the Western Legal Tradition* (Berkeley, Los Angeles and Oxford 1993), 205ff. The debate now appears closed thanks to J. Canning, 'Italian juristic thought and the realities of power in the fourteenth century', *Political Thought and the Realities of Power in the Middle Ages*, ed. J. Canning and O.G. Oexle (Göttingen 1998), 229–39.

realities and obsessions of Italian politics.[60] More generally, it is not the least of his achievements that he has injected some normative value into the tired vocabulary of *populus*, *civitas* and the like. This is exactly what we find, and with it, we encounter the final, insuperable problem of Bartolus' thought. The *civitas sibi princeps* is, as we have seen, a synonym for *ipsa res publica* from which the *res publica* may be detained, the purpose of which, in turn, was to provide a stronger legal reason for proceeding against insurgents; thanks to this abstraction their crime was against a public, not a private person. The difficulty resides precisely in the fact that Bartolus differentiates between just and unjust rule not simply on the grounds of what governments actually do, but also (indeed, chiefly) on the grounds of who forms the government.

When reviewing Giles of Rome's list of typically tyrannical measures, which include, most significantly, expulsion, Bartolus actually ratifies most of them.[61] A just government will occasionally have to exile prominent citizens, for it is they who are best placed to foment unrest. Similarly with the use of spies and informers, with the prohibition of lawful public and private assembly, with the use of foreign bodyguards: a just government has good reason to adopt all of these heavy-handed measures. And this is the point. A just government has *good* reason, the tyrant has an evil reason.[62] What, then, is a just government? In the case of cities recognising a superior such as the emperor, the question practically answers itself, for the existence of such an universal superior lord as good as defines tyrannical behaviour: 'For just as the king or emperor of the Romans is a true, just and universal king, so it is that if someone wants to detain that place unjustly he is properly called a tyrant ...'[63] By 'unjustly' Bartolus means without title, that is, without

[60] *De guelphis et gebellinis*, 114ff, beginning: 'Circa tertium, scilicet utrum habere istas affectiones sit licitum ...'.

[61] *De tyranno*, 483–544. Consider, by way of example, Bartolus' robustly practical comment on discrimination against the prominent citizens at 486: 'Quis enim dubitat, quod si aliquis esset in civitate potens, rixosus et seditiosus, iste debeat de civitate expelli a quolibet iusto iudice?'

[62] *Ibid*, immediately following: 'Tunc cum iusta causa fieret, non esset actus tyrannicus.' This is repeated in relation to the persecution by the tyrant of the learned and educated (492), and the disbanding of a city's educational institutions, concerning which Bartolus is much too much the lawyer to countenance the teaching of Roman law at simply any location (497: 'Si vero prohibetur studium ad quod civitas non est apta, non est actus tyrannicus, ut in i. constitutione ff. orum ...'). Most instructively, Bartolus' qualified sanction of a prohibition of assembly concludes (503): 'Ex qualitate ergo personarum comprehenditur, an istas sodalitates turbare sit actus tyrannicus.' The difficulty of deciding on the qualities of persons had already prompted many cities to compile lists of the politically unreliable, the kind of list which we have already seen failing to achieve its end in the case of the Lambertazzi of Bologna.

[63] *De tyranno*, 65–9: '... Sicut enim rex seu imperator Romanorum proprie est verus et iustus rex et universalis, ita si quis illum locum vult iniuste tenere proprie appellatur tyrannus.'

grant or delegation from the emperor. Similarly, all acts committed by a usurper are null because such a tyrant 'cuts himself off from the communion of the universal empire, which is clear enough because he transgresses against the *Lex Iulia maiestatis* . . .'[64]

What, however, could be the criterion in the case of a free city which benefits from Bartolus' *de iure–de facto* distinction? This city is already an usurper. What allows Bartolus to argue that one way of governing this city – by an elected assembly – is legitimate, whereas another way of governing it – by a single person – is not? After all, both governments will be behaving in similar fashion. The answer might be thought to reside in the common good, with which Bartolus makes free play throughout his three treaties on civic politics, but with the common good we return to the initial problem: whose good is the common one? Bartolus' practical good sense has already led him to claim as just tools of a just government most of the methods employed by a tyrant. In the same vein he admits: 'For there is nothing against calling someone a tyrant with respect to certain persons, but a just judge with respect to the community . . .'[65] Who is the community if this is (as it appears to be) a typical city governed in the typical manner, that is, by means of expropriation, expulsion and other forms of political discrimination, a city where the alpha and omega of constitutional debate will be embraced by the question: who is the community? Further, and even more candidly, he notes: 'One rarely comes across any government which attends entirely to the public good and in which there is no hint of tyranny . . .'[66] In the end, there is little conviction even in that most movable of medieval feasts, the greater and weightier part of the people, on which Bartolus falls back towards the end of *De tyranno*.[67] Who are the people?[68]

The greatest and entirely unacknowledged weakness of Bartolus'

[64] *Ibid.*, 288–90: 'Sed tempus tyrannidis potest dici tempus scismatis. Scindit enim tyrannus se et separat se a communione universalis imperii: quod patet, quia incidit in legem Iuliam maiestatis . . .'.

[65] *Ibid.*, 743–45: 'Nichil enim prohibet, quod quis respectu certarum personarum dicatur tyrannus, respectu vero communitatis iustus iudex . . .'.

[66] *Ibid.*, 747–49: '. . . raro reperitur aliquod regimen, in quo simpliciter ad bonum publicum attendatur et in quo aliquid tyrannidis non sit.'

[67] Lines 734–35: 'Et predicta vera, quando maior pars populi opprimitur, gravatur vel male contentatur.'

[68] It will be clear, therefore, that I regard Ullmann's endorsement of Bartolus' majoritarian method of establishing the moment at which consent is deemed to be given by the people as wide of the mark. It is one thing to insist that Bartolus' apparent endorsement of majority voting presupposes the equality of the people and therefore represents 'an important advance towards a properly conceived individualism' (Ullmann, '*De Bartoli Sententia*', 719), but quite another to treat as the people only those with the right to vote. See, in any case, the passage cited at the end of note 62 above for a more qualitative assessment of civic and uncivic contribution by Bartolus.

justification of independent cities is also an indirect result of what has most endeared him to modern commentators: his willingness to argue *de facto* instead of formally or *de iure*. The attractions of such a method are manifest, especially when measured against the earlier medieval jurisprudence discussed in the foregoing pages. However, a *de facto* theory will perforce take the fact as primary by deriving normative positions from the facts. If the facts change, the theory loses credibility. In other words, Bartolus' argument verges on brittle empiricism because it leaves no room for dynamic. When the Cardinal Legate Gil Albornoz sanctioned the right of the Malatesta to rule over Rimini, Pesaro, Fano and Fossombrone,[69] those who by Bartolus' definition had previously been *tyranni ex defectu tituli* could henceforth only be described as tyrants by the suspiciously *ad hominem* argument that the papacy frequently had to suffer the lesser evil for want of means to eradicate the greater by direct confrontation.[70] The tendency of the powerful to reach terms over the heads of cities like Perugia, the comparative ease with which universal authorities re-established what Bartolus had long abandoned, the *de iure* ordering of Italy, lends redoubled urgency to the question of what constitutes a people, for a theory deriving powers of self-government from the people in Aristotelian terms would then have been open to him. But he is too concerned with things as they are to make systematic use of Aristotle on this point at all attractive. As a result, his appeal to the common good is little more convincing than an appeal to any other sectarian interest. Consider, for example, his discussion of which forms of government best suit settlements of different sizes.[71] No energy is devoted to defining the difference between, say, Perugia, a city with a *populus* legislating for itself, and those peoples subject to Perugia. A puny and debilitated human body may not govern itself without the help of a tutor or curator; 'little peoples' cannot rule themselves in any way, but must submit to another or ally with another. This is hardly an argument calculated to defend Perugia against the same charge which Perugia, in ever more obsolete republican-Guelf tradition, levelled at, say, the Visconti or the Malatesta, least of all once those men had put themselves on the side of legitimacy by negotiating with the empire or papacy. *De facto* argument of this nature smacks more of empiricism than scholasticism, of convenience rather than rigour. The rapacity with which Perugia defended its rule over its own *signoria* of subject peoples sits ill with the highly charged vocabulary of

[69] Colliva, *Albornoz*, 113–17.

[70] *De tyranno*, 607–11.

[71] *De regimine civitatis*, 441–48: 'Et videmus in civitatibus et castris, que sunt sub protectione huius civitatis Perusine. Sicut enim corpus humanum debile et parvum non potest per se regi sine auxilio tutoris et curatoris, ita isti populi parvi per se nullo modo regi possunt, nisi alteri submittantur vel alteri adhereant.'

the common good with which Bartolus upholds the *regimen ad populum* in which he so passionately believes. Bartolus needs a justification for the self-government of a free people, but only *one* free people.

The success of Bartolus' theory is, therefore, open to some doubt. If we take the *civitas sibi princeps* as an argument against the emperor, then we shall stop reading Bartolus at the outset, for as an argument it will not stand. Its strength lies in justifying government once the legal, formal source of jurisdiction has been by-passed. But this by-passing operation requires a suspension of critical faculties in order to work: we have to assent to *de facto* instead of *de iure* argument. If we do, then we must admit that the readiness to accept what we find and accord it legitimate status commits us to accepting the tyrant as well as the council. The irony of Bartolus' achievement is that if the *civitas sibi princeps* works for anybody, it works for everybody, including those whom Bartolus could only suffer to rule as grotesque travesties of all that is good, expedient and just.

COURT CASES AND LEGAL ARGUMENTS IN ENGLAND, *c*.1066–1166

By John Hudson

READ 21 MAY 1999 AT THE UNIVERSITY OF READING

THE relationship between law, the power of participants in disputes, and the structure of society and politics is always a complex one. It is also, not surprisingly therefore, controversial in writings on jurisprudence, modern law, and legal history. In this paper I argue for the importance of legal norms in the conduct of disputes in England in the period between the Norman Conquest and the early Angevin legal reforms. This importance is certainly related to the extent of Anglo-Norman royal power. However, in a wider context I shall argue against any necessary, simple, and direct link between political structure and the existence and influence of legal norms.

My arguments therefore run contrary to many recent treatments of mediaeval disputing, initially focusing on France but now stretching at least as far east as Poland and northwards to the British Isles and well beyond.[1] These emphasise activity outside court and involving force or

[1] See esp. G. Duby, 'The evolution of judicial institutions', in his *The Chivalrous Society* (1977), tr. C. Postan, 15–58, a highly influential article which concentrates primarily on jurisdiction and the administration of justice and on disputes and settlements. [Hereafter Duby, 'Judicial Institutions'.] F.L. Cheyette, '*Suum Cuique Tribuere*', *French Historical Studies*, 6 (1970), 287–99 [Hereafter Cheyette, 'Suum Cuique']; S.D. White, ' "*Pactum ... Legem Vincit et Amor Iudicium*": the Settlement of Disputes by Compromise in Eleventh-Century Western France', *American Journal of Legal History*, 22 (1978), 281–308 [Hereafter White, 'Pactum']; P.R. Hyams, 'Henry II and Ganelon', *Syracuse Scholar*, 4 (1983), 22–35 [Hereafter Hyams, 'Henry II']; P.J. Geary, 'Living with Conflicts in Stateless France: a Typology of Conflict Management Mechanisms, 1050–1200', in his *Living with the Dead in the Middle Ages* (Ithaca, NY, 1994), 125–60; M.T. Clanchy, 'Law and Love in the Middle Ages', in *Disputes and Settlements: Law and Human Relations in the West*, ed. J. Bossy (Cambridge, 1983), 47–67 [Hereafter Clanchy, 'Law and Love']; P.H. Freedman, *The Diocese of Vic* (New Brunswick, NJ, 1983), ch. 5 on 'the informal system'; P. Gorecki, '*Ad Controversiam Reprimendam*: Family Groups and Dispute Prevention in Medieval Poland, c. 1200', *Law and History Review*, 14 (1996), 213–43. For related works, placing more emphasis on legal argument in court, see W.I. Miller, *Bloodtaking and Peacemaking: Feud, Law and Society in Saga Iceland* (Chicago, Illinois, 1990), esp. ch. 7 [Hereafter Miller, *Bloodtaking*]; S.D. White, 'Inheritances and Legal Arguments in Western France, 1050–1150', *Traditio*, 43 (1987), 55–103, esp. 84. [Hereafter White, 'Inheritances'] Note further the articles in *The Settlement of Disputes in Early Medieval Europe*, ed. W. Davies and P. Fouracre (Cambridge, 1986), although the overall conclusions of that volume pay rather less attention to types of norms which concern me here; their focus, e.g. at 218, is on procedural rules. [Hereafter *Settlement of Disputes*, ed. Davies and Fouracre.] For another article questioning the model laid out in this paragraph, see J.

mediation. Within court, they tend to stress the following points.[2] Apart from formal claims and denials, procedure and argument displayed considerable informality and flexibility. Personality and power, honour and shame came into play, implicitly or explicitly. Argument did not focus on legal rules; indeed the legal was not clearly distinguished, if distinguished at all, from the social or the religious. Disputes in general were settled by compromise, from which no one left empty-handed. Often, but not always, these various elements are seen as closely inter-related, for instance forming part of the so called *mutation féodale*. Implicit in many such analyses is a contrast drawn between the 'political' nature of early medieval disputing and a highly rules-based version of later law and disputing.[3]

The aptness of such views can be assessed in various ways. One might, for example, survey the conduct of disputes, in and out of court, from start to finish.[4] Here, however, I work outwards to the discussion of the nature of law and the practice of disputing from analysis of argument in courts in England *c.*1066–1166. More can be said of the nature and use of norms within such argument than has sometimes been believed, in ways that are revealing of the ideas and practices of

---

Martindale, '"His Special Friend"? The Settlement of Disputes and Political Power in the Kingdom of the French (Tenth to mid-Twelfth Century)', *TRHS* 6th Ser. 5 (1995), 21–57. [Hereafter Martindale, 'Special Friend'.] I would like to thank Rob Bartlett, Paul Brand, George Garnett, Bill Miller and Esther Pascua for their comments on drafts of this article, and Dan Klerman for wide-ranging advice.

[2] See e.g. Hyams, 'Henry II', 27, 35; Duby, 'Judicial Institutions', 55, 58; Cheyette, '*Suum Cuique*', 288–9, 293; White, '*Pactum*', 283.

[3] The debate concerning the relationship of law and politics is made more problematic by the instability of both terms. Historians of mediaeval law and disputes have tended to use political in a particular sense: 'Early medieval court cases were political ... That is to say, they fitted into the network of local social relationships that preceded each case, and indeed succeeded it, slightly modified by the case itself' (*Settlement of Disputes*, ed. Davies and Fouracre, 233). However, other possible senses of political seem to underlie their writings, and these become apparent in theoretical writings on modern law. Some would categorise politics simply in terms of what politicians, as opposed to lawyers, do; e.g. R.A. Posner, *The Problems of Jurisprudence* (Cambridge, Mass., 1990), 130–1. Others would see politics as entering into law whenever a judicial decision is grounded on 'policy'; e.g. R.M. Dworkin, *Law's Empire* (1986). Others see law as inherently political because of the power and ideological bias inherent within society; e.g. M. Kelman, *A Guide to Critical Legal Studies* (Cambridge, Mass., 1987), 3–4, and ch. 9; D. Kennedy, *A Critique of Adjudication* (Cambridge, Mass., 1997), chs 3 and 4. [Hereafter Posner, *Problems*; Kelman, *Guide*; Kennedy, *Critique*] It is not therefore that a particular period or area is unusual in the existence of a mingling of law and politics; rather what must be investigated is the particular nature of that mingling.

[4] I adopted something of this approach in 'La Interpretación de Disputas y Resoluciones: el Caso Inglés, 1066–1135', *Hispania*, 57 (1997), 885–916, which included discussion of issues further developed here, and also, at p. 913, a brief consideration of the consequences outside court of my reassertion of the importance of the normative. [Hereafter Hudson, 'Interpretación'.]

participants in disputes. At the same time, the conclusions are important in explaining later legal development.

Some of these norms decided cases, others had more restricted influence. Some were precise, others general. Moreover, some can be classified as legal as distinct from being elements of common social practice or belief. For example, ecclesiastical insistence on life grants returning to the church clashed with lay social norms, which accepted the principle of inheritance. Sometimes churches caved in by allowing a succession of life-tenures, all granted with the specification that the church would take back the land on the tenant's death. Such instances show a clear and significant differentiation between law and social practice.[5] The Becket *miracula* demonstrate a related point. In the early 1170s, a certain Ailward faced trial by ordeal for theft. However, Ailward had been baptised on the eve of Whitsun and, according to popular opinion [*sicut uulgaris habet opinio*], in ordeal he could not go under water nor be burnt by iron; thus he was sure to be convicted by the former, acquitted by the latter. Popular opinion appears clearly distinguished from formal law on ordeal.[6]

It is important to note what I am not arguing. Factors other than norms, for example money and favour, often played an important part in disputes and court cases.[7] Contemporaries sometimes willingly employed these, sometimes saw them as a common part of court procedure, sometimes condemned them as corrupt. But it remains notable that such factors were distinguished from norms, particularly when litigants claimed that favour or antipathy produced injustice. The vindictive reeve's decision to ensure conviction by sending Ailward to ordeal by water is presented by the writer as an abuse of justice, not a legal act; it contradicted a broad norm: the accused should have some chance of success in making proof.

Records of disputes and of legal arguments survive in various sources, but certain immediate problems must be noted. We rely upon written records from a largely oral culture. The records are almost entirely Latin versions of largely vernacular proceedings. Except in Domesday Book or when the king was one party in the dispute, there are very

[5] See J.G.H. Hudson, 'Life-Grants of Land and the Development of Inheritance in Anglo-Norman England', *Anglo-Norman Studies*, 12 (1990), 67–80.

[6] *English Lawsuits from William I to Richard I*, ed. R.C. van Caenegem (2 vols., Selden Soc. 106, 107; 1990–1), no. 471; see also below, p. 97. For the sake of brevity, where possible, I cite non-Domesday cases by reference to *Lawsuits*, whilst sometimes modifying translations and referring to additional material.

[7] For appearance or reputation, see e.g. *Lawsuits*, nos. 204, 416; for money, see *Lawsuits*, no. 390; also Richard Fitz Nigel, *Dialogus de Scaccario*, ed. and tr. C. Johnson, F.E.L. Carter, and D.E. Greenway (Oxford, 1983), 120, arguing against the king's detractors that payment was to hasten, not to purchase, justice.

few recorded cases where both litigants were laymen. The need to draw upon all the meagre evidence risks neglecting variation between types of court or change within the period. Models of court proceedings drawn from a limited type of disputes, particularly those unusually problematic cases which left some of the fullest accounts, can mislead.[8] It is impossible to answer quantitative questions, for example what proportion of cases were settled by judgment or by compromise, let alone to make quantitative comparisons between countries or periods.

Collections of norms, be they urban customs in Domesday, other urban collections, or the various sets of *Leges*, are instructive as to some men's thinking concerning law, but they are of limited scope, and are not clear and direct indications of the nature of argument in court.[9] Whereas studies of disputing in France have been written from charters which contain long narratives of disputes, English charters tend to be more formulaic. However, many English cases were recorded in monastic chronicles, such as those of Abingdon, Battle, Ely, and Peterborough, devoted in large part to the estates of the house. Amongst these chronicles, the prevalence of those combining charter and narrative is peculiar to twelfth-century England. However, they do raise difficulties. The most useful texts are from abbeys with close ties – historical, institutional, and sometimes personal – to the king, and are from southern and central England. Moreover, they are of course ecclesiastical texts, displaying, for example, the influence of canon law. They therefore need comparison with secular sources, and here Domesday reports a great mass of disputes and related legal material. The procedures used in the Domesday inquest need not have been typical of all court cases, but they were not unique, and are certainly revealing of assumptions about law and disputing. However, its information is almost invariably highly compressed, and as Fleming has pointed out 'detailed descriptions are rare, but they do suggest that behind the more typically laconic accounts of disputes in Domesday lay angry argument and loud, heartfelt opinion'.[10]

In fact, with all our sources, we need to consider the varying significance of silences. The makers of records, the recounters of stories, were less interested in forms of pleading and reasons for decisions than

[8] See further Hudson, 'Interpretación'.

[9] For a positive assessment of the value of the *Leges Edwardi Confessoris*, see B. O'Brien, *God's Peace and King's Peace: the Laws of Edward the Confessor* (Philadelphia, Penn., 1999); for a negative assessment of the *Leges Henrici*, see J.G.H. Hudson, *The Formation of the English Common Law* (1996), 249–50. [Hereafter O'Brien, *God's Peace*; Hudson, *Formation*.]

[10] R. Fleming, *Domesday Book and the Law* (Cambridge, 1998), p. 1 [Hereafter Fleming, *Domesday*]; see also P. Wormald, 'Domesday Lawsuits: a Provisional List and Preliminary Comment', in C. Hicks, ed., *England in the Eleventh Century* (Stamford, 1992), 61–102. [Hereafter Wormald, 'Domesday'.]

in the subject of the dispute, the form of proof, and the outcome of the case.[11] They favour the sensational over the routine. Their case narratives are not modern law reports; in many ways they more resemble newspaper stories, and their form and content is of considerable consequence for analysis.

Cases were heard by courts made up of suitors, presided over by a lord or official. They began with a formal accusation or claim, followed by a formal denial. Wider-ranging pleading followed, citing evidence, using a variety of arguments, and drawing implicitly or explicitly on a variety of norms.[12] At the same time other considerations could play a part: the relative power of the parties or their supporters; their reputations; the attitude of the court president.[13] If the case was not terminated during such pleading, there followed a 'mesne judgment' as to the form of proof. There might then be a pause in proceedings, before proof was made by one or both parties, and lastly a final judgment was reached on the basis of that proof.

The pattern of disputing and court procedure was likely to vary with the type of case and the status of those involved. So one must distinguish the easy case from the difficult, difficult because of some problem of law, or a lack of available evidence, or the antagonism of the parties, or blocked access to the usual sources of justice.[14] In addition one should distinguish between disputes concerning offences against the person, moveable goods, or land. Historians tend to have a preconception that regular courts would spend their time hearing in full a series of significant cases, for example a lord's court would have a

[11] Note how the two accounts of the case of Bricstan differ in the amount of space devoted to court proceedings, the version in the *Liber Eliensis* showing how easily details might be omitted; *Lawsuits*, no. 204 – cf. pp. 169 and 173. For likely abbreviation of pleading, see also *Lawsuits*, no. 286 ('et alternatis rationamentis utentes.') For pleading involving the retelling of past events, see e.g. *Lawsuits*, no. 223. For a record of pleading concentrating on the claim and offer of proof, see e.g. *Lawsuits*, no. 15.

[12] Note *Lawsuits*, no. 135: Lanfranc 'opened his case with an introductory statement which to everyone's surprise seemed far removed from the matters which had been or were to be dealt with, [but] proceeded thus that he utterly demolished what had been said against him on the previous day and showed them to be without substance, with the result that henceforth for the rest of his life no one would stand up and say a word to oppose him.'

[13] See e.g. above, fn. 7.

[14] See e.g. *Chronicon Monasterii de Abingdon*, ed. J. Stevenson (2 vols., 1858), II, 37–40 (part of which is printed as *Lawsuits*, no. 147); note that the earliest surviving version of the chronicle dates from the 1160s, although this probably should not lead one to conclude that the phraseology is anachronistic for William II's or Henry I's reign. [Hereafter *Abingdon*.] The mockery of Bricstan of Chatteris's appearance might not have occurred, or have been ruled improper, had the royal officials in the court not been against him, *Lawsuits*, no. 204 (p. 169).

steady supply of land claims to settle. Yet such disputes may well have been untypical; an occasion when three land cases were dealt with in one day stands out as unique in the Abingdon *Chronicle*.[15]

The frequency with which certain questions arose could determine the clarity and influence of relevant norms. It is therefore plausible that norms were clearest and most influential in matters of procedure, in the type of routine business which was later to be so evident on the royal plea rolls. Some such norms concerned people other than the litigants, for example those regarding suit of court or the carrying of summons.[16] Others concerned those linked to the litigants, for example their sureties.[17] Others still concerned the litigants themselves. Some would be general – as against hasty judgment *in absentia*[18] but others much more specific. For example, norms concerning essoins, whilst not necessarily standardised between courts, may at least have been routine within courts. The law would be clear, the problem would lie in the matter of fact: was the person making the essoin really ill? A man whose opponent in a land case had failed to answer a proper summons was to enjoy seisin of the disputed land, but had the opponent received such a summons?[19]

Another set of procedural norms concerned jurisdiction and financial benefit from court proceedings. These feature in the urban customs preserved in Domesday: 'If a thief is captured in Dunwich, he shall be judged there. Corporal justice shall be made in Blythburgh, and the adjudged's goods shall remain to the lord of Dunwich.'[20] Such norms

[15] *Lawsuits*, no. 164.

[16] *Domesday Book*, ed. A. Farley (2 vols., 1783), I, 179r, 269v; II, 312r. [Hereafter *DB*.] See also below, pp. 102–3, on hearsay.

[17] See e.g. *Lawsuits*, nos. 204, 209. For bail being provided 'more patrio', see *Lawsuits*, no. 350; on the giving of pledges for ordeal, *DB*, II, 207v–208r.

[18] See e.g. *Lawsuits*, no. 321 at p. 270; for this widespread principle, note also e.g. Beroul, *The Romance of Tristan*, tr. A.S. Fedrick (Harmondsworth, 1970), 67. For some such general principles, the first explicit written record is Magna Carta, or the grants to specific beneficiaries which are precursors of some of its clauses; see J.C. Holt, *Magna Carta* (2nd edn; Cambridge, 1992), esp. ch. 3. For enforcement of legislation by Henry II against individual accusation by archdeacons, see *Lawsuits*, no. 371.

[19] In later law it may only have been in the case of essoins for bed-sickness that there was any real interest in ascertaining the facts, as opposed to concern with more free-standing rules, for example concerning whether essoins had to be warranted; I owe this point to Paul Brand. For early evidence of the essoin of illness, see *DB*, II, 449r; for summons, see e.g. *DB*, II, 423v–424r. There may also, for example, have been set procedures for dealing with the handing over of a man's goods to the king (see e.g. *Lawsuits*, no. 204).

[20] *DB*, II, 312r–v. Cf. the customs referred to at the trial at Penenden Heath, *Lawsuits*, no. 5, and in the enquiry concerning customs of York cathedral, *Lawsuits*, no. 172; also no. 167. Such matters of procedure and privilege also characterise the type of knowledge Hervey de Glanville displayed in the shire court of Norfolk and Suffolk in Stephen's reign; *Lawsuits*, no. 331; see also *Lawsuits*, no. 135.

may not have been followed in every case, but deviation from them would require some reason.[21] Changes to practice, notably at the start of Henry II's reign and for example concerning the transfer of cases between courts, would have heightened awareness of procedural norms.[22]

The other main concern of the Domesday customs was offences against the person or concerning moveable goods. These customs were usually very concrete in their form, specifying offence, penalty, and recipient of any fine: thus if anyone in Wallingford killed a man in the king's peace, he forfeited his body and all his property to the king.[23] Occasionally they are more general, notably the prohibition that no one except the king could restore peace to an outlaw. In York, a further significant distinction is drawn: if anyone is outlawed according to the law, only the king shall give him peace. However, if the earl or sheriff shall have expelled anyone 'from the province [*de regione*]', they can if they wish recall him and give him peace.[24] Norms also occasionally appear explicitly in other texts, suggesting what must elsewhere be hidden. Thus the Abingdon chronicler recorded that a thief should have lost both his goods and his life, 'by custom of the judgment of England [more judicii Anglie].'[25]

Throughout the medieval period, the easiest case involving criminals concerned those caught red-handed. These were dealt with by summary trial, and were unlikely to develop any very sophisticated law. However, certain norms do emerge which may have governed these and other cases. A man accused of homicide could plead a simple form of exception, that he had indeed killed the victim, but that it was an accident or in self-defence.[26] The value of goods stolen determined the seriousness of theft. One aspect of such a distinction appears in Huntingdonshire Domesday, where the sokemen of Broughton claimed thefts up to 4d, whilst allowing the abbot of Ramsey forfeitures for thefts of larger amounts. In the early 1170s the persecutors of Ailward, mentioned above, had to heap further goods upon him beyond the penny's worth he had taken, since so small a theft would not lead to mutilation. In the thirteenth century, *Bracton* would state in notably general terms, 'if a thief has been convicted, depending upon the kind

[21] See below, p. 109, on default setting. On the need for precision as to the financial beneficiaries of legal rights, note also the *Battle Chronicle*'s account of the law of wreck in the first half of the twelfth century; *Lawsuits*, no. 303.

[22] See *Lawsuits*, no. 420; also below, p. 103, on the need to prove seisin at Henry I's death or after.

[23] *DB*, I, 56v; see also e.g. *DB*, I, 56v, 262v, 268r.

[24] *DB*, I, 298v; cf. *DB*, I, 262v, 280v, 336v. See also J. Goebel, *Felony and Misdemeanor* (New York, 1937), 419–23.

[25] *Lawsuits*, no. 193; note also *DB*, II, 7r.

[26] *Lawsuits*, no. 139.

of thing stolen and its value let him either be put to death or abjure the realm or the *patria*, the county, city, borough or vill, or let him be flogged and after such flogging released.'[27]

More difficult cases generally presented the most interesting material for narratives. Take the case of the alleged thief, usurer, and concealer of treasure-trove, Bricstan of Chatteris.[28] Bricstan was contemplating entering the abbey of Ely as a monk, but was accused of the aforementioned offences by a malicious royal official, Robert Malarteis. He was tried before a royal justice, Ralph Basset, in the shire court, which was meeting 'as the custom is in England [*ut mos est in Anglia*]'. His denial was rejected, his wife's offer of ordeal made no difference, and he was mocked by his persecutors. He was handed over to royal custody, and only saintly intervention saved him. Particularly given that the detailed recording of the case may owe something not just to its miraculous outcome but also to Ely's desire to defend its privileges, the case certainly illustrates the impact of power and personality.

However, it is also notable that on the key issue of whether Bricstan was a usurer, the two surviving versions differ. According to one, he had slipped into a life of usury; according to the other, he merely retained pledges from his debtors because of the untrustworthiness of men. One account may simply be lying. Alternatively there may have existed

(i) a factual problem as to what Bricstan actual did;
(ii) conflicting perceptions of his actions;

or, perhaps in addition,

(iii) a legal difficulty as to the difference between usury and the taking of sureties.

In any of these ways, his may have been a difficult case, and hence especially open to the influence of a wider range of considerations.

Some general principles and legal norms underlie court arguments and judgments, as well as other transactions, concerning land. For example, at the most general end of the scale is King Arthur's statement of principle in reaction to Roman aggression: 'Nothing which is acquired

[27] See *DB*, I, 204r; *Lawsuits*, no. 471; 'Henry de Bracton', *De Legibus et Consuetudinibus Regni Anglie*, fo. 151b, ed. and tr. S.E. Thorne (4 vols., Cambridge, Mass., 1968–77), II, 427–8; note also T.A. Green, *Verdict According to Conscience* (Chicago, 1985), 60–1.

[28] *Lawsuits*, no. 204. One account was preserved in Normandy at Saint Evroul by Orderic Vitalis in his *Ecclesiastical History*, the other at Ely in the *Liber Eliensis*. The Ely account is the one which makes Bricstan guilty of usury, and also omits some of the procedural material.

by force and violence is justly possessed by anyone.'[29] Somewhat less general, more specifically legal is the distinction drawn between inheritance and acquisition: the latter was more freely alienable in relation to the tenant's kin, if perhaps also more tightly bound to his lord. And certainly by Henry II's reign, a distinction between property and possession,. seisin and right, was informing some arguments and judgments in court.[30]

The Norman settlement itself must have stimulated comparison of land-holding practice, and hence thinking about norms.[31] Domesday describes few customs concerning land-holding,[32] but it records a multitude of disputes. Sometimes we have a formal accusation and denial, together with offer of proof, but little further indication of arguments used:

> Count Alan claims these bovates [in Kesteven, Middlesex], and his man Algar has given the king's barons a pledge to confirm through ordeal or through battle that Aethelstan was not seised of these fourteen bovates in the time of King Edward. Against this, Aelfstan of Frampton Guy [de Craon]'s man, has given his pledge that he has been seised of this land with sake and soke, and that Guy was seised of them from the time of Ralph the staller until now, and that he holds them now.[33]

This may be all that was said, or just the limited information that Domesday supplies. On other occasions the basis of the claim was made clear in terms of justified descent or transfer of land; the dispute might turn on a matter of fact, for example the existence or non-existence of a royal writ and seal.[34] Elsewhere we have parties pleading

[29] *The Historia Regum Britannie of Geoffrey of Monmouth, i. Bern, Burgerbibliothek MS 568*, ed. N. Wright (Cambridge, 1985), 114. For relevant mentions of force in Domesday, see below, fn. 85.

[30] Inheritance: acquisition: see J.G.H. Hudson, *Land, Law, and Lordship in Anglo-Norman England* (Oxford, 1994), esp. chs 6 and 7; [Hereafter Hudson, *Land, Law, and Lordship*] *Abingdon*, II, 39; property/possession: see e.g. *Lawsuits.* no. 393; M. Cheney, '"Possessio/Proprietas" in Ecclesiastical Courts in mid-Twelfth-Century England', in *Law and Government in Medieval England and Normandy: Essays in Honour of Sir James Holt*, ed. G.S. Garnett and J.G.H. Hudson (Cambridge, 1994), 245–54. [Hereafter *Law and Government*, ed. Hudson and Garnett.] Further on the principles underlying land-holding in the Anglo-Norman period, see G.S. Garnett, 'Royal Succession in England, 1066–1154', (Ph. D. thesis, Cambridge, 1987); S.F.C. Milsom, *The Legal Framework of English Feudalism* (Cambridge, 1976).

[31] See the suggestions of Hudson, *Land, Law, and Lordship*, 105–6, and Fleming, *Domesday*, 83–5.

[32] Note *DB*, I, 56v (relief in Wallingford), 262v (taking of land in Chester); see also below, fn. 51.

[33] *DB*, I, 377v; note also cases involving vouching a warrantor: esp. *DB*, II, 290v; *DB*, I, 1r, 111v, 132r, 137v, 227v, 276v, II, 6r–v, 18v, 31v–32r, 59v–60r, 103r, 110v, 125v, etc.

[34] See e.g. *DB*, I, 57v, 59r, 215r, II, 299r–v.

fuller explanations of what underlay their claims, and on occasion supporting this with strong evidence:

> Bishop Osbern showed his charters for [the manor of Crediton], which testify that the church of St Peter had been seised of it before King Edward reigned. In the time of King William, moreover, the bishop deraigned before the king's barons that this land was his.

Here we have a story composed of facts, but facts charged with a strong normative under-pinning.[35] Most notable are cases where rival claimants, and witnesses, told such stories:

> Another of the carucates outside Lincoln was attached to the church of All Saints in the time of King Edward, also 12 tofts and 4 crofts. Godric son of Garwine had this church and the church's land and whatever pertains to it. But he has become a monk, and the abbot of Peterborough holds [*obtinet*]. But all the burgesses of Lincoln say that he has them unjustly, since neither Garwine nor Godric his son nor anyone else could give them outside the city or outside their kin, except by grant of the king. Earnwine the priest claims this church and what pertains there by inheritance of his kinsman Godric.[36]

Land cases outside Domesday reveal a similar recounting of a brief history of the estate and the related claim in terms which appeal to underlying norms.[37] Let us examine one unusually extensive narrative in depth. As Grenta of North Stoke lay dying in *c.*1120, both his son-in-law Modbert and the monks of Bath cathedral priory were seeking his land in North Stoke, Somerset.[38] Soon after Grenta's death, Modbert may have made an initial and unsuccessful claim to the land in the bishop of Bath's court, but the source makes no mention of this. Rather, the recorded hearing opens with the reading of a royal writ in the bishop's court, composed of his 'friends and barons', assembled for the preceding day's feast of the Apostles Peter and Paul: 'William, the king's son, to John, bishop of Bath, greeting. I order that you justly seise Modbert of the land which Grenta of Stoke had held, to which he made him heir during his lifetime. Witness: the bishop of Salisbury.' The bishop's reaction displays an awareness of the detail of the written word and a desire for the matter to be settled by discussion in court; he would 'do what has been ordered by the son of my lord through

[35] *DB* I, 101v; see also esp. *DB*, I, 48v, 264r; also for stories *DB*, I, 43v, 80r, 83r, II, 62v, 187v.

[36] *DB* I, 336r. See also e.g. *DB*, I, 44v, II, 176v–177r, 185v.

[37] For an unusually lengthy telling of a story, see *Lawsuits*, no. 223.

[38] *Lawsuits*, no. 226. The account, from a Bath cartulary, favours the church's case. For further consideration of the dispute, see Hudson, *Formation*, 105–8.

this letter, if it is just. However, my friends and lords ... I beg you to discuss what is more just in this matter.'

After taking counsel with the monks, the prior responded with the following arguments:

(i) 'It is agreed that this land ... had been given from early days to the brethren of this holy house of the Lord for their own use and free possession and has never come under military right by the decision of any king, bishop or abbot.' By implication, 'military right' is equated with heritability.

(ii) Grenta on his deathbed had stated that 'This is the inheritance of the servants of the Lord, which I have been permitted to hold as long as I live for payment and not by law of inheritance.'

(iii) And Grenta concluded 'now that I am dying, I leave myself with the land to the brethren to whom it belongs by right.'

Thus the prior is arguing that Grenta neither could nor did leave the land to Modbert. He supported his argument with

(i) Lawful witnesses of Grenta's testament

(ii) a charter in the name of the Saxon King Cynewulf, with a ferocious curse against anyone harming his gift.

Modbert put forward counter-arguments:

(i) that 'he was married to the daughter of the deceased (who during his lifetime had adopted him as his son)'

(ii) that Grenta 'had held the land ... freely and hereditarily'.

Various questions of fact and law had thus emerged: for example, if the land had been given in perpetuity to the church, could a later grant to a layman over-ride the earlier one? However, as in the Domesday cases above, the essential issue is presented as a choice between two arguments, each resting on a legally charged fact:

(i) the land was held for life;
or (ii) the land was held heritably.

The bishop resorted to the judgment of those known 'to be neither advocates nor supporters of the parties.' Distinguished by their age and legal learning [*majores natu et juris peritiores*], they weighed the arguments they had heard, and came to a judgment. Their decision was that Modbert must prove his claim 'by at least two free and lawful witnesses from the "familiars" of the church, who shall be named today and produced within a week, or by a signed and credible cirograph. If he fails in either, he shall not be heard again.' Modbert's ensuing silence, as far as we can tell, meant that he abandoned his claim.

It may be that other elements entered into this dispute. Henry I later sent a writ to the bishop ordering that the monks hold the land to which they had proved their right against Modbert. This perhaps suggests that there were underlying problems between bishop and monks over the land. However, there was no recorded discussion of, say, Modbert's personality, of his worthiness as a potential tenant. The case as presented in the record suggests a concentration on legal argument and evidence.[39]

Such a combination of legal argument and evidence was common. Although parties to disputes were with some frequency prepared to offer proof by ordeal or battle, the actual performance of such proof seems largely reserved for cases which could be settled in no other way.[40] Elsewhere evidence was brought to support claims.[41] In disputes over lands or other rights, charters or witnesses might be produced and examined,[42] or an inquest made by a group of local men.[43] Further norms dealt with evidence and proof, as was particularly necessary since power and influence could be brought to bear here as well.[44] There are signs of attempts, perhaps through questioning, to assess the quality of evidence, for example differentiating hearsay from direct

[39] *Regesta Regum Anglo-Normannorum, 1066–1154* (4 vols., Oxford, 1913–69), II, no. 1302; alternatively simple concern lest Modbert revive the dispute may explain why the priory obtained this confirmation.

[40] P.R. Hyams, 'Trial by Ordeal: The Key to Proof in the Early Common Law', in *On the Laws and Customs of England: Essays in Honour of Samuel E. Thorne*, ed. M. Arnold *et al.* (Chapel Hill, NC, 1981), 90–126; R.J. Bartlett, *Trial by Fire and Water: The Medieval Judicial Ordeal* (Oxford, 1986); note the cautionary words of S.D. White, 'Proposing the Ordeal and Avoiding It: Strategy and Power in Western French Litigation, 1050–1110', in *Cultures of Power*, ed. T.N. Bisson (Philadelphia, Penn., 1995), 89–123, on the use made of offers of ordeal, aimed, for example, at persuading parties to settle; also Martindale, 'Special Friend', 47–9.

[41] For Domesday evidence of offers of ordeal being confronted by witnesses testifying, see *DB*, I, 336r, II, 213r, 332r. For physical proof, see e.g. *Lawsuits*, no. 415.

[42] See e.g. *Lawsuits*, nos. 3, 189, 226, 243, 377 at pp. 339–40; also no. 257 for a cirograph being shown to be false. For eloquent argument being insufficient without documents or witnesses, see *Regesta Regum Anglo-Normannorum: the Acta of William I (1066–1087)*, ed. D. Bates (Oxford, 1998), no. 39. [Hereafter *Acta of William I.*] For the written word's importance in disputes in Burgundy, see Duby, 'Judicial Institutions', 52.

[43] E.g. *Lawsuits*, no. 254; in this period such juries seem often to have been used in cases concerning a variety of rights, such as tolls, rather than in land disputes.

[44] See Fleming, *Domesday*, 17–28, on Domesday jurors. For an interesting example of witness intimidation from an early thirteenth century ecclesiastical court, see *Select Cases from the Ecclesiastical Courts of the Province of Canterbury c.1200–1301*, ed. N. Adams and C. Donahue (Selden Soc., 95; 1981), A12. [Hereafter *Canterbury Cases.*] For fear and testimony, see *Lawsuits*, no. 3; note also no. 19.

witnessing or assessing the value of documentary evidence.[45] Early in Henry II's reign it was established that an Englishman claiming right to land had to base his claim on his own or his ancestor's seisin on the day Henry I died or thereafter.[46]

The bringing of evidence or the use of an inquest focused attention on the particular facts of the case. In Domesday, testimony was generally a statement of the supposed facts, sometimes extending to a brief story, and on occasion revealing or raising questions concerning the normative underpinning of the facts:

> Concerning the six bovates of soke which are claimed between the bishop of Durham and Eudo [son of Spearhavoc] ... the men of Wraggoe wapentake say that in the time of King Edward the two brothers – Harold and Guthfrith – held the soke equally and in parage, but in the year in which King Edward died, Guthfrith's sons had all of the soke, but they do not know for what reason they had it – whether through force or by gift of their uncle.[47]

The testimony therefore fails at the stage where the normative underpinning of the facts becomes important – had they gained the land illegitimately by force or legitimately by gift? In a few instances, the testimony is presented explicitly as a process of reasoning, the justification resting on the norms of land-holding and transfer:

> Alvred of Lincoln claims a carucate of land ... against Count Alan. The men of Holland agree with Alvred, *because* [*quia*] it was his ancestor's and he was seised of it in the time of Earl Ralph.

> They testify that all of Asa's land ought to be Robert Malet's, because she had her land separate and free from the lordship and power of her husband Beornwulf, even when they were together, so that he could make neither a donation nor a sale of land, nor a forfeiture.

[45] Hearsay: see e.g. *DB* I, 208r–v. Such a distinction is clearly drawn in ecclesiastical cases, in a way that suggests questioning of the witness; see e.g. *Canterbury Cases*, nos. A.4, A.10. The Domesday case just cited suggests that such procedure may also have occurred in secular courts. For further evidence from ecclesiastical courts of common-sense assessment of evidence, of a type which was probably common to all courts, see *Canterbury Cases*, no. A.6 (p. 22), on a witness who 'seemed to speak lukewarmly, and not constantly, and to offer a premeditated speech'. On documents, see above, fn. 42. One should, however, compare these norms with the development of much more detailed rules discussed by T.P. Gallanis, 'The Rise of Modern Evidence Law', *Iowa Law Review*, 84 (1999), 499–560. [Hereafter Gallanis, 'Evidence Law'.]

[46] See Hudson, *Land, Law, and Lordship*, 256–7.

[47] *DB* I, 375r. For briefer statements of fact, see e.g. *DB*, I, 203r, 208r, 376v; also the Yorkshire *clamores*, *DB* I, 373r ff. Note also e.g. *DB*, II, 124v, a hundred rejects a claim that land had belonged to the claimant's *antecessor*. For examples of conflicting testimony in Domesday, see *DB*, II, 285v, 337v, 338r–v, 392v–393r.

> After their separation she withdrew with all her land and possessed it as lord [*ut domina*]. All the men of the county, moreover, saw William seised of all her land until the castle was attacked.[48]

At the very least, therefore, the records reveal a distinction between, on the one hand, testimony as to facts and, on the other, the claims and arguments which rest heavily on normative ideas of proper practice: these are respectively the *testes* and the *rationes* whereby Lanfranc triumphed at Penenden Heath.[49]

Let us look more closely at the form in which appeal was made to norms. The reasoning is not presented as a syllogism, as modern legal reasoning sometimes can be: rule, instance, claim/outcome.[50] Rather, the first two elements are combined in what I earlier called a 'legally charged fact'. In Domesday, we do not have arguments in the form that

(i) land held in alms was inalienable,
(ii) the land concerned had been alms, and therefore
(iii) it should not have been alienated.

Rather we have statements such as 'Neither of them could sell because their lands always lay in alms in the time of King Edward and all of his ancestors, so the shire testifies.'[51] The reasoning in Modbert's case was presented in a similar fashion, and this is true of many other records of Anglo-Norman cases.[52] It was probably their skill in constructing such arguments which made so valuable men such as the priest Alfwi, *causidicus* of Abingdon abbey. His knowledge was not simply factual, he was no mere witness; rather, the abbey's chronicler characterised him

[48] *DB* I, 377v, 373r respectively; see also *DB* I, 62r, 377v.

[49] *Lawsuits*, no. 5B; see also no. 12 ('rationatione et plurimorum testimonio sapientum'). For words based on *ratio* being used elsewhere for arguments in court, see *Lawsuits*, no. 286 – both sides produced their 'rationamenta'; also no. 5H 'ualida ratione subnixa'; 303 'ratione usus premeditata'. Note also the last element of no. 164: the tenant restores land 'which abbot Reginald had unjustly given him, because [*quia*] they were of the demesne'.

[50] Posner, *Problems*, 42; but see below p. 108.

[51] *DB* I, 137v; note also *DB*, I, 209r. A similar norm underlies *DB*, I, 212r, land which had been the abbey's 'of their supplies TRE. [*de uictu eorum*]' Note also *DB*, I, 210r, implicit appeal to the norm of inheritance; *DB*, I, 216v, failure to pay rent justifies forfeiture. See also the interesting instance of a carucate in Plumstead, Norfolk, *DB*, II, 199r: after 1066, Bishop Æthelmær annexed [*invasit*] it for a forfeiture, because the female tenant married within a year of her husband's death; it is unclear to us, although probably not to people at the time, whether this records a just action based on breach of a norm, or an unjust seizing, as is suggested by the word *invasit*. For appeal to other norms, without their being stated in the abstract, see e.g. *DB*, I, 77r, 211r, 211v, 218v.

[52] Note also *Lawsuits*, no. 18D, where a writ of William I asks a litigant 'quomodo eam reclamat', that is upon what legally charged fact is his claim based.

by his memory of past events, his eloquence concerning worldly matters, and his knowledge of the laws of the land.[53]

How conscious were courts and disputants of norms in the abstract? How far is it justified to unwrap the 'legally charged fact' into abstract rules of law and matters of fact to which such rules should be applied?[54] The extreme rarity of cited abstract norms in case records and dispute accounts arises for various reasons, some to do with our surviving evidence, some to do with the issues of disputes and practice in court. As already noted, the nature of the sources is an initial problem. A helpful analogy is with modern reporting on sports which certainly have authoritative rules. Domesday's minimalist accounts may resemble the cryptic form of the slightly expanded cricket score-card which appears in some newspapers: 'England batsman X, lbw Australian bowler Y, 0; played no shot to ball outside off stump.' Or turn to the narrative sources. Just as a soccer report states simply that 'X was offside', or more allusively that 'Y was on his own when the linesman's flag was raised', rather than stating the rules of offside, so too might a dispute record state simply that 'X held the land unjustly' or more allusively that 'Y was deprived of his land, which he and his family had held for longer than any could remember'. These analogies of course do not *prove* the existence of acknowledged underlying norms, but do show the difficulty of writing from sources not designed with the legal historian in mind.

Secondly, in many cases argument concerning norms was not central. Perhaps particularly in the period shortly after 1066 many land cases were likely to turn on straightforward questions of fact; 'had the land been granted to Robert or to William?'; 'did an English freeman belong to one fee or to another?'[55] And cases of offences against the person or involving moveables were always likely to be of this type; not 'did Thomas's deed constitute theft', but 'was it Thomas who had taken the stolen goods?' Even in some more complicated cases, the parties may simply have assumed knowledge of norms, or not cited them because the parties agreed upon them. If a case arose, for example, over who was the closest heir to an inheritance, it may simply have been a

[53] *Abingdon*, II, 2 (= *Lawsuits*, no. 4), 27.

[54] Such a distinction is clearly made in some ecclesiastical disputes in England, and also occasionally appears in French documents; Eadmer, *Historia Nouorum in Anglia*, ed. M. Rule (1884), 45; White, 'Inheritances', 78 fn. 113. Note also S.F.C. Milsom, 'Law and Fact in Legal Development', in his *Studies in the History of the Common Law* (1985), 171: 'This essay is about the beginnings of the common law as an intellectual system, and its premiss is that legal development consists in the increasingly detailed consideration of facts.' [Hereafter Milsom, 'Law and Fact'] See also White, 'Inheritances', 86 fn. 150, and 97; I perhaps lay greater significance than White does on the effect of the nature of the record in obscuring the role of norms and the capacity to distinguish norm and fact.

[55] *DB* II, 447r.

question of fact, based on a shared view of inheritance custom. In such instances, explicit statement of norms need not have formed part of pleading, but their implicit role remained. Compared with the complexities of modern law and society, such must have formed a greater proportion of cases in earlier periods.

Yet people could obviously think and speak in terms of abstract norms, as is apparent from records of law-giving such as Henry I's Coronation Charter or the *statutum decretum* of the 1130s requiring inheritances to be divided between heiresses.[56] Orderic wrote of treason that 'English law punishes the traitor by beheading, and entirely deprives his whole progeny of their just inheritance . . .' whilst Earl Roger 'was judged according to the laws of the Normans, and condemned to perpetual imprisonment after losing all his worldly inheritance'.[57] Some norms were alluded to in judgments in more ordinary cases. The Abingdon chronicler says the following of a man who had failed to serve his lord, the abbot, in the king's army: 'it had been decided according to the law of the country [*lege patrie*] that he deservedly ought to be deprived of the land'.[58] If such law determined judgments it must at least have formed arguments, and may well have been explicitly referred to within them. However, the clearest evidence of all comes from a letter of John of Salisbury concerning the famous Anstey case early in Henry II's reign.

> Richard, kinsman and nephew of William de Sackville, instituted a claim of inheritance to obtain his uncle's goods. In reply, Mabel, William's daughter, asserted in the court of secular judges where the suit was being tried, that a daughter must be preferred to a nephew for her father's inheritance. Richard denied that she had any hereditary right, since she was not born of a lawful marriage, but was the child of an adulterous union.[59]

[56] See J.C. Holt, 'Feudal Society and the Family in Early Medieval England: (iv) the Heiress and the Alien', *TRHS*, 5th Ser. 35 (1985), 1–28 at 9–14; for an alternative interpretation, see J.A. Green, 'Aristocratic Women in Early Twelfth-Century England', in *Anglo-Norman Culture and the Twelfth Century Renaissance*, ed. C. W. Hollister (Woodbridge, 1997), 81–2. At approximately the same time, the *Leges Edwardi Confessoris* can persuasively be taken as an attempt to abstract generalities from practice: see O'Brien, *God's Peace.*

[57] *Lawsuits*, no. 7; cf. William of Poitiers, *Gesta Guillelmi*, ed. and tr. R.H.C. Davis and M. Chibnall (Oxford, 1998), 42, on the Norman 'lex transfugarum'. Note also William I's legislation concerning proof in cases between Englishmen and Frenchmen: *Acta of William I*, no. 130.

[58] *Lawsuits*, no. 164. Note also *Abingdon*, II, 118 on an offence 'contra legem consuetudinariam'; *Lawsuits*, no. 421 on Becket's trial at Northampton in 1164: 'all his moveable goods were quickly declared to be confiscated unless by chance royal clemency was willing to mitigate the judgment, i.e., as the popular saying goes, he was judged to be in the king's mercy for all his moveable goods'.

[59] *Lawsuits*, no. 408B.

Here we have a claim, a counter-argument stating a general point of inheritance law, and further argument as to why the general point did not apply to this particular case. Thus even prior to Henry II's reforms, we have court arguments involving abstract norms, or at the very least arguments which a John of Salisbury could recount in abstract fashion for the benefit of the pope.

So norms were both consciously held and influential. How far did their form, use, and influence differ from later periods? There is certainly a danger of exaggerating the difference between the early and later middle ages. If a case went contrary to certain decisive norms, participants were aware that the case was not being decided according to law, and the disappointed party might look to the king to correct such a 'default of justice'.[60] Furthermore, the use of norms in pleading continued sometimes to be implicit rather than explicit. The following are later thirteenth-century pleadings, in the form of legally charged facts:

> The prior says that he cannot answer them on this writ because someone else holds half an acre which is part of the appurtenance of this land.
>
> Henry readily acknowledges that the charter is the deed of his father Henry but says that he is not obliged to warranty by that charter because the charter was made while his father was kept in chains in Roger's prison.[61]

This was also true of, for example, thirteenth-century ecclesiastical courts, which operated against a background of considerably more extensive written law.[62] Very general principles, too, entered into arguments put forward by litigants or justices.[63] And when records beyond the official plea rolls recount later medieval disputes, they

[60] See *Leges Henrici Primi*, 10.1, ed. and tr. L.J. Downer (Oxford, 1972), 108 [hereafter *Leges Henrici*, ed. and tr. Downer]; also e.g. Hudson, *Formation*, esp. 114.

[61] *The Earliest English Law Reports*, ed. and tr. P.A. Brand (2 vols., Selden Soc. 111–12; 1996), nos. 1268.1, 1276.4 (Plea roll). [Hereafter *Law Reports*, ed. Brand.] Note also the form of count and defence presented in *Brevia Placitata*, ed. G.J. Turner and T.F.T. Plucknett (Selden Soc. 66; 1951). [Hereafter *Brevia Placitata*.] Moreover, Milsom, 'Law and Fact', 180–3 argues that after the thirteenth century there was a move away from the type of examining of facts which stimulates legal development; 182, 'the lawyers have retreated from the facts by going back to the ancient pattern of law-suit'.

[62] For a case where rules are not explicitly cited, but where they clearly play a crucial implicit role, see *Canterbury Cases*, no. A6; note also e.g. nos. A1, A5, and introduction p. 53. See further *Canterbury Cases*, no. A15, which mixes an at times notably rhetorical telling of a story with references to the *ordo judiciarius* and allusion to canon law.

[63] See e.g. the justice's remarks in *Law Reports*, ed. Brand, no. 1275.3.

reveal the continuing importance of, for example, favour, money, and reputation.[64]

Some comparisons with modern law are also instructive. Writers on jurisprudence have developed ideas on the nature of legal rules with notable resonance for historians, and which may soften, although not deny, the contrast between mediaeval and modern law. Rules do not provide certain answers for all cases; they have an 'open texture'.[65] Some writers even argue that in routinely decided cases, rules are only producing regular rather than definitive answers.[66] Not all legal reasoning works syllogistically; cases uncertain enough to reach decisive litigation may require more general forms of argument and reasoning.[67] Most obviously, in cases perceived as difficult by the parties and courts involved, a variety of considerations beyond defined legal rules are likely to intrude explicitly, for example general considerations of morality or of policy.[68]

Particularly notable are certain rules, sometimes referred to as standards, which use terms and notions such as 'reasonable', 'negligent' or 'significant'.[69] These notions demand the involvement in legal argument and decision-making of ideas, customs, and practices which are in no discrete sense 'legal'. Moreover, the ideas and customs thereby involved are generally unwritten, just like the mass of early mediaeval custom. Reliance on the unwritten can encourage greater flexibility. Such notions, and such norms, may have been more widely prevalent, more influential in the workings of mediaeval courts, but the modern parallel does raise the question of how far the distinction between the mediaeval and the modern is quantitative, how far qualitative.

Likewise, much modern disputing goes on against a background of legal rules, and sometimes through the use of legal rules, but not in the

[64] See esp. M.T. Clanchy, 'A Medieval Realist: Interpreting the Rules at Barnwell Priory, Cambridge', in *Perspectives in Jurisprudence*, ed. E. Attwooll (Glasgow, 1977), 176–94.

[65] E.g. H.L.A. Hart, *The Concept of Law* (Oxford, 1961), 121–32, esp. 124; also e.g. Kelman, *Guide*, 50. Hart's argument rested on linguistic analysis, which distinguished a core of certainty from a less certain penumbra. The relationship of core to penumbra is affected by the oral or written nature of the rule; for brief comment on this relationship, see below, p. 110.

[66] E.g. Kelman, *Guide*, 3–4, 12–13, 258; Kennedy, *Critique*, 159–60.

[67] Posner, *Problems*, 73, 78.

[68] For one controversial version of this argument, see the works of Ronald Dworkin; R.M. Dworkin, 'Is Law a System of Rules?', in *The Philosophy of Law*, ed. *idem* (Oxford, 1977), 38–65 provides easy access to some of his ideas; for a fuller and more recent view, one must look e.g. at his *Law's Empire*.

[69] Note Posner, *Problems*, 44; Kelman, *Guide*, ch. 1, esp. pp. 15–16; Kennedy, *Critique*, 39, 61. On writing and precision, see e.g. M.T. Clanchy, *From Memory to Written Record* (2nd edn.; Oxford, 1993); J. Goody, *The Logic of Writing and the Organization of Society* (Cambridge, 1986).

form of court cases being determined by legal rules. William Miller has drawn an analogy between modern American commercial law and mediaeval Icelandic law which can apply just as well elsewhere. Using the metaphor of computing he states that such law acts as 'a default setting that would govern unless the parties to the transaction preferred to bargain out of the ambit of the rule.'[70]

One must not, however, jump to the simple assumption that the role of norms in eleventh-or twelfth-century courts was very similar to their later mediaeval or modern equivalents, if not as clear cut, efficient, or effective. First, I have sought to reveal the workings of some of the strongest Anglo-Norman norms.[71] Others, whilst significant in court, were less clear or less powerful. An issue might be complicated by different parties seeing different norms as representing correct practice in a case. Take the question of succession to castles. It may well be that the king felt they were his to give at will, whereas custodians saw them as their own hereditary property. Similar conflicts of perception might exist over inheritance of land by distant relatives. In the absence even in England of a routine appeal system to a royal court enforcing one interpretation of custom, such divergent views might long survive. When there was no single generally accepted norm, power could obviously intrude as the parties strove to have their version of law accepted.[72]

Secondly, to return to modern rules: jurisprudence does not describe the typical workings or the typical perception of the role of rules in the most common cases; rather it usually focuses on appellate jurisdictions, difficult cases, and the 'true nature' rather than the general perception of rules. But for historians such routine cases and common perceptions are very important. It therefore remains significant that in the majority of modern cases, rules play a much more explicit role, are seen as much more definitive than in all but a few early mediaeval ones. Rules are more numerous and cover more areas.[73] Despite the importance of the 'standards' referred to above, many modern legal rules are more precise, so the scope for other considerations routinely to become involved is more restricted.

Further, early medieval case records do not reveal other elements

[70] Miller, *Bloodtaking*, 228.

[71] On standardisation between courts, see below, p. 114.

[72] On inheritance of castles, and by distant relatives, see Hudson, *Land, Law, and Lordship*, ch. 4. The fundamental treatment of the multiple perceptions of custom is S.D. White, 'The Discourse of Inheritance in Twelfth-Century France: Alternative Models of the Fief in *Raoul de Cambrai*', in *Law and Government*, ed. Garnett and Hudson, 173–97. For arguments which would make this a characteristic less peculiar to early mediaeval law, see Kennedy, *Critique*, Kelman, *Guide*.

[73] For very stimulating analysis of developments in a later period, see Gallanis, 'Evidence Law'.

characteristic of modern legal discourse: the interplay of norm and fact through argument based on precedent; rules being explicitly contrasted, incompatibilities pointed out in court. These difference may simply be a product of the evidence, but there is certainly no sign, for example, that if one rule were preferred to another, the latter might lose its validity.[74] Nor were secular courts recorded creating new, explicit rules to justify their judgments, as modern courts sometimes do.

Thirdly, developments of this type are apparent in the later middle ages. Evidence even from the later thirteenth century shows norms being of a more technical nature, being stated more explicitly, and being applied with greater strictness.[75] Whilst manuals such as *Brevia Placitata* generally present pleading in terms of legally charged facts with reference to particular instances, they also contain some statements of general rules.[76] The very increase in the use of writing, in legal educational works and in statutes, could produce greater rigidity in norms. Records reveal more judgments being stated in a reasoned fashion, with distinct reference to law and fact:

> Because William [II] the son of Simon [I] had entered the tenements after the death of his uncle Nicholas [I], on whose seisin the claim was brought, and had held them all of his life and died in seisin of them without bastardy ever having been alleged against him and Nicholas [II] had asserted in his count that Simon [I] had died without issue and no proof of this was admissible as under English law and custom no one can be bastardised after their death, it is adjudged that Simon [III] hold the land quit of the claim of Nicholas [II] and his heirs in perpetuity etc.[77]

Legal thinking could increasingly work according to its own logic, through subtle and technical development, as Milsom argues in his analysis of legal thinking outstripping legal form in the case of debt and detinue.[78] The types of argument used in Anglo-Norman courts were likely to be comprehensible to all members of that court, the rationale of norms explicable if necessary in everyday terms. In the professionalised law of the later middle ages, at least in some areas of

[74] Note also White, '*Pactum*', 306–7, who argues that a 'later medieval court would have formally taken into account some ... obligations but not others, because it would have regarded only some of them as legal obligations arising out of legal rules. Second, in the event that some of those having legal force pointed towards different ways of deciding the case, the court would have normally had at its disposal some accepted way of deciding which rule should take priority and control its decision in the case.'

[75] See e.g. *Law Reports*, ed. Brand, no. 1272.1.

[76] See the general rule given in a rubric concerning the writ *praecipe in capite* in *Brevia Placitata*, 11, in a form contrasting with that of writ, count, or defence.

[77] *Law Reports*, ed. Brand, no. 1276.5.

[78] Milsom, 'Law and Fact', 176–9.

law, the development of technicalities and related language meant that this was no longer the case.[79]

Was England before the Angevin reforms peculiar in the importance of norms and in the nature of disputing more generally?[80] Here I shall limit myself to a few comments, beginning with a comparison of the image of disputing presented by three mid-twelfth century texts concerning abbeys enjoying strong royal links: Suger's description of his administration of St Denis, Henry of Blois' account of his resumption of Glastonbury's lands, and the Abingdon chronicler's history of the church and its abbots.[81] Certain differences are immediately noticeable. In Suger's story oppressive lords are the predominant opponents; at Abingdon and Glastonbury, they are recalcitrant tenants, grantees of earlier abbots or custodians of the house, or covetous royal officials.[82] Henry of Blois and abbots of Abingdon, most notably Henry I's physician Faritius, generally responded to challenges by starting court proceedings, and at Abingdon in particular the chronicle also often records the associated royal writ. Outside the reign of the Conqueror direct forceful action by abbots was rare. Suger more frequently looked to use the influence of his many connections, or to buy off his oppressors, or to confront them forcefully, for example by building defences or – to the disquiet of his conscience – by military action. Even when the king became involved on Suger's behalf, it was not in disputes involving the abbey's ordinary tenants.[83] Most notably, Louis VI operated militarily against oppressors of the church such his brother Philip and

[79] Cf. the development, certainly by 1217, of legal devices being used to circumvent the rules of law in order to achieve desired ends; see Magna Carta (1217), c. 43.

[80] I here treat England as a realm with common practices; in fact, patterns of disputing may have differed in certain areas, for example the borders with Scotland.

[81] Suger, *Œuvres Complètes*, ed. A. Lecoy de la Marche (Paris, 1867); see also L. Grant, *Abbot Suger of St-Denis* (1998), 220–5. [Hereafter Suger, *Œuvres Complètes*; Grant, *Suger*.] Henry's account appears in Adam de Domerham, *Historia de Rebus Gestis Glastoniensibus*, ed. T. Hearne (2 vols., Oxford, 1727), II, 305–15, [hereafter Adam of Domerham] and *English Episcopal Acta, VIII: Winchester, 1070–1204*, ed. M.J. Franklin (Oxford, 1993), 205–11; see also N.E. Stacy, 'Henry of Blois and the Lordship of Glastonbury', *EHR*, 114 (1999), 1–33. [Hereafter Stacy, 'Henry of Blois'.] For further signs of contact with the king in disputes, see also the charters noted in Suger, *Œuvres Complètes*, 366, 371, 373; also Grant, *Suger*, 212, 221. I emphasise that I am looking at the *image* of disputing presented by these texts, rather than analysing in full the disputes partially revealed by the texts.

[82] Also amongst Henry's opponents was Roger, bishop of Salisbury; see Adam of Domerham, 312–13, Stacy, 'Henry of Blois', 8–9. For Suger and vexatious royal officials at Beaune-la-Rolande, see *Œuvres Complètes*, 175, Grant, *Suger*, 221; also *Œuvres Complètes*, 184 which concerns Normandy in the time of Henry I.

[83] Confronting opponents: *Œuvres Complètes*, 160, 172; charter at 350. Payment to opponents, e.g. *Œuvres Complètes*, 182. Royal involvement: e.g. *Œuvres Complètes*, 168, charter at 372; see Grant, *Suger*, 220; note also *Œuvres Complètes*, 171.

Hugh of le Puiset, whilst observing such forms as summoning his opponents to court.[84]

Other evidence confirms the impression that the use of force, which is a common focus of studies of disputing in areas of France, was relatively limited in Anglo-Norman England, except under Stephen. Domesday Book reveals few violent local conflicts which – had they existed – might well have been central to jurors' testimony.[85] Among historians, it is a common-place – and probably justified one – that private war was not permitted in Anglo-Norman England. Some may have ignored the prohibition, others known that the king would turn a blind eye. Disputants might use limited violence in order to escape it being classified as private war, whilst much which continental charters described as *guerra* could be presented as the vigorous exercise of distraint, the effective assertion of firm lordship. Yet such activities do seem distinct from many continental instances, and may not have differed very greatly from those used in the classic Common Law period after the time of Henry II.[86]

So at least in some aspects of the conduct of disputing England does seem to have differed from areas of France, for example. However, such limits of violence need not correspond to a greater importance of norms and normative arguments in disputing. Other countries too had a culture in which numerous and detailed legal norms played a very significant part.[87] Miller has written of Iceland that

[84] *Vie de Louis le Gros*, cc. 17–18, printed in *Œuvres Complètes*, 66–80.

[85] Note e.g. *DB*, I, 32r 'inimicitia'; for taking by force, see *DB*, I, 41v (half a virgate), 78v, 166r, 203r, 208r, 216r, 228r, 236v, 247v, 373r, 375r (where it is uncertain whether a party held by force, suggesting that any violence cannot have been sufficient to be notorious), 376v; cf. Harold's actions by force, *DB*, I, 30v–31r, 133r, or even violence, *DB*, I, 2r; Godwin's wife, *DB*, I, 136v–137r; Earl Gyrth, *DB*, II, 210r–v. Note also *Acta of William I*, no. 129, for sheriffs taking lands violently from churches. For disputes involving the abbey of Abingdon during Stephen's reign, see e.g. *Abingdon*, II, 200–3 (included in part in *Lawsuits*, no. 378). For the harassment of William of St Calais in 1088, see *Lawsuits*, no. 134 (p. 104). For mention of a man committing violence against a church, see *Lawsuits*, no. 163D. For a man 'by force' holding onto land which his opponent claimed had been granted for only one year, see *Lawsuits*, no. 220. For wrongfully received tolls being taken away 'violenter per justiciam; see *Lawsuits*, no. 254.

[86] For the continuing use of extra-legal methods of disputing and enforcement of custom well beyond the mediaeval period, see e.g. E.P. Thompson, *Customs in Common* (Harmondsworth, 1993).

[87] For some parallel uses of norms in western France, see White, 'Inheritances', 88–9. Note also the case of the county of Barcelona, where the influence of the Visigothic *Liber Judiciorum* had lasted into the eleventh century; in the twelfth century we have court records which contain parallels with written compilations of customary law, such as do not exist for Anglo-Saxon or Anglo-Norman England – see *The Usatges of Barcelona*, tr. D.J. Kagay (Philadelphia, Penn., 1994), 26, 115. Note the comment by Posner, *Problems*, 319, that heavy reliance upon norms by judicial authorities may in fact be a sign of strong social pressure towards a more personally, less rules-based justice: again advocacy

> Grágás' style and its bulk evidence a cultural predisposition for law and lawmaking. Some of the rules themselves display a rococo complexity that suggests sheer pleasure in the formulation of law almost as if it were for law's sake alone. The propensity for lawmaking, however, was not just the theoretical musings of juristically inclined people. The society backed its laws with courts to hear claims arising from their breach. And what is especially remarkable is that Iceland developed a legal system – courts, experts in law, rules clearly articulated as laws – in the absence of any coercive state institutions.[88]

At the same time Miller has much evidence of feuding; detailed norms need not be associated with an absence of violent disputing.

Likewise, it is very difficult to relate a preference for compromise to a prevalence of out-of-court disputing or a limited reliance upon norms.[89] In England, as elsewhere, out-of-court and compromise settlements continue into the later middle ages and to the present day, but both before and after *c.*1200 were shaped *inter alia* by norms. Similarly compromises were arranged in ecclesiastical courts, where the role of written law and specialist lawyers was more significant at an earlier date than in lay courts.[90]

Furthermore, decision and compromise co-existed in a variety of ways. One might succeed the other in the process of disputing, for example according to a party's tactical choice.[91] Concession over a specific incident might be outweighed by the victory in a matter of lasting principle.[92] Clearly, one must be very cautious in making any

of norms cannot be equated with a powerful state. For example, some Continental Peace and Truce of God legislation, including that issued under powerful lay authority, may present an attempt to impose a wide range of norms on a situation where authority may have been weakening; e.g. Comital peace assembly of Barcelona, 1064, in *Usatges*, 103–5.

[88] Miller, *Bloodtaking*, 224; see also 228, and, on legal experts, 226.

[89] For a position on compromise close to the one taken in this paper, see *Settlement of Disputes*, ed. Davies and Fouracre, 235–6; for further comments on settlement patterns, see Hudson, 'Interpretación'. Miller, *Bloodtaking*, 233 shows that the 'hyperlegalization' of Icelandic society could encourage disputing out of as well as within court. For problems of diplomatic, note also e.g. White, '*Pactum*', 294. See Wormald, 'Domesday', 69ff. for some statistics on Domesday disputes, or rather the stages of disputes recorded in Domesday. For some fifteenth-century English statistics, see E. Powell, 'Arbitration and the Law in England in the Late Middle Ages', *TRHS*, 5th Ser. 33 (1983), 49–67 at 51.

[90] See *Canterbury Cases*, Introduction, 55–6 for a preference for out of court and compromise settlements in ecclesiastical disputes, where a distinct body of law definitely was available.

[91] E.g. *Lawsuits*, no. 163; note also *DB*, II, 377r. For the co-existence of law and arbitration, see also Powell, 'Arbitration', 57. For courtroom and violent disputing co-existing, see e.g. Miller, *Bloodtaking*, 233.

[92] See e.g. *Lawsuits*, no. 12; note also cases of non-performance of homage and service, where the lord might have enforced forfeiture, but rather accepts the homage and service which had been his original aim: see e.g. *Lawsuits*, no. 164, 206; also *DB*, II, 383r, 385r–

simple determinist connection between form of settlement and type or role of norms. Likewise, the continuation to the present day of the prevalence of non-judicial, and out-of-court, settlements precludes associating in any simple way a preference for settlements with any particular judicial or political system.

These points appear part of a wider crisis of explanation. The type of functionalist view which underlies many recent studies of disputing seems so riddled with exceptions – each individually admitted within the studies but not confronted collectively – that the underlying view must be questioned.[93] It is not that links do not exist, for example, between the nature and importance of norms, the form of judicial organisation, and the process of disputing. Rather, the relationships are complex, may well be particular to certain situations, and may include a variety of factors – notably cultural ones – which are too often excluded in functionalist analysis. Hopes of explanation need not be abandoned, nor need we have been looking in the wrong areas for them. But the combination of factors underlying disputing and legal development may be less necessarily inter-related than they have recently seemed.

In England, the period from Henry II's reign brought many developments which increased the number, variety, and role of decisive norms. Access to royal justice became more routine, making norms more rigidly enforceable. Royal justices played a greater role in controlling argument and deciding cases.[94] The centralised system of courts, intent on enforcing a single set of norms, a common law, ensured a standardisation of norms which did not occur when royal justice was extended in France, for example.[95] Formal and informal legal education

v; cf. Clanchy, 'Law and Love', 48. Note that decisions tempered by mercy or charity still could reinforce the norm on which the main decision was based.

[93] For criticism of such direct and causal links between the various elements, see e.g. Martindale, 'Special Friend', 24–5, 50; *Settlement of Disputes*, ed. Davies and Fouracre, 235–6; D. Barthélemy, *La Société dans le Comté de Vendôme* (Paris, 1993), 652–80; White, 'Inheritances'; C. Wickham, 'Property Ownership and Signorial Power in Twelfth-Century Tuscany', in *Property and Power in the Early Middle Ages*, ed. W. Davies and P. Fouracre (Cambridge, 1995), 222–3.

[94] See e.g. *Law Reports*, ed. Brand, nos pre-1273.2, 1276.7.

[95] See e.g. *Etablissements de Saint Louis*, ii 23, tr. F.R.P. Akehurst (Philadelphia, Penn., 1996), 143: 'When my lord the king orders his *bailli* to give a hearing to some plaintiff, he gives the order in this form: "We order that you give a good and speedy trial to the bearer of this writing, according to the custom of the area and the district" '; also ii 16 (p. 133): king's court reviewing judgments: 'if it is against the law, then he should have it annulled; and if it is not against the law, then he should have it executed and confirmed by the custom of the area'. Philippe de Beaumanoir, *Coutumes de Beauvaisis*, Prologue 7, tr. F.R.P. Akehurst (Philadelphia, Penn., 1992), 4: 'the customs of France are so varied that you could not find in the kingdom of France two castellanies which used the same

encouraged argument and decisions according to set norms.[96]

However, the importance of judgments, courts, and legal norms before the mid-twelfth century was essential to Henry II's reforms and the development of the Common Law. Most notably, at the core of the reforms, and one of their most popular elements, were the assizes, for example those of *novel disseisin* and *mort d'ancestor.* These worked in terms not of the explicit application of abstract rules, but rather of a set of questions posed to those making the recognition. The answers they were seeking were to take the form of legally charged facts: yes, William had died seised in demesne as of his fee, yes he had died since the king's coronation, and yes Henry was his closest heir.[97] Upon similar thinking rested pleading and other procedures in the Angevin courts. It was a collection of such procedures that *Glanvill* in the late 1180s could present as a body of law to rival the Romano-canonical tradition.

customs in all cases'. In England, matters concerning procedure may have shown particular variation beyond the Anglo-Norman period; this may be the meaning of 'Glanvill', *Tractatus de Legibus*, xiv 8, ed. and tr. G.D.G. Hall (Edinburgh, 1965), 177: 'thefts and other pleas belonging to the sheriff, which are heard and determined according to the varying customs of different county courts'. This does not mean that such norms could not have a decisive effect within that court, but does distinguish them from the greater proportion of standardised norms after Henry II's reign.

[96] P.A. Brand, *The Origins of the English Legal Profession* (Oxford, 1992).

[97] Hudson, *Formation*, 198–201. Note also the process whereby presenting juries sifted communal accusations: R.D. Groot, 'The Jury of Presentment before 1215', *American Journal of Legal History*, 26 (1982), 1–24.

THE DIVERGENCE OF ENGLAND: THE GROWTH OF THE ENGLISH ECONOMY IN THE SEVENTEENTH AND EIGHTEENTH CENTURIES

The Prothero Lecture

By E.A. Wrigley

READ 7 JULY 1999

THAT something remarkable was happening in England in the quarter millennium separating the late sixteenth century from the early nineteenth is plain. In Elizabeth I's reign the Spanish Armada was perceived as a grave threat: the English ships were scarcely a match for the Spanish, and the weather played a major part in the deliverance of the nation. By the later eighteenth century the Royal Navy was unchallenged by the naval forces of any other single country, and during the generation of war which followed the French revolution, it proved capable of controlling the seas in the face of the combined naval forces mustered by Napoleon in an attempt to break the British oceanic stranglehold.[1] Growing naval dominance was a symbol of a far more pervasive phenomenon. In the later sixteenth century England was not a leading European power and could exercise little influence over events at a distance from its shores. The Napoleonic wars showed that, even when faced by a coalition of countries occupying the bulk of Europe west of Russia and led by one of the greatest of military commanders, Britain possessed the depth of resources to weather a very long war, enabling her to outlast her challenger and secure a victory.[2] The combination of a large and assertive Navy and dominant financial and commercial strength meant that, in the early decades of

[1] Or, as J. Brewer put it, 'From its modest beginnings as a peripheral power – a minor, infrequent almost inconsequential participant in the great wars that ravaged sixteenth and seventeenth-century Europe – Britain emerged in the late seventeenth and early eighteenth centuries as the military *Wunderkind* of the age.' J. Brewer, *The Sinews of Power: War, Money and the English State 1688–1783* (1989), xiii. What was true in the early eighteenth century was true *a fortiori* by its end.

[2] The fact that it is accurate to refer to England when describing events in the sixteenth century, but to Britain when attention is transferred to the eighteenth and nineteenth centuries is, of course, itself highly significant. I shall be less than punctilious in this regard in this essay, normally referring to England when it might be more accurate to refer to Britain or even to the British Isles, but since much of my discussion is concerned with long periods of time, I hope it is an acceptable simplification to write of England rather than to attempt greater precision.

the nineteenth century, Britain was able to impose her will over large tracts of every continent. But her dominance did not grow out of the barrel of a gun. It derived chiefly from exceptional economic success: it grew out of the corn sack, the cotton mill, and the coal mine.

In a long-settled area which largely shares a common culture and technology it is unusual for one political entity substantially to increase its relative 'weight' compared with other political units unless it expands territorially in the manner of the Chinese or the Roman empires. This is likely to be especially true of pre-industrial political entities because every such economy had an 'organic' base.[3] The land provided almost all material products of value to man. Density of settlement and ability to produce material goods were closely linked to the productivity of the soil. Hence the tendency on the part of a rising power to seek territorial expansion both to symbolise and to consolidate a temporary advantage: Prussia in the late seventeenth and eighteenth centuries is an example of this mode of expansion. There will be exceptions to any generalisation of this kind but few more striking than the experience of England in the early modern period. The remarkable relative increase in English power sprang principally from what might be described as an intensification rather than an extensification of her territory.[4]

My intention in this essay is draw attention to some features of English history between the later sixteenth and the early nineteenth centuries which exemplify the exceptional character of English development relative to that of most neighbouring continental countries. Economic success was at the heart of the differential success of England and it is with this aspect of the period that I shall be chiefly concerned, though I shall also touch on wider questions about capitalism and modern economic growth.

To provide a perspective for subsequent discussion, consider the following crude calculation of changing relative gross national product. The population of England grew by approximately 280 per cent between 1550 and 1820 while the population of western Europe minus England grew by about 80 per cent. All the major countries of continental western Europe grew by roughly similar percentages over this period.[5] Attempting to estimate changes in output per head over

[3] The concept of an organic economy is described in E.A. Wrigley, *Continuity, Chance and Change: the Character of the Industrial Revolution in England* (Cambridge, 1988), 17–32.

[4] In a more extended discussion of this question, it would be necessary to take into account the complex issues associated with the extension of English power within the British Isles and, especially towards the end of the period, the acquisition of colonies on other continents. Hence the qualification implied by using the adverb 'principally'.

[5] E.A. Wrigley, 'The Growth of Population in Eighteenth-Century England: a Conundrum resolved', *Past and Present*, 98 (1983), 121–5. Countries such as Italy or Germany were not, of course, united political entities in this period. Even those, such as France, which were already nation states in the sixteenth century experienced boundary changes

the same period is subject to much wider uncertainties than the estimate of population change, but it seems certain that the pace of increase was higher in England than elsewhere. Maddison's calculations suggest that in 1820 English output per head was about 40 per cent higher than that of France or Holland and even further ahead of that of continental Europe as a whole.[6] If, for argument's sake, we assume that there was little difference between England and the continent in the mid-sixteenth century, the implication of this exercise is that the gross national product of England was three times larger relative to that of continental countries by the end of the period than it had been at its beginning.[7] An exercise of this kind is subject to many uncertainties, and can make no claim to precision. The result, however, is as likely to understate as to overstate the relative economic advance of England. In any case it leaves no room for doubt that her relative advance was exceptional. How did it come about?

A first point to stress is that the relative advance was in train long before the period which has conventionally been assigned to the

---

during the early modern period. The estimated growth rates are intended to refer to the areas now occupied by the states in question, though all are subject to significant margins of error.

[6] At first sight Maddison's work does not suggest large differences among England and advanced continental countries at the beginning of the nineteenth century. For example, his estimates of gross domestic product per head in 1820 for France, the Netherlands, and the United Kingdom fall within quite a narrow range: that for France (expressed in 1970 US dollars) is $377, for the Netherlands $400, and for the United Kingdom $454. But the UK figure includes Ireland, and Maddison estimated Irish output per head at only half the British figure. Since Irish population was 32.6 per cent of the UK total in 1821, this implies that the British figure for GDP per head would be $542 rather than $454, or 36 per cent higher than the Dutch and 44 per cent higher than the French, rather than 14 and 20 per cent as suggested by a comparison using UK GDP estimates. Since Scottish output per head was lower than English, a figure for England only would be still higher and the advantage over France and the Netherlands therefore still more pronounced: A. Maddison, *Phases of Capitalist Development* (Oxford, 1982), tab. 1.4, 8 and 167; B.R. Mitchell, *British Historical Statistics* (Cambridge,1988), tab. 1.2, 9–10. Unless Maddison's work can be shown to be deeply flawed, therefore, the scale of the contrast between England and other European countries at the end of the early modern period suggests a substantially different structure of aggregate demand in England, and reinforces the likelihood of a distinctive prior history. If data for European countries other than France and the Netherlands were available, the contrast would, in general, be still more pronounced.

[7] To be more concrete, by way of illustration, suppose that output per head in a 'typical' continental country rose by one-third between 1550 and 1820 and that its population increased by 80 per cent, then its gross national product would have risen by about 140 per cent ($1.33 \times 1.8 \times 100 = 239$). Over the same period the English population rose by 280 per cent and we have made the assumption that its output per head moved from parity with a continental average in 1550 to an advantage of 40 per cent by 1820. Therefore gross national product would have risen by about 600 per cent ($(1.33 \times 1.4) \times 3.8 \times 100 = 708$). And 708/239 = 2.96, or approximately a threefold relative increase.

industrial revolution. The change was cumulative and progressive rather than abrupt. It was largely the product of developments within the period often termed pre-industrial; the period when the land was the source not simply of the food of the nation but of the great bulk of its raw materials also, and when therefore the productivity of the land was the key to the possibility of increasing the output of material goods: the period of an organic economy.

Since an almost exclusive emphasis on the land as the source of the material products needed to satisfy human wants is an unfamiliar idea today, it may be helpful to exemplify the point somewhat. Many of the largest industries of the twentieth century are freed from any dependence on animal or vegetable raw materials. Capital goods are constructed predominantly from metal, concrete, and bricks. Most consumer durables are made from metal or plastics. Ceramics and glass are widely used and are produced in great quantity. Transport vehicles, ships, planes, trains, lorries, and cars are made of metal, plastics, and glass. Even articles of clothing, once made exclusively from vegetable or animal raw materials, are now often made from nylon, polyester, or similar materials. Footwear is no longer exclusively made from leather. The supply of mineral ores, clays, oil, and coal, the raw materials from which so many products are manufactured, is not unlimited. Some may become exhausted in the foreseeable future. All must eventually be worked out or at least become increasingly inaccessible. Converting them for human use entails expending a huge quantity of energy. This, too, in time may give rise to grave difficulties, either because no cheap and effective alternative to fossil fuels is developed, or because of the pollution to which their use gives rise. But all such problems are quite different from those which faced organic economies.

The nature of such economies is immediately suggested by their employment structures. In England the most numerous employment groups outside agriculture even as late as 1831 were trades such as shoemakers, carpenters, tailors, blacksmiths, masons, butchers, bricklayers, and bakers, or service occupations such as publicans and shopkeepers.[8] A couple of centuries earlier, if equivalent information were available, it is unlikely that shopkeepers or bricklayers would have been so prominent, but the other occupations, though many fewer in absolute number, would have retained much the same relative positions.

[8] These ten occupations were the largest in the general category of 'handicraft and trade' at the taking of the 1831 census: E.A. Wrigley, 'Men on the Land and Men in the Countryside: Employment in Agriculture in Early-Nineteenth-Century England', in *The World We Have Gained: Histories of Population and Social Structure*, eds. L. Bonfield, R.M. Smith and K. Wrightson (Oxford, 1986), tab. 11.2, 300–1. The list of trades is shown in descending order of size. If all ten occupations were to be treated as a single list, publicans would rank fourth and shopkeepers fifth in size.

With the exception of masons, all these were occupations which depended on animal or vegetable raw materials either as inputs into the production process or, in the case of the service occupations, as the ultimate source of the material goods which they were making available to the public. Blacksmiths and bricklayers were only apparent exceptions to the rule, since the smelting of metals and the baking of bricks were traditionally dependent upon wood as a fuel source, and this was the reason for the modest scale of the output from iron foundries or brickworks in the pre-industrial era. The first stirrings of change in regard to fuel supply, however, were already taking place in early modern England, a development which will require further examination in due course.

If, for simplicity's sake, and as a first approximation, it is agreed that England for most of the early modern period may be regarded as an organic economy, then the nature of the limitation imposed upon it, in common with all other such economies, is clear. All animal and vegetable life is ultimately dependent upon photosynthesis, the process by which a small fraction of the incident energy pouring down upon the earth each year from the sun is converted into a form which either itself constitutes life or affords a basis for other life forms. Animate life is normally in a sense a zero sum game. A square kilometre of forest occupied by pine trees cannot also sustain oaks. A tribe of neanderthals who succeed in securing the bulk of the annual 'crop' of deer will put pressure on a local wolf population which had been heavily dependent upon deer for its food. Symbiosis greatly complicates any such over-simple picture but there is nonetheless a substantial element of truth in viewing competition for the finite products of photosynthesis as a defining feature of animate life. Organic economies constantly juggled with the same problem. Fodder for livestock represented the product of land which might otherwise have been used to grow food for people. The woollen industry could not expand indefinitely without limiting wheat output. Sheep did eat up men.

This point underlies the well-known principle, formulated to greatest effect by Ricardo, which has come to be known as the law of diminishing returns. This principle follows directly from the nature of any organic economy. If the base of all material production lies in the process of photosynthesis and the land surface is finite, there must be limits to the expansion of the quantity of raw materials which can be made available to mankind. The neolithic food revolution, by substituting plants of use to man for the natural vegetation cover, vastly increased the proportion of the products of photosynthesis annexed by man for his own use at the expense of those plants and animals which did not serve his purposes. But once the limits of convenient cultivation had been reached, additional output had either to be won from soils rendered relatively infertile by altitude, steep slope, or poor drainage; or from the more intensive farming of land already in cultivation. In either case, so Ricardo argued, each additional unit of output could be secured only by an increasing proportional input of labour, or capital, or both. As a result the returns to capital and labour must both fall and, at some point, further expansion would become impossible.[9]

All organic economies faced these difficulties, but England proved exceptionally adept at overcoming them. It is a crude but convincing measure of the extent of her achievement to note that by the beginning of the nineteenth century, when the country was still largely self-sufficient in food, only about 40 per cent of the adult male labour force was engaged in agriculture, whereas in continental Europe the comparable figure characteristically ranged between 60 and 80 per cent.[10] An unusually small proportion of the labour force in agriculture, of course, also implies an unusually large proportion in secondary industry and tertiary occupations. Or again, in 1800 England was the most heavily urbanised country in Europe other than Holland, even though in the mid-sixteenth century she had been amongst the least urbanised.[11] London became the largest city in Europe during the seventeenth century.[12] Urban growth in England accelerated so dramatically that during the second half of the eighteenth century 70 per cent of all the urban growth taking place in Europe as a whole occurred in England alone, even though the population of England was only about 8 per cent of that of Europe.[13] Gregory King had been concerned about the ability of England to provide a strong enough tax base to sustain a prolonged conflict with France or Holland, the two countries

[9] For a fuller discussion of the treatment of this issue by the classical economists, Adam Smith, Ricardo, and Malthus, see E.A. Wrigley, 'The Classical Economists and the Industrial Revolution', in *idem*, *People, Cities and Wealth: the Transformation of Traditional Society* (Oxford, 1987), 21–45.

[10] In Finland in 1805 82.1 per cent of the total labour force was engaged in agriculture. In Italy in 1871 61.2 per cent of the male labour force was in agriculture, and the comparable percentages in Ireland (1841) and Sweden (1860) were 68.5 and 64.6. The percentages for Italy, Ireland, and Sweden would certainly have been higher at the beginning of the nineteenth century. In England in 1800 comparable percentage was only about 38 per cent. Mitchell, *British Historical Statistics*, tab. C1, 161–73; Wrigley, 'Men on the Land', tab. 11.12, 332.

[11] J. de Vries, *European Urbanization 1500–1800* (Cambridge, Mass., 1984), tab. 3.2, 30; tab. 3.6, 36–7. Also E.A. Wrigley, 'Urban Growth and Agricultural Change: England and the Continent in the Early Modern Period', *Journal of Interdisciplinary History*, XV (1985), 683–728.

[12] The population of London in 1600, 1700, and 1800 was approximately 200,000; 575,000; and 865,000: the population of Paris, her chief rival in size, at the same three dates was 220,000; 430,000; and 581,000: de Vries, *European Urbanization*, app. 1, 269–78.

[13] Wrigley, 'Urban Growth', tab. 7, 709.

whose power gave most concern to Englishmen in his day.[14] Yet the course of events in the eighteenth century showed that the English economy was able to cope with a substantially heavier tax burden, both in times of peace and war, than that imposed by the French government. Moreover, the weight of taxation did not prevent a continued and sustained expansion of the economy contrary to the fears expressed by King and many others.[15]

Although no comprehensive agricultural production statistics are available until well into the nineteenth century, it may be taken as certain not only that there was a very large rise in the output of English agriculture between the late sixteenth and the early nineteenth centuries, but also that output per head increased greatly.[16] The first point follows directly from the fact that the population tripled while the country remained broadly self-sufficient in basic foodstuffs.[17] The second follows from the first if combined with the probability that the workforce engaged in agriculture increased only slightly between 1600 and 1800.[18] The second point is the more remarkable of the two since it signifies that for a quarter-millennium England succeeded in escaping from the ineluctable pressures which Ricardo had described.[19]

[14] See, for example, G. King, *Natural and Political Observations and Conclusions upon the State and Condition of England 1696*, reprinted in *The Earliest Classics: John Graunt and Gregory King*, with an introd. by P. Laslett (Gregg International, 1973), 227–30. His concern with this issue surfaces repeatedly in the many calculations reproduced from his notebooks in this work.

[15] An extended discussion of the scale of the tax burden in England, of its nature, and of the relation between the tax yield and military success, together with a comparison of England and her main rivals, France and the Dutch Republic, in these respects, may be found in Brewer, *The Sinews of Power*. See also P.K. O'Brien, 'The Political Economy of British Taxation, 1660–1815', *Economic History Review*, 2nd ser., XLI (1988), 1–32 and P. Mathias and P.K. O'Brien, 'Taxation in England and France 1715–1810', *Journal of European Economic History*, 5 (1976), 601–50.

[16] Official series for agricultural acreages and livestock numbers for Great Britain began in 1867, though production series are available only from 1885. Mitchell, *British Historical Statistics*, section III.

[17] Nor was the population ill nourished. There is persuasive evidence that the English population was better nourished than populations in continental Europe at the end of the eighteenth century, though much less well fed than those who lived in the newly independent United States. R.W. Fogel, 'The Conquest of High Mortality and Hunger in Europe and America: Timing and Mechanisms', *Working Paper Series on Historical Factors in Long Run Growth*, no. 16, National Bureau of Economic Research (Cambridge, Mass., 1989), tab. 4, 30 and fig. 5, 38.

[18] Wrigley, 'Urban Growth', tab. 4, 700–1.

[19] It is relevant to note in this connection, however, that unlike many other European countries, the population of England in 1600 was probably still substantially smaller than it had been at its medieval peak at the beginning of the fourteenth century. In 1600 the population was approximately 4.2 million; *c.*1300 it is widely thought to have exceeded 6 million. The pressure of population. on agricultural resources may therefore have been significantly less pronounced in early seventeenth-century England than in many other

How should one seek to explain this phenomenon? In an extended discussion of this issue it would be natural to begin by reviewing in detail the changes which occurred. For example, there is clear evidence that cereal yields doubled between *c.*1600 and *c.*1800. This change, combined with the fact that new rotational systems made it possible to reduce the proportion of the land which was fallowed from perhaps 30 per cent of the arable area at the beginning of the period to a figure of about 12 per cent at its end, goes far towards establishing the proximate reasons for the country's ability to cope with a growing population without any large percentage increase in the area in cultivation.[20] Or again, the nitrogen content of the soil is now widely seen as the key immediate determinant of crop yields. The introduction of leguminous plants into crop rotations helped in this connection both directly by the fixing of nitrogen in their root systems and indirectly by enabling a larger livestock population to be sustained and hence a larger quantity of nitrogen in the form of animal manure to be returned to the soil. Since there is a trade-off between the number of draught animals available on the farm and the number of men whom it is necessary to employ, and it is demonstrable that the ratio of draught animals to men in agricultural employment was substantially higher in England than in France, a part of the rise of manpower productivity

---

countries and population growth may have been accommodated more easily. For the population in 1600: E.A. Wrigley, R.S. Davies, J.E. Oeppen and R.S. Schofield, *English Population History from Family Reconstitution 1580–1837* (Cambridge, 1997), tab. A9.1, 614–15. The size of the population 300 years earlier is subject to much wider margins of uncertainty, but Smith concluded, after a critical review both of the available empirical evidence and of the views of leading scholars, that they strongly suggested 'that the English population total prior to 1310 is very unlikely to have been less than 5.0 million and most probably exceeded 6.0 million': R.M. Smith, 'Demographic Developments in Rural England, 1300–48', in *Before the Black Death: Studies in the 'Crisis' of the Early Fourteenth Century*, ed. B.M.S. Campbell (Manchester, 1991), 49. He noted that this may imply that not until the 1760s was the medieval peak exceeded (50). There are, however, those who stand out against the consensus. Campbell *et al.*, for example, basing their view on the area sown to grain crops each year, net yield per acre, and assumptions about average calorie intake, conclude that the population of England may have been no higher than between 3.4 and 5.6 million and make it clear that their sympathies lie with a figure towards the lower end of the range: B.M.S. Campbell, J.A. Galloway, D. Keene, and M. Murphy, *A Medieval Capital and its Grain Supply: Agrarian Production and Distribution in the London Region c.1300*, Historical Geography Research Series no. 30 (1993), 43, and, more generally, 37–45.

[20] The figure of 30 per cent for the sixteenth century is probably an underestimate. In different parts of the country arable land was fallowed every second, every third, or every fourth year. The overall figure is therefore a function of the relative importance of the three different predominant rotations. The position is much clearer for the beginning of the nineteenth century when the data available in the county surveys suggests that the ratio of fallow to crops was about 1:7. B.A. Holderness, 'Prices, Productivity, and Output' in *The Agrarian History of England and Wales*, VI, 1750–1850, ed. G.E. Mingay (Cambridge, 1989), 133.

taking place in England can probably be attributed to an increase in this ratio.[21] An abundance of draught animals also makes it more readily possible to perform the large number of ton-miles of effort needed if lime and marl are to be applied assiduously to improve soil quality.[22] However, since this discussion must be brief, I intend to concentrate upon some wider issues that are repeatedly raised when attempting to specify the features of English society and economy that gave the country for a time a marked advantage over neighbouring countries.

The first point to consider is whether what happened in England was *sui generis*, or whether there were precedents for it. The question can be made more explicit. In what respects, if any, were developments in England in the seventeenth and eighteenth centuries different from those which took place in Holland in the sixteenth and seventeenth centuries? Was English success merely Dutch success writ large because of greater resources and a bigger population? Holland in its heyday had developed a productive commercial agriculture; had urbanised to the same extent as that attained by England about 1800; had achieved dominance of the international oceanic carrying trade; had succeeded in raising Dutch real incomes to a level substantially higher than that of her rivals; and had enjoyed technical superiority in many branches of manufacture. Yet the momentum of growth in the Dutch republic had faded before the end of the seventeenth century, giving way during the eighteenth to a lengthy period of virtual stagnation. Alone among the nations of western Europe the population of Holland failed to grow during the eighteenth century and her economy ceased to expand.[23] The standard of living did not plummet. Real wages fell moderately during the eighteenth century, but they remained higher than those of most other European countries.[24] The Dutch economy, however, ceased to display what is often taken as a defining characteristic of a modern economy, that over any considerable period both gross output and output per head will rise. In this respect, English experience was different since the two centuries of expansion before 1800 were followed not by stagnation but by a further acceleration in the rate of growth. Focusing on this feature of English experience compared with Dutch points to a distinctive aspect of the divergence of England. It also makes it possible to approach a question of fundamental importance in shaping

[21] E.A. Wrigley, 'Energy Availability and Agricultural Productivity', in *Land, Labour and Livestock: Historical Studies in European Agricultural Productivity*, eds. B.M.S. Campbell and M. Overton (Manchester, 1991), 323–39.

[22] Wrigley, *Continuity, Chance and Change*, 43–4.

[23] J. de Vries and A. van der Woude, *The First Modern Economy: Success, Failure and Perseverance of the Dutch Economy, 1500–1815* (Cambridge, 1997), 665–93.

[24] Ibid., 627–32.

our view of the nature of the modern world, since it is inextricably intertwined with the related question of the propriety of treating the development of capitalism as a valid explanation of the unprecedented economic dynamism of west European countries in this period.

The question at issue is whether the very nature of the capitalist system, which had developed greatly in the seventeenth and eighteenth centuries, ensured that growth would be constant and progressive, if at times productive of severe hardship and social tension, or whether capitalist economies, on the model of eighteenth-century Holland, might enter a phase of stagnation, which might prove as long lasting as any previous period of expansion, or even possibly indefinite. If the former were the case, the whole sequence of growth from Tudor times to Edwardian England and beyond may be seen as a unitary phenomenon, each phase a natural, even an inevitable development from earlier phases. If the Dutch case is not treated simply as an aberration, however, the advent of capitalism is not in itself a sufficient explanation of the course of events.

Since the chances of securing exponential growth may appear very differently *ex prae facto* from *ex post facto*, it is illuminating both to consider the views of contemporaries and of more recent scholarship in this connection.

Adam Smith considered the sources of growth and the limits to growth at length, often turning to Holland in the course of his discussion of the question. He opened the *Wealth of Nations* by analysing with great clarity the possibilities for increasing productivity per head afforded by the division of labour, and then explained the close connection between gains achieved in this fashion, the extent of the market, and the scale of capital accumulation. The example which he chose to illustrate the scope for productivity gains has subsequently acquired the status of a secular parable. He asserted that 20 pinmakers combining to maximise the efficiency of pin production were capable of raising productivity per head 240 times when compared with what a single pinmaker could achieve operating on his own.[25] Even when allowance is made for the fact that he regarded the comparable opportunities in agriculture, by far the largest employer of labour, as slighter,[26] the world which he depicts might appear to offer immense opportunities for progressive gains in productivity, intimately connected with capitalist enterprise. But Adam Smith himself saw matters differently. He was convinced that opportunities for raising production per head were finite and limited, remarking:

[25] A. Smith, *An Inquiry into the Nature and Causes of the Wealth of Nations*, ed. E. Cannan, 2 vols. (Chicago, 1976), I, 8–9.

[26] Ibid., I, 9–10.

> In a country which had acquired that full complement of riches which the nature of its soil and climate, and its situation with respect to other countries, allowed it to acquire; which could, therefore, advance no further, and which was not going backwards, both the wages of labour and the profits of stock would probably be very low.[27]

Although Smith did not suppose any country had yet reached this state, it is clear that he believed that Holland was close to it. It had largely exhausted the range of opportunities for profitable local investment. Smith, using the prevailing interest rate as a surrogate measure of the return on capital, noted that in Holland the government could borrow at 2 per cent and individuals of good credit at 3 per cent and remarked that 'the diminution of profit is the natural effect of its prosperity [that is, the prosperity of Holland], or of a greater stock being employed in it than before'.[28] With investment opportunities so limited close to home, and capital abundant and cheap, Dutch capitalists increasingly turned to other countries and to the carrying trade.[29] Smith, in other words, in common with the other great classical economists, Malthus and Ricardo, envisaged growth as giving way eventually to what they termed the stationary state, an unpromising situation in which neither those who depended on their labour for a livelihood, nor those who depended on capital, were well rewarded for their contributions to the production process.[30] In short, Adam Smith not only regarded it as possible that the advent of capitalism might, after a period of growth and prosperity, be followed by a much darker situation, but expected that the very dynamism of the capitalist system in seeking out opportunities for profitable investment must eventually bring about the stationary state. On this view, what happened subsequently in England was against all expectation.

That Smith's pessimism was unjustified is plain. Rather than deceleration occurring, later generations experienced rates of growth without precedent. Before the nineteenth century the low level of productivity

[27] Ibid., I, 106.

[28] Ibid, I, 102.

[29] 'The carrying trade,' he remarked, 'is the natural effect and symptom of great national wealth; but it does not seem to be the natural cause of it.' Ibid., I, 395. See also ibid., I, 108.

[30] Labour and capital could both enjoy good returns during the phase of expansion made possible by the division of labour, an extensive market, and a steadily rising supply of capital, but this would not last. Smith wrote, 'It is in the progressive state, while the society is advancing to the further acquisition, rather than when it has acquired its full complement of riches, that the condition of the labouring poor, of the great body of the people, seems to be the happiest and most comfortable. It is hard in the stationary, and miserable in the declining state.' Ibid., I, 90–1.

per head universally experienced in fully settled countries meant that the idea of abolishing poverty was a utopian dream. By the end of the century, this possibility no longer seemed out of reach. The outrage expressed by Marx that the means of production existed to enable poverty to be abolished, but that the vastly increased flow of wealth was being concentrated in fewer and fewer hands, fired socialist politics for several generations. The classical economists proved mistaken in their forebodings, but perhaps they were mistaken not from any flaw in their logic, but because, as so often in history, events took a turn for which there was no precedent and which was therefore impossible to foresee.

The other classical economists followed Adam Smith's lead, adducing additional arguments in reaching the same conclusion. Malthus, though in his later years less pessimistic than Smith about the future, was nevertheless oppressed by the thought of what must follow if a rising population bore harder and harder on a fixed and limited supply of land.[31] Ricardo, in formulating the doctrine of declining marginal returns, was the most categorical of all in ruling out any possibility of a prosperous future for mankind, insisting that the problem ultimately arose from the laws of nature rather than the dispositions of man:

> Whilst the land yields abundantly, wages may temporarily rise, and the producers may consume more than their accustomed proportion; but the stimulus which will thus be given to population will speedily reduce the labourers to their usual consumption. But when poor lands are taken into cultivation, or when more capital and labour are expended on the old land, with a less return of produce, the effect must be permanent. A greater proportion of that part of the produce which remains to be divided, after paying rent, between the owners of stock and the labourers, will be apportioned to the latter. Each man may, and probably will, have a less absolute quantity; but as more labourers are employed in proportion to the whole produce retained by the farmer, the value of a greater proportion of the whole produce will be absorbed by wages, and consequently the

[31] Malthus' model of the characteristic behaviour of an economy included long-term 'oscillations' during which for considerable periods of time the secular tendency of real wages might be either upwards or downwards. During an upswing, as he envisaged the matter, one of two results were possible: 'one, that of a rapid increase in population, in which case the high wages are chiefly spent on the maintenance of large and frequent families; and the other, that of a decided improvement in the modes of subsistence, and the conveniences and comforts enjoyed, without a proportionate acceleration in the rate of increase'. In the latter case, the benefits accruing were not necessarily dissipated by excessive population growth but might facilitate the establishment of a new and higher plateau of living standards. T.R. Malthus, *Principles of Political Economy*, 2nd edn. (1836) in *The Works of Thomas Robert Malthus*, ed. E.A. Wrigley and D. Souden (1986), v, 183.

value of a smaller proportion will be devoted to profits. This will necessarily be rendered permanent by the laws of nature, which have limited the productive powers of the land.[32]

The event which escaped contemporary notice was the coming into existence alongside the organic economy of a new and different economy based not on the produce of the land, and thus ultimately on the limits set by the annual quantum of photosynthesis, but on minerals and on fossil fuels which, in contrast to output derived from the soil, were not necessarily subject to declining marginal returns. Production in this mode could be expanded immensely, and often enjoyed increasing marginal returns. Negative feedback could be replaced by positive feedback. But was the course taken by events implied by the very nature of the new economic system, the capitalist system, which had grown up in the past two or three centuries, or might capitalist economies, as Adam Smith supposed, pass from growth to stagnation? To express the same idea using differing terminology, was capitalist growth intrinsically exponential or might it equally well be asymptotic?

There can be no final resolution of this issue, given its nature and the uncertainties which surround it. Yet, since the answer to these questions must affect our appreciation of the nature of capitalism, they cannot be ignored. Marx, whose influence has been pervasive both among those who have shared his political views and among those who have not, may be taken as the weightiest advocate of the former view. A capitalist economy, in his analysis, moved inevitably from the handicraft period through manufacture to modern industry. Manufacture developed out of the handicraft system either 'from the union of various independent handicrafts, which become stripped of their independence and specialised to such an extent as to be reduced to mere supplementary partial processes in the production of one particular commodity' or because it split up a 'particular handicraft into its various detail operations, isolating, and making these operations independent of one another up to the point where each becomes the exclusive function of a particular labourer. – But whatever may have been its particular starting-point, its final form is invariably the same – a productive mechanism whose parts are human beings.'[33] During the manufacturing period machinery played only a subordinate role to the

[32] D. Ricardo, *On the Principles of Political Economy and Taxation* in *The Works and Correspondence of David Ricardo*, I, ed. P. Sraffa with the collaboration of M.H. Dobb (Cambridge, 1951), 125–6.

[33] K. Marx, *Capital: a Critical Analysis of Capitalist Production*, ed. F. Engels, trans. S. Moore and E. Aveling from the 3rd German edn. (2 vols., 1887), I, 329.

division of labour in securing more efficient production.[34] It was an organisational form rather than a particular embodied technology which defined manufacture. Such an organisational form required the concentration of larger and larger amounts of capital in the hands of capitalist entrepreneurs, converting the labourer into what Marx termed 'a crippled monstrosity'.[35] 'As the chosen people bore in their features the sign manual of Jehovah,' he concluded, allowing himself a flight of fancy, 'so division of labour brands the manufacturing workman as the property of capital.'[36]

The critical difference between the era of manufacture and the era of modern industry, in Marx's eyes, lay in the nature of the machine. The capitalist strives constantly to reduce production costs because, by shortening that fraction of the working day in which the labourer works for himself, that is to supply his maintenance, the fraction of the day during which he works for the capitalist is increased.[37] 'In short,' as Marx put it, 'it is a means of producing surplus-value.'[38] The emphasis shifts from labour power itself to the instruments of labour. The crucial distinction, between the two eras, in his view was that between a tool and a machine. 'The machine proper is therefore a mechanism that, after being set in motion, performs with its tools the same operations that were formerly done by the workman with similar tools. Whether the motive power is derived from man, or from some other machine, makes no difference in this respect. From the moment that the tool proper is taken from man, and fitted into a mechanism, a machine takes the place of a mere implement.'[39] He explicitly rejected the view that the crucial distinction had to do with motive power. He noted that it had been argued that in the case of a tool the motive power was supplied by the worker himself whereas in the case of a machine the motive power was supplied by an animal, the wind, or a water fall, but he suggested, as an insuperable obstacle to this view, that it would entail accepting that production by machinery preceded production by handicraft, since animals had been used to provide mechanical energy in the production process from a very early date.[40] Elaborating the same point, he wrote,

[34] 'But, on the whole, machinery played that subordinate part which Adam Smith assigns to it in comparison with the division of labour.' What Marx termed the 'collective labourer, formed by the combination of a number of detail labourers' was 'the machinery specially characteristic of the manufacturing period.' Ibid., I, 341.

[35] Ibid., I, 354.

[36] Ibid., I, 355.

[37] Ibid., II, 365.

[38] Ibid., II, 366.

[39] Ibid., II, 368.

[40] Ibid, II, 366.

> The steam-engine itself, such as it was at its invention, during the manufacturing period at the close of the 17th century, and as it continued to be down to 1780, did not give rise to any industrial revolution. It was on the contrary, the invention of machines that made a revolution in the form of steam-engines necessary. As soon as man, instead of working with an implement on the subject of his labour, becomes merely the motive power of an implement-machine, it is a mere accident that motive power takes the disguise of human muscle; it may equally well take the form of wind, water or steam.[41]

For Marx, therefore, the transition between manufacture and modern industry was unproblematic. The nature of capitalism determines the characteristics of both economic systems and ensures that there will be a transition from one to the other. The technological changes which occurred were equally unproblematic since they were induced by the necessities of the two systems. Capitalism, unlike any earlier socio-economic form, brought into being a dominant class whose nature committed them to promoting changes which tended to increase productivity. 'The bourgeoisie,' he wrote, 'cannot exist without constantly revolutionising the instruments of production, and thereby the relations of production, and with them the whole relations of society. Conservation of the old modes of production in unaltered form, was, on the contrary, the first condition of existence for all earlier industrial classes.'[42] There was a continuum between the forces which had first turned independent craftsmen into what would now be termed a proto-industrial workforce and those which substituted powered machinery for hand-held tools.[43]

Marx's conviction that development was essentially continuous has been echoed by many others. One of the two economic historians to be awarded a Nobel prize in 1993, Douglass North, for example, comes to the same conclusion, though by a different route. Since he regards change in institutional structures as the key development which made possible a capitalist economy and facilitated rapid and persistent economic growth, he focuses on the importance of the appearance of a legal framework within which rational decisions can be taken and implemented and treats the subsequent growth, whether occurring

[41] Ibid., II, 370. Finally, in summary, he wrote, 'The machine, which is the starting point of the industrial revolution, supersedes the workman, who handles a single tool, by a mechanism operating with a number of similar tools, and set in motion by a single motive power, whatever the form of that power may be.' Ibid., II, 370–1.

[42] K. Marx and F. Engels, *The Communist Manifesto*, trans. S. Moore (London and Chicago, 1996), 16.

[43] Marx's manufacturing phase closely resembles the proto-industrial period as defined by Mendels, who coined the term. F.F. Mendels, 'Proto-Industrialization: the First Phase of the Industrialization Process', *Journal of Economic History*, XXXII (1972), 241–61.

before or after the changes which we term the industrial revolution, as essentially downstream from the creation of such a framework. 'The technological change associated with the industrial revolution required the *prior* development of a set of property rights, which raised the private rate of return on invention and innovation.'[44] Further, 'our stereotyped views of the industrial revolution are in need of revision. The period that we have come to call the industrial revolution was not the radical break with the past that we sometimes believe it to have been. Instead, – it was the evolutionary culmination of a series of prior events.'[45] Or again, 'The most convincing explanation for the industrial revolution as an acceleration in the rate of innovation is one drawn from straightforward neoclassical theory in which a combination of better specified and enforced property rights and increasingly efficient and expanding markets directed resources into new channels.'[46]

The list of those taking a similar view of the continuity in the nature of change before, during, and after the industrial revolution could be extended almost indefinitely. The increasingly clear consensus amongst economic historians intent on measuring aggregate economic growth that any acceleration which took place during the classic period of the industrial revolution was minor has tended to underwrite this viewpoint.[47]

[44] D.C. North, *Structure and Change in Economic History* (New York, 1981), 147. The same, he argued, had been true of the earlier growth surge in the Netherlands. 'The merchants of the Low Countries in recognition of this situation paid their rulers through the States General to establish and enforce property rights and end restrictive practices. The Netherlands as a result became the first country to achieve sustained economic growth.' Ibid., 154.

[45] Ibid., 162.

[46] Ibid., 166. Further, 'Particularly significant to the developing of more efficient markets, however, is the better specification and enforcement of property rights over goods and services; and in many cases much more was involved than simply removing restrictions on the mobility of capital and labour – important as those changes were. Private and parliamentary enclosures in agriculture, the Statute of Monopolies establishing a patent law, and the immense development of a body of common law to better specify and enforce contracts are also part of the story.' Ibid., 167. Or again, '– an increase in the rate of technological progress will result from either an increase in the size of the market or an increase in the inventor's ability to capture a larger share of the benefits created by his invention'. Ibid., 165–6.

[47] There is an enormous literature on this issue and a substantial remaining dispute about the weights to be attached to individual output series and the best methods of dealing with sectors of the economy, such as services, for which the direct empirical evidence is very limited. It is symptomatic of the scale of the revision which has taken place that Crafts, who has been a leading figure in urging the case for much more modest estimates of growth rates, concluded that in none of the four sub-periods into which he divided the period 1700–1830 did the rate of growth of national product per head exceed 0.5 per cent per annum and in one period (1760–80) he estimated that there was no increase at all in this figure, a very marked contrast with the earlier estimates of Deane and Cole. N.F.R. Crafts, *British Economic Growth during the Industrial Revolution*

The 'traditional' view that the industrial revolution represented a marked discontinuity with the past and that it occurred during the later decades of the eighteenth century and the early decades of the nineteenth century has not, however, disappeared from recent literature on the subject. Few scholars have taken a more wide-ranging interest in the question than Mokyr. He leaves no doubt about his view of the importance of the industrial revolution. 'Examining British economic history in the period 1760–1830 is a bit like studying the history of the Jewish dissenters between 50 B.C. and 50 A.D. At first provincial, localized, even bizarre, it was destined to change the life of every man and woman in the West beyond recognition and to affect deeply the lives of others . . .'.[48] And Mokyr is explicit that capitalism alone is no guarantee of change as fundamental as that which occurred in Britain in this period. 'Holland,' he pointed out, 'was an urban, capitalist, bourgeois society, indicating that having the "right kind of society" is not a sufficient condition for a successful Industrial Revolution.'[49] Nor does he accept the kind of argument advanced by North, once again by drawing attention to the Dutch case.[50]

To dispose of one common source of misunderstanding about the industrial revolution, and to underline its transformative power, Mokyr undertook two simple modelling exercises. The first relates to the absence of a sharp acceleration in *aggregate* growth rates during the 'classic' period of the industrial revolution. If there is a small 'modern' sector of the economy with a very high growth rate and a much larger 'traditional' sector where the growth rate is low, it will take a long time for the former to contribute sufficiently to the overall growth rate to produce a marked general acceleration. For example, if, at a given date, the modern sector comprises 10 per cent of the whole and is growing at 4 per cent per annum, while the remainder, the traditional sector, is growing at 1 per cent per annum, the combined growth rate will be 1.3 per cent per annum. Assuming that both sectors continue to grow at the stated rates, it will take 74 years for the two sectors to become of equal size, at which point the overall growth rate will have increased to no more than 2.5 per cent per annum.[51] The second

(Oxford, 1985), tab. 2.11, 45. On the potential significance of the services sector in this context, see R.V. Jackson, 'Government Expenditure and British Economic Growth in the Eighteenth Century: some Problems of Measurement', *Economic History Review*, 2nd ser., XLIII (1990), 217–35.

[48] J. Mokyr, 'Editor's Introduction: the New Economic History and the Industrial Revolution', in *The British Industrial Revolution: an Economic Perspective*, ed. J. Mokyr (Boulder, San Francisco, Oxford, 1993), 131.

[49] Ibid., 39.

[50] Ibid., 44–5.

[51] Ibid., 12.

exercise was designed to establish what might have happened to living standards if growth had continued within the constraints obtaining before the cluster of technological changes which Mokyr regards as the key to explaining what happened. He addressed the question by means of a counterfactual exercise assuming that there were no technological advances, that labour and resources changed at their actual historical rates, and that productivity growth was constrained to zero. He then made three different assumptions about the rate of capital accumulation. The result on the most optimistic assumption was an estimated fall in real income per head of 6 per cent between 1760 and 1830. On the least optimistic assumption the fall was 19 per cent. Mokyr gives reasons to suppose that his calculations probably understate the fall which would have taken place in the absence of an industrial revolution.[52] Both these econometric exercises and the more conventional arguments which he also deployed, therefore, confirmed Mokyr in his view that something exceptional took place in late eighteenth-century England.

It is noteworthy that the Dutch experience should have attracted attention both in Adam Smith's time and still at the end of the twentieth century. To Adam Smith the history of the Dutch Republic was his warrant for expecting growth rates generally to falter. To Mokyr it supplied good reasons to look for a feature peculiar to England to account for the industrial revolution. Recently two very distinguished economic historians have returned to the issue of the 'modernity' of the early modern Dutch economy and have delivered a clear verdict. Their work bears closely on the 'divergence of England' question, since de Vries and van der Woude are intent on demonstrating that in her 'golden age' Holland was subject to opportunities and constraints essentially similar to those which determine the behaviour of advanced economies in the twentieth century; that it was, indeed, in their phrase, the 'first modern economy'.

Four main criteria were employed by de Vries and van der Woude in deciding whether or not a 'modern' economy existed. They were:

1. that markets both for commodities and for the three factors of production, land, labour, and capital, should be reasonably free and cover the bulk of productive activity.
2. that agricultural productivity should be sufficiently high to support a complex social and occupational structure, thus making possible an extensive division of labour.
3. that the state should be attentive to property rights and freedom of movement and contract, while not neglecting the material needs of the bulk of the population.

[52] Ibid., 119–20.

4. that a level of technology and organisation should exist capable of supporting a material culture of sufficient variety to sustain market-oriented consumer behaviour.[53]

The defining characteristics of what de Vries and van der Woude term a modern economy, therefore, are essentially those which might equally well be employed to define a capitalist economy, though they prefer to conduct their discussion in terms of modernity.[54] It is convenient briefly to summarise their key findings. Enumerating them will also underline the closeness of the parallels between the Dutch experience and events in England a century or so later.

That the economy of the Netherlands made extraordinary progress between the middle decades of the sixteenth century and *c.*1680 has never been in dispute. De Vries and van der Woude emphasize that, although the achievements of the Dutch Republic in commerce and industry have attracted most attention, agriculture was an equally dynamic sector of the economy. The physical output of Dutch agriculture was increasing on average by between 0.7 and 0.8 per cent per annum during the sixteenth and early seventeenth centuries.[55] Yields rose sharply, especially in the maritime zone where they were double the continental norm.[56] Output per worker engaged in agriculture was far in excess of the European average and this was the basis for a beneficial relationship between the agricultural sector and the rest of the economy.[57] These developments were a prerequisite for the rapid urban growth which took place in the Republic and for the transformation of the occupational structure of the country which anticipated that found in England by 150 years.[58] They insist on the immense benefits conferred on the Dutch economy through the creation of an excellent transport infrastructure and the availability of an abundance of cheap energy, again anticipating two of the main stimuli to growth

[53] De Vries and van der Woude, *First Modern Economy*, 693.

[54] I have discussed a very similar range of issues in E.A. Wrigley, 'The Process of Modernizaton and the Industrial Revolution in England', *Journal of Interdisciplinary History*, III (1972), 225–59.

[55] De Vries and van der Woude, *First Modern Economy*, 232.

[56] Ibid., 230.

[57] They refer to 'the integral part it played through interaction with commercial and industrial activity in creating the dynamic qualities of the seventeenth-century economy'. Ibid., 195.

[58] The percentages in agriculture, industry, and other forms of employment in the Netherlands in the eighteenth century are given by de Vries and van der Woude as 41, 32, and 27, which may be compared with figures of 36, 30, and 34 for England for the same categories in 1801. Ibid., tab. 11.5, 528. Since, if anything, agriculture increased in relative importance in the Netherlands in the eighteenth century, it is probable that if comparable data existed for the mid-seventeenth century, they would show a lower percentage in agriculture and higher percentages in the other two categories.

in England at a later date.[59] The role of cheap and abundant energy supply in the Dutch golden age is of particular interest.[60] It is noteworthy, however, that energy use in the Netherlands had already peaked before the end of the seventeenth century and thereafter declined irregularly down to the beginning of the nineteenth century.[61]

De Vries and van der Woude seek to demonstrate the modernity of the early modern Dutch economy, by showing that the same influences which shape the success or failure of a twentieth-century economy were dominant in the seventeenth-century Netherlands, and that the same modes of analysis which can throw light on these issues today are applicable to the Dutch economy three centuries ago. They insist that the period of stagnation which began before the end of the seventeenth century and lasted for a century-and-a-half must also be understood as modern in nature. 'To suggest that the Republic suffered a "modern decline"', they write, 'must seem perverse, but this is our argument. The economy did not suffer a Malthusian crisis, nor did it revert to some preindustrial norm after a brief, "accidental" boom. In sector after sector – the economy struggled with the modern problems of profit, employment, market access, and costs.'[62] They then go on to make explicit the conclusions implicit in their earlier analysis: 'This formulation harbors an implicit claim about modern economic growth. It is not self-sustained, exponential, and unbounded.'[63] The view that an economy having the hallmarks of modern capitalism is not *ipso facto* assured of exponential growth is persuasive, both in the form to be found in Adam Smith and in its most recent guise, as expounded by de Vries and van der Woude. Accepting it implies that because English growth continued unchecked, explaining her success entails directing attention to some features of English experience not represented in the

[59] Ibid., 338.

[60] De Vries and van der Woude note that in the seventeenth century many of the export-orientated industries, including bricks, tiles and ceramics, pipes, beer, spirits, sugar, salt, soap, whale oil, and glass, '... shared a pronounced energy intensivity, which suggest their common debt to the Republic's uniquely low-cost energy supplies. It appears that energy use in the Republic, both household and industrial, stood far above the levels common to the rest of Europe until the end of the eighteenth century.' Ibid., 338–9. They remark that the foundation of the Republic's 'technological superiority was its effective utilization of energy supplies (peat, wind, and water), which took expression in the development of specific applications of the available energy sources to the needs of the economy', and note that 'The Republic's peat deposits provided a uniquely large supply of heat energy – in excess even of England's coal output until well into the eighteenth century.' Ibid., 344, 694. See also J.W. De Zeeuw, 'Peat and the Dutch Golden Age: the Historical Meaning of Energy Attainability', *A.A.G. Bijdragen* (1978), XXI, 3–31.

[61] De Vries and van der Woude, *First Modern Economy*, 710.

[62] Ibid., 711.

[63] Ibid., 720.

history of the Dutch Republic. This issue is the focus of the balance of this article.

I start with a platitude. The answer to any question is heavily conditioned by the way in which it is posed. I propose to discuss the divergence of England by treating the secular trend in real income per head as the most important single measure of economic growth. If this definition is adopted, there is a clear and vitally important distinction between the period since the industrial revolution and any earlier period in capitalist societies. Even though the early decades of the industrial revolution brought terrible hardship and uncertainty for many people, thereafter, and as a result of its occurrence, a larger and larger fraction of the population of the world has enjoyed a degree of freedom from material deprivation, from malnourishment, and from disease which has no earlier precedent. Pre-industrial capitalism, for reasons which have never been more clearly expressed than in the *Wealth of Nations*, was capable of leading to a more effective deployment of capital and labour than alternative systems, and, since it facilitated the division of labour, it could give rise to substantial improvements in output per man hour. Yet, again for reasons which were spelled out by Adam Smith, this did not imply that progress in this regard would be prolonged, or universal. Rather, with the exhaustion of opportunities for the profitable employment of capital, it was likely that the stationary state would supervene and that 'corn wages', that is the purchasing power of the average worker, would be driven down to a low level. This is a realistic assessment of the possibilities open to an organic economy, but not to an economy which has ceased to be organic.

It was in early modern England that a new base for economic activity began to appear for the first time on a substantial scale, emerging initially so inconspicuously that the classical economists mistook England still for what all societies had been previously, a country constrained by the limitations from which an organic economy cannot free itself. Adam Smith accounted for the initial divergence of England, indicating how she achieved a striking degree of success in making the most of the possibilities of an organic economy, though in this England had been anticipated by Holland. English agriculture succeeded not only in raising food output to keep pace with population increase at rates much higher than those found on the continent; output of animal and vegetable raw materials to sustain a rapid growth of industry; and output of energy in the form of fodder for a rising population of draught animals to bolster both agriculture and transport, but achieved this with little or no increase in the agricultural labour force. Thus for several centuries there was a benign conjunction of rising aggregate output and rising output per head in agriculture which both permitted and fostered a great expansion in the demand for the products of secondary industry and for the services supplied by the tertiary sector, paralleled by major changes in the occupational structure of the labour force. The same developments also underpinned a notable surge in urban growth.

These changes would have sufficed to bring about a major reordering of England's rank within the nations of Europe, economically, politically, and militarily, as indeed they had already done in the case of the Dutch Republic. They would not, however, have sufficed on their own to engender an industrial revolution. England was not simply successful in making the most of the possibilities of an organic economy; the first beginnings of a more radical change were in train. No matter how assiduously Icarus may strive, human flight is not possible if the energy employed in the attempt is muscular. Yet what will always elude the flapping of artificial wings is readily achieved with the assistance of mechanical power. An organic economy suffers from certain necessary limitations which are, as Ricardo asserted, ultimately related to physical constraints. An economy which is increasingly based on inorganic raw materials is not so constrained. Its advantages spring partly from the fact that harnessing the stored energy of innumerable past millennia of insolation in the form of coal, oil, and natural gas places at the disposal of mankind vastly greater quantities of energy than can be secured when the annual quantum of energy is limited by the process of photosynthesis. But the change confers the further advantage that the input of raw materials into the production process, which in an organic economy always creates competition for the use of land, can be achieved from the mouth of a mine rather than from a cultivated field.

Between Elizabethan and Victorian times England moved gradually from dependence upon a purely organic base to a mixed economy in which a steadily increasing fraction of the output of secondary industry was based on minerals. In so doing she also eased herself clear of the problems which would otherwise have led to increasing difficulties. The significance of the change was not apparent to the classical economists. Yet the fact that in 1800 British coal output was providing as much energy as would otherwise have required the devotion of about 15 million acres to the production of wood for fuel on a sustained yield basis is a telling instance of the scale of the changes which had been taking place.[64] When Arthur Young travelled the length and breadth of France in the years 1787, 1788, and 1789 he frequently remarked upon the absence of glazing even from the windows of houses which were otherwise well-built. This was something which was, as he put it, an 'extraordinary spectacle for English eyes' at the time.[65] The fact that

[64] Wrigley, *Continuity, Chance and Change*, 54–5.

[65] 'Pass an extraordinary spectacle for English eyes, of many houses too good to be

sheet glass had become a commonplace in England reflected the availability of cheap thermal energy. Brick became the normal building material for the same reason. Similarly, once a means had been found to use the thermal energy of coal to smelt iron ore without introducing unwanted impurities in the process, the output of iron could reach a multiple of what had previously been possible, given the extravagant amount of heat needed to produce iron or steel and the limited area of forest available as a source of charcoal. A tree may store the energy acquired from the sun by photosynthesis for a century. A coal mine can tap the stored energy of the sun accumulated over millions of years. Further illustrations of the same point abound. The history of the advent of the steam engine, the blast furnace, the railway, the steamship, and of power-driven machinery of all types, for example, has been told many times and from many viewpoints. In the context of this essay the significance of these developments can be simply expressed. The move away from an exclusively organic economy was a *sine qua non* of achieving a capacity for exponential growth. As a result of the advent of energy-intensive and mineral-based sectors in the economy, for the first time in human history poverty became problematic: problematic because the *capacity* to satisfy human material needs was transformed, leaving uncertain only the question of whether the will and the institutional structure existed to banish it. These changes were largely an English phenomenon in their early stages, and the same changes which were transforming her productive potential were also reinforcing the divergence of England from other countries.

The gradual emergence of a new kind of economy in England during the period between the late sixteenth and the mid-nineteenth centuries raises many questions which remain controversial. Why, for example, should access to coal as a source of energy have led to the progressive transformation of so many sectors of industrial production in England but not in China, where coal usage was common in certain areas as early as the fourth century and may have reached a peak about the eleventh century?[66] But for present purposes the significance of these

called cottages, without any glass windows.' A. Young, *Travels in France and Italy during the Years 1787, 1788 and 1789*, Everyman's Library (London and Toronto, n.d.), 22. He was referring to houses encountered en route between Limoges and Brive. He made similar remarks made about cottages near Pont-de-Rodez in the Dordogne and about 'a large village of well-built houses, without a single glass window' near St Gaudens (ibid., 25, 30). Brittany provoked a rash of comparable comments when he passed through Combourg, Guingamp, and Auray (ibid.,101, 103, 105, and again at Aix-en-Provence (ibid., 208) and at Cuges-les-Pins near Toulon (ibid., 213). In the last he complained that there was no glass in the windows of his room in the *auberge* even though he had one of the best rooms.

[66] P.J. Golas, *Mining* in *Science and Civilisation in China*, ed. J. Needham, v, pt. XIII (Cambridge, 1999), 186–201, esp. 195–6.

developments lies in the additional impetus which they gave to the divergence of England and the part which they played in ensuring that the growth process did not lose momentum in England as it had done in Holland. It is idle to speculate about what might have happened if, for example, there had not happened to be abundant coal close to the surface in England, but it would be rash to assume that in its absence an alternative base would have been found upon which the momentum of growth might have been sustained. Seventeenth-century Holland was plainly a highly successful capitalist economy, enjoying rapid growth. But the Dutch economy lost its earlier momentum in the eighteenth century. For well over a century it trod water. It did not fulfil the worst fears expressed by Adam Smith. But, on the other hand, when growth resumed it was not generated by a renewed domestic dynamism but rather as part of the process by which the whole of western Europe began to conform to the new path of economic growth first traced out by England. Indeed de Vries and van der Woude regard Dutch earlier success as having been an obstacle to the adoption of new production technology, arguing that the 'nineteenth-century industrial development of the Netherlands was not held back by its backwardness but rather by its very modernity'.[67]

There is an instructive irony about the industrial revolution in England. The great bulk of the advance made relative to continental countries before 1800 was due to much the same causes as had earlier allowed a much smaller country to achieve a brilliant period of commercial and economic dominance and a notable degree of naval and military success. It sprang from expertise in making the most of the possibilities of an advanced organic economy. In this period, the sources of increased economic efficiency were in the main institutional rather than technological, and institutional structures are often difficult to transfer to different political and social environments. Other countries both admired and feared the growth of English power, as they had earlier admired and feared Dutch success, without finding it easy to emulate. But when the sources from which growth derived themselves changed, when the new mineral-based and energy-intensive sector of the economy became the driving force of the economy as a whole, when the attention of the world was drawn to the steam engine, the puddling furnace, the railway, gas lighting, the mule, and the power loom, when, in other words, the sources of growth were technological rather than institutional, other countries found it far less difficult to recover lost ground. England's continental neighbours soon narrowed

[67] De Vries and van der Woude, *First Modern Economy*, 713. They note that the country possessed a large stock of capital but that this was invested in obsolete plant, equipment, and skills. Ibid., 712.

the gap between themselves and their island rival. Before the end of the nineteenth century, it was England which was observing German industrial, technological, and educational excellence with increasing concern, rather than the reverse. The same developments which had allowed England to escape the constraints of an organic economy also made it comparatively easy for others to match and later to surpass her achievements. As a result, the divergence of England rapidly came to an end.

REGIONAL DIVERSITY IN THE LATER RUSSIAN EMPIRE[1]

By David Saunders

READ 22 OCTOBER 1999 AT THE UNIVERSITY OF HUDDERSFIELD

WERE tendencies in the direction of regional difference in the later Russian Empire outweighing tendencies in the direction of homogeneity? In view of the fact that the empire fell apart in 1917, it looks as if the emphasis ought to be on difference. A good case, however, can also be made for homogeneity. I shall therefore be proposing that the regions of the Russian Empire occupied a more or less constant position on an imaginary 'divergence–coalescence spectrum'. Admittedly, the contest between divergence and coalescence ceased to be equal during the First World War and the empire collapsed. This imbalance, however, turned out to be temporary. The empire re-emerged under a new name at the end of 1922 and for sixty-nine years thereafter occupied more or less the same place on the divergence–coalescence spectrum that it had occupied before it collapsed. So I shall be arguing that, except under extreme duress, the empire was stable. It is this stability I wish to draw to your attention. One's natural inclination is to think of the later Russian Empire as a hotbed of change. I have argued in a recent article that the inclination should be resisted in analyses of work-patterns.[2] I shall argue today that it should also be resisted in the field of regional diversity. To make the case, I shall divide what I have to say into three parts, the first on divergence, the second on coalescence and the third on the First World War.

I

I begin, then, by conceding for the moment that the best way to look at the question of regional diversity in the later Russian Empire may indeed be to think in terms of divergence.

There are at least two good reasons for emphasising the diversity of

[1] I am indebted to the British Academy and the Leverhulme Trust for supporting the research on which this essay is based and to Dr Caroline Brooke for commenting on an earlier draft.

[2] David Saunders, 'The static society: patterns of work in the later Russian Empire', in *Reinterpreting Russia*, ed. Geoffrey Hosking and Robert Service (1999).

the later Russian Empire. First, the potential for diversity that resulted from size, distance, and diversity of environment was so great that progress in the direction of uniformity could only be slow. Second, in the course of the nineteenth and early twentieth centuries the empire ran up against sources and types of disparity which it had not encountered earlier in its history.

On size, distance, and diversity of environment much might be said. In 1914 the empire occupied about 21.8 million square kilometres,[3] which is more than twice the size of the modern United States, more than two-thirds the size of Africa, just over a seventh of the total land surface of the world, and only a little less than the area of the British Empire in the 1870s.[4] Size is not enough on its own, of course, to imply diversity. It is tempting, for example, to say that what was really remarkable about Siberia, the largest of the empire's regions, was not the extent to which it differed from the western part of the empire but the extent to which it resembled it. In ethnic terms, after all, nineteenth-century Siberia was more Russian than many of the European parts of the tsars' domains. Russians constituted just under 69 per cent of the population of Siberia in 1795 and just under 78 per cent in 1917.[5]

It is unwise, however, to think of the Russian colonisation of Siberia as an unqualified success. In 1894 advocates of the foundation of a 'Siberian Society for Agriculture, Industry, and Trade' argued:

> We are used to reading self-satisfied assertions of our extraordinary success in Siberia and Central Asia, but it is enough to recall the civil and social history of Siberia and compare it, for example, with the English colonisation of Australia (not to mention the North American colonisation) to get an impression of the real cultural measure of our Siberian success.[6]

Although Russians constituted the majority of the population of the western part of Siberia as early as the beginning of the eighteenth century, they did not become the majority in the eastern part for another 150 years.[7] The construction of the Trans-Siberian railway in the 1890s did only a little to bring the eastern part closer to the heartland. St Petersburg was unable to fight a successful war in the Far

[3] *Rossiia 1913 god: Statistiko-dokumental 'nyi spravochnik*, ed. A.M. Anfimov and A.P. Korelin (St Petersburg, 1995), 14 (square versts converted to square kilometres).

[4] *Philip's Atlas of the World*, 6th edn (1996), x, xiv (USA, Africa, world); Iu. E. Ianson, *Sravnitel 'naia statistika Rossii i zapadno-evropeiskikh gosudarstv* (2 vols., St Petersburg, 1878–80), 1, 3 (British Empire in the 1870s).

[5] S.I. Bruk and V.M. Kabuzan, 'Dinamika chislennosti i rasseleniia russkogo etnosa (1678–1917gg.)', *Sovetskaia etnografiia*, 4 (1982), 17.

[6] St Petersburg, Rossiiskii gosudarstvennyi istoricheskii arkhiv [hereafter RGIA], *fond* [hereafter f.] 391, *opis'* [hereafter op.] 1, *delo* [hereafter d.] 47, *list* [hereafter l.] 143.

[7] Bruk and Kabuzan, 'Dinamika', 22.

East in 1904–5. When the Duma asked the tsar's Minister of Trade and Industry in 1913 whether he could find better ways of supplying the Far East with salt (for lack of which local fishermen were having to sell their catch as fertilizer), he replied that he could not.[8] Running such a place from distant St Petersburg was never likely to be easy. The intensive process of colonisation which began in the 1890s created almost as many problems as it solved. Non-Russians, for example, sometimes obliged Russian incomers to abandon their efforts to establish themselves. Thus the Governor of Nizhnii Novgorod reported in 1894 that one Mikhail Liagunovskii had been unable to recover the horses and bulls he had lost to Siberian nomads and had decided to return to the province of Poltava in Ukraine.[9] Since, moreover, the Siberian climate militated against immigration at the best of times (a peasant in Vologda, in the European part of the empire, acknowledged in 1918 that it was cold in Siberian Iakutiia, which, coming from a peasant in Vologda, was acknowledgment indeed[10]), the full integration of the region into the empire looked likely to remain a distant prospect even if the problems posed by distance, climate, and the relations between old and new inhabitants could be resolved.

In view, however, of the fact that Siberia contained so few inhabitants, perhaps, in the context of the empire as a whole, its intractability hardly mattered. Consider this table:[11]

Component Parts of the Russian Empire on 1 January 1914

	Area (% of the total)	Population (% of the total)	Population Density (people per sq km)
European Russia	22.19	72.24	26.64
Poland	0.52	6.87	107.96
Caucasus	2.15	7.24	27.54
Siberia	57.41	5.61	0.80
Central Asia	16.24	6.22	3.14
Finland	1.49	1.82	9.96
Whole empire	100.00	100.00	8.18

[8] RGIA, f. 395, op. 2, d. 2959, *listy* [hereafter ll.] 1–3.

[9] RGIA, f. 391, op. 1, d. 47, l. 192.

[10] *Dnevnik totemskogo krest'ianina A.A. Zamaraeva: 1906–1922 gody*, ed. V.V. Morozov and N.I. Reshetnikov (Moscow, 1995), 196.

[11] Calculated from the absolute figures for area and population in Anfimov and Korelin, *Rossiia 1913 god*, 11–14, 16 (square versts again converted to square kilometres for the purposes of the third column).

Siberia took up more than half the empire's area but contained only about one-eighteenth of its population. Whatever the degree of its intractability, it would not have troubled St Petersburg very much if the heartland of the empire had been a unity.

But the heartland was not a unity. If it had been, it might be easier to say where it was. Clearly it lay somewhere to the west of the Urals (it is hard to think of Central Asia as a candidate), but since the area west of the Urals was far from being a coherent whole it cannot all have been the heartland. Today this area contains eleven countries and part of a twelfth. Around 1900 its four component parts (Poland, Finland, 'European Russia', and the Caucasus) were divided into seventy-nine tsarist provinces. Pinpointing a group of these that could be called the heartland is difficult. One might begin the attempt by excluding from the reckoning the ten that made up the Kingdom of Poland, the eight that constituted the Grand Duchy of Finland, and the eleven that administrators dubbed 'The Caucasus'. On geographical, ethnic, and to some extent administrative grounds this looks reasonable, but it is risky on economic grounds in respect of the Kingdom of Poland (whose industrial output was crucial to the economic performance of the empire as a whole) and it is risky on ethnic grounds in respect of the three Caucasian provinces that lay to the north of the Caucasus mountains because, by 1900, the indigenous populations there had been greatly outnumbered by Russians and Ukrainians.

The main reason, however, for not consigning the twenty-nine Polish, Finnish, and Caucasian provinces to the periphery is that cutting them out does not leave a coherent residue. Nineteenth-century bureaucrats called the fifty provinces that were left 'European Russia', a practice adopted by many historians, but if the term is taken to mean that the fifty provinces possessed a substantial degree of homogeneity, it obscures more than it illuminates. Today, the fifty provinces make up all or part of seven countries; and as we shall see, the differences among them were not merely of the kind that can be employed to justify pretensions to political independence.

From the point of view of the economic activities they supported, it is tempting to think of the fifty provinces as a unity on the grounds that they constituted a more or less undifferentiated zone of agricultural activity. Since, however, only about 20 percent of the area they occupied was under the plough in 1861,[12] the characterisation seems not to work very well. Roughly speaking, the terrain of the fifty provinces fell into five broad east–west strips: scrub in the far north, then, moving south, coniferous forest, mixed coniferous and deciduous forest, purely

[12] A.V. Dulov, *Geograficheskaia sreda i istoriia Rossii: konets XV – seredina XIXv.* (Moscow, 1983), 12.

deciduous forest which, after most of the trees had been felled, came to be known as 'forest-grassland' or 'forest-steppe', and grassland or steppe on which trees had hardly ever grown.[13] Only the 'forest-grassland' contained high-grade agricultural land, the so-called 'black soil'.[14] Elsewhere, the inhabitants had to combine agriculture with off-farm earnings. The effect was to generate regional variety.

Two key eighteenth-century developments, moreover, had implanted centrifugalism in the territory that was to become the fifty provinces. First, the rulers of the empire had shifted their administration northward. Moscow, the long-time capital, had owed much of its original and continuing authority to its ecological centrality. It was at the heart of the mixed forest zone, not far from the sources of the rivers Volga, Dnieper, and Western Dvina, and at the intersection of the imaginary horizontal line which divides surplus from sufficient moisture and the imaginary vertical line which marks the boundary between moderately cold and really cold winter temperatures.[15] St Petersburg, on the other hand, the centre of the empire's administration from 1712, was peripheral indeed. Until Helsinki and then Reykjavik displaced it in the twentieth century, it was the most northerly capital in the world. It was not connected to Moscow by metalled road until 1833 or by railway until 1852.[16] Even then, educated people seem to have wondered whether improved communications would bring about a deterioration rather than an improvement in the fortunes of the city, for in January 1870 the tsar's Minister of Internal Affairs was apparently relieved to be able to conclude his report on the recent city census with the reflection that 'At any rate, [it has] undoubtedly demonstrated that the construction of railways has not yet led to the reduction in the well-being of the capital which many predicted.'[17] But although better communications brought about an increase rather than a diminution in the population of St Petersburg they also served to perpetuate the extreme transience of the city's population, to which a celebrated book entitled *The Belly*

[13] For a map of these strips before they had been significantly altered by human intervention see Marek Zvelebil and Paul Dolukhanov, 'The Transition to Farming in Eastern and Northern Europe', *Journal of World Prehistory* 5 (1991), 244.

[14] For a list of the provinces and parts of provinces which contained 'black soil' see Ianson *Sravnitel'naia statistika*, I, 10–12.

[15] The maps on which this sentence is based are to be found in R.E.F. Smith, *Peasant farming in Muscovy* (Cambridge University Press, 1977), 220, and Simon Franklin and Jonathan Sheppard, *The Emergence of Rus 750–1200* (1996), 404–5.

[16] On the road, see A.A. Beliakov, 'Vedomstvo putei soobshcheniia: Ot Siversa do Kleinmikhelia (1798–1855gg.)', in *Sankt-Peterburgskoe nauchnoe obshchestvo istorikov i arkhivistov: Ezhegodnik*, ed. L.E. Shepelev *et al.* (St Petersburg, 1997), 108, 113; on the railway, see William L. Blackwell, *The Beginnings of Russian Industrialization 1800–1860* (Princeton, 1968), 279–302.

[17] RGIA, f. 1290, op. 2, d. 59. l. 64.

of St Petersburg referred in the 1880s and which scholars have been commenting on ever since.[18]

Meanwhile, the tsars' eighteenth-century conquest of the Black Sea coastline had brought about a southward shift in the fifty provinces' economic centre of gravity. Odessa, the city founded by Catherine the Great at the southern end of the fifty provinces in the 1790s, owed its explosive nineteenth-century growth to an economic orientation on the Mediterranean. St Petersburg and Odessa looked out on quite different parts of the world.[19]

Because of the new centrifugalism it is necessary, at the very least, to think of the area of the fifty provinces as two large swathes of land either side of an east–west fault-line not far south of Moscow. To the north of the line (the area of scrub, coniferous, and mixed forest) peasants could only scratch a living from the soil and depended heavily on non-agricultural means of supplementing their incomes. To the south, in the area of forest–grassland, they had the advantage of the 'black soil', 'a soil whose fertility [was] unparalled in western Europe and which, outside Russia, [was to be found] ... only in India and North America'.[20] Peasants farmed on both sides of the line, but their reliance on farming was much greater in the south than the north. The exposure of the east–west fault-line in the eighteenth century had broken the European part of the empire into two great economic regions, a northern industrial and a central and southern agricultural. 'Each of these regions,' wrote a famous early twentieth-century commentator, 'constituted a market for the other, and the development of seigneurial agriculture in central and southern Russia could rest only on the success of non-agricultural production in northern Russia.'[21]

Dividing the fifty provinces into two parts is by no means enough, however, to express the full extent of their diversity. In November 1901 the regime established a commission to investigate what was known in debates of the time as 'the impoverishment of the centre'. The three volumes of data published by the commission in 1903 concluded that the economic 'black hole' which had indeed emerged between north and south embraced not only 'the entire centre' but also 'the whole of the east and even part of the south'.[22] The strains imposed by the

[18] A.A. Bakhtiarov, *Briukho Peterburga: Ocherki stolichnoi zhizni* (St Petersburg, 1994, first published in 1887), 155–62; James H. Bater, *St Petersburg: Industrialization and Change* (Montreal, 1976), esp. 313; Barbara Alpern Engel, *Between the fields and the city: Women, work, and family in Russia, 1861–1914* (Cambridge, 1994), 64–99.

[19] On Odessa see Patricia Herlihy, *Odessa: A History 1794–1914* (Cambridge, Mass., 1986).

[20] Ianson, *Sravnitel'naia statistika*, I, 9.

[21] Petr Struve, *Krepostnoe khoziaistvo: Issledovaniia po ekonomicheskoi istorii Rossii v XVIII i XIX vv.* (n.p. [Moscow], 1913), 33.

[22] Anon, *Materialy Vysochaishe uchrezhdennoi 16 noiabria 1901g. kommissii po issledovaniiu voprosa*

centrifugalism of the eighteenth century were coming home to roost; by the beginning of the twentieth century the fifty provinces had to be divided into at least three broad regions rather than two.

But even three is too few. In 1881 the regime announced an across-the-board reduction in the former serfs' redemption payments. A year later it went on to consider which serfs ought to be granted a further reduction on the basis of special economic need. To establish a basis for the second reduction it produced not a two- or a three- but a four-way classification of the 350 districts of the thirty-four affected provinces: those with black soil, those with mixed black and non-black soil, those with non-black soil in which local crafts were well developed, and those with non-black soil where local crafts were not well developed.[23] Even this apparently sophisticated classification gave rise to disagreement between central and local authorities on the question of categorising particular parts of particular provinces.[24]

It is easy to continue this game of increasing the number of regions into which the fifty provinces of 'European Russia' may be divided. A modern book on rural–urban relations in the second half of the nineteenth century speaks of five.[25] A modern demographic study detaches a 'Baltic' group of provinces and so turns the five into six.[26] Maps in various modern western publications depict nine, eleven and twelve.[27] Soviet scholars usually spoke of thirteen,[28] though they came up with different reasons for their classifications and drew slightly different borders between the regions. Thirteen was also the number into which V.P. Semenov planned to divide the fifty provinces at the time he began publishing a *Complete Geographical Description* of the Russian Empire in 1899.[29] Some evidence makes the possible number of regions

---

o dvizhenii s 1861g. po 1900g. blagosostoianiia sel'skogo naseleniia srednezemledel'cheskikh gubernii, sravnitel'no s drugimi mestnostiami Evropeiskoi Rossii (3 vols., St Petersburg, 1903), III, 280.

[23] RGIA, f. 1290, op. 2, d. 145, ll. 47–8.

[24] See, for example, RGIA, f. 1290, op. 2, d. 146, for the determination of additional reductions in the province of Viatka.

[25] P.G. Ryndziunskii, *Krest'iane i gorod v kapitalisticheskoi Rossii vtoroi poloviny XIX veka* (Moscow, 1983), 22–3 and *passim.*

[26] A.G. Vishnevskii, 'Rannie etapy stanovleniia novogo tipa rozhdaemosti v Rossii', in *Brachnost', rozhdaemost', smertnost' v Rossii i v SSSR: Sbornik statei*, ed. A.G. Vishnevskii (Moscow, 1977), 109 and *passim.*

[27] *Die Nationalitäten des Russischen Reiches in der Volkszählung von 1897*, ed. Henning Bauer, Andreas Kappeler, and Brigitte Roth (2 vols., Stuttgart, 1991), II, 35; Maureen Perrie, *The agrarian policy of the Russian Socialist-Revolutionary Party from its origins through the revolution of 1905–1907* (Cambridge University Press, 1976), xii; Seymour Becker, *Nobility and Privilege in Late Imperial Russia* (DeKalb, Illinois, 1985), endpapers.

[28] See, for example, the table in Bruk and Kabuzan, 'Dinamika', 17, and note the authors' statement at the end of this article that they consider their regional division to be 'accepted in scholarly literature' (*ibid.*, 25).

[29] Calculated from the projected contents of the twenty-two volumes Semenov was

seem almost infinite. A government enquiry of 1882 into the question whether peasant migration from the European part of the empire ought to be managed rather than resisted began its work with an eleven-point questionnaire to provincial governors which elicited so many conflicting descriptions of local circumstances that dividing the fifty provinces into well-defined regions on the basis of them would be impossible.[30]

Different provincial groupings result, of course, from the use of different criteria for classification. So far I have employed or hinted at climatic, environmental, economic, and, very much in passing, ethnic considerations. Others may be readily imagined. Social criteria would involve distinguishing between the central part of the fifty provinces where serfdom had arisen and the fringes where it was either absent or less well-developed or did not take the form of manual labour on land owned by noblemen. The abolition of serfdom in 1861 required a general and four regional statutes.[31] Linguistic criteria would involve noting that at the end of the nineteenth century ten languages in the fifty provinces were spoken by more than a million people and another fifteen by more than 100,000.[32] Religious criteria would involve drawing attention to differences between Orthodox, Catholics, Protestants, Muslims, and Jews (not to mention a few Buddhists). Cultural criteria would involve explaining why northern soups tended to be green and southern red; why northern peasant huts were brown and southern white; why, to quote some well-known demographers, 'marital fertility is often more uniform within regions, and more varied from region to region, than would be expected on the basis of the social and economic characteristics of the provinces that constitute the region';[33] why family size was larger in the southern part of the fifty provinces than the northern; and why there were slightly more women than men in the north, slightly more men than women in the south.

It is important here, finally, to emphasise the point I have touched on already that in some respects the fifty provinces were becoming more rather than less diverse with the passage of time. The cen-

hoping to publish: *Rossiia: Polnoe geograficheskoe opisanie nashego otechestva*, ed. V.P. Semenov (11 vols., St Petersburg, 1899–1914), I, vi–vii.

30 RGIA, f. 391, op. 1, d. 4, ll. 1–5 (the questionnaire); ibid., d. 9 (summary of the governors' responses); ibid., d. 47, ll. 314–5, 338–9, 384–6 (typical responses *in extenso* from the governors of Livland, Vitebsk, and Minsk).

31 *Polnoe sobranie zakonov rossiiskoi imperii* [hereafter PSZ], 2nd series (55 vols., St Petersburg, 1830–84), XXXVI, part I, 141–69 and 231–372 (statutes 36657 and 36662–5, 19 February 1861).

32 Calculated from *Obshchii svod po imperii rezul'tatov razrabotki dannykh pervoi vseobshchei perepisi naseleniia, proizvedennoi 28 ianvaria 1897 goda*, ed. N.A. Troinitskii (2 vols., St Petersburg, 1905), II, 2–19.

33 Ansley J. Coale, Barbara Anderson, and Erna Härm, *Human Fertility in Russia since the Nineteenth Century* (Princeton, 1979), 53.

trifugalism implicit in the foundations of St Petersburg and Odessa in the eighteenth century found many manifestations in the nineteenth century apart from the 'impoverishment of the centre'. As urbanisation took off, towns were to be found at the centre and on a number of peripheries of the European part of the empire, but not in large swathes of territory between them.[34] The coming of railways in the later nineteenth century had disintegrative as well as integrating consequences in view of the fact that things not produced locally could now be more or less readily procured elsewhere (which encouraged regional specialisation). The growth in the area of arable land which took place in the twenty years after the abolition of serfdom in 1861 occurred in the 'black soil' provinces rather than in the north (where, except in the Baltic provinces, the area of arable diminished).[35] Perhaps as a result, the patriarchal family declined at a faster rate in the north than the south.[36] So even if one could come up with a satisfactory way of breaking down the European part of the empire into regions, it would work only for a particular point in time. As time passed, the distinguishing features of regions changed.

This point about change over time is crucial if one is trying to embrace regional diversity not just in the fifty provinces but in the empire as a whole, for imperial expansion continued more or less throughout the nineteenth and early twentieth centuries. Russia took over eastern Georgia in 1801, Finland in 1809, Bessarabia in 1812, most of Azerbaidzhan in 1813, Napoleon's Grand Duchy of Warsaw in 1815, Armenia and the rest of Azerbaidzhan in 1828, the eastern shore of the Black Sea in 1829, the northern part of what the 1897 census called Central Asia in the first half of the nineteenth century (by gradually pushing a line of forts across the steppe), the northern Caucasus at the end of the 1850s and in the early 1860s, the southern part of Central Asia between the mid-1860s and the mid-1880s, the Kars region of eastern Turkey in 1878, the lower part of the river Amur in the extreme east of Siberia in 1858, the western shore of the Sea of Japan (otherwise known as the Ussuri region) in 1860, and the island of Sakhalin to the north of Japan in 1875. Admittedly, the empire sold Alaska to the United States in 1867 and gave up half of Sakhalin to Japan in 1905, but Alaska had become a liability (many Americans thought that buying

[34] See the remarkable diagram in Veniamin Semenov-Tian-Shanskii, *Gorod i derevnia v evropeiskoi Rossii* (St Petersburg, 1910), 207.

[35] V.K. Iatsunskii, 'Izmeneniia v razmeshchenii zemledeliia v evropeiskoi Rossii s kontsa XVIII v. do pervoi mirovoi voiny', in *Voprosy istorii sel'skogo khoziaistva, krest'ianstva i revoliutsionnogo dvizheniia v Rossii: Sbornik statei k 75-letiiu akademika Nikolaia Mikhailovicha Druzhinina*, ed. V.K. Iatsunskii *et al.* (Moscow, 1961), 125–7.

[36] Helena Chojnacka, 'Nuptiality Patterns in an Agrarian Society', *Population Studies*, 30 (1976), esp. 212–13.

it was a bad idea) and the surrender of the southern half of Sakhalin was involuntary (a result of defeat in the Russo-Japanese War). Although, in the nineteenth and early twentieth centuries, Russia sometimes drew in its horns, and although in this later period of the history of the Russian Empire some government agencies (above all the Ministry of Foreign Affairs) seem to have been doves rather than hawks, one has only to point to the empire's forward moves in Manchuria immediately prior to the Russo-Japanese War and to the establishment of a protectorate over the Mongolian region of Tuva in April 1914 to demonstrate that the idea of expansion still had influential supporters in St Petersburg until at least the outbreak of the First World War.[37]

This constant expansion brings me to my second reason for highlighting the diversity of the later Russian Empire. The first was that the degree of diversity was so great that one could not reasonably expect progress in the direction of uniformity to have been anything other than slow. The second is that in the course of the nineteenth and early twentieth centuries the empire ran up against sources and types of disparity which it had not encountered earlier in its history. The new sources were the newly acquired lands which I have just been listing. These I shall pass over, on the grounds that if the new disparity been merely geographical, it might have been manageable. The imperial administration had been finding ways of dealing with the sort of disparity which resulted from the acquisition of new territory since at least the point in the middle of the sixteenth century when a tsar first took over large numbers of non-Slavs.[38] The new types of disparity, on the other hand, need to be highlighted. In the nineteenth century tsars had to respond to the ideologically driven sort of diversity which stemmed from the central and west European notion of ethnic identity. This caught them unawares.

In 1819 the liberal Russian poet and literary critic P.A. Viazemskii pointed out in a private letter from Warsaw, capital of the tsar's newly acquired 'Congress Kingdom of Poland' (Napoleon's former Grand Duchy of Warsaw) that Poles had come up with a neologism, *narodowość*, 'people-ness', to translate the French word *nationalité*. Why, Viazemskii

[37] The specialist literature on Russia's nineteenth-and early twentieth-century annexations is too voluminous to cite, but for studies which cover many of them see Andreas Kappeler, *Russland als Vielvölkerreich: Entstehung, Geschichte, Zerfall* (Munich, 1992), 87–93, 137–76, and *Russian Colonial Expansion to 1917*, ed. Michael Rywkin (1988), esp. 139–256. For a good example of the occasional caution of the central government see David MacKenzie, 'Expansion in Central Asia: St Petersburg vs. the Turkestan Generals (1863–1866)', *Canadian Slavic Studies*, 3 (1969), 286–311. On Tuva see now E.A. Belov, *Rossiia i Kitai v nachale XX veka* (Moscow, 1997), 181–96.

[38] Administrative matters are now well covered in *Natsional'nye okrainy Rossiiskoi imperii: Stanovlenie i razvitie sistemy upravleniia*, ed. S.G. Agadzhanov and V.V. Trepavlov (Moscow, 1998).

asked, could he not employ the equivalent neologism, *narodnost'*, in Russian? 'If the word is needed, it will take root.'[39] The word did take root. Its strong anti-statist and proto-populist connotations appealed not only to Poles but also to Russians who felt at odds with their authoritarian government and to educated non-Russian (and non-Polish) inhabitants of the empire, who latched on to it to point out that the tsar ruled not one 'people' (*narod*) but many. Up to a point, Nicholas I undermined the anti-authoritarian implications of the word when he permitted his Minister of Education, Sergei Uvarov, to make it the third plank of the celebrated governmental ideological platform of 1833 ('Orthodoxy, Autocracy, Nationality'). The word's ethnic implications, however, continued to attract explorers. In the 1840s a handful of educated Ukrainians proposed converting the imperial monolith into a federation.[40] Twenty years later the paranoid Russian nationalist Mikhail Katkov took the view that enthusiasm for federalism was all around him. In March 1866 he devoted a leader in his influential newspaper *Moscow News* to the proposition that it was gaining ground even at the heart of the imperial government. The authorities seemed not to take the charge seriously and merely served a formal warning on the newspaper for the strength of its language, but by the 1880s they too began responding obviously to the possibility that minority nationalism was gaining ground. The policy of 'Russification' on which they insisted in the 1880s seems to indicate that what had been only a word in 1819 had become as big a threat to the regime as the empire's size and diversity.[41]

II

In view of everything I have said so far, it may look as if the case for the significance of centrifugalism in the later Russian Empire is overwhelming. Even the older parts of the empire differed substantially from each other. New lands and new ideas were complicating matters. Why didn't the empire fall apart sooner?

Perhaps the first point to make on the 'centripetal' side of the fence is that the element of ethnic threat which I was trying to convey at the end of the first part of the paper needs to be set in context. Not many of the Russian Empire's ethnic minorities were large, or rather, non-

[39] *Ostaf'evskii arkhiv kniazei Viazemskikh*, ed. V.I. Saitov (5 vols. in 8, St Petersburg, 1899–1913), I, 357–8.

[40] For the documents to which their prosecution gave rise see *Kyrylo-Mefodiivs'ke tovarystvo*, ed. P.S. Sokhan' *et al.* (3 vols., Kiev, 1990).

[41] On the Katkov affair of 1866 see V.G. Chernukha, *Pravitel'stvennaia politika v otnoshenii pechati: 60–70-e gody XIX veka* (Leningrad, 1989), 160–1. I return to Russification below.

Russians were numerous in absolute terms but constituted a much smaller proportion of the total population of the empire than, for example, non-German speakers did of the Austrian. People whose first language was Russian made up between 43 and 44 per cent of the total population of the Russian Empire at the end of the nineteenth century and were nearly two-and-a-half times more numerous than the next-largest ethnic group (Ukrainians). In the Habsburg Monarchy, by contrast – the one European state which, by common consent, really was challenged by ethnic diversity in the nineteenth century – German-speakers made up only some 23 per cent of the total population in 1910 and were not much more numerous than the ethnic group in second place (Hungarians). Five ethnic groups below the top two in the Habsburg Monarchy made up larger proportions of the total population of the state than any of the ethnic groups below the top two in the Russian Empire. German and Hungarian, furthermore, belong to quite unrelated groups of languages, whereas Russian, Ukrainian, and Belarusian – the languages of the first-, second-, and fourth-largest ethnic groups in the Russian Empire – are all East Slavonic.[42]

Admittedly, Russians in the nineteenth century were spread out over a larger area even than they had been in the eighteenth century. But Russians who migrated to the peripheries of the empire seem to have been good at retaining the cultural identity of their forebears. Indeed, to judge by the late-imperial examples of the future White general Anton Denikin (who was half-Polish and brought up in Poland), the extreme Russian nationalist Vladimir Purishkevich (who came from Bessarabia), and members of the Russian Nationalists' Club in Kiev, some Russians from the borderlands came to insist even more strongly on their Russian identity than Russians who stayed at home.[43]

And if Russians maintained or insisted on their culture, did they also, directly or indirectly, persuade the non-Russians around them to adopt Russian culture? Insofar as some non-Russians adopted the Russian language, the answer is undoubtedly yes. The imperial census-takers of 1897 were certain that significant numbers of the empire's many Finnic inhabitants as well as of its Greek, gypsy, and native

[42] For the Russian Empire, the calculations in this paragraph rest mainly on the linguistic results of the 1897 census (the source for which is given in n. 32, above). Since, however, Finland was not included in the census, one must add 2.2 million Finns and 300,000 Swedes (Kappeler, *Russland*, 325). For the main nationalities of the Habsburg Monarchy in 1910, see the table in István Deák, *Beyond Nationalism: A Social and Political History of the Habsburg Officer Corps, 1848–1918* (New York and Oxford, 1990), 13.

[43] A.A. Denikin, *Put' russkogo ofitsera* (New York, 1953), esp. 17–57; Prince Serge Dmitriyevich Urussov, *Memoirs of a Russian Governor* (1908), 71–2 (on Purishkevich); and Olga Andriewsky, 'The Politics of National Identity: The Ukrainian Question in Russia, 1904–12' (Ph. D. thesis, Harvard University, 1991), 227–48.

Siberian communities had become Russian-speaking.[44] Although they acknowledged, citing the Irish as their main example, that 'many nationalities long retain the memory of the nationality to which they used to belong after having adopted as a result of physical and spiritual assimilation the culture, language and up to a point the physical characteristics of more numerous or culturally stronger peoples',[45] it is hard not to believe that at least some of the non-Russians who adopted Russian as their native language also began to adopt Russian culture as a whole.

Non-Russians who belonged to privileged estates of the realm certainly tended to adopt Russian culture, for this was the best way of retaining their privileges. The various individual Armenians, Georgians, Kazakhs, and even Poles who identified themselves with their Russian masters were not alone.[46] Cultivated by the regime, local nobles worked for it enthusiastically in many parts of the borderlands. It is true that the German-speaking barons of the Baltic provinces managed to convey their loyalty to St Petersburg without losing their cultural distinctiveness, but most non-Russian gentry who welcomed Russian rule went the way of the Ukrainian gentry on the east bank of the river Dnieper, who Russified well-nigh completely.[47]

Russia may also have had a good deal to offer the lower echelons of non-Russian communities. Because no one was debarred from government service on grounds of ethnic origin,[48] the empire offered all of its subjects employment. Indirectly, empire probably offered the unprivileged other economic benefits. Whether or not one accepts the view that the European part of the empire possessed a unified internal market as early as the middle of the nineteenth century,[49] regional differences in the prices of rye and wheat certainly came down in the wake of the rapid expansion of railways from the 1860s.[50] The question

[44] S. Patkanov, 'K tablitsam XIII, XIV, XV i XVI', in *Obshchii svod* (n. 32, above), II, i.

[45] Ibid.

[46] The individuals I have in mind include the Armenian M.T. Loris-Melikov (Alexander II's Minister of Internal Affairs in 1880–1), the Georgian Prince P.I. Bagration (who died of the wound he received at Borodino in 1812), the Kazakh Chokan Valikhanov (on whom see Petr Petrovich Semenov, *Travels in the Tian'Shan' 1856–57* [1998], 26), and the Poles Viktor Artsimovich (liberal Governor of Kaluga at the time of the abolition of serfdom) and Petr Rachkovskii (head of the tsarist secret police in Paris in the 1880s and 1890s).

[47] On these Ukrainians see Zenon Kohut, *Russian Centralism and Ukrainian Autonomy: Imperial Absorption of the Hetmanate 1760s–1830s* (Cambridge, Mass., 1988).

[48] Stephen Velychenko, 'Identities, Loyalties and Service in Imperial Russia: Who Administered the Borderlands?', *Russian Review*, 54 (1995), 188–208.

[49] For the possibility that it possessed one even earlier see B.N. Mironov, *Vnutrennii rynok Rossii vo vtoroi polovine XVIII – pervoi polovine XIX v.* (Leningrad, 1981).

[50] Jacob Metzer, 'Railroad Development and Market Integration: The Case of Tsarist Russia', *Journal of Economic History*, 34 (1974), 529–50.

whether it is legitimate to consider the economy of the late Russian Empire as an integrated whole seems to be one of those that divides the specialists in the field most strongly,[51] but it is still possible to discern at least some advantage for the non-Russians in respect of improved access to markets, products, capital, and investment. It is true, of course, that Russia benefited from empire too, especially in respect of markets and raw materials. Drawing up a profit-and-loss account is therefore difficult; but it is doubtful, for example, whether an electric tram service would have opened in Tashkent in 1912 if General Cherniaev had not conquered the city in 1865.[52]

To the extent, therefore, that some non-metropolitan subjects of the tsar saw advantages in their incorporation into the empire, centripetalism in the later Russian Empire may have been popular. To the extent, furthermore, that the regime did not press its ambitions too hard, centripetalism may not have been blatantly obvious. Much of the time tsars and top imperial officials gave the appearance of not seeking the furtherance of ethnically Russian culture but of asking merely for loyalty to the dynasty. They seem to have been careful, moreover, not to give themselves too many problems of integration at the same time. One of the major features of the Russian Empire which differentiate it from the other two enormous empires of world history, the Mongol and the British, is that it was put together very slowly.[53] This may be an important part of the reason why it lasted.

It is not possible, however, fully to explain how the Russian Empire held together without acknowledging that, much of the time, its central authorities fostered centripetalism deliberately. The empire did not remain a single unit simply because all its inhabitants wanted it to or because tsars were careful, but also because the authorities were determined that it should do so. Although St Petersburg expressed its determination in different ways – de-centralising in the provincial reform of 1775, re-centralising in the establishment of central government ministries in 1802, attempting to improve the capacity of some of the new ministries to reach out to the countryside under Nicholas I,[54] de-centralising again in the introduction of provincial and district local government assemblies in 1864, re-centralising once more in the promulgation of the Law on Reinforced Safeguard of 1881 and the

[51] Precluding, for example, resolution of the longstanding debate about the condition of the peasantry after the abolition of serfdom: see especially James Y. Simms, 'More Grist for the Mill: A Further Look at the Crisis in Russian Agriculture at the End of the Nineteenth Century', *Slavic Review*, 50 [199l], 1004, n. 7.

[52] The opening is reported in RGIA, f. 23, op. 17, d. 539, l. 17.

[53] See the graph of comparative imperial growth in Rein Taagepera, 'An Overview of the Growth of the Russian Empire', in *Russian Colonial Expansion*, ed. Rywkin, 5.

[54] O.V. Moriakova, *Sistema mestnogo upravleniia Rossii pri Nikolae I* (Moscow, 1998).

introduction of Land Captains in 1889 – its object was nevertheless, at every turn, to increase the extent to which the edicts of the central government took effect on the ground. The ratio of government officials to the population as a whole went up seven-fold between 1796 and 1903.[55] Although frequent changes of tack on the part of the central authorities often succeeded only in making confusion worse confounded, although some of their innovations turned out to be positively counter-productive (notably the introduction of local assemblies in 1864, which provided outlets for local initiatives which conflicted with the policies coming down from on high), and although, however hard it tried, St Petersburg could never get right down to the local level, the authorities' aspiration to establish complete control over everything that happened in the empire is clear.

This aspiration, it seems to me, applied to the empire as a whole, not just to the ethnically Russian parts of it. We return here to the controversial question of the extent to which the imperial authorities engaged in the 'Russification' of their non-Russian possessions. Andreas Kappeler, the leading expert on inter-ethnic relations in the Russian Empire, plays Russification down.[56] Echoing him, Boris Mironov argues that the phenomenon is really discernible only in the later nineteenth century, when the authorities were trying to modernise the empire in order to put themselves in a better position to compete with their rivals and found that they had to standardise the way in which they ran it in order to achieve their objective.[57] Theodore Weeks, meanwhile, minimises Russification even in the last years of the empire's history. 'In general,' he says (in an essay on the years 1905–14), 'the Russian government did not pursue a consistently nationalistic or "Russifying" policy.'[58]

The views of these scholars go too far in the direction of exculpating the imperial government from the charge of attempting to steamroller the non-Russians. Mironov, whose concern is to establish that Russia was not an imperially minded power at all, suppresses evidence which does not fit his case. He overlooks, for example, a key part of the instructions Catherine the Great gave Prince A.A. Viazemskii on appointing him Procurator-General of the empire in 1764. The empress wrote:

[55] P.A. Zaionchkovskii, *Pravitel'stvennyi apparat samoderzhavnoi Rossii v XIXv.* (Moscow, 1978), 221.

[56] Kappeler, *Russland, passim*, but esp. 134–8, 203–4, and n. 1 on 359.

[57] Boris Mironov, *Sotsial'naia istoriia Rossii perioda imperii (XVIII – nachalo XX v.)* (2 vols., St Petersburg, 1999), I, 41.

[58] Theodore R. Weeks, 'Defending Our Own: Government and the Russian Minority in the Kingdom of Poland, 1905–1914', *Russian Review*, 54 (1995), 540.

> Little Russia [Ukraine to the east of the river Dnieper], Livland and Finland are provinces which are ruled on the basis of confirmed privileges. To destroy these by abolishing them all overnight would be very unseemly, but to call them [the provinces] foreign countries and deal with them on that basis is more than a mistake, one can justifiably call it foolish. It is necessary by the easiest means to bring these provinces (and Smolensk) to the point where they Russify and stop looking like wolves to the forest.[59]

The twenty-five years in which P.A. Rumiantsev ruled 'Little Russia' (1764–89) testify to the efficiency with which the Russian administration implemented the empress's policy in at least one of the provinces to which she referred.[60]

It is true that, in the first quarter of the nineteenth century, Alexander I took a different view of the way in which non-Russian lands ought to be administered and conferred constitutions on Finland, Bessarabia, and the former Grand Duchy of Warsaw (and even commissioned a draft federal constitution for the empire as a whole). Under Nicholas I, however, the regime reverted to the practice of Catherine. Having undermined the libertarian implications of 'nationality' (*narodnost'*) by yoking the concept to 'Orthodoxy' and 'Autocracy' in 1833, the tsar proceeded, in 1847, to attack its ethnic implications too. After the suppression of the Ukrainian 'Kirillo-Methodian Society' in that year, his Minister of Education, the same person who had promulgated the doctrine of 'Orthodoxy, Autocracy, Nationality' fourteen years earlier, announced the government's abandonment of the third of the platform's three elements. 'Russian Slavdom,' Uvarov wrote, 'must in its pure form express unconditional allegiance to orthodoxy and autocracy; everything which passes beyond these bounds [i.e. nationality] represents the admixture of alien concepts.'[61] Thus the imperial government re-established its antipathy to non-Russians as early as the second quarter of the nineteenth century. Despite the views of Kappeler, Mironov, and

[59] 'Sobstvennoruchnoe nastavlenie Ekateriny II kniaziu Viazemskomu pri vstuplenie im v dolzhnost' general-prokurora (1764 goda)', *Sbornik imperatorskogo russkogo istoricheskogo obshchestva* (148 vols., St Petersburg, 1867–1916), VII, 348.

[60] Kappeler (*Russland*, 97) downplays the significance of Catherine the Great's instructions of 1764, but fails to point out that, because Ukrainians were much the largest non-Russian group in the empire, the central government's treatment of them may have been a better indicator of what it really thought about the problem of ethnic diversity than its more emollient treatment of smaller non-Russian peoples.

[61] P. B[artenev], 'Ob Ukraino-slavianskom obshchestve (iz bumag D.P. Golokhvastova)', *Russkii arkhiv* 7 (1892), 348. The head of the empire's secret police wrote in the same vein at the same time: Dm. Bahalii, 'Novi dzherela pro Kyrylo-Metodiivs'ke bratstvo', *Nashe mynule*, 2 (1918), 178–9.

Weeks, Russification in the later nineteenth and early twentieth centuries was not new. Mironov's notion that late-imperial Russification was one of the prerequisites of modernisation may even put the cart before the horse, for it is just as easy to see modernisation as a prerequisite of more determined Russification – it gave the administration more efficient means of pursuing a policy it was pursuing already. As for Theodore Weeks's view that 'the Russian government did not pursue a consistently nationalistic or "Russifying" policy', it is necessary only to say that the regime did not often behave consistently in any area of policy. Governor Urusov of Bessarabia remarked to the King of Romania in 1903 that the Russian Empire had 'as many governments as there were ministries'.[62] Some ministries certainly did pursue Russification with a degree of resolution. My own specialist work has attempted to show the determination with which the Ministries of Education and Internal Affairs (through the medium of censorship) sought to prevent the emergence of a separate Ukrainian identity in the period 1847–1905.[63] The Ministry of Education's adoption of the Russian language as the more-or-less exclusive medium of instruction in primary schools in the law on the subject of July 1864 arose out of a conscious desire to prevent cultural diversification.[64] Even in some of the cases when late-imperial St Petersburg did not insist on the use of Russian in primary education, it could still be said to have been pursuing an integrationist or centripetalist policy. The point of the introduction of the 'Il'minskii system' in the Kazan' educational district was not to promote the languages of the Muslim minorities for their own sake, but to undermine the Tatar language of the largest local Muslim group.[65] David Rich, meanwhile, has emphasised the overwhelming importance which the War Ministry attached to keeping a firm grip on Poland in the later nineteenth century.[66] One of the goals of the 'Migration Department' of the Ministry of Internal Affairs in the later nineteenth and early twentieth centuries was certainly to Russify the peripheries of the empire.[67] When the

[62] Urussov, *Memoirs*, 137.

[63] David Saunders, 'Russia's Ukrainian Policy (1847–1905): A Demographic Approach', *European History Quarterly*, 25 (1995).

[64] V.Z. Smirnov, *Reforma nachal'noi i srednei shkoly v 60-kh godakh XIX v.* (Moscow, 1954), 141–2.

[65] Wayne Dowler, 'The Politics of Language in Non-Russian Elementary Schools in the Eastern Empire, 1865–1914', *Russian Review*, 54 (1995), 518 ('Linguistic diversity served as a bulwark against Tatar universalism').

[66] David Rich, 'Imperialism, Reform and Strategy: Russian Military Statistics, 1840–1880', *Slavonic and East European Review*, 74 (1996), 637.

[67] In September 1889, for example, the Minister of Internal Affairs pointed out to the head of the civil administration of the Caucasus that 'Russia possesses peripheries in

government dissolved the Second Duma and changed the basis on which its successor was to be elected on 3 June 1907, it declared 'the State Duma must be Russian ... in spirit', and that although 'Other nationalities ... must have representatives of their needs in the State Duma ... [they] must not and will not be represented in it in numbers which enable them to decide on purely Russian questions'.[68] This preference for Russians, it seems to me, was the culmination of a longstanding and rarely modified policy.

The numerical imbalance between Russians and non-Russians, the willingness on the part of some non-Russians to accept Russian rule, the economic benefits of inclusion in a large imperial unit, the enlargement of the imperial administration, and St Petersburg's attachment to the idea of extending the culture of the Russians succeeded, to a very large degree, in offsetting the centrifugal impulses to which I devoted the first part of this paper. The nineteenth-century Russian Empire saw nothing like the four 'risings of the borderlands' with which tsars had been confronted in the seventeenth and eighteenth centuries.[69] Very few subordinate inhabitants of the empire took up arms against the authorities between the last of those risings in the 1770s and 1914. At the beginning of the twentieth century the realisation of the subversive potential of ethnic centrifugalism was still a long way off in the Russian Empire. Centrifugalism was not yet a doctrine to which the majority of any of the empire's ethnic groups subscribed (with the possible exception of the Poles of the Congress Kingdom). In a recent survey of all the empire's national minorities in the last twenty years of its life Theodore Weeks points out: 'It should be remembered that with rare exceptions (the Polish Socialist Party being one), no significant movement among *any* of the Russian Empire's major ethnicities called for outright independence before the empire's collapse in 1917.'[70] Scholars seem to agree that, even after the empire had collapsed, non-Russians hesitated to insist on their separate identity or to declare their complete independence of Russia. If circumstances had been slightly different, they might have been satisfied by the Provisional Government's espousal of autonomy and democratisation.[71]

which the strengthening of the Russian population would not only meet the agricultural needs which have arisen but also constitutes a matter of state necessity': RGIA, f. 391, op. 1, d. 27, l. 27.

[68] PSZ, 3rd series (33 vols., St Petersburg, 1885–1916), XXVII, 320 (statute 29240).

[69] For the suggestion that the expression 'risings of the borderlands' best describes what Soviet scholars used to call 'peasant wars' see G.-G. Nol'te, 'Russkie "krest'ianskie voiny" kak vosstaniia okrain', *Voprosy istorii*, 11 (1994), 31–8.

[70] Theordore R. Weeks, 'National Minorities in the Russian Empire, 1897–1917', in *Russia under the Last Tsar: Opposition and Subversion 1894–1917*, ed. Anna Geifman (Oxford, 1999), 130 (italics in the original).

[71] See, for example, Mironov, *Sotsial'naia istoriia*, I, 64; Stephen Jones, 'The Non-Russian

III

Having placed the emphasis on centrifugalism in the first part of this paper, I now seem to be saying that centripetalism was in the ascendant. Did regional diversity play no part whatever, then, in the collapse of the Russian Empire in 1917? I would confine its part to the sort of diversity that turns on economic rather than ethnic relations. It is true that the First World War made some sorts of ethnic relations fraught in the Russian Empire. Hostility to the local Germans reared its head on the southern shore of the Baltic; in 1915 St Petersburg deported some 800,000 Jews and Germans from the western frontier and began to liquidate German landholdings there; the perennially troublesome Poles had to be promised post-war autonomy; a handful of Ukrainian activists appear to have done shady deals with Austrians and Germans; large numbers of Central Asians rebelled in 1916 when the state attempted to subject them to the draft.[72] It has been one of the theses of this paper, however, that these shifts in inter-ethnic relations were not enough significantly to weaken the regime. The authorities had always had a good sense of the piebald character of their country and could live with it. They seem not to have panicked in the ethnic sphere. They did not, for example, accompany their anti-Jewish and anti-German measures with 'similarly aggressive russification measures elsewhere in the Russian Empire'.[73] And in making the acquisition of Constantinople and the Straits one of their principal war aims they showed that they were perfectly willing to contemplate further additions to the diversity of their possessions.[74]

What they could not cope with, however, was the sort of regional diversity that turned on the economic relations of the various parts of the empire. Just after the outbreak of war, members of the Vladivostok

Nationalities', in *Society and Politics in the Russian Revolution*, ed. Robert Service (1992), 35–63; Ronald Grigor Suny, 'Nationalism and class in the Russian revolution: a comparative discussion', in *Revolution in Russia: Reassessments of 1917*, ed. Edith Rogovin Frankel, Jonathan Frankel, and Baruch Knei-Paz (Cambridge University Press, 1992), 219–46.

[72] N.S. Andreeva, 'Pribaltiiskie nemtsy i pervaia mirovaia voina', in *Problemy sotsial'no-ekonomicheskoi i politicheskoi istorii Rnssii XIX–XX vekov: Sbornik statei pamiati Valentina Semenovicha Diakina i Iuriia Borisovicha Solov'eva* (St Petersburg, 1999), 461–73; Terry Martin, 'The Origins of Soviet Ethnic Cleansing', *Journal of Modern History*, 70 (1998), 818–19 (deportations of Jews and Germans); Oleh Fedyshyn, 'The Germans and the Union for the Liberation of the Ukraine, 1914–1917' in *The Ukraine, 1917–1921: A Study in Revolution*, ed. Taras Hunczak (Cambridge, Mass., 1977), 305–22; Piotr S. Wandycz, *The Lands of Partitioned Poland, 1795–1918* (Seattle, 1974), 335; Kappeler, *Russland*, 286–7, 294 (Central Asian uprising).

[73] Martin, 'Origins', 825, n. 57. (It should be noted, however, that 'aggressive russification' did take place when the tsar's forces were in the Ukrainian part of Austrian Galicia in 1914–15.)

[74] On Russian enthusiasm in this regard see the autobiography of the empire's last significant foreign minister: S.D. Sazonov, *Vospominaniia* (Paris, 1927), esp. 299.

stock exchange pointed out that because goods took four or five months to reach them by sea and two or three by rail, local wholesalers risked either not being in a position to provide them when they were wanted or having to hold on to them when they were not wanted and consequently being unable to pay off the debts they had incurred in procuring them.[75] This difficulty was going to get worse in the situation in which the country now found itself. To judge by the anecdotal evidence of Vera Broido's recently published memoirs, the Siberian economy as a whole, if not that of the Far East, managed reasonably well during the First World War,[76] but in the European part of the empire new economic trends greatly exacerbated the regional differences that existed already. Cities grew at the expense of the countryside (and St Petersburg grew at the expense of all other cities). In February 1915 the Chairman of the Moscow Stock Exchange wrote to the Minister of Trade and Industry to complain about the 'ever increasing intervention of [provincial] Governors, the military authorities, and town councils in the business of the regulation of the conditions of production and trade, which is absolutely none of their business'. As a result, he felt, the empire was almost literally falling apart. Because provincial governors were taking decisions on economic matters on their own initiative, 'every province is turning into a sort of independent state'.[77] In May 1915 M.V. Chelnokov, Mayor of Moscow and head of the Union of Towns, wrote to the Ministry of Agriculture on behalf of the Moscow town council to call for the establishment of a 'Central Imperial Committee' to monitor supplies and distribution throughout the empire. If such a body were not established, he said, 'Complications may arise in the future which neither governmental agencies, nor the towns, nor the zemstva, acting in an uncoordinated manner, have the capacity to foresee or predict.'[78] In February 1916 the 'Council of Ministers on Providing Needy Parts of the Empire with Food and Fuel' (headed by the Minister of Trade and Industry) decided that it was 'necessary, for the duration of the war, wholly to prevent the further development of factory industry in Petrograd'.[79] This remarkable edict, whose provisions the government publicised in the press in April and extended, in May, to Novgorod, Pskov, Vitebsk, and the three Baltic provinces, arose out of the fact that, owing to pressure on the railway network, not enough fuel and raw material could be brought north to make possible the efficient execution of orders placed with the factories there. Thus the problem inherent in the longstanding division of the

[75] RGIA, f. 395, op. 2, d. 2959, ll. 84–7.
[76] Vera Broido, *Daughter of Revolution: A Russian girlhood remembered* (1998), 51–2, 65, 80.
[77] RGIA, f. 395, op. 2, d. 2961, ll. 31–6.
[78] Ibid., ll. 48–9.
[79] RGIA, f. 23, op. 17, d. 503, l. 4.

European part of the empire into northern and southern regions (industry in the north, raw materials and fuel in the south) began to look crucial. Official correspondence later in 1916 showed that the government was failing to make its edict stick.[80] Purchasers of factory-made goods (i.e. the military) had no choice but to place their orders where appropriate factories existed already or where the expertise was available to make possible the construction of new ones. An old fault-line was widening. Petrograd continued to grow. Shortage of supplies there was to be one of the major reasons for the eruption of February 1917.

Although, therefore, the ethnic variant of regional diversity was relatively unimportant in the downfall of the Russian Empire, the economic variant may be said to have played a significant part in it. It is important to note, however, that even the economic variant seems to have been too poorly developed to resist the Bolshevik version of centripetalism which took root after October 1917. By 1922, after all, most of the former empire was again in Russian hands. Despite what I have been saying about the First World War, therefore, my conclusion is that over the long term the relationships among the regions of the empire centred on the interplay between multiple centrifugal and centripetal impulses which were usually – collectively – of more or less equal weight. In this analysis, the collapse of 1917 looks like the product of what a historically inclined evolutionary biologist might be tempted to think of as a bout of 'punctuated equilibrium'.[81]

[80] Ibid., ll. 53–5.

[81] For reflections on this term by the palaeontologists who invented it in 1972 see Stephen Jay Gould and Niles Eldredge, 'Punctuated equilibrium comes of age', *Nature*, 366 (1993), 223–7.

THE BRITISH–IRISH UNION OF 1801

THE UNION IN A EUROPEAN CONTEXT

By William Doyle

AT THE PUBLIC RECORD OFFICE OF NORTHERN IRELAND, BELFAST

READ 10 SEPTEMBER 1999

FOR anyone so improbable as a historian of France to presume to address a conference about a landmark in British and Irish history requires some explanation. It lies in a bizarre twist of professional history which left me, for the best part of twenty years, teaching late eighteenth-century Ireland as a special subject. My research interest, however, has always lain in the *ancien régime* in France.

One of the most striking, fundamental, and – to my mind – exhilarating characteristics of that old order is its sheer institutional variety, that baffling chaos which later revolutionaries tried to replace with something simpler, more rational, and more uniform. My initial subject of research was the parlement of Bordeaux, one of those 'sovereign' courts of law which exercised final appellate jurisdiction over part of the king's realms, and enjoyed certain legislative powers there too, including the right to criticise proposed new laws. The jurisdictional area of this parlement was extensive: scarcely smaller, perhaps, than Ireland. But there were others as big, or bigger, and a number a good deal smaller too. Roughly, it corresponded to the old duchy of Aquitaine, that Plantagenet fief finally reconquered from English rule in the mid-fifteenth century. Those of other provincial parlements corresponded similarly to other formerly independent or semi-independent counties, duchies and even kingdoms (in the case of Navarre) accruing over the centuries to the king of France. And in a number of these there was a further complication not present at Bordeaux. Parlements like those of Languedoc, Brittany or Burgundy shared, or vied for, authority with estates. In these provinces there were representative bodies with powers to grant taxes and loans to the monarch, and to administer various public works.[1] Posterity conventionally thinks of pre-revolutionary France as an absolute monarchy, where rulers did not share their power. Kings habitually claimed as much, and those who later overthrew them found self-justification in

[1] The most convenient general survey of these complexities is M. Bordes, *L'Administration provinciale et municipale en France au xviii*[e] siècle (Paris, 1972).

accepting their claims, if only for the purpose of triumphant repudiation. But in practice, for both sides, this was more a matter of assertion than objective description. The reality of the *ancien régime* was intense confusion of powers and perpetual overlaps of unequal jurisdiction, in which the king, so far from imposing an unchallengeable authority, was constantly bargaining with his subjects at a number of different levels. And one way of bargaining with subjects, especially new ones, was to grant or confirm on an ad hoc basis the very powers which were later seen to impede royal authority. The parlements of most provinces, or their estates, owed their new or continued existence to 'capitulations' or confirmations at the moment when the king of France became their ruler. Nor were these concessions invariably shrouded in the mists of the middle ages. When Lorraine finally fell to Louis XV in 1766, a parlement was almost automatically established at Nancy. Later still, newly annexed Corsica was endowed with a sovereign court (1768) and with estates (1770).

The results were chaotic, inconsistent, and self-contradictory, but this was the institutional *ancien régime*; and for several centuries it worked. Nor (although the term *ancien régime* was invented by the French revolutionaries who destroyed it) was this pattern exclusively French. Early modern Europe was largely made up of what John Elliott has called composite monarchies, built up, and sometimes in turn split up, by a complex process of dynasticism or conquest.[2] When territories changed rulers, they seldom changed institutions. Only denial of a new ruler's legitimacy through physical resistance was likely to result on his part in denial of his new subjects' claims to distinctive treatment and particular privileges, as when Philip V of Spain cancelled the *fueros* of the crown of Aragon in 1707.[3] But this was rare. In a Europe where dynastic right was generally acknowledged to be the best entitlement to authority, few subjects felt justified in rejecting the ruler whom God had given them, however apparently random His methods. When they did so, as in the case of the Dutch rebels against Philip II, or indeed the inhabitants of these islands twice in the seventeenth century, it was because religious differences made it less than clear what God had actually intended. But that vast majority who never did contest a change of ruler usually found themselves rewarded by respect for their institutions, including representative ones. At the level of provinces, or sub-kingdoms in composite monarchies, representative bodies were more widespread than is often recognised among observers dazzled by the apparent progress of 'absolutism'. What they overlook is a complex and infinitely diverse set of public practices, a continent-wide

[2] J.H. Elliott, 'A Europe of Composite Monarchies' *Past and Present* , 137 (1992), 48–71.
[3] H. Kamen, *The War of Succession in Spain, 1700–17* (London, 1969), 299–307.

institutional *ancien régime*, or what a late seventeenth-century writer described as Europe's 'noble gothic constitution'.[4]

Two hundred years ago, a century after the writer's death, the phrase would have struck instant chords in Belfast. For he was of course William Molyneux, whose *Case of Ireland* of 1698 was one of the sacred texts of Irish legislative independence.[5] Every educated Irishman would have heard of an author invoked by Henry Grattan in his famous speech celebrating the achievement of legislative independence in 1782. Molyneux's argument (at this point in his text at least) was that Ireland's separate legislature, with its independent powers under the Crown, was an example of a 'universal' pattern in Europe of parliamentary government, a pattern which he though should be preserved *'Sacred and Inviolable'* wherever it was found. Ireland, then – although Molyneux could not have conceived of a term invented only 90 years after his death – was a typical enough specimen of a Europe-wide *ancien régime.*

Over the past fifteen years or so there has been extensive discussion of the idea launched by Jonathan Clark that there was an English *ancien régime* which came to an end between 1828 and 1832.[6] But it was largely about England alone that Clark advanced the idea, and the key to his conception of an *ancien régime* state was that it was 'confessional', the central characteristic being a politico-religious exclusivism. This was certainly typical enough of eighteenth-century European states; but it should be remembered that by then England was no longer a state in itself. It was part of a wider composite monarchy under the British crown; and this made it not less but even more typically an *ancien régime* entity. In statutory legal terms from 1707 England did not exist at all, although Englishmen, as they always have, tended to use the word to include everybody else on the island of Great Britain. Technically, after the Act of Union, the former England was merely South Britain.[7] And North Britain, if it gave up its separate parliament for a share of the representation at Westminster, retained its own legal system, a distinct religious establishment, and a whole host of other peculiar institutions which had remained unaltered, just as England's had, when dynastic fate brought the two crowns onto a single head in 1603. It is true that Scotland's distinct institutions survived as the result of a treaty between jurisdictionally equal partners, whereas under a continental monarch they would have figured as a confirmation of privileges. They remained

[4] J.G. Simms, *William Molyneux of Dublin, 1656–1698* (Dublin, 1982), 108.

[5] W. Molyneux, *The Case of Ireland's being bound by acts of parliament in England, stated* (Dublin, 1698).

[6] J.C.D. Clark, *English Society 1688–1832* (Cambridge, 1985).

[7] Although not enshrined in the Act of Union, the terms North and South Britain were regularly employed in eighteenth-century Acts of Parliament.

privileges all the same, in the sense of an entitlement to special, separate treatment that conferred advantages.

The material value of those advantages for Scotland become obvious soon enough, and it was foreseen from the start by Irish observers. Molyneux was dead by the time the crisis broke which precipitated the Act of Union of 1707; but in a passage dropped from the 1782 edition of the *Case of Ireland*, he spoke wistfully of a legislative union with England as the best of all solutions for Ireland, but one which was 'an happiness we can hardly hope for'.[8] As it became clear under Queen Anne that a union between England and Scotland was likely to happen, the Irish parliament itself began to petition for inclusion in it, and went on doing so for some time after the Scottish union became a reality.[9] But Scotland had blackmailed England in a way that Protestant Ireland as represented in the Dublin parliament never could, by threatening to restore the Stuarts. It was only when, almost a century later, an even more alarming threat of independence came from across the water that the rulers of Great Britain were prepared to contemplate a widening of the union to include Ireland.

And meanwhile the Irish parliament carried on, a legislative body representing a substantial part of the king's dominions, the separate realm of Ireland. Was it so different, in the British composite monarchy, from, say, the Hungarian Diet under the Habsburgs, or the parliament of Sicily under the Neapolitan Bourbons, or the estates of Cleves and Mark under the Hohenzollerns, or the estates of French *pays d'états* like Languedoc or Brittany? It was often enough compared, in the 1760s and 1770s, and many a time since by historians right down to Roy Foster, to the colonial legislatures of North America.[10] But unlike them it was practically coeval in age with the English parliament, and by Molyneux's day there was an extensive mythology, upon which he liberally drew, about its origins and early powers and development.[11] Similar cherished myths shrouded the origins of other European legislatures. In Poland and Hungary, they traced the freedom which they claimed to symbolise to conquerors, Sarmatians or Magyars, who by virtue of their conquests enjoyed a monopoly of representation and alone had the right to speak for all the inhabitants of their territories.[12] Molyneux explicitly invoked the Polish comparison, perhaps more appositely than he consciously intended, for throughout most of its

[8] Simms, *Molyneux*, 106.

[9] W.E.H. Lecky, *A History of Ireland in the Eighteenth Century*, 5 vols., London 1902) I, 443–4.

[10] R.E.F. Foster, *Modern Ireland 1600–1922* (London, 1988) ch. 8.

[11] Simms, *Molyneux*, 104–6.

[12] R. Butterwick, *Poland's Last King and English Culture* (Oxford, 1998), 26–7. H. Marczali, *Hungary in the Eighteenth Century* (Cambridge, 1910) 102–6.

history down to 1793 the Irish parliament, too, was happy to represent only a minority which owed its power to conquest, English-speaking exclusively from the start, and Protestant exclusively for all but the briefest periods throughout the seventeenth and eighteenth centuries. In real, though not strictly jurisdictional terms, the Polish comparison could be pushed even further, since for most of the eighteenth century the Polish–Lithuanian Commonwealth was in effect a Russian substate, and the real ruler not the elected monarch, but the Russian ambassador. In Polish historiography the period from 1773 to 1788 is known as the proconsulate – a term not far removed from viceroyalty[13]...

There are other contemporary parallels. It has often been pointed out, for example, that there was little that modern eyes would regard as representative in the way members of so-called representative bodies were chosen under the *ancien régime*.[14] Where elections took place, as in Poland or Sweden, they were seldom open contests, and were dominated by magnate influence. Would it be fair to say anything else of Ireland? Notoriously, no general election at all took place between 1727 and 1761. Many Irish seats were in effect the private property of noble patrons, and all members of the upper house sat, like many members of continental estates, by right of office. None of this was identical to any other legislature, even Westminster. If Dublin undeniably mirrored Westminster, the mirror was a distorting one. But the whole essence of the institutional *ancien régime* was that nothing *was* quite like anything else. Everything was, in a legal sense, particular and peculiar, and the Irish parliament did not differ more from, say, the estates of Brittany than they in turn differed from the assembly of communities of Provence. Some French provincial estates sat annually, others biennially just like the Irish parliament. They had intermediary commissions to see that their business got done when they were not sitting, which it is surely not altogether fanciful to compare to the Lords Justices who administered Ireland between parliaments before the viceroyalty of Townshend. In France, as in Ireland, the sitting of a provincial legislature required the presence of the king's representative, the governor, who would open the proceedings in the sovereign's name. One of his duties was to see that business was smoothly managed, and he needed reliable managers for that – what in Ireland were called undertakers. These systems seldom malfunctioned in France. And in Ireland, until Townshend's attack on the undertakers after 1768, there

[13] King Stanislas Poniatowski himself described Stackelberg, the Russian ambassador, as 'the proconsul': S. Goryainov *et al.* (eds.), *Mémoires du roi Stanislas – Auguste Poniatowski* (St Petersburg/Leningrad, 1914–1924), II, 298. I am grateful to Richard Butterwick for this reference.

[14] R.R. Palmer, *The Age of the Democratic Revolution 1769–1800* (2 vols., Princeton, 1959–64), I, chs. 2–4.

were only two serious parliamentary crises in the eighteenth century – Wood's Halfpence in the 1720s and the Money Bill furore in the 1750s. It was a record a good deal less turbulent than that of the estates of Brittany, for instance, or the Hungarian Diet.

In point of powers, continental parallels were even closer. The prime function of all those representative institutions was to authorise taxation by giving a semblance of consent from those who had to pay it. By the eighteenth century (appearances in the Money Bill crisis to the contrary) the days of refusing supply were long gone. The king's ministers decided what they needed, and secured it by a process of backroom bargaining with the local power-brokers before any formal proposal reached the floor. And who were those power-brokers? Office-holders and prelates, who were rewarded for their co-operation with patronage. These words, apart from the irresistible reference to the Money Bill, have been carefully chosen; they could apply equally well to the parliament of Ireland, or to the estates of Languedoc. Both raised their revenue from a specific pattern of fiscality, quite distinct from that falling on most of the king's other subjects: in Ireland there was no land tax; in Languedoc the *taille*, the basic direct tax, fell on land rather than on persons. Both legislatures made themselves responsible for an extensive range of public works, such as roads and canals. Both took a special interest in excluding religious dissidents from any power or influence within their jurisdiction, for, in both, religious civil war was something within living memory.[15] What neither did, and no comparable body elsewhere tried to do either, was to challenge the king's right to make general policy for all his dominions. In Ireland Poynings' Law made sure of that, reinforced from 1720 by the Sixth of George I – even if most of the English statutes applicable to Ireland between then and 1782 were quite uncontentious.[16] The occasion for that notorious Act had actually been jurisdictional rather than legislative, to establish the overriding appellate authority of the British House of Lords over all the king's dominions. The French comparison here is more aptly with the parlements, whose 'sovereign' authority was theoretically final in their areas but who found themselves struggling constantly against the 'evocation' of sensitive cases to the Privy Council.[17]

In yet another area of the Irish parliaments' competence, there is an obvious comparison with the estates of the Habsburg hereditary

[15] Languedoc was the centre of French Protestantism, and the *guerre des Camisards*, in which some of the Protestant rebels invoked William III as their potential saviour, lasted from 1702 to 1705. See E. Le Roy Ladurie, *Les Paysans de Languedoc* (2 vols., Paris, 1966), II, 619.

[16] G. O'Brien, *Anglo-Irish Politics in the Age of Grattan and Pitt* (Dublin, 1987), 31–2.

[17] See M. Antoine, *Le Conseil du Roi sous le règne de Louis XV* (Paris–Geneva, 1970), 292–6, 515–18.

dominions. This was in raising troops, and paying for their upkeep. The crisis of the European *ancien régime*, out of which the age of revolution was born, began when states of military ambition sought to expand their capacities and find new ways of paying for it. The first power to confront this problem was the House of Habsburg, which in the aftermath of the loss of Silesia in the Austrian Succession War sought to upgrade and expand its armed forces by removing their financing and recruitment from the control of the various provincial estates. It dressed this up as a boon to them, demanding in return a ten-year 'recess' in which the estates surrendered their freedom to grant taxes. Those contesting this dubious bargain had it forced upon them by an assumed 'royal right'.[18] The British state in its turn felt the need for enhanced military readiness, this time to defend its gains from the Seven Years War. This was the purpose of George Grenville's ill-fated Stamp Tax of 1763, which inaugurated the movement towards American independence. It was also the brief given to Townshend when he became Lord-Lieutenant of Ireland in 1767. He was instructed to carry an increase of troops on the Irish establishment from 12,000 to 15,000; and he forced it through, if not by some royal right, at least by a ruthless resumption of royal patronage that rewrote the ground rules of Irish parliamentary politics and paved the way for the struggles of 1778–82.[19]

With those struggles we enter the age of revolution proper, which culminated for Ireland in the loss of the representative institutions which so far this paper has been attempting to set in a structural context. What now about the developments which brought the Irish parliament to such a momentous end in 1800–1? Were they *sui generis*, or can they be seen as part of wider processes affecting *ancien régime* states in general? The most immediately striking aspect of the history of the Irish parliament between 1767 and 1801 is surely the way that its extinction followed a quarter of a century in which its power and independence had seemingly grown. There are certain parallels for this. Poland again offers one of the most obvious. In 1788, with the Russian power distracted by a Turkish war, the Polish legislature, the *seym*, began a four-year session in which Russian tutelage was thrown off, and a new constitution adopted on 3 May 1791 designed to secure Polish autonomy.[20] All this built on a generation of vigorous national consciousness-raising since the partition of 1772.[21] In Ireland the so-

[18] P.G.M. Dickson, *Finance and Government under Maria Theresia 1740–1780* (2 vols., Oxford, 1987), I, chs. 10–11; II, 1–35.

[19] T.W. Bartlett, 'The augmentation of the army in Ireland, 1767–1769', *English Historical Review*, xcvi (1981), 540–59.

[20] D. Stone, *Polish Politics and National Reform 1775–1788* (Boulder, Col., 1976).

[21] Butterwick, *Poland's Last King*, ch. 7.

called constitution of 6 April 1782 was equally the culmination of a generation of patriotic rhetoric at a time when the dominant power was weakened and distracted by foreign war.

What happened in Poland was all too dangerous in a Europe threatened by the French Revolution. Attempts to curb it by the surrounding powers, indeed, led to a national rebellion in 1794 which acknowledged the inspiration of the French Revolution, and vainly appealed to Paris for help.[22] It was put down, largely by the Russians, with appalling slaughter, and in the aftermath the *seym* was compelled to vote itself out of existence and Poland disappeared as a distinct entity from the map of Europe. The Commonwealth's separate existence, and its peculiar institutions, had simply become more trouble that they were worth. An independent Poland, controlled in fact from St. Petersburg but handling its own internal affairs through the representative institution of its social elite, had seemed since the days of Peter the Great the best way to ensure the stability of Eastern Europe. By the 1790s, however, it was repeatedly endangering that stability, and flirting too with a movement – the French Revolution – which challenged the legitimacy of all established authorities. A lot of this ought to sound familiar. As in the comparison made earlier with Languedoc, only a word or two needs to be changed to make this a description of what happened in Ireland. Authority devolved to a local aristocracy, and its representative assembly, eventually provoked more trouble that it had first been tolerated in order to dispel. In both cases the struggle against the French Revolution exacerbated matters. Eventually the threatened power only felt safe in absorbing these troubled dependencies into a system of more direct control.

In both cases, too, there was an outcry; because this absorption ran against what those who witnessed or experienced it had been educated to expect. The effect of the age of revolution, for all its rhetoric, was to destroy representative institutions wholesale, not consolidate them – but the expectations out of which it developed were quite the opposite. The roots of late-eighteenth-century revolutions can be found in mid-century 'patriotism' – the sentiment that a country was being ill-served by its existing, established, form of government (or at least those who were running it) and that the solution lay in making institutions more representative of those with the true interests of the country at heart. There was nothing unique about the Irish self-styled patriots who opposed undertaker or castle influence in parliament, demanded an Irish habeas corpus and Militia Bill, sought regular general elections, and denounced Poynings' Law or the Sixth of George I. When the Americans rebelled, Irish patriots saw instant parallels between colonists

[22] B. Lesnodorski, *Les Jacobins polonais* (Paris, 1965).

protesting at being taxed without representation under the British crown, and their own subordinate situation. But there were plenty of continental parallels, too. In addition to the Poles, there were Dutch patriots who denounced oligarchy and the ambitions of the Prince of Orange,[23] Belgian patriots who resisted the rationalising despotism of Joseph II,[24] Hungarian patriots outraged by the same monarch's refusal to acknowledge their peculiar institutions and privileges,[25] or French opponents of Louis XV's attempts to remodel and silence the parlements, who called themselves patriots eighteen years before the term became synonymous in France with revolutionary.[26] Nor were Irish patriots unique in their readiness to take up arms in furtherance of their convictions. The Volunteers had counterparts in the Dutch Free Corps, the Belgian *Pro Aris et Focis* militias (this motto was adopted by some Volunteer companies),[27] and most spectacularly in the French National Guard of 1789.

The Irish patriots believed, perhaps justifiably, that their activity, once they became an armed mass movement among Protestants, had brought about British agreement first to 'free trade', then to the repeal of Poynings' Law and the Sixth of George I, which made Ireland a notionally equal partner to Great Britain under the crown of George III. But was what made Pitt (whose ministry was almost co-terminous with Grattan's Parliament) prepared to tolerate Irish legislative independence perhaps a genuine receptivity to the potential of devolved representation?[28] If he was indeed open to such possibilities, he was certainly not alone in Europe. Necker, the ministerial miracle-worker who had paid for French involvement in the American War of Independence without new direct taxes, was a professed believer in the representation of taxpayers in the processes of government. In 1778 he had introduced two provincial assemblies in areas hitherto without estates and was projecting a third when he fell from power in 1781. He was proud of their achievements, and did not cease to trumpet them through his well-oiled publicity machine in subsequent years.[29] In 1787 Calonne, whose reform plan precipitated the pre-revolutionary crisis,

[23] The classic survey is in chs. 3 and 4 of S. Schama, *Patriots and Liberators. Revolution in the Netherlands, 1780–1813* (London, 1977).

[24] J. Polasky, *Revolution in Brussels 1787–1793* (Brussels, 1986).

[25] B.K. Kiraly, *Hungary in the Later Eighteenth Century* (New York, 1969).

[26] D. Echeverria, *The Maupeou Revolution. A Study in the History of Libertarianism. France, 1770–1774* (Baton Rouge, La., 1985), 37–122.

[27] In the Ulster Museum there are buttons from Volunteer tunics with these words inscribed.

[28] O'Brien, *Anglo-Irish Politics*, 166.

[29] R.D. Harris, *Necker, Reform Statesman of the Ancien Regime* (Berkeley, Los Angeles, London, 1979) 176–91. See also M. Léonce de Lavergne, *Les Assemblées provinciales sous Louis XVI* (Paris, 1879), *passim*.

proposed the generalisation of such provincial assemblies. Several of them actually sat and began work under his successor Brienne.[30] But from the start it was feared that such assemblies, which, despite their names, did not sit in historic provinces but in generalities (the administrative districts of the agents of absolute monarchy, the intendants) would be bodies of stooges, with neither the power nor the courage to resist the demands of authority. Since mid-century, in fact, there had been growing support for an alternative representative model – the generalisation of provincial estates. Some parlements in provinces which had lost them had begun to call for their restoration from the 1750s onwards, and others joined them once Louis XVI was on the throne.[31] These demands were reinforced when Corsica was given new estates, and existing ones such as those of Languedoc or Brittany managed to increase their powers in various ways over the same years.[32] The pre-revolutionary crisis brought the movement to a head when Brienne capitulated to the demands of two provinces to be represented by estates rather than by his projected assemblies. Provence was allowed the full form of its old estates, last assembled in 1639. Dauphiné was granted the first assembly of any kind since 1628. And once these concessions were made, the movement snowballed, and every province was soon clamouring for its own estates, whether or not it had enjoyed them historically. Not only that. Many of them based their claims in the rhetoric of distinct national identity. The Dauphinois, whose example did most to inspire this movement, started calling themselves the Dauphinois 'nation', it came as no problem to the Bretons to call themselves a nation, and soon less probable areas were claiming nationhood. The first important thing ever written by Robespierre, which doubtless he was happy enough soon to forget, was a pamphlet addressed *A la Nation artésienne*, about the form to be taken by restored estates in Artois.[33]

In the event, all this came to nothing. Once Louis XVI conceded that the Estates-General, themselves defunct since 1614, would meet in 1789, attention throughout his realms became concentrated on them, and the form they should take. Although there was a widespread conviction, especially among the nobility, that the deputies to the Estates-General should be chosen by provincial estates, that was only allowed to happen in the case of Dauphiné, Béarn and Navarre. The

[30] P.M. Jones, *Reform and Revolution in France. The Politics of Transition, 1774–1791* (Cambridge, 1995), 139–56.

[31] W. Doyle, *The Parlement of Bordeaux and the end of the Old Regime 1771–1790* (London 1974), 227.

[32] Jones, *Reform and Revolution*, 37–8.

[33] J.P. Jessenne, G. Derégnaucourt, J.P. Hirsch, H. Leuwers (eds.), *Robespierre: de la Nation artésienne à la République at aux Nations* (Lille, 1994), 73–104.

decision of December 1788 to opt for other methods stopped the movement for revived provincial estates dead in its tracks; and despite considerable continued support for them in the *cahiers* of the following spring, it was an idea that the National Assembly showed no interest in when it embarked later in 1789 on its reform of French administration. It is true that the constitution of 1791 enshrined a considerable measure of devolution, but it was of a standard, uniform sort which took no account of historic provinces and their privileges. In any case, it did not last. The 'Jacobin' pattern of representation bequeathed to France by the Revolution was to be posited on a nation 'one and indivisible', whose only legitimate representatives sat in a single national legislature, directly elected. It is a pattern that has only begun to be diluted under the regional devolution set in train since the 1960s by the Fifth Republic.

It was to such a Jacobin regime that the desperate Polish patriots appealed for help in 1794, seeing in its aspirations a parallel to their own doomed constitution of 3 May 1791. The heirs to the Dutch patriots, whose hopes had been snuffed out by Prussian invasion in 1787, also worked after their emancipation by the French in 1795 to give the new Batavian Republic a French style unitary representative constitution quite distinct from that of the old loosely federal United Provinces. And that was certainly the aspiration of the United Irishmen after 1795 – help from the French to establish in Ireland an independent legislature for a republic one and certainly indivisible. What they most emphatically did not want, having begun themselves in 1791 as a movement for parliamentary reform, was the Irish parliament – as constituted at any time in its history, remote or recent. However much they failed to achieve, they were certainly instrumental in securing this end, at least.

Other papers at this conference have explored the precise way in which the Irish parliament met its end, and the local implications for the conduct of British and Irish public life. The purpose of this paper is to try to see the Union from a much greater distance, and in a much wider setting. The key must lie in the French Revolution. Part of its origin lay in a desire for greater representation in government through devolution, that same desire which fuelled Irish demands for greater autonomy under the British crown. And if this aspect of the Revolution's origins is now largely forgotten, it is because for a complex set of reasons the settlement which emerged was committed to a single, centralised form of representation. That commitment entailed the abandonment of the rich and varied luxuriance of *ancien régime* institutions, including parlements and provincial estates. They were now seen as more likely to impede than to promote the legitimate activity of government. The behaviour of the Irish parliament, both before and after 1782, confronted George III's ministers with the same conundrum.

Even as they made concession to patriot demands on free trade or legislative independence, both Lord North and Shelburne's Whigs pondered whether Ireland might not be more easily governable under 'an union'.[34] Pitt was more agnostic. He thought legislative independence could be made to work, given the right reforms;[35] but what finally made such reforms impossible, again, was the revolution in France, in the manifold ways in which it impacted upon the Irish body politic.

Above all, the revolution helped to revive the Catholic question. The one area for comparison with the continent scarcely touched upon so far is the religious one, and this is because there was no true continental parallel to a legislative assembly which only represented a religious minority. Even in Languedoc, where sectarian antagonism was as strong as in Ireland, the oppressed Protestants were only in a majority in a few districts. Even so, what the French revolutionaries did to give Protestants civil and political equality[36] was instrumental in reviving the question of Catholic equality in Ireland; both by highlighting the intrinsic injustice of anything else, and by showing that Catholics in power were not natural oppressors.[37] And then, when the new regime in France began to quarrel with the Catholic Church, the prospect opened up in the British body politic, for the first time since the Reformation,[38] that Catholicism under the British Crown might be turned into a fund of loyalty rather than potential treason. Accordingly, the years between 1791 and 1793 became, as it were, a race between the United Irishmen and the British government to capture the support of the Catholics of Ireland. The Dublin parliament found itself sidelined, even though it would have to bear any immediate consequences. It was now that the term *Ascendancy* was first coined – rather like the term *ancien régime* in France – to describe an order assumed to be on the verge of extinction.[39]

Yet the encounter with the French Revolution was to produce a further twist. When the French invasion of the Austrian Netherlands pitched Great Britain into war, reform of any sort was put on hold.

[34] G.C. Bolton, *The Passing of the Irish Act of Union. A Study in Parliamentary Politics* (Oxford, 1966), 6–7; O'Brien, *Anglo-Irish Politics*, 50.

[35] O'Brien, *Anglo-Irish Politics*, ch. 6.

[36] See B.C. Poland, *French Protestantism and the French Revolution. A Study in Church and State, Thought and Religion, 1685–1815* (Princeton, 1957), *passim*.

[37] T.W. Bartlett, *The Fall and Rise of the Irish Nation. The Catholic Question 1690–1830* (Dublin, 1992), chs. 8 and 9; D. Keogh, *'The French Disease', the Catholic Church and Irish Radicalism 1790–1800* (Dublin, 1997).

[38] In Europe at least; the same strategy had of course underlain the Quebec Act of 1774, itself passed to reinforce the loyalty of Catholic French Canadians at a time when Protestant subjects of the king were on the verge of rebellion in the thirteen colonies.

[39] Bartlett, *Fall and Rise*, 151.

This gave the Irish parliament a last chance to prove its value in what had always been its primary function from the perspective of London, which was to keep Ireland under control in the British interest. It failed. Within five years its ineffectual intransigence had helped to provoke a rebellion, largely among the very Catholics whom Pitt had hoped to turn into a bulwark of resistance to the menace from France. Instead, driven to desperation by the savage though supposedly pre-emptive tactics of the Ascendancy's executive, Catholics positively begged the French to intervene as their ancestors had a century earlier. And, even though the French response was poor compared with that sent by Louis XIV to support James II, the Ascendancy could not cope with it. It had to be rescued from General Humbert and his peasant auxiliaries by money and troops from across the water. Parliament, meanwhile, now boycotted even by the very Whigs and patriots who had previously trumpeted its independent pretensions, had lost all relevance to what was happening in Ireland.

And so the French revolutionaries, who destroyed the institutional *ancien régime* first in their own country, and then wherever else they went, were also instrumental in destroying it even where they did *not* go – or at least not in significant numbers. In his classic analysis of *The Ancien Régime and the Revolution*, Tocqueville argued that the historic mission of the French Revolution was to destroy the remaining obstacles to the power of the centralised state. More recently this perception has been reformulated by Tim Blanning into the proposition that the Revolution liberated not so much the people as the state.[40] But once that had been done in France, and the energies thus released channelled into war against all major powers of Europe, sooner or later those powers, if they were to survive, had to liberate themselves in the same way from the shackles of their own *ancien régime* structures. Napoleon, the Revolution's heir, was defeated in the end not by the *ancien régime* – which he completed the Revolution's work by destroying outside France as well as within – but by states reformed and remodelled along parallel lines. The great exception to this generalisation is supposed to have been Great Britain, secure and untouched beyond its natural moat. From an anglocentric perspective I suppose that it is just about sustainable – although even here the extent of administrative reform during those supposedly frozen years has often been underestimated.[41] And this is to overlook the elimination of the most glaring of *ancien régime* aspects of the British state, the separate sub-kingdom of Ireland

[40] T.C.W. Blanning, *The Origins of the French Revolutionary Wars* (London, 1986), 211.

[41] See P. Harling, *The Waning of 'Old Corruption'. The Politics of Economical Reform in Britain, 1779–1846* (Oxford, 1996), 104–6, 261–2.

and its distinct legislature, Britain's Achilles heel in its life-or-death struggle with the sworn enemy of all *ancien régime* institutions. Whether that elimination strengthened the British body politic for any other purpose that the defeat of France is, of course, a very different question.

THE UNION IN BRITISH HISTORY[1]

By J.G.A. Pocock

READ 9 SEPTEMBER AT THE QUEEN'S UNIVERSITY OF BELFAST

'BRITISH history', or 'the new British history' – a field which the present writer is over-generously credited with inventing some twenty-five years ago – seems to have reached a point of takeoff. At least two symposia have appeared in which the method and practice of this approach are intensively considered, and there are monographs as well as multi-author volumes – though the latter still preponderate – in which it is developed and applied to a variety of questions and periods.[2] Its methodology remains controversial, and it may be in its nature that this should continue to be the case; for, in positing that 'the British isles' or 'the Atlantic archipelago' are and have been inhabited by several peoples with several histories, it proposes to study these histories both as they have been shaped by interacting with one another, and as they appear when contextualised by one another. There must be tensions between such a history of interaction and the several 'national' histories that have come to claim autonomy, and it is probable that these tensions must be re-stated each time a 'British history' is to be presented – as is the case in the present paper.

For a variety of reasons, the emphasis of 'new British history' has so far fallen on the early modern period preceding the formation of a unitary state and its disruption in the twentieth century. The Union of 1800–1 is of course cardinal to the latter process, and may be placed on the hinge or *Sattelzeit* marking the transition from early modern to

[1] An earlier version of this essay was delivered as a paper to the conference in Belfast. It has been revised in the light of that conference, but contains little that was not heard there.

[2] To the bibliography attempted on p. 491, n. 2, of David Armitage, Jane Ohlmeyer, Ned C. Landsman and Eliga H. Gould, '*AHA* Forum: the New British History in Atlantic Perspective', *American Historical Review* (IV, 2, April 1999) there should now be added that symposium itself; Tony Claydon and Ian McBride (eds.), *Protestantism and National Identity: Britain and Ireland, c. 1650–c.1850* (Cambridge University Press, 1998); Glenn Burgess (ed.), *The New British History: Founding a Modern State, 1603–1715* (London: I.B. Tauris, 1999); S.J. Connolly (ed.) *Kingdoms United: Great Britain and Ireland since 1500* (Dublin: the Four Courts Press, 1999); Laurence Brockliss and David Eastwood (eds.), *A Union of Multiple Identities: the British Isles, c. 1750–c.1850* (Manchester University Press, 1997); Alexander Murdoch, *British History, 1660–1832: National Identity and Local Culture* (London: Macmillan, 1998); Keith Robbins, *Great Britain: Identities, Institutions and the Idea of Britishness* (London: Longman, 1998).

modern 'British history'. In this paper I attempt to review and re-periodise the earlier period as leading to the formation of the Union, so as to suggest some ways in which the modern phase of this history may be pursued. The bibliography reveals that the 'new history' has advanced beyond the seventeenth into the eighteenth century, and is venturing into the nineteenth; the history of the twentieth century awaits perspective. In this sequence the Union must appear a pivotal event, though its claim to that role cannot be exclusive of others.

The 'Age', 'War' or 'Wars' of the 'Three Kingdoms' are concepts that dominate our understanding of the early modern period, in which dynastic and parliamentary unions precede the formation of a comprehensive state. There has however begun to appear a new multi-volume 'history of the British Isles', which valuably proposes subdividing the early modern period under the headings of 'the two kingdoms' and 'the double crown' – the transformation of the one into the other falling at 1603.[3] Useful as this suggested re-periodisation is, the series displays the guiding hand of the late Geoffrey Elton, for whom (it sometimes seemed) only the sovereign state was real and had a history. Scotland and England were sovereign kingdoms; Ireland was not, and seems likely to appear in the new series only as part of the 'empire' which the English and their British state exerted over realms not included in its structure.[4] In this essay an attempt will be made to recognise a greater autonomy of 'Irish history' within the 'British' pattern and contributing to its shaping; and partly to that end, but also for larger reasons, there is proposed a somewhat different conceptualisation of the relations between 'state' and 'empire'.

The 'two kingdoms' may be seen entering on an 'early modern' history if we focus for the moment on the English kingdom and its marcher lordships. There are three crucial statutes enacted at Westminster and Dublin during the fourth decade of the sixteenth century. First must stand the Act in Restraint of Appeals (1533), which defines England as an 'empire', less in the sense that it exercises dominion over others – as of course it does – than in the sense that it exercises sovereignty over itself: that unshared sovereignty both ecclesiastical and civil, which the crown exercises both in parliament and out of it, and

[3] *A History of the Modern British Isles* (founding editor: Sir Geoffrey Elton; general editor: John Stevenson). Mark Nicholls: *1529–1603; The Two Kingdoms*; David L. Smith: *1603–1707; The Double Crown* (Oxford: Blackwell, 1999). Other volumes are to follow.

[4] The volumes in preparation for the Blackwell series are listed as three further volumes on 'the History of the British Isles' to the present, a further volume on '*The British Empire, 1500–1997*' and 'in association with the series: *A History of Ireland, 1798–1998*.' Keith Robbins (above) also, though for other reasons, relegates Ireland to separate treatment. It should perhaps be emphasised here that 'national' histories can, should and will be written alongside cross-national histories and co-exist with them.

which must from now on be agreed upon and exercised if England is to be a sovereign kingdom and define itself as a Christian community. 'Empire' is henceforth a precarious and deeply contested term, to be exercised in dynasty, parliament and church all together if 'England' is to be governed and have meaning. It is exercised by England over England, as well as by England over subordinate realms; but failures of 'empire' in the latter sense may entail failures of 'empire' in the former, and for this reason no separation between internal 'state' and external 'empire' is satisfactory.

The subordinate realms must now be brought into the picture, and allowed historic autonomy, if 'British' history is not to be collapsed into 'English'. The Statute of Wales in 1536 liquidates the marcher lordships and completes the incorporation of 'Wales' into 'England' – an assimilation of a society still Celtic to an Anglo-Norman model so uniquely successful that Welsh nationalist historiography consists largely in examining the costs of its success. Since there had at no time been a functioning kingdom of Wales, this union does not figure in the sequence of Unions punctuating the history of the 'Three Kingdoms,' and the statute of 1536 is therefore antithetical with that enacted at Dublin in 1541, which erected the English king's 'lordship of Ireland' into a 'kingdom'. This inaugurates a history of the Three Kingdoms, and at the same time renders it problematic, for the reason that 'Ireland' is at best a subordinate kingdom and may not be one at all. The English monarch is king in Ireland, but this does not necessarily mean that he has there a kingdom in the sense of a body politic of which he is the head. There are, however, from an early date elite groups in Ireland who desire that status for themselves – these are as likely to be settler as indigenous, loyalist as rebellious – and there is a history, and a historiography, turning on the question whether Ireland is a colony undergoing conquest or a body politic shaping itself within a multiple monarchy.[5]

It is crucial that, whereas the elites within Wales by and large accepted the Anglican church-state brought into being by the Act in Restraint of Appeals – and were in the next century divided by it along lines not unlike those dividing the English – the elites and the governed classes of Ireland did not. There exists a literature which enquires, with respect to both the Gaelic Irish and the Old English, why it was that they remained Catholic and what kinds of Catholic they remained.[6]

[5] See, classically, Brendan Bradshaw, *The Irish Constitutional Revolution of the Sixteenth Century* (Cambridge University Press, 1979), and the ensuing debate among Irish historians.

[6] The Welsh and Irish cases are compared by Bradshaw, 'The English Reformation and identity formation in Ireland and Wales', in Brendan Bradshaw and Peter Roberts (eds.), *British Consciousness and Identity: the making of Britain, 1533–1707* (Cambridge University Press, 1998).

The persistence of a Catholic majority deeply separates the history of the Irish from that of the two other Kingdoms, and is of course inseparable from the continued status of Ireland as a kingdom imperfectly conquered and still undergoing conquest. A crucial process in the history of the 'Two Kingdoms' of the island properly termed 'Britain' is the occurrence in Scotland of a Protestant Reformation more sharply Calvinist and presbyterian than was the Anglican. This gives the relations of church and monarchy, and therefore the structure of the Scottish kingdom, a distinct and ultimately unassimilable character; but for a hundred years it was not unreasonable to imagine a convergence of the two monarchies along episcopalian–presbyterian lines. This was imaginable to the Protestant churches in Ireland, but not to the Catholic majority. The Old English who so resolutely proclaimed their loyalty to James VI and I at the conclusion of the Nine Years War must either imagine him as their secular protector, or imagine that the Catholic aspects of his Anglican kingship might be extended to a point where they came close to the Gallican formula of empire over the church coupled to communion with Rome. James's ecumenical interests held out hopes which were to prove delusive.[7]

In 1603 a dynastic union replaces the 'Two Kingdoms' with the 'Double Crown', leaving the status of the Third Kingdom more ambiguous than before – but not (it is important to stress) to be excluded on those grounds from 'British history'. The fall of the Gaelic-Tudor earldoms leaves the Old English exposed to competitors from the Protestant New English influx, while promoting that momentous innovation, the colonisation of Ulster by Scottish and English Protestants. This is an event in the history of all three kingdoms, and could not have come about but for King James's interest in consolidating his properly British realms. The history of early modern Scotland is imported into that of Ireland, but is so by the authority of the Crown of Westminster rather than that of Scone. Taken in conjunction with events in Argyll and the Hebrides, it may properly appear that the colonisation of Ulster was part of an attempted Protestantisation of the northwestern Gaeltacht which had always bridged the North Channel; but it occurred in the further context of a kingdom of Ireland which was a realm of the English crown, and the Scottish colony in Ulster was not a colony of the Scottish kingdom. Simultaneously, the colonies of settlement which were extending the empire of the Crown to the

[7] W.B. Patterson, *King James VI and I and the Unity of Christendom;* (Cambridge University Press, 1997). The nature of Irish Catholic royalism has been explored in a number of studies. The proposition of Brendan Fitzpatrick (*Seventeenth-Century Ireland: the Wars of Religion*, Dublin, Gill and Macmillan, 1988) that Old English Catholicism was para-Gallican, Gaelic Catholicism Franciscan and ultramontane is suggestive, though his understanding of both Anglicanism and Calvinism is deeply flawed.

North American seaboard and the West Indian islands were deemed to be English and the Scots had none of their own; it might have been otherwise.

We now enter upon the problems of church and state – of empire as defined by the Act in Restraint of Appeals – in the multiple monarchy of a single dynasty, and may look forward, at the usual risks of foreshortening and telocentricity, to the Fall of the British Monarchies and the Wars of the Three Kingdoms. The coupling of these terms is the most trenchant move which has yet been made towards a 'British history' of the English themselves, since it entails the assertion that their internal dissensions would never have led them to civil war, and that this was a consequence of a breakdown of government and a failure to control the sword first in Scotland and then in Ireland – in each case produced by attempts to impose English modes of 'empire' in church and civil government.[8] While it is intensely salutary that we have ceased using 'the English Civil War' as a term comprising the wars in all three kingdoms, it should not be forgotten that there was such a war, discussed in great intellectual depth precisely because it had been undesired and unexpected and was desperately hard to understand;[9] or that the memory of this conflict, and the operation of institutions designed to prevent its recurrence, governed English history to the end of the eighteenth century. This is a fact of 'British' as well as 'English' history; we have arrived at a point where 'empire' in the sense of governance of realms beyond England is capable of devastating 'empire' in the sense of England's civil sovereignty over itself. The Cromwellian union of 1651–60 was imposed on Scotland and Ireland largely to ensure that these realms should have no power over the settlement of a dispute the English were having with themselves.

No revolutionary settlement being available, the year 1660 sees a partial return to empire in the government of all three kingdoms. In Ireland the defeat of the Confederation underlines the hopeless position of the kind of Catholicism represented by the Old English; to that extent, Protestant rule is on the way. In Scotland, the willingness of the aristocracy to consider episcopacy as a means of controlling the clergy opens a road to Erastianism and Enlightenment. In England, a separate

[8] The bibliography may be summarised by mentioning Conrad Russell, *The Fall of the British Monarchies, 1637–1642* (Oxford: the Clarendon Press, 1991); John Morrill, *The Nature of the English Revolution* (London: Longman, 1993); and Martyn Bennett, *The Civil Wars in Britain and Ireland* (Oxford: Blackwell, 1997).

[9] J.G.A. Pocock, 'The Atlantic Archipelago and the War of the Three Kingdoms,' in Brendan Bradshaw and John Morrill (eds.), *The British Problem, c. 1534–1707* (London: Macmillan, 1996), pp. 172–91; 'Thomas May and the Narrative of Civil War', in Derek Hirst and Richard Strier (eds.), *Writing and Political Engagement in Seventeenth-Century England* (Cambridge University Press, 1999, pp. 112–44).

periodisation is necessary; we embark on 'the long eighteenth century', lasting till 1832 and marked by parliamentary determination to maintain an established church.[10] This is the form in which Tudor 'empire' was maintained through the Hanoverian era; but it took time and a revolution to bring the Stuart monarchy back to support of the church of which it was the head. In 1688–9 a 'glorious revolution' which was also a 'second Restoration'[11] achieved this end at the high cost of expelling James VII and II from all three of his kingdoms. The war cycle that moved from Torbay through Killiecrankie to Limerick was not a Second War of the Three Kingdoms of the same order as the First, since it was not a breakdown or dissolution of government in all three realms as much as a re-ordering of government in the face of a European power struggle threatening to engulf the multiple monarchy. King William landed at Torbay and crossed the Boyne in order to enlist the island kingdoms in his war against Louis XIV in Flanders, and the War of the English Succession was the archipelagic face of the War of the League of Augsburg or Nine Years War. On the other hand, the enlistment of the Three Kingdoms transformed European power politics by consolidating that parliamentary and military fiscal state, the Kingdom of Great Britain, capable of exercising empire in the archipelago, intervening at times decisively in the power politics of the peninsula, and pursuing empire in the modern sense on the oceans and in America and India.[12] This was the true revolution achieved in the quarter-century following the Dutch intervention of November 1688.

With the Kingdom of Great Britain we may begin to write 'British history' in more than a conceptual sense, but there remains the difficulty that the state of which it is the history is preponderantly English and activated by English politics in a sense nearly exclusive of all others. The kingdom was formed by the parliamentary Union of 1707, largely the result of a Scottish decision that their kingdom could no longer maintain a separate political economy and that a merger with the English parliamentary fiscal structure was the only recourse. On the English side, however, there were reasons, some of them religious in character, why the maintenance of empire in the Tudor sense required

[10] J.C.D. Clark, *English Society, 1688–1832* (Cambridge University Press, 1986; revised edition, 2000).

[11] For 1688 as 'second Restoration', see Jonathan Scott, 'Radicalism and Restoration: the shape of the Stuart experience', *Historical Journal*, XXI, 2 (1988), and *Algernon Sidney and the Restoration Crisis, 1677–1683* (Cambridge University Press, 1991).

[12] Jonathan I. Israel (ed.), *The Anglo-Dutch Moment: Essays on the Glorious Revolution and its World Impact* (Cambridge University Press, 1991), Dale Hoak and Mordechai Feingold, *The World of William and Mary: Anglo-Dutch Perspectives on the Revolution of 1688* (Stanford: Stanford University Press, 1996); John Brewer, *The Sinews of Power: War, Money and the English State, 1688–1783* (New York: Knopf, 1989).

a union of king and parliament so close that there could be no thought of a federal relationship in which the king would be responsible to more parliaments than one. For the same reasons, however, what had to be an incorporating union of parliaments had to be a federative union of church-states. The year 1689 had seen a presbyterian revolution in Scotland, where the extrusion of the Episcopal Church kept the kingdom in a state of latent civil war till 1746; and the Kingdom of Great Britain, in which theoretically the Kingdoms of England and Scotland ceased to exist, remained one in which the sovereign was head of the church in England and something other than that in Scotland. Theoretically again, this entailed a drastic separation of civil and ecclesiastical sovereignty; practically, it entailed no such thing, since the maintenance of established religion continued to be vital in both kingdoms.[13]

The ecclesiastical dimension can never be omitted from the study of early modern history; nor can 'Enlightenment' – defined as the subordination of religion to civil society – be omitted from that section of it denoted by the term 'ancien regime'.[14] In English history, 'the long eighteenth century' is the period during which an established church, with an apparent monopoly of civil office, must be maintained by king-in-parliament, but the purpose of doing so is to ensure that neither orthodoxy nor dissent can disturb the civil order. This is the late form taken by Tudor 'empire', the national sovereignty in church and state, and its purpose within England is to prevent any recurrence of the disorders of the seventeenth century. In the larger fields of British, archipelagic and as we shall see Atlantic history, this objective merges with that of maintaining empire in the sense of sovereignty over the larger system (this is the commonest meaning of 'empire' in eighteenth-century anglophone discourse). It is with 'empire' in all these senses, including the ecclesiastical and Enlightened, that the Scottish kingdom is merged by the Union of 1707, and this is the point at which to introduce a periodisation of British history moving from an Age of the Three Kingdoms to a First Age of Union, lasting from 1707 to 1801. The Anglo-Irish Union can be considered in the setting this provides, as inaugurating a Second Age of Union from 1801 to 1921; this will be succeeded by an age or ages to which it would be premature to give a name, since the end is not yet and it is not our business to foresee it.

All such periodisations are verbal devices intended to focus our attention in selected ways, and it is not inappropriate to employ a

[13] John Robertson (ed.), *A Union for Empire: political thought and the Union of 1707* (Cambridge University Press, 1995).

[14] J.G.A. Pocock, *Barbarism and Religion, volume I: The Enlightenments of Edward Gibbon* (Cambridge University Press, 1999).

diversity of them in conjunction. In English history, 'the long eighteenth century' overlaps 'the First Age of Union'; in Irish history, an age of 'Protestant ascendancy' has a beginning and end of its own. There is also imperial history, in which it has been customary to distinguish between a 'First British Empire' and a 'Second', the moment of transition occurring about 1783, when the recognition of American independence coincides with the acquisition of massive state power in India. The various meanings assigned to the term 'empire' in this essay may suggest some modifications in the last of these, but several periodisations may be employed in interpreting the Union of 1800–1.

The ecclesiastical-Enlightened dimension sketched above is far from explaining everything that happened, but provides a useful key that may be employed in setting the events in order. In the English kingdom it accounts for significant tensions within the Church of England; in so far as the regime needed to rest upon a church universal, that church must be apostolic and maintain the fulness of catholic tradition, but in so far as it was a pillar of civil society it upheld rational and sociable concepts of the Christian life which might move in directions Arian, Socinian or crypto-deist.[15] A current of non-trinitarian thinking persisted within the Church of England, and about 1772 emerged in alliance with a more radical unitarianism of nonconformist origin, to form the peaceable yet subversive movement which we know as Rational Dissent.[16] In its extreme development, conspicuous if not representative, this reduced all worship to freedom of opinion; it called for an actual separation of church and state, a goal attainable only under revolutionary and millennial conditions; and in denying any ecclesiastical character to political authority, it encouraged radically and even democratically Lockean views of the latter. Though it had little revolutionary potential within the kingdom of Great Britain, Rational Dissent was vocally and disturbingly active in its support of both the American and French Revolutions, and joined with other currents of discontent, Whig and Tory in origin, to act as progenitor of that British Left whose language has always been more revolutionary than its practice.

It plays this not insignificant role in a cycle of rebellions, revolutions and reconstructions, datable from 1776 through 1801, which may be compared with the War of the Three Kingdoms and the War of the English Succession for the way in which it brought to a close both the First Age of Union and – if we retain the term – the First British

[15] For the former, see Clark, *English Society*, 1985; for the latter, B.W. Young, *Religion and Enlightenment in Eighteenth-Century England; theological debate from Locke to Burke* (Oxford: the Clarendon Press, 1998).

[16] Knud Haakonssen (ed.), *Enlightenment and Religion: Rational Dissent in Eighteenth-Century Britain* (Cambridge University Press, 1996).

Empire. In this critical period the Irish crisis of 1782–1800 is conspicuous and important, but we should approach it by way of a detour though the other provinces of the Hanoverian multiple monarchy and empire. In Scotland, the last war fought within the Kingdom of Great Britain – the reconquest of the northwestern Gaeltacht following the Anglo-Lowland victory of 1746 – is to be viewed alongside the relative peace of the Protestant kingdom within the Union of 1707. There is some potential for radical Covenanting and perhaps proto-nationalist discontent with the abandonment of the militancy of the seventeenth century, but this is checked and pacified by that combination of lay patronage, Moderate oligarchy and civil philosophy known as the Scottish Enlightenment.[17] The remarkable success of this experiment in containing the ecclesiastical within the civil can be measured by comparing it with the case of the Scottish colony in Ulster, where Moderate control did not take shape and New Light anti-trinitarianism joined with Old Light Calvinism in the rebellious societies of Belfast.[18]

Before turning to the Irish aspects of the story, we must take account of an American dimension, in which the politics of the archipelago are enlarged into those of the Atlantic and the cis-Appalachian seaboard, and there appear new areas in which the problems of empire endanger the stability of the kingdom in church and state. The colonies and conquests in North America and the Caribbean had not been organised into viceroyalties or subordinate kingdoms on either the Spanish or the Irish model. They were largely, and considered themselves to be, English; though their populations contained – additional to large numbers of enslaved Africans – sizeable ethnic minorities including Scots-Irish (as Presbyterian emigrants from Ulster were beginning to be known in American historiography). These colonies were of diverse and often ill-defined juridical and political status, and from one point of view their history in the eighteenth century is that of their search for a more clearly defined political character, entailing demands for political autonomy greater than can be met within the existing structures of empire, so that in the end they take the revolutionary step of proclaiming themselves independent states.[19] We may look on these events as phenomena in the history of settler nationalism, if by that term – 'settler' is preferable to 'colonial', though 'nationalism' may not be preferable to 'patriotism' – we denote the processes which occur when settler populations begin to make claims against the state, and

[17] Richard B. Sher, *Church and University in the Scottish Enlightenment: the Moderate Literati of Edinburgh* (Princeton University Press, 1985).

[18] I am greatly indebted here to Ian McBride, *Scripture Politics: Ulster Presbyterians and Irish Radicalism in the Late Eighteenth Century* (Oxford: the Clarendon Press, 1998).

[19] Jack P. Greene, *Peripheries and Center: Constitutional Development in the Extended Polities of the British Empire and the United States, 1607–1788* (New York: Norton, 1990).

sometimes the people, that originally sent them forth: claims to conduct their own relations with the sovereign, claims to be enracinated in the land they have conquered from, or now share with, indigenous cultures from whom they sometimes derive part of their legitimacy. Phenomena of this kind are ancient in Irish history, where Old English, New English and Ulster Scots constitute three settler populations and as many religions; it is a key to medieval history that the Old English and Gaelic populations interacted, a key to early modern history that they remained Catholic and did not fully accept Anglican empire.

Publicists writing on behalf, first of the Old and then of the New English, had developed the argument that the Irish parliament was or should be subject to the English crown but not the English parliament – a contention increasingly unacceptable in England as the crown increasingly became a crown-in-parliament. It was taken up, during the 1760s and 70s, on behalf of American colonial assemblies claiming a similar autonomy, and claiming to be representative of bodies politic which they rendered autonomous by representing them. It is a question whether this claim to autonomy and sovereignty constitutes a 'nationalism' or not; but had it been systematically developed, it would have had the effect of converting the empire into a confederation of states held together by autonomy under a single crown. It is one of the keys to 'British history' that English history rendered this impossible.[20] Not only was there an ancient tradition of regarding Ireland as a conquered realm subordinate to the English king in parliament; in order to govern themselves, and resolve the deep tensions inherent in their polity, the English had effected so close a unity between crown and parliament that it could scarcely be shared with any confederate equals. If the king were responsible to any parliament but the English (British), his unity with that parliament would be broken and the twin spectres of absolutism and rebellion would rise again. That unity, furthermore, was never free from threat. No sooner had George III been freed of the challenge from Jacobitism than he had found both aristocratic politicians and enemies of aristocratic politics accusing him of delegitimising his rule in new ways, so vehemently as to challenge his own legitimacy. The American crisis grew as part of what Edmund Burke called 'the present discontents'. In these circumstances the King was no more likely to listen to American claims to autonomy early in his reign than

[20] J.G.A. Pocock, 'States, republics and empires: the American Founding in early modern perspective', in Terence Ball and J.G.A. Pocock, (eds.) *Conceptual Change and the Constitution* (Lawrence, KS: University of Kansas Press, 1988), pp. 55–77; 'Empire, state and confederation: the War of American Independence as a crisis in multiple monarchy', in Robertson (ed.), *A Union for Empire*, pp. 318–48; *La Ricostruzione di un Impero: sovranità britannica e federalismo americano* (Macerata: Biblioteca del Laboratorio di storia costituzionale Antoine Barnave, 1996).

to Catholic claims to emancipation towards the end of it; he was insufficiently secure in his position at the apex of empire in state and church.

The imperfect legitimacy of the Hanoverian dynasty may help explain the ease with which figures as diverse as George Washington and Theobald Wolfe Tone found themselves patriots in arms against a monarchy and empire they might otherwise have served; though due weight must be allowed to an ideology of universal right to rebellion which had conservative ideologues asking how any government could persist in face of 'the rights of men'. This, however, did not simplify all problems out of existence. The Americans by 1776 were reduced to proclaiming the empire a confederation in order to proclaim that confederation dissolved by reason of the crown's refusal to recognise it. This entailed proclaiming the absolute independence of thirteen states; at the same time, however, the Declaration of Independence announced the purpose of dissolving the ties which had bound 'one people' to 'another'. In a certain sense, both 'the American people' and 'the British people' are American inventions, though it remains possible that processes more complex than invention were bringing both into existence. The former, held to consist of thirteen states and one people, was by the Declaration committed to entering upon a discourse of federalism, precluded by the nature of parliamentary monarchy from forming part of a British discourse. At the same time, however, the completeness of the separation pronounced between American and British history meant that the Declaration had nothing further to say about the latter and uttered no call to revolution within it. However great the shock of American independence to British empire, the first great secession from British history left the latter's politics much as they had been before it. The second great secession, that of the Irish in the twentieth century, is a very different story.

The crisis of empire in the last quarter of the eighteenth century was the crisis of an empire in church as well as state. Since the American colonies had not been organised as subordinate kingdoms, like Ireland in one sense and post-Union Scotland in another, the Crown had not been obliged to consider an establishment of religion in them, and the Anglican and even Catholic confessions – where these existed and were sometimes strong – had something of the character of sects in a multi-congregational ecclesiastical polity. Though the Crown had no sustained intention of erecting American bishoprics, the fear that it might do so was remarkably persistent, especially after the Quebec Act of 1774 seemed to establish the Catholic church in newly conquered French Canada. If religion cannot be considered a major cause of the American Revolution, it did much to determine the character of the society that emerged from it.[21] The English-speaking United States were a model of late-Enlightened Protestant culture, unitarian, liberal and deist at one extreme, sectarian, evangelical and millenarian at another; and the separation of church and state, achieved by these forces in combination, seemed to Rational Dissenters in Birmingham and New Light Presbyterians in Belfast the revolutionary fulfilment of a dream. Antitrinitarian enmity to all establishments is a recurrent if not a necessary feature of the revolutionary ferment in the British ecumene.

If the wars of America were not wars of religion, those of Ireland notoriously have been and are of that character. The 'new British history', precisely because it views each particular history in the context afforded by some other, leans away from regarding national identities as primordial, while accepting that there are good reasons for their formation where this has successfully occurred. The history of the Irish response to the imperial crisis, the American Revolution and later the French, culminates with the United Irishmen's attempt to put together a national republicanism which, after its failure and the imposition of the Union, became the foundation of a republican nationalism; but the pluralist approach of the new British history tends to treat this story in terms of the convergences and divergences of three ethnic groups confessionally defined. The strongly Whiggish leadership of the Church of Ireland ascendancy reacted to the ineffective government of the American war by seeking greater autonomy for their own parliament, and by organising a national Protestant militia for the patriot purpose of demanding it; a programme natural to what we are calling settler nationalism. In proportion as they came close to achieving a confederal status unattainable by the Americans with whom they sympathised, they faced the problems generated by church ascendancy: the denial of many and various rights to those not of the Church of Ireland, first those significantly known by the English term 'Dissenters' – though they were Scottish Presbyterians, 'Covenanters' and 'Secessionists' when they dissented from their own kirk, as some but not all of them did – secondly the Catholic majority, no longer distinguishable into 'Old English' and 'Gaelic', and beginning to enter into new forms of middle-class and peasant organistation. There was an underlying problem of empire: was the government of Ireland by means including an established church so narrowly based that it would lead to revolutionary resistance, or could it be broadened and legitimised by measures of relief and emancipation? In England and Scotland, Enlightenment was a means of moderating established religion, but there was also an Enlightenment which attacked it at its root.

[21] J.C.D. Clark, *The Language of Liberty, 1660–1832: political discourse and social dynamics in the Anglo-American world* (Cambridge University Press, 1994).

There appeared radicals within the Protestantism that was not Presbyterian who aimed to break with both established religion and the executive's control of the Dublin parliament – with 'empire', therefore, in both Tudor senses of the term – and were attracted to American and later French revolutionary models. They came to propound an Enlightened republicanism which offered to include, but at the same time to assimilate, all three confessions. The parallel developments within Belfast and Ulster Presbyterians appear of a special character once we begin seeing them as produced by a history peculiar to that people – as the pluralism inherent in 'British history' encourages us to do. A history Scottish but not Moderate turns first towards a revolutionary pursuit of religious and civil emancipation – as 'the Scots-Irish' among others in America are doing already – but there remains the alternative of a hard-core or Old Light Calvinism that either rebels against the state or joins in supporting it.[22] To see this as key to the journey of Northern Protestants from rebellion towards loyalism is to say that they have a history of their own, unshared with others; but it has become the aim of republican nationalism to deny them such an autonomy.

The crucial encounter at all levels is that with a reorganised, largely lay, Catholicism; and here we ourselves encounter a problem in historical demarcation. There were levels, British and Canadian as well as Irish, at which relief and recognition of Catholics could be discussed as matters of public policy and the Catholic hierarchy and laity might negotiate with the state. Here the state might be moved to reconsider its own history, as built upon a repudiation of papal sovereignty so strong as to exclude Catholics from civil society and history condemning them as inherently disloyal to both. Enlightenment very often inherited this condemnatory attitude from Protestantism before it. The state was under strong pressures to continue a rigorous exclusion of Catholics from both state and society, resting on an established church. On the other hand, Enlightenment, the absorption of religion by civil society, might mitigate the rigors of both establishment and its opposites, Catholic and Dissenting; and in the last third of the eighteenth century, that delusive interval between the fall of the Jesuits and the Bonapartist captivity of the papacy, it was possible on both sides of the divide to believe that civil society and Catholic authority could come to terms. The Gallican strategy of separating civil sovereignty from sacramental communion was one which Enlightenment continued and with which the Church might perhaps negotiate, and the Protestant empire of the Hanoverians made offers of conciliation and concession to which the hierarchy responded. There was, however, a Catholic history going on,

[22] For all of this see McBride, *Scripture Politics*.

in which such offers were sometimes embraced and sometimes rejected, and neither statesmen in the eighteenth century nor historians in the twentieth have always known that history well enough to respond to it in the ways demanded of them.

The revolutionary response to the same question, when it appeared, was not other than a more radical version of Enlightenment. The offer to divorce the state from all recognition of religion, granting equal civil rights to those of all confessions, carried the implication that all were equally in harmony with civil society; and Catholics, like other Christians, had to decide whether they were content with the status of civil beings with a set of beliefs peculiarly their own. It is notorious that neither hierarchy nor laity, nor both in dialogue with each other, have been of one mind in this matter, and the debate is continuing. In Irish history this meant that the programmes favoured by Wolfe Tone rested on the assumption that Irish like French Catholics would accept the status offered them by the Civil Constitution of the Clergy; it was the Enlightened, not the Catholic, view of Catholicism. In the larger pattern of British history as the history of empire, the debates leading to Union in 1801 and Emancipation in 1829 turned on how the Westminster if not the Dublin parliament was to handle relations with a Catholic majority that must somehow be modified.

At other levels, a Catholic resurgence took the form of peasant organisation which was met by responses, escalating towards violence, of two kinds. The first was Protestant counter-organisation at the same social levels, which in due course shaped the evolution of the Northern Presbyterians towards a loyalism initially Orange, in which they had not shared; it is of interest that the turn towards loyalism was connected with a great debate resulting in the condemnation of Arianism, though that was many years later.[23] The presence of conditions intermittently anticipatory of ethnic cleansing is a reminder that political development in Ireland had a character of its own, imperfectly controlled by the state which might either co-opt or be co-opted by it. This points to the second quasi-violent response, that of the state, which at one level develops machinery of police and espionage slower to develop in the island of Britain, where conspiracy is less endemic; but at another helps bring about the rebellions of 1798 through responding to Catholic agitation by dragonnades, that is by military repression supported by regular soldiers but carried out by sub-regular forces, militia, yeomanry and fencibles. It recurrently occurs in the nineteenth and twentieth centuries that the state in Ireland is not perfectly in command of its own military responses. This, however, is a phenomenon of the Second

[23] McBride, ibid., pp. 219–22.

Age of Union, when empire is no longer being exercised in senses confined to the early modern.

If American independence – the first revolutionary outcome of the crisis of the late eighteenth century – leaves the structures of empire in church and state much as they had been before it, the Union with Ireland is revolutionary in the sense that it deeply transforms them (as the Revolution of 1688–89 had begun doing a century before). The Union has certainly to be seen in the context of other transformations, brought about by war with revolutionary France and the growth of Indian and maritime empire;[24] but from the perspective adopted in this paper, it is desirable to focus on the interval between Union and Emancipation. That the former made little sense without the latter was known to Pitt and Cornwallis, but it was delayed nearly thirty years – setting on foot processes which acted in the ultimate failure of the Union – due in some measure to the opposition of George III. It is a useful exercise to take the King's attitude seriously. Would he have had so much difficulty granting Emancipation if it had been unaccompanied by Union? Queen Anne had had fewer problems with her coronation oath over the Union of 1707, but that had been a union of parliaments, not of churches, which left the Church and Kingdom of England intact (since no one believed for a moment that they had disappeared). 1801 was a union of parliaments, not of administrations; but Ireland was being united with the Kingdom of England, of which it had been an appanage, and if the Church of Ireland was being more closely linked with the Church of England, Emancipation meant, as it did in 1829, a major modification of that special position of the Church within the Kingdom that the King was sworn to uphold.[25] 1829 was in a real sense the end of the Tudor church-state established four centuries before, the 'national apostacy' of the Oxford Tractarians; it is unhistorical to employ the language of Enlightenment to suggest that this is without significance.

The Union, then, foretells what does not happen until 1829–32: the end of 'the long eighteenth century', that *ancien regime* period in which the Crown governs through the historic parliament and church, and 'empire' in the English sense of the Act in Restraint of Appeals is modified by the exercise of 'empire' meaning sovereign dominion over realms other than England. As an experiment speedily resolved and carefully planned by practical politicians too busy, as usual, to consider the meaning of what they were doing, the Union entailed Emancipation but not Reform; there was no reason to anticipate the conjunction of

[24] C.A. Bayly, *Imperial Meridian: the British Empire and the World, 1780–1880* (London, Longman, 1989).

[25] Clark, *English Society*, pp. 383–408.

repeal of the Test and Corporation Acts with reconstruction of the system of parliamentary representation. Yet what came about in 1800–1 both was and was not a powerful extension of parliamentary, if no longer of ecclesiastical, empire. The Second Age of Union was one in which a post-revolutionary parliamentary state confronted, and helped engender by way of reaction against itself, a modern democratic nationalism (and, by way of reaction against the latter, a counter-nationalist loyalism in the distinctive history of the North). A romantic republicanism with its roots in 1798 maintained a tradition of political violence, which it succeeded in legitimating after 1916; while this was going on, however, the Union established in Ireland a parliamentarism (the parliamentarism of Parnell) more effective and deeply rooted than any achieved by the parliament of the pre-Union kingdom. Republicanism, which had to contend with the Catholic Church, had also to contend with a parliamentary style of politics; and this is one reason why the revolution of 1916–22 did not result in a fascist revolution like its Italian contemporary – as it might have done – but in a middle-class Catholic democracy. The Union was an extension of parliamentary empire which ended in revolution within that empire and independence from it (complicated by the Protestant North); but there is a history in which we continue to study 'empire' as the distribution of sovereignty shaped by forces operating within the Atlantic archipelago. At the time of writing, there are two sovereign states joining to contain the violent politics of a border province which can no longer be allowed to destablise either of them.

BRITAIN AND THE UNION, 1797–1801

By Peter Jupp

READ 9 SEPTEMBER AT THE QUEEN'S UNIVERSITY OF BELFAST

STUDENTS of the Union and the Irish and British contexts in which it was shaped owe G.C. Bolton and his study of the subject, *The Passing of the Irish Act of Union*, a considerable debt. By 1966, the year of its publication, J.C. Beckett, E.M. Johnston and R.B. McDowell had laid the foundations for a re-evaluation of Irish politics and British–Irish relations in the later eighteenth century, but for many aspects of those subjects, including the Union, Lecky's near-eighty-year-old history still remained the principal source. Bolton's was therefore a pioneering book and not only in the sense that it was the first to be based on an exhaustive study of the available evidence: it also broke new ground in its attempt to measure Irish elite and popular opinion on the issue and in the techniques that were used to do so. For these and other reasons, Bolton's study has had a strong influence on more than a generation of undergraduates at Queen's, some of whom have become major historians of the period; his study is, and will remain, an essential guide to the subject.

That said, we know much more now about the British dimension of Bolton's account than we did in 1966. The purpose of this essay, therefore, is to discuss the impact of subsequent research on our understanding of the making and the passing of the Union in Britain, adding here and there some findings of my own. It begins with a brief outline of Bolton's analysis of British policy, 1797–1801 – so that the groundwork can be laid – and then continues with a discussion of three of the contexts in which that policy was shaped: the executive, parliamentary politics, and public opinion.

Bolton's starting-point is that the 1782 settlement led to a series of well-known clashes between the British and Irish governments and from then on until 1797 Pitt, Dundas and a number of other politicians, both British and Irish, had considered in private the merits of a Union.[1] Pitt, however, had not applied himself consistently to Irish policy and had no 'long-cherished scheme of Union'.[2] The decision to create a Union was taken by Pitt after discussion with Grenville on or about

[1] This summary is based on G.C. Bolton, *The Passing of the Irish Act of Union* (London, 1966), *passim*. References for specific points are given below.
[2] Ibid., 217.

2 June 1798 following probable discussions with 'a few intimates' in April and May.[3] The reasons, Bolton suggests, were as follows: the Irish executive's growing financial dependency on Britain, which was made apparent in 1797; the rapid deterioration of the security situation in Ireland during April and May; and the possibility that a French expeditionary force was on its way from Toulon. Once the decision had been taken, British policy passed through two stages. The first lasted from the summer of 1798 to the spring of 1799 when the objective was to hammer out the terms of a Union which would be acceptable to the British and Irish parliaments. Pitt was inclined (and Bolton puts it no higher than that)[4] to make concessions to Catholics a part of a Union, but he dropped the idea in November under pressure from Irish ministers, particularly Lord Clare. The second stage lasted from the spring of 1799 until the summer of 1800, when the objective was to establish the precise terms of the Union and have them accepted by the two parliaments – in the case of the Irish, by using every means of persuasion that were available. In both stages, Bolton suggests, Pitt relied heavily on Irish ministers for the details of the Union provisions and apart from some concerted opposition to the clause allowing the free export of English wool to Ireland, encountered little interest and minimal opposition in the British Parliament.

There was, of course, a third stage, to which Bolton devotes less space – understandably so, given his concentration on the passage of the Union in Ireland. This took place between the summer of 1800 and February 1801 when Pitt turned to the way Ireland was to be governed after the Union. Various matters were discussed but the key decision was to make Catholic relief and a state endowment of the Catholic and Presbyterian churches the first policy to be presented to the new imperial Parliament. It was George III's opposition to this which persuaded Pitt to resign.

The executive

In the case of the operation and the thinking of the executive between 1797 and Pitt's resignation in 1801, a number of post-1966 publications have a bearing on Bolton's history. Several distinguished and highly influential long-range studies of the British state have appeared, two of which were written by contributors to this conference. Taken together,

[3] Ibid., 53–4.
[4] Ibid., 56.

they suggest, first, that we should not underestimate the persistent power and influence of monarchy, aristocracy and anglicanism in what is best described as an *ancien regime* state;[5] second, that eighteenth-century governments were keen to integrate Scotland and Ireland into a unitary 'European empire' with a strong military and financial base;[6] third, that a sense of Britishness developed as an accompaniment to this 'empire';[7] and, fourth, that notwithstanding these hegemonic forces and centralising tendencies, it would be foolish to underestimate the substantial authority that remained with local government in what might be best described as a 'parish state'.[8] As for publications with a more direct bearing on events, there are a number which illuminate both the specific contributions of the key politicians on the British side and the general policies of the government after 1797, particularly those related to military strategy and diplomacy.[9]

What then, are the conclusions that we can draw ? With regard to the question of *who* made the decisions on the British side, there are some amendments and additions to be made to Bolton's account. It is now generally accepted, for example, that from at least 1791 the mainspring of the government was the 'triumvirate' of Pitt, Dundas and Grenville and that from the outbreak of war in 1793 this constituted an inner cabinet similar to the war cabinets of Lloyd George and Churchill. Thus, although there is no doubt that Pitt occupied the leading role in decision-making, more emphasis is now placed on the contributions of the other members of the triumvirate to war policy in general and to Irish policy in particular. This point has a bearing on the questions of the timing of the decision to proceed with a union and the circumstances surrounding it. The evidence that is now available therefore establishes that Pitt first broached the subject openly on 28 May (with Camden, the Lord Lieutenant);[10] that his first substantive

[5] J.C.D. Clark, *English Society 1688–1832* (Cambridge, 1985).

[6] C.A. Bayly, *Imperial Meridian. The British Empire and the World 1780–1830* (London, 1989). J. Brewer, *The Sinews of Power: War, Money and the English State 1688–1783* (London, 1989) also touches on this theme.

[7] L. Colley, *Britons* (Yale, 1992).

[8] D. Eastwood, *Government and Community in the English Provinces 1700–1870* (London, 1997).

[9] The list includes: J. Ehrman, *The Younger Pitt* (3 vols., London, 1969–96); P. Jupp, *Lord Grenville 1759–1834* (Oxford, 1985); M. Fry, *The Dundas Despotism* (Edinburgh, 1992); P. Mackesy, *The Strategy of Overthrow, 1798–99* (London, 1974) and *War Without Victory. The Downfall of Pitt, 1799–1802* (Oxford, 1984); E. Ingram, *Commitment to Empire: Prophecies of the Great Game in Asia, 1797–1800* (Oxford, 1981); C. Emsley, *British Society and the French Wars 1793–1815* (London, 1979); J.E. Cookson, *The British Armed Nation 1793–1815* (Oxford, 1997); T. Bartlett, 'Defence, counter-insurgency and rebellion: Ireland, 1793–1803' in T. Bartlett and K. Jeffery, *A Military History of Ireland* (Cambridge, 1996), 247–93; D. Wilkinson, '"How Did They Pass the Union?" Secret Service Expenditure in Ireland, 1799–1804', *History*, vol. 82, no. 266, April 1997, 223–51.

[10] Ehrman, *Pitt*, III, 170 and n. 2.

discussions with a colleague took place with Grenville four or five days later;[11] and that Grenville himself had been privy for some time to the view of his brother and former-Lord Lieutenant, the Marquess of Buckingham, that a union was essential.[12] It is also relevant, in this respect, that Dundas had been drawn into the decision-making circle by August.[13]

Newly discovered archives (or more extensively researched established ones) have also underlined the fact that in the crucial decision-making period from May to November 1798, each of these three had their own networks of communication on Irish matters. In Pitt's case, this included, on the British side – apart from Grenville and Dundas – Auckland (a former Chief Secretary), Hobart (Auckland's father-in-law and another former Chief Secretary), Thomas Pelham (the incumbent Chief Secretary), Camden (the outgoing Lord Lieutenant), and two under-secretaries at Dublin Castle, Edward Cooke and William Elliot; and, on the Irish side, Clare, Castlereagh and John Beresford. Grenville's circle was naturally smaller and included Camden, Auckland, Buckingham, Carysfort (his brother-in-law), Cooke, and, amongst the Irishmen, Clare and Sir John Newport. As for Dundas, his sole regular correspondent was Cornwallis, Camden's successor as Lord Lieutenant.

A consideration of these networks leads to several observations. The first is that the triumvirate appear to have restricted their regular correspondence within the senior and junior ranks of London-based ministers to just one other cabinet member – Camden – and to one junior minister (but senior figure) -Auckland. Thus, although there is evidence of Pitt consulting with Portland, the Home Secretary, and Canning, it is not strong enough to lead to the conclusion that these were regular confidants.[14] This is evidence of Pitt's *ad hoc* methods of doing business and Grenville's and Dundas's compliance with it. The second is that Auckland appears to have played a more crucial role than Bolton suggests. Although occupying the near sinecure post of Joint Postmaster General, Auckland had considerable experience of Irish matters and was closely involved from the start with both Pitt and Grenville in the decision and its implementation.[15] Finally, the circles of correspondents suggest that there was no significant departmental input from London and that the only bureaucratic expertise that was brought to bear on the decision emanated from Cooke and Elliot in

[11] *The Times*, 31 May 1798 reports a cabinet meeting on Irish affairs on the 30th which started at about 2.00 pm and lasted for some 30 minutes.

[12] Jupp, *Grenville*, 265 and n. 12.

[13] Ehrman, *Pitt*, III, 172 n. 3.

[14] Ibid.

[15] Castlereagh acknowledges Auckland's role in his letter to him, 13 Dec. [1799], PRONI, Sneyd Tss. T.3229/2/45.

Dublin. This is not in itself surprising but it underlines the fact that so important a decision rested on the shoulders of a relatively small number of hard-pressed politicians. It is also relevant to Professor Cookson's argument that the absence of a bureaucratic contribution to major policies is a feature of an *ancien regime* state.[16]

With regard to the practicalities of decision-making, Bolton stresses that Pitt only turned his mind to Ireland when he had to, with the implication that the Union period was one of those occasions.[17] Today, however, we would draw attention to the fact that Pitt, and, more particularly, Grenville and Dundas, had accumulated very considerable experience of governing Ireland since 1782 and that with the exception of Cornwallis this was also true of many of their British confidantes listed above. Further, we also have a much better understanding of the stresses and strains bearing down upon them. More will be said below about the war, but the key point to make is that in 1797 and 1798, each member of the triumvirate was shouldering an immense burden of work, largely alone. In Pitt's case, besides overseeing the whole, it was the raising of the new income tax; in Dundas's, the mobilisation of a massive defence force; and in Grenville's, the creation of the second allied coalition. The burden had taken its toll of their health and personal relationships. Pitt was seriously ill in May 1798 and Dundas only just recovered from exhaustion.[18] Grenville was physically fit but obsessed with devising an allied military strategy that would earn him his place in the history books. He and Dundas were diverging on war policy, with the result that each of them were developing their own priorities, with Dundas focusing on defence and Grenville on a continental offensive. In addition, we now have strong evidence that from about this time (and perhaps earlier), the King became increasingly dissatisfied with his government's policies and with slights to his authority on the part of its leading members.[19]

It is also possible to add a little more detail to Bolton's general view that the government's conduct of the Union business was not as efficient as it might have been. A key issue here was the contemporary litmus test of real friendship and confidence – private, as opposed to official, correspondence between ministers. Pitt, as was his custom, wrote very little to Cornwallis and indeed to Clare between 1799 and 1801, and

[16] Cookson, *Armed Nation,* 245.

[17] Bolton, *Union,* 11.

[18] B[ritish] L[ibrary] Add. Mss. 41582 fos. 22–3, Lord Grenville to Thomas Grenville, 30 May 1798; evidence of Dundas' weariness earlier in the year can be found in PRO, Chatham Mss. 30/8/157, Dundas to Pitt, 10 Feb. 1798.

[19] A. Aspinall, ed., *The Later Correspondence of George III* (5 vols., Cambridge, 1962–70), III, xv–xvii.

both thought they were badly neglected.[20] Portland, the Home Secretary, wrote very little to Cornwallis, with the result that the latter's only confidant in the cabinet was Dundas.[21] We should also not overlook the fact that the government left the Irish executive very ill-prepared for the first debates on the Union in the Irish Parliament and that the decision to proceed with Catholic relief in 1801 was made by ill-attended and ill-prepared cabinets.[22] Overall, the evidence now suggests that the Union decision was made by three men under considerable mental and physical strain who, although they were well versed in Irish affairs, did not develop a coherent method of managing the enterprise in London.[23]

The most important addition to our knowledge concerns the thinking behind the Union. In broad terms, the war, and the associated issues of military strategy, military resources and internal security, are much more prominent than they once were in explaining the decision taken in May–November 1798, that is, to proceed with a Union *and* Catholic relief. The situation, as seen from London from January to June 1798, was as follows:[24] the peace negotiations with France in 1797 had failed, leaving France in occupation of the Low Countries and the three other major continental powers either in states of uneasy peace with her or, in the case of Russia, on the defensive. Britain was therefore encircled and alone. From January onwards it seemed likely that the Directory would attempt an invasion of Britain and Ireland – either across the Channel where large transports were being assembled in sight, on a clear day, of Dover; or from Toulon; or from both simultaneously.[25] The problem was that Britain had insufficient regular troops to participate in any counter-offensive and at the same time defend her European empire – in the Channel Islands, in Ireland and in Britain itself.

In these circumstances, the triumvirate devised two short-term and two long-term strategies. The two short-term strategies consisted of

[20] N[ational] A[rchives of] S[cotland], Melville Mss. GD 51/1/331/28, Lord Cornwallis to Henry Dundas, 26 June 1800; B.L., Add. Mss. 37416, fo. 74, W. Wellesley Pole to Lord Wellesley, 10 Feb. 1801.

[21] NAS, Melville Mss. GD 51/1/331/22, Lord Cornwallis to Henry Dundas, 19 Feb. 1800.

[22] On the question of the Irish executive being inadequately prepared for the Union debates in 1799 see Ehrman, *Pitt*, III, 180–1 and PRONI, Sneyd Tss. T.3229/1/16, Lord Clare to Lord Auckland, 5 Feb. 1799.

[23] Lord Minto was very critical of the management of Irish affairs at this time, see NLS, Minto Mss., 11052 fos. 13–16, 88–9, 124–7, Lord Minto to Lady Minto, 16 June, 22 Nov., 15 Dec. 1798. In the first of these letters Minto alleges that Pitt failed to tell Portland of his sending of Cornwallis to Ireland.

[24] This summary is based principally on the studies by Cookson, Ehrman, Ingram, Jupp and Mackesy referred to in note 9.

[25] Fears of an invasion were particularly strong in the first three weeks of May, see leader comment in *The Times*, 18, 21 May 1798.

launching raids against the French coast to forestall a channel invasion and to reinforce the Mediterranean fleet under Lord St Vincent. In the last week of May it was known that a raid against the Ostend canal locks had been successful, but that the French fleet had set sail from Toulon on the 19th – its destination unknown. The two long-term strategies were as follows. The first, largely in Grenville's hands, was to create a second coalition with Russia, Austria and Prussia that would take the offensive against France in Europe. By May 1798, much to everybody's amazement, there seemed a chance that this would come into being and that the two great German armies would be united, and, in the mind of Grenville, decisively, for the first time since 1794. Indeed, a four-power conference was due to open in Berlin on the 28th of that month.[26] This would have disposed Grenville to argue that if Britain was to participate with money and troops in such a grand design, it could not afford distractions in Ireland. Hence, in Grenville's view, there had to be a Union and, if necessary, Catholic relief.

The second strategy rested largely in the hands of Pitt, Dundas and their military advisor, Cornwallis. The most recent analysis of this strategy is by Professor Cookson, who argues that Britain's Irish policy from 1778 onwards was firmly placed in the context of the increasing demands of war.[27] This meant Catholic recruitment and the conciliation of Catholic grievances. This central point, Cookson suggests, lies behind the views that Pitt, Dundas and Grenville took on the great Anglo-Irish disputes of 1782, 1783, 1785, 1792–3, and 1795. By 1797–8, however, Britain itself was under severe threat. Pitt, Dundas and Cornwallis therefore planned and executed a massive mobilisation of volunteers for home defence – 'the armed nation', to quote Cookson's title. This mobilisation would have strategic advantages because the regulars, one-third of whom, he speculates, were by this time Irish, could be used in any offensive operations; and it would have political advantages in so far as it would bind the gentry, the volunteers and their families to the war effort and the political status quo. However, it was precisely at the time when Dundas was overseeing the huge increase in the volunteer establishment from 54 to 116,000, that is, between April and July 1798, that 'open' rebellion broke out in Ireland, and forces that could have been used for home defence and a continental offensive had to be diverted to crush it. This left the number of serviceable regulars on the ground dangerously low. Pitt and Dundas therefore concluded that their ideal of an armed nation with loyal Catholic support in Ireland

[26] For additional information on this point see J.M. Sherwig, *Guineas and Gunpowder. British Foreign Aid in the Wars with France 1793–1815* (Cambridge, Mass., 1969), 103–4.

[27] Cookson's study draws on arguments put forward earlier by C.A. Bayly and T. Bartlett – see above.

should no longer be frustrated by what they saw as the narrow interests of the Irish ruling class – hence a Union accompanied by Catholic relief.[28]

Although it may be questioned how far the conciliation of Catholic grievances for military purposes was the central preoccupation of government policy in all the previous crises in Anglo-Irish relations, there can be little doubt that the problems of home defence as part of the war strategy played a significant part in Pitt's and Dundas' thinking in 1798.[29] Overall the post-Bolton version of events looks like this: policy was shaped by the triumvirate of Pitt, Dundas and Grenville and had been since at least 1791; each of them shouldered immense burdens of work and two were either ill or very tired in May 1798. The minds of all three were focused almost exclusively on the war, the state of which was critical from the British point of view in the first six months of 1798. Each one took a different view of the priorities of future war policy but whatever that priority was, it did not take account of the need to manage a rebellious and near bankrupt Ireland within existing constitutional arrangements. In these circumstances, a union with Catholic relief could suit each of their respective long-term war policies.

The parliamentary context

In his analysis of the passage of the Union through the British Parliament, Bolton makes two main points. The first is that it passed 'with remarkable smoothness' – in fact with average minorities of just twenty-seven in the Commons and only eight in the Lords. The second, made as a response to the 149 v. 24 Commons' vote in favour of the Union resolutions on 31 January 1799, is that the 'thinness' of the turnout 'perhaps reflected the usual apathy shown by many members towards Irish and colonial affairs'.[30]

Subsequent research provides us with a greater understanding of the context in which the Irish debates took place and modifies Bolton's bleak assessment. In the case of the easy passage of the measure, a fuller explanation can be found in recent work on the political state of the Commons and on the extraordinary growth of loyalism and patriotism in the constituencies. The introduction to the relevant

[28] See, in particular, Cookson, *Armed Nation*, chapters 1–3 and 6.

[29] It is notable that other ministers (Grenville excepted) placed most stress on the political advantages of a Union in Ireland and rarely mention the impact on war policy.

[30] Bolton, *Union*, 116–8, 200–1.

volumes of the *History of Parliament*, for example, shows how the 1796 general election produced 424 supporters for Pitt, 95 for the Whigs and just 39 MPs of an 'independent' or 'doubtful' persuasion – a net gain for the government over the Opposition of 182 seats.[31] Moreover, this huge majority was enhanced when Fox and a sizeable proportion of the Whigs seceded from Parliament in May 1797. Apart from any other result, the secession strengthened the government's superiority in debate. In the Commons, its leading spokesmen in the Union debates were Pitt, Dundas, Canning and Hawkesbury. Despite the fact that apart from the debatable case of Canning, these four were notably short of any first-hand knowledge of Ireland, yet they easily outshone the principal Whig spokesmen, Sheridan, Dr Laurence, Grey, Tierney and General Fitzpatrick, most of whom had. The government's superiority was even more striking in the Lords. There, Grenville could call not only on his first-hand knowledge of Ireland but also on that of a succession of ex-lords-lieutenant and chief secretaries, each of whom pledged their support. The Whigs, by comparison, could rely only on Holland, who knew little of Ireland, and the semi-detached Fitzwilliam.

Another reason was the growth of loyalism and what Cookson refers to as 'national defence patriotism'.[32] The former was sponsored, encouraged or manufactured by the government from 1792 on an unprecedented scale. By 1797 there were approximately 2,000 loyalist associations in England and Wales.[33] The latter, Cookson argues, arose from the mass volunteering that developed after 1794 and led to a force 100,000 strong – 'easily the largest requisition of military manpower' so far made by the British state.[34] In addition, the years from 1797 to 1800 were filled with events other than the Irish rebellion which encouraged a sense of a 'nation under siege' and a 'battle for Britain': the imposition of an income tax; the national thanksgiving for the naval victories at Camperdown and Cape St Vincent; the sight of Bonaparte's invasion batteries across the channel; volunteering on an unprecedented scale; the massive voluntary monetary contributions to the war effort; Nelson's great victory in the Nile; the Anglo-Russian military expedition to Holland; the assassination attempt on the King; and the severe food shortages of 1800. All these developments served to bolster Pitt's apparent hegemony and to weaken further the position of the Whigs.

Bolton's suggestion that Parliament had little interest in Irish affairs also deserves some reconsideration. In this regard it is important not

[31] R.G. Thorne (ed.), *The History of Parliament: the Commons, 1790–1820* (5 vols., London, 1986), I, 149.

[32] Cookson, *Armed Nation*, chap. 8, partic, 211–19.

[33] Ibid., 26, referring to H.T. Dickinson, 'Popular Conservatism and Militant Loyalism 1789–1815' in idem. (ed.), *Britain and the French Revolution 1789–1815* (London, 1989), 115.

[34] Cookson, 36 (for the quotation): 7.

to underestimate the Irish presence in Parliament before the Union. According to one contemporary estimate there were forty-one Irish peers who sat as British peers in the Lords in 1800, another seventeen who sat in the Commons and an estimated seventy or so who lived in Britain.[35] In addition there were perhaps as many as twenty-five other MPs with Irish ancestry, including some of the front-bench spokesmen on the Union – Canning, Sheridan, Tierney, Laurence and Fitzpatrick.[36] The Irish presence in Parliament before the Union was by no means negligible.

It also appears that a substantial amount of parliamentary time and interest was devoted to debates on Ireland. During the 1797 and 1798 sessions – that is, before the Union debates began in 1799 – there were thirteen debates that dealt solely with Irish issues and two in which Ireland figured prominently. Unfortunately, the newspapers were unable to report four of the most important ones due to strangers being excluded, but the evidence suggests that taken as a whole they accounted for some 20 per cent of total debating time and attracted a fair level of interest.[37] In 1799 and the first session of 1800 the Union occupied nearly 40 per cent of the recorded debates in both houses – much more than is recorded for any other single issue.[38] Further, the division figures and the number of speakers do not support Bolton's contention. The division figures suggest that in 1799 attendance at the debates in the Commons was, on average, about 150 members, rising to well over 200 in 1800, when they were inflated by Grey's introduction of the issue of parliamentary reform and when members were exercised about the commercial aspects of the measure. The comparable figure for the Lords in 1800, interestingly enough, gives a similar proportion of that House – seventy-four members.[39] Finally, although neither house was overwhelmed with would-be speakers, at least forty-five members of the Commons and twenty-seven in the Lords are recorded as getting to their feet. Overall, these figures do not suggest a lack of interest

[35] *The Times*, 7 Aug. 1800.

[36] Calculated from Thorne, *The Commons*.

[37] The unreported debates took place on 14, 15, 22 and 27 June 1798. My estimate is based on the number of columns of debate recorded in *The Parliamentary History of England* (hereafter *Parl. Hist.*). In the case of the unreported debates, there were at least 48 speakers, for whom I have made an allowance which is included in my overall estimate. The number of members who voted in divisions on these motions varied between 83 and 126 in the Lords and 165 and 225 in the Commons and these suggest a moderately high degree of interest.

[38] The calculation hs been arrived at in the same way as cited in n. 37. The Union occupied 795 of the 2,055 columns of debate recorded in *Parl. Hist.*

[39] These figures are based on the following divisions: in the Commons, on 7, 11, 14 Feb. 1799 and 21, 25 Apr., 1, 2 May 1800; and in the Lords on 21, 28 Apr., and 7, 8 May 1800.

relative to other issues, even though, in retrospect, it might be said that the issue did not create a level of interest commensurate with its importance.

A reading of the recorded debates in their entirety also reveals a considerable degree of interest in the issue on the part of those who did speak. Here we enter dangerous and surprisingly uncharted waters. In the case of the executive, we can rely on reasonably reliable evidence in the form of private correspondence. In the case of parliamentary debate, we have to remind ourselves not only that the reports are partial and defective, but also that members said things first and foremost to influence others rather than make statements of principal or reveal their real intentions. To use modern jargon, there were several different Union discourses. That said, even Lecky's analysis, which, understandably, is more extensive than Bolton's, is not comprehensive and this justifies a re-examination of the debates with a view to establishing the principal arguments.

The government's case on Ireland was certainly not a static one. In both the Commons and the Lords, arguments were adopted to suit circumstances: to fend off Whig arguments in 1797–8; to woo the Irish Parliament in the first months of 1799, when the details of the measure had not been worked out; and to deal with specific criticisms of those details in April and May of the following year.

In 1797–8, the Whigs and others put forward a series of motions arguing that disorder in Ireland was due to the failure of the Irish executive and the Irish Parliament to proceed with Catholic relief and parliamentary reform and calling upon the government to insist on their passage. Pitt and others responded by arguing that the independence of the Irish Parliament could not be violated and drew attention to the improvements that had been made under its auspices, both commercially and politically.[40]

The decision to proceed with a Union, however, required different arguments. Thus in 1799 and 1800 a particular interpretation of Anglo-Irish relations was advanced persistently, albeit with variations, by a series of ministers and their closest supporters. The essence of this was as follows. Ireland's problems were deep-rooted and, in the view of several ministers, lay in the fact that she had been conquered by England and then subjected until 1690 to several hundred years of oppression – the exact number varied from speaker to speaker. This was followed, until 1782, by the 'very narrow policy'[41] of subcontracting

[40] *Parl. Hist.*, xxxiii, clms. 157–65; see also Grenville's similar argument, xxxiii, clms. 142–3.

[41] Pitt's words, Parl. Hist., xxxiv, clm. 250. Pitt said he did not agree that there had been 300 years of oppression, ibid.

power to the Protestant elite, at which point political and commercial concessions had been made to the elite's parliament. English mismanagement prior to 1782 was therefore ultimately responsible for the glaring inequalities in the distribution of property, a Protestant constitution that 'rested upon the foundation of Catholic exclusion',[42] the want of commerce and capital, the lack of a middle class that could connect the interests of the upper and the lower classes, and for the ignorance and poverty of the peasantry. It was this ignorance that explained the misguided infatuation with jacobinism and the involvement in the rebellion and not, by implication, Catholicism. Further, the Protestant elite in Ireland was entirely wrong to think that 1782 was meant to be a final settlement of the relationship between the two countries. On the contrary, said Pitt (with the support of the Lord Lieutenant at the time, the Duke of Portland, and all his other colleagues) it was recognised even by Fox that a more precise definition of the relationship would have to follow. The fact that this had not happened was the root cause of the frequent differences between the two Parliaments and the recent articulation of the distasteful concept of a Protestant ascendancy.

The other key arguments for a Union were deployed more tactically. In the debates in the early months of 1799, for example, emphasis was placed upon the advantages of a Union from the Irish point of view. Dundas produced the often-repeated argument that Scotland had benefited substantially in commercial and other terms since the Union of 1707. The relationship between the British executive and the Irish Parliament was analysed and shown to be defective on the grounds that the Irish Parliament could not scrutinise the executive and that the executive could not rely on the Irish Parliament in crucial matters affecting both kingdoms, such as declarations of war and peace. The commercial advantages of a free trade were advanced, as were the political advantages of a settlement of the issue of Catholic exclusion without endangering Protestantism and a reduction of tithes coupled with state salaries for the Catholic clergy. Moreover, there was a frequently stated cultural argument: namely that barbarism and ignorance would be done away with by the infusion of what were referred to by a number of speakers as British 'habits, customs, and morals'.[43]

In 1800, on the other hand, it is noticeable that much more emphasis was placed on the question of security. In Pitt's speech on 21 April, for example, he placed particular emphasis on the security advantages, telling the house that the Union was a 'great national policy' whose object was 'effectually to counteract the restless machinations of an

[42] Pitt's words, ibid., clm. 292.
[43] Ibid., xxxiv, clm. 306.

inveterate enemy'.[44] This made sense. In 1799 Pitt and his colleagues were trying to persuade the Protestant and Catholic interests in Ireland to support the Union on the grounds that it would be beneficial to all. In 1800, with the Union accepted in Ireland, it was politic to emphasise the security aspects to supporters who were sceptical of the advantages for Britain. It is also possible that the strategic argument was particularly relevant, given the collapse of the second coalition and the possibility that Russia and the other Baltic powers would prevent Britain from defending herself in the North Sea.[45]

The Whigs also thought tactically and, in some respects, agreed with the government. In 1797 and 1798 they called upon Pitt to impose reform on a corrupt Irish Parliament, calling the 'independence' of 1782 a sham. In 1799 and 1800, however, they replaced this refrain with another. They, like the government spokesmen, believed that there had been several hundred years of English misrule and that this was the root cause of the poverty and ignorance of the Irish masses. They also regarded an harmonious connection between the two countries as vital to the security and prosperity of the empire. Their reading of recent history, however, was now very different. Given that they were responsible for the settlement of 1782, they insisted time and time again that it was not only accepted as final on the British side, but more importantly, had been regarded as final on the part of the Irish. The subsequent clashes between the two countries and the rebellion could therefore not be laid at the door of that settlement. Rather, these were due to oppressive British policies and the refusal to promote parliamentary reform and Catholic relief. Several admitted that a genuinely voluntary Union might be desirable at some stage in the future but they all argued that it was inappropriate in 1799 and 1800, given the highly charged state of Irish opinion and the initial rejection of the measure by the Irish Commons. Pitt, they alleged, had been forced to bribe the Irish parliament into submission against the wishes of the majority of the population and the majority of the men of property; and that the result would be a Union which would probably add to the animosity between the two countries. The only certain result was that the majority of the 100 Irish MPs would support whatever party was in power and therefore would undermine further the balance of power between King, Lords and Commons. These were the arguments which justified Grey in the Commons and Holland in the Lords introducing motions for parliamentary reform and Catholic relief on

[44] Ibid., xxxv, clm. 39.

[45] This summary is based on the following speeches: Canning (23 Jan. 1799); Pitt (31 Jan. 1799; 21 Apr. 1800); Hawkesbury (31 Jan. 1799); Dundas (7 Feb. 1799); Windham (7 Feb. 1799); Sir John Mitford (Sol.-Genl., 14 Feb. 1799); Grenville (19 Mar. 1799); Auckland (11 Apr. 1799).

behalf of the depleted party during the debates on the Union Bill in 1800.[46]

As might be expected, the independent members expressed a wide variety of views. Most of these were the same as those of the principal government and Opposition speakers, although they were usually linked in unusual combinations. Some had particularly pointed comments to make. Henry Bankes thought that English policy towards Ireland had been 'barbarous and narrow' for three hundred years, with the result that Catholics hated the English as much as they did the Irish Protestant elite.[47] Robert Peel took the view in 1799 that the silence of the British trading interests on the subject meant that they were anxious to lend a helping hand to their Irish colleagues; and in 1800 thought that the substantial petitioning campaign against the commercial clauses of the measure by the English wool manufacturers exaggerated the supposed disastrous effects of the free export of wool to Ireland.[48] Lord Sheffield said that it was nonsense for the English 'colony' in Ireland to refer to itself as a nation,[49] while Robert Buxton predicted that without a Union, Ireland would soon become a province of France.[50] Some of the most interesting speeches were by three loose canons in the Lords: Lansdowne, Moira and Darnley – all landowners in Ireland. Lansdowne, for example, said that although he did not think ministers knew much about Ireland, he supported their Union and argued that there should be one army, one navy, one legal system – including Habeas Corpus and trial by jury – one system of commerce, Catholic relief, the abolition of tithes and a stop put to the spread of pastureland in order to ease the plight of the peasantry.[51]

Overall, the debates suggest the following conclusions. First, that the British Parliament exhibited a fair degree of interest in the condition of Ireland and the Union. Second, that the government and the remnants of the Opposition approached the question tactically. Third, that the arguments focused primarily on historic English guilt, the historic culpability of the Irish elite, the consolidation of resources, and the advantages and disadvantages to each country. And, fourth, the references to the specific security advantages that the triumvirate had in mind are very rare indeed. In short, this was a different discourse

[46] This summary is based on the following speeches: Sheridan (23 Jan. 1799); Laurence (31 Jan.; 11 Feb. 1799); C. Grey (7 Feb.1799; 21, 25 Apr. 1800); Tierney (7, 11 Feb. 1799); R. Fitzpatrick (11 Feb. 1799); B. Hobhouse (14 Feb. 1799); Holland (19 Mar. 1799; 21, 30 Apr. 1800).

[47] Ibid., xxxiv, clms. 446–8.

[48] Ibid., xxxiv, clms. 478–82; xxxv, clms. 123–5.

[49] Ibid., xxxiv, clm. 948.

[50] Ibid., clm. 956.

[51] Ibid., cols. 672–80.

from that which took place in the executive when the scheme was hatched.

Public opinion

The third and final context to be discussed is British public opinion – a subject which Bolton says very little about but which has recently attracted a great deal of scholarly attention. One of the factors that shaped public opinion was first-hand knowledge of Ireland and Irish people. In the case of people there were plenty about, including one Mr O'Brien, a celebrated 'Irish Giant' nearly 9 feet in height who, claiming lineal descent from 'Brian Boreau', toured Britain in 1796.[52] The personal connections between the British and the Irish aristocracies were extensive and many Irish were to be found in London during the parliamentary and social seasons or in the watering holes of Cheltenham and Bath. Irishmen were well represented in Parliament and increasingly in the merchant communities of London, Bristol and Liverpool. A particular focal point for the well-heeled Irish and friends of Ireland in London were the St Patrick's Day dinners of that saint's London Benevolent Society.[53] The Society itself appears to have played a highly successful role in supporting the collection raised in 1797 by John Julius Angerstein to help the Dublin poor. It was said that the funds raised were soon feeding 25,000 in the city. In addition, parts of Britain were no strangers to the Irish poor. London and other cities had Irish quarters and thousands travelled to Britain for work during harvest time. Personal knowledge of the Irish in Britain probably accounts for the two most common stereotypes found in contemporary literature and images: the upper-class Irish adventurer and 'Paddy', the latter usually being depicted as a wild-looking labourer, in contrast to the portly and slightly bemused stockman or shopkeeper, 'John Bull'.[54]

The other important conditioning factor was printed material: books,

[52] *Lincoln, Rutland and Stamford Mercury*, 4 Mar. 1796. He appeared at Stamford Fair in that month, the entrance fee being 1 shilling for ladies and gentlemen and sixpence for their servants.

[53] Held at the Freemasons' Tavern, tickets 10 shillings and sixpence in 1800, *The Times*, 15 Mar. 1800.

[54] I have in mind here Isaac Cruikshank's 'An Irish Union' pub. 30 Jan. 1799 (BM 9344) where Pitt and Dundas are portrayed trying to tie the hands of 'Paddy' who is asking Dundas, 'Now is it Blareying you at' and 'John Bull' with the latter saying 'This may be Nation good Fun – but dang my buttons if I know what it is about! & Cousin Paddy dont seem quite clear in the case neether.' Paddy and John Bull were represented in various ways during this period.

pamphlets, periodicals, cartoons and newspapers. Measuring how far these were inclined, or able, to present a full range of opinion and what audiences they reached are, of course, difficult issues to resolve. The government was very active in sponsoring favourable comment on its war and Irish policies, and subsidised publishers and authors of all the various forms of printed material in both Britain and Ireland – activities which coincided with the promotion of loyalism and patriotism.[55] In addition, there is the obvious problem of distinguishing between what was published, what was purchased, and consequently, what was read in sufficient number to have had had any impact on opinion. On this issue, my method was to construct a database of books and pamphlets advertised by booksellers and publishers in the London press – the argument being that this would provide a reliable guide to what was actually purchased and, with less reliability, read.

On this basis there appear to have been about ten books (as opposed to pamphlets) published or re-published between 1797 and 1800 which were clearly directed at the Irish question and the Union.[56] A number of these were reprints of works with a bearing on the issue, such as Sir John Davies' *Historical Tracts*, Defoe's *The History of the Union between England and Scotland*, de Lolme's *The British Empire in Europe* and George Chalmers' *An estimate of the Comparative Strength of Great Britain*, while others were special compilations such as Woodfall's *Debates on the Irish Propositions* (of 1784–85). Taken together they were strongly unionist in their emphasis and some of the information they contained was certainly used by pro-unionists in the parliamentary debates.

The pamphlet war was less extensive than in Ireland and was much more one-sided.[57] So far, forty-four pamphlets advertised in the London press have been identified, a much lower number than of those published in Ireland. Seventeen of these were of Irish origin and consisted of speeches in the Irish Parliament and a number of especially authored works such as Edward Cooke's *Arguments for and against an Union*, which was published almost simultaneously in both capitals and was the official government publication. In addition, nine speeches in

[55] The principal source on press subsidies remains A. Aspinall, *Politics and the Press c.1780–1850* (London, 1949). On loyalism see L. Colley, *Britons* (Yale, 1992), chaps. 4 and 5. J.E. Cookson, in *Armed Nation*, chap. 8, suggests that the national thanksgiving for the naval victories of Camperdown and Cape St Vincent in Dec. 1797 and the collection of the voluntary contributions of Feb.–May 1798 and thereafter mark the beginning of state-sponsored patriotism.

[56] Ten is the number I have found so far.

[57] So far I have identified 171 Union pamphlets from the catalogues of the Linen Hall Library, Belfast, the Local History Section of the Belfast Central Library, the search facilities of COPAC and the London newspapers. My guess is that this is about the total number that were published.

the British Parliament were advertised, virtually all of them being by government spokesmen or pro-unionists.[58] The remainder were authored works, the following of which appear to have been particularly popular: four by James Gerahty published in January–February 1799 – his *Present State of Ireland considered in a letter to Lord Cornwallis*, *Consequences of an Union*, *Necessity of an Union*, and *Utility of an Union*; Drs Tucker and Clark's *Union or Separation* – which went through at least three editions by April 1799, Clark being Chaplain to the Prince of Wales; the same Clark's *The Rt. Hon. Mr. Foster's misconceptions and misstatements before the Irish House of Commons*, published in January 1800; and Dr John Gray's *Practical Observations on the proposed Treaty of Union*, published in the following March. The majority of these were pro-union.

Periodical literature has not been assessed because there were only three periodicals of significance, but caricatures are worthy of consideration.[59] The British Library Catalogue lists some 360 political caricatures published in London from 1797 to 1800, thirty-seven of which deal with the rebellion and the Union.[60] The proportion of Irish subjects may have been low but many of the images are extremely powerful. In 1798 the most striking images were produced by Gillray, who was then at his most active in attacking French republicanism in conjunction with Canning's *Anti-Jacobin Review*. The dominant theme of his caricatures in that year (and that of other artists) was the savagery of the rebels coupled with a pillorying of their misplaced faith in the support of the French who are portrayed as more interested in plunder than the advance of liberty. The Whigs are also lampooned for their patronage of rebels such as Fitzgerald and O'Connor.[61] In 1799–1800 Gillray produced fewer plates and the work of Rowlandson and Isaac Cruikshank is more notable on Irish subjects. Moreover their themes are different. Thus Pitt and the government are satirised for going to

[58] A comparatively rare unsolicited testimonial to the positive effect in Ireland of a speech made in the British parliament (Lord Minto's) can be found in NLS., Minto Mss. William Elliot to Lord Minto, 14 Aug. 1799.

[59] It is worth noting a change of tack by the *Annual Register*. The edition for 1798 contains no comment on Ireland. The 1799 edition prefaces a section on the Union debates with the view that it was agreed in 1782 that a new constitutional relationship would have to be formed between the two countries and that at the moment there was no 'unity of power' or 'unity of defence', 202–4. The 1800 edition, however, introduces a section on the Union debates in the Irish Parliament in 1799 and 1800 with the observation that 'self-continuance' or 'self-preservation' and a determination to retain 'a consciousness of identity' was the first 'law of nature' and particularly so in small nations. The author then suggests that popular anti-Unionism had been subdued by force of arms, 112–13.

[60] M. D. George, *British Museum Catalogue of Political and Personal Satires* (vol. vii, 1793–1800, London, 1942).

[61] Two examples are Gillray's 'Meeting of Unfortunate Citoyens', 12 May 1798 (BM 9205) and his 'United Irishmen Upon Duty', 12 June 1798 (BM 9228).

extraordinary lengths to secure the Union, while an impoverished 'Paddy' and a bemused 'John Bull' are depicted as equally unwilling bedfellows.[62] However, a notable feature of all the caricatures of this period is that there is no sympathetic treatment of the anti-Union cause in Ireland: any criticism of the measure is based on the probable unfortunate impact on Britain.

Finally, what did the newspapers say? Of all the media under discussion, these were the most widely read. Hannah Barker has shown that there were about twenty-six daily, tri-weekly and weekly newspapers published in London in the 1780s, with a readership of about 250,000 – that is, about one in three of the city's total population. Readers therefore included artisans and shopkeepers as well as some from lower down the social scale. In addition, there were at least fifty English provincial and largely bi-weekly newspapers in 1780 reaching another 500,000 readers, principally those living in the towns. Overall, she argues that the English press was very unusual in a European context in that it 'defined public opinion largely and overtly in political terms'.[63]

The research for this paper has concentrated on the immediate pre-Union period, from 1797 to 1800, and is based on a reading of five of the London dailies and twenty-six provincial newspapers from all parts of England as well as one from Scotland – that is, about one-third of the total number by that date. The London dailies chosen are fairly representative of the various shades of political opinion with the *Sun* and *True Briton*, which were subsidised by the government, representing the right wing, *The Times*, which had its government subsidy stopped in July 1799, and the *Morning Post*, the right of centre, and the *Morning Chronicle*, the Whig organ, the left wing. In the case of the provincial papers, the selection was more random being simply all those in the British Library's newspaper collection. However, these were published in all parts of England.

In general terms, all these newspapers are similar in that they consist of two pages of advertisements and two pages of news. Further, as far as news is concerned, there are two common features. The first is the dominance of the London press in determining much of the 'international' and 'national' copy of the provincial newspapers. The latter usually divided their news into separate columns distinguishing international and national matters from those of purely local interest – the national often being headed 'London'. Much of the non-local material was drawn from the London press. The second, not surprisingly, is the

[62] The best-known example is Cruikshank's 'An Irish Union' of 30 Jan. 1799 referred to above n. 54 (BM 9344).

[63] H. Barker, *Newspapers, Politics, and Public Opinion in Late Eighteenth Century England* (Oxford, 1998), *passim* but partic., 23, 111, 115 and 181 (for the quotation).

dominance of the war and the key domestic events that have been listed earlier and that were associated with it.[64] Most attention was paid to this extraordinary succession of crises, victories and defeats: in particular to the voluntary subscriptions to the war effort raised in the area of circulation. Column after column of the provincial newspapers contain the names and sums of money donated by village after village – some of the donations being no more than a penny-farthing. The dominance of the war effort is underlined by the *Sun*'s lengthy retrospectives on the principal events of 1798 and 1799. In these, the war and associated matters took up all but *two* sentences – those two being devoted, briefly, to the '98 rebellion and at rather more length, to the Union.[65] In general terms, the overwhelming impression created by reading all these newspapers – particularly the provincial newspapers – is of a nation under siege.

Nevertheless, there was considerable coverage of certain Irish matters in both the London and the provincial press. The rebellion attracted widespread notice: partly because of the sensational and usually grisly character of events; partly because of the ready supply of information from Dublin Castle, the *London Gazette*, the Irish press and various Irish correspondents;[66] and partly because of the involvement of British regular troops and the twenty-six volunteer militia regiments that were sent – especially if the newspaper concerned happened to circulate in one of the twenty-four widely scattered counties in England and Wales from which these were recruited.[67] Further, equal attention was paid to the debates on the Union in both the Irish and British Parliaments in 1799, with particularly fulsome reporting of the former. It was only after it became clear that the Irish Parliament would accept the Union that interest fell away, although there was pretty extensive reporting of the debates on the measure in the British Parliament in April 1800.

Overall, the allocation of space to Irish issues and the general way they were reported leads to the following general conclusions. First, there is much more space allocated to Irish affairs than to any other part of the empire, or for that matter, any part of England other than London and the area within the circulation of the newspaper concerned. There are very few references to the affairs of Wales, Scotland, Canada, the West Indies or India although it is interesting that there are notices of debates in the US Congress. Second, the way Irish affairs are

[64] See above p. 205.

[65] *The Sun*, 4 Jan. 1799, 2 Jan. 1800.

[66] The whiggish *Chester Chronicle* printed a remarkable series of columns from late 1798 to April 1799 under the heading 'Ireland. Private Letters'. They seem to have been written by one person who, to judge by the contents, was extremely well informed: see, for example, 25 Jan. 1799.

[67] *The Leeds Intelligencer*, 9 July 1798.

reported suggest that Ireland was seen as a 'sister kingdom', whose principal places and leading political figures would be reasonably well known to readers. Thus no editor seemed to think it necessary to explain the peculiar religious and commercial features of Belfast before commenting upon its politics; or to give an introduction justifying the importance of the views of John Foster. It is as if editors were preparing copy for well-informed readers to whom Wexford was as familiar as Glasgow – perhaps more so.

With regard to the views of these newspapers on Irish issues, the first point to make is that editorial comment is much more frequent, partisan, and fulsome in the London dailies than in the provincial press. In the majority of the last, it is either infrequent and muted, or absent. Further, there are clear cases of provincial newspapers following the lead of their London associates. It should also be borne in mind that there was a tradition of support in the right-wing British press for Irish Catholicism. Thus the principal authority on this subject, Professor Sack, shows how the newspapers which supported George III and Lord North in the 1770s called for a relaxation of Penal Laws against Irish Catholics, but the strictest enforcement of them against Irish dissenters, whom they saw as infected with republican and democratic principles. Sack refers to the 1790s as the 'anni mirabili' for the pro-Catholic right-wing press and argues that it was the publication in 1799 and 1801 of Musgrave's vivid description of Catholic atrocities during the rebellion which converted this section of the press to an anti-Catholic stance in the early nineteenth century. In this respect it is interesting that the government-sponsored *Sun* re-printed some of Musgrave's articles in the Irish press that appeared under his pseudonym, 'Camillus'.[68]

Sixteen of the sample of thirty-two newspapers supported the Union with an enthusiasm which ranged from the ardent to the moderate. Three, the *Sun*, *True Briton* and *The Times* were London dailies and the other thirteen consisted of twelve English provincial newspapers and the *Edinburgh Evening Courant*.[69] As far as editorial comment is concerned, a wide variety of opinions were expressed but, at the risk of over-simplification, they had the following narrative in common. The Irish Parliament was dominated by a selfish faction which some newspapers

[68] James J. Sack, *From Jacobite to Conservative. Reaction and orthodoxy in Britain c.1760–1832* (Cambridge University Press, 1993), 226–7, 240. For the evidence of Musgrave's articles in *The Sun*, B.L. Add. Mss. 35731 fo. 298, Musgrave to Lord Hardwicke, n.d. [? 1801].

[69] The twelve English pro-Union newspapers were: *Berrow's Worcester Journal*, *Coventry Mercury*, *Derby Mercury*, *Felix Farley's Bristol Journal* (4 Jan. 1800), *Hampshire Chronicle* (4 Feb. 1799), *Ipswich Journal*, *Jackson's Oxford Journal* (4 Feb. 1799, 3 Jan. 1801), *Kentish Gazette* (5 June, 3 July 1798, 22 Jan. 1799), *Leeds Mercury* (2, 9 Feb. 1799), *Leeds Intelligencer*, *Manchester Mercury* (15 Jan. 1799), *Portsmouth Gazette* (4 Feb. 1799). Material in the editions cited above support the content of this paragraph. Where no edition is cited, I have made a judgement based on the way the news was presented.

referred to repeatedly as 'Orangemen'. This faction had taken advantage of the 1782 settlement to feather its own nest, despite the fact that it was obvious that the British government of the day had never meant it to be a final settlement. It was these 'Orangemen' who were largely responsible for the rebellion, which was not a religious conflict but the result of the humble peasant being deluded by the false principles of the French Revolution. The incapacity of the Irish Parliament to debate issues rationally and dispassionately was demonstrated by the unruly behaviour that took place in the debates of January 1799. The Union was therefore bound to be beneficial to Ireland as a whole. It would be taken out of the hands of a narrow faction and brought under British protection. Catholic emancipation might follow. In addition, and in the words of *The Times*, it would consolidate 'our strength and resources' and lead to a 'long, successful and glorious resistance to the crimes, the rancour, and the ambition of the enemy'.[70] This, as we can see, bears a close resemblance to the line of the government in Parliament.

The London daily, *The Morning Chronicle*, and five provincial newspapers expressed various degrees of opposition to the Union with a narrative that in one particular respect was similar to that of the pro-Union press.[71] Thus all these papers were strongly critical of the faction that had for so long dominated the Irish Parliament by what they alleged were corrupt means. Thereafter, however, they had their own particular line. The principal cause of the rebellion, they argued, was not French principles but the avariciousness of landlords, middlemen and the system of land-tenure. Further, they all expressed varying degrees of criticism of the brutality of the British army, believing that conciliation, not coercion, was the answer. As for the Union, they believed that the majority in Ireland did not support the measure and that the Irish Parliament had been won over by corruption. The Union, they felt, would not conciliate Ireland in the short or medium term and was doomed to failure. In addition, some expressed the fear that the incoming Irish MPs would quickly become the lackeys of any party in power and therefore undermine further the 'balanced constitution'. Here again, the similarity with the Whig line in Parliament is notable.

Finally, the *Morning Post* and eight provincial papers were equivocal on the issue while one, the *Sussex Weekly Advertiser*, changed its mind.[72]

[70] *The Times*, 1 Jan. 1801.

[71] The five provincial anti-Union papers were: *Cambridge Intelligencer* (2 June 1798, 2 Feb. 1799), *Chester Chronicle* (8 June 1798), *Kentish Chronicle* (8 June 1798), *Newcastle Chronicle* (28 July, 11 Aug. 1798, 16 Feb. 1799), and *Sheffield Iris* (23 Feb., 2 Mar., 23 Nov. 1798). Material in the editions cited above support the content of this paragraph.

[72] The eight other papers are: *Bath Journal*, *Ipswich Journal*, *Lincoln, Rutland and Stamford Mercury*, *Northampton Mercury*, *Norwich Mercury*, *Nottingham Journal*, *Salopian Journal*, and *York Courant*.

The lines taken by the two named newspapers are worth adumbrating. The *Post*'s view in 1798 and 1799 was that Ireland and Britain were two different 'nations': that Ireland had been misgoverned but Pitt, the Whigs and John Foster were colluding to use the rebellion to crush liberties in both, and a Union could only be carried by corrupt methods.[73] However, in 1800 the editor offers no comment on the actual terms of the Union and spends all his time commenting on Bonaparte's Italian campaign. The *Sussex Advertiser* told its readers on 2 July 1798 that the Union was openly being talked of in Dublin as Cornwallis's principal policy (the first time, as far as I can tell, that it was mentioned in the English press). Later, on 21 January 1799, it took the view that the overbearing Irish aristocracy and the 'monopolising' Dublin Corporation would be forced to sell Ireland's independence as 'a nation' and bow to the 'fiat' of Pitt, the tyrant. The losers would be the broken Irish peasantry. However, once the debates on the Union had taken place, the editor began to wonder whether there would be some benefits and whether the anti-Unionists in Ireland were not being blinded by pride and prejudice.[74]

Thus, in addition to providing about 750,000 Englishmen and women with a substantial amount of information about the rebellion and the Union, and presenting it in a way that seems to have assumed that most would be familiar with the principal Irish places and politicians, the English press was almost wholly hostile to the Irish elite and largely supportive of the Union. Most editors in the provinces seem to have taken the view that given their existing masters in Ireland, the Irish, so to speak, had nothing to lose.

To sum up: the union was discussed at three different levels and in three somewhat different ways during a time when most of Britain was convinced it was under siege . Within the executive, the decision was made by the triumvirate, aided and abetted by about half-a-dozen other British politicians but no London-based bureaucrats. The threat of invasion and future war strategy played a much more prominent part in their decision than Bolton suggests, with all three having their own reasons for supporting a union. Contrary to the impression conveyed by Bolton, a substantial amount of time was taken in debating Irish matters in Parliament by a larger number of members than is usually referred to. Interpretations of history as well as party considerations were to the fore in the arguments put forward, but there was very infrequent reference to the specific strategic advantages related to the war which the triumvirate had in mind. Further, the print media, particularly the newspapers, gave three-quarters of a million readers a

[73] *The Morning Post*, 13 June 1798, 22 Jan. 1799, are good examples.

[74] *Sussex Weekly Advertiser; or Lewes Journal*, 28 Jan. 1800.

running commentary on the rebellion and a record of a substantial proportion of the debates in both parliaments. The weight of the opinions that were expressed were largely supportive of British policy, largely critical of the Protestant elite, and moderately sympathetic to the circumstances of Catholic Ireland. Once again, there was very little reference to specific security advantages. In short, the Irish question was discussed in three different but interconnected ways.

ALLIANCES AND MISALLIANCES IN THE POLITICS OF THE UNION

By L.M. Cullen

READ 9 SEPTEMBER 1999 AT THE QUEEN'S UNIVERSITY, BELFAST

THE Union has been little studied; its undoing on the other hand has been much debated. One reason for the contrast is of course that the Union was later seen by many as uncongenial; another was that the methods of securing it seemed on a universal telling clear cut: it was, or so it was said, achieved by corruption and was intensely unpopular. In Lecky's view, for instance, 'The measure was an English one, carried without a dissolution and by gross corruption, in opposition to the majority of the free constituencies and to the great preponderance of the unbribed intellect of Ireland.'[1]

The reality is that the story was much more complex. The politics of the Union was a case at national level of a misalliance, which lacked a real common purpose, and which projected its unconvincing nature to contemporaries themselves. There were cleavages in late eighteenth-century Ireland at the centre of both orthodox political opposition and government support. One of these divides was among Whigs. The decision to withdraw from parliament in May 1797 and to refuse to contest the general election was not shared, nor acted on, by all Whigs. In 1800, one section of the secessionist Whigs of 1797 was vehement in opposition to Union, and was able to draw some but not all of the other Whigs with them. Likewise the handpicked and hard-line government supporters who had made up the participants in the two secret committees of parliament in 1798 fractured: in essence the split was between those who felt that the protestant interest was best served by alliance with England and others who felt that the defeat of the rebels in 1798 proved the ability of protestants to defend themselves and to guide their own destinies without concessions to rebels or to London.

[1] Lecky, *History of Ireland*, vol. v, 422. There is in Lecky's writing a very evident tendency to magnify the significance and scale of hostility expressed against the Union. Thus, meetings in January 1800 against the Union were described by him as 'great', and as lacking a denominational character (ibid., pp. 353, 354). Large numbers signing petitions against the Union have been stressed by him, and by others, and Lecky claimed that except in Galway pro-Union supporters did not take the initiative in organising a county meeting (ibid. pp. 313, 314, 354).

The alliance against Union was one of reckless elements on both sides, an improbable combination of a confederacy of Whigs under the leadership of Grattan, Ponsonby and others who had self-destructed in 1797, and of a hard-line group of loyalists such as Foster and Downshire who put the domestic circumstances of Irish protestants ahead of either conciliation of rebels or the interests of Britain. Union itself apart, the secessionist Whigs of 1797 and the hard line protestants of 1799 had nothing in common: this was noted at the time by Drennan, for instance, and later by Barrington, but, though obvious to contemporaries, the incongruity has been too little recognised in modern writing. The numerous and overt associations of Whigs in 1797 and 1798 with United Irishmen, glossed over in Lecky and post-Lecky historiography, had added to their cumulative discredit. Likewise anti-unionists, however influential in Dublin and in narrow reaches of Louth, Down, Monaghan and Tyrone, were isolated from other committed loyalists like Lord Shannon or John Beresford who were closer to a central tradition of seeing Irish Protestant and English interests as converging.

This strange grouping of Whigs and loyalists has been turned in the historiography into a broad alliance against the government. Lecky argued that county members normally supported the government:[2] this, if true, would have given opposition by county members a special significance in 1799 or 1800. However the truth of the matter is that county members had frequently opposed the government, and it had been unlikely in any event that county politicians would lightly consent to the demise of the Irish parliament. The divide in the counties was more complex than a simple one of an abstract common stance on the Union, and often hinged not on broad national alliances or misalliances, but on responses to local circumstances. Roscommon, Down, Wexford, Tipperary, Armagh for instance represented such circumstances more than they did the straightforward Union issues which have been read into their politics.

Corruption was argued by the opposition to the Union, and while superficially plausible, the repetition of the mantra at the time reflected political weakness rather than the strength of the anti-union case. The anti-unionists lacked real staying power in 1800 and, after the vote on the Union resolutions in February, as even Lecky was forced to admit, opposition fell away.[3] Uncommitted political opinion in the country had doubted the good faith of the old Castle group, and was ready to lend support to the Cornwallis administration in finding common national ground. The political debate had already become unreal in 1797: the loyalist argument that the situation was so desperate that

[2] Ibid., p. 289.
[3] Ibid., p. 414.

measures beyond the law had become necessary as a declared policy rather than just the sordid connivance of government with low standards, and the Whig position that there was no problem except in so far as government measures created one, were both public stands for a narrow party political purpose.[4]

The Union has had a poor press. Indeed, even more, it has been assumed that because it proved a failure, the seeds of its future destruction were already sprouting in its seed-bed in its very first days. There is a contradiction at the heart of this. It means that if we accept that the Union was unpopular, the old Castle administration is vindicated. That is of course the position at the time of Barrington, and much later even of Lecky, whose Union thoughts are based on a series of unhistorical suppositions and on his own keenly felt concerns related to the politics of the 1880s.[5] The heroes of the opposition to the Union have at various points of time become so for unhistorical reasons. Barrington, Orangeman and opponent of Grattan, later regarding Grattan as a hero for his opposition to the Union, lamented that on his death he was buried in Westminster Abbey, not in Dublin.[6] Later still, those who opposed the Union have become national heroes to the left of the Irish political spectrum, as, for instance, Foster did in 1920 for Sinn Fein in Louth.[7] The suppression of the parliament became a

[4] The political thrust of the campaign against brutalities is reflected in an inability to enumerate the irregularities, and, even more pertinently, in an evident difficulty in using the evidence in court proceedings in the March assizes of 1798. Despite statements by Moira and by Sampson about thousands of cases, Moira in the House of Lords in England referred simply to 'upward of a hundred affidavits which I have brought down with me this day' (*Cobbett's Parliamentary History*, vol. XXXIII, 26 March). In the papers in Castleforbes there are a hundred affidavits relating to a single place in Donegal (I am grateful to Dr Anthony Malcomson for this information). It is hard to avoid assuming that this was all that Moira had to hand, that the sweeping statements had preceded the gathering of evidence, that its collection either began late or proceeded slowly, and that one of the problems in February and March was that the Whigs could not show their full hand for this very reason, only too aware that a public display of evidence confined to a single locality would weaken rather than strengthen their case. Tone had been quick to advert at the outset of March 1798 to the weaknesses of Moira's earlier and more general speech in Dublin in February (*Life of Theobald Wolfe Tone*, ed. T. Bartlett (Dublin, 1998), 827–9), from which in advance great things had been expected and which was intended to relaunch the general Whig campaign.

[5] The narrow and contemporary perspective of Lecky can be seen on the last page of the fifth volume of his *History of Ireland* where he reflected, with his own era in mind, on 'the folly of conferring political power, in the interests of any political theory or speculation, and of weakening those great pillars of social order, on which all true liberty and all real progress ultimately depend' (494).

[6] Jonah Barrington, *Personal sketches and recollections of his own times* (Glasgow, 1876), 187–90.

[7] I remember well as a young graduate student in Galway Liam O'Buachalla, professor of economics, speaking warmly of Foster and of his legacy to his descendants. As a young man Liam O'Buachalla collected money for Dail Eireann: he recalled in the mid-1950s

great tragic theme in Irish history. Barrington's writings and those put together with filial loyalty by Grattan's son are self-serving sources for this version of the Union. These themes were then further confirmed in the ranting of O'Connell, and in the deification of Grattan by Lecky. The praises of the parliament were later still sung by the arch nationalist ideologue Sigerson in his *Last Independent Parliament of Ireland.*

The case against Union at the end of the 1790s was made neither by a broad band of Irish society, nor by well-defined political categories: it came from smaller segments within wider categories of political society, both the more irresponsible or more highly politicised among Whigs (what we would to-day call professional politicians) and the more extreme loyalists. The loudest shouts were made by them; the most vigorous campaigns were made by them; if we make a head-count of pamphlet titles, a majority of pamphlets were anti-Union. However, it can be looked at differently. To Drennan, not hostile to Union, the pamphlet writing was that of 'pamphleteering barristers', discussing the issue 'without a spirit of hibernicism'.[8] Less-literary opposition in many parts of the country was muted; politicians who changed their minds were few, and not so much corrupt as weak figures, struggling to cope with local circumstances. There was little firm opposition outside Dublin and rather well-defined reaches of the north-east dominated by the hand of Foster or the nod of Downshire. The discrediting of the Whigs as a political force can be seen in the fact that in the Whig reaches of the country action was singularly ineffective. It is taken for granted that anti-Union feeling was strong among merchants in Dublin. A meeting of merchants which took a stand against the Union was chaired by David La Touche. Was David La Touche a merchant in any meaningful sense, had he ever been popular with merchants, and how much in common did La Touche have with merchants, or with how many merchants? That question can be answered, but this is not the place to do so. In any event, the meeting was summoned by the Corporation, which further reduces its mercantile character.

There are two central preliminary propositions which have to be taken into account. The first was that the existing Castle administration was already discredited.[9] It had never acted in the 1790s from a position of strength; its security policy was catastrophic, and the courts,

---

and proudly that he got a contribution from the Foster of the time who remarked that 'Dail Eireann must have money'. Whether the custodian of Mount Oriel made a donation by conviction or simply by prudence because a new order was in the making is another question.

[8] D.A. Chart, *The Drennan letters* (Belfast, 1931), 285.

[9] See L.M. Cullen, 'The politics of crisis and rebellion 1792–1798', in *Revolution, counter-revolution and Union: Ireland in the 1790s*, proceedings of 1998 Notre Dame conference forthcoming from Cambridge University Press, ed. J. Smyth.

imperfectly but effectively, upheld the rule of law amid circumstances in which the government forces could only intermittently and uncertainly interfere with it. There was powerful anti-government feeling in 1797, and many in the counties remained untainted by loyalist frenzy. Even after the rebellion, they held to their view that, while subversion was intended by the United Irishmen, the government itself had created much of the problem. The secret committees of both houses of parliament, which questioned the state prisoners in August, were a vital part of the effort by the loyalist interest in Dublin Castle to convince this powerful and critical constituency. The committees' reports were rushed into print widely and cheaply at the outset of September.

The ultras themselves were divided. The committees had been masterminded by Fitzgibbon, the law and order man of the Castle, and who more than any other man was eager to have a justification of its methods from admissions by rebels. He himself seems to have been the main questioner in the Lords; the Commons committee took its lead from the lords committee, being consciously guided by the line of questioning in the higher house, and the speaker, Foster, led the questioning in the lower committee. The superficial unity, however, quickly unravelled. Foster became an open opponent of Union. The general divide among old government supporters took months to be clearly identified, and can most conveniently be illustrated in the uncertainty of the Castle about the intentions of Downshire and in his gradual drift into open opposition or warfare. Fitzgibbon's own pro-Union position became more complex, as his soft line on an arrangement with state prisoners for *raison d'état*, did not reach to catholic concessions. Inevitably all this strengthened the hand of Cornwallis, and provided the basis for the advancement of the apparatchik politicians, Castlereagh, who made his name and career out of the Union negotiations, and the chameleon figure of Cooke, half-bureaucrat, half-politician.

Protestants have too often been seen as a single group. Hardy and Charlemont, for instance, have been seen as 'more or less anti-catholic' in the same way as figures such as Lords Enniskillen and Farnham were,[10] and Castlereagh and his father as reflecting 'the shift of the presbyterians towards conservatism'.[11] While to later generations of Protestants the Union may be summarised in the phrase that 'The promise of security for protestants largely explains the Anglo-Irish acquiescence in the act of Union',[12] at the time the dominant issues

[10] Bolton, *The passing of the Irish action of Union: a study in parliamentary politics* (Oxford, 1966), 140.

[11] Ibid., 135.

[12] Oliver MacDonagh, 'Introduction: Ireland and the act of Union 1801–70', in *New History of Ireland*, vol. v, ed. W. Vaughan (Oxford, 1989), liv.

were concrete ones: attitudes to the rebels, the Catholic question, and in Armagh at least assertion of the traditional independency of the county. Even those who favoured the Union were made up of politicians like Fitzgibbon opposed to concessions to Catholics, others who conceded the English government's central position and could accept change, and those already publicly committed, by past action or current views, to support of the Catholic question.

If the discredit of the Castle, its internal weakness, and the public division among its former denizens is the first preliminary proposition about Union politics, the second is the necessity to appreciate how strong was dislike of the old Castle clique in the countryside, and how in fact the rebellion of itself did not lead protestants to change their opinion. The argument that political apathy had reigned in 1797, and that a largely uncontested general election is a further proof of indifference, is of course widely held. So also is the argument that, as news came in of Wexford events, a unity of Protestants was created by reports of massacres. If we look at the reporting however, its credibility was dented by the fact that massacres had been reported even before they had occurred. The real events were reported slowly enough in Dublin and in both the Belfast and Scottish press, and their stressing was necessary precisely because the mind of the protestant, or at least of many protestants, had to be won over. The stressing in July and August, after some original lag in reporting, of the sectarian elements of the rebellion in Wexford was part of a desperate effort to win favour for the old regime and to draw the unconvinced out of their skeptical position. So were the allegations which peaked in September of a divide between the Defenders and United Irish men in the north. All formed part of a thrust which included the rushing of the committees' reports into print.

To understand all this, it is necessary to go back to the politics of 1797. The county meetings organised by Whigs in April and May 1797 had once more spelled out widespread opposition to government policy, even in Armagh, the county where almost two years earlier the Orange Order had been born. Government desperation, culminating in the inclusion in the proclamation of 17 May of powers to ban further meetings by the use of military force and in the speedy issue of orders by the commander-in-chief to his troops the following day, could have had a high political cost. It was saved only by the actions of its opponents. On 15 May the Irish Whigs – or at any rate Grattan at 5.30 a.m. on the 16th – had decided in protest to withdraw from politics. This also entailed a decision not to contest the election, a decision which, contrary to what is usually said preceded the decision by Charles Fox (itself, unlike the Irish decision a purely personal one and not a party one). As a result the government did not face in the general election the sustained challenge that it had greatly feared, and it hastened rather than deferred, as it had first thought of doing, the holding of the election. A fall in the number of registered electors in some instances is not due to apathy, as so often suggested: radical Whigs chose not to register their freeholders. That explains a mere 300 voters in Kildare, and in Wexford, the largest interest, Cornelius Grogan, had registered a bare 19 freeholders.[13] The government were down-faced with some defiance in Dublin, even without the radicals contesting the election. A public meeting was held on the eve of the poll, ringed by troops who dared not intervene to prohibit it, despite defiance of the terms of the proclamation 1797. Lame public statements at the time about the popularity of the two indifferent candidates, John Claudius Beresford and Arthur Wolfe, reflected the loyalist weakness (the contemporary rumour of a Foster candidacy itself had illustrated the Dublin desperation). The Whig policy of withdrawal, though far from popular with all Whigs, usually prevailed in Whiggish strongholds. Dublin itself is the best example of that. Outside Dublin, the radicals prevailed over the wishes of the moderates in the two bastions of Kildare and Antrim, precisely because of the closeness of the links between Whigs and United Irishmen: a candidate had wanted to context the election in Kildare, and a candidate withdrew early in the poll in Antrim. In Wexford, the Whigs divided, in part because of the peculiar allure Mountnorris had for the propertied Catholics on his own estate and in part because north-county Whigs, in contrast to south-county Whigs, did not stand aside from the contest, and backed Mountnorris's candidate.

Anti-government feeling remained widespread, and is made to vanish in modern accounts only through the false premise of electoral apathy. Liberal gentry also stood up to the pressures on them to get rid of the catholic members of their yeomanry corps. The argument that magistrates were supine was a catchword of loyalists who wanted activist partisanship. Those who ran to the towns were not the magistrates at large, but loyalist figures of rabid political disposition. Far from the prospect of rebellion generating a general fear among protestants at large, it divided protestants even further. Moreover, and ironically because of the alleged fears of 1797 and 1798, it was precisely the ultras, alleging a United Irishman reign of terror and favouring hard line methods who, after the rebellion, least feared the challenge of ruling an island of murderous papists.

On both these fronts – Union and catholic rights – there was a divide. It was very clear in parliament. In 1799 amid the Union politics of the year, the debate on Judkin Fitzgerald and the methods he

[13] Bolton, *Union*, 153; PRONI, McPeake papers.

employed in Tipperary in 1798 became the central issue for a time in the spring. It commanded much attention in the press, and raised the whole question of the legitimacy of the methods pursued by the old government. In January 1800, Arthur Browne, a liberal of the 1790s and an opponent of the Union at the outset of 1799, instancing the circumstances of Tipperary, and the indemnification of Fitzgerald, asserted his personal change of opinion:

> Had I seen, after the rejection of the Union last year, any measures brought forward to conciliate the people, to heal the distractions of the country, had I seen any reminiscences of that spirit, which produced the constitution of 1782, coming forward to preserve it, I should not have listened to proposals of Union, nor would you have again heard them now ... Because then the parliament had the warm affection of the nation, now it has not.[14]

The Union, when not seen as a historic injustice, has sometimes been studied as a Namierite exercise. One of the striking things about Bolton's book, in itself, especially for its time, a highly competent study of the politics of the Union, is that the rebellion scarcely occurs as a theme. It does not feature in the chapter headings, and in the index it obtrudes in a mere six entries. The rather good passages on pp. 57–61 seem to have no effect on the general analysis. The Catholic question, Catholic emancipation so called, is overemphasised: pro-Union support is represented as a mechanistic response based on the presence of a Catholic vote summoned into existence in 1793. In comments on this paper at the conference on the Union in Belfast last year, several speakers said that its approach was itself Namierite, emphasising the political interests and calculation of politicians. That may be. However, there is a difference. Political outlook had been greatly influenced by Volunteering and by the divides in Volunteering which opened up in the 1780s, and the issues raised at the time were even more central to public life in the 1790s. There was an active public opinion, of which politicians had to take account, and the responses of politicians were not simple ones of calculating political advantage, and even less of responding like autonomons to either catholic voters or to the spectre of them. The question – and the challenge – remains as to what extent a 'popular' political opinion existed or can be measured. Moreover, at gentry level itself, the county divides of the 1790s had antecedents, and one of these – Volunteering – had raised questions of principle as well as of immediate advantage.

There are three questions which have to be adverted to. The first is that opposition by politicians to the Union has to be recognised as

[14] Bolton, *Union*, 172.

representing by its nature an impossible and untenable alliance. The second is that there are real difficulties as to how meaningfully to measure opposition. The third is that within constituencies the catholic question reflects more than the question of catholic emancipation, *tout court*.

First, there was nothing in common between the groups which made up the anti-Union alliance. The extreme example of this is of course the series of meetings taking place in Charlemont House, with Downshire in the chair, to orchestrate opposition to the Union. The incongruity of this was a fundamental weakness of the anti-Union case. While some historians have seen a relative absence of county meetings as reflecting the weakness of the pro-Union side, the fact is that a demand for meetings was not greatly in evidence on either side. In a sense that is surprising because they had acquired a new momentum from 1782–3 onwards. However, there is a reason. The proclamation of 17 May 1797, one of whose principal clauses was intended to halt the gathering pace of the Whig-inspired campaign of public meetings, and which was later used in February–March 1798 by Castle politicians in a confrontation with the commander-in-chief to embarrass Abercromby who had assumed that it had lapsed, had not been revoked. Force was displayed to overawe a proposal of a King's County meeting in 1799, ironically a repetition of the pattern in 1797 of interference, even before the proclamation of 17 May had been issued, by the high sheriff in the King's County meeting.[15] Drennan speculated on the legality of the Downshire-inspired meeting of January 1800.[16] County meetings presented novel problems; quite apart from the danger of meetings highlighting local divisions of opinion, the side opposed to government was, given the proclamation of May 1797, at a tactical disadvantage, and in 1799–1800 as in 1797 government was prepared to turn a blind eye to meetings whose outcome was likely to favour it.

Secondly, the question remains of weighing the strength of opinion for and against the Union. The merits of grand jury resolutions, county meetings, and petitions sighed by people were discussed by Bolton. The import of petitions is sometimes doubtful, as it was possible to have conflicting petitions in a county. Some counties, as Bolton observed, had no petition at all: Antrim, Kerry, Waterford, and Londonderry.[17]

[15] The attempted meeting in May 1797 was reported in the press; on the May 1799 event see Bolton, *Union*, 188. See also Sir Jonah Barrington, *Personal sketches*, 270. In King's county, the events reflected also the longstanding government effort to contain Whig dominance of the county's politics, and had also been coloured by the county's Volunteering politics: King's County alone of Leinster counties maintained in the 1780s a county review of Volunteers, one attended, moreover, by Whig politicians.

[16] Chart, *Drennan letters*, 298.

[17] Bolton, *Union*, 156.

Overall, petitions favouring the measure came in from nineteen counties. From these counties came 23 of 26 Unionist MPs; on the other hand, 23 of 38 anti-Unionist MPs represented counties from which no Unionist petition came. On this basis, in compressed arithmetic, he assumed that 'It seems reasonable to assume that a minority of articulate public opinion favoured the Union, a rather larger group, perhaps half as many again, opposed the measure and the rest were apathetic.'[18] At the time both sides professed that they had support for their view. Thus Edgeworth claimed that 28 of 32 counties, and 38 of 64 county members declared against the Union.[19] Government supporters had a different view, and Castlereagh was of course to state with confidence on 5 February 1800 that 'the property of those, who have declared in favour of it in the two Houses of Parliament, is in comparison with those who oppose it, nearly in the proportion of three to one; nineteen counties, whose superficial contents form five-sevenths of the island, have come forward in its support'.[20]

The third point is the complex pattern of constituency politics. We can advance our understanding somewhat if we look at the counties which had two county members voting against the Union in 1799. In thirteen counties two members had opposed the Union.[21] In seven counties they had supported the Union. However the position in the opposition counties is varied. First, there is a bias to the northern half of the country, and to counties which had assumed a distinctly hard-line profile throughout the 1790s. Second, the counties were far from homogeneous: Kings, Wicklow, Carlow and Armagh reflected Whig dominance, Roscommon had a sharp internal divide in its politics, and Donegal was both Whiggish and outside the mainstream of politics.

The pattern in some counties, whether returning two members against the Union or having a divided representation, was very complex. Armagh is the outstanding instance, because despite its proximity to the anti-Union politics of west Down and Tyrone and the fact that the Orange Order had been started there, its politics were older. They were driven not by Protestantism, but by the tradition of independence (an attitude strengthened by the county's prominence in Volunteering): it was this spirit which prevailed in the alliances which in 1799 left Gosford, the *eminence grise* of government politics in the county, on the other side of the political fence. The fact that in 1799 both Roscommon members voted against the Union conceals the divides separating the

[18] This conclusion has been accepted by McDowell in, 'Revolution and the Union, 1794–1800', in *New History of Ireland*, vol. IV, *Eighteenth-century Ireland*, ed. T.W. Moody and W.E. Vaughan, 368.

[19] Bolton, *Union*, 151.

[20] *The speech of the Rt. Hon. Lord Viscount Castlereagh, 5 Feb.* (Dublin, 1800), 5.

[21] Bolton, *Union*, pp. 129n., 130n.

two men. With his mechanistic explanation, Bolton accounted for this in terms of a failing Catholic power: 'where, as in Roscommon, their reaction was more tardy or divided, the Unionists failed to make their expected gains'.[22] Roscommon, of course, had long been polarised on the Catholic issue, with one faction favouring hard line opposition to Catholic rights and brutal repression of Defender unrest. Even Bolton conceded that 'Camden commented on the illiberality of the Roscommon landlords'.[23] To the point in illustrating the anti-Catholic animus was Lord Dillon, who though a cretinous supporter of establishment, was an assiduous questioner in the Lords secret committee.[24] There is also the fear of intimidation adverted to by Myles Keon in collecting signatures.[25] However, the politics of the county were less catholic politics than the politics of two groups, the King and French interests. Both members had voted against the Union, but their relationships with Catholics was entirely different. While both grand jury and county meeting had adopted an anti-unionist posture,[26] the fact that 11 out of 23 favoured Union pointed to a sharp divide which augured badly for the more marginal politicians. Mahon shifted from opposition on the Union in 1799 as a borough member into support when sitting in early 1800 as a fresh county replacement for King, and then back to opposition. He finally withdrew from the house after opposing the Union in the vote in February 1800 in order to avoid offending constituents by opposing the subsequent votes anticipated.[27]

In Tipperary, shifts by John Bagwell, a county member, represented not only local political circumstances but the row over law and order in the county made topical by the parliamentary debates in 1799 on Judkin Fitzgerald's irregularities. Bagwell was at this stage anti-unionist: however in April 1799 in the debates in parliament he had already taken care not to be seen as supporting Fitzgerald (a stance in which he was supported by another Bagwell, both from the family associated with the sectarian violence of thirty years previously in the 1760s).[28] A county meeting in August 1799 routed the anti-Unionists. Aware of pro-Union opinion in the county, he then shifted to favour the Union; later, in the face of resolutions from anti-Unionists in the north of the county and gaining little personal backing in the south of the county,

[22] Ibid., 154.
[23] Ibid., 147.
[24] On Dillon, see a slightly later comment from *Memoirs and correspondence of Viscount Castlereagh*, ed. Charles Vane, marquess of Londonderry, iv, 32.
[25] *Castlereagh corr.*, vol. III, p. 223.
[26] Bolton, *Union*, 148.
[27] Ibid., pp. 147, 168.
[28] *The trial of T.J. Fitzgerald ... with the proceedings in parliament ...* (Dublin, 1799). R.I.A., Halliday pamphlets, vol. 785.

he slipped into opposition in February 1800. Lord Donoughmore had observed that the outlook of some was more motivated by an anti-Bagwell stance than by Union politics.[29] One can also recall readily the scornful words of Edmund Burke years earlier on Bagwell.

The politics of January and February 1800 actually pointed to a weakening anti-Unionist position. There was a flurry of opposition at the outset of 1800: a crescendo or more accurately a damp squib building up to the first vote of 1800 which occurred on 5 February. Three counties were at the centre of this episode, Roscommon, Tipperary and Carlow. The shifts of Mahon and Bagwell in Roscommon and Tipperary respectively, reversing anti-Unionist stances into a pro-Union one, then back into opposition at the outset of February, was due to pressure brought to bear, with a crucial vote in the offing, on two politicians who held a marginal place in county politics.

In Carlow events were closely linked to Lord Downshire's unsuccessful agitation in Down by the authorising by Downshire of signatures among his Co. Down militia, at the time stationed in Co. Carlow, the sole county of south Leinster in which the Orange Order implanted itself strongly. Whig politics had fractured in the county in the 1797 Whig shenanigans. Burton, the leading Whig in the county, dissented from the Ponsonby-Grattan line, on withdrawal from politics; moreover, though a whig stronghold, the county gentry moved firmly to the right on law and order in 1797, and Carlow was one of the few counties in which a county meeting in 1797 took a pro-government line, a fact soon reflected both in Orange organisation and in magistrate activism. The county had a tense general election in 1797, and a stormy grand jury session in March 1798, poisoned by a duel between Sir Edward Crosbie and Burton's son. However, the Burtons at least were strongly anti-Union, and the presence of Downshire's regiment in Carlow can only have added to a curious blending of Whig and Downshire views, and to a heady sense of opposition to Union at the end of 1799. The other county member elected in 1797, Sir Richard Butler, did not have a strong family base, a fact which explains why he opted for a pro-Union line at first, and then buckled under pressure in January. A circular had been sent out on 20 January from Lord Charlemont's house, under the names of Downshire, Charlemont and W.B. Ponsonby to stimulate a wave of anti-Union petitions.[30] Issued at this late stage it was a manoeuvre of desperation. Downshire, who in 1797 acted swiftly to prevent a Down county meeting, was not only reversing his stance, but in his own county summoning a meeting which was as illegal as the meeting he had prevented in 1797. The meeting took place at a

[29] Bolton, *Union*, 149.
[30] Ibid., 187.

mere week's notice. It gave birth to a petition, and, desperate for signatures, he was reduced to canvassing in his regiment, which would provide 600 or 700 captive signatures.[31] The contradictory evidence of the arithmetic of signatures to the petition itself hints at weakness.[32] The opposition in his own county to Downshire was formidable, including the improbable combination – another of the strange alliances of Union politics – of Lord Londonderry and the Whig bishop of Down.[33]

If Down provided a significant instance of the ineffectiveness of anti-Union agitation, Wexford provided an other example. Though the campaign there unlike the one in Roscommon, Tipperary or Down was driven by a liberal circle around Carew and Alcock in the north of the county, it came to nothing. The person writing to Castlereagh warning of the manoeuvres in the county was no less than James Gordon, wrongly identified by both the editor of the Castlereagh papers and by Bolton as a gentleman. He was of course the celebrated clergyman, sympathetic to Catholics and a supporter of the Cornwallis line.

> I took the liberty, a few days ago, to give you an instance, in the address of Mr Carew's tenantry, how little the public opinion can be readily known by such addresses. The most respectable Protestants here have refused signing it, though they may suffer the enmity of Mr Carew and his Romanist agents ... Another petition is going about of the same nature; and wretches, who had signed in favour of a Union before, are now, for fear of their landlord, signing against it.[34]

Bolton overrated the anti-Union manoeuvres of January and February. He did not give much prominence to the political destruction of Downshire which was under way, and to the reassertion of the liberal faction, aided by improbable allies, in the traditional fashion of county Down politics against its arch-enemy. In the case of Roscommon and Tipperary, he went so far as saying that 'in the last two counties government complacency had underrated the effect of the last-minute petitioning campaign by the anti-unionists'.[35] In emphasising the firmness of Cornwallis's action, he chose to see it as halting 'further deterioration in the government's parliamentary situation'.[36] The three members who changed their stance were marginal figures in the politics

[31] *Castlereagh corr.*, vol. III, 233; Bolton, *Union*, 189.
[32] Bolton, *Union*, 188n.
[33] Ibid., 188.
[34] Bora Lodge, near Enniscorthy, 31 Jan. 1800, *Castlereagh corr.*, vol. III, 229.
[35] Bolton, *Union*, 190.
[36] Ibid., 192.

of their counties, two of them Mahon and Bagwell, lightweight and discredited figures respectively, and the third, Sir Richard Butler, was somewhat in the same position if he was to turn his circumstances of 1797 to greater advantage. He was in the same position as Robert Camden Cope, whose family for decades had lacked sufficient backing to gain a county seat, and for whom the government side seemed tempting in 1800. The pressures in Tipperary and Roscommon, Wexford and Down and more obscurely in Carlow where Downshire's regiment was stationed, arose from this last fling. In Tipperary, Lord Landaff reported on emissaries in the county, seeking out 'to obtain signatures to another counter address from every hole and corner'. The pro-Union address however, as Landaff said, 'stands in so respectable a light, supported by almost all the estated interest in the county, by the personal appearance of the gentlemen at the meeting, property convened (upwards of £300,000 per annum landed property in that county being present), and, on the other side, excepting Lords Mount-cashel and Lismore, representatives of the Ponsonby family, no property of any consideration'.[37]

Armagh is one of the key constituencies in contradicting the facile model of fears as the driving force of Protestants. The county's behaviour in 1799 was consistent with its lofty sense of independence, and the repute of the shining white knights, Brownlow, Richardson and the first Lord Charlemont, of its politics of the 1780s. The county's politics had been coloured more than those of any other county by the breach over the Volunteers. It was the only rural region in which after 1783 a body of gentry and Anglicans backed the continuance of the Volunteers. If that created at one level a divide between pro-and anti-Volunteer gentry, it resulted at another level in a growing embitterment between deep radicals (who had followed the earl Bishop of Bristol in 1783) and the gentry-led moderate or Charlemont-Brownlow volunteers.[38] So sharp was the divide that in late 1783, as Charlemont later recalled, in passing through Armagh on the way back from the November convention in Dublin, the earl bishop and 'his drunken companions had the impudence to insinuate something which was deemed disrespectful, they were saluted with a volley of stones, and the populace was with difficulty restrained from farther mischief'.[39] However, a year later, Blackhall, agent of the Cope estate, not only revived the Loughgall Volunteer corps, but dallied with radical issues. Volunteer politics proved far more of a problem for Charlemont in his home county than

[37] *Castlereagh corr.*, vol. III, 228.

[38] Cullen, 'The United Irishmen: problems and issues of the 1790s', *The Turbulent decade: Ulster in the 1790s, Ulster local studies*, vol. 18, no. 2 (Spring 1997), 7–27.

[39] HMC, Charlemont Mss, vol. I, p. 134.

in Down, Antrim or Derry, where the internal fractures in surviving volunteering were fewer. If the Armagh city reviews seem to have fallen by the way side in the 1780s (members of surviving corps going to the reviews in Newry or Belfast), they were revived late in the decade, when efforts by the government interest in the county to discredit the Volunteers by arguing that resort to the terms of the 1787 Police Act would make volunteering redundant, actually led to the revival of parading variously by new and revived corps, and finally to the flourish of a large review in Armagh city in the summer of 1791.[40] The impetus for the recovery was radical, and groups in seven parishes were radical enough as late as 1793, in the face of universal gentry disavowal of the Dungannon Convention of 1793, to elect representatives.

However, a revival, unique in its occurrence in a largely Anglican as well as a rural community, was solidly on the side of the Established Church: modern commentary has had difficulty in coping with the concept of being both politically radical and solidly attached to a Protestant constitution. Already alienated from the more advanced radicals, Charlemont and the grand jury now incurred opprobrium in their effort to steer a middle course in 1788 on sectarian tensions in the county. These tensions soon helped conservatives to achieve a quite unique outcome to faction in freemasonry politics in the county in 1792. At one level, they helped to lay the basis for the rise of the Orange Order. At another level, they began to leave the Charlemont–Brownlow interest increasingly isolated in the county, losing support on both the right and left of the centre. The consequence was that when Brownlow junior ran for the county in January 1795, Robert Camden Cope was able to make a formidable bid for the county seat, losing by a mere 80 votes in a contest which took a month. So poor was the image of Brownlow and Charlemont that the *Northern Star*, instead of

[40] There is no evidence of the admission of Catholics into Volunteer units in Armagh in the 1780s, or that the declaration of the Loughgall Volunteers in October 1784, had any practical outcome. Parading by Volunteer units caused offence not because Catholics were either excluded or had their Volunteer firearms seized, but because, however radical the impetus to the reactivation of Volunteering, revival anachronistically advertised a public activity which was confined to Protestants: hence the emphasis by Catholics on also assembling and on parading, and the importance assumed by privately held firearms either as an assertion of effective equality or, in the eyes of others, as a blatant violation of the law. The terms of Grand Jury resolutions, the pastoral letter in 1788 by the Roman Catholic primate, O'Reilly, and the letters of the Presbyterian clergyman Campbell and Anglican clergyman Hudson to Charlemont, are instructive on the underlying issues. William Campbell's letter of 10 August 1788 to Rev. Benjamin McDowell, Dublin, is particularly informative (see PRONI, 'Extracts from the Bruce letters, N.L.I.'). The urge to activate Volunteer corps was entirely political; the argument that landlords valued the Volunteers as a defence force is contradicted by the opposition of conservative gentry and clergy to them, and by the eagerness even of the gentry supporters of volunteering that Volunteers should maintain a low and unprovocative profile.

supporting Brownlow, put Cope and Brownlow on a par, counselling people against involvement in electoral contests, advice which could only advantage the weaker party, Cope.[41] Pitching for the support of the paper's radical readers, Cope advertised his candidature in it, and a notice also appeared from him formally denying rumours which had been circulated.[42] Cope shrewdly had secured in advance the backing of Acheson (whose own son was under age, and whose political future could only be helped by the defeat of Brownlow), and the weakness of Brownlow's appeal for radicals, combined with support from Gosford, meant that Cope just failed to take the seat.

The novel situation – the dramatic fall from grace of Brownlow – resulted in unprecedented politicking over the next two years with the 1797 general election in prospect.[43] In April 1797, at the county meeting, through electoral calculation few wanted to oppose the radical position: in a three-way split, the radical resolution carried the day against both Caulfield and Gosford resolutions. Despite the government wish to avoid contests as far as possible,[44] a solid contest seemed in prospect in the general election between Acheson, Caulfield, Richardson and Cope. The latter two candidates withdrew early in the contest, given the lead taken by the other candidates.[45] The partisan role of the high sheriff (brother-in-law to Acheson), Richardson's reluctance to spend money, and what Charlemont described as 'apathy' (but a term which in 1797 could have many connotations) all played a part in the story.[46] Whig opposition in the April meeting to the radical motion and Whig readiness to participate in the election contrasted with the emerging and quite open alliance of United men and Whigs in Leinster in favour of an abstentionist policy there. The general lack of gentry sympathies with the United Irishman in Armagh (in contrast to the position taken up by many Whigs elsewhere) may help not only to explain why the county avoided serious trouble in 1798, but also why its upper classes had a cohesiveness in 1798 which was lacking in Leinster or even in

[41] See *Northern Star*, 'A card', 15–18 Dec. 1794; 'An old Whig', 18/22 Dec. 1794; address 'to an Armagh freeholder', 22–26 Dec. 1794; and an item on 22–26 Jan. 1795.

[42] The *Northern Star* carried Cope's address throughout November, December and January. The issue of 29 Dec.–1 Jan. 1995 carried Cope's reply to a rumour, and he called for support 'against a combination of interests that threatened the independence of this county'.

[43] Scattered letters from Dalrymple, the general in charge of east Ulster, in the Pelham papers, have some comments on the politicking and its unhelpful effects.

[44] In Wicklow on the other hand against the hated Fitzwilliam interest the government persisted suicidally in opposition to the point of an embarrassing withdrawal on the morning of the opening of the hustings.

[45] For details of the poll, I am indebted to my former student Ms Deirdre Lindsey.

[46] See PRONI, letters from Charlemont to Stewart, Cookstown, 13 July and 10 August 1797, 1/67, 1/68, for some interesting comments.

adjacent Down. That explains in turn why a degree of common ground could be found on an anti-Union stance:[47] Gosford, the leader of the government interest in the county, was in effect isolated in 1799, as indeed was the traditional county interest itself, and Cope, by running as an anti-Unionist, this time swung his narrow defeat in the 1795 by-election in the county into a victory. The high politics of Armagh, *pace* the *Northern Star* and its caustic comments in the mid-1790s, displayed some of their traditional character, and neither the Orange Order nor the government interest played the central role they did in the conflict in the high politics of neighbouring Down.

Wexford, cockpit and bloodbath of rebellion, is equally and perhaps still more apposite in illustrating the dangers of falling into a simple explanation. Catholics were not automatically in favour of Union, nor did Protestants, in the county in which Protestant loss of life had been largest, necessarily share any of the views of George Ogle, in bitter exile in Dublin. He had feared to face the Wexford electorate in 1797, and his progressive discrediting over the 1790s represented the weakness of the government interest in the county. Stances on the Union repeated those in the general election in 1797. In 1797 the Whig interests in the north of the county, in defiance of the Grattanite call, had lent their support actively to Mountnorris's candidate. The radical southern Whigs, *hors de combat* through the Whig call to abstain from politics, gave their interest passively to one of the candidates or split their vote; in any event, Grogan, the county's largest landowner, did not register his tenants. Two years later the north county Whig gentry, who had participated in the election in 1797, opposed the Union; the southern gentry seem to have favoured Union. Among loyalists, Ely – whose political interest had fared well in the general election of 1797 simply because of the divides among the opposition – could not afford to adopt an anti-Union line if he wished to turn his chance good fortune in the general election into a permanent constituency inheritance. He maintained ties with Catholics. Remarkably, as early as July 1798, he had supported Philip Hay at his trial. Years later George Kingston in his vendetta against Hay was reduced to referring lamely but inaccurately to Ely, 'who though for the only time in his life opposed his interest to those of the loyalists of Ireland'.[48]

[47] See PRONI, D3030/1028, mxxviii, October 1799. The calculations in this document suggest a majority were pro-Union; however, a large number were undecided, and the election in the same month suggests that the assessment was rather optimistic from a government point of view.

[48] *A narrative of the proceedings of the commissioners of suffering loyalists in the case of captain Philip Hay, with remarks thereon by George, earl of Kingston* (Dublin, 1808), 3. However, he put forward a Catholic petition from New Ross in 1799, and he had correspondence with Caulfield, the Roman Catholic bishop of Ferns.

Gordon, himself a liberal partisan and not the middle-of-the-road man that Lecky took him to be, observed:

> The protestants, as far as I have had an opportunity of knowing it (and I took much pains), are in general in favour of the Union and if the measure could be carried, would almost universally acquiesce in it.

Fear does not appear to have been the calculus, nor opposition to emancipation (though undoubtedly and with ample reason many like Gordon himself would without a Union, be fearful of Romanist or demagogic rule). The liberal interest in the county had been strengthening over the 1790s as Ogle's betrayal of his old ideals and ever closer identification with government destroyed his former standing in the county. His rivals from old Volunteer activity, radical in politics and sympathetic to the Catholics, grew in status. While moderate Whigs contested the election in the sense of throwing their active backing behind Mountnorris's candidate, only the passive electoral profile in 1797 of the more radical Colcloughs and Grogan block made possible the success of Lord Ely's party, who, even if borough-rich, had only the modest acres in the county of the Tottenham and Loftus families to help Ely's minions win the two prestige county seats. Hence, the practical problems of Ely in 1799: where did the future interest of the family lie: in pleasing the anti-union Whigs or backing government? The electoral upshot of Ely's uncertain and short lived ascendancy was that a Whig interest was restored in the county for almost twenty years. Of course, a Whig revival brought its old divides with it: the famous and tragic duel between Alcock and Colclough in 1807 reflects less bad blood individually than bitterness that grew out of the 1797 electoral divide among Whigs. What has to be stressed is that Wexford politics were surprisingly unaffected by the rebellion: the leading interests had been liberal in the 1790s, and their new grip of politics faltered only in the 1820s. Cloney's pamphlet in 1832 was not a history of the rebellion, but a recital of Whig politics in the county, part of an effort both to restore Whig dominance, and to bring it under the banners of repeal.[49] It touched on the rebellion at some length, but primarily in terms of Cloney's own role, and as a rebuttal of attempts by hardliners to revive the memories of the ambiguous past of a man who was not only a prominent partisan of the policy but for a while in the wake of the 1829 emancipation act a possible candidate.

An effective Catholic vote in the form of registered freeholders emerged slowly, and its importance in county politics was often late or

[49] T. Cloney, *A narrative of those transactions in the county of Wexford in which the author was engaged* ... (Dublin, 1832).

varied, as Peter Jupp showed many years ago.[50] Within counties, the key issues in the 1790s were not new voters, but the existing and known sympathies of politicians. The Union was relevant in Co. Roscommon by introducing an extra-county divide to further complicate existing politics. The French family had always been supporters of the Catholics. They had in the past provided postal franks to Charles O'Conor and his friends for instance. Outside intervention was necessary to detach Catholics from French: this is the point of the observation by Altamont, friend of both government and Catholics in neighbouring Mayo, who had told Castlereagh as early as March 1799 that 'if you will give me the *least assistance*, I will shake Roscommon'.[51] The Myles Keon petition, got up by a Catholic activist from neighbouring Leitrim, was the form that interference took.

In fact, the ultras worked well only in Dublin and in a swathe of landlord dominated society from Louth through Down to Tyrone, a phenomenon which the shrewd John Beresford recognised. They could not reach adjacent Armagh or distant Wexford. The anti-Unionist foray in January and February 1800 into the politics of several counties was a desperate last fling, and while it turned the heads or votes of four known vulnerable members, in overall terms it had no consequence on parliamentary arithmetic. Dublin borough alone was the constituency in which the politics of 1797 and 1800 made permanent inroads. The Whig withdrawal in 1797 ceded the day to government politicians and to their creation of a firm base in the capital: it nullified the advances associated with Travers Hartley's election in the by-election in 1782 or the great triumph of Grattan and Henry Fitzgerald in 1790. The defeat of the Whigs was all the greater because of their close identification with the United Irishmen; their withdrawal from the election advertised the influence of their dubious associates, and if anyone entertained doubts about the alliance, they had only to recall the Whig faces standing beside United Irishmen at the meeting on the eve of the general election. For the next forty years politics was dominated by a new and loyalist interest (with some La Touche and Guinness trafficking in a pretence of Catholic sympathies), even if the failure of Ogle to be elected in 1802 showed that an overtly anti-catholic posture was not good electoral politics.

The assumption that the Union was unpopular has informed all study. The scheming of January–February 1800 however was a pale reflection of past politicking, and lacked the momentum that the great

[50] P. Jupp, 'Irish parliamentary elections and the influence of the catholic vote', *Historical Journal*, vol. x (1967). Bolton himself, despite his emphasis on the Catholic vote, came close to making this point at one stage (*Union*, 34).

[51] Bolton, *Union*, 147.

Whig meetings of 1797 had threatened to hold. In other words, whatever the strength of the parliamentary position of the anti-unionists (and the opposition to the Union had both numbers and talent), the call to public opinion was its weakest arm. The weakness of the anti-Union campaign lay not only in the very nature of the coalition, but was compounded by isolation from their fellows within each of the two coalition components. The violent loyalists of Dublin, Louth and Downshire districts were isolated from much Protestant opinion. The significance of the 86 or so members who supported Catholic relief in 1795 has been underplayed. At that time, anti-Catholic opinion had to dismiss its significance by suggesting that it was merely the consequence of promises in the past to a now-discredited lord-lieutenant (though if this were true, against all Namierite concepts of political behaviour, politicians would emerge as faithful to past undertakings in defiance of both personal and political self-interest). The anti-Union Whigs of 1799 were in the main a group who papered over the cracks which had shown in the Whig politics of 1797. However, they failed to bring with them the more committed abstentionists, such as Bishop Dickson in county Down,[52] or the Colclough/Grogan interest in Wexford. Even more decidedly they had lost the United Irishmen who instigated the withdrawal policy in 1797: in the main the United Irishmen supported the Union. A sign too of where the most radical sympathies lay is the virtually mute state in 1799–1800 of what had been the two politically most radical counties of the 1790s, Antrim and Kildare (Kildare moreover as its solid involvement in the preparations for Emmet's rising in 1803 was to show was at popular level far from politically dormant in the wake of '98). However, ironically, even if the anti-Union Whigs had forfeited the compromising goodwill of the United Irishmen, they were still tarred with the brush of their multiple indiscreet associations in 1797 and 1798 with United Irishmen. Thus, like the extreme loyalists who were isolated from other and well-got loyalists, the anti-Union Whigs were a visibly wounded group, in a sense sheep in wolves' clothing.

Overall, the story of the Union has been written from the future into the past. It would be better to see it in terms of the weight of the past – itself defined at most as the preceding decade or two – on events in 1799 and 1800. The Rebellion raised momentous issues. It had been a near-civil war; invasion had occurred and was still a possibility. Hence, gentry realism could not afford the luxury of perpetuating rejection, and, when the issue was finally decided, opponents as well as supporters

[52] On Dickson, see the warm comment in Barrington, *Personal sketches*, 57. He had also the distinction of being singled out for attack by Lord Clare in his speech on the Moira address in the Irish Lords in February 1798.

of Union had no difficulty in accepting office. They could still differ on the Catholic Question: Emancipation, depending on the views of the proponent, either threatened the safety of the state or helped to secure it. Pragmatically, acceptance of the Union progressed, and it strengthened with the granting of Emancipation in 1829 which belatedly completed the Union compact. For others, acceptance of the Union rested less on pragmatism than on an essentially negative approach, the rejection of the 'rotten' administration of the 1790s. The Union in popular catholic outlook quickly came to be represented as 'the second betrayal' (i.e. a repetition of the story of the treaty of Limerick), and its appeal inevitably declined. The fact that a prospect of opposing catholic relief existed as a political option until 1829 fanned the hopes of orangeism and gave it a coherent purpose that it lacked in 1798; protestant evangelicanism before and after 1829 was beginning to give a flagging post-Reformation anti-catholicism a new ethos; and the withholding of emancipation for three decades after the Union nurtured the resentments of Catholics now increasingly imbibing an ultramontane Catholicism singularly unsuited for the mixed society and unhappy history of Ireland. By 1829 the Union was already in effect doomed, even if nearly a century was still necessary to complete its death throes.

THE CATHOLICS AND THE UNION

By Patrick M. Geoghegan

READ 10 SEPTEMBER 1999
AT THE PUBLIC RECORD OFFICE NORTHERN IRELAND

IN late-1800, after the passing of the Union, Lord Cornwallis wrote a carefully argued paper on Catholic emancipation in which he posed the chilling question:

> What then have we done? We have united ourselves to a people whom we ought in policy to have destroyed.[1]

That Cornwallis, one of the leading proponents of both the Union and Catholic emancipation, should have put the question in such stark terms is revealing. For him, Union without emancipation was worthless; the government would not secure the loyalty of the country, and there would never be a genuine uniting of the peoples on the two islands. The lord-lieutenant's analysis summed up the challenge facing the government towards the end of 1800: how to reconcile the claims of the Catholics with the fears of the Protestants before the beginning of the united kingdom on 1 January. This was a critical issue, because over the previous two years the government had tried to make the Union appear all things to all men, and all creeds. For some, the Union was supported because it seemed to be the best mechanism for securing Catholic emancipation; for others it was welcomed as a way of closing the door on the Catholics for ever. The political crisis of 1801 was a direct result of this confusion and culminated in both the collapse of the ministry and the end of Cornwallis's hopes of making the Union complete.

It is necessary to examine two complex areas to fully understand the nature of the relationship between the Catholics and the Union. The first, is the status of the Catholic question in the Union deliberations; the second (and related) area, is the response of the Catholic leadership to the measure during the various shifts in policy. Only by examining these aspects simultaneously is it possible to explore the reaction of the largely Catholic Irish population to the Union, influenced as they were by both.

A legislative Union had been something Prime Minister William Pitt

[1] Cornwallis to Portland, 1 December 1800 (*The correspondence of Charles, 1st Marquess Cornwallis*, ed. Charles Ross, 3 vols. (1859), III, 307).

had long been considering for Ireland. He saw it as the only way of resolving the ambiguities in the Anglo-Irish relationship that had existed since legislative independence. But, despite what Thomas Bartlett and others have argued, the Union was not predicated in a desire to pass Catholic emancipation. Rather it was conceived to bring about an imperial security and allow a stable framework to address the Catholic question, either then or at a future date.[2] Emancipating the Catholics, giving them the right to sit in parliament and serve in the higher legal offices, was seen by some observers (like Cornwallis) as the only way of keeping Ireland tranquil. But many others (like Pitt) were unwilling to allow emancipation as long as the Irish parliament remained independent. A Catholic parliament in Dublin risked too much, but allowing them to sit in a united parliament (where their influence would be diluted) offered one solution to this problem.

Discussing a Union with Pitt as early as 1792, the viceroy of the time, Lord Westmorland, gave a precise assessment of opinion in Ireland that was still valid in 1798. Westmorland shrewdly observed that the Irish Protestants would prefer a Union to conceding emancipation, and that likewise the Catholics would prefer a Union rather than continue as they were. In his response, Pitt admitted, that the idea of a legislative Union followed by the civil emancipation of the Catholics was one that had 'long been in my mind'.[3] He explained how

> the admission of catholics to a share of the suffrage could not then be dangerous – the protestant interest in point of power, property and church establishment would be secure because the decided majority of the supreme legislature would necessarily be protestant.

The arch-conservative, and resolutely anti-Catholic, Westmorland was not impressed with this analysis and asked Pitt if he meant 'to force the Protestants to a Union'.[4] His advice encapsulated the Union dilemma: he warned Pitt to 'choose between the Catholic or the Protestant interest', refusing to be drawn into a discussion about the question.

As ever, the focal point for many of the concerns in this period was the French revolution. The fear of revolutionary fervour sweeping Britain was intensified once the countries went to war in 1793. As Bartlett has shrewdly noted, it is no coincidence that the Catholic relief

[2] See Thomas Bartlett, *The Fall and Rise of the Irish Nation* (Dublin, 1992).

[3] Pitt to Westmorland, 18 November 1792 (quoted in G.C. Bolton, *The Passing of the Irish Act of Union* (London, 1966), 12).

[4] Westmorland to Pitt, 10 January 1793 (Cambridge University Library, Add. MS 6958, f. 1199).

acts of the late-eighteenth century were always passed in times of war. The government's reasoning for this was obvious: the support of the Irish Catholics was critical in any wartime situation, both because Catholic troops were necessary for any war effort, and also because relief measures helped neutralise the threat of insurrection in Ireland, thus securing the weak flank of the empire.

The French Revolution also helped to define the Catholic bishops' response to political events in Ireland. The natural response of the hierarchy to the events of 1789 was one of deep distrust and suspicion. Many of the bishops and priests had been educated in France; they retained a strong affection for the country, and had genuine fears about the revolutionary contagion reaching Ireland. This was not helped by the revolutionaries recent imprisonment of Pope Pius VI. One case study is worth mentioning, to illustrate just how real the French revolution was to some leading Catholic figures. During the September massacres in France in 1792 a middle-aged Irish priest, Peter Flood, narrowly escaped death at the hands of an angry mob. Rescued by two municipal officers, he was imprisoned for a time, as his appeal to be allowed to return to Ireland was rejected by the national assembly. A professor of moral theology, Flood had been regarded as the 'finest scripturist and casuist in France', but had been dismissed from his position after refusing to take the oath for the civil constitution of the clergy in 1791. Eventually released, Flood returned to Ireland where he became a parish priest in Co. Longford. However in January 1798 he was elected the second president of Maynooth College, and was in charge during the rebellion in the summer, and the subsequent passing of the Act of Union. Perhaps unsurprisingly, Flood was a vehement opponent of the 1798 rebellion, and refused to allow expelled students to return. He also supported the Union in 1799 and 1800, grateful that the government had not ended its grant to Maynooth. The chief secretary, Viscount Castlereagh, praised him as 'a very worthy and respectable man' and noted that he was 'a zealous supporter of the great measure in contemplation'.[5]

Of the twenty-two Catholic bishops and four archbishops in Ireland, almost all were unambiguous in their condemnation of the rebellion. The challenge that faced them was to try and maintain their fragile relationship with the British government while simultaneously avoiding the alienation of their flock. Unquestionably, their main objective was to secure Catholic emancipation, and this influenced both their response to the 1798 rebellion and the subsequent Union. Determined to be loyal, and to be seen as loyal, they did not wish to give any opportunity

[5] Quoted in Richard Hayes, *Biographical Dictionary of Irishmen in France* (Dublin, 1949), 99.

to the Protestant reactionaries to make their extravagant claims that the Catholics could never be trusted.

The subtle nuances in the Catholic hierarchy's leadership was best epitomised by the behaviour of the archbishop of Dublin, John Thomas Troy. Although a strong advocate of loyalty to the state, he had also courted controversy, especially in 1793 with his *Pastoral on the duties of Christian citizens* when he had referred to the Catholics as 'an enslaved people' and provoked outrage by his use of the word 'citizens' in the title.[6] Troy's overriding concern was to disassociate the rebellion from Catholicism, and he prepared various addresses and pastorals proclaiming the church's loyalty while simultaneously attempting to ensure that loyalty throughout the country. On 27 May he published short instructions that were uncompromising in their attack on the rebels and which threatened excommunication unless they desisted. As a result Troy found himself assailed from all sides, regarded with suspicion by the government, mistrust by many of his own clergy, and hostility by the rebels; in July Castlereagh placed him under government protection for his own safety.[7]

Other bishops had similar experiences during the rebellion. William Coppinger, the bishop of Cloyne and Ross, was publicly opposed to the rising, and produced a controversial social pastoral against insurrection which argued that the poor would remain poor no matter what type of government was in power. Coppinger had been educated in France, and had even applied for a commission in the French army, before deciding on the priesthood. In Cork his uncompromising opposition to the rebellion was not well received and during the summer of 1798 he was forced to flee from his home in Youghal, and settle in Middleton. Unlike almost all the other bishops, however, he refused to acknowledge the potential benefits of a legislative Union, and resolutely opposed it in 1799 and 1800, despite some pressure. He was, he insisted, 'little in the habit of bowing at the castle'.

Acting as a counterpoint to Coppinger, was the bishop of Killala, Dominic Bellew. A somewhat controversial figure, his loyalty to the state was questioned in 1798 because of his perceived sympathies for the rebels. It was in his diocese that Humbert landed, and Bellew served as president of a committee of public safety in Ballina. His brother, Thomas Bellew, a former soldier, became a rebel general, and was hanged for his part in the rising, casting more suspicion on the bishop. After the rebellion was extinguished Bellew was summoned to Dublin to defend himself, and he insisted that he had remained neutral to avoid trouble; satisfied, the castle dropped the charges. However,

[6] See Dáire Keogh, *The French Disease* (Dublin, 1993), 62–4.
[7] Ibid., 158.

perhaps because of this taint on his reputation, Bellew became an uncompromising supporter of the Union, and between 1799 and 1801 was determined to prove his loyalty.

The response to the rebellion in London made the Catholic question assume a major significance in Anglo-Irish politics. On 28 May, upon hearing news of the outbreak of the rising, Prime Minister Pitt decided to introduce a legislative Union as soon as the rebellion was crushed. One of the first key decisions made about the measure was the replacement of Earl Camden with Marquess Cornwallis as viceroy. This change is usually only seen as a minor point of the Union business, but as Bartlett correctly notes it showed that Pitt was, at a minimum, keeping an open mind on the Catholic question.[8] Unlike Camden, who had once admitted that he was 'quite possibly, a very prejudiced Englishman', Cornwallis was a firm proponent of Catholic emancipation. Indeed he had refused the office of lord lieutenant on a previous occasion, because there was to be no alteration in the government's policy towards the Catholics. The threat to the empire in 1798 saw him accept the position without any such assurances, although he was determined to see that the benefits of the Union reached the entire Irish population.

Crucially, it seems certain that Pitt, in the summer of 1798 shared Cornwallis's sympathies towards the Catholics. He and Lord Grenville, the foreign secretary, wrote an important paper on the Union in early June that contained interesting insights about the status of the Catholic question. Although this paper has proved elusive for historians, there is sufficient internal evidence to show that it is the undated document, 'Points to be considered with a view to an incorporating Union of Great Britain and Ireland'. In the section on parliamentary representation, the paper suggested 'giving to Catholics, as well as Protestants, the right of eligibility', to stand for election to the united parliament. Pitt and Grenville both admitted in the autumn that they had initially supported the idea of accompanying the Union with emancipation.[9]

In October 1798 the first serious shift in the Union policy occurred. The occasion was the visit to London by the Irish Lord Chancellor, the Earl of Clare. This consultation on the Union is credited by Peter Jupp, Grenville's authoritative biographer, with persuading the foreign secretary to reconsider his support for emancipation. It also appears to have shaken the opinion of Pitt, who decided to keep the issues separate so as to avoid unnecessary conflict. Arriving in England, Clare was horrified to find that the ministers were 'as full of their popish projects

[8] Bartlett, *Fall and Rise*, 246.

[9] See P.M. Geoghegan, *The Irish Act of Union* (Dublin, 1999), for a wider analysis of the significance of this document.

as ever'. However after some lengthy discussions he won the argument and it was decided to go for 'a Union strictly Protestant'.

In Ireland, Cornwallis, realising that the Catholic question was about to be sacrificed, entered the debate with a forceful letter to Pitt that transformed the discussions in England. The intervention was a nasty shock for Clare, who noted with horror that 'some untoward devil must have taken his station in my accursed country ... Nothing more unfortunate and ill-timed could have happened than the letter of Lord Cornwallis'.[10] Accepting that even with emancipation the Catholics would not immediately become good subjects, the lord lieutenant argued that if the

> most popular of their grievances is removed (and especially if it could be accompanied by some regulation about tithes) that we should get time to breathe, and at least check the rapid progress of discontent and disaffection.[11]

Cornwallis's timely letter ensured that the Catholic question was left open, 'for a full demonstration of what is right upon it at a proper season'. The government meetings then ended with much 'drunkenness at Bellamy's'.[12]

The only minister who retained a full belief in the necessity of emancipation accompanying the Union was Henry Dundas, the secretary of state for war. Interestingly enough, he was also a close friend of Cornwallis, soon to be his only friend in cabinet. Unfortunately for the Catholics, however, he was in Scotland when the deliberations with Clare occurred, and returned to find the question decided. This led to 'some dryness' between him and Pitt, and Cornwallis speculated that had his friend been present he might have 'been able to carry the point of establishing the Union on a broad and comprehensive line' although he accepted that 'things have now gone too far to admit of a change'.[13]

The abandonment of the Catholic emancipation principle caused some discontent in the Irish administration. William Elliot, the castle under-secretary for the military department, came close to resigning over the issue. A shy, reserved man, the English-born (but of Scottish descent) Elliot had become a supporter of emancipation under the influence of Edmund Burke, and had acted as Cornwallis's envoy during the discussions in England. Privately accepting that the Irish

[10] Clare to Auckland, 28 October 1798 (Public Record Office Northern Ireland, Transcripts 3287/7/22).

[11] Cornwallis to Pitt, 8 October 1798 (National Library Ireland, Manuscripts 886, ff. 385–6).

[12] Canning to Windham, 23 October 1798 (British Library, Additional Manuscripts 37844, f. 274).

[13] Cornwallis to Ross, 15 November 1798 (*Cornwallis correspondence*, II, 433).

Catholics had justifiable grounds for complaint,[14] Pitt's weakness was much criticised. Elliot felt that a little more firmness in London might have enabled the Catholic claims to have been incorporated into the Union. Instead, the prime minister's 'lamentable facility, yielded the point to *prejudice*, without I suspect, acquiring a support in any degree equivalent to the sacrifice'.[15] Some historians, like Bartlett, have dismissed these criticisms as being 'wide off the mark',[16] but Elliot had had long discussions with Pitt on the Catholic question and was fully aware of the prime minister's new position on the subject. As Pitt himself wrote to Cornwallis at the time, Elliot had not convinced him 'of the practicability of such a measure at this time [n]or of the propriety of attempting it'.[17] In the end Castlereagh, who had struck up a close friendship with Elliot, persuaded him to withdraw his resignation, but the very fact the a senior member of the administration came so close to resigning on the Catholic question is significant.

With Catholic emancipation definitely to be excluded from the terms of the Union, Cornwallis's task in persuading the Catholic leadership to support the measure became much more difficult. However he was soon pleasantly surprised to discover that Lords Fingall and Kenmare (he referred to them as 'my' lords) were favourable to the Union. With the disbandment of the Catholic committee, Fingall, Kenmare and Troy were the three most influential Catholic leaders in the country, and all shared a close relationship with the lord lieutenant. They also had personal reasons for being friendly with the castle. Kenmare, whose title had been a disputed Jacobite creation, finally received a new viscountcy from the king on 12 Feb. 1798 and was anxious for an earldom; similarly Fingall also wanted his position recognised in any new arrangement. Both men were therefore willing to give a cautious support to Cornwallis and the Union. Desperate to remove the remaining restrictions on the Catholics through peaceful means, and disillusioned with the ascendancy Irish parliament, Troy was also 'perfectly well inclined'[18] to the measure, provided the Catholic question was left open for a future date.

On 15 December 1798 forty prominent Catholics met in Dublin to discuss the Union – comprising 'respectable persons, gentry, and principal merchants of the city'. It followed on the heels of a meeting of the Irish bar, which had been almost unanimous in its opposition to the measure. The meeting of the Catholics saw far more uncertainty

[14] Elliot to Castlereagh, 28 November 1798 (*Memoirs and correspondence of Viscount Castlereagh*, ed. Marquess of Londonderry, 12 vols. (1848–53), II, 29).

[15] Ibid.

[16] Bartlett, *Fall and Rise*, p. 248.

[17] Pitt to Cornwallis, 17 November 1798 (*Cornwallis correspondence*, II, 440).

[18] Bartlett, *Fall and Rise*, 249.

about how to proceed; some thought the opposition of the orangemen was enough of a reason to support the Union, while others remained suspicious about the exclusion of the Catholic question from its terms. The meeting was adjourned for a week, during which time Cornwallis canvassed some leading sceptics, and in the end the participants decided to leave the subject open. As Troy informed Castlereagh, the Catholics decided 'not to deliberate on the Union as a question of empire, but only as it might affect their own peculiar interests as a body'.[19] Thomas Bartlett in his chapter on this period in his book *The fall and rise of the Irish nation*, probably the finest account of the status of the Catholic question during the Union, argues that this was the best possible result for Cornwallis. There is much truth to this. A declaration in favour of the Union from the Catholics would have alienated many Protestants, and weakened the measure in the month before the Irish parliament was to meet. Conversely, a declaration against the Union would have risked alienating the Catholic population from the measure completely. The Catholics were not powerful enough to guarantee the success of the Union, but they were capable of preventing it ever passing; and this distinction helps explain their importance during the different attempts to bring about the measure.

The role of Cornwallis during these negotiations is worth examining. During his viceroyalty he acted as an unofficial spin-doctor for the Catholics, always writing up their support and loyalty in his official despatches, but privately despairing about their likely conduct. Therefore Cornwallis's various statements about having enlisted the support of the Catholics should never be read unquestioningly. At the end of December many of the Dublin Catholics were becoming increasingly cynical about the Union, and Cornwallis received a report that they were even considering joining with the Protestants to defeat the measure if this would best serve their interests. Nevertheless the lord lieutenant refused to pass on this distressing (and probably exaggerated) intelligence to London, merely warning that the Catholics appeared to be hardening against the measure. In private, he was consumed by doubts, and darkly admitted that he thought 'from the folly, obstinacy, and gross corruption which pervade every corner of this island, that it is impossible that it can be saved from destruction'.[20]

The Irish parliament was due to meet on 22 January 1799, and ten leading bishops met a few days before to discuss a proposal from Dublin castle. Their meetings took place on 17, 18, and 19 January, and the four archbishops, Richard O'Reilly of Armagh, Edward Dillon of Tuam, Thomas Bray of Cashel, and John Thomas Troy of Dublin all

[19] Troy to Castlereagh, 24 December 1798 (*Castlereagh correspondence*, II, 61).
[20] Cornwallis to Ross, 12 December 1798 (*Cornwallis correspondence*, III, 16).

attended. It seems Cornwallis had offered the hierarchy a government stipend for the clergy, in exchange for the concession of a veto on the future appointment of bishops, an issue that was to become increasingly contentious in the decades ahead. It was probably implicitly understood that the bishops would also support the Union in return for this deal. Somewhat reluctantly, the bishops decided to accept the government's offer, although the proposal did not get any further. When George III discovered the overture later in the month he was furious, and ordered an immediate end to the negotiations.

In any case, the status of the Catholic question had changed anyway, after the extraordinary events in the Irish parliament. Attacking the implicit mention of a Union in the king's address, the opposition inflicted an important defeat on the government, which saw its support haemorrhage in the commons. Castlereagh was forced to inform the house that the Union would not be introduced that session, and that the government would wait until the mood of the country and the parliament had changed before attempting it again. The week after this defeat was critical for the government. For a time it appeared that the Catholics would join with the anti-Union Protestants in opposition to the measure, forming a powerful coalition that would have virtually blocked any future attempts. On the day the parliament met, as Kenmare later informed Cornwallis, George Ponsonby, a leading anti-Unionist, had promised the Catholics that emancipation would be granted at a future date if they presented a petition against the Union. This offer had been rejected, but the castle feared that such an alliance would be formed in the wake of the defeat in parliament. Indeed on 26 January a story circulated that a deal had been done, causing great despair, but this was soon shown to be an unfounded rumour.

The refusal of the Protestant opposition to negotiate with the Catholics proved to be a fatal mistake. But in many ways any such alliance was impossible. To understand the delicate negotiations during the Union debate, it is necessary to examine the four major groups that existed. The first comprised those who were pro-Union, and pro-Catholic (for example Cornwallis), the second, was those who were pro-Union but anti-Catholic (for example Clare), the third was those who were anti-Union, but pro-Catholic (for example Henry Grattan), and the final group was those that were anti-Union and anti-Catholic (for example, John Foster, the speaker). It is pointless to speculate about what would have happened if the Foster faction had joined with the Catholics to oppose the Union in return for emancipation. One of the chief reasons why so many opposed the Union, was because they wanted to protect the ascendancy, not break it. Others, like John Beresford, supported the Union for the very same reason.

For their part, the position of the Catholics in 1799 was no different from what it had been in 1792 when Westmorland had explained it to Pitt. This was plain to see for Cornwallis, who advised Portland, the home secretary, about their likely conduct at the end of January. It was clear the Catholics would prefer equality without a Union to equality with one. Cornwallis accepted that 'in the latter case they must ever be content with inferiority; in the former, they would probably by degrees gain ascendancy'.[21] The problem was that this analysis was equally obvious to Foster, and explains why no alliance was formed. When the chief opponents of the Union met in February 1799 they passed politically insensitive resolutions espousing high Protestant principles.

On 28 January the Catholic hierarchy met to discuss their position on the Union a second time. They decided to postpone the question 'for the present' and thus avoid embarrassing the government, something Cornwallis (who was close to being sacked) was very grateful for. Thus, as Bartlett notes, 'if the castle refused to race, so too did the opposition',[22] and the support of the Catholics remained in limbo. However, the Catholic leadership remained in an strong negotiating position. Three figures, Archbishop O'Reilly, Archbishop Troy, and Bishop Patrick Joseph Plunkett of Meath, were authorised 'to treat with Lord Castlereagh on the subject [of the Union], when[ever] he may think expedient to resume' their discussions.[23]

Of the four Catholic archbishops, the two most senior, Richard O'Reilly and John Thomas Troy, both gave a steady support to the Union. Of the men, Troy was the most committed to the measure and was probably the government's strongest ally amongst the hierarchy. For example, in February 1799 he helped persuade recalcitrant Catholics to vote for Isaac Corry, the new chancellor of the exchequer in his by-election, and Matthew Lennan, the local bishop of Dromore, observed that 'the Catholics stuck together like the Macedonian phalanx'.[24] If Pitt supported Union as the best means of achieving an imperial security, then Troy supported the measure as only means of achieving a Catholic security. For Troy, Union represented the only protection for Catholics against 'a faction seemingly intent on their defamation and destruction'.[25] Troy had many private discussions with Castlereagh about the measure and agreed to enlist the support of the bishops and clergy as far as was practicable. With this in mind he wrote to Thomas Bray, archbishop of Cashel, who was less sure on the question, asking him to 'discreetly exert' his influence 'in the counties of Tipperary and

[21] Cornwallis to Portland, 28 January 1799 (*Cornwallis correspondence*, III, 54).
[22] Bartlett, *Fall and Rise*, 254.
[23] Troy to Hippisley, 9 February 1799 (*Castlereagh correspondence*, II, 172).
[24] Bartlett, *Fall and Rise*, 255.
[25] Ibid., 256.

Waterford' to procure Catholic petitions in favour of the Union.[26] Bray was cautious in his response, and warned that the instructions of an archbishop would not necessarily be followed by the people. This is an important caveat to bear in mind. The power of the Catholic leadership chiefly derived from the control they were able to exert over the people. But it was never likely that the Catholics would follow blindly the advice from the altar; 1798, if nothing else, had shown that many were prepared to disagree with the instructions of their bishops even if it risked excommunication. As Bray reminded Troy in July 1799 'what little influence we have over them [the Catholics] in political matters', should not be risked, and he advised against acting publicly in favour of the Union 'to avoid censure'. However he did intimate that the Union would have his 'good wishes' and 'the whole of my little mite of assistance'. Bishop Plunkett of Meath expressed similar sentiments, and refused to support a pro-Catholic petition in his diocese until the mood of the country had changed. Repeating Bray's analysis, he admitted that 'in political questions it becomes us rather to *follow* that to *lead*'.[27]

The fourth, and most junior archbishop, Edward Dillon (he had only succeeded Boetius Egan in 1798) was also canvassed by Troy to come out publicly in favour of the Union in July. Dillon was unsure about how to proceed and asked both Bray and O'Reilly for advice; O'Reilly advised him to sign the resolutions in favour of the Union.[28] If Troy was the most enthusiastic of the archbishops about the merits of a Union, then Dillon was the most suspicious, but it is interesting that within the space of two months he had come to share Troy's sentiments. The reasons for his change of heart reveal much about the status of the Union with the Irish people in general. After a summer of visiting his dioceses, Dillon revealed that he had observed 'how little averse the public mind is to that measure'. He also admitted that he had 'an opportunity of acquiring the strongest conviction that this measure alone can restore harmony and happiness to our unhappy country'.[29]

Francis Moylan, the bishop of Cork, and one of the most influential members of the hierarchy, confirmed Dillon's findings. In September 1799 he declared that 'the Roman Catholics in general are avowedly for the measure', and prayed that 'with the blessing of God, it will be effected'.[30] It is more than possible, though, that the bishops were exaggerating the support in the country for the Union. The following year would show that it was not as solid as they claimed, and it suited

[26] Bray to Troy, 1 July 1799 (*Castlereagh correspondence*, II, 345).
[27] Bartlett, *Fall and Rise*, 256.
[28] Dillon to Troy, 9 July 1799 (*Castlereagh correspondence*, II, 347).
[29] Dillon to Troy, 1 September 1799 (*Castlereagh correspondence*, II, 387).
[30] Moylan to Hippesley, 14 September 1799 (*Castlereagh correspondence*, II, 399).

their interests to make it appear that the people were friendlier to the government than they actually were.

A distinction must also be made between the Catholics of Dublin and those in the rest of the country. The inhabitants of the capital were even less willing to take instructions from the hierarchy than those elsewhere. But ultimately even they were unwilling to press too strongly against the measure. As Cornwallis reported to the British government in August 'little more is to be expected than neutrality'. In the end the Union secured 79 petitions from the country in favour of the measure, and as Bartlett shows 11 were exclusively from Catholic bodies; and of the 50 petitions that were against Union, none was from Catholic groups.[31]

To re-emphasise, the support of the Catholics in 1799 for the Union should not be exaggerated. In some instances they were indifferent to the proposed measure because the Irish parliament had little effect on their lives. In other cases they gave it a grudging support only because they held out an expectation that Catholic emancipation would accompany it. With the Union about to be reintroduced in 1800 its success was still largely dependent on the support of the Catholics. The government were in no doubt about the precariousness of their position. As long as the Catholics remained friendly, or at least neutral, towards the measure it would pass, but if they became alienated from the government the entire policy would hang in the balance. This danger was made even more apparent to the castle when an unfounded rumour was 'industriously propagated' in Ireland that the passing of the Union would:

> preclude for ever the Roman Catholics of this kingdom from the hopes of further emancipation, that, under the imperial parliament, the junto who opposed them would still prevail, and hold the reins of the government of this country.[32]

The propaganda war for the support of the country was now turning nasty, and with this in mind, Castlereagh was sent to London in September to receive firm instructions on the Catholic question. His mission was to force the cabinet, which had been discussing the problem with some regularity, to come to a decision, and end the debilitating uncertainty in Ireland.

Thus, in November 1799, the most serious shift in the status of the Catholic question took place. Distracted by foreign policy, and other concerns, it was only in that month that the cabinet were able to have a thorough examination of the Union question. On two consecutive

[31] Bartlett, *Fall and Rise*, 257.

[32] Moylan to Hippesley, 14 September 1799 (*Castlereagh correspondence*, II, 400).

days, either the 15th and 16th, or the 16th and 17th November, the ministers heard Castlereagh explain just how precarious the support in Ireland for the Union actually was. The cabinet heard from the chief secretary how:

> we had a majority in parliament composed on very doubtful materials; that the protestant body was divided on the question with the disadvantage of Dublin and the orange societies against us – and that the Catholics were holding back under a doubt whether the union would facilitate or impede their object.[33]

With the sides so evenly matched, Castlereagh explained that the decision of the Catholics would prove decisive. Success hinged on their support. The ministers were told bluntly that: the measure could not be carried if the Catholics were embarked in an active opposition to it.[34] As it seemed inevitable that the Catholics would be 'unanimous and zealous' in their opposition to the Union if it excluded emancipation, Castlereagh warned that a radical shift in policy was unavoidable. As Cornwallis would not hold out false promises to the Catholics, whose trust and goodwill he had carefully nurtured, some direct assurances were necessary from Whitehall. Unwilling to risk the entire Union strategy being defeated, the ministers decided to accept the advice of Cornwallis and his chief secretary. At the second cabinet meeting, Castlereagh was informed that

> as far as the sentiments of the cabinet were concerned, his excellency need not hesitate in calling forth the Catholic support in whatever degree he found it practicable to obtain it.

The ministers even debated whether or not they should make a public statement on their support for the Catholic question. This was decided against, mainly because of fears that it might alienate Protestants in both countries against the Union, 'in a greater degree than it was calculated to assist the measure through the Catholics'. Castlereagh returned home with instructions that the castle could do whatever was necessary to win the support of the Catholics, preferably without having to make any explicit promises, but these were authorised in the event that they were unavoidable.

As it turned out Cornwallis did not have to make any explicit promises to the Catholics. But he did allow the Catholic leadership to implicitly understand that emancipation would soon accompany the passing of the measure. The change in the status of the Catholic question was kept a secret, hidden even from key supporters of the

[33] Castlereagh to Pitt, 1 January 1801 (C.U.L., Add. MS 6958, f. 2827).
[34] Ibid.

Union. Clare was not told of the new policy, and was later furious that he had been deceived by the castle. This deception was only to be expected, for Clare had informed Cornwallis earlier in the year that if emancipation was to accompany the Union he would put himself at the head of all the Irish Protestants in opposing it. Upon hearing this, Cornwallis discreetly changed the subject.

The new policy on the Catholics appealed greatly to the lord lieutenant. Cornwallis was glad he did not have to make any official pledges on the controversial question. Doing so would have weakened the authority of the Union, as it would be believed that the government had bartered emancipation for the Catholics' support. For Cornwallis, 'a gratuitous concession after the measure' was far more preferable. But, again, the support of Troy and the bishops, and the approval of leading gentry like Fingall and Kenmare, did not guarantee the support of the people. As the Union was debated in the Irish house of commons in the first half of 1800 the position of the Catholic population remained unclear. It was a nervous time for the castle, because even though they had a majority in the commons, they realised that popular disturbances could still defeat the measure out of parliament. As Cornwallis warned Whitehall, it was reckless to think that 'a measure so deeply affecting the interests and passions of the nation can be carried against the voice of the people'.[35] In late January it appeared that the Catholics would refuse to support the Union. This was Cornwallis's own opinion, although he carefully shielded it from the ministers in London. Privately, however, he regretted that he had not been able to 'obtain the smallest degree of favour' from the Catholics who had been increasingly alienated by the 'imprudent speeches and the abuse cast upon them by our friends'.[36] The following months, however, would reveal that the lord lieutenant had become a victim of his own neuroses; the support in the commons held firm, and the Catholics remained aloof from any unconstitutional attempts to prevent the measure. The extraordinary declamation of the young barrister, Daniel O'Connell, in 1800 did not come to pass. In an early example of O'Connell's great gift for extravagant rhetoric and hyperbole, he had confidently insisted that the Catholics would rather see the return of the penal laws than achieve emancipation through supporting a Union. This was nonsense. O'Connell could not claim to know what the Irish people would prefer, and the indifference in the country to the passing of the Union, showed the foolishness of his pronouncement.

In the first half of 1800 the Union passed inexorably through the commons, and in June the bill went through its final reading. Cornwallis

[35] Cornwallis to Ross, 21 January 1800 (*Cornwallis correspondence*, III, 167).
[36] Cornwallis to Ross, 31 January 1800 (*Cornwallis correspondence*, III, 174).

attributed much of the success of the Union to his relationship with the Catholics. Archbishop Troy was full of praise for his handling of the delicate negotiations, and wrote to the Home Office to congratulate the lord lieutenant for being 'all benevolence, all liberality'.[37]

However, with the United Kingdom of Great Britain and Ireland due to come into effect on 1 January 1801, the second half of 1800 became a tense time for Dublin castle. Both Cornwallis and Castlereagh were under no illusions about the likely opposition to emancipation in England, and feared that their honour would be compromised by vacillating ministers in London, who were afraid of provoking their king. The Catholic bishops were quietly confident about the start of the new year, and felt that they had done their part in the success of the Union. Cornwallis was less sanguine, and spent months trying to force the cabinet into honouring their commitments towards the Catholics. In a carefully argued letter in December, he reminded the ministers that even if the Roman Catholics were full 'of obstinate and irreclaimable disaffection', this would be ended once they were 'no longer the objects of suspicion and are relieved from their present mortifying and degrading exclusions'.[38] As far as Cornwallis was concerned the cabinet had to decide whether the Catholics could ever be good subjects. If they believed they could, then emancipation must logically follow the Union. If they did not, if they agreed with 'the hereditary prejudices' of the Protestants in Ireland, then the Union had been a foolish measure: 'what then have we done? We have united ourselves to a people whom we ought in policy to have destroyed.'[39]

The arguments had little effect. The cabinet was disintegrating in England, over a combination of foreign and domestic policy concerns, and the Catholic question became one issue too many. With a divided ministry, Pitt had little hope of persuading the king to relent on his coronation oath. In any event, the question was soon taken out of his hands. A public levee on 28 January saw George III react furiously to the presence of Viscount Castlereagh. Having heard of the planned Catholic emancipation policy, through other sources, he rounded on Henry Dundas, and declared:

> What is this catholic emancipation which *this young lord, this Irish secretary* has brought over, that you are going to throw at my head? I will tell, that I shall look on every man as my personal enemy who proposes that question to me.[40]

[37] Troy to Home Office, 26 April 1800 (N.L.I., MS 5027).

[38] Cornwallis to Portland, 1 December 1800 (*Cornwallis correspondence*, III, 307).

[39] Ibid.

[40] Camden, 'Memorandum' in Richard Willis's 'William Pitt's resignation in 1801: Re-examination and document' (*Bulletin of the Institute of Historical Research*, xliv, no. 110 (1971), 252).

There was no way around this impasse. A broken man, Pitt tendered his resignation, the ministry collapsed, the king went mad, and a new government was formed on high Protestant principles. The emancipation policy was dead. To preserve calm in Ireland, Cornwallis met with Fingall and Troy on 13 February and explained the current crisis. With Pitt's help, two papers were also prepared for the Catholics to prevent any violent response, and encourage the people not to become disillusioned from the Union. Both the viceroy and Castlereagh resigned along with Pitt, explaining that to have remained would have constituted a 'breach of faith' with the Catholics. Bitterly disappointed, there was little Troy could do. Having come so close to securing emancipation, it was demoralising to have had it prevented by the prejudices of leading figures in England. It was obvious that the Catholic question would have to sleep for the remainder of George III's reign. The Catholic leaders continued with the only strategy they had – demonstrating their loyalty to the crown, proving that the Catholics could be trusted, and hoping that some day this would be recognised and that their remaining restrictions would be lifted.

In a wonderful, but largely meaningless, soundbite Professor Bartlett has said that 'the Catholics carried the Union; the rest is detail'. A former viceroy, Lord Buckingham, had insisted that the Catholics were the 'sheet anchor' in the Union project. The reality is that the Catholics had had the power to frustrate the Union, but chose not to for a combination of reasons. The main one is that, prompted by the bishops and the gentry, they were encouraged to see the Union as the best means of relieving them from their civil restrictions. The political crisis of 1801 ensured that the loyalty of the Catholics was not secured, and a genuine opportunity for creating a new imperial security was lost. Without emancipation accompanying it, the Catholics soon became alienated from the measure. As a unifying security mechanism, the act of Union was stillborn. It is very difficult, on this occasion, to disagree with the conclusion of Sir Jonah Barrington, who summed up the treatment of the Catholics at this time in one sentence:

> In 1798 they were charged; in 1799 they were caressed; in 1800 they were cajoled; in 1801 they were discarded.[41]

[41] Jonah Barrington, *Historic memoirs* (1833), II, 332. I would like to thank Rory Whelan and Michael Brown for their excellent assistance with earlier drafts of this paper, and Anthony Malcomson for his kind comments and advice at the conference.

POPULAR POLITICS IN IRELAND AND THE ACT OF UNION

By James Kelly

READ 10 SEPTEMBER 1999 AT THE PUBLIC RECORD OFFICE OF NORTHERN IRELAND

THE most striking features of the popular political response in Ireland to the attempts between mid-1798 and mid-1800 to bring about the legislative union of Britain and Ireland are its comparative uneventfulness and traditional character. On first encounter, this observation may appear provocative since it is still commonly perceived, the work of G.C. Bolton notwithstanding,[1] that the Act of Union was imposed upon a reluctant parliament and an antipathetic people. Moreover, it does not sit easily with what we know of popular anti-unionism in eighteenth-century Ireland, the most celebrated manifestation of which was the anti-union riot of 3 December 1759 when the Dublin mob invaded both houses of parliament and assaulted a number of leading officeholders arising out of a rumour that a legislative union was intended.[2] Arising out of such manifestations of popular attachment to a domestic Irish parliament, and the high level of political, social and criminal violence during the 1790s, it is hardly surprising that leading figures in the Irish administration anticipated that serious public disorder would be a feature of the opposition to a union in 1798–1800. In point of fact, the decisive defeat of the 1798 rebellion and the strenuous efforts of United Irish leaders to minimise the extent of their revolutionary involvement thereafter ensured that there was no overt popular resistance from a quarter which, during the 1790s, treated every reference to a union with disdain.[3] As a consequence, Lord Castlereagh noted with satisfaction in January 1799 that 'the lower orders are naturally indifferent to the question'. Whether a populace, the extent of whose politicisation, it is now commonly argued, increased greatly in the 1790s, were quite as disinterested as he and Lord Cornwallis, who was

[1] G.C. Bolton, *The passing of the Irish Act of Union* (Oxford, 1966).

[2] Sean Murphy, 'The Dublin anti-union riot of 3 December 1759' in G. O'Brien, ed., *Parliament, politics and people* (Dublin, 1989), pp. 49–68; James Kelly, *Henry Flood: patriots and politics in eighteenth-century Ireland* (Dublin, 1998), pp. 72–4.

[3] Marianne Elliott, *Partners in Revolution: the United Irishmen and France* (London, 1982), chapter eight; for United Irish opposition to the idea of a union see, *inter alia*, *The Beauties of the Press* (London, 1800), pp. 340–45

equally persuaded that 'the people neither think or care about the matter', averred is contestable.[4] James Woodford, a percipient military officer who saw service in Ireland in the late 1790s, suggested that 'the people' scarce gave 'the question of union' any thought because they had another agenda; they were 'persuaded ... of the French making another and successful invasion'. [5] The pervasiveness of this conviction remains to be established, but there is no gainsaying that the failure of the rebellion, by enfeebling radicalism and discrediting the republican ideology it presented, ensured there was no popular resistance to a union from that quarter in the late 1790s.

Nor were radicals the only political interest with a diminished capacity to generate a vigorous popular response to the proposal to abolish the Irish parliament. The credibility of the whig-patriots was weakened by the withdrawal from the House of Commons in 1797 of a number of their most eminent voices, as well as by revelations of their contacts with leading United Irishmen. As a result, the patriots were ill-positioned organisationally and politically to spearhead a successful campaign to ensure the survival of the parliament whose legislative authority they had done so much to increase. This was true also of the Catholic interest had they been so-minded. The potential political influence of Catholics was greatly augmented by the extension to them of the franchise in 1793 and by the emergence subsequently of what was termed 'Catholic emancipation' as a political aspiration. However, the dissolution of the Catholic Committee and the question marks posed against Catholic loyalty as a consequence of the 1798 Rebellion put the Catholic leadership so firmly on the defensive they did not even consider recreating the popular ferment that had proved so advantageous in 1792–3, to extract concessions as part of a union settlement.[6]

The cumulative effect of recent events, therefore, was either to negate or to confine the capacity of radicals, whig-patriots and Catholics to orchestrate a popular response to the proposal to unite the British and Irish parliaments. Of the three interests, the whig-patriots were possessed of the greatest room to manoeuvre because of the continuing appeal of their arguments in favour of Irish parliamentary government. However, they were obliged to contend for the political limelight with ideological conservatives, whose political star was in the ascendant in

[4] Marquess of Londonderry, ed., *Memoirs and correspondence of Viscount Castlereagh* (4 vols., London, 1848–54), II, 81; Sir Charles Ross, ed., *Correspondence of Charles, first Marquis Cornwallis* (3 vols., London, 1859), III, 93. For the issue of popular politicisation see Kevin Whelan, *The tree of liberty* (Cork, 1996).

[5] Woodford to Portland, 22 Sept. 1799 (National Library of Scotland (henceforth NLS), Minto papers, Ms. 11195 ff. 13–14).

[6] The fullest account of Catholic politics in the 1790s is contained in T. Bartlett, *The fall and rise of the Irish nation: the Catholic question 1690–1830* (Dublin, 1992).

the late 1790s, and whose grounds for opposing a union differed from theirs in several fundamental respects. If, as a result, popular opposition to a union lacked ideological coherence, it also meant that it followed a familiar eighteenth-century pattern, and that it is to the *ancien regime* world of aggregate meetings, resolutions, petitions and addresses rather than to the revolutionary world of mass protests, public disorder and political intrigue that one must look to establish the impact on popular politics of the implementation of the Act of Union.

I

When the idea of a legislative union was floated by William Pitt following the outbreak of rebellion in late May 1798, he was assured of a positive response from the 'leading people' in Ireland, many of whom had concluded in 1792–3, when the question of Catholic enfranchisement was at issue, that this offered the best long-term security for the Irish 'Protestant interest'.[7] This was not, as Pitt acknowledged at the time, sufficient to neutralise the formidable opposition to any such initiative that would ensue from the anticipated coalition of metropolitan, popular and parliamentary interests that would gather to defend their historical right to make law for Ireland, who continued to argue during the early and mid-1790s that a union was not in Ireland's strategic, political or economic interest.[8] At the same time, he and other proponents of a legislative union could take comfort from the fact that the heightened revolutionary activity in Ireland from 1795 increased the parliamentary appeal of a union above the figure of eighty MPs claimed following Lord Fitzwilliam's dramatic recall in February 1795.[9] Despite this, Pitt would not have contemplated terminating his policy of governing Ireland by 'expedients' in favour of a union but for the outbreak of rebellion on 23 May 1798. Convinced that a union alone provided the basis for a 'permanent settlement, which may provide for the internal peace of the country and secure its

[7] James Kelly, 'Public and political opinion in Ireland and the idea of an Anglo-Irish union 1650–1800' in D. George Boyce and R.R. Eccleshall, eds, *Political discourse in early modern Ireland* (forthcoming); Westmorland to Pitt, 28 Nov. 1792 (National Library of Ireland (henceforth NLI), Union correspondence, Ms. 886 ff. 17–26); A.C. Kavanaugh, *John Fitzgibbon, Earl of Clare* (Dublin, 1997), p. 256.

[8] Westmorland to Pitt, 28 Nov. 1792 (N.L.I., Union correspondence, Ms. 886 ff. 17–26); *Dublin Evening Post* (henceforth *DEP*) 21 Apr., 30 May 1795, 3 May 1796; [Lord Cloncurry], *Thoughts on the projected union between Great Britain and Ireland* (Dublin, 1797), pp. 33–42; Drennan to McTier, 26 Mar. [1793] in D.A. Chart. ed., *The Drennan letters* (Belfast, 1931), p.145; *The Beauties of the Press*, pp. 340–45

[9] *DEP*, 18 Apr. 1795; Clare to Mornington, 20 Apr. 1797 (British Library, Wellesley papers, Add. Ms. 37308 f. 34).

connection with Great Britain', he promptly set matters in train to make his decision reality.[10] Significantly, his decisiveness was not mirrored by public and political opinion in Ireland. There, the rebellion dominated the political horizon, and with 'extermination' and 'disqualification' foremost on the minds of a majority of Protestants, there was no groundswell of public support for a union though it was favoured by what the Rev. Charles Warburton termed 'the sensible party' as the means most likely to ensure long term 'peace and security'.[11]

As this suggests, the most significant short-term effect of the rebellion upon Protestant political opinion in Ireland was to strengthen its already powerful conservative strand. Sensitised by the regular recollection of the events of 1641, reports from Counties Wicklow and Wexford of 'massacres' perpetrated upon Protestants by rebels, fixed Protestant perceptions of the rebellion as a sectarian effusion inspired by an unholy combination of Catholic thirst for 'heretic blood' and 'the adoption of French principles'.[12] Arising out of this, it took no great leap of imagination to present the rebellion as 'a monstrous combination of anarchy and religious bigotry' and to conclude that events vindicated conservatives like the MP for Dublin city, John Claudius Beresford, who maintained that it was 'folly' either 'to temporise or to maintain a war of half measures with conspirators'. By extension, most felt reflexively that condign punishment should, as a matter of justice, be meted out to those responsible.[13] They also found ideological comfort in substantial numbers in conservatism, as manifested by the detectable increase in support, most observable in Dublin, during the summer of 1798 for the rhetoric of Protestant ascendancy.

Throughout the eighteenth century, Irish Protestants of all political hues demonstrated a near-pavlovian eagerness to express their commitment to uphold the 'Protestant constitution in church and state'. Such professions attained heightened ideological potency as a result of the elaboration of the language of 'Protestant ascendancy' in the mid-

[10] F. Bickley, ed., *The diary of Sylvester Douglas* (2 vols., London, 1928), I, 35; Pitt to Camden, 28 May, 11 Jun. (Kent Archives Office (henceforth KAO), Camden papers, U840/0190A/6, 79); Pitt to Auckland, 4 June 1798 in Bishop of Bath and Wells, ed., *The correspondence of William Eden, first Lord Auckland* (4 vols., London, 1861–2), IV, 2.

[11] Warburton to Bentinck, 11 July 1798 in [A.P.W. Malcomson, ed.,], *Eighteenth-Century Irish official papers in Great Britain, I* (Belfast, [1973]), p. 188; Cornwallis to Pitt, 20 July 1798 (Public Record Office, 30/8/327 ff. 183–4); Castlereagh to Camden, 9 July 1798 (K.A.O., Camden papers, U840/C98/2).

[12] See James Kelly, "We were all to have been massacred: Irish Protestants and the experience of rebellion' in David Dickson *et als* eds, *The 1798 Rebellion* (forthcoming, 2000); *Freeman's Journal* (henceforth *FJ*), 22, 26, 29, 31 May, 2, 7, 12 June, 10 July 1798, 16 Nov. 1799.

[13] *FJ*, 24, 29 May, 21 June, 10 July; Cornwallis to Ross, 8, 24 July 1798 in *Cornwallis Corres.*, II, 358, 369.

1780s. This became so well-established during the 1790s that it had many adherents in the summer of 1798.[14] In one aspect, it is identifiable in the preparedness of bodies like Dublin Corporation and the Aldermen of Skinner's Alley to honour known conservatives with complimentary addresses and approbatory resolutions.[15] Another, more significant, manifestation central to an understanding of the antipathy with which many conservatives regarded a union is detectable in their readiness to profess their commitment to the maintenance intact of the Protestant constitution. This was defined as their object by the Orangemen of Dublin when, towards they end of June, they called upon all 'loyal subjects' to 'rally round the constitution'.[16] As the timing and content of this pronouncement emphasise, the horizon of those who shared this outlook was dominated by the desire to restore to Protestants the rights afforded them by their 'inestimable constitution'. In other words, they assumed that the defeat of the rebellion was about maintaining the *status quo*. Indeed, in so far as the future of the Irish parliament was even contemplated, the impression generated by conservative champions such as George Ogle and John Claudius Beresford was that 'a Protestant House of Commons' was as intrinsic to the maintenance of their 'happy establishment in Church and State' as a Protestant monarchy.[17] Some, the Protestant inhabitants of Bandon most notably, went a step further and pronounced explicitly against 'the fatal love of innovation'. They justified this stand by reference to the desolation revolutionaries had brought to the continent of Europe and 'traitors' to the Irish countryside. And it was a short step from there to the conclusion that since they possessed a constitution that approached 'perfection', it was incumbent upon them, as the corporation of Dublin pronounced, to ensure its 'preservation and protection'.[18] The strength of this conviction was affirmed by the conclusion of the parliamentary committees of inquiry into the rebellion that the United Irishmen had aspired to the subversion of 'the existing establishments in church and state', and by continuing disorder in the countryside.[19] As far as popular Protestant opinion, as expressed in the summer and autumn of 1798, was concerned, Irish Protestants had by their recent actions demonstrated their commitment to the preservation of the constitution and

[14] See, *inter alia*, James Kelly, 'The genesis of Protestant ascendancy' in O'Brien ed., *Parliament, politics and people*, pp. 85–129; 'The development of political parading' in T.G. Fraser, ed., *Political parading in Ireland* (London, 2000); W.J. McCormack, *The Dublin paper war of 1786–1788* (Dublin, 1993).

[15] Lady Gilbert, ed., *Calendar of Ancient Records of Dublin*, xv (Dublin, 1911), pp. 52–3, 55–6; *FJ*, 12 July 1798.

[16] *FJ*, 23 June, 12 July, 2 Aug. 1798; Gilbert, ed., *Ancient records of Dublin*, xv, 54–5.

[17] *FJ*, 2 Aug., 28 Aug. 1798.

[18] *DEP*, 13 Oct.; *FJ*, 22 Sept. 1798; Gilbert, ed., *Ancient Record of Dublin*, xv, 64.

[19] *FJ*, 6, 8 Sept. 1798.

the British connection,[20] and priority must be given to penalising those who threatened them. This certainly was the view of Dublin Corporation, which responded to the evidence in the report of the Commons' committee that Henry Grattan was *au fait* with United Irish plans by disfranchising him and others implicated in 'the late horrid rebellion'. This punitive disposition was further demonstrated during the exceptionally animated celebration of the anniversary of William of Orange's birthday on 4 November, when the sole piece of green silk in evidence among the profusion of orange ribbons decorating the statue of King William on College Green was placed under the feet of his mount in a symbolic affirmation by loyal Protestants of their continuing commitment to their 'unrivalled constitution'.[21]

By the time this demonstration of loyalism took place, reports that a union was in contemplation were the subject of 'general conversation'.[22] Anticipating 'considerable opposition' the Irish administration aspired both to discourage public debate and to wrong foot their political opponents by declining to comment while the details of the measure were worked out and officeholders and likely supporters were briefed.[23] This did not deceive Lord Charlemont, a veteran of many patriot campaigns, who interpreted the chief secretary's silence, when he enquired on 16 October if a union was intended, as an admission that this was indeed the case. Charlemont wasted no time circulating this information with a view to galvanising resistance among like minded peers and commoners. Despite this, the administration's reserve generated enough uncertainty during the months of October and November to cause some elements of the popular press and a number of leading patriot MPs, Lawrence Parsons notably, to conclude optimistically that the scheme had been abandoned. More consequently, it inhibited the emergence within the depleted, disorganised and demoralised ranks of the whig-patriots of a coherent plan of opposition.[24]

The consensus among commentators was that public opinion was 'generally against' a union and that this posed a major question as to 'whether the measure can be carried in Ireland'. Edward Cooke, the

[20] As they observed routinely in complimentary addresses to vacating officeholders and others in the late autumn (*FJ*, 13 Oct. (Corporation of Shoemakers), 27 Oct. (Corporation of barbers, surgeons etc), 8 Nov. 1798 (Loyal Dublin Cavalry)).

[21] Gilbert, ed., *Ancient record of Dublin*, xv, 66–7; *DEP*, 6 Nov., *FJ*, 6 Nov. 1798.

[22] DEP, 13 Oct.; Patrick to James Clancy, 31 Oct. 1798 (NLI, Clancy papers, Ms. 20626).

[23] Cornwallis to Pitt, 1 Nov. 1798 in *Cornwallis Corres.*, II, 427; *FJ*, 8 Nov., 1 Dec.; *DEP*, 17 Nov.; Tighe to Ponsonby, Nov. in E.M. Bell, *The Hamwood papers* (London, 1930), p. 304; Cooke to Castlereagh, 9 Nov. in *Castlereagh Corres.*, I, 432.

[24] Charlemont to Parsons, 16 Oct. (NLI, Rosse papers, Ms. 13840/4); Parsons to Charlemont, 5 Nov., Hardy to Charlemont, 6 Nov., Stewart to Charlemont, 12 Dec. 1798 in H.M.C., *Charlemont*, II, 337–8, 338–9, 342; *DEP*, 28 Nov. 1799.

experienced under-secretary, contended that union legislation would only be ratified if it were 'written up, spoken up, intrigued up, drunk up, sung-up and bribed up'.[25] This was a formidable agenda, but it applied equally to the opponents as well as to the proponents of a union if they were intent on victory and each side exaggerated the preparations of the other. The perception of Lord Castlereagh in mid-November was that 'the opponents of the union' were prepared and laying in wait for the administration. In practice, matters were not so clear cut. William Conyngham Plunket, the MP for Charlemont, did seek to inaugurate a display of public opposition by encouraging a meeting of the bar in late October, but despite the expected hostility of a majority of its members to the idea of a union, there was little sense of urgency, and reports that strong resistance could be anticipated from that quarter were vitiated by reports that Cork was 'strongly for' and Ulster apathetic.[26]

Matters had become clearer by the end of November when Castlereagh informed Cornwallis that 'the principal opposition' was to be anticipated from Dublin.[27] The city's legal establishment expectedly was to the fore. Spurred on by William Saurin, captain of the Lawyers' Corps of Yeomanry, who sought initially, and inappropriately, to persuade the corps to address the matter, a meeting of the full bar was called on 9 December. It amply fulfilled the hopes of anti-unionists in the city by pronouncing that 'the measure of a LEGISLATIVE UNION of this KINGDOM and GREAT BRITAIN is an INNOVATION, which it would be HIGHLY DANGEROUS and IMPROPER to propose at the present juncture'. Moreover, the majority in favour of the existing constitution was so decisive and the language and arguments appealed to in its defence derived from familiar patriot and corporate concerns, it was warmly welcomed in the city at large.[28] The fact that that venerable political club, the Aldermen of Skinner's Alley pronounced against a union on the same day provided its opponents with further encouragement and prompted expectations that 'the rest of the kingdom will follow this example'. This certainly was the wish of the liberal press. The *Dublin*

[25] Cooke to Castlereagh, 9 Nov. in *Castlereagh Corres.*, I, 432; Patrick to James Clancy, 21 Oct., 24 Nov. 1798 (NLI, Clancy papers, Ms. 20626); Elliot to Elliot, 19 Nov. in Countess of Minto, ed., *Life and letters of Sir Gilbert Elliot, Earl of Minto* (3 vols., London, 1874), III, 27–8; Cooke to Auckland, 27, 30 Oct. 1798 (Public Record Office of Northern Ireland (henceforth PRONI), Sneyd papers, T3229/2/27, 40).

[26] Cooke to Auckland, 30 Oct. 1798 (PRONI, Sneyd papers, T3229/2/ 40); Castlereagh to Wickham, 19 Nov., Castlereagh to Beresford, 24 Nov., in *Castlereagh Corres.*, II, 8–9, 16–7; Castlereagh to Wickham, 23 Nov. in *Cornwallis Corres.*, II, 443–4.

[27] Castlereagh to Cornwallis, [late] Nov. 1798 in *Castlereagh Corres.*, II, 26–7.

[28] Castlereagh to Portland, 30 Nov., 5 Dec. in *Cornwallis Corres.*, II, 453–4, III, 5–6; *FJ*, 1, 6, 13 Dec.; *DEP*, 1,6, 11 Dec.; M'Clelland to Corry, 9 Dec., Cooke to Castlereagh, 10 Sept (recte Dec.) 1798 in *Castlereagh Corres.*, II, 37–9, I, 343–4.

Evening Post urged freeholders and freemen to prepare addresses to their representatives instructing them not to sanction a 'dangerous experiment' that must ultimately bring about 'the final separation of the two countries'.[29] As this suggests, though they existed in largely separate liberal and conservative camps, the opponents of a union had reason to feel optimistic in early December. They had grasped the initiative in the battle for public opinion, and their advantage in the public sphere was enhanced when they also claimed the initiative in the 'paper war' inaugurated by the publication late in November of Edward Cooke's pamphlet, *Arguments for and against an Union*. Cooke's tactic was to persuade the public of the logic of a union by presenting the arguments for and against in a manner than demonstrated the validity of the former over the latter. Though ostensibly impartial, his style and approach was too transparent to achieve its aim and his intervention was effectively neutralised by a salvo of replies and rebuttals that served merely to consolidate the anti-unionist argument in the public mind's eye within weeks of its appearance.[30]

While this debate was taking place, public opposition intensified, particularly in Dublin. At its most basic level, it was manifested in the appearance of anti-union ballads and emblematic ribbons bearing the slogan 'no union, freedom and independence to Ireland'.[31] Of greater import were gatherings of metropolitan interests to formulate anti-union resolutions. These, inevitably, reflected the prevailing conservative and patriot ideology of their membership. Following on the bar, the first notable body to assemble were the bankers and merchants, and their resolution of 18 December that a union was not in the commercial or legislative interest of the kingdom of Ireland because the country had enjoyed enviable prosperity since the concession of legislative independence in 1782, represented a firm endorsement of the patriots' position. Though the administration would have preferred it if they had followed the example of the Orange Order and declined to offer an opinion, the resolution of this body did not discommode them

[29] Patrick to James Clancy, 11 Dec. 1798 (N.L.I., Clancy papers, Ms. 20626); *DEP*, 4 Dec. 1798; *FJ*, 10 Jan. 1799; Beresford to Castlereagh, 19 Dec. 1798 in *Castlereagh Corres.*, ii, 50.

[30] [Edward Cooke], *Arguments for an against an union between Great Britain and Ireland considered* (Dublin, 1798). For a selection of responses to Cooke see *DEP*, 6, 13, 22, 29 Dec. 1798, 12 Jan. 1799; [John Humphrey], *Strictures on a pamphlet entitled arguments for an against an union* (Dublin, 1798); Joshua Spencer, *Thoughts on an union* (Dublin, 1798); *An address to the people of Ireland against an union* (Dublin, 1798); *Reasons against the Union* (Dublin, 1798); *A reply to a pamphlet entitled Arguments for and against an union* (Dublin, 1798); *Observations on a pamphlet supposed to be written by an Englishman entitled arguments for an against an union* (Dublin, 1799).

[31] Patrick to James Clancy, 11 Dec. 1798 (NLI., Clancy papers, Ms. 20626).

greatly.[32] The Corporation of Dublin was a quite different proposition, particularly when it opted for the more stridently ideological stand, at a post assembly on 17 December, of linking its opposition to a union to its defence of the constitution when the county was in rebellion:

> Resolved unanimously, that having boldly defended the constitution in King, Lords and Commons, against the open and secret abettors of Rebellion, we are determined steadily to oppose any attempt that may be made to surrender the free legislation of this kingdom by uniting it with the legislature of Great Britain.[33]

The 'manly and spirited' stand taken by the conservatives who dominated Dublin Corporation mirrored the prevailing mood of the city, as a host of metropolitan bodies demonstrated by following its lead in the winter of 1798–9.[34] The language and tone of their addresses and resolutions did not replicate those of the Corporation in all instances. But there is a striking ideological symmetry in the tone and content of the sentiments ratified by interests as diverse as the attorneys who determined on 27 December that a legislative union would be 'an innovation ... dangerous to the kingdom'; the feltmakers company which decreed that advocates of a union should be 'treated as rebels to the constitution'; and the guild of tallow chandlers, which vowed to defend the

> constitution and oppose by every legal means the destruction thereof, whether attempted by internal rebellion, foreign foes, or those domestic traitors who would surrender the free legislation of this kingdom by uniting it with the legislature of any other country.[35]

Across the municipal spectrum, equivalently defiant pronouncements were offered by trade guilds, notably the merchants, cutlers, cooks, hosiers, butchers, weavers and dyers, reprobating a union as subversive of the constitution, as well as destructive of trade, and condemning anyone who took a contrary view as 'an enemy' to the constitution and

[32] Cornwallis to Portland, 15 Dec., in *Cornwallis Corres*, III, 18–9; Cooke to Castlereagh enclosing resolutions, 18 Dec., in *Castlereagh Corres.*, II, 47–8; *DEP*, 18, 20 Dec., *FJ*, 20 Dec. 1798.

[33] Gilbert, ed., *Ancient records of Dublin*, XV, 80–81. This argument had been articulated by 'a country yeoman' earlier in the month (*DEP*, 8 Dec. 1798) when it had elicted a concerned reaction by Cornwallis (*Cornwallis Corres.*, iii, 5–6).

[34] *DEP*, 22, 24 Dec. 1798. The tide of opposition to a union was running so strong in the city of Dublin by the middle of December 1798 that, Patrick Duigenan reported, 'some of the first and most popular characters who are perfectly convinced of the ... necessity of the measure' declined 'to proclaim their opinions' (Duigenan to Castlereagh, 20 Dec. 1798 in *Castlereagh Corres.*, II, 52–3).

[35] *DEP*, 27 Dec., 1798, 8 Jan. 1799; H.F. Berry, 'The records of the feltmakers company of Dublin 1687–1841', *Journal of the Royal Society of Antiquaries of Ireland*, 41 (1911), p. 28.

the country.[36] Moreover, such sentiments were not the exclusive preserve of metropolitan commercial interests eager to reinforce their quotidian commercial anxieties with a constitutional imperative. Meetings of the freeholders of county Dublin, of the freeholders and freemen of Dublin city, the County Dublin grand jury, the quarter assembly of Dublin Corporation and the electors of the boroughs of Swords and Trinity College resolved against the idea of a union in only marginally less forceful terms as hostile to 'the rights, liberties and interests of Ireland'.[37]

The collective thrust of these anti-union pronouncements offered a clear statement of what John Claudius Beresford described as 'the universal disgust' abroad in Dublin 'at the idea of a union' in the winter of 1798–9.[38] The problem for anti-unionists was that public opinion elsewhere was not equally aroused. This was due in part at least to the fact that commercial interests outside the capital did not identify their continuing commercial prosperity as intimately with the presence of a national parliamentary assembly. Equally importantly, they did not possess the organisational infrastructure that gave ideological conservatives such a powerful voice in the capital. As a result, popular opposition to a union elsewhere was more likely to be stoked by patriot interests and to be expressed in the language of patriotism at aggregate meetings of freeholders. The comparative lethargy of patriots when compared with the alertness of commercial bodies in the metropolis in the winter of 1798–9 was a source of such anxiety to supporters of the anti-union cause that the *Dublin Evening Post* chided the public outside Dublin for their inactivity and exhorted freeholders to assemble to instruct their representatives to vote against any such proposal in parliament.[39] Such exhortations were not without effect, but the response was decidedly spotty. In County Louth, the public opposition of John Foster, the most eminent local politician, ensured a meeting of local freeholders in mid-January at which it was resolved that 'an independent Irish legislature is as necessary as [the] British connexion to the prosperity of Ireland'. Significantly, Foster was not content with this. He observed in his reply that as well as many substantive economic reasons for opposing a union, the example of France 'teach[es] us the danger of innovating on the established constitution'. The responses of the local MPs, John Ball and Edward Hardman, to the request of the freemen and freeholders of Drogheda to oppose a union were less assertive. But their readiness to comply

[36] *DEP*, 8, 12, 17, 19, 22 Jan.; *FJ*, 10, 17 Jan. 1798; W.J. Battersby, *The Repealer's manuel* (Dublin, 1837), pp. 331–2, 333–4.

[37] *DEP*, 1, 5, 10, 12, 19, 22 Jan.; *FJ*, 5, 10, 12, 19 Jan. 1799; Battersby, *Repealer's manuel*, p. 332; Gilbert, ed., *Ancient records of Dublin*, xv, 81–2

[38] Beresford to Castlereagh, 19 Dec. 1798 in *Castlereagh Corres.*, II, 51.

[39] *DEP*, 1, 17, 19 Jan. 1799.

ensured that, after Dublin, County Louth was one of the main popular bastions of anti-unionism.[40] There were few others. The high profile anti-unionism of patriots such as Lawrence Parsons in Kings' and Sir John Parnell in Queen's County ensured the approval of resolutions at meetings of freeholders that condemned a union as 'highly dangerous' and 'a virtual surrender of our constitution'. The freeholders of Meath, Westmeath, Carlow, Monaghan and the freeholders and inhabitants of Galway city likewise focussed on the implications of a union for the 'constitution of 1782', though the Galway meeting was also attracted by the argument, expressed in some quarters in Dublin, that MPs did not possess the power 'to vote away their independence'.[41] It was a modest list, all things considered, which accurately reflected the lack of enthusiasm throughout much of the country for the anti-unionist campaign in the early months of 1799.

Popular opposition to a union was at its weakest in Munster. In Cork, the Corporation fulfilled expectations by determining on 5 January that 'an union . . . grounded upon just and equitable terms, will be the most effectual and decisive means of establishing and preserving the peace and prosperity of this kingdom'. Further expressions linking their support for a union to 'the unprovoked rebellion, which has lately disgraced certain quarters of this kingdom, and the treachery, which invited a foreign enemy to its shore' underlined the appeal of political integration in this quarter. But optimistic expectations in official circles that Waterford and Limerick would emulate Cork proved misplaced.[42] Despite this, the absence of overt opposition caused the administration to conclude, somewhat rhapsodically, that the whole province was 'well disposed' when the reality was less certain.

Matters were certainly less than clear cut in Ulster which was, Cornwallis maintained on 21 January, 'in a state of neutrality'. It is true that attempts by anti-unionists in several Ulster counties, Armagh and Cavan notably, to orchestrate addresses calling upon representatives to oppose a union did not bear fruit, but there was little evidence of strong unionist sentiment either. The fact that a number of MPs from the province declared publicly their intention to oppose a union registered less with the administration than the information that 'all the thinking people' and the linen trade were well-inclined and that the influential Orange Order in the province was content to follow the

[40] *DEP*, 8, 17, 19 Jan.; *FJ*, 19 Jan.; Hudson to Charlemont, 21 Jan. 1799 in H.M.C., *Charlemont*, II, 343–4.

[41] *DEP*, 8, 10, 15, 17, 19, 22, 24 Jan.; *FJ*, 17 Jan. 1799.

[42] Richard Caulfeild, *The council book of the Corporation of Cork* (Guilford, 1876), p. 1131; *FJ*, 13, 18 Dec., 1798, 17, 19 Jan.; Castlereagh to Portland, 9 Jan. 1799 in *Castlereagh Corres.*, II, 85–6.

example of the Dublin lodges and refrain from expressing an opinion.[43]

The preparedness of the leaders of Catholic opinion to do likewise was also interpreted positively by the administration arising from their anxiety that the failure to include a provision to allow Catholics the right to parliamentary representation as part of the union settlement might generate resistance from that quarter. In truth, the Catholic leadership had not recovered from the fright of the rebellion and, like the Orange Order, was anxious to avoid the embarrassment of exposing the different attitudes within the Catholic communion on the issue of a union. For these reasons, a meeting of Catholic leaders determined prudently in December that they did 'not wish the question of the Catholics being admitted into the representation to be agitated at this time', and that they 'judged it inexpedient to publish any resolution or declaration'.[44]

The sharp variation in public attitudes towards a legislative union – ranging regionally from support in the south, to disinterest in the north and hostility, to hostility in Dublin, Galway and the midlands – suggested that the administration stood an excellent chance of securing parliamentary approval for a union at the first time of asking because it meant that only a minority of MPs were under intense public pressure to oppose from within their constituencies. By the administration's calculations, the opposition was unlikely to muster much more than one hundred, but both Cornwallis and Castlereagh acknowledged that the impact of public 'clamour' in Dublin and the self-interest of borough proprietors meant they could not be certain.[45] As is well known, though their assays of the likely size of the opposition were not substantially in error, the administration failed to convince enough of the two-thirds of MPs not committed to opposition to join with them. In two divisions, on 23 and 25 January, appertaining to the inclusion of a reference to a union in the address to the king, the united opposition first pushed the administration to within two votes and then defeated them, 111 to 106, thereby preventing the advancement of union legislation at this time. It was an embarrassing outcome for Castlereagh who admitted that he had not anticipated that 'the question would have been fought on the

[43] Cornwallis to Ross, 21 Jan. in *Cornwallis Corres.*, III, 40; *DEP*, 3, 15, 17, 22, 24 Jan.; Castlereagh to Portland, 2 Jan., Alexander to Knox, 17 Jan., Lyle to Castlereagh, 23 Jan., Castlereagh to Portland, 21 Jan. 1799 in *Castlereagh Corres.*, II, 80, 123–4 , 127–8, 128.

[44] Cornwallis to Ross, 8 Dec., Cornwallis to Portland, 24 Dec 1798, 2 Jan. 1799. in *Cornwallis Corres.*, III, 9, 22, 28–9; Cooke to Castlereagh, 17 Dec., Troy to Castlereagh, 24 Dec., in *Castlereagh Corres.*, II, 46–7, 61; Lord to Lady Minto, 10 Dec. 1798 in *Life and letters of Minto*, III, 35.

[45] Cooke to Auckland, 12 Dec., Castlereagh to Auckland, 13 Dec. 1798 (PRONI, Sneyd papers, T3229/2/44, 45); Cornwallis to Portland, 11 Jan., Castlereagh to Portland, 21 Jan. 1799 in *Castlereagh Corres.*, II, 89–90, 126; Castlereagh to Portland, 5 Jan., Cornwallis to Ross, 21 Jan. 1799 in *Cornwallis Corres.*, III, 30–32, 40.

address'.[46] By contrast, the opponents of the measure were delighted, and the celebrations that followed on the streets of Dublin indicated that as far as the populace of the city was concerned it was a victory for public opinion.

The assessment by Lord Camden on 8 February that the 'agitation is so great at Dublin and in various part of Ireland' that consideration of a legislative union should be postponed to a future session suggests that the decision not to press forward at this time was influenced by public disorder on the streets of the capital.[47] This was not the case; there was little disorder of any consequence. The debate in the House of Commons on 22 January did provoke some 'hissing, ... groaning, and clapping' from the public gallery. But this only became a matter of controversy subsequently because of an unsubstantiated report in the London *Sun* that 'above a dozen members' who supported a union had 'quitted the house in disgust'.[48] Similarly, the public's response to the divisions of 23 and 25 January was exuberant celebration rather than riotous discontent, as a brief account will bear out. It began in the afternoon of 23 January when Speaker Foster, who was widely applauded by the public for his opposition to a union, was accorded the traditional honour of having his carriage unhorsed and being drawn by a number of 'respectable' citizens from College Green to his home in Molesworth Street. When darkness fell, the citizens further manifested their pleasure at events by organising a general illumination that was the occasion of some anti-social behaviour when a mob broke the windows of anti-unionists who declined to join in the euphoria of the moment. Matters only became serious when an attempt was made to force an entry into the house of a prominent unionist, which obliged him and his family to quit for a time, but no great damage resulted. However, when a further illumination was called two days later to celebrate the vote of 25 January the authorities took immediate steps to ensure that they and not the mob gained control of the streets. Once again, they could not prevent darkened windows being broken, but they did ensure there was no sustained disorder by calling out the military who demonstrated their intent by firing on and killing two people when a mob threatened to get out of control.[49]

The rapture of the Dublin populace that fuelled such demonstrations

[46] Bolton, *The passing of the Irish Act of Union*, chapter four, provides a full account; Cornwallis to Portland, 30 Jan. in *Cornwallis Corres.*, III, 58–9; Castlereagh to Portland, 28 Jan. 1799 in *Castlereagh Corres.*, II, 142.

[47] Camden to Clare, 8 Feb. 1799 (PRONI, Camden papers, T2627/4/226).

[48] This account is based on a report of a debate on the matter in the House of Commons on 8 February (*FJ*, 12 Feb. 1799).

[49] *DEP*, 24, 26 Jan.; *FJ*, 26 Jan.; Cornwallis to Portland, 25 Jan. 1799 in *Cornwallis Corres.*, III, 51.

mirrored the delight of more mainstream opposition interests, such as the bar, which met on 24 January to applaud the stand of anti-union MPs. The patriots had, in similar circumstances in 1785 rallied the public to frustrate William Pitt's plan for a commercial union.[50] Eager to replicate this success they conceived that they could best insure against the introduction of union legislation by affirming the strength of public opposition through public votes of thanks to 'the glorious and virtuous' one hundred and eleven MPs who had represented their position on 25 January. It was a strategy that paid some dividends. Many of the bodies that met in the spring of 1799 to approve resolutions and addresses either to prominent members of the opposition such as John Foster, Sir John Parnell and James Fitzgerald or to the full complement of MPs that had carried the day on 25 January had previously expressed anti-union views, but for many more it was the first time and the process did provide an opportunity for a broader demonstration of popular anti-unionism.[51]

However, it was not long before the energy that characterised the popular response to the union in the winter of 1798–9 began to dissipate. Extensive reports of proceedings at Westminster where William Pitt advanced what even some of its opponents accepted was an impressive case in favour of a legislative union, and the failure of repeated attempts by anti-unionists 'to consolidate their party' and present a united front in the House of Commons were manifestations of the lack of coherence and purpose within their ranks which not even the realisation that the administration was intent on reintroducing the union could redress.[52] Lord Charlemont was one of the first on the anti-union side to recognise that the victory registered in January 'though glorious' was 'not decisive', and convinced that the country had to be *seen* to pronounce against a union in order to dissuade the government from taking up the measure once again, he redoubled his efforts to promote an anti-union address in his home county of Armagh and to encourage friends and allies to do likewise elsewhere.[53] The response initially was encouraging. Reports from Ulster suggested that the apathy that had prevailed in the province earlier in the winter had evaporated, while resolutions against a union were secured from, among other places, the city of Cork. However, it was apparent before the end of February that the momentum was fast draining from the opposition's campaign. This was highlighted by the fact that various initiatives, such as the suggestion that a 'public

[50] James Kelly, *Prelude to Union: Anglo-Irish politics in the 1780s* (Cork, 1992), pp. 210–21.

[51] *DEP*, 26, 29, 31 Jan., 2, 7, 9, 12, 16, 19, 26 Feb., 5, 16, 28 Mar.; *FJ*, 29, 31 Jan. 1799.

[52] *FJ*, Jan.–Feb. passim; *DEP*, 4 Feb.; Cornwallis to Ross, 28 Jan., Cornwallis to Portland, 28 Feb. in *Cornwallis Corres.*, III, 56, 68–9; Troy to Coxe Hippesley, 9 Feb., Castlereagh to Portland, 9 Feb.1799 in *Castlereagh Corres.*, II, 170–71, 172.

[53] Charlemont to Haliday, 2 Feb. 1799 in H.M.C., *Charlemont*, II, 345.

memorial' should be erected to the peers and commoners who had opposed a union in January, failed to elicit the requisite support and that the flow of anti-union resolutions slowed appreciably.[54] The anti-union cause was given a welcome, but short-lived, boost in April when John Foster delivered his long anticipated reply to Pitt's argument in favour of a union. The response across the anti-union spectrum was enthusiastic, which enhanced further the Speaker's reputation in that quarter and reinforced committed opponents to the measure in their positions. Supporters of a union were palpably less complimentary. But of greater consequence that the *ad hominem* disparagement of Foster that many indulged was the realisation that for all the passion of his rhetoric and the logic of his argument the Speaker did not, Bishop Euseby Cleaver noted approvingly, leave 'the cause of the union weaker in the House of Commons than he found it'.[55] This was critical because in the country there were already signs that the public attitude to the union was beginning to soften and that the combined forces of popular conservatism and patriotism that had ignited and sustained public opposition to an act of union in the winter of 1798/99 would have to compete for support if it was to retain its dominance in the public arena.

II

In mid-February, at the height of the anti-unionist campaign to obtain addresses congratulating the 111 MPs who had voted against a union, the second Earl of Shannon advised a worried Earl Camden not to be too impressed by the number of anti-union statements that were forthcoming because many of them were trumped up or procured by dubious means.[56] There is little evidence to sustain this, but the implication that the unlikely combination of conservatives and patriots that orchestrated the popular campaign against a union did not fully represent public opinion was correct. One small pointer to this, from which unionists took considerable comfort, was provided by the re-election in February of the newly appointed chancellor of the exchequer, Isaac Corry, and prime serjeant, St George Daly, for the 'populous'

[54] Hudson to Charlemont, 3 Feb, 9 Mar., Boyd to Charlemont, 20 Feb., in H.M.C., *Charlemont*, II, 345–6, 347; *DEP*, 23 Feb., 2 Mar. 1799.

[55] *Speech of the rt hon John Foster ... delivered in committee on Thursday 11 April 1799* (Dublin, 1799); Buckingham to Grenville, 12 Apr. in H.M.C., *Fortescue*, V, 10–11; Haliday to Charlemont, 15 Apr., Charlemont to Haliday, 19 Apr., Hudson to Charlemont, 1 May in H.M.C., *Charlemont*, ii, 349–50; Cornwallis to Ross, 15 Apr. in *Cornwallis Corres.*, III, 89; Cleaver to Egremont, 17, 29 Apr. 1799 (Petworth House, Egremont Papers).

[56] Shannon to [Camden], 17 Feb. 1799 (KAO, Camden papers, U840/081/7).

and 'independent' boroughs of Newry and Galway respectively.[57] Another, more reliable index, was provided by the preparedness of discrete bodies of unionists in a variety of jurisdictions to publish pro-union addresses. The decision of thirty-six eminent freeholders in County Antrim, who were alarmed by a sudden rise in disorder locally, to call on their MPs to request that the question of a legislative union 'be fairly investigated ... as the best means of securing the country from ... threatened ruin' represented an early tentative step.[58] Others followed. Before the end of February, a group of forty-one freeholders from County Galway, headed by the Church of Ireland Archbishop of Tuam and Ardagh, William Beresford, dissatisfied with the anti-union address sanctioned at a meeting of freeholders at Loughrea, pronounced that

> a legislative union with Great Britain, established on terms of perfect equality, would invigorate the resources, encrease the wealth and add materially to the security of both countries, enabling them to oppose their common enemy with encreased strength and power – and most effectually to defeat their object of dividing the empire, for the purpose of subsuming it.[59]

The logic of this argument was compelling to many within the Protestant community, and the town of Galway and the grand juries of both Cork county and city had pronounced in favour of a union on similar grounds by the beginning of April. The most impressive demonstration of support in the country for a union came from County Cork where the success of the anti-unionist camp in securing as address to which some seven hundred names were appended, was countered by a pro-union address with five hundred and sixty signatories headed by most of the main noblemen and gentlemen of the county.[60]

The ability of unionist interests in Cork, Galway and Antrim to secure addresses signed by sizeable numbers of freeholders with substantial property interests allied to the inability of the anti-union cause to capitalise on the assizes to secure additional declarations in favour of their position was a source of encouragement to Castlereagh, Cornwallis and other unionists who observed 'the change of feeling in regard to the Union' that took place throughout the country in the late

[57] Ibid.; Pelham to Minto, 22 Feb. 1799 (NLS, Minto papers, Ms. 11195 f. 3).

[58] *DEP*, 16 Feb. 1799. Somewhat earlier a number of unionists in County Monaghan had made known their discontent with an address congratulating the majority of 25 January (*DEP*, 9 Mar. 1799).

[59] *DEP*, 7 Mar. 1799.

[60] *DEP*, 2, 16, 18 Apr.; Garde to Devonshire, 20 Mar. 1799 (PRONI, Chatsworth papers, T3158/1788); public addresses and declarations in favour of union, 2 Apr. 1800 (Public Record Office (henceforth PRO), Chatham papers, 30/8/327). I wish to thank Dr P.J. Jupp. for the latter reference.

spring and early summer with unalloyed pleasure.[61] The administration did not have enough parliamentary or popular support to risk reintroducing the measure into the Irish parliament during the 1799 session, not least because there were no defections, a worried Lord Charlemont observed with some relief, from the anti-union side. This was due, among other reasons to the impact of the distribution of Foster's speech in pamphlet form, but there was no masking the drift among the doubtful and undecided in parliament and in society at large towards a union.[62] The appeal of union was enhanced by alterations to its terms that won over nervous parliamentary interests, by the continuing extensive reportage of proceedings at Westminster and by the impact of pro-union propaganda subsidised or paid for with money illegally secured from the British secret service list.[63] The publication that best served the union cause in the summer of 1799 was the speech by Lord Minto in the British House of Lords on 11 April. Prepared for the presses with the aid and advice of William Woodfall, who had also overseen the publication of William Pitt's speech of 31 January, the balanced manner in which Minto addressed the subject 'produced more effect and impression than any publication ... yet ... circulated', as even anti-unionists conceded. Minto's speech was particularly suited to mass circulation in Ireland because it endorsed the principal of 'political equality' for Catholics in a manner that did not alarm Protestants, and the Irish administration got a good return for sponsoring an edition of 5,000 copies 'for general circulation throughout the kingdom'.[64]

The slowly growing momentum supportive of a union to which this

[61] *FJ*, 14, 23 Mar.; Garde to Devonshire, 20 Mar. (PRONI, Chatsworth papers, T3158/1788); Castlereagh to Portland, 27 Mar., Alexander to Castlereagh, 28 Mar. in *Castlereragh Corres.*, II, 240, 242; Cornwallis to Dundas, 14 Mar., Cornwallis to Ross, 20, 28 Mar., Cornwallis to Portland, 29 Mar. in *Cornwallis Corres.*, III, 77, 80–81 83; Shannon to Boyle, 10 Apr. in E. Hewitt, ed., *Lord Shannon's letters* (Belfast, 1983), p. 188; Woodford to Minto, 29 April., Elliot to Minto, 23 May (NLS, Minto papers, Mss. 11195 ff. 9–10, 11229 ff. 152–3); Cooke to Camden, 7 May (KAO, Camden papers, U840/081/3); Hill to Barnard, 22 May 1799 in A. Powell, ed., *Barnard letters 1778–1824* (London, 1928), p. 107.

[62] Shannon to Boyle, [post 10 Apr.] in Hewitt, ed., *Shannon's letters*, p. 188; Cornwallis to Portland, 29 Mar. in Cornwallis Corres., III, 82–3; Cooke to Camden, 7 May (KAO, Camden papers, U840/081/3); Charlemont to Haliday, 10, 14 May. 1799 in H.M.C., *Charlemont*, II, 351–2.

[63] Cornwallis to Portland, 27 Mar., Cornwallis to Ross, 28 Mar. in *Cornwallis Corres.*, III, 80–81; Cleaver to Egrement, 9 Apr. 1799 (Petworth House, Egremont papers); David Wilkinson, 'How did they pass the Union: secret service expenditure in Ireland 1799–1804' , *History*, 80 (1997).

[64] Woodfall to Minto, 12 Apr. Elliot to Minto, 23 May, Day to Douglas, 28 May, Douglas to Minto, 17 Sept., 1799, 5 Jan. [1800] (NLS, Minto papers, Ms. 11195 ff. 5–6, 11129 f. 152, 11130 ff. 92, 98, 113); Shannon to Boyle, 9 July in Hewitt, ed., *Shannon's letters*, p. 200; Cornwallis to Portland, 20 July 1799 in *Castlereagh Corres.*, II, 353.

contributed took tangible form in the shape of further pro-union addresses during the summer months. The administration was not overwhelmed by the number presented. But the impact of the changing mood and the success of Cornwallis's policy of 'earnestly' recommending 'to the friends of government' that they should 'exert themselves during the summer in their several counties' to obtain declarations 'similar to those of Cork and Galway in favour of the measure' allowed them to seize the initiative in the battle for public opinion.[65] Proceeding by 'private application rather than by public meeting', unionists in counties Meath, Kerry, Kings', Mayo and the town of Ballyshannon, had come forward by the first week of July with a variety of addresses, declarations and statements professing their conviction that a union must help 'remove every cause of distrust and jealousy between the two countries', secure the Anglo-Irish connection, reduce sectarian animosity, promote economic growth and 'consolidate the power and resources of the empire'. The number of signatories to these documents was sometimes not large but, as Justice Robert Day boasted of the Kerry declaration, they represented 'the weight of property of the ... county'.[66] More importantly, as far as the administration was concerned, they helped increase the number of unionists in the House of Commons to an estimated 165 by 22 June and boosted their confidence and that of their supporters by declaring they would triumph when the measure was presented again in 1800.[67]

Though he was encouraged by these developments, by the anticipation of further declarations from counties Clare, Derry, Tipperary, Waterford and Wexford, and by the prospect of declarations from counties Antrim, Armagh, Donegal, Down, Kilkenny, Leitrim, Longford, Monaghan, Meath, Queen's, Roscommon, Sligo, Tyrone and Westmeath, Lord Cornwallis could not claim with any confidence that public opinion was on his side. He noted with satisfaction that it was now 'impossible to excite any popular commotion against the Union in any part of the Kingdom except in Dublin', and eager to improve his position with public opinion still further, he undertook a three-week tour of the 'south' in late July 'for the purpose of obtaining declarations, &c, in favour of the Union'.[68]

[65] Cornwallis to Portland, 22 June 1799 in *Castlereagh Corres.*, II, 368–9.

[66] Knowlton to Heaton, 10 July (PRONI, Chatsworth papers, T3158/1791); O'Beirne to Castlereagh and enclosure, 14 May, Altamont to [ ], 5 June, Cornwallis to Portland, 22 June, Castlereagh to Portland, 6 July in *Castlereagh Corres.*, II, 309–10, 327–9, 336–9; Shannon to Boyle, 5 July in Hewitt, ed., *Shannon's letters*, p. 199; *DEP*, II, 14 May, 6, 9 July ; Day to Douglas, 28 May 1799 (NLS, Minto papers, Ms. 11130 ff. 92–3).

[67] Cornwallis to Ross, 19 June, Cornwallis to Portland, 22 June in *Cornwallis Corres.*, III, 103–4; Moore to Castlereagh, 22 June, Abercorn to Castlereagh, 2 July in *Castlereagh Corres.*, II, 343–4; Shannon to Boyle, 22, 23 July 1799 in Hewitt, ed., *Shannon's letters*, p. 207.

[68] Cornwallis to Ross, 2, 21 July in *Cornwallis Corres.*, III, 111, 118; Cornwallis to Portland, 22 June, 20 July 1799 in *Castlereagh Corres.*, II, 338–9, 352.

Cornwallis' tour of Munster had a galvanic effect on the popular pro-unionist campaign. At every location the lord lieutenant visited, local unionists ensured that as well as the warm welcome normally accorded a personage of his eminence he was presented with addresses supportive of the principle of a legislative union. The tone and content of a majority of the addresses did not differ greatly from location to location. Most pronounced that a union 'founded on equal and liberal principles' would ease domestic tensions and benefit the empire commercially and politically. However, a number from locations in County Cork, reflecting deep-seated conservative concerns, dwelled with more deliberation upon the security a union would provide against 'the fatal effects of anarchy'; whilst those from the clergy of the Church of Ireland in particular expressed a wish that the Protestant 'constitution in Church and state' would be preserved intact.[69] Significantly, Cornwallis did not encourage such declarations. Quite the contrary; everywhere he went 'he paid equal attention to the papists as to the protestants', and the result was better than he could have hoped for. Not alone did 'the people of the south seem to wish more for a union' on his departure for Dublin in mid-August, he had addresses from a variety of interests in most major towns (Kilkenny, Waterford, Cork, Youghal, Bandon, Carrick-on-Suir, Tipperary, Cahir and Limerick) to prove it. No less consequently, his avowed determination to treat Catholics fairly persuaded members of that communion throughout the province of Munster to accept the advice of Archbishops Troy and Bray and come forward in large numbers with addresses professing their enthusiasm for a union.[70]

The momentum Cornwallis' tour of Munster gave the unionist cause at popular level was sustained following his return to Dublin, as the number of supportive public addresses continued to appreciate through August and September. In tone and content, they bear close comparison with a majority of the addresses presented to the Lord Lieutenant from Munster, but they emanated from a wider geographical catchment. Thus, there were addresses from Catholics (frequently chaired by the local bishop) as well as Protestants from counties Wexford, Tipperary, Kerry, Galway, Leitrim, Longford and Clare, the baronies of Tyrawly and Tyrenagh in the Catholic diocese of Killala and the towns of Galway, Athlone, Monasterevin and Dundalk. With 'the Union ...

[69] Shannon to Boyle, ca 18 July in Hewitt, ed., *Shannon's letters*, p. 205; *DEP*, 25, 30 July, 3, 8, 13, 15, 20 Aug.; *FJ*, 8, 10, 13 Aug.; Troy to Marshall, 6, 13 July, Bray to Troy, 1 July 1799 in *Castlereagh Corres.*, II, 344–5, 349.

[70] Knowlton to Heaton, 11 Aug. (PRONI, Chatsworth papers, T3158/1794); Cornwallis to Portland, 13 Aug. in *Castlereagh Corres.*, II, 372–4; *DEP*, 8, 10 Aug.; *FJ*, 10 Aug. 1799; Public addresses and declarations in favour of a union, 2 Apr. 1800 (PRO, Chatham papers, 30/8/327).

daily gaining ground', expectations rose accordingly that it would become law when the Irish parliament reconvened. According to Edward Cooke, this was a commonly expressed opinion in Dublin's coffee houses before the end of September.[71]

His success in Munster confirmed, Cornwallis turned his attention to Ulster from where few pro-union addresses had originated during the summer of 1799. While he was in Munster, Lord Castlereagh had visited Ulster with the dual purpose of discouraging anti-union declarations in County Down, and of encouraging positive pronouncements elsewhere.[72] His presence at the County Down assizes was not without impact, but it took until the end of September for addresses to arrive in any number. Guided by John Beresford, the Grand Jury of County Londonderry set the trend. The freemen and freeholders of the city and county followed suit within days, and County Antrim joined them before the end of the month. The language of the declarations in each case was reasoned and moderately turned, but the most striking feature was the number of freeholders prepared to append their names. Though on record as preferring 'in general, resolutions of the men of property' to the pronouncements of 'county meetings', it was impossible for Cornwallis and others not to be impressed by the numbers of signatures, amounting respectively to over 2230 and 1600, included with the addresses forthcoming from Counties Londonderry and Antrim.[73] They certainly provided Cornwallis with good reason to believe that a trip to Ulster would achieve an equally positive result as his tour of Munster when he set out in early October. The response was encouraging. Following a visit to Belfast that elicited an address from the sovereign and burgesses of the corporation stating that 'a legislative union with Great Britain founded upon equal and liberal principles will be productive of interior concord and tranquillity to this nation and of general power, happiness and consequence to the empire', he was presented with equally welcome addresses elsewhere. Among those forthcoming were the clergy and people of Armagh, the clergy of the diocese of Dromore, the burgesses and principal inhabitants of Limavady, the electors and principal inhabitants of the borough of Antrim, the mayor, noblemen, clergy, freemen, freeholders and inhabitants of Londonderry, the mayor aldermen and burgesses of Coleraine, the corporation and inhabitants of Lifford, the merchants and inhab-

[71] *DEP*, 8, 13, 15, 20 Aug., 7, 10, 12, 19 Sept.; *FJ*, 13, 17 Aug., 7, 10, 26, 28 Sept., 3, 10 Oct.; Cornwallis to Ross, 22 Sept. in *Cornwallis Corres.*, III, 133; Cooke to Castlereagh, 18 Sept., Dillon to Troy, 1 Sept. in *Castlereagh Corres.*, II, 403, 386–7; Douglas to Minto, 15 Sept. 1799 (NLS, Minto Papers, Ms. 11130 f. 97).

[72] Castlereagh to Portland, 5 Aug. 1799 in *Castlereagh Corres.*, II, 367–69.

[73] Cornwallis to Ross, 4 Sept. in *Cornwallis Corres.*, III, 129; *FJ*, 19, 21 Sept.; *DEP*, 24, 26 Sept., 10 Oct.; Marsden to Castlreagh, 28 Sept.1799 in *Castlereagh Corres.*, II, 406.

itants of Castlefin and the provost, burgesses and inhabitants of Strabane. In addition, addresses were received subsequently from the grand jury of Monaghan and, with more than 3,000 signatories in each case, from Counties Tyrone and Donegal.[74]

These were impressive demonstrations of popular as well as propertied support for a union, and they ensured that Cornwallis's initial assessment that there was 'reason to entertain very sanguine hopes of the good disposition of the people' of Ulster towards a union understated the reality. Moreover, the example set provided a stimulus to others, and further addresses or supplementary lists of signatures were forthcoming from the towns of New Ross and Kinsale and from 3000 Catholics, headed by Bishop Caulfield, from County Wexford and 1,386 Catholics from County Leitrim.[75]

III

Based upon the ample evidence with which he was provided that the Catholics were 'decidedly' pro-union, Lord Cornwallis was prepared to venture that the union 'cannot fail of success' by the beginning of winter.[76] By contrast, the mood in the anti-union camp was downbeat. Unlike the administration, their cause had atrophied during the summer of 1799. A number of diehard opponents – Jonah Barrington, Thomas Osborne and Capel Molyneux – kept the press supplied with a thin corpus of anti-union commentary but it was poor compensation for a vigorous popular campaign. Moreover, the death of Charlemont in August weakened the patriot wing of the anti-unionist cause, and there was little occasional articles in the press could do to mask the dramatic downturn in public support. This was highlighted when the corporation of Dublin was unable, on 17 July, to agree an address to William Saurin because of his opposition to the union.[77]

In the absence of a visible anti-union movement, the popular press sought to impugn the legitimacy of the pro-union declarations of their

[74] Littlehales to Castlereagh, 9, 18 Oct. in *Castlereagh Corres.*, II, 414–5, 430; Cornwallis to Portland, 22 Oct. in *Cornwallis Corres.*, III, 138–40; E.M. Boyle, *Records of the town of Limavady* (Londonderry, 1912), pp. 115–6; *DEP*, 5, 10, 17, 19 Oct., 16 Nov., 3, 26 Dec; *FJ*, 12, 15, 17, 19, 22 Oct., 5, 17 Dec. 1799.

[75] *DEP*, 31 Oct. *FJ*, 12, 22, 31 Oct., 12, 19 Nov.; Cornwallis to Portland, 22 Oct., Cornwallis to Ross, 24 Oct. in *Cornwallis Corres.*, III, 138, 141; Elliot to Castlereagh, 19 Oct. 1799 in *Castlereagh Corres.*, II, 431–2.

[76] Cornwallis to Ross, 7 Nov. in *Cornwallis Corres.*, III, 143; see also Musgrave to Cooke, 1 Nov. in ibid., 143–4;

[77] *FJ*, 15 Jun., 20 July; *DEP*., 15 Jun, 4, 6, 16 Jul., 13 Aug., 5 Sept., 1, 3 Oct.; Gilbert, ed., *Ancient records of Dublin*, XV, 115; Castlereagh to Portland, 20 July 1799 in *Castlereagh Corres.*, II, 353–4.

opponents. It accused them of having recourse to 'forgery' and undue influence, alleged that they were the work of the 'dependent and self-interested', and gleefully highlighted any evidence of impropriety that came its way.[78] The anti-union cause was not without popular support, of course, but compared with its opponents the few public declarations it elicited during the later months of 1799 from Dublin Corporation, the Grand Jury of County Dublin, the Grand Jury of the City of Dublin and the freeholders of County Roscommon merely served to emphasise its current problems.[79] This was not lost on the anti-union movement,[80] but they had little success in generating renewed momentum behind their campaign until January 1800. Their cause was helped by the launch on 9 December 1799 of a newspaper entitled *The Constitution, or Anti-Union* dedicated to the elaboration of the anti-union case. With space to fill, the *Anti-Union* provided critics of a legislative union with an opportunity to make their case at length. However, since most of the relevant issues had been debated thoroughly already, and most people had already determined where they stood on the larger question, its impact was modest. To compound matters, its editorial direction lacked flair and imagination. As a result, though a wider range of issues were dealt with in the newspaper than in the mainstream press, the influence of the *Anti-Union* was less than the anti-union cause required. This was a relief to the Irish administration, as Edward's Lees made clear when he observed on 20 December that 'scarcely anything has appeared deserving notice in the anti-union newspaper that has not been refuted'.[81]

The administration could not afford to take public opinion for granted at the same time. With the *Anti-Union* on the streets, the volume of anti-union propaganda abroad increased manifold. So too did the number of voices calling upon freeholders across the country 'to arouse from their criminal supineness' and emulate the example of County Roscommon and come out against a union.[82] The response was markedly less than it had been the previous winter. But the efforts of committed anti-unionists, and unease 'among the middling and lower order people' enabled them to generate further addresses, petitions and other declarations hostile to a union from counties Limerick, Galway, Roscommon, Leitrim and Westmeath, and from a faction of liberal middle-class Catholics in Dublin in the run-up to the opening of

[78] *DEP*, 3, 8, 27 Aug., 14 Sept., 10, 29 Oct. 1799.

[79] Elliot to Castlereagh, 19 Oct. in *Castlereagh Corres.*, II, 431–2; *DEP* , 14, 30 Nov., 14 Dec.; *FJ*, 19 Dec. 1799.

[80] See *DEP*, 12, 14 Nov., 14 Dec. 1799.

[81] *Constitution or Anti-Union*, 9 Dec. 1799–30 Jan. 1800; Lees to Auckland, 20 Dec. 1799 in A.P.W. Malcomson, ed., *Eighteenth-century Irish official papers*, II (Belfast, 1992), p. 303.

[82] *DEP*, 24 Jan. 1800; *Constitution or Anti Union*, 7, 11 Jan. 1800.

parliament on 15 January.[83] Pro-union interests also sought actively at this time to sustain the public momentum in their favour. They remained confident that they would be victorious, and their expectations were buoyed by the presentation of three addresses from County Roscommon that enabled them to counteract the emphasis currently being attached to anti-union declarations from the same quarter. It particularly gratified the administration that the addresses crossed the denominational divide. Two – one from the bishop and ten parish priests attached to the diocese of Elphin, the other organised and presented by Myles Keon which came with 1500 signatures – were from Catholics, while, the third featured most of the major Protestant property owners in the county. In addition, further addresses or additional signatures were presented from the freeholders of County Wexford, from the mayor, burgesses and freemen of Wexford town, and from a thousand plus noblemen, gentlemen, clergy, merchants and freeholders in County Armagh.[84]

With this evidence of public support for a union, the administration had little reason to apprehend the presentation of union legislation to the House of Commons though the re-election of Henry Grattan increased the expectations in patriot ranks that 'the father of the constitution' of 1782 might yet provide them with a trump card. It did not prove to be so. The administration's comfortable numerical preponderance in the debate on the address to the king in which mention of a union was made suggested that the die was cast for the session if the opponents of a union could not generate a public outcry of sufficient scale to cause a substantial number of MPs to alter their vote.[85] With this in mind, the leaders of the parliamentary opposition prepared a circular for distribution to people of influence throughout the country urging them to get up petitions for presentation to the House of Commons. Their goal was to procure moderate anti-union declarations from more than the eighteen or nineteen counties Castlereagh claimed had pronounced in favour of a union, and they urged their supporters to take advantage of the early session recess to set this process in train.[86]

[83] *Constitution or Anti-Union*, 7, 11, 16, 21 Jan. 1800 ; *DEP*, 31 Dec. 1799, 2, 7, 14, 16 Jan.; Hamilton to Abercorn, 5 Jan. in J.H. Gebbie, ed., *The Abercorn letters* (Omagh, 1972), p. 210; Bradshaw to Castlereagh, 13 Jan. 1800 in *Castlereagh Corres.*, III, 224–5; Battersby, *Repealer's manuel*, pp. 352–3.

[84] Cornwallis to Ross, 4 Jan. in *Cornwallis Corres.*, III, 157; Keon to Castlereagh, 8 Jan. in *Castlereagh Corres.*, III, 222–3; *FJ*, 2 7, 30 Jan.; *DEP*, 9, 14, 25 Jan. 1800.

[85] *Constitution or Anti-Union*, 14, 16, 18 Jan.; Bolton, *The passing of the Union*, pp. 185–6; Cornwallis to Portland, 16 Jan., Cornwallis to Ross, 21 Jan. in *Cornwallis Corres.*, III, 163–5, 167–8; Agar to Townshend, 21 Jan. 1800 (Beinecke Library, Townshend papers, Box 8).

[86] Copies of printed circular and petition, 20, 29 Jan., Cooke to Auckland, 20 Jan. ,

With the active support of the popular press, which needed no convincing that the existence of the Irish parliament depended on the public's response, the getting up of petitions commenced. As the bastion of popular anti-unionism, Dublin was held up as 'the patriotic example'. The moderate tone of the declarations forthcoming from that quarter, when compared with those approved in 1798–9, indicates that anti-union interests there were as anxious as their parliamentary leaders to maximise support for their cause. Dublin Corporation set the tone with a series of resolutions (agreed on 17 January) and a petition (agreed on 31 January) in which it singled out its 'abhorrence of the indirect modes which have been adopted to carry into effect the measure of a legislative union', and drew attention to the impoverishment, the loss of 'chartered rights and the 'surrender of the birthright of Irishmen' it must of necessity involve.[87] The city's guilds were no less eager that this should not come to pass, and they came forward in even greater numbers than they had the previous winter to profess their opposition. John Beresford described the resolutions approved by the guild of merchants on 15 January as 'very strong', and while this is a fair assessment in this instance, the resolutions originating with the guilds reflected more traditional patriot and corporate concerns than had been the case the previous the year. They were not without impact for all that, and the strength of the opposition they articulated was given added weight by separate pronouncements by the grand jury, and by the freemen and freeholders of the city that a union could not possibly advantage the kingdom.[88]

Public endorsement for this position was less forthcoming from outside Dublin.[89] This did not inhibit anti-unionists for when parliamentary business resumed on 3 February they had successfully 'raised a powerful clamour against the measure in many parts of the kingdom

Castlereagh to Auckland, 25 Jan. (PRONI, Sneyd papers, T3229/2/55, 56, 52, 54); Castlereagh to Portland, 20, 27 Jan., Castlereagh to King, 25 Jan. in *Cornwallis Corres.*, III, 166–7, 170–71, 173

[87] *DEP*, 23 Jan.; Cornwallis to Lichfield, 24 Jan. in *Cornwallis Corres.*, III, 169; Gilbert, ed., *Ancient records of Dublin*, XV, 127–8, 135–9.

[88] The resolutions of the various guilds and corporations (merchants, cutlers and stationers, chandlers, barbers and surgeons, goldsmiths, hosiers, tailors, butchers, joiners, weavers, carpenters, saddlers and upholsterers, shoemakers, bricklayers and plasterers, smiths, coopers) are conveniently printed in Battersby, *Repealer's manuel*, pp. 334–50; see also Berry, 'Records of the feltmaker's company', p. 28; Beresford to Auckland, 20 Jan. (PRONI, Sneyd papers, T3229/2/53); Cornwallis to Portland, 21 Jan. 1800 in *Cornwallis Corres.*, III, 168; J.R. Hill, *From patriots to unionists* (Oxford, 1997), pp. 260–61; *FJ*, 18, 30 Jan. 1800.

[89] One noteworthy exception is the Roman Catholics of Limerick who resolved at a general meeting on 23 January that a union must bring 'ruin and degradation to a country, which since the glorious epoch of 1782 has been rapidly improving in commerce, manufacturers, industry and population' (*DEP*, 28 Jan. 1800).

and put the capital in an uproar'. Optimists within their ranks were hopeful they could yet overturn the administration's majority in the Commons. The administration, by contrast, was worried that the 'clamour against the union' might escalate into violence.[90]

The prospect of the campaign against the union turning violent was greater in early February 1800 than at any other time because of the palpable increase in the political temperature in the latter part of January. The mood of the public was manifestly more volatile on the resumption of the House of Commons on 3 February than it was on the opening day of the session when the large crowds that filled 'the streets about the houses of parliament' had observed 'good order'. The administration apprehended tumult, and their worst fears seemed about to be realised when supporters of a union were attacked leaving the precincts of parliament on Thursday, 5 February, and attempts were made to throw a number of carriages into the river Liffey. The timely intervention of the town major prevented any escalation in the disturbance on this occasion, and there were no further incidents of this kind while the union was being debated.[91]

This was a great relief to the administration as some MPs showed signs of weakening in the face of public pressure, but once they had steadied their nerve and secured a few Common's victories they made rapid progress. Unable to make an impression in the division lobbies, and aware, as Edward Cooke observed, that 'any attempt to move government without a general cry of popular discontent is folly' the only tactic left to the opponents of a union was 'to bring forward the mass of the people'.[92] The preparedness of substantial numbers of Catholics in counties Longford and Louth to endorse the controversial anti-union stand urged by Daniel O'Connell in Dublin in December, and the unwillingness of many lodges, who rejected the directive of the Grand Lodge of Ireland that the Orange Order should 'continue silent', to do as requested suggested this was still possible.[93] This prospect was improved by reports from around the country that anti-union interests were busy organising petitions for presentation to parliament and that twenty-five counties and eighteen corporate and commercial interests had done precisely this by the end of February.[94] However, for all their

[90] Cornwallis to Ross, 31 Jan, 4 Feb. in *Cornwallis Corres.*, III, 175, 177; *DEP*, 25 Jan. 1800.

[91] Cornwallis to Portland, 18 Jan. in *Cornwallis Corres.*, III, 165; Cooke to Auckland, 18 Jan. in Malcomson, ed., *Eighteenth-century Irish official papers*, II, 304; *FJ*, 16 Jan.,15 Feb.; Cooke to Grenville, 14 Feb. 1800 in H.M.C., *Fortescue*, VI, 128.

[92] Cooke to Grenville, 22, 25, 29 Feb. 1800 in H.M.C., *Fortescue*, VI, 139, 145, 149.

[93] *DEP*, 25 Jan., 1, 4, 6,11, 13, 25, 27 Feb., 4, 8, 20 Mar., 3, 19 Apr. 1800.

[94] *DEP*, 1, 4, 6, 13, 15, 18, 20, 22, 27 Feb. By 7 March, the number of county petitions had risen to 26 (*Cornwallis Corres.*, III, 205).

success in this sphere, the campaign against the union in the spring of 1800 proved disappointing because, Dublin perhaps excepted, it failed to generate a sufficient popular outcry against a union to cause MPs to consider changing their vote. Indeed, the fact that the administration received addresses from the gentlemen and freeholders of counties Meath, Westmeath, Down and Mayo, from the Catholic and Protestant freeholders of County Kilkenny, and professions of support from sundry MPs during the early spring indicated that the opposition had failed even to eclipse the support for a union in the country at large.[95]

Arising out of the failure of their petitioning campaign to provide them with the decisive momentum they needed, the opposition in the House of Commons contrived in March 'to fix upon the most unpopular points of the measure' in the hope that they could thereby 'inflame the country'. The tactic proved only modestly successful, not least because of disunity within their ranks on specific points. Further, defeats on the articles of the union convinced them that there was no advantage to be obtained pressing every aspect of the measure to a division and they effectively gave up the contest on the union resolutions in the Commons.[96]

With no prospect of success in the Lords, there seemed few options available to the opponents of a union. They resolved to soldier on, however, and perceiving that the spring assizes provided them with their last opportunity to rally public opinion they determined to petition the king directly. This troubled Pitt, who instructed the Irish administration to secure 'counter-declarations' in order to demonstrate that the people of Ireland were not solidly 'against the measure' lest it should devalue the decision of parliament.[97] Precipitated, as a result, into a further test of public opinion on an act of union, the opponents and proponents each contrived to rally support. Not surprisingly, given the course of the parliamentary session, this was a contest for which unionists no longer had much enthusiasm. The anti-unionists, by contrast, saw it as their last chance and the motivational advantage this provided enabled them to secure a substantially larger number of petitions than their opponents. In some instances, Cork being the most notable, the success of the local popular anti-unionists in securing the support for a petition to the king of five thousand freemen, freeholders, merchants, traders and manufacturers, was impressive. However, neither this nor the petitions from counties Sligo, Fermanagh, Kings, Cavan, Roscommon, Longford, Dublin or elsewhere influenced

[95] *DEP*, 1, 6 , 15, 22, Feb.; *FJ*, 8 Mar. 1800.

[96] Cornwallis to Portland, 11, 12, 22 Mar. in *Cornwallis Corres.*, III, 210–11, 214–5; Cooke to Grenville, 5, 10, 22 Mar. in H.M.C., *Fortescue*, VI, 152, 159–60, 172.

[97] Cornwallis to Portland, 22 Mar. in *Cornwallis Corres.*, III, 217; Cooke to Castlereagh, 5 Apr. 1800 in *Castlereagh Corres.*, III, 261.

Cornwallis who observed that in so far as the public mind had shifted it was to favour the measure.[98] The balance of evidence certainly suggests that by now there were established pro- and anti-union interests in every part of the country and that as in Dublin, where John Giffard's defence of a union on 16 April was more remarked upon that the Corporation's contrary pronouncement, dissenting opinions sometimes had a greater impact.[99] At the same time, the campaign energised the anti-union cause once more, which excited alarm in some that 'there will be some violent attempt by a general rising or some other means' to prevent the union becoming law. There was little prospect of this, or of the union being lost, as more experienced politicians appreciated.[100] Nonetheless, the intensification of popular anti-union sentiment encouraged the parliamentary opponents of a union to make a final stand against the union bill in the House of Commons. It was not the most refined of parliamentary engagements, and it was never destined to succeed. Moreover, its chances were diminished by the sudden and unexpected outburst of loyalism that erupted in late May–early June following an attempt to assassinate George III.[101] This served both to ease the final passage of the act of union and to facilitate its acceptance. The result of a by-election in County Londonderry, when a pro-union candidate triumphed over the anti-union nominee of the Ponsonbys, suggested this was likely in any event. But of equal significance are the statements of opponents of the union who observed as soon as its enactment was secured that they not alone accepted the decision they would encourage others to do likewise.[102] Given this context, it is not surprising perhaps that Lord Cornwallis should observe of the Act of Union following its final ratification by the Irish parliament that it was 'received throughout the nation, and even in the metropolis, with less ill-humour than could have been expected'.[103]

[98] *DEP*, 3, 10, 15, 17, 19, 29 April, 3, 13, 15, 22 May; F.H. Tuckey, *The County and City of Cork Remembrancer* (Cork, 1837), pp. 213–4; Cornwallis to Ross, 22 Apr. 1800 in *Cornwallis Corres.*, III, 229–30.

[99] For Dublin, and John Giffard's celebrated stand in favour of a union, see Gilbert, *Ancient Records of Dublin*, XV, 143–4; J.R. Hill, 'Religion, trade and politics in Dublin' in L.M. Cullen and P. Butel, eds, *Cities and merchants* (Dublin, 1986), pp. 248–9; *FJ*, 17 Apr. 1800.

[100] Garde to Heaton, 23 Apr. (PRONI, Chatsworth papers, T3158/1801); Lees to Townshend, 22 Apr. (Beinecke Library, Townshend papers, Box 6); Shannon to Boyle, 3 May 1800 in Hewitt, ed., *Shannon's letters*, p. 215.

[101] Cornwallis to Portland, 20 May in *Cornwallis Corres.*, III, 236; Gilbert, ed., *Ancient records of Dublin*, XV, 159; *DEP*, 10, 12, 17, 21, 28 June 1800.

[102] *FJ*, 31 May–5 June; Cornwallis to Portland, 9 June in *Cornwallis Corres.*, III, 251; Barnard to Barnard, 12 June in Powell, ed., *Barnard letters*, p. 122; *FJ*, 19 June 1800.

[103] Cornwallis to Portland, 17 June in *Cornwallis Corres*, III, 262.

IV

Though it cannot be said that the fate of the act of union was determined at the level of popular politics, the struggle for public opinion was a major feature of the history of its enactment. Aided by the lack of preparation of the Irish administration, the anti-unionist interest capitalised on the disposition of Protestant conservatives to maintain existing political structures and the well-established devotion of the whig-patriots to self-government to generate a vocal popular campaign against a union in the winter of 1798–9 that helped to ensure that it did not become law in 1799. The strength of the popular campaign against a union was sustained during the early spring of 1799 with the result that the slight possibility that the Irish administration might have sought approval for a union towards the end of the 1799 session came to nothing. However, as the momentum of the opposition's campaign decreased in the late spring and summer of 1799, the unionist cause demonstrated that it was not without public support. Appeals to concerns for the future security of Protestants as well as to the prospect of a more generous and inclusive style of government struck a cord with a substantial section of the public, and elicited supportive declarations that enabled the advocates of a union to gain the initiative with public opinion by the autumn of 1799.

The contribution major figures in local and national politics, in civil and religious life, in the Catholic as well as the Protestant establishments, made to this was enormous. Throughout the country, peers such as Lord Shannon, Protestant churchmen like Archbishop William Beresford, Catholic churchmen such as Archbishop Bray and eminent commoners like John Beresford played a critical part in convincing others of lesser stature to stand forward and pronounce their support for a union. The preference of the Irish administration was for the support of property rather than democracy, but the unionist cause did not only attract support among the propertied. Some addresses were signed by thousands of freeholders. Consequently, when a legislative union came to be considered by the Irish parliament for a second time in 1800, the supporters of a union could claim that they were as representative of public opinion as their opponents. This was a contestable claim, but it did ensure that public opinion did not determine the outcome. The Act of Union was carried because Dublin Castle had the numbers to ensure it victory in all the divisions that mattered. Its opponents were still capable of generating an impressive display of opposition as their petitioning campaign in the spring of 1800 attests, but they could no longer summon up public emotion. Bishop Barnard's observation in March that 'Dublin streets are much quieter than ever I remember to have seen them in ... peaceable times' is revealing in this respect.[104] Indeed, it is a measure of how resigned the public had become to the idea of a legislative union that 'there was not a murmur in the street, nor ... an expression of ill-humour throughout the whole of the city of Dublin' on 1 August when Cornwallis gave the act the royal assent, or when the legislative union came into being five months later.[105]

[104] Barnard to Barnard, 24 Mar. 1800 in Powell, ed., *Barnard letters*, p. 117.

[105] Cornwallis to Ross, 2 Aug. 1800 in *Cornwallis Corres.*, III, 285; Cornwallis to Castlereagh, 2 Jan., Cooke to Castlereagh, 2 Jan. 1801 in *Castlereagh Corres.*, IV, 13, 14.

THE IRISH PEERAGE AND THE ACT OF UNION, 1800–1971

By A.P.W. Malcomson

READ 10 SEPTEMBER AT THE PUBLIC RECORD OFFICE OF NORTHERN IRELAND

THERE was always an important, though varying, distinction between the Irish peerage and the Irish House of Lords. The former dated from the late twelfth century, and the latter, or at least something discernible as its forerunner, from the late thirteenth. From then until the early seventeenth century, because men who were neither temporal nor spiritual peers attended the House of Lords (though in decreasingly significant numbers) by virtue of a writ of summons only, the House of Lords was a larger body than the Irish peerage.[1] Thereafter, due to the number of non-Irishmen and/or non-residents who were created Irish peers, the House of Lords became the smaller body, because such people seldom or never attended.

The Act of Union terminated the existence of the Irish House of Lords, but established arrangements for the representation of the Irish peerage in the new House of Lords of the United Kingdom. So the Irish peerage survived the Union, and exists today. Not so the Irish representative peerage: it was declared defunct by a controversial decision of the committee for privileges in 1966, and formally wiped off the statute book in 1971. Under the Peerage Act of 1963, the Scottish representative peerage had also been abolished, but on the (to Scottish peers) favourable basis that the remaining Scottish peers without hereditary seats were absorbed into the House of Lords.[2] Between 1963

[1] Francis G. James, *Lords of the Ascendancy: the Irish House of Lords and its Members, 1600–1800* (Dublin, 1995), pp. 20–2; T.W. Moody, 'The Irish Parliament under Elizabeth and James I: a General Survey', in *Proceedings of the Royal Irish Academy* (hereafter, *Proc. RIA*) vol. XLV (1939), 55; R.P. Gadd, *The Peerage of Ireland, with Lists of all Irish Peerages, Past and Present* (Irish Peers Association, 1985), 7–10 and *passim*, together with Gadd, *Errata: Addenda* (1987).

[2] For information about the campaign mounted by the Irish peers without hereditary seats and their sympathisers, 1963–71, I am indebted to the then (1972) chairman of the Irish Peers' Association, who kindly allowed me to examine and make extracts from printed matter contained in one of the association's minute books (PRONI, D/3312/19, and see also PRONI, T/2956). The aim of the campaign was not to achieve the absorption of all the Irish peers without hereditary seats, but to prove that the representative peerage system had not been affected by the government of Ireland act of 1920 and partition in 1922. For an excellent recent survey of the constitutional and legal position, 1920–95, see Charles Lysaght, 'The Irish Peers and the House of Lords: the Final Chapter', *Burke's Peerage and Baronetage* (106th ed., 2 vols., Chicago, 1999), I, xli–xliii.

and 1999, therefore, the Irish peerage was the only one of the five peerages in the British Isles which enjoyed neither an hereditary nor an elective right to sit in the House of Lords; and now the other four peerages are about to join it. These twentieth-century developments are crucial to an understanding of the Act of Union as it affected the Irish peerage.

There is no point in covering the same ground as Professor Bolton did in his admirable (and for 1966 precociously perceptive) book on the passing of the Act of Union. His conclusions about the comparative irrelevance of honours, bribes and Sir Jonah Barrington have almost become a new orthodoxy.[3] So, too, have his conclusions about the regional concentration of the so-called 'Act of Union peerages' on people from the west, particularly Cork and Connaught, who felt distanced from Dublin and regarded London as not much further away. The actual figures for all 'Act of Union peerages', which need to be set slightly higher than Professor Bolton did, are as follows: of twenty-five creations made just after the passing of the measure, only some fifteen were rewards for votes for the Union, and the rest had nothing or virtually nothing to do with it. Likewise, of the sixteen promotions in the Irish peerage, at least two were irrelevant to the Union. A number of the others (for example, the marquessate of Thomond) were made solely or mainly for the purpose of preserving existing precedence – in this case, preventing newer earls from becoming marquesses ahead of Lord Thomond.[4] This principle, though laudable, inflated the number of promotions in the Irish peerage at the time of the Union. Finally, there were five creations of British peerages, for the benefit of Lords Carysfort, Clare, Drogheda, Ely, and Ormonde, one of which was not really Union-related.

Professor Bolton's conclusion that the bill was not exorbitant is therefore valid. For example, the Irish general election of 1776 had been marked by eighteen peerage creations, ten of them in favour of Irishmen who had probably strengthened their claims by providing the government with seats in the house of commons, but eight of them in favour of non-Irishmen or Irishmen being rewarded for other things.

[3] G.C. Bolton, *The Passing of the Irish Act of Union: a Study in Parliamentary Politics* (Oxford, 1966), 153, 167–72, 197–9, 205–7 and 218–22. This new orthodoxy has been challenged by recently discovered evidence about the illegal use made of secret service money. For a discussion of this issue which puts it back into perspective, see Patrick M. Geoghegan, *The Irish Act of Union: a Study in High Politics, 1798–1801* (Dublin, 1999), 87 and *passim*.

[4] PRONI, Portland Papers, T/2905/7/2 and 7, earl of Inchiquin (later marquess of Thomond) to duke of Portland, the Home Secretary, 23 Sep. 1794, and Portland to Inchiquin, 6 Oct. 1795.

A 'pay-off' also quite frequently occurred at the close of a parliament or parliamentary session and has to be taken into account: for example, five peers were created and eleven promoted at the close of the exceptionally tempestuous session of 1779–80.[5] These practices were not peculiar to Ireland. Pitt had created more than fifteen British peerages to facilitate the British general election of 1796. So the Act of Union creations and promotions begin to look like a bargain price for 'the fee simple of Irish corruption'.[6] Obviously, a higher price would have been necessary if the government had not had the new patronage of the twenty-eight representative peerages to play with.

Yet even these figures do not tell the full story. It is important not to confuse the underlying cause of a man's elevation to or promotion in the peerage with the proximate. In 1816, the Hon John William Ward, son and heir of the British Viscount Dudley, described his father as '... according to the usual "tariff" a perfectly earlable man'.[7] Some men were 'earlable', indeed 'peerable',[8] and some were not. The almost invariable qualification in late eighteenth-century Ireland was sizeable landed income, combined almost invariably with at least respectable lineage. The proximate cause of a man's elevation to the peerage was more often than not political, and in Ireland, where peers controlled a very much higher proportion of the seats in the house of commons, and where electoral influence was a much more common cause of ennoblement, than in England, the proximate cause was usually something to do with electioneering. Moreover, it was a convention of some standing that major parliamentary events, such as a general election and of course an Act of Union, should be marked by the creation of peerages, because at this time there were coronation, but neither birthday nor new year's honours. The existence of this convention means that ennoblement, even when unconnected with trafficking in seats, usually looks as if it was.

However, in the many instances in which such trafficking did occur, it was almost always no more than a makeweight in the scale of the already peerable men. When making his recommendations for 'Act of Union peerages', the Lord Lieutenant, Lord Cornwallis, meticulously itemised the rent rolls of the various aspirants, and all were satisfactory

[5] T.J. Kiernan, *History of the Financial Administration of Ireland to 1817* (Dublin, 1930), 224.

[6] *Memoirs and Correspondence of Viscount Castlereagh* ... (4 vols., 1848–9), III, 333, Castlereagh (chief secretary for Ireland) to Edward Cooke (under-secretary in Dublin Castle), 21 June 1800.

[7] *Letters to 'Ivy' from the 1st Earl of Dudley*, ed. S.H. Romilly (1950), 301, Ward to Mrs Helen Stewart, 7 Jan. [1816].

[8] For a contemporary use of this term, see an article on a proposed peerage bill in *The Cork Hibernian Chronicle* of 27 May 1776.

(between £5,000 and £12,000 a year or more).[9] The only ennobled Irishmen of the last decade of the eighteenth century who did not possess a landed income of at least £5,000 a year were some of the judicial peers – notably Lords Avonmore, Carleton and Kilwarden, who were all comparatively poor men. But insufficiently rich judicial peers were a problem in Great Britain as well as Ireland; and the honest poverty of Avonmore, Carleton and Kilwarden was preferable to the suspicious riches of two other judicial peers, Lords Clonmell and Norbury. With all the attention focussed on those who were made peers – at the Union and at other times – too little has been focussed on those who were not: the poorer men who controlled single boroughs, such as the Blakeneys of Castle Blakeney, Co. Roscommon, the Hores of Harperstown, Co. Wexford, the Lambarts of Beauparc, Co. Meath, the Lowthers of Kilrue, Co. Meath, and the Ruxtons of Ardee, Co. Louth – whose boroughs were their principal financial asset. For such men, the very fees on patents of peerage would have been 'a serious consideration'.[10]

The only proposition advanced by Professor Bolton which should perhaps be questioned is his suggested correlation between indebtedness and anti-Unionism.[11] This relies too heavily on the extreme case of Speaker John Foster (who is relevant to this discussion because his wife was an Irish viscountess), to whom the opposition to the Union was, according to Lord Chancellor Clare, 'principally, if not altogether,' due.[12]

[9] *Correspondence of Charles, 1st Marquess Cornwallis* ... (2nd ed., 3 vols, 1859), III, 252–6, Cornwallis to Portland, 9 June 1800. For earlier investigations into the level of landed income possessed by aspirants to the Irish peerage, see, for example: Public Record Office of Northern Ireland (hereafter PRONI), Bedford Papers, T/2915/10/32, duke of Bedford, the lord lieutenant, to earl of Shelburne, 15 Sep. 1760; *H.M.C. Stopford-Sackville Mss.*, I, 243, William Tonson to Lord George Germain, 18 Feb. 1776; National Library of Ireland (hereafter NLI), Talbot-Crosbie Papers, earl of Glandore to Thomas Pelham, the chief secretary, 9 Oct. 1795; PRONI, Macartney Papers, D/572/7/72, Sir Edward Leslie of Tarbert, Co. Kerry, to Earl Macartney, 7 Aug. 1801; PRONI, FitzGerald (Knight of Kerry) Papers, MIC/639/17/16, fragmentary reminiscences of Maurice FitzGerald, Knight of Kerry, 3 Oct. 1848.

[10] PRONI, Foster/Massereene Papers, D/562/3383, Lord Oriel to Viscount Ferrard, 2 Oct. 1825. In the third quarter of the eighteenth century, fees on Irish peerages were as follows: a barony, c.£250; a viscountcy, c.£320; and an earldom, c.£390 – BL, Add. Ms. 23711, fees on Irish patents, 1752–83. Fees on special remainders were particularly high: in 1790, the fees on a barony were c.£280, rising to £468 for one special remainder and to £663 for a second – PRONI, D/562/4952 and 7518. In the mid-nineteenth century the fees on investitute as a knight of St Patrick (the highest order of chivalry in Ireland) were over £530 -D/562/3484, receipt from Ulster king of arms to Viscount Massereene and Ferrard, 2 July 1851.

[11] Bolton, *Union*, 182–4.

[12] Malcomson, *John Foster: the Politics of the Anglo-Irish Ascendancy* (Oxford, 1978), 15–16 and 323–7; British Library (hereafter BL), Wellesley Papers, Add. Ms. 37308, ff. 283–5, Clare to Marquess Wellesley, 9 Mar. 1800.

Debt is relative. Assets are needed to run it up, and all aristocratic families incurred debt (rather than sell assets, especially land) in order to provide for their children and dowagers, build houses and (more questionably) fight elections. The Unionist Lord Abercorn probably had no debts to speak of, but he was still a poorer man than the heavily indebted but very rich anti-Unionist, Lord Downshire.[13] If indebtedness was a factor at all, it surely would have operated in favour of Unionism (after the disastrous failure of 1799 and once the compensation arrangements for boroughs and – quite as important – *offices* were made known)? Recipients of compensation money were compulsorily assisted to clear or reduce debt, and did not incur the loss of face and status which inevitably accompanied sales of land.

Apart from these few, preliminary comments, this paper takes Professor Bolton's conclusions as axiomatic and seeks to explore different territory, starting with some general comments on the Irish peerage and on Irish peers. The Irish peerage is a purely legal concept, and Irish peers were not necessarily characterised by birth, residence or landownership in Ireland, or even by the common denominator that their patents of peerage had all passed the great seal of Ireland.[14] They were a group in only a technical sense, can never have felt any sense of group identity, and certainly were never capable of group action. Certain sections of them, it is true, proved capable of concerted action – the Irish peers without British titles at the time of the princess royal's wedding in 1734 and of George III's wedding and coronation in 1761,[15] the absentee Irish peers in

[13] Malcomson, 'A Lost Natural Leader: John James Hamilton, 1st Marquess of Abercorn (1756–1818', *Proc. RIA*, vol. 88, sec. C, no. 4 (1988), 68–9; W.A. Maguire, *The Downshire Estates in Ireland, 1801–45* (Oxford, 1972), 1–8 and 85–92; and Malcomson, 'The Gentle Leviathan: Arthur Hill, 2nd Marquess of Downshire, 1753–1801, in *Plantation to Partition: Essays in Ulster History in Honour of J.L. McCracken* (Belfast, 1981), 103, 105 and 107.

[14] Sir John Sainty, the retired clerk of the parliaments and an authority on the history of the House of Lords, informs me that numerous cases of patents passing the great seals of England or Great Britain are listed in the *Forty-Seventh Report of the Deputy Keeper of Public Records* (1886), *Appendix VI.* Sainty has himself noted thirty such patents in the Crown Office Docket books during the period 1660–1707. Surprisingly, a Committee of the House of Lords reported in February 1803 that there were no such instances – *Journals*, vol. XLIV, 52a.

[15] F.G. James, 'The Active Irish Peers in the early Eighteenth Century', *The Journal of British Studies*, vol. XVIII (Spring 1979), *passim*; *H.M.C. Egmont Mss.*, I, 403–40, II, 60 and 452–6, and III, 138, diary of the 1st earl of Egmont; [Egmont or, more probably, his son, later the 2nd earl], *The Question of the Precedency of the Peers of Ireland in England, Fairly Stated in a Letter to an English Lord by a Nobleman of the other Kingdom* (Dublin, 1739 [and reprinted at the time of George III's coronation in 1761]), *passim.*

1773[16] and 1797–8,[17] and the Irish peers who had seats, on one basis or another, in the House of Lords, at various points in the nineteenth century.[18] Yet each of these sections counted for only a small proportion of the total number of Irish peers, and all but the first acted in concert with other interest groups who were not Irish peers. This lack of concert and of group identity among the Irish peers derived from the fact that the honours system was British Isles-wide.

In the pre-1801 period the most clear-cut example of an Irish peer is the man whose only title or titles was or were Irish; who was a member of no other legislative assembly than the Irish House of Lords; and who, from his ancestry, his place of residence and the location of all or most of his estates, can be called an Irishman. However, it is probable that only about half the Irish peers of the period fell into this clear-cut category. Some had no land in Ireland, never set foot in the Irish House of Lords and had no Irish ancestry – for example Lords Auckland, Delaval, Fife, Lisburne, Melbourne, Milford, Muncaster and Newborough. Some can be called Irishmen, on grounds of ancestry, property and, in the main, residence, but had subsidiary British titles which entitled them to sit in the British House of Lords – for example, the dukes of Leinster and Lords Donegall, Downshire and Waterford – or had no British title and sat in the British house of commons – for example, Lords Arden, Clanbrassill, Farnham and Palmerston. Some had land in Ireland and were in part Irish by ancestry, but were seldom in Ireland because they also had land and higher titles in Great Britain – for example, Lords Abercorn, Hertford, Lansdowne and Rockingham. Even these loose categories are not loose enough to accommodate all the Irish peers. Also, there were a number of English or British peers who had land in Ireland and were in part Irish by ancestry, but happened to have no Irish title – for example, the dukes of Devonshire, and Lords Courtenay, Dacre, de Clifford, Derby, Egremont (from 1774), Portsmouth, Sandwich, Stanhope (from 1765), Uxbridge and Weymouth/Bath. This last category cannot, on technical and legal grounds, be counted as Irish peers, although in reality they had much more to do with Ireland than the many Englishmen whose connection with the country was, as one of them put it, 'merely nominal and

[16] *The Correspondence of Edmund Burke*, ed. Lucy S. Sutherland, II (Cambridge, 1960), 464–510; Thomas F. Moriarty, 'The Irish Absentee Tax Controversy of 1773 ...', *Proceedings of the American Philosophical Society*, vol. CXVII, no. 4 (Sep. 1974), *passim*.

[17] Public Record Office (hereafter PRO), Home Office Papers, HO 100/69, ff. 115–18, and /70, ff. 23–4, Earl Camden, the lord lieutenant, to duke of Portland, the home secretary, 1 Mar. 1797, and Portland to Camden, 7 July 1797; West Sussex Record Office, Petworth House Archives, PHA/1270/55, Earl Fitzwilliam to earl of Egremont, 28 Jan. and 4 Feb. 1798.

[18] For examples, see PRONI, D/3078/3/27, 33–5 and 44, 1837–9, 1846–8 and 1860, correspondence of the 3rd duke of Leinster, the leader of the Irish whigs.

titular'.[19] Reducing this extremely complex situation to something resembling statistics is no easy task. But the following is a crude attempt.

In 1809–11 there were as many as 219 Irish peers to 302 English and British peers (excluding royal dukes).[20] These figures are not realistic, as some thirty-eight of the Irish peers were English or British peers as well. To obtain a fair comparison, it is reasonable to deduct from the Irish peers the eleven or so who had no remaining connection, if indeed they had ever had any, with Ireland, and whose English or British peerages were higher than or equal to their Irish; also, the ten or so who were connected with Ireland through property and even occasional residence, but whose English or British peerages were likewise higher than or equal to their Irish. From the other side of the comparison, the English or British peers, it is then reasonable to deduct the seventeen or so who had property in both Great Britain and Ireland, but whose Irish peerages were higher than their British (or in one case, Lord Fitzwilliam, of equal degree). A problem, however, arises over five of these seventeen – Lords Carysfort, Fitzwilliam, Moira, Upper Ossory and Wellesley. The first four had very extensive English property, on which they resided; the last, having sold his family estate near Trim, Co. Meath, had little property anywhere and lived in England. Retaining these five in the scale of the English or British peers, the figures now stand at 197 Irish peers to 290 English or British – a slightly more defensible ratio. Yet, there still remain in the scale of the Irish peers some forty-five non-Irishmen, with no connection with Ireland whatever except for their peerages,[21] but with Irish peerages which ranked higher than their British (if indeed they had a British peerage, which only five had). Since these people had all become Irish peers on purely British grounds, it is reasonable, for the sake of argument, to deduct them from the Irish peers and, indeed, to add them to the English or British (except of course for the five of them who are there already). The resulting figures are 152 Irish peers to 330 English or British – an

[19] PRONI, Leinster Papers, D/3078/3/27, Viscount Melbourne, the Prime Minister, to Duke of Leinster, 13 Jan. 1837.

[20] These figures are taken from William Playfair, *British Family Antiquity* ... (9 vols., 1809–11), vols. I, II, IV and V, *passim*, and inevitably are approximate because of the two-year period over which *Playfair* was published, and also because it is not a wholly reliable source. In the case of the Irish peerages, it is unreliable to the extent that its table of contents omits four (the earldom of Antrim, and the viscountcies of Downe, Lumley and Strabane). Its figures have been adjusted accordingly. However, it does possess the advantage – as a source – of making possible almost contemporaneous comparison between the two peerages and, as will be seen, the two baronetages.

[21] Excluded from the 45 is one Dutchman, the earl of Athlone; since his ancestor, General Ginckel, had been ennobled for his services on the Williamite side in the Williamite war, it is appropriate that he should remain in the scale of the Irish peers. See PRONI, Pery Papers, T/3087/2/18, Athlone to E.S. Pery, 14 Dec. 1777.

unexceptionable ratio in regard to the contemporary populations of Ireland and of England and Wales.

Moreover, regard should be had to the next, and lower, tier of hereditary honours – baronetcies. In the period up to the Union, when Ireland had its separate baronetcy,[22] baronetcies seem to have been less esteemed in Ireland, and therefore less viable as substitutes for peerages, than was the case in England. After the Union, in 1811, there were only 103 Irish baronetcies in existence, compared to 438 English or British (i.e. excluding in both cases UK baronetcies created post-1800).[23] There were a number of Irishmen who were baronets of Great Britain or baronets of both kingdoms, and one Englishman who was a baronet of Ireland. Otherwise, these figures – in conjunction with the previous re-casting of the figures for peerages – suggest that hereditary honours had not been conferred with disproportionate profusion on Irishmen.

The non-Irishmen who were made Irish peers in the eighteenth century were highly respectable, apart from some half dozen temporarily unacceptable, but soon to be accepted, Jews and Jacobites (one of the former, Lord Huntingfield, being described encouragingly by Pitt in 1796 as 'a very zealous convert'[24]). If the nineteenth-century 3rd Viscount Palmerston, who in terms of landownership was predominantly Irish,[25] is anything to go by, they valued Irish peerages because such honours combined much of the social prestige of the upper house with continued eligibility for the lower.[26] In a sense, resident Irish politicians, for example Foster, played the same game. If they wished their families to be ennobled while a friendly government was still in power, but were

[22] PRO, Home Office Papers, HO 100/105, f. 106, Edward Cooke, under-secretary in Dublin Castle to John King, 20 Feb. 1801.

[23] NLI, Vesey FitzGerald Papers, Ms. 7835, pp. 227–87, Ross Mahon of Castlegar, Co. Galway (who was soon to accept a UK baronetcy), to William Vesey FitzGerald, 24 Nov. 1814; Playfair, *British Family Antiquity*, vols. VI, VII and IX, *passim*.

[24] PRONI, Pratt Papers, T/2627/4/48, Pitt to Earl Camden, 9 June 1796. This letter also explains the circumstances of the creation of the Irish barony of Carrington in favour of an Englishman.

[25] *Portrait of a Whig Peer, Compiled from the Papers of the 2nd Viscount Palmerston (1739–1802) by Brian Connell* (1957), 352 and 402–4.

[26] I am indebted for this point to the late Professor J.C. Beckett. Palmerston came near to making it in a letter to Sir George Shee, Bt, of 9 Feb. 1841 (Shee Papers, BL, Add. Ms. 60341, ff. 205–6). (For help with this reference, I am indebted to Mr Robert A.H. Smith of the BL Department of Manuscripts.) It was specifically made in the lengthy correspondence about 'Mr Pennington's tedious business', which ran from April 1782 to July 1783 (Bury St Edmonds Branch of the Suffolk Record Office, Grafton Papers, 141, 668–81 and 749–54). The 3rd duke of Grafton had promised John Pennington of Muncaster Castle, Ravenglass, Cumberland, that an honour or office, compatible with his seat in parliament would be found for him, and repeatedly threatened to resign from the Rockingham and Shelburne cabinets if this promise was not fulfilled. Pennington, a highly respectable county MP and the heir to an English baronetcy created in 1676, was made Lord Muncaster in the Irish peerage in October 1783.

not yet ready to leave the house of commons themselves, they obtained peerages for their wives with remainder to their male issue. On this basis, Mrs Foster was created Baroness Oriel in 1790 and Viscountess Ferrard in 1797. The main difference was that the Fosters' son had no option but to go to the lords, whereas the options of the descendants of Irish peers in the British house of commons remained open. In 1829, Lord Tyrconnel, an Englishman whose ancestor had been made an Irish peer in 1761, attributed this to the fact that '... in former times peerages were not so common as now, and my family was rewarded by an Irish peerage merely ...'[27] Events and conventions in one part of the British Isles thus had repercussions for others. For example, between the Scottish Union in 1707 and the 1780s, English prejudice against Scots was so strong that few Scots received British peerages. Those who did were debarred from taking their seats and, by an inconsistency of injustice, from voting in Scottish representative peerage elections.[28] In these circumstances, it is surprising that no more than four Scots were made Irish peers between 1707 and the 1780s. It was English prejudice, rather than the unsuitability of the Scots concerned, which accounts for these four creations.[29]

William Duff, one of the already-mentioned four Scots, who is sometimes quoted as an example of the doubtful status of the Irish peerage and of the non-Irishmen promoted to it, will serve as a case study which demonstrates the contrary. It never seems to have been a reason for ennoblement that men had built great houses; but Duff had built a house of enormous grandeur, Duff House, Banff. Duff House is the Scottish Houghton, even though it was never completed because of a dispute between Duff and his architect, William Adam. The only possible objections to Duff were that, although his family was 'ancient', the current extent of his estate and wealth was recent;[30] also, that his choice of Irish titles – Viscount Macduff and Earl Fife – was Gilbertian, or rather Shakespearean. The wording of the egregious duke of Newcastle's recommendation of him to the lord lieutenant in 1735 was unduly defensive: '... he lives altogether in Scotland, hardly known anywhere else, even by name; and I should hope that such a man, at such a distance, who never can come to interfere with the peers of Ireland in any degree, ... would not give them any uneasiness ...'.[31]

[27] PRONI, Rossmore Papers, T/2929/5/11, Tyrconnel to Lord Rossmore, 4 Sep. 1829.

[28] A.S. Turberville, *The House of Lords in the Age of Reform, 1784–1837* (1958), Chapter Six, *passim*.

[29] Of the four (Lords Fife, Macdonald, Panmure and Seaforth), the last two were politically less respectable, as their ancestors had been Jacobites and the titles they chose in the peerage of Ireland were actually under attainder in the peerage of Scotland.

[30] Ian Gow and Timothy Clifford, *Duff House* (Edinburgh, 1995), 29 and *passim*.

[31] *Correspondence of John, 4th Duke of Bedford, 1742–70*, ed. Lord John Russell (3 vols., 1842–6), II, 347, Newcastle to Bedford, 21 July 1758.

By 1787, the 2nd Earl Fife was credited by a neighbour with a rental of £18,000 a year;[32] in the first quarter of the nineteenth century, the prime minister, the 2nd earl of Liverpool, thought it no disgrace to live for most of his political life in Fife House, Charing Cross (now demolished), rather than in Downing Street, and did not change its name; and in 1889, the then Lord Fife was regarded as good enough to marry the prince of Wales's daughter and in 1899 was created a UK duke.

Had the non-Irishmen selected for Irish peerages been any less respectable (except in a very few isolated incidents) than Duff, the result would not just have been offence to the resident peers of Ireland, but that the Irish peerage would have ceased to be a viable agency of British patronage. There is no evidence that this happened. Two of the non-Irishmen concerned, Lords Westcote and Radstock, who were made Irish peers in 1776 and 1800 respectively, were the younger brothers of English peers and scions of ancient and distinguished English families. (Westcote was perhaps a special case, because his wife was an Irish heiress.) Such men would never have accepted rank in a peerage which was of 'equivocal value'[33] in British currency.

Part of the mythology about unsuitable non-Irish entrants to the Irish peerage dated from early Stuart times. In 1603 there were only twenty-five Irish peers, but between then and 1641 the crown created (and generally sold) eighty new peerages.[34] The choice of Irish titles by non-Irishmen in this period was pretty much a case of 'Agatha has found it on the map'. Many of these non-Irishmen had certainly been dubious. But so had some of the Irishmen. In 1616, when Gerald

[32] PRONI, Hart Papers, D/3077/D/1/10, General James Grant of Ballindalloch (near Banff) to Major G.V. Hart, 15 Oct. 1787.

[33] Bolton, *Union*, 198. Some contemporary comments, from various periods, which apparently confirm this view, will be found in: *The Orrery Papers*, ed. Countess of Cork and Orrery (2 vols., 1903), I, 148, earl of Orrery to Viscountess Allen, 8 Feb. 1735/6; Robert Halsband, *The Life of Lady Mary Wortley Montagu* (Oxford, 1956), 282, quoting Lady Mary to her daughter, 22 June 1750; Earl Stanhope, *The Life of the Rt Hon. William Pitt* (4 vols., 1862), III, 233, Marquess Wellesley to Pitt, 28 Apr. 1800; Hartley Library, Southampton University, Palmerston Papers, Ms. 62, GC/BR/14/1, Henry Brand to Viscount Palmerston, 24 Aug. 1862 (I am indebted for this reference to Sir John Sainty); and *Hansard, Third Series*, vol. 219, 1585, speech of Lord Dunsany on representative peerage reform, 1874. This, however, is a somewhat anecdotal way of looking at the matter. In purely legal terms, the Irish peerage is the 'purest' of the five, in that it exists solely by patent and was never adulterated by the admission, on an hereditary basis, of men who (or whose ancestors) originally sat in a House of Lords by virtue of a writ of summons – Lord Dunboyne to Malcomson, 7 Feb. 1976, PRONI, Irish Peerage Papers, D/3312/17; J.H. Round, 'The Barony of Arklow', *Collectanea Genealogica* (1881), 44–6; and Bodleian Library, Oxford, Talbot Papers, b.6:c.10, case papers in an unsuccessful attempt to prove the existence of a twelfth-century Talbot de Malahide barony by writ, 1833–7.

[34] C.R. Mayes, 'The Early Stuarts and the Irish Peerage', in *English Historical Review*, LXXIII (1958), 247. This excludes creations made after the outbreak of the civil war.

Moore, ancestor of the marquesses of Drogheda, had been created Baron Moore of Mellifont, this creation had proved one too many for Archbishop Ussher, then dean of St Patrick's, who is alleged to have preached a sermon on the occasion which took for its text *Acts, XVII*, 2 – 'There were more noblemen than they which were at Thessalonica'.[35] Hard cash had certainly changed hands in early Stuart times and, ironically, had been paid by the ancestors of many of the Irishmen who counted as old nobility in the late eighteenth century – for example, Lords Antrim, Barrymore, Cork, Drogheda, Fingall and Westmeath. Most ironical of all, the 1st earl of Charlemont, who was as much priggish as whiggish, who loudly denounced the sale of peerages and who, on being made an earl in 1763, asked that his patent should state that the earldom was unsolicited, owed his oldest title to a down payment of £2,000 in 1620.[36]

These Stuart peers were not very progenitive. In the earl to mid-eighteenth century so far from there being the 'mob of nobility' which Horace Walpole deplored in 1776, there was a distinct dearth of temporal peers in the Irish House of Lords, because many of the then Irish peers were Englishmen, absentees or bad attenders.[37] The number of resident peers in 1751 was twenty-eight, rising to sixty-seven in 1776.[38] Some of them however, although possessed of comparatively ancient peerages, no longer had the money to live up to their rank or even to attend parliament and were dependent on an 'aristocratic dole' (such as existed in contemporary Great Britain, and was certainly not exclusive to Ireland).[39] The desperate search for peerable natives in mid-eighteenth century Ireland is well illustrated by the case of the Dublin brewer, Joseph Leeson (another builder of a great house,

[35] PRONI, Rossmore Papers, T/2929/5/76, incomplete copy of a printed squib called *The Spectator's Anatomy of the Peerage*, c.31 Dec. 1831.

[36] Mayes, 'Early Stuarts and the Irish Peerage', 349–43; *H.M.C. Charlemont Mss.*, I, 136–7. Sir John Sainty points out that, by 1763, preambles to British patents of peerage had long since ceased to recite the merits and services of the patentee. Visually, Irish patents of peerage of the last third of the eighteenth century were also much more elaborate, and beautiful, than British.

[37] G.E. Cockayne, *The Complete Peerage*, ed. Vicary Gibbs and others (13 vols, 1910–40), III, 643; BL, Nicolson Papers, Ms. 6116, f. 127, Bishop Nicolson to Archbishop Wake, 14 Dec. 1723; BL, Newcastle Papers, Add. Ms. 32704, f. 394, earl of Chesterfield, the lord lieutenant, to Newcastle, 29 Nov. 1745.

[38] PRONI, Hotham Papers, T/3429/1/8, earl of Buckinghamshire, the lord lieutenant, to Sir Charles Hotham Thompson, Bt, 26 Dec. 1776.

[39] BL, Newcastle Papers, Add. Ms. 32690, f. 448, duke of Devonshire, the lord lieutenant, to Newcastle, 2 Dec. 1737; *The Letters of Philip Dormer Stanhope, Earl of Chesterfield*, ed. Lord Mahon (4 vols, 1847), III, 173, Chesterfield to Newcastle, 11 Mar. 1745/6; and BL, Lansdowne Papers, Add. Ms. 24138, ff. 60 and 73, duke of Portland, the lord lieutenant, to earl of Shelburne, 8 Aug. 1782, and memorial of Viscount Ranelagh, [1782?].

Russborough, Co. Kildare). Writing to urge Leeson's claims to a barony, George Stone, archbishop of Armagh, remarked apologetically: 'I am sorry to say, I cannot think our House of Lords would be dishonoured by ... [him]. A man with a great estate, who pays his debts and commits no act of violence and is well affected to the government, does very well in ... [this impure republic] ... His demerits are the common failings of a *bourgeois gentilhomme* ...'.[40] What is also significant is that Leeson had no parliamentary interest, apart from his own, purchased seat for Rathcormack borough, Co. Cork. He had to wait for his barony until 1756, but was earl of Milltown by 1763.

Various coinciding events in Ireland from the mid-eighteenth century onwards enabled Ireland, not only to operate an indigenous, as opposed to an indigent, House of Lords, but increasingly to participate in the system of honours and honourable employments which was common to the empire as a whole. The multiplication of Irish peerages, particularly in the period 1770–1801 – 'profuse creations', as *The Complete Peerage* disdainfully describes them[41] – was dramatic (though no more dramatic than the contemporary multiplication of British peerages under Pitt between 1784 and 1801[42]): there were some 115 Irish peers in 1750, some 150 in 1783 and some 240 in 1801 (including royal dukes with subsidiary Irish earldoms). Of the 240 Irish peerages in existence in 1801, 135 had been created since the accession of George III, and only fifty-nine of the Irish peers of 1801 had not been further ennobled in some way by that monarch.[43] These creations – apart from the thirty-six made in favour of non-Irishmen – were largely a recognition of a changing economic and political situation. It is clear that there was a dramatic rise (in real and non-inflationary terms) in the rental income of Ireland between the mid-eighteenth century and 1815.[44] Since landed income was the basis for all creations of Irish peerages in this period, except a very few for distinguished legal, military or naval services, it is not surprising that peerage creations too increased dramatically. By 1801, nearly all the great landowners of Ireland had become peers, and to that extent the peerage creations of the previous

[40] PRONI, Wilmot Papers, T/3019/1012 and 1063, Stone to Sir Robert Wilmot, 25 Apr. and 29 June 1748.

[41] III, 643.

[42] Turberville, *House of Lords, 1784–1837*, Appendix III. In this context creation means the bestowal of British or U.K. peerages, whether by a new creation or a special remainder, on commoners and Irish or Scottish peers.

[43] *The Gentleman's and Citizen's Almanack* (Dublin, 1751), 40–41; David Large, 'The Wealth of the Greater Irish Landowners, 1750–1815', *Irish Historical Studies* (hereafter IHS), xv (1966–7), 27; and G.E. Cockayne, 'The Peerage of Ireland', *The Genealogist. New Series*, v (1888), 1–16, 82–9, 145–52 and 180–205. All subsequent figures for Irish peers will be taken from this last source, unless otherwise attributed.

[44] Large, 'Greater Irish Landowners', 28–9.

half century were a simple recognition of economic reality. One or two great landowners held aloof, refusing to perform the political services which were the proximate cause of ennoblement – Thomas Conolly of Castletown, Co. Kildare, is the obvious example. But most went to the Irish House of Lords, including old nobility like the 'titular' 17th earl of Ormonde in 1791 (who, as Lord Chancellor Clare was the first to point out, was not 'titular' at all, because parliament had in error omitted to include the Irish honours of the 2nd duke of Ormonde in his attainder in 1715[45]). Lord Ormonde cannot have objected to associating with the supposedly 'mushroom' or 'pitch-fork' nobility of late eighteenth-century Ireland.[46]

Political change also favoured this process. From the early 1750s onwards, the Irish house of commons became increasingly difficult to manage. With the increased expense of electioneering consequent on the octennial act of 1768 and the increased intrusion of extra-parliamentary organs of opinion on the work of parliament, MPs who fought for the government necessarily demanded higher bounty. Also, the government's deliberate policy from the late 1760s onwards of dealing direct with the political interests in the house of commons, down to the possessors of single votes, undoubtedly had an inflationary effect in the matter of patronage, peerages of course included. The winning of the so-called 'Constitution of 1782' enhanced the prestige of both houses of parliament, particularly that of the House of Lords, which recovered from its British counterpart the appellate jurisdiction in all Irish cases. Still, the constitution of 1782 provided no constitutional safety-valve for the defeat of the Irish government in the Irish parliament. Defeat had therefore to be averted by all possible means, including advancement *to* the Irish peerage and advancement *in* the Irish peerage. The 'profuse creations' which took place reflected a coincidence of economic change and political need.

But the expansion of the resident Irish peerage and the increasingly flourishing state of the Irish ruling class were also a reflection of Ireland's expanding share in the good things of the British Isles and of the empire at large; also its expanding share in the good things of Ireland itself. The archbishoprics of Armagh and Dublin remained

[45] BL, Dropmore Papers, Add. Ms. 59252, f. 36, paper by Clare (then FitzGibbon) on the Ormonde attainder, 6 May 1790.

[46] Neither term of abuse seems to be contemporary, and both gained currency in late nineteenth-century polemics, notably J.G. Swift McNeill's *Titled Corruption: the Sordid Origins of some Irish Peerages* (1894). The earliest reference to a mushroom peer which I have come across is NLI, Tottenham of Ballycurry, Co. Wicklow, Papers, positive microfilm 4937, John de [?Renzy] to Major Hugh Eccles, 22 Dec. 1834, referring to Lord Carew, newly raised to the Irish peerage by the whigs, as 'that mushroom, half-created peer'. For period-piece strictures on 'pitch-fork' peerages, see M.A. Hickson, *Old Kerry Records: Second Series* (1874), 278.

sacred to Englishmen (and so continued for twenty years after the Union), but the lord chancellorship of Ireland went (temporarily) to an Irishman in 1789, as did most of the other offices hitherto regarded as within the English spoils system. Englishmen and even members of the royal family slowly faded from the Irish pension list, and Ireland was not called upon to make any compensatory contribution to the king's civil list.[47] English lords lieutenant and chief secretaries continued to fare well at Ireland's expense. But in the period 1764–1800, two of the former, Lords Hertford and Fitzwilliam, were Irish peers (among other things) and five of the latter, the 6th earl of Drogheda, Theophilus Jones, Sir George Macartney and Viscounts Milton and Castlereagh, were Irishmen. There were even two British prime ministers, Rockingham and Shelburne, who were Irish earls. Meanwhile, Irish peers entered the British house of commons in significant numbers: seventy-two sat there between 1754 and 1790, although half of these were non-Irishmen, some twenty-six were Irish absentees and only some ten were regular or periodical residents in Ireland.[48] (It is noteworthy that so few residents should have sat. This continued to be the case after the Union; there were about a dozen Irish peers per parliament between 1800 and 1820, mostly non-Irishmen.)

More important, Irish peers who were wholly or partially resident in Ireland began to be admitted in even greater numbers to the British peerage. These included: Lord Kildare (1747), who had to borrow his territorial designation of Taplow, near Beaconsfield, from his cousin, Lord Inchiquin, because he himself owned not a square inch of land in England; Lord Bessborough (1749); Lord Hillsborough (1756); Lord Shelburne (1760); Lord Milton (1762); Lord Ligonier (1763); Lord Moira (1783); Lord Abercorn (1786); Lord Shannon (1786); Lord Tyrone (1786); Lord Donegall (1790); Lord Macartney (1796); Lord Courtown (1796); Lord Mornington (1797); etc, etc. Some of these were made British peers for services to the empire at large. However, the Irishman who was perhaps the most distinguished for services to the empire during the last third of the eighteenth century, General Sir Guy Carleton, was a commoner; he was created a British peer as Baron Dorchester in 1786. Many other British peers came from the ranks of the major non-

[47] Malcomson, *John Foster*, 237–42; Surrey History Centre, Woking, Midleton Papers, Ms. 1248/17, ff. 9–10, Charles Brodrick, Bishop of Kilmore, to Viscount Midleton, 15 Mar. 1797. The bishop remarked (inaccurately as far as the army was concerned): '... excepting our own jobs, what expenses have we? England pays for the navy, for the whole diplomatic arrangements and for foreign garrisons.'

[48] These figures are compiled from L.B. Namier and John Brooke, *The History of Parliament: the Commons, 1754–90* (3 vols., 1964), II and III, *passim*. By contrast, only one English, Scottish or British peer sat in the Irish house of commons over the whole period 1692–1800.

resident magnates in the Irish peerage – the 2nd earls of Egmont and of Upper Ossory granted British baronies in 1762 and 1794 respectively, and the 2nd earl of Shelburne promoted to the British marquessate of Lansdowne in 1784. There was thus, long before the Union, an increasing convergence in the peerages of England/Britain and of Ireland.

From the point of view of the resident Irish peers, the objections to the introduction of non-Irishmen into the Irish peerage were not to the individuals concerned but to the principle of '*English recommendations*' – as the harassed lord lieutenant wrote in 1783,[49] when the king was refusing to grant British peerages at the recommendation of the Fox-North coalition, and was only prepared to grant Irish ones. In 1797, another general election year in Ireland and therefore the occasion for a flurry of peerage-creations, the king was making no such difficulties. But there were so many instances of '... bestowing the honours and advantages of the country upon individuals who have no interest [in] or connection with it whatever ...', that the Irish government protested strongly to the British, and the chief secretary contemplated resignation.[50] However, there was not much logic in this Irish prejudice against '*English recommendations*'. Many resident Irish peers, for example the 1st Lords Leitrim and Somerton and Lord Downshire, by-passed the lord lieutenant and sought 'English recommendations' by direct approach to the British home secretary, the prime minister or even the king himself. Many more resident Irish peers, and upper-class Irishmen generally, constantly solicited '*English recommendations*' in favour of sons and other relatives for whom they wanted commissions or promotions in the *British* armed services, or in the higher parts of the Church of Ireland which the recommendations of the lord lieutenant could not reach.

Ireland, it is true, deserved its fair share of military patronage, because in peacetime it accommodated, and moreover paid for, most of the British army – between 12,000 and 15,000 men. But it contributed nothing to the British navy, in spite of the proposal that it should do so as part of the abortive commercial propositions of 1785. Ireland also had no East India Company (unlike Scotland it had never even attempted anything resembling a Darien Scheme). So it was thanks to the *British* East India Company that James Alexander of Derry acquired

[49] BL, Northington letter-book, Ms. 38716, ff. 25–9, earl of Northington to duke of Portland, the prime minister, 23 June 1783; *The Rolliad* (Dublin ed., 1796), 76.

[50] PRONI, Normanton Papers, T/3719/C/31/55, Lord Arden (an absentee Irish peer and proprietor, who nevertheless was moved to indignation on this subject) to Charles Agar, archbishop of Cashel (and Lord Somerton), 19 May 1797; BL, Pelham Papers, Add. Ms. 33113, ff. 97–9, Thomas Pelham, the chief secretary, to duke of Portland, the home secretary, 1 Aug. 1797.

possibly one of the four largest 'nabob' fortunes of the last third of the eighteenth century, bought the Caledon estate, Co. Tyrone for £96,400 in 1776, and died as earl of Caledon in 1802.[51] Lord Castlereagh himself, the chief secretary who helped to botch the Union in 1799 and did much to carry it in 1800, owed the origin of his family's fortune to a collateral 'nabob' ancestor of the 1730s, whom '*English recommendations*' had made governor of Bombay.[52] Under such circumstances, could the Irish peers reasonably object to the fact that Clive of India, a bird of gorgeous if slightly spotted Eastern plumage, made the Irish peerage his sole habitat, between 1762 and his suicide in 1774, as Baron Clive of an imaginary Plassey, Co. Clare?[53]

Such was the confluence of the system of honours and recommendations in Great Britain and Ireland, and such, it must be admitted, was Irish provincial avidity for English honours, that in 1761 Lord Kildare chose to walk in George III's coronation procession as a British viscount instead of walking as the only Irish marquess; that in 1783, when his son, the 2nd duke of Leinster, was offered the foremost place in the new order of St Patrick, he made this the pretext for advancing his pretensions to the Garter; and that in the same year, the 6th earl of Antrim declined St Patrick so that he could hold on to his knighthood of the Bath.[54] In general, there was a tendency for Irish peers to choose titles which dissociated them from Ireland, associated them with England, Scotland or Wales, or simply sounded grand. Thus, there were earls of Aldborough (who was also Viscount Amiens), Altamont, Belvedere, Brandon (who was actually a countess in her own right), Carhampton, Clermont, Darnley, Egmont, Gosford, Grandison, Kingston, Landaff and Mount Cashell, a Viscount de Vesci, and Lords Arden, Clarina (who was nearly Niagara), de Montalt, Harberton,[55] Lisle,[56] Mount Charles, Mountflorence (briefly), Somerton and Tem-

[51] P.J. Marshall, *East India Fortunes: the British in Bengal in the Eighteenth Century* (Oxford, 1976), 238–9; PRONI, Caledon Papers, D/2433/A/1/91–2, sale particulars of the Caledon estate and deed of sale, 5 Sep. 1775 and 18 Jan. 1778.

[52] H. Montgomery Hyde, *The Rise of Castlereagh* (1933), 10–11.

[53] A myth is gaining currency that Clive's peerage was called after Plassey, Co. Limerick, and that he owned that estate – *cf.* Mark Bence-Jones, *A Guide to Irish Country Houses* (revised ed., 1988), 232. But this is incorrect. The Plassey estate, Castletroy, outside Limerick City (and now the nucleus of the university of Limerick), was acquired by a lesser 'nabob' called Maunsell, who re-named it after Clive's great victory.

[54] *H.M.C. Charlemont Mss.*, I, 137; PRONI, Leinster Papers, D/3078/3/4, duke of Leinster to Earl Temple, the lord lieutenant, 15 Jan. 1783; PRONI, Foster/Massereene Papers, D/562/2718, Hon. Chichester Skeffington to his wife, [11 Feb. 1783].

[55] PRONI, Abercorn Papers, T/2541/IA1/13/227, Arthur Pomeroy (soon to be created Lord Harberton, 'a place in Devonshire where my family formerly had some concern') to earl of Abercorn, 21 July 1783.

[56] Lisle was an island in Cork harbour belonging to the first peer of that name, John Lysaght, although grandiloquence undoubtedly had more to do with his choice than

pletown. In 1785, the Irish baron who was compelled to accept the title of 'Sunderlin' had wanted to be 'Sunderland', and the Irish earl who become 'Portarlington' had wanted to be 'Arlington'.[57] The facetious English clergyman in Ireland who in 1779 recommended his brother to solicit an Irish peerage as Lord Clonbullock of Swineford[58] was actually being less insulting than de Latocnaye in 1797, who claimed to have heard of an Irishman who wanted to be created 'Lord Peloponessus and earl of Greece'.[59] There was, however, one good example of uncompromising Irishness. When offered a British barony in 1786, the 2nd earl of Tyrone chose 'Tyrone' as his title. When he was told that his territorial designation had to be on the British mainland, he refused to opt for some obscure English hamlet associated with his family, the Beresfords, but grumpily chose 'Baron Tyrone of Haverfordwest', because the latter was the point on the east Pembrokeshire coast which was closest to his native Co. Waterford.

These examples suggest that, to many members of the Irish House of Lords, it seemed a provincial institution. The fact that '... The houses of parliament [were] much more grand than in England ...' in 1782, and were made grander still in c.1784–9,[60] is attributable, not to self-confidence, but insecurity. Even Barrington could muster up only the following faint praise: 'As a body the Irish lords were not particularly prominent in the affairs of their country; but they were dignified ...; their conduct, if not spirited, was firm and respectable.'[61] Unionist commentators on the Irish House of Lords did not have Barrington's motive for mincing their words. Judge Robert Day, writing in 1802, described it as '... an assembly ridden, and with very little ceremony, by the poor chancellor [the late Lord Clare], which served only to register the acts of the lower house or as the chancellor's organ to affirm his own decrees. ... [Compared to] the imperial house of peers, ... the Irish was no better than a parish vestry.'[62] Prior to the constitution

---

geography. He declared to the lord lieutenant: '... If it should be thought to savour anything of the French, which I utterly disclaim, yet I would waive it for that of Crumlin in the county of Dublin ...' – a considerable come-down in the world! See PRONI, Bedford Papers, T/2915/5/24, Lysaght to duke of Bedford, 24 Aug. 1758. A number of these high-falutin titles, e.g. 'Clarina', had similar geographical justification.

[57] *H.M.C. Rutland Mss.*, III, 205, Lord Sydney, the home secretary, to duke of Rutland, the lord lieutenant, 7 May 1785.

[58] PRONI, Hotham Papers, T/3429/2/6, Rev. Dr John Hotham to Sir Charles Hotham Thompson 7 July [1779].

[59] *A Frenchman's Walk through Ireland, 1796–7. Translated from the French of [the Chevalier] de Latocnaye by John Stevenson, 1917, with an Introduction by John A. Gamble, 1984* (Belfast, 1984), 153.

[60] *Lord Fife and his Factor: being the Correspondence of James, 2nd Lord Fife, 1729–1809*, ed. Alistair and Henrietta Tayler (1929), 141–4, especially Lord Fife to William Rose, 30 May 1782; Edward McParland, *James Gandon: Vitruvius Hibernicus* (1985), 76–84.

[61] Quoted in Constantia Maxwell, *Dublin under the Georges, 1714–1830* (1956), 127.

[62] NLI, Talbot-Crosbie Papers, Judge Robert Day to Lord Glandore, 13 Mar. 1802.

of 1782, the Irish House of Lords actually played a lesser part in Irish legislation than both the Irish and the British privy councils.[63] After 1782, it made little use of its enhanced power over legislation. Its debates were, presumably, regarded as of so little public interest that, with the mysterious exception of the 1783–4 session, they were not included in the seventeen-volume *Irish Parliamentary Register*, which covered the period 1781–97. The House of Lords, though ready enough to tangle with the house of commons,[64] seldom went against the government.[65] However, they were criticised in 1786 for being 'rather too much disposed to exercise their new power', when they threw out a bill which the chairman of committees had failed to make clear was a government measure; in 1788, led by the redoubtable Charles Agar, archbishop of Cashel, they wrecked a tendentious measure of supposed tithe reform called the barren lands bill, which the government had countenanced from opportunistic motives; and in 1789 there was an anti-government majority in the lords under the exceptional circumstances of the regency crisis.[66] In spite of these infrequent gestures of defiance, the lords gave overwhelming support to the principle of a Union in 1799, even though no mention had yet been made of monetary compensation for disfranchised boroughs.

Because the House of Lords possessed little collective consequence and derived its importance from the individual importance of its members, and particularly their influence in the house of commons, those members had good reason for consenting to its extinction. Able and ambitious Irish peers, like the 2nd Lord Glentworth, who as 1st earl of Limerick (the first post-Union promotion or creation in the Irish peerage) was to prove a minor political success-story in the UK House of Lords, must have looked forward to graduating from the 'parish vestry' in College Green. If the cases of Lords Abercorn, Downshire, Ely, Shannon and Waterford, the 'big five' borough owners and political magnates, are studied, what clearly emerges is that genuine difference of opinion, influenced quite as much by age, principle and rebellion-induced panic as by self interest, determined their conduct at the time

[63] *H.M.C. Various Collections*, VI, 57, Baron Wainwright to George Dodington, 2 Jan. 1733/4.

[64] Trinity College, Dublin, Crofton Papers, W. Disney to Christopher Henry Earbery, 4 Aug. 1787; PRONI, Sheffield (Gage) Papers, T/2965/148, Thomas Pelham to Lord Sheffield, 10 June 1797.

[65] Midleton Papers, Ms. 1248/16, f. 44, Bishop Brodrick to Viscount Midleton, 20 Apr. 1795.

[66] PRO, Home Office Papers, HO 100/18, ff. 158–61, Thomas Orde, the chief secretary, to Evan Nepean, 31 Mar. 1786; PRONI, Pery Papers, T/3052/207, Orde to Viscount Pery, 31 Mar. [1786]; and PRONI, Normanton Papers, T/3719/C/22/8, 24 and 31, bishop of Killala to Archbishop Agar, 30 Mar. [1788], and Welbore Ellis to Agar, 12 June and 25 July 1788.

of the Union. 'Self-interest' in their case must be defined as meaning more than the immediate rewards obtained by the four Unionists among the 'big five' for their support of the measure. Compensation for the disfranchisement of their boroughs[67] was not an inducement to any of them, because they had never sold seats and had always made more money in the long term, and gained more prestige, than their seats were worth on the open market. But what *was* an inducement was the prospect of having their remaining constituency influence transferred to the more important forum at Westminster, where one seat was deemed the equivalent in importance (and a saleable seat in value) of two in the Irish parliament. Only Lord Shannon – though this did not deter him from supporting the Union – could not look forward with confidence to any post-Union constituency influence. He must have realised that the sleeping giant of Lismore Castle, the duke of Devonshire (successor to 'the great earl of Cork'), would come to life once borough and county interest in Cork produced seats and votes in a London, as opposed to a Dublin, parliament – which is exactly what happened.[68]

Lord Ely, though Wexford-based, had a relatively small estate in Co. Wexford, and of his borough interest only his alternate nomination for Wexford borough was due to survive the Union. But he owned the largest, though not the most valuable, estate in Co. Fermanagh, and this northern interest offered considerable political potential (which his descendants signally failed to realise). If he bargained hardest at the time of the Union (as Professor Bolton demonstrates that he did[69]), it must be remembered in fairness that he started from a lower base than the other four. He had been born a commoner and had succeeded in 1783 to none of the titles of his childless uncle and predecessor. He was the only one of the big five who was not already a British peer and was not, or had not had the opportunity to become, an Irish marquess.[70] He was the child of an era when peerage and other honours mattered more to many people of his class than major political issues. As he was ambivalent on the issue of catholic emancipation, and dependent in Co. Wexford election politics on the support of emancipationist interests,[71] he had no principled motive for refusing to support the Union on terms which brought his family back up to the level of the rest of the big five.

[67] Significantly, the top scorer in borough compensation money was the one *anti*-unionist among them, Lord Downshire – see Malcomson, 'The Gentle Leviathan', 115 and 267.

[68] Malcomson, 'Lord Shannon', in Esther Hewitt (ed.), *Lord Shannon's Letters to his Son ... 1790–1802* ... (PRONI, Belfast, 1982), xxvi and xxxii–xxxvi.

[69] Bolton, *Union*, 173–5.

[70] Malcomson, 'Lord Abercorn', 63–4, and 'Lord Shannon', xlvii–xlviii.

[71] See Cullen, *supra*, pp. 221–42.

Interestingly, the Irish House of Lords resembled the thane of Cawdor in that nothing in its life became it like the leaving it. Nearly all the debating power in favour of the Union resided in the House of Lords, and the government – uneasy, like all eighteenth-century governments, when numbers alone were on its side – published these speeches in newspapers and pamphlets as a counterweight to the effusions of the slick young lawyers in the house of commons. Lord Clare's magnificent orations were intellectually the most powerful. But Archbishop Agar was wooed and won on account of his debating skill and mastery of detail, in return for which he obtained important securities for the Church of Ireland (to which the Irish house of commons had been no friend), to say nothing of important advantages for himself. Great symbolic significance attached to Lord Avonmore, the former Barry Yelverton, whose claims to have obtained the constitution of 1782 were more solid than Grattan's. Avonmore's was therefore one of a number of speeches in the House of Lords published by the government in pamphlet form.[72] The fact that Cornwallis, the lord lieutenant, regularly reported to Portland, the home secretary, the course of debates in the House of Lords and the prodigies performed by the leading government spokesmen there,[73] is proof in itself of the propaganda value attached to the deathbed utterances of that body.

In spite of the limited incentive of the resident Irish peers to fight for the survival of the Irish House of Lords, they fought hard and successfully to obtain favourable terms for themselves in the brave, new world of the United Kingdom; and as a result the resident Irish peers were treated most handsomely under articles iv and viii of the Act of Union in a number of (to them) very important respects.[74] The first was their influence over returns to the lower house. In 1707, the Scottish peers lost the very great influence which they had possessed in the unicameral Scottish parliament, and – in spite of the best endeavours of a few of them – did not obtain the concession that their eldest sons would be eligible to sit for Scottish constituencies.[75] The Irish peers lost a much less significant influence deriving from their house of the Irish

[72] *The Speech of the Rt Hon. Barry, Lord Yelverton, Chief Baron of His Majesty's Court of Exchequer, in the House of Lords of Ireland on Saturday, March 22, 1800 ... Published by Authority* (Dublin, J. Milliken, 1800). Yelverton was promoted to the viscountcy of Avonmore later in 1800.

[73] See, for example, *Cornwallis Correspondence*, III, 184–6, Cornwallis to Portland, 11 Feb. 1800 (two letters, one 'official' and one 'private', of the same date).

[74] 40 George III, cap. 38 [in the Irish *Statutes*], Articles Four and Eight. See also 40 George III, cap. 29.

[75] Turberville, *House of Lords, 1784–1837*, Chapter Six. I am also grateful to Dr D.W. Hayton for steering me out of error on this issue.

parliament, and their eldest sons continued to be eligible to sit for Irish constituencies. As a result, in the house of commons of the United Kingdom, the Irish representation was markedly more aristocratic than the representation of England and Wales or of Scotland, at least until catholic emancipation in 1829 and parliamentary reform in 1832. The Irish peers themselves continued to be eligible to sit for constituencies outside Ireland – which the Scottish peers were *not* for constituencies outside Scotland. This latter concession was regarded by peerage-purists as lowering the status of the Irish peers, and the particular members of the order who pressed for the concession were the English, not the Irish, peers of Ireland.[76] Nevertheless, the latter – in small numbers (the 2nd Baron Dufferin, for example, until elected a representative peer in 1820) – availed themselves of it.

The peerage-purists had some other causes for cavil about article iv. Until 1857, all Irish peers who had not taken their seats in the former Irish House of Lords, had to establish their right to vote in Irish representative peerage elections (and thus their claim to their peerages) by a similar process as 'claimants to *contested peerages*' (as one of them indignantly observed in 1804[77]). The most bizarre mode of establishing such a claim was that adopted accidentally by the 2nd Lord Cloncurry. He was anxious to vote in a representative peerage election which took place in the summer of 1811, but had never gone through the process of proving his father's death and his own succession. However, he had just divorced his wife by private act of parliament for committing adultery in 1806 with a notorious libertine more-or-less in full view of a mural painter called Gaspare Gabrielli. As the 2nd earl of Charlemont

[76] PRONI, Castlereagh Papers, D/3030/420, Lord Sheffield to Castlereagh, 18 Dec. 1798; BL, Egmont Papers, Add. Ms. 47141B, ff. 1–10, Lord Arden to [Lord Clare?, late? 1799?]; NLI, Talbot-Crosbie Papers, Lord Glandore to Charles Bragge, 23 Jan. 1803; Hampshire Record Office, Normanton Papers, 21 M 57, earl of Shaftesbury to earl of Normanton, 24 Sep. 1838, and Lord Dunsany to Normanton, 3 Apr. 1860.

[77] PRONI, Caledon Papers, D/2433/C/5/57, Lord Clonbrock to earl of Caledon, 13 Aug. 1804. In fact, a claimant to a contested peerage petitioned the crown, which referred the matter to the attorney-general, whereas the successor to an Irish peerage presented his claim direct to the House of Lords. The former was a costly procedure, the latter virtually free, unless doubt about the succession emerged. In both types of claim, the committee for privileges decided the matter: after 1857, the lord chancellor was empowered to decide claims except in cases of doubt. I am grateful to Sir John Sainty for this exposition of the procedural position. For the House of Lords' rulings on this matter, 1802 and 1810, see *Journals of the House of Lords*, XLIII, 493a, 514a and 607a, and XLVII, 533b. For the simple proofs of descent required of the 2nd Viscount Ferrard (whose claim was of above-average complexity and was badly mishandled), see PRONI, Foster/Massereene Papers, D/207/74/246 and T/2519/4/2085 and 2070, J.L. Foster to Ferrard, 17 May 1827 and 12 Apr. 1828, and Lord Dufferin to Ferrard, 20 May 1827. See also: ibid., D/2681/66, J.P. Benvan [?] to Viscount Massereene and Ferrard, 8 Feb. 1843; and PRONI, Howard Bury Papers, T/3069/E/14, minutes of evidence heard by the committee for privileges on the Charleville peerage claim, 26 Apr. 1836.

wittily observed: '... the chancellor [of Ireland, Lord Manners] ... *himself* recollected that the *legislature*, in passing his bill of divorce under the name of Lord Baron Cloncurry, has in fact established the point – the first time a man's *having a whore* as his wife was of service to him in the proof of his pedigree. ...'[78]

However, these minor indignities apart, the provisions of article iv considerably upgraded the precedence of the Irish peers, in much the same way as the provisions of the Scottish Union had considerably upgraded the precedence of the Scottish peers. Since Charles I's reign, Irish peers had taken precedence in England *after* all English, Scottish and British peers of the same rank.[79] Even this rearward place in the pecking order had often been disputed, and once denied – in the already-mentioned royal wedding of 1734. The Act of Union not only confirmed the less unflattering interpretation of existing precedence, but also placed the precedence of the Irish peers of 1800 on an unassailable footing for the future. From 1801 onwards, Irish peers then in existence were to take precedence over all subsequently created UK peers; and subsequently created or 'promoted' Irish peers were to take precedence along with UK peers of the same rank, in strict chronological order of creation or 'promotion'. This provision seems to have dissuaded Lord Fitzwilliam from accepting the marquessate of Rockingham when offered it in 1806, because such a promotion would place him 'at the tail of a marquess of Sligo, etc, etc'.[80]

As far as numerical representation in the House of Lords was concerned, the Irish peers fared better than the Scottish. On the face of things, this would seem to be the reverse of the truth: in 1707 there were eighty or so Scottish peers, whose representation had been set at sixteen (or 19.2 per cent); in January 1800 (prior to any of the Union creations), there were 213 Irish peers, whose representation was set at twenty-eight (or 11.8 per cent); and in 1801 (following all the Union creations), there were 239 Irish peers (8.9 per cent).[81] At the start of the 1800 session of parliament, in January, only 126 Irish peers had taken

[78] Clements Papers, Killadoon, Celbridge, Co. Kildare, Q/2/5, Charlemont to earl of Leitrim 11 July 1811; *Deirdre Phelan and others, Lyons Demesne: a Georgian Treasure Restored to the Nation* (privately printed, Dublin, 1999), 22–3 and 29–31; and NLI, Cloncurry Papers, Ms. 8492/8, Cloncurry to Thomas Ryan, 17 Mar. 1811.

[79] BL, Egmont Papers, Add. Ms. 47099, ff. 1–16, petition to the king from the peers of Ireland, [1732–3].

[80] E.A. Smith, *Whig Principles and Party Politics: Earl Fitzwilliam and the Whig Party, 1748–1833* (Manchester, 1975), 289 and 298 (quoting from Fitzwilliam to Howick, 27 Sep. 1806). The 3rd earl of Altamont had been created marquess of Sligo in 1800 for his services in promoting the Union in his native Connaught and elsewhere.

[81] House of Lords Record Office (hereafter HLRO), Main Papers, 5 June 1806, list of the Irish peerage as it stood on 15 Jan. 1800, with particulars of who had and had not taken their seats.

their seats in the Irish House of Lords, and therefore were qualified to vote.[82] This figure had presumably not changed much, or at all, by August when the first 28 representative peers were elected. Of the 126, seven were non-Irishmen (like the 2nd Earl Fife), who had taken their seats out of curiosity or because they were passing through (for example, on military service in Ireland).[83] They would not have had 'any chance of success' had they stood as candidates for the representative peerage; so Portland was right in estimating 'that one out of very little more than four [of the mainly resident Irish peers] must be returned'.[84] Omitted from the 119 were half a dozen women (whose peerages were remaindered on men), half a dozen Roman catholics (who would become eligible both to vote and sit in 1829[85]) and the resident Irishmen (or Irishwomen) who were waiting to be created 'Act of Union peers'. Nevertheless, in practical terms, the chances of being elected a representative peer remained higher for an Irish than for a Scottish peer.

This was because virtually all governments went out of their way to ensure that only Irishmen with a reasonable record of residence in Ireland ever succeeded in being elected.[86] Of the 159 Irish representative peers elected during the duration of the system (the years 1800–1920)[87] there is only one definite example of a non-Irishman or non-resident being elected; this was Lord Curzon in 1908, who wanted to go to the House of Lords and whom the liberals would not create a UK peer. Curzon is the exception who proves the rule. In spite of all the influence which the conservative party could bring to bear, and circular letters from leading Irish conservatives like the 2nd duke of Abercorn, the candidature of an outsider was so resented by the largely conservative Irish peerage that Curzon got in by a majority of only two after a fierce, three-cornered contest the like of which had not been seen since

[82] Cockayne, 'The Peerage of Ireland', 5–6.

[83] NLI, Talbot-Crosbie Papers, earl of Clare to Glandore, 27 Sep. 1801; Hartley Library, Palmerston Papers, Ms. 62, BR 137/65, Thomas Bourchier, deputy clerk of the crown in Ireland, to Viscount Palmerston, 29 Sep. 1801. For help with this latter reference I am grateful to Dr C.M. Woolgar.

[84] *Cornwallis Correspondence*, III, 213–14, Portland to Cornwallis, 15 Mar. 1800.

[85] Nothing came of the sensible suggestion that they should be allowed to vote as soon as the Union became law – PRO, HO 100/87, ff. 258–9, Cornwallis to Portland, 22 Nov. 1799. This would have put them on the same footing as Roman Catholics with votes in elections to the house of commons.

[86] BL, Hardwicke Papers, Add. Ms. 35712, f. 33, Charles Abbot, the chief secretary, to earl of Hardwicke, the lord lieutenant, [Sep./Oct. 1801]; PRONI, Donoughmore Papers, T/3459/D/11/5, Lord Howden to earl of Donoughmore, 5 Feb. 1824; and PRONI, Howard Bury Papers, T/3069/E/17–18, duke of Wellington and Sir Robert Peel to earl of Charleville, 28 Nov. and 2 Dec. 1839.

[87] For the names of those returned at the 159 elections, see Sainty, *A List of Representative Peers for Scotland, 1707 to 1963, and for Ireland, 1800 to 1961* (HLRO, memorandum no. 39, 1968).

1825.[88] Surprisingly – since there were proportionally far fewer non-Scotsmen in the Scottish peerage than non-Irishmen in the Irish – elections of non-Scotsmen to the Scottish representative peerage were more frequent (various viscounts of Falkland and Lords Fairfax, and the 9th Viscount Irvine, are cases in point).[89]

Again, the non-Irishmen in the Irish peerage were not only virtually disqualified as candidates; they also participated much less prominently than the Irishmen in representative peerage elections.[90] This was partly because some of them thought it a matter of principle that the decision should be left to the Irishmen, partly because article iv precluded Irish peers who were members of the house of commons from participating in representative peerage elections, and partly because article viii *implied*, though it did not actually stipulate, that an Irish peer had to go to Ireland in order to take the oaths which would qualify him to vote.[91] The imprecision of article viii in this last respect gave rise to the questionable practice of Irish JPs administering the necessary oaths in England and, in one extreme case in 1825, in St Petersburg, where the British ambassador, the 6th Viscount Strangford, was an Irish peer.[92] However, this questionable and probably short-lived practice did not affect the general position that the resident Irishmen in the Irish peerage monopolised the returns and dominated the electorate.

In fact, because of the already-mentioned emphasis on residence and good works as criteria for election to the representative peerage, as also for creation and promotion as Irish or UK peers and for admission to

[88] HLRO, Main Papers, 21 Jan. 1908; R.B.P. Jennings, 'The Unionists and Ireland, 1886–1906: the House of Lords and the Irish Peers' (University of Liverpool Ph.D. thesis, in preparation in 1975, but subsequently abandoned). I am indebted to Mr Jennings for lending me in the early 1970s a draft of his chapter on the Irish representative peers (PRONI, D/3312/19), which included a detailed study of the Curzon election. See also earl of Midleton, *Records and Reactions, 1856–1939* (1939), 209–10.

[89] Sir James Ferguson, Bt, *The Sixteen Peers of Scotland* (Oxford, 1960), 30, 42, 82, 86 and 153.

[90] This can be seen from the returns for the representative peerage elections in HLRO, which will be analysed shortly.

[91] PRONI, Caledon Papers, D/3433/C/13/6 and C/5/47, 44 and 58, Lord Radstock to 3rd earl of Caledon, 6 June 1840, and Lord de Blaquiere and Viscounts Chetwynd and Harberton to 2nd earl of Caledon, 9 (two letters) and 13 Aug. 1804. Immediately after the passing of the Act of Union, the government was not in any doubt of the necessity for taking the oaths *in Ireland* – PRO, HO 100/104, f. 45, Sir George Shee to Charles Abbot, 21 Aug. 1801.

[92] Midleton Papers, Ms. 1248/18, ff. 40–41, Bishop Brodrick to Viscount Midleton, 14 Nov. 1801; NLI, Farnham Papers, Viscount Downe to Lord Farnham, 14 Sep. 1825, and Farnham to Viscount Strangford, 4 Nov. 1825; PRONI, Rossmore Papers, T/2929/5/50, Lord Radstock to Lord Rossmore, 18 Sep. 1829. One Irish peer living in Brighton and anxious to qualify himself to vote at an election in 1831, found that 'An Irish justice of the peace is a rara avis here', and in the end had to drag an aged invalid out of his bed (Farnham Papers, Lord Decies to Lord Farnham, 20 Feb. [1831]).

the order of St Patrick, these honours were in practice a means of aristocratic social control and of encouraging the Irish peers to live on their estates and do their duty.[93] The Union, thought it depopulated Dublin of Irish peers and depreciated the value of aristocratic town-houses,[94] had the opposite effect on the Irish countryside. Because it left all thirty-two Irish counties as two-member constituencies, it encouraged the Irish peers and the non-peerage families who were major county interests, to build or rebuild 'big houses' as focal points for their electoral influence.[95] In 1883 (not a congenial time for residence in the Irish countryside), it was calculated that, out of a total of 182 Irish peers, only forty-eight had neither house nor land in Ireland (even though many of the 134 had their principal places of residence elsewhere).[96]

The Irish method of election to the representative peerage was also more dignified than the Scottish because, being primarily postal, it was not liable to the personal confrontations and wrangles which often disturbed the Scottish conclaves in Edinburgh.[97] The election of the original twenty-eight Irish representative peers was a travesty, partly because it was conducted *viva voce* (including proxies[98]) in the Irish House of Lords according to an elaborate procedure laid down in article viii, and mainly because the election – or rather the government's selection – was part and parcel of the bargaining over the passing of the Act of Union. The government so botched the business that printed lists of its nominees, corresponding precisely to those who were elected on 2 August 1800, were circulated in advance of the election.[99] Thereafter, the procedure for electing an Irish representative peer, as specified by article viii, was that within fifty-two days from the test of the writ stating that the previous representative peer had died, each qualified Irish peer returned two duplicate writs of return to the crown office of

[93] Malcomson, review of the Rev. Peter Galloway's *The Most Illustrious Order of St Patrick, 1783–1983* (Chichester, 1983), in *IHS*, xxv, no. 99 (May 1987), 326–7. For a typical statement, in a canvassing letter for the representative peerage, see PRONI, Belmore Papers, D/3007/J/19, Lord Crofton to earl of Belmore, 18 June 1872.

[94] McParland, *James Gandon*, 71–2; NLI, Clifden estate papers, Ms. 8796/2, report on Viscount Clifden's Dublin City estate, [c.1870?]. This latter report concludes snobbishly: '... This city is declining rapidly. There is only one lord who keeps a house in it....'

[95] Malcomson, 'Absenteeism in Eighteenth-Century Ireland', *Irish Economic and Social History*, I (1974), 26–7 and *passim*; Bence-Jones, *Irish Country Houses*, xvii–xix.

[96] Malcomson, 'Belleisle [Co. Fermanagh] and its Owners', *Clogher Record* (1998), 38.

[97] Ferguson, *The Sixteen Peers*, Chapters Four and Five, *passim*; PRONI, Castle Stewart Papers, D/1618/14/2, *Minutes of the Election of the Peers of Scotland, July 24, 1790, with an Appendix containing Copies of the Protests, etc; Printed by the Direction of All Concerned.*

[98] NLI, Talbot-Crosbie Papers, Glandore to earl of Darnley, 16 July 1800.

[99] A copy survives among the Netterville Papers which, until 1987, were in the possession of Mr David Synnot at Furness, Naas, Co. Kildare. Prior to 1987, it was photocopied by PRONI (T/3430/1).

chancery in Ireland, having filled in the blanks on both writs with the name of the peer of Ireland for whom he voted, and having signed both writs with his title of honour and affixed to them his seal of arms. There were considerable complications about these arrangements.[100] For example, following the almost simultaneous deaths of no less than three representative peers, the three ensuing writs were all returnable on the same day, 2 March 1816, and a number of peers, quite understandably, got their writs mixed up, and voted for somebody who was not a candidate to fill that particular vacancy.[101] In September 1915, at the election of General the 10th earl of Cavan, Lord Cavan himself wrote: 'On active service. No seal available.'[102]

However, the main problem is, not that electors were on active service, drunk at the time, had lost their seals or their marbles, had left their returns blank, had voted for somebody who was dead, already elected or not a candidate, etc, etc, but rather that the records of parliament relating to representative peerage elections are defective. The 'bipartite' writs of return were issued by and sent back to the lord chancellor of Ireland, who routinely sent one set to the House of Lords, retaining the other in the hanaper office in Dublin, where they were destroyed in the four courts fire in 1922. Of the sets sent to the House of Lords, six are missing altogether, and some are either slightly or seriously incomplete. As part of a general, futile flurry of representative peerage reform proposals in the period 1869–77,[103] a return was made of the results of Irish representative peerage elections, 1800–74, to a select committee of the House of Lords. Where comparison can be made between the original returns and the printed results furnished to that committee, the latter have been found to contain errors and omissions, and of course they do not list the names of the peers who voted for each candidate. They do, however, cover all five of the elections during that period for which the original returns are missing or incomplete.

The following conclusions are therefore based on the surviving, original, parchment writs of return.[104] Between 1800 and 1920 there

[100] This is a paraphrase of the text of a writ issued for the election of a representative peer. It was alleged in 1819 that 'The clerk of the crown neglects to send the writs [to each qualified peer] unless they are asked for ...' – PRONI, Belmore Papers, D/3007/H/3/21, Lord Arden to earl of Belmore, 1 Mar. 1819. If this is true, and was not peculiar to the c.1820 period, it would help to explain some of the suspiciously low polls.

[101] HLRO, Writs, box 25.

[102] HLRO, Main Papers, 24 Sep. 1915. This, incidentally, is a reminder that the system allowed peers to vote for themselves.

[103] For examples of this, see PRONI, T/3430/10–13.

[104] These will be found, in chronological order of return up to and including 1849, in HLRO, Writs, boxes 23–6 and 21–2: thereafter, they are filed in the Main Papers series,

were 159 elections of Irish representative peers. Of these, sixty-two were unanimous (assuming that the original twenty-eight were unanimous, although the entry in the Irish *Lords' Journals*[105] states that the twenty-eight were elected 'by a majority – a stock phrase which may or may not mean what it says). Forty-five elections were seriously contested (i.e. more than six votes, not necessarily for the one peer, were cast against the successful candidate). Ten were 'technical' contests (i.e. only a technicality prevented them from being unanimous). Forty-two were 'crank' contests (i.e. six votes or less were cast for the unsuccessful candidate/s). The election of 12 April 1914 is undocumented, because the original returns are missing in their entirety (though the voting figures may be given in contemporary newspapers). The forty-five contests (out of a recorded total of 158 elections) are therefore a conservative estimate, the more so as all or some of the initial, rigged twenty-eight elections may well have been contested. In particular, there were high polls and often narrow victories at the elections of 1825, 1831, 1833, 1835, July 1845, 1854, January 1855, 1865, September 1868, February and April 1873, January 1908 (Lord Curzon), November 1908, 1909, April and November 1911, 1912 and 1915.[106]

Between 1800 and the 1820s, when British parties became clarified and classified as whig and tory, Irish representative peers 'were always mere nominees of the government' of the day, which usually signified its wishes unsubtly by a circular to the electors.[107] There then occurred, in December 1825, a furious contest between the 3rd earl of Mount Cashell and the 5th Baron Farnham. Lord Mount Cashell, an emancipationist, was the government candidate, or at any rate the candidate of the then lord lieutenant, the emancipationist 1st Marquess Wellesley:

under the date of return. I have compiled lists of the voting in every election for which at least some returns survive (PRONI D/3312/17), arranging the voters for each candidate in alphabetical order according to their highest peerage title. Originally, the returns were bundled according to precedence in the peerage of Ireland. But some of the bundles have become disassembled and disarranged, and it would be a laborious task to rearrange the voters according to then precedence. In any case, alphabetical order is much easier to follow than precedence, and a peer's highest title is usually the one by which he is best known. Baron 'Conway and Killultagh' has therefore been recorded as the marquess of 'Hertford', though 'Hertford' has been placed in brackets to denote the fact that that was not the title by virtue of which he voted and with which he signed the return.

[105] *Journals of the House of Lords of the Kingdom of Ireland* (8 vols, Dublin, 1780–1800), VIII, 543–4.

[106] In the election of Nov. 1908, an equal number of postal votes (forty-one) was cast for two candidates; which meant that, uniquely, a new *viva voce* election had to be conducted by the clerk of the parliaments in the House of Lords on 4 Nov.

[107] PRONI, Erne Papers, D/1939/21/5N/68, earl of Clancarty to earl of Erne, 19 May 1845; Killruddery, Bray, Co. Wicklow, Meath Papers, J/3/24/1, duke of Leinster to earl of Meath, 25 Sep. 1804; PRONI, Belmore Papers, D/3007/H/3/7, earl of Roden to earl of Belmore, 26 Feb. 1819.

Lord Farnham was also a government supporter, but an anti-emancipationist.[108] Lord Mount Cashell relied on the support of the lord lieutenant, while Lord Farnham exerted himself energetically and spent a great deal of money (which Lord Mount Cashell did not have). The result was that Lord Farnham obtained forty-nine votes, Lord Mount Cashell forty-three, and the Marquess of Westmeath (who was not a serious candidate in any case) four. Eleven peers did not vote. Since those qualified to vote at that date numbered only 107, this was a huge turnout.[109] It was also a great humiliation for the government, or rather for Lord Wellesley, who voted as an Irish peer for Lord Mount Cashell.[110]

Until the Curzon election of 1908, there was no other contest like that of 1825. The 1830s were characterised by vigorous combats between whig supporters of the government, tory opponents, and independents, complicated by permanent switches from whig to tory by peers such as the 3rd marquess of Downshire on the issue of Irish church reform in the mid-1830s.[111] Thereafter, representative peerage elections calmed down. But as they occurred fairly frequently, they often coincided with political crises of one sort or another; and, therefore, even when the voting was not close or the election unanimous, the accompanying correspondence about the election, when it survives, can be revealing, and is a neglected source. According to a well informed calculation in 1837, only thirty-three Irish peers at that time were whig; and from 1833 on tories were invariably elected, regardless of what government was in power.[112] However, every tory prime minister or leader of the opposition allowed the Irish peers freedom of choice, based on the aforementioned criteria of residence and good works, and merely acted as arbitrators in cases of dispute, so that an agreed waiting-list was drawn up and a split in the tory vote avoided.[113] There were not too

[108] BL, Peel Papers, Add. Ms. 40381, f. 367, Farnham to Peel, the home secretary, 24 Sep. 1825. I am indebted for this reference to Professor P.J. Jupp.

[109] Farnham reckoned (correctly) that the usual turnout was 'thirty or forty' – PRONI, Foster/Massereene Papers, D/207/52/60, Farnham to Lord Oriel, 8 Sep. 1825.

[110] HLRO, Writs, box 26, election of Lord Farnham, 17 Dec. 1825; PRONI, Foster/Massereene Papers, D/562/3478, Farnham to Viscount Ferrard, 5 Jan. 1826. For an analysis of the causes of Farnham's victory, made later by a cousin who had probably been an activist in the Farnham campaign, see PRONI, Erne Papers, D/1939/21/5N/47, Charles Fox to earl of Erne, 2 Mar. 1845.

[111] David Large, 'The House of Lords and Ireland in the Age of Peel, 1832–50', *IHS*, IX (1954–5), *passim*; PRONI, Downshire Papers, D/671/C/12/526, Downshire to earl of Roden, 18 Sep. 1834.

[112] PRONI, Arran Papers, T/3200/6/1, printed petition from the liberal Irish peers to the king, Apr.–May 1837; HLRO, Writs, box 26, election of Lord Downes, 30 Mar. 1833.

[113] For evidence of how these matters were arranged between the conservative Irish peers and the conservative leadership, see: PRONI, Downshire Papers, D/671/C/12/719

many examples of good works which made an impact outside Ireland, but the 'astronomical' 3rd earl of Rosse, who was elected in 1845, is a case in point.

While this may seem a convenient arrangement from the point of view of the Irish tory peers, it was actually the reverse. Because the whigs/liberals had to make their supporters UK peers in order to reward them and/or get them into the House of Lords,[114] the key to permanent preferment was not to be a tory. This applied particularly to the 1830s, when most of the translations of whig Irish peers into whig UK peers took place. By the end of the decade, the whigs were precipitating Irish commoners and supporters straight into the UK peerage – for example, Lords de Freyne, Lurgan and Stuart de Decies. At a later period, Lord John Russell, Gladstone and Lord Granville usually liked to have a tame and token Irishman (such as the 3rd Lord Cremorne, the 5th Lord Dufferin, the 1st Lord Emly and the 2nd Lord Lurgan) somewhere about the government, if only as a lord-in-waiting.[115] The whig John Wilson Fitzpatrick, illegitimate son and part-heir of the 2nd and last earl of Upper Ossory, was made a UK baron as Lord Castletown in 1869, although (in addition to being illegitimate) he had succeeded only to the *Irish* estates of his father. Finally – and this is a later example – under the post-1905 liberal administration, the 8th earl of Granard, who had no money but possessed the rare assets among

---

and 723, earl of Dunraven to marquess of Downshire, 12 Apr. 1839, and reply, 16 Apr. 1839; PRONI, Caledon Papers, D/2433/C/13, 2–3 and 8, Peel and Wellington to earl of Caledon, 11 Apr. 1840 (two letters of the same date), and earl of Lucan to Caledon, 7 June 1840; PRONI, T/3069/E/18, Peel to earl of Charleville, 2 Dec. 1839; PRONI, Erne Papers, D/1939/21/5N/5, 45, 67 and 79, Lord Farnham to earl of Erne, Erne to earl of Belmore, and earl of Wicklow to Erne (two letters), 20 Nov. 1842, [pre-2 Feb. 1845], and 19 May and [late May] 1845; Hampshire R.O., 21 M 57, Charleville to earl of Normanton, 11 Apr. 1839, and earl of Derby to Normanton, 19 June 1854; PRONI, Belmore Papers, D/3007/J/7 and 11, Derby to Belmore, 15 Oct. 1862 and 2 Jan. 1864; Birr Castle, Co. Offaly, Rosse Papers, M/3/1–10, correspondence of earl of Rosse about his election, 21 Nov. 1867–25 Aug. 1868; Belmore Papers, J/62–3, Viscount Bangor to Belmore, [pre-12 Jan. 1886], and earl of Kingston to Belmore, 12 Sep. 1887; ibid., J/126–7 and 131, Lord Cloncurry to Belmore, 27 Jan. and 9 Feb. 1898, and duke of Abercorn to Belmore, 30 Jan. 1898.

[114] PRONI, Leinster Papers, D/3078/3/35, earl of Clarendon, the whig lord lieutenant to duke of Leinster, the leader of the Irish whigs, 24 Dec. 1848. This was also true of the Scottish peerage: of 18 Scottish peers who were made UK peers between 1830 and 1874, 17 were liberals (PRONI, T/3430/10).

[115] PRONI, Rossmore Papers, T/2929/11/14, Lady Rossmore to earl of Carlisle, the whig lord lieutenant, 25 Mar. 1857; A.T. Harrison, 'The 1st Marquess of Dufferin and Ava: Whig, Ulster Landlord and Imperial Statesman' (unpublished D.Phil. thesis, New University of Ulster, 2 vols, 1973), I, 44–8; *The Political Correspondence of Mr Gladstone and Lord Granville, 1868–76. Edited for the Royal Historical Society by Agatha Ramm, MA, Camden [Society] Third Series*, LXXXI (1952), 9–10, and LXXXII, 389 and 395, Gladstone to Granville, 9 Jan. 1869, and Granville to Gladstone, 14 Jan. 1869 and 6 Aug. and 18 Aug. 1873.

Irish peers of being both a home ruler and a Roman catholic, was given various appointments in the Asquith government, as a result of which he made a financially and socially dazzling marriage to an American heiress in 1909. The operation of the Irish representative peerage system, often stated as being a sorry reflection on the integrity and independence of the Irish peers, therefore reflects some credit upon them. At considerable sacrifice, to themselves and to their descendants, the great majority of the Irish peers stuck to their tory guns.

The provision of article iv that an Irish representative peer should be elected for life was undoubtedly wise and a marked improvement on the Scottish system. But it should have been accompanied by a proviso that he should be replaced in the event of his receiving or inheriting an hereditary seat.[116] In actual practice, the Scottish representative peers changed little from parliament to parliament - certainly in the period 1784–1837 (they changed not at all in the latter year); and a Scottish representative peer vacated his seat if he obtained an hereditary title (though only since 1787).[117] As a result of the failure to insert a parallel provision in article iv, the absurd situation had been reached by 1831 that seven of the twenty-eight Irish representative peers were UK peers as well, to the great indignation of the two contemporary pamphleteers on the subject, the 2nd Lord Rossmore and the 2nd Lord Langford, who were neither.[118] Lord Rossmore unwisely admitted that an Irish representative peer was never truly a representative because of his life-tenure. The logic of that argument was that his subsequent elevation to the UK peerage made no difference to his position, as it certainly did to that of a Scottish Representative peer elected only for one parliament. If the Scottish precedent was not relevant in this case, it was positively fatal in the similar case of Irish peers with hereditary seats in the House of Lords retaining the right to vote in Irish representative peerage elections. As Langford pointed out, this was a legal absurdity, as a man could not be represented by someone else in an assembly in which he sat in person. Unfortunately for the Irish peers without hereditary seats, the British House of Lords had ruled in 1793 that Scottish peers who had British peerages as well, had the right to vote in Scottish representative peerage elections. Article

[116] This was suggested in January 1800, but nothing was done about it –PRONI, Castlereagh Papers, D/3030/679, queries about the representative peerage.

[117] Turberville, *House of Lords, 1784–1837*, Chapter Six.

[118] Ibid., PRONI, Anglesey Papers, D/619/28A, pp. 73 and 76, marquess of Anglesey, the lord lieutenant, to Earl Grey, the prime minister, 16 and 21 Feb. 1831; PRONI, Rossmore Papers, T/2929/5/70, printed draft petition from the Scottish and Irish peers without hereditary seats to the king, 3 April 1831, circularised by Rossmore round the entire Scottish and Irish peerage; PRONI, Arran Papers, T/3200/6/1, Lord Langford to earl of Arran annexing a printed petition to the king, 3 May 1837.

iv of the Union with Ireland was founded on this dubious decision.

The reality was that the complicated distinctions between the situations of the Irish and Scottish peers without hereditary seats, made any form of collective action on their part very difficult, the more so as their brethren who were fortunate enough to possess the advantage of hereditary seats never showed much enthusiasm for their cause. This was the disheartening experience of Lord Rossmore. In 1829, he addressed a circular letter to all the Irish and Scottish peers, to which one Scottish peer, the 9th Lord Napier, replied tartly that the Scottish peers had not been degraded like the Irish, because they had had '... the precaution to secure the dignity and integrity of their body as a peerage, by depriving the crown of the power of ever adding to their numbers in times to come'.[119] This was indeed a very important distinction between the Scottish and the Irish peerages. The Scottish Act of Union had not mentioned the possibility of further Scottish peerages being created after its passing, so that it was assumed that the Scottish peerage had come to a halt with the extinction of the separate parliament of Scotland. The Irish Act of Union, by contrast, had expressly provided for further additions to be made to the Irish peerage after the extinction of the separate parliament of Ireland. Indeed, it was only after the Irish House of Lords had shown itself to be uncharacteristically unmanageable,[120] that the British government had consented to limit these additions by providing that no new Irish peerage could be created until three which had existed at the time of the Union had become extinct. This was the famous 'one-for-three' rule. It was to apply until such times as the total number of Irish peers without hereditary seats had dwindled to below 100, in which event the crown was empowered to create Irish peers up to, but not beyond, the 100 mark. Also, the crown retained a limitless right to 'promote' existing Irish peers to a higher rank in the peerage, in spite of the fact that it was a nonsense in peerage law to regard a so-called 'promotion' as anything other than the creation of a new peerage.[121]

The first exercise of the one-for-three rule was the worst. In 1806 Peter Isaac Thelusson, a banker of Swiss extraction with no conceivable connection with Ireland, was created an Irish peer as Lord Rendlesham, thus prompting the wags to call him 'a Rendle-*sham*'.[122] This whig

[119] Rossmore Papers, T/2929/5/1 and 37, Rossmore's duplicated circular, 24 Aug. 1829, and Lord Napier to Rossmore in reply, 11 Sep. 1829.

[120] PRONI, Sneyd Papers, T/3229/1I28, Lord Clare to Lord Auckland, 6 Mar. (1800).

[121] Cockayne, 'The Peerage of Ireland', 5–6. The rest of the information for this and the next four paragraphs is drawn from this source, unless otherwise attributed.

[122] Chatsworth Papers, Derbyshire (transcript made by the late Professor A. Aspinall, and kindly placed at my disposal by Professor P.J. Jupp), Duchess of Devonshire to Dowager Countess Spencer, [17 Feb. 1806); Shee Papers, C/22, Lord Pelham to Sir George Shee, 17 Nov. 1805.

creation was particularly unfortunate, because it cast doubt on the perfectly good intentions of the Pitt government at the time of the Union. At that stage, there had been a genuinely held apprehension that, in an age when titles were still regarded as forms of social control, uplifting example and general ornamentation in the localities, the sheer quantity of peers resident in Ireland would diminish to a worrying extent. Scottish peerages differed from English, Irish, British and UK peerages, because they passed through women: the other species of peerage did not, unless they were accompanied by a special remainder, were baronies by writ or, in the solitary Irish instance of the 1661 viscountcy of Massereene, were remaindered on 'heirs general'. So, in spite of occasional problems in determining the sex or legitimacy of a Scottish peer, there was no possibility of the Scottish peerage dying out.[123] The other important point is that, had the Act of Union arrested the development of the Irish peerage by enacting that no further Irish peerages were to be created, it would have brought about a situation in which bearers of ancient Irish titles would have been leap-frogged over by new men, who would have had to be created UK peers because there was no other peerage into which to put them. It is more than doubtful that Lord Napier was correct in his smug satisfaction that the Scottish was a dead peerage.

The real problem – apart from Lord Rendlesham – was the defective drafting of article iv.[124] It failed to take account of the fact that one man could hold more than one peerage and that each peerage he held might have different remainders. The commonsense interpretation of the act was that, at his death, an extinction for purposes of the one-for-three rule did not occur unless *all* his peerages died with him. '... The *reverse*, however, of this interpretation was sought to be established by the extinctions used for the creation of the barony of Fermoy ...' in 1855, when a major *furore* broke out over the creation of a new Irish peerage when only *two* old ones had become extinct. Perhaps because of doubts about the interpretation of this part of article iv, it was little acted upon thereafter – nor indeed had it been acted upon very sweepingly since c.1840. All told, only twenty-two Irish peerages were created under the one-for-three rule, the last being Curzon in 1898, for the politically expedient but still unprincipled reason that he had to be a peer in order to go to India as viceroy, but wanted back to the house of commons on his return. All the others, Rendlesham and Curzon apart, were wholly unexceptionable Irishmen. Even Lord

[123] PRONI, Castlereagh Papers, D/3030/619, memo. about the representative peerage, [1799?].

[124] PRONI, Resdesdale Papers, T/3030/7/34, Lord Redesdale, lord chancellor of Ireland, to Spencer Perceval, 5 Jan. 1806.

Bloomfield (who was made an Irish peer for being a lickspittle of George IV's) had been born in Co. Meath and owned land, and retired to a country house, in Tipperary. In other words, the one-for-three rule notwithstanding, the Union marked the end of the 'profuse' creations of Irish peerages, and virtually the end of the practice of bestowing them on non-Irishmen. Nor were the post-Union 'promotions', which were not limited by the one-for-three rule, particularly numerous: there were only thirty-one promotions, the second-last in 1831, and the last in 1868; and all those promoted were resident, or largely resident, Irishmen, with the exception of the non-resident John Baker Holroyd, 1st Lord Sheffield in the peerage of Ireland, who was 'promoted' to the Irish earldom of Sheffield in 1816.

In fact, in the period 1801–c.1840, it was not the British government's selection of Irish peers, but the Irish peers' choice of titles, which tended to undermine the existence of a separate, genuinely Irish peerage of Ireland. The pre-Union tendency to grandiosity became more marked. Honest Irish towns, baronies and counties were largely ignored when it came to choosing new titles, and the emphasis fell heavily on the non-Irish and the grand. Thus, the Irish peers created or 'promoted' at or after the Union tended to choose *opéra buffe* names, many of them double-barrelled (as if two Irish titles were needed to equal in status one UK[125]): Dufferin and Claneboye, Dunraven and Mountearl, Dunsandle and Clanconal, Fitzgerald and Vesey (formerly Mr William Vesey Fitzgerald), Frankfort de Montmorency,[126] Oranmore and Browne, Talbot of Malahide, and so on. The patronymics of Irish peerage families likewise underwent some adornment: Wesley became Wellesley (admittedly, just before the Union), Cradock became Caradoc, and Mullins became de Moleyns. Worst of all, when Irish peers were given UK titles, they usually chose a title which associated them with England or Scotland, in spite of the fact that, after the Union, Ireland was legally as much a part of the United Kingdom as the British mainland itself. Thus, Lords Boyne, Clanricarde, Conyngham, Enniskillen, Gosford, Longford and Meath resorted to mostly obscure English and Scottish towns and villages for their UK titles. Few Irish peers had the dignity and common sense of Lords Clanwilliam, Fingall, Gormanston, Kenmare, Lismore, Powerscourt and Rossmore, who chose UK titles which were the same as their Irish, or the enterprise

[125] This sort of double barrel is to be distinguished from the other – two peerages with two distinct creations which, by the accidents of descent, have become vested in the one individual. The best-known example of the second sort of double barrel is Viscount Massereene and Ferrard.

[126] C.M. Tenison, 'Cork MPs, 1559–1800', *Cork Historial and Archaeological Journal*, II (1896), 37.

of Speaker Foster[127] and Lord Headfort, who chose UK titles which were derived from the Gaelic. If all the Irish peers raised to the UK peerage had chosen UK titles which were the same as their Irish, they would have been known both socially and senatorially by the same title,[128] and they would have asserted the continuing existence of a distinct peerage of Ireland in which they took pride.

For their part, successive British governments, if they had a consistent approach or gave much thought to the matter, seemed to favour the absorption of the Irish peerage into that of the UK. The reason for this was, partly, the attitude of at least one British prime minister, Lord Liverpool, who held that office from 1812 to 1827 and considered that the Irish (and Scottish) peers without hereditary seats were in a special category when it came to creations of UK peerages (because they already possessed virtually all the other privileges of peerage, provided they did not sit in the house of commons)[129]; partly, the already-mentioned creativeness of whig governments, particularly in the 1830s; and, partly, the jitteryness of all governments, especially post-1855, about how to interpret the opaque drafting of article iv in such a way as to create Irish peerages of indisputable legality. Between 1801 and 1887, seventy-eight Irish peers became UK peers, some by succession but most by creation; and in 1887 (allowing for twenty extinctions among the seventy-eight and for the thirty-one Irish peers whose hereditary seats in the House of Lords pre-dated 1801), there were eighty-nine Irish peers with hereditary seats there – just over half of the whole Irish peerage at that date. The number of Irish peers not possessing hereditary seats was quietly allowed to fall below the 100 mark (it stood at eighty-eight in 1887), and the number of Irish peers generally fell from 239 in 1801 to 177 in 1887. Against the creation of twenty-one peerages is to be set the extinction, between 1801 and 1887, of no less than seventy-six (the seventy-six all being cases where every peerage formerly in the family had ceased to be). This process of extinction was not kept up: in 1963, the number of Irish peers without hereditary seats in the house, of lords still stood at roughly seventy – double the number of the Scots and too many to be, like them, absorbed. However, the fact that there were too many to be absorbed is not to be attributed to post-Union creations – quite the contrary; nor is it to be attributed to any failure to absorb Irish peers on an hereditary footing into the nineteenth-century House of Lords.

After the Fermoy fiasco in 1855, it actually began to look as if the

[127] PRO, HO 100/72, f. 137, Foster to [a Dublin Castle clerk], 23 July [1797].

[128] It was a twentieth-century development that peers were designated in the order papers by their highest title, not by the title in right of which they sat in the lords.

[129] Large, 'House of Lords and Ireland', 368–9.

Irish peerage was as closed and dead an order as the Scottish. There was a flicker of life in 1868. In that year, the conservatives created John McClintock of Drumcar, Co. Louth, a veteran supporter and former MP, Lord Rathdonnell in the peerage of Ireland. In the same year, they 'promoted' the 2nd marquess of Abercorn to the Irish dukedom of the same name. It was an appropriately Irish dukedom because it was a recognition of services as lord lieutenant of Ireland; but Abercorn could presumably have asked for it to be a UK dukedom, and did not do so because he had the social assurance deriving from ancient lineage and the practical advantage of a British marquessate conferred by Pitt in 1790. In all subsequent instances, however, the public services of Irishmen were rewarded with UK peerages.[130] This had usually been, and continued to be, the case in respect of Irishmen who were members of the British cabinet or government – Lords Maryborough (1821), Congleton and Monteagle (both 1839) and Carlingford and Emly (both 1874), and in their case it may have had something to do with strengthening the government in the House of Lords. But this consideration was not a factor in most of the post-1855 cases of leapfrogging. For example, Sir John Young of Bailieborough, Co. Cavan, the first governor-general of the newly confederated Canada, was created Baron Lisgar of Bailieborough and Lisgar, Co. Cavan, in the peerage of the UK in 1870; and all the 5th Lord Dufferin's rewards for his distinguished proconsular and ambassadorial services, culminating in the marquessate of Dufferin and Ava in 1888, were in that peerage, not the Irish. The two great soldiers of the queen in the late nineteenth century, the warring Field-Marshals Wolesley and Roberts, were both Irishmen, but both went straight into the UK peerage, in 1885 and 1892 respectively. Only Roberts, whose territorial designation was 'of Kandahar and Waterford City', preserved – however incongruously – a link with Ireland in his choice of title.

Quite as important, new blood and, particularly, new or newish money, were not introduced into the Irish peerage. Henry White, the son of a millionaire who had started life as an itinerant bookseller in Belfast in the 1770s,[131] went straight into the UK peerage as Lord Annaly in 1863. The Guinness brothers followed suit, as Lords Ardilaun and Iveagh, in 1880 and 1891 respectively. In 1892, the Belfast businessman, John Mulholland of Ballywalter Park, Co. Down, who had risen to landed prominence through the improvidence of the already mentioned Lord Dufferin, was created a UK baron as Lord

[130] PRONI, Abercorn Papers, T/2541/VR/330/3, Sir Michael Hicks-Beach, Bt, the chief secretary, to duke of Abercorn, the lord lieutenant, 28 Apr. 1874.

[131] See Malcomson, 'Introduction to the Annaly/Clifden Papers', PRONI, Register of Irish Archives.

Dunleath. In 1906, the head of the Belfast shipbuilding firm of Harland & Wolff was created Baron Pirrie, also in the peerage of the UK. All of these men could have been translated to the UK peerage in due course, in recognition of their wealth and/or public services (for example, Lord Ardilaun's celebrated gift of St Stephen's Green to the city of Dublin). But Guinness would have been good for the Irish peerage, and should in the first instance have flowed into it. From 1885 to 1911, it has been estimated that twenty per cent or more of new entrants to the UK peerage had commercial or industrial connections and that at least sixteen per cent came from backgrounds other than nobility and gentry.[132] There was not a vast amount of commercial or industrial wealth in Ireland; but there were in Belfast other possessors of it as peerable as Lords Dunleath and Pirrie, and more of it should have been embodied in the Irish peerage. Certainly, the few Irishmen of the type who were ennobled should not have contributed exclusively to the UK statistics.

An Irish peerage which had been kept up to the 100 mark and regularly topped up by a correctly interpreted one-for-three rule and by new blood and new money, would have been in a much stronger position to maintain its representative peerage rights at the time of the government of Ireland Act of 1920 and partition in 1922. These rights could not reasonably have remained on their existing footing: provision should have been made for both electors and candidates in Irish representative peerage elections to be resident in the new United Kingdom of Great Britain and Northern Ireland, and for the figure of twenty-eight to be reduced proportionately.[133] However, both the government of Ireland act of 1920 and subsequent amending legislation were entirely silent on the subject, and therefore left the representative peerage system in *statu quo*. They did, however, make provision for any residual, unspecified powers exercised by the former lord chancellor of Ireland to be transferred to the governor of Northern Ireland, who should thus have replaced the lord chancellor as the functionary who initiated the process of election.

What was to becloud the issue was the phrase 'to sit and vote on the part of Ireland', which had been introduced into the Act of Union by inept drafting, and seemed to lend colour to the notion that the representative peerage system was connected with the continuing existence of a kingdom of Ireland. This phrase should have been interpreted in the light of article viii, sec 5, and 40 Geo III, cap. 29,

[132] Ralph E. Pumphrey, 'The Introduction of Industrialists into the British Peerage: a Study in Adaptation of a Social Institution', *The Americal Historial Review*, LXV, no. 1 (Oct. 1959), 8 and *passim*.

[133] See PRONI, Kilmorey Papers, D/2638/119/3, for an anonymous memorandum suggesting some such provision, [c.1922–5?].

sec 4, both of which state that the representative peers not only 'sit and vote on the part of Ireland', but also 'represent the peerage of Ireland': a construction borne out by three specific statements that the Irish representative peers were to represent the Irish peerage, made in correspondence between the home secretary and the lord lieutenant in 1800.[134] The same phrase – 'to sit and vote on the part of Ireland' – had also been applied by the Act of Union to the archbishop and three bishops who were to sit by rotation in the House of Lords. Yet, if there had been no disestablishment and the rights of the bishops had still existed in 1920, no one would have argued that they represented 'Ireland' as opposed to the Church of Ireland. Whatever may have happened to 'Ireland' as a result of the government of Ireland act, there can be no question that the Irish peerage still existed and still exists. In spite of this, the representative peerage system was declared defunct by the Committee for Privileges in 1966 and cleared off the record by a statute law (repeals) act of 1971.[135]

A statute law (repeals) act ought to be confined to non-controversial matters. However, it so happened that the then lord chancellor, Lord Hailsham, was the son of the attorney-general, Sir Douglas McGarel Hogg, who, jointly with his fellow law officer, W.H. Inskip, had misadvised the government in June 1925 about the continuing existence, or otherwise, of the Irish representative peerage system. In that year, the 3rd Lord Oranmore and Browne, an Irish representative peer, acting on sounder legal advice,[136] had sought to initiate a representative peerage election. When this move was opposed by the government, he argued that, if the governor of Northern Ireland had no transferred power to act, and if the Irish representative peers were supposed to represent a defunct kingdom of Ireland rather than an extant peerage of Ireland, why were those elected pre-1920 still sitting in the House of Lords. This question is unanswerable, since the life-tenure of Irish representative peers must be construed as incidental to and contingent

[134] *Cornwallis Correspondence*, III, 260–61 and 265, Portland to Cornwallis, 13 June 1800, and Cornwallis to Portland, 17 June 1800. As Lord Dunboyne points out, this construction was in effect acknowledged to be the correct one by the committee for privileges on 20 Oct. 1999.

[135] Lysaght, 'Irish Peers and the House of Lords'.

[136] By F.H. Maugham (later lord chancellor) and W.A. Greene (later master of the rolls). Their opinion was published by Lord Dunboyne under the title 'Irish Representative Peers: Counsel's Opinion, 1924', *Public Law* (Winter 1967), 314–22. Lord Dunboyne wrote to *The Times* on 3 June 1971 warning in vain against the 'injustice' and 'perfidy' of the statute law (repeals) bill, which would set the precedent for depriving British citizens of their constitutional rights by means of a measure which parliament had not had the opportunity of considering. The Hogg-Inskip opinion, of 10 June 1925, will be found in the Public Record Office, Law Officers' Department Papers, Box 35, no. 57 G.25 (photocopy in PRONI, T/3430/18).

upon their representative character. Lord Oranmore's question was answered by an incorrect legal decision followed, by a strange coincidence, by the conferring on Lord Oranmore of a UK barony in 1926. So, the Irish representative peers elected pre-1922 continued to sit until, one after the other, they dropped off their perches, the last being the 4th earl of Kilmorey in 1961. Similar illogicality was observed towards the knights of St Patrick and indeed towards Ulster king of arms, who were left to linger in a legal limbo and to die from natural causes.[137]

To conclude: the Irish House of Lords supported the Union for a variety of reasons, of which so-called 'Act of Union peerages', representative peerages and general exertions of patronage, were not the most important. The members of that House participated in the general, recent and alarming realisation of Ireland's financial and military dependence on Great Britain. Moreover, the terms offered to them, like the financial and commercial terms offered to Ireland as a whole, were generous in respect of all those matters of status, precedence and representation which weighed so heavily with eighteenth-century aristocrats, and were made more so following negotiation. After the Union, Irishmen regained almost exclusive possession of the Irish peerage, just as they had already regained, or rather, gained for the first time, possession of a high proportion of the patronage of Ireland. The Union, by throwing the emphasis of the Irish representation at Westminster on the county constituencies, and post-Union British governments by operating the Irish representative peerage system on the basis that resident Irish peers were left to elect fellow-residents of their own choosing, almost certainly had the effect that more Irish peers built or rebuilt country houses, and spent longer, on their Irish estates than had been the case in the eighteenth century.

What went wrong was that, from the 1850s onwards, the post-Union Irish peerage was allowed to dwindle numerically, new public services performed by Irishmen were not rewarded by admission to it, new Irish blood and money were not infused into it, and the constituency which elected the representative peers became too small and too redolent of an anachronistic *élite*. With the erosion of the Irish peers' influence in county elections, the erosion of their estates and wealth through the progressively more inequitable and expropriatory provisions of successive land acts, and their growing exclusion from a local administrative role following the local government act of 1898, they became an increasingly irrelevant group. In particular, the Irish peers were not a body which carried sufficient weight in 1922, at the time

[137] Galloway, *Order of St Patrick*, 53–78.

this was vitally needed, to ensure that the representative peerage system survived partition, as legally and constitutionally it ought to have done. The relevant part of article viii was not formally repealed. But the representative peerage system, one of the few post-1920 vestiges of the Act of Union, was left to fade away, thanks to muddled thinking, double standards and ultimately, breach of faith, on the part of post-1920 British governments.[138]

[138] For permission to draw on manuscript material in their keeping, I should like to thank the various repositories listed in the footnotes, especially the Public Record Office of Northern Ireland, and also the following which are not listed: the Derbyshire Record Office (in respect of the Wilmot Papers photocopied by PRONI), the Gloucestershire Record Office (in respect of the Redesdale Papers), the Hampshire Record Office (in respect of the Normanton Papers), the Hull University Library (in respect of the Hotham Papers), and the Keele University Library (in respect of the Sneyd Papers), the Centre for Kentish Studies (in respect of the Pratt Papers) and the Nottingham University Library (in respect of the Portland Papers). I should also like to thank the following owners and depositors of manuscripts: the marquess of Anglesey, the late Mr Walter Armytage, the late Mr Rex Beaumont, the trustees of the Bedford estates, the earl of Belmore, the earl of Caledon, the Marquess Camden, the Earl Castle Stewart, Mr Charles Clements, the Lord Egremont, the earl of Erne, the Lord Farnham, Mr Adrian FitzGerald, the duke of Grafton, the Lord Hotham, the late and present Viscount Massereene and Ferrard, the late and present earl of Meath, the Viscount Midleton, the Earl of Normanton, the earl of Rosse and the Lord Rossmore. In addition to the various authorities, living or dead, whose contribution to this paper is acknowledged in the footnotes, I should like to record a more general debt of gratitude to Professor P.J. Buckland, His Honour the Lord Dunboyne, Mr Robin-Eyre-Maunsell, Professor P.J. Jupp, Mr Charles Lysaght and Sir John Sainty. My greatest debt is to PRONI. In the early 1970s, when I had responsibility for PRONI's publications, PRONI financed my work on the representative peerage election returns (in the unfulfilled hope that it would be published jointly by PRONI and HLRO). In 1997, this paper was conceived as part of PRONI's contribution to the RHS conference in Belfast on 'The British–Irish Union of 1801'. In the event, I had retired as deputy keeper of the records of Northern Ireland by the time the conference took place. But PRONI continued to give me very practical support in producing the final text of the paper. For this I wish to record my gratitude to my successor, Dr G.J. Slater, and to his resourceful and long-suffering personal secretary, Mrs Lisa Nelson.

THE UNION AND THE MILITARY, 1801–c.1830

By Allan Blackstock

READ 10 SEPTEMBER 1999 AT THE PUBLIC RECORD OFFICE OF NORTHERN IRELAND

WHEN writing his monumental history of the British army, Sir John Fortescue devoted just two paragraphs to the military implications of the Union. He noted that Union greatly simplified British military affairs in general and that this was an excellent thing for historians, driven to distraction by the confusing archival situation produced by the pre-Union military relationship of the two countries.[1] The Irish military historian, Sir Henry McAnally, was equally succinct, merely remarking that 'military matters had not bulked largely in the Union debates'.[2] In ways they were both right. Although none of the eight articles of the Union refer to the army, it was understood that the assimilation principle, which regulated other branches of the public service and the church, would apply to the army. Yet, beneath and perhaps because of the delusive brevity of these bare facts, lies a seriously under-researched subject with wider ramifications, both in the short and longer term. Before these issues can be developed, it is first necessary to set the context by describing the pre-Union military background Ireland and then outlining the formal changes wrought by the Union.

The Irish military system in the eighteenth century

The origins of the eighteenth-century Irish military system go back to the Nine Years War (1689–97) between England and her allies and France. The scale of this conflict made it necessary to retain some of the army in peacetime. Following the Glorious Revolution of 1688, such a suggestion was bound to raise objections from whigs who equated a large standing army with European absolutists rather than with English liberty and limited monarchy. A compromise between ideology and military strategy was reached and Ireland chosen as a

[1] Sir John Fortescue, *A History of the British Army*, (13 volumes, 1899–1930), IV, 886–7.
[2] Sir Henry McAnally, *The Irish Militia, 1793–1816*, (Dublin and London, 1949), 159.

natural garrison for the peacetime standing army. In 1699 an English act of parliament set the limits of this peacetime force at 12,000 troops.[3] Given the turbulent history of Ireland in the seventeenth century, this force was seen as having a more important internal peacekeeping role than its British counterpart.[4] Although financed from Irish revenues, the Irish parliament had no authority to vary troop numbers which were set by the English legislation. This Irish establishment also functioned as a strategic reserve for Britain and the Empire and could be increased when the demands of overseas war required it.[5] Britain's imperial expansion meant more men were needed overseas and an augmentation in 1769 increased the Irish establishment to over 15,000, with the guarantee that 12,000 would always remain for home defence. The demands of warfare were ever increasing though and the Irish parliament accepted additional men going abroad during the American war.[6]

This dual role of wartime reserve and peacetime garrison meant that Ireland could be left with a seriously depleted garrison whenever overseas war or, as during the 1745 rebellion, domestic British crisis, required units to move. From 1715 this deficiency was supposed to be counterbalanced by the arraying of an Irish militia. However, although this force was mobilised during the various Jacobite and invasion scares, as it was financed by the respective counties, it was seldom adequately equipped. It continued in statuary existence up to 1775, but in practice fell into neglect from mid-century.[7] The militia legislation had lapsed by the time of the American war and was not renewed. When France entered the war in 1778, the demands on the Irish establishment were so severe that only 8,500 regular troops were left in Ireland.[8] This serious shortfall was made up by the voluntary service of citizens organised in independent Volunteer corps, the famous Irish Volunteers whose interference in politics helped obtain 'legislative independence' for the Irish parliament in 1782.

From 1701 it was decreed that neither Catholic or Protestant Irishmen could serve in the ranks, though Protestants could become officers. This was both a legacy of the conflicts of the previous century and an attempt to further increase the Protestant interest, as the regiments on

[3] K.P. Ferguson, 'The Army in Ireland from the restoration to the Act of Union, (Ph. D. thesis, Trinity College Dublin, 1980), 54–5, 60; 10 William III, c. 1.

[4] S.J. Connolly, *Religion, Law and Power: the making of Protestant Ireland, 1660–1760* (Oxford, 1992), 200.

[5] Alan Guy, 'The Irish Military Establishment, 1660–1776', in *A Military History of Ireland*, ed. Thomas Bartlett and Keith Jeffery (Cambridge, 1996), 216.

[6] Ferguson, 'The Army in Ireland', 62.

[7] Jim O'Donovan, 'The Militia in Munster, 1775–78', in *Parliament, Politics and People: Essays in Eighteenth-Century Irish History*, ed. G. O'Brien, (Dublin, 1989), 31–47.

[8] Guy, 'Irish Military Establishment', 229.

the Irish establishment recruited English Protestants. However, here too the increasing pace of eighteenth century warfare rendered such restrictions potentially self defeating and the embargo on Irish Protestants was relaxed.[9] During the Seven Years' War (1756–63) though Catholic enlistment was still technically illegal under the penal laws, there is evidence that the authorities were prepared to wink at officers who recruited Irish Catholics where the regiment was to go abroad.[10] Irish Catholic manpower represented a potentially enormous recruitment resource, but there were strings attached. Their assistance in the war effort could be represented as a demonstration of loyalty by those pushing for relaxation of the penal code. In 1762, the Catholic aristocrat, Lord Trimleston, sent an address to the lord-lieutenant noting that the hierarchy had instructed prayers to be said for British success and offered to raise Catholic soldiers.[11] A legal loophole was suggested, in that the Catholic soldiers could have enlisted in the service of Portugal, Britain's ally. Though the Irish parliament refused, the fact that such a proposal was seriously considered was a significant straw in the wind. The relief bills which passed the British and Irish parliaments in 1778 were intended to secure Catholic, particularly Irish Catholic support and manpower for the American war.[12]

The conflict which started with revolutionary France in 1793 was warfare on an unprecedented scale in manpower terms. France set the standard. The pre-revolutionary French army totaled around 150,000, but Carnot's 1793 *Levee en Masse* raised half a million 'citizen soldiers'.[13] This had implications in Britain where militia, fencibles[14] and volunteer infantry and mounted yeomanry corps were raised to help boost Britain's home defences and free up the regular army. In Ireland Hobart's Catholic relief act was passed in 1793 which, *inter alia*, permitted Catholic service in the army on the Irish establishment and allowed them to hold officer's commissions up to the rank of general. This was complemented by the raising of a new Irish militia which was mostly Catholic in its ranks but largely Protestant at officer level, despite the relief act. A further home service force, the Irish yeomanry, was raised in late 1796. In contrast with the militia, the yeomanry was predominantly Protestant in all ranks.

[9] Guy, ibid., 218–9.

[10] Thomas Bartlett, 'A weapon of war as yet untried: Irish Catholics and the armed forces of the Crown, 1760–1830', in *Men, Women and War*, ed. T.G. Fraser and Keith Jeffrey (Dublin, 1993), 60.

[11] Petworth House Archive, West Sussex Record Office, PHA/1270/1, Viscount Trimleston to Lord Egremont, 5 March 1762.

[12] Bartlett, 'A weapon of war as yet untried', 70–71.

[13] Major-General J.F.C. Fuller, *The Conduct of War, 1798–1961*, (1972), 31.

[14] Author's note: fencibles were full-time soldiers raised for home defence for the duration of the war. They were confined to service within the British Isles.

Increases in manpower notwithstanding, Ireland by 1796 was facing a deepening security crisis caused by the insurrectionary plans of the United Irishmen backed by France's promise of military assistance. British ministers had for some time been worried about the potential strategic dangers of an Irish parliament which, since its 'independence' of 1782, could now legally determine how many troops it would vote for the war. Although in practice there had not been any official reticence by the Irish parliament the dangerous potential inherent in a divided authority played on Pitt's mind. When the long-dreaded insurrection came in 1798, it had the effect of overturning the logic upon which the eighteenth-century Irish military system was based. Instead of functioning as a strategic reserve for Britain and the Empire, Ireland became a drain on British manpower and a danger to her security. The diversion of thousands troops to help with the suppression of the 1798 rebellion was one of the major factors influencing Pitt's final decision in June 1798 to create a Union.

Despite this strategic imperative, actual military issues featured little in the debates in either the British or the Irish parliaments. Government spokesmen frequently claimed that Ireland, as it stood, with an 'independent' parliament, and a partly disaffected population rank with religious faction was a weak link in the war. Opponents of Union did utilise more specifically military arguments, though they were anything but coherent. The British opposition claimed weakly that the post-rebellion reinforcements were kept in Ireland to impose Union, with Sheridan ridiculously proclaiming: 'You should not publish the banns of such a marriage by the trumpets of your 40,000 men'. Lord Moira, a serving general, more practically reminded Grenville that 'there was no such thing as a separate Irish regular army' and that in reality the military establishments of Britain and Ireland were so interdependent that formal Union was superfluous.[15] In Ireland, anti-Unionist military arguments were taken rather more seriously, not so much for logic, but because they could and were intended to re-activate proud memories of the Volunteers. Indeed the example of the Volunteers' political intervention in 1782 featured both in and out of parliament and in the pamphlet literature.[16] The wealthy anti-Union magnate Lord Downshire tried to use his militia regiment as a platform for his political views, while key Dublin figures like William Saurin, who led the influential Dublin Lawyer's yeomanry corps, held that as native forces suppressed the worst of the rebellion before reinforcements arrived, Ireland could

[15] *The Parliamentary History of England, 1780–1803* (hereafter: *Parliamentary History*) , XXXIV, 217, 223–4, 689.

[16] Robert Holmes [pseud. 'Eunomous'], *An Argument to the yeomanry of Ireland,* (Dublin, 1800).

still defend herself without being a drain on Britain. The government had to address these arguments and commissioned the civil under-secretary, Edward Cooke, to write a pamphlet arguing that Union would achieve the same end as the Volunteers of 1782 aimed at: namely Ireland's prosperity and happiness.[17] Pitt himself was well aware of the emotive handle that could be made of the military exertions of Irish loyalists, both in the Volunteers of 1782 and the yeomanry in 1798, and tried spike the anti-Unionists' guns by tactfully recognising yeomanry service during the rebellion, which he linked to the British voluntary military effort, calling the loyalists 'the brethren of Britons'.[18]

The immediate military implications of Union

The actual changes in military organisation wrought by the Union can be summarised quickly. Under the assimilation principle the Irish military establishment was merged with the British and the Irish ordnance and artillery were amalgamated with their British counterparts. The post of Irish commander-in-chief was suppressed and replaced by a commander-of-the-forces. With the demise of a separate Irish military establishment, the lord lieutenant lost most of his military patronage to the British commander-in-chief, retaining only the 'small change' of issuing commissions for ensigns and cornets. This essay will first examine the immediate impact of this military assimilation in the period up to 1803 and then consider some longer term military implications of the fact that Union passed without Catholic emancipation.

Military assimilation overlaid a context of ongoing re-definition of civil-military relationships in both Britain and Ireland. In Ireland there was a background of periodically strained relations between the civil and military hierarchies. For most of the eighteenth century, Irish commanders-in-chief were decidedly subservient to the lord lieutenant who had extensive military powers and patronage. Eighteenth-century lord lieutenants would select a Board of General Officers from the commander-in-chief and the staff to provide advice to help determine the more important aspects of military policy. The lord lieutenant's primacy was such that the Irish establishment's efficiency could suffer as many incumbents had little military experience.[19] In the 1750s, the

[17] E. Cooke, *Arguments for and against an Union … considered* (Dublin, 1799), 7, 48.
[18] *Parliamentary History*, XXXIV, 269.
[19] Guy, 'The Irish Military Establishment', 224.

reforming ideas of the then British commander-in-chief, the duke of Cumberland, were largely thwarted by Dublin Castle's reticence to forward military information to London.[20] Up to the 1770s most military administration was the lord lieutenant's responsibility. His chief secretary, as well as having civil duties, was the functional equivalent to the British secretary at war. From this time, however, Irish commanders in chief began to reside at the Royal Hospital Kilmainham where they gradually began to develop a parallel administration. The Castle regained its position in 1777 when the chief secretary's office was divided into civil and military branches, the latter known as the Irish War Office. The development of Kilmainham encouraged Irish commanders-in-chief to assert their independence and tension developed on several occasions.[21] In Britain similar developments were ongoing since 1795 when the duke of York replaced the aged Lord Amhurst and quickly saw that the whole military system needed professionalisation in its administration and training.[22] Here too these reforms led to tension between the respective civil and military hierarchies based at the War Office and the Horse Guards.

In addition to this difficulty, military assimilation also impacted on a wider developments as the political fall out from Union cast an ominous cloud over Dublin Castle, where the powers of the lord lieutenancy were left exceedingly vague. This problem, like so much else, had not been addressed by the framers of the Union. The fact that Cornwallis, the lord lieutenant who oversaw the passing of Union, was, uniquely, joint viceroy and commander-in-chief, while it undoubtedly helped him concentrate on crushing the rebellion, also allowed the issue of viceregal powers to be swept under the carpet of expediency. The first post-Union lord lieutenant the earl of Hardwicke, in an early version of political correctness, took up post on Saint Patrick's day 1801. However he walked into a situation that was dangerously vague regarding his authority. Hardwicke's consistent line regarding the relationship between the lord lieutenant and the army was that the pre-Union division of power was inherent in the office. He had known from February that the army patronage would go to the duke of York, but the situation regarding the actual command of the army was far from resolved when he arrived in Dublin.[23] Indeed there was no military commander at all until the appointment on 8 May 1801 of Sir William Medows, after the first choice, Lord Howe, had perhaps wisely turned

[20] Alan Guy, *Oeconomy and Discipline: Officership and Administration in the British Army, 1714–63*, (Manchester, 1985), 36–7.

[21] Ferguson, 'The Army in Ireland' , 64–66.

[22] P. J. Haythornthwaite, *The Armies of Wellington* (1994), 14–15.

[23] *The Diary and Correspondence of Lord Colchester*, ed. Lord Colchester, (3 vols.), I, 254.

it down.[24] Medows's military powers in relation to the lord lieutenant remained ill defined to the extent that he initially did not even have an official title. This embarrassing situation had implications for Hardwicke's task governing post-Union Ireland. His military under-secretary, Colonel Littlehales, warned him that 'the anti-Unionists would rejoice to see their idea realised of a government without power and splendour and an army without a commander-in-chief.'[25]

Hardwicke complained to his brother Charles Yorke, Addington's secretary for war, about the position of the new military supremo. He was told that the old title of commander-in-chief was withheld because it was now Union policy to consider the British army as the same army with one commander-in-chief, and that in consequence the Irish commander could not have the same title. Medows's title therefore was to be commander-of-the-forces.[26] Charles Yorke reassured Hardwicke that his viceregal position as head of the army in Ireland would be the same as his predecessors, except for the loss of military patronage. On 8 July Hardwicke's chief secretary Charles Abbot met the home secretary Thomas Pelham to discuss the problem of division of post Union military power. Matters seem to have been smoothed over. On 17 July Charles Yorke optimistically told his brother he was 'glad ... that many things which threatened difficulty have turned out so well ... I allude particularly to the affair of Kilmainham.'[27] However events arising from ongoing political and military developments in Britain would soon prove his optimism misplaced as Union meant Ireland became less insulated from events in the sister kingdom. Two parallel developments in London had particular significance for Hardwicke in Dublin.

Firstly the tension between the Horse Guards and the War Office over the duke of York's reforms had, since 1799, been resolved in favour of the former. The military shake up in Ireland following Union gave the duke opportunities for further centralisation. The second development was at the Home Office. In the late eighteenth century, Ireland had been the responsibility of this department. The same arrangement continued after Union but Addington's home secretary, Thomas Pelham, wanted to build up the powers of his office. With the position of the Irish lord lieutenant left vague after Union, he saw loaves and fishes up for grabs in much the same way as the duke of

[24] *Colchester Correspondence*, I, 265–8.

[25] British Library (hereafter B.L), Hardwicke papers, add. mss. 35701, Hardwicke to Yorke, 13 June 1801.

[26] Public Record Office of Northern Ireland (hereafter PRONI), Hardwicke papers, T3451/6, Yorke to Hardwicke, 16 June 1801.

[27] *Colchester Correspondence*, I, 274; PRONI, Hardwicke papers, T3451/8, Yorke to Hardwicke, 17 July 1801.

York did. In short Pelham wanted the Home Office to directly assume much of the Irish lord lieutenant's power and reduce him to the status of an English county lord lieutenant. Pelham advocated that the lord lieutenant's patent be altered in all details but 'especially in military concerns' and argued that, with Union assimilation, 'the duties which a distinct military establishment created, should leave the viceroy', leaving him only the power of ordering the troops for domestic peacekeeping.

Hardwicke resolutely contested this, complaining to Addington that he simply could not govern Ireland if 'the lord lieutenant is reduced to a mere superintendent of police'. In September and October 1801 Pelham and Hardwicke drew up papers outlining their opinions on what the status of the lord lieutenancy should be and Littlehales was sent over to London to negotiate. In the event, Addington determined in favour of Hardwicke and Pelham's invasion of Ireland was halted. Charles Abbot noted in a memo at the end of the year that 'Sir William Medows [was] cordially cooperating with the lord lieutenant.'[28] However Pelham's ambitions remained undiminished and he waited another opportunity.

This came in 1802 when the Peace of Amiens led to reductions in the armed forces. These cuts had particular implications for the auxiliary forces in both countries which were raised only for wartime: the volunteers, yeomanry and militia. An increasingly acrimonious correspondence began between Dublin Castle and Whitehall which shows that the Irish yeomanry became a bone of contention between Hardwicke and Pelham. From Pelham's perspective, aside from financial retrenchment, he had departmental reasons to press for the full disbandment of the force. As the Castle's full control of the Irish yeomanry and its patronage remained intact after Union, Pelham's arguments for disbandment can be interpreted as a continuation of his earlier attempts to asset-strip the Irish lord lieutenancy. Hardwicke, on the other hand, fought hard to retain as much of the yeomanry force in peacetime as he could. Although some cuts were inevitable, Hardwicke, along with Wickham and Littlehales kept suggesting ways to keeps parts of the force intact, even forwarding the kind of local magistrate's state of the country reports to Whitehall that at other times would have been dismissed in Dublin as alarmist. Hardwicke needed proof that domestic disaffection meant that the yeomanry had to be maintained at some level.

There was another dimension to Hardwicke's struggle against yeomanry disbandment. Since taking up office, he had had to deal with a substantial residue of Protestant opinion, which still resented the loss

[28] *Colchester Correspondence*, I, 287, 303–330.

of their parliament. Anti-Union Dublin yeomen, led by the influential lawyer William Saurin, had threatened mutiny in 1800. Hardwicke knew little of Ireland before his arrival and the gentry-raised, gentry commanded yeomanry were a link to both pro-and anti-Union opinion, because of their associations with Irish Protestants, particularly since 1798. Soon after his arrival Hardwicke made every effort to conciliate them by taking every opportunity to treat the yeomen well and even creating occasions, such as the lavish banquet he threw in July 1801 for 96 yeomanry captains, to celebrate the year of their inception 1796.[29] Therefore the retention of pre-Union yeomanry patronage, allied to the fact that the yeomanry could function as a ready-made instrument to build political bridges, made them an important component in the governance of post-Union Ireland.

Addington again came down on Hardwicke's side and he succeeded in retaining the best of the yeomanry. Legislation was passed in both countries allowing for the continuation of some voluntary service, but the Irish legislation gave Hardwicke crucial additional controls, with discretion for any reductions and authority to continue yeomanry pay. The renewal of war in May 1803 obviated the need for reductions and stimulated a huge increase of offers for yeomanry and volunteer service in both countries. May 1803 also saw a renewal of 'the affair of Kilmainham' with the arrival of a new commander-of-the-forces to replace Medows. Given the background of political tension and functional ambiguity surrounding this post, problems were again likely, come the man, come the moment. The man General Henry Edward Fox arrived on 28 May, selected after much combing of the army lists. The moment came in Thomas Street, Dublin on the evening of Saturday 23 July 1803 when Robert Emmet's insurrection suddenly flared.

Although Hardwicke and Wickham were both initially enthusiastic about General Fox,[30] given the background of civil and military difficulties since Union, in reality he had all the credentials to be a disaster in Ireland. He was Charles James Fox's brother and a relative of the duke of Leinster. Some Irish eyebrows were raised about these perceived opposition connections, though Hardwicke blithely reassured himself that consanguinity did not necessarily mean political association.[31] However, Fox had another influential connection which was soon to cause Hardwicke consternation: he was a personal favourite of the duke of York. When trouble came, it came not from Holland House or even Leinster House but from the Horse Guards.

[29] BL, Hardwicke papers, add. mss. 35701, Hardwicke to Yorke, 31 July 1801.

[30] Hampshire Record Office (hereafter HRO), Wickham papers, 38M.49/1/46, Wickham to Addington, 29 Jan. 1803.

[31] BL, Hardwicke papers, add. mss. 35772, 28 May 1803.

After the initial difficulties under Medows, the civil and military hierarchies had developed a pragmatic cooperation, even though the duke of York had significantly refused to reply to Hardwicke's suggestions to set this on an official footing.[32] Matters took a sudden and dramatic turn under General Fox. Hardwicke's objections notwithstanding, instructions were issued to make the commander-of-the-forces independent of the Irish government, and Fox's behaviour soon made it obvious that he was not going to answer to the Castle.[33] Whenever cooperation with the civil government was unavoidable, he made things as difficult as possible. Alexander Marsden, the civil under-secretary, told Castlereagh that almost from the day of Fox's arrival, 'we at the Castle could not get a couple of soldiers to escort a prisoner 100 yards without a letter to the Royal Hospital, and orders going from [there] to [the garrison commander] General Sir Charles Asgill in Rutland Square and [then] back again to General Dunne at the Barracks.' He markedly contrasted this with the more relaxed situation which had developed under Medows when 'a note from one of the secretaries procured us what we wanted.'[34] This communication breakdown and the power struggle which drove it was brought to a head when Robert Emmet's followers staged their insurrection on 23 July 1803. Without going into a full re-construction of Emmet's rising, it is sufficient to say that neither the Castle or Fox were without blame.

The fact that some of Emmet's powder exploded prematurely in Patrick Street on 16 July points to a defect in the Castle's intelligence system; though Hardwicke insisted that he had written to Fox, who later claimed to have missed the letter.[35] The Irish government stated that, although they knew an outbreak was coming, they did not know exactly when. Marsden claimed that they only discovered on the evening of Friday 22 July that the insurrection was planned for the following day, and that Fox was summoned to the Castle at 2 o'clock on the Saturday, and told the rising was imminent. Hardwicke saw this as tantamount to giving him orders – which of course was the crucial point.[36] Fox delayed taking action till nine-thirty in the evening, and when he did so, he summoned the garrison commanders to Kilmainham to receive orders and almost had them killed when they passed Thomas Street on their return to barracks. Word of the turmoil spread like

[32] HRO, Wickham papers, 38M.49/1/55, Hardwicke to Charles Yorke, n.d. [autumn 1803].

[33] PRONI, Redesdale papers, T3030/7/7, Redesdale to Spencer Perceval, 16 August 1803.

[34] PRONI, Castlereagh papers, D3030/1841, Marsden to Castlereagh, 22 Nov. 1803.

[35] PRONI, Castlereagh papers, D3030/1799/1, Précis of correspondence on General Fox, 23 Sept. 1803.

[36] PRONI, Castlereagh Papers, D3030/1840, Marsden to Castlereagh, 14 Nov. 1803.

wildfire and the Dublin yeomen hurried to the Castle to get their arms, several of them being killed on their way. Wickham caustically noted that 'there was not a cartridge at the Castle'.[37] Fox, without communication with the lord lieutenant, had ordered all yeomanry arms to be removed to the Ordnance department which, since Union, was outside the Castle's control.

The Emmet affair had wide repercussions and led to the Irish government's capability being questioned in parliament. Castlereagh publicly defended Hardwicke in the Commons, but privately believed that there was also negligence on the Irish government's part.[38] The fact was that Hardwicke had ultimate authority over the yeomanry, including the power to call them out on permanent duty. This could easily have been done, given that he had intelligence of the insurrection the night before the outbreak. It was rather weakly claimed that the Castle did not want to create panic by the public step of calling out the yeomanry, but given the total breakdown in civil-military relations, a much more likely explanation is that yeomanry, when called out on permanent duty, were under full military law and therefore under the sole authority of General Fox.[39]

Whatever way it is examined, the response to Emmet's insurrection is redolent of a catastrophic break-down in communications. For two dangerous hours, the gap between the Castle and Kilmainham was occupied by Emmet's insurgents. Fox was blamed, but surely the real blame for what Hardwicke euphemistically dubbed this 'dangerous misunderstanding' must reside with those who had so far failed to tie up the loose ends left by military and political Union. Although Emmet's rising was jocularly dismissed as 'the affair in Thomas Street', he intended to attack the Castle, the centre of government. Coups d'etat do not require field armies, but they do need the unpreparedness of the authorities. With substantial disaffection lingering in Dublin and the surrounding counties, and with French invasion a serious possibility, the consequences of such a symbolic gesture, even if it failed, could have been drastic.

Fox's Dublin days were numbered. There was speculation that Cornwallis would return as commander-of-the forces. Lady Hardwicke told Abbot's wife that 'the undefined situation of lord lieutenant and commander of the forces, would never have been at odds with such temperate men as Lord Cornwallis and Lord Hardwicke.[40] However, personality alone could never overcome the difficulties created by the

[37] *Colchester Correspondence*, Wickham to Abbot, 12 Aug. 1803, I, 438.

[38] A.P.W. Malcomson, *John Foster*, (Oxford, 1978), 440.

[39] Unsigned memorandum on the state of Ireland from 1798 to 23 July 1803, Public Record Office (hereafter PRO), Home Office (hereafter HO) papers, 100/115/ff. 134–58.

[40] *Colchester Correspondence*, Lady Hardwicke to Mrs. Abbot, 10 Sept. 1803, I, 440.

ill-defined post-Union situation. Cornwallis was ruled out. Although Hardwicke wanted him, and reckoned he would be acceptable in a solely military capacity, his support of emancipation and his sour relations with the yeomanry after the 1798 rebellion and Union were important factors.[41] After consideration, a Scot William Schaw Cathcart was appointed. The omens were not good. Edward Cooke remarked on Cathcart's reputedly hot temper, saying he would not be surprised 'if the Castle and the Hospital shall still be like Protestants and papists.'[42]

Cathcart arrived in early October and when his instructions from the duke of York were known, another unholy row erupted. These instructions appeared to underwrite Fox's approach, assuming that the army in Ireland was independent of the Castle. Hardwicke and Wickham felt that Cathcart's orders, if implemented, would make it 'impossible for the lord lieutenant to be responsible for the peace and safety of the country'. He consulted Irish lord chancellor, Redesdale, for an opinion on the legal standing of the lord lieutenancy since the Union and whether the duke of York's instructions infringed Hardwicke's royal patent. Redesdale felt they did and, with typical hyperbole, branded them 'grossly insulting ... illegal and unconstitutional' and claimed that Cathcart would be technically guilty of high treason if he implemented his instructions to the letter. Redesdale criticised the duke of York saying that when he first became commander-in-chief, he knew the limits of his authority, but now assumed 'a great deal which does not belong to his department.'[43] Hardwicke sent a confidential memorandum for Charles Yorke setting out the legalities of his viceregal position. Like his eighteenth-century predecessors, Hardwicke considered the viceregal office to have complete responsibility for Ireland's internal and external security and 'supreme powers' in the king's name, which meant in consequence that 'the military force must necessarily be obedient to him.'[44] At one stage, Charles Yorke actually advised his brother to resign the viceroyalty and apply to be re-instated as joint civil and military governor.

We have to remind ourselves that while this acrimonious wrangling was going on, the danger of French invasion was never more acute. Wickham sounded the clarion note of reality in December 1803 saying

[41] BL, Hardwicke papers, add. mss. 35703, Hardwicke to Yorke, 24 Aug. 1803.

[42] Centre for Kentish Studies, Pratt papers, U840/C/104/5, Cooke to Camden, 13 Sept. 1803.

[43] PRONI, Redesdale papers, T3030/5/19, Redesdale to [?Addington], 14 Oct. 1803; T3030/7/9, Redesdale to Spencer Perceval, 20 Oct. 1803; PRO HO100/114/f. 89, Hardwicke to Yorke, 'Private', 18 Oct. 1803; *Colchester Correspondence*, Wickham to Abbot, 25 Dec. 1803, I, 473.

[44] HRO, Wickham papers, 38M.49/1/55, Hardwicke to Charles Yorke, n.d. [autumn 1803].

that 'with the enemy at our gates, we ought not to be fighting among ourselves.'[45] Eventually Hardwicke again got his way. Assurances were received from both Addington and Charles Yorke that neither Cathcart nor the duke of York intended to supersede Hardwicke's authority. Ruffled egos were soothed as the affair was represented as a mistake arising from the stupidity of war office clerks who completely misunderstood the constitutional position of the lord-lieutenant.[46] It was determined that the relationship of the Irish commander-of the-forces and the lord lieutenant was to be the same as that of the British commander-in-chief with the king. Matters improved after this; a situation symbolised in June 1804 by a joint review of yeomanry and regular army in the Phoenix Park presided over by Cathcart himself. The ostensible reason for the review was to celebrate the king's birthday; however, given the background the real meaning had more to do with the Royal Hospital than with royalty. General Fox had once spared himself the political embarrassment of a yeomanry review, excusing himself on the militarily dubious grounds of having a boil on his thigh. By 1805, the chief secretary Charles Long, commenting on the reconciliation between the Castle and Kilmainham, said, 'I hear on all sides it was very bad, it is now excellent.'[47]

Perhaps it had taken Robert Emmet to focus minds on the reality that these power struggles meant a dilution or misdirection of actual military power. Union did not cause these clashes of authority, they would have happened anyway given the ebb and flow of power inherent in the ongoing administrative developments and military reforms in both countries. However the fact that Union left so much ill-defined in military affairs, as it did in legal and ecclesiastical matters, created a battle-ground for these conflicts to be fought out on. The crowning irony was the dangers of divided authority had been one of the major grounds on which Union measure was promoted in the first place.

The question of religion in the armed forces after Union

One thing the Union arrangements did not hinder was the flow of Irishmen, both Protestant and Catholic, into the various branches of

[45] *Colchester Correspondence*, Wickham to Abbot, 25 Dec. 1803, I, 473.

[46] PRONI, Redesdale papers, T3030/3/13, Addington to Redesdale, 23 Oct. 1803; T3030/6/10, Eldon to Redesdale, n.d. [pre-January 1804].

[47] BL, Hardwicke papers, add. mss. 35702, Hardwicke to Yorke, 11 Aug. 1803; PRO, HO100/128/f. 313, Long to King, 1 Dec. 1805.

the armed services. Given that Union passed without emancipation, and that religious questions had featured prominently in the pro-Union arguments,[48] what impact had this issue for the military in the longer term? Historians have examined this question both at the level of the military policy of governments and the actual experience of the men under arms. Thomas Bartlett has convincingly demonstrated the linkages between Irish Catholic relief and Britain's growing military needs from as early as 1760. He has also argued that 'militarisation' – the various home defence levies between the American and the Napoleonic wars was a crucial element in 'politicisation'. Focusing on the home service experience of Catholics in the militia and Protestants in the yeomanry, Bartlett argues that this led to the politicising of each group by the 1820s during the final struggle for emancipation, as their prior military experience had exposed them to Ireland's residual sectarianism. He concludes that 'the yeomanry and the militia can best be regarded as the military expression of two rival "nations" that emerged in Ireland in the years after 1800'.[49]

John Cookson's excellent study of mass mobilisation also examines the 'armed nation'. Like Bartlett, Cookson stresses the connection between Irish Catholic relief and Pitt's war policy. He detects a change of emphasis when Addington replaced Pitt in 1801. In Cookson's view, Pittites and Addingtonians both agree on the necessity of drastically increasing Britain's military capability, but differ as to means. Pittites believe volunteering helps the war effort by inculcating loyal service and hatred of the French. Addingtonians, on the other hand, see political and military danger in arming the English volunteers, many of whom come from the new industrial working classes and enjoy considerable local independence from central authority. They prefer militia to volunteers as the former are under military control and can also provide recruits for the regular army. Cookson extends this interpretation to Ireland, where it is cut across by the religious question. He notes the Pittite policy of using Catholic relief to encourage Catholic loyalty and recruitment, a policy epitomised in the Irish militia of 1793. However, when Union passes without emancipation and Pitt resigns, the incoming Addingtonians, pledged against relief, suspect the Irish militia because they are largely Catholic. In this perspective, Ireland becomes an Addingtonian looking-glass world where the militia appear as the English volunteers, politically dangerous and militarily dubious. On the other hand, there is what he calls 'an equally strong affirmation

[48] Cooke, *Arguments for and against an Union*, 23–4; *Parliamentary History*, xxxiv, 273–4.

[49] T. Bartlett, 'A weapon of war as yet untried.'; 'Militarisation and Politicisation in Ireland, 1780–1820', *Culture et Pratiques Politiques en France et en Irelande*, (Paris, 1988), 135.

of the Irish yeomanry as indispensable for the defence of the Protestant Ascendancy and British sovereignty over Ireland.'[50]

In many respects both historian's views fit with what we know of post-Union Ireland. At the level of military policy, the Irish yeomanry seem custom-made to address Addingtonian opposition to emancipation and fear of uncontrolled volunteering. Hardwicke once admitted, 'although it is desirable to have a Protestant yeomanry, the least said about it the better.[51] The yeomanry were indeed predominantly Protestant by 1801 and the yeomanry system, pragmatically devised in 1798, offered military integration and safeguards through a system of brigade majors which the English volunteer system did not at this stage possess. To turn to the militia, there certainly were several occasions during Addington's administration when interchange between the Irish and English militias was advocated on the grounds of the perceived untrustworthiness of Catholic militiamen.[52] Cookson's thesis of the alternating Pittite-Addingtonian responses to the armed nation can be applied to Grenville's 'Ministry of all the Talents' which revived the Pittite notion of Catholic relief benefiting recruitment. Indeed it was the Catholic issue in another form which toppled the 'Talents' in 1807. Grenville had attempted to resolve yet another post-Union military anomaly by trying to extend to Britain the provisions of the Irish relief act of 1793, which permitted Catholics to hold commissions up to the rank of general and allowed Catholic soldiers to practice their religion.[53] Portland's incoming 'no popery' administration can be seen as resurrecting the 'Addingtonian' approach. Portland's Irish lord lieutenant, Richmond, the northern yeomanry's military utility with their Protestant spirit.[54]

Similarly, at the level of service in the ranks, evidence of 'politicisation' in both yeomanry and militia, is not hard to find. In 1811, when the Catholic Board were raising the temperature in the push for emancipation, the interchange of British and Irish militia was seen as removing from the Board 'a strength on which they much depended.'[55] At the same time, the Catholic activist, Denys Scully, criticised the government's use of the yeomanry, claiming 'the yeomanry were on

[50] J.E. Cookson, *The British Armed Nation*, (Oxford, 1997), 167.

[51] HRO, Wickham papers, 38M49/5/10/90, Hardwicke to Wickham, 12 Nov. 1802.

[52] BL, Hardwicke papers, add. mss. 35771, Hardwicke to Pelham, 7 April 1802; *The Memoirs and Correspondence of Viscount Castlereagh,* ed. C. Vane (4 vols., 1848–53), Wickham to Castlereagh, 19 Nov. 1802; Wickham to Castlereagh, 14 Aug. 1803, IV, 296–8, 244–6.

[53] P.J. Jupp, *Lord Grenville, 1759–1834* (Oxford, 1985), 401–12.

[54] *The Supplementary Despatches, Letters and Memoranda of Arthur Wellesley, first Duke of Wellington,* (5 vols., 1860), Richmond to Wellesley, 5 Jan. 1808, V, 283–4.

[55] PRO, HO100/163/ff. 319–20, W.W. Pole to Richard Ryder, 27 May 1811.

duty and the Protestants every day receiving assurances that something would be done for them.'[56]

However, there are important aspects, at both policy and actual service levels, in which these overarching theories do not fit. As we have seen, official attitudes to the Irish yeomanry during the Peace of Amiens had more to do with post-Union administrative power-struggles than with resisting emancipation, which only re-emerged as a major issue with the 1805 petition. Hardwicke's dealings with the Irish yeomanry had more to say about the practicalities of governing post-Union Ireland than about emancipation. Moreover, religion or politics aside, the yeomanry had practical uses as a wartime alternative to regulars. Though Grenville's government certainly resurrected the Pittite Catholic relief–Catholic service paradigm, his Irish lord lieutenant, Bedford, also used yeomanry permanent duty against the 'Threshers'[57] in Connaught in late 1806. Indeed yeomanry numbers reached 82,000 under the 'Talents', the third highest total of their institutional life of almost 40 years.[58] Indeed the yeomanry policy of successive Irish governments goes well beyond gesture politics to Protestants. The retention of yeomanry patronage assumes great significance when set in the context of the loss of military patronage with the Union.

It is not fully appreciated just how severely this loss impacted upon landed families who had traditionally looked to Dublin Castle for military advancement for younger sons. A recent study of the political use of military patronage during Wellesley's chief secretaryship sees the patronage deficit as emanating from the lavish use rewards to secure the passage of Union, booth by the creation of honours or the tying up of future vacancies through Union 'engagements'.[59] The decimation of military patronage at Union is not mentioned, yet convincing evidence exists that this was sorely missed by both the Irish government and the gentry. The haemorrhage of governing power it entailed extended beyond the actual issuing of commissions. Even the lord lieutenant's recommendations for commissions were ignored at the Horse Guards. Hardwicke told his brother he was 'greatly mortified' at the duke of York's total neglect, which meant that 'the office is wonderfully lowered and degraded when the lord lieutenant has not

[56] The Catholic Question in Ireland and England, 1798–1822: the Papers of Denys Scully, ed. B. MacDermott, Worcester, 1988), P. Hussey to Scully, 31 March 1813, 128.

[57] Author's note: Threshers were an agrarian secret society directed against tithes, priests' fees, and the exploitation of large farmers.

[58] A. F. Blackstock, *An Ascendancy Army, the Irish Yeomanry, 1796–1834* (Dublin, 1998), 114.

[59] K. Robson, 'Military Patronage for Political Purposes: the Case of Sir Arthur Wellesley as Chief Secretary for Ireland', in ed. C.M. Woolgar, *Wellington Studies I* (Southampton, 1996), 115–38.

the same chance of being attended to as . . . Messrs. Cox and Greenwood [presumably army agents].'[60] Wickham received a letter from the younger son of a government supporter and large Tipperary landowner, Colonel Bagwell, which reflects the disgust felt by landed families. Young Bagwell complained that there 'did not appear the remotest prospect of finding employment for an officer of his rank'. Wickham told the prime minister that it was 'very material, tho' the patronage of the army is taken from the lord lieutenant, that the gentlemen of this country should be taught to make their applications for preferment and employment through the king's government and that the same attention should be paid to them at the Horse Guards as . . . English gentlemen of equal rank. . .'. In 1803 Wickham noted that Colonel Archdall had been passed over in a promotion of brigadiers and that 'though resident in Ireland he could not serve with his own regiment though stationed here'. This time he bluntly spelled out the political implications. 'His family has been very friendly to this government. His connexions are extensive, and his voice, if given against us, might at this moment be particularly hurtful. . .'. Hardwicke himself remarked that if a stringent letter he received from the marquess of Sligo's brother, Denis Browne, 'could have convinced the duke of York and the ministers by urging the same arguments, he would have done some service, [as] at present the Irish gentlemen have certainly reason to complain that [illegible] and the military service are hardly open to them'.[61]

The grievance was highlighted when the Army of Reserve was levied in 1803.[62] Many Irish gentlemen objected to it on the understandable grounds that, as the selection of officers was no longer mediated through the Castle, their traditional authority in their own localities was undermined. Wickham told Addington of the problem. 'Obstacles have been thrown in the way of our levy here which I foresaw when in London, and pointed out to the secretary at war who transmitted my letter . . . to the duke of York, but unfortunately it was not attended to.'[63] Hardwicke significantly noted that unreconciled anti-Unionists were exploiting this to prove 'that the removal of the Irish parliament had lessened the chance of promotion for Irish families in the regular army'.[64] With yeomanry patronage still in the gift of Dublin Castle,

[60] BL, Hardwicke papers, add. mss. 35701f. 164–5, Hardwicke, Dublin to Yorke, 13 Nov. 1801.

[61] HRO, Wickham papers, 38 M.49/1/46, Wickham to Addington, 5 Dec 1802; 22 Aug. 1803; 38 M.49/5/30, Hardwicke to Wickham, 5 Oct. 1803.

[62] Author's note: A reserve force to be raised by ballot with quotas set for each part of the United Kingdom.

[63] HRO, Wickham papers, 38 M.49/1/46, Wickham to Addington, 22 Aug. 1803.

[64] PRO, HO100/112/f. 248, Hardwicke to Pelham, 17 Aug. 1803.

some key Irish magnates saw in this, if not a total solution, at least a means of saving face locally. The marquess of Abercorn decided to raise large bodies of yeomen as a 'supplementary legion' in Tyrone and Donegal, which he believed would shield him from the disgrace to his standing with his own tenants. It is notable that Hardwicke, notwithstanding Addingtonian fears of plebeian armament,[65] fully backed Abercorn.[66]

The lack of military patronage was a long term problem. In 1806 it was contemplated that Bedford should regain the Irish military patronage, but eventually rejected on the grounds that he would be overwhelmed with applications. On the eve of the 1807 general election, and battling to strengthen the government interest, Wellesley tried to claw back some influence by asking the duke of York to be allowed to mediate by filtering commission applications through the Castle before forwarding them to the Horse Guards. He met with a ambivalent reply, and a caustic reminder of the profligacy of pre-Union lord lieutenants.[67] Despite this, and possibly because Wellesley was a soldier, there was some amelioration during the period 1807–8.[68] However, there was no reversion to the pre-Union position. In 1815 a War Office memorandum confirmed that since the Union no lists for commissions, promotions or exchanges were received from Dublin Castle, and that the accepted practice was for notifications for all commissions, regardless of their origin, to issue direct from the Horse Guards to the War Office from where they went to the secretary of state.[69]

Wickham had admitted that the yeomanry system 'was full of job' and the potential rewards so alluring that a wary eye was always kept open for fraud.[70] Given its lucrative and mutually beneficial nature, it is not surprising that yeomanry patronage remained important in the long term. Unlike British auxiliary forces, the Irish yeomanry were retained after the end of the Napoleonic war, though with some rationalisation. Following the announcement that county brigade majors were to be reduced by half, Robert Peel, as chief secretary, was inundated with requests by county magnates either wanting their

[65] Author's note: Supplementaries were an un-uniformed, largely untrained reserve for the 'regular' yeomanry who undertook to do duty during emergencies.

[66] PRONI, Abercorn papers, D623/A/81/68, Abercorn to Littlehales, 2 Sept. 1803; D623/A/82/14, Abercorn to Hardwicke, 25 Feb. 1804; PRO, HO100/111/f. 166, Hardwicke to C. Yorke, 2 Sept. 1803.

[67] *Wellington, Supplementary Despatches*, Wellesley to Gordon, 9 May 1807, v, 39–40.

[68] Robson, 'Military Patronage', 135.

[69] PRO, HO100/183/f. 184, 'Opinion of War Office', 18 Jan. 1815.

[70] HRO, Wickham papers 38M.49/5/3/10, Wickham to Lord Liverpool, 13 Dec. 1802; PRONI, Castlereagh Papers, D3030/1432, Sir George Shee, Treasury Chambers to Castlereagh, 22 Aug. 1800.

nominees retained or granted fat pensions.[71] Apart from commissions and places, yeomanry pay was important. Pay was issued from Dublin to the yeomanry captains in virtually every barony and town in Ireland to distribute to their men. In the days before the development of local government bureaucracy, the pay system supplemented direct patronage by creating a channel from the centre to the localities, a political conduit along which the complimentary tides of patronage and indebtedness could flow. Surviving yeomanry pay books show that paternalist landlord-captains could arrange loans to their tenants to be offset against future pay, or even dock the pay of those who misbehaved.[72] The controls such a patronage system gave cannot be divorced from the Catholic question, particularly after growth of Catholic electoral interests in some counties from 1807. Nonetheless, as Hardwicke had shown with the Dublin anti-Unionists in 1801, this complex net which the Castle could cast out over the country surely had a wider political and governing utility than simple resistance to emancipation.

To turn from policy to the question of yeomanry service and the 'politicisation' of lower-class Protestants, here too matters are less than straightforward. Bartlett argues that politicisation originated, empirically and spontaneously, in the militarisation of Irish society, and that, although it is less well-known than the Catholic experience, Protestant Ireland, by participating in this process, also shared in the mobilisation and politicisation of the 1820s.[73] This question of popular Protestant political awareness is indeed an intriguing one which can be examined from various perspectives. A comparison between yeomanry pay lists and the membership lists of Brunswick Clubs, the Protestant equivalent to O'Connell's Catholic Association, may shed some light on this issue. However, given the strong traditional paternalism in the yeomanry, such a comparison would not reveal whether the motivation sprung from service experience or landlord direction. Viewed through the lens of the ordinary yeoman's service, it could be argued could be made that their understanding of this experience was very different than from the politicisation Bartlett describes.

The terms of service of the yeomanry and militia were very different. Unlike the latter, which served outside their home county, the yeomanry was essentially a static force, the corps taking their names from the area they were raised in. Whereas militiamen were full-timers, yeomen served part-time who lived and worked in their home district. Their service was restricted to their own or adjoining baronies and, although

[71] BL, Peel papers, add. mss. 40291 f. 112, Peel to the Earl of Enniskillen, 16 July 1816.
[72] PRONI, Morrow papers, D3696/A/4/1, Lurgan Yeomanry Detail Book, 9 Sept. 1801.
[73] Bartlett, Militarisation and Politicisation', 126.

they could and did volunteer wider service during emergencies, most duty was strictly local. It is a moot point whether such service, even when it brought conflict with Catholic groups like the Ribbonmen, translated into the very 'modern' phenomenon of proletarian political mobilisation. An alternative argument could be advanced that such local service, rather than impel its participants towards democracy, actually threw them back into a pre-democratic interpretation of Protestant-Catholic relations. The Orange Order, to which many yeomen belonged, helped inculcate interpretations of organisations like the Ribbonmen and even the Catholic Board which represented them as being unrelated to contemporary politics. Instead they were represented in a completely different context. Everything, whether political organisation or rural incendiarism, was traced back to the 1798 rising, which itself was seen as another manifestation of the Catholic plots, conspiracies and rebellions of the seventeenth century.[74] Moreover local service itself may well have underwritten such regressive interpretations. In some parts of Ulster the first yeomanry corps were raised on the basis of much earlier proletarian Protestant groups based on parish or townlands, who had traditions of faction fighting and tenuous gentry links. As sectarian tensions rose in parts of Tyrone in the 1820s, when the government had severely curtailed yeomanry duty, it is perhaps significant that similar groups spontaneously appeared, carrying arms but without gentry leadership.[75] In terms of their aims and methods and lack of structure, such inchoate, atavistic proletarian groups were polar opposites from both the Catholic Association and the Brunswick Clubs.

Other qualifications can be advanced for Catholic politicisation in the militia. Inevitably, with the sources naturally biased in favour of the exceptional, the ordinary soldier's experience is going to be hard to access. Given that various 'state of the country reports', form the central core of the historian's source material, it is not difficult to find evidence of Catholic militiamen being involved in sectarian incidents with both civilians and other soldiers. However, the ordinary routine existence of a Catholic militia private – the men were often accompanied by their families on their peregrinations around Ireland[76] – is less visible precisely because it was unexceptional. Moreover, where there were violent incidents, one wonders what role regimental clannishness played. In 1806 an incident between militiamen and soldiers of the King's German Legion began when one of the Germans snatched a switch or

[74] *Resolutions of the Honourable, the Protestant Loyal Society of County Down*, (North Shields, 1813).

[75] PRO, HO100/214/ff. 38–9, Egerton to Goulburn, 1 Jan. 1825.

[76] McAnally, *Irish Militia*, 265–77.

stick from the Monaghan militia's drummer boy. From this apparently trivial incident a full-scale riot developed in which each party attacked the other with musket and bayonet causing one death and many injuries.[77] If the obviously symbolic switch had been a political ribbon the incident could be interpreted as a 'politicising' experience. However the fact that the familiar pattern of collective insult and retaliation occurred in an apolitical incident, and the fact that the militiamen were light company detachments from the Monaghan, Sligo, Londonderry and Limerick regiments, a mixture which from their counties of origin would mean Protestant and Catholics serving together, at least raises qualifications about militarisation and politicisation. Such incidents do not diminish the impact of the sectarian clashes and attitudes that some Catholic militiamen undoubtedly faced, but they do at least caution against assuming that militia units were religiously homogenous entities, a qualification which, in spite of their overall Protestant and orange composition, could also be applied to the yeomanry in some southern and western counties. Nor indeed can we discount regimental, group or regional loyalties which, if challenged by outsiders of any ilk, would be seized as a pretext for a fight.

To turn briefly to the impact of religion on the thousands of Irishmen who served as regular soldiers in the post-Union British army, again we find a vexed question full of contradictions. One can speculate on how Irish religious divisions, when carried overseas in the British army, impacted on the lives and consciousness of these servicemen both when abroad and, more importantly, when they returned. John Cookson recognises the difficulty of definitive statements, noting that the heaviest recruiting areas were those most troubled by sectarianism, yet he also astutely raises the possibility that a combination of communal solidarity in Irish regiments, serving against a common enemy along with English and Scottish soldiers, plus a decline in religious observance on campaign may have led to an Irish regimental identity superseding religious divisions.[78] The scattered evidence about returned veterans is equally contradictory. In the early 1820s the government were prepared to raise veteran battalions in the south to boost the regular garrison and help them cope with disturbances amongst the Catholic peasantry of Munster. Yet, during the 1828 Clare election campaign, the authorities stopped military pensions being distributed at a central point in the county as so many pensioners were gathering that the Catholic Association were mobilising the crowd for electoral purposes. Even the pro-Catholic lord lieutenant, Anglesey, told the commander-of-the-forces, that he had received 'some official reports and many vague rumours

[77] Ibid., 199–200.
[78] Cookson, *Armed Nation* , 170–1.

... that the Roman Catholic soldiers of the army are not to be depended upon' and noted that though he had been in the habit of dismissing such claims until recently, he now credited them 'such is the power of the priests'.[79] Obviously, for each category of Irish serviceman, yeoman, militiaman or regular soldier, further research is necessary before the post Union impacts of the issue of religion can be further refined.

Conclusions

What conclusions can be drawn from this examination of the immediate and longer term military implications of Union? Certainly in the short term, the decision to let military assimilation evolve in practice was potentially disastrous. It created instability, not because leaving things to evolve is necessarily a bad thing, but rather because it left important aspects of the governing of Ireland at the mercy of ongoing British military and governmental developments. Given that Napoleon was preparing an invasion fleet, this cannot be seen as anything other than dangerous neglect. Although the clash of civil and military authorities was resolved, echoes were still discernible years later and the position of Irish commander-of-the-forces remained a sensitive one. On two occasions, in 1816 and 1819, General George Nugent, was considered for the post. Nugent had a high reputation as a soldier, was high in the confidence of the duke of York and had experience in serving in Ireland in 1798 when he won praise for his handling of the northern rebellion and his ability to work with the yeomen. Militarily, he was undoubtedly the man for the job. However, on both occasions, he was passed over because he privately supported emancipation.

With the passage of Union without emancipation, the question of religion in the armed forces is an important issue in the longer term. However, from the perspective of Dublin Castle's policy on the yeomanry, there is evidence that it is not the only, and at times not the major, determining factor. With the loss of military patronage after Union, yeomanry patronage and pay assume great importance as a substitute political cement to binding the centre to the localities. Contradictions abound when we consider the politicising effect of the experience of military service between the Union and emancipation for the large numbers of Irishmen, Protestant and Catholic, who enlisted in the yeomanry, militia and regular army. The very pervasiveness of

[79] PRONI, Anglesey papers, D619/26/C/67–8, Memo transmitted [by Anglesey] to Sir John Byng, 21 July 1828.

these contradictions perhaps points to an ultimate reality that the relationship between military experience and Ireland's religious divisions cannot be generalised and fluctuated according to the contexts of time and place. The quicksilver nature of these contractions was dramatically illustrated in 1831, when Anglesey re-armed the yeomanry, moribund for years, and used them in the 'tithe war'. The effect was explosive, literally. One yeomanry corps fired on Catholic protesters in Newtownbarry killing about 14 people. As petitions rained into parliament, Anglesey explained himself by saying he had wanted to stop some northern yeomen and orangemen, disgusted after emancipation, from joining with Catholics to support O'Connell's campaign for repeal of the Union.[80]

[80] PRONI, Anglesey papers, D619/27B/26–7, Anglesey to Holland, 4 July 1831; I am grateful to the following individuals and institutions for permission to publish from material in their keeping: The Deputy keeper of the records, PRONI; the British Library; the Hampshire Record Office; the Centre for Kentish Studies. The Home Office papers are Crown copyright.

POLITICS, PUBLIC FINANCE AND THE BRITISH–IRISH ACT OF UNION OF 1801

By Trevor McCavery

READ 11 SEPTEMBER 1999 AT THE QUEEN'S UNIVERSITY OF BELFAST

BEFORE the smoke of the Irish rebellion of 1798 had cleared, the British prime minister William Pitt was convinced of the necessity of a legislative union between Britain and Ireland.[1] He broached the subject seriously with his cabinet colleague, Lord Grenville, on 2 June and by 4 June the joint post master general, Lord Auckland, an expert on Irish commercial affairs, was brought into Pitt's confidence. Pitt told Auckland that he and Grenville had been able to: 'see daylight in almost everything but what relates to trade and revenue.'[2] The subject of this paper is to discover how matters of trade and revenue were arranged in the Act of Union and to discuss some of the political difficulties which arose from implementing these arrangements. As the evolution of ministers' thinking is documented, the authorship of some points can be precisely identified and the thinking and tacit economic forecasting brought to light. This paper will suggest that the arrangements were intended to be generous to Ireland and contrasts with an Irish nationalist interpretation of the subject articulated in the early decades of the twentieth century.[3] Then the difficulties that politicians experienced in executing policies within the framework laid down by these articles are considered. The whole vice-regal system of government was by no means guaranteed in the immediate post-Union period as it worked against the chancellor of the Irish exchequer in his attempts to manage Irish public finance. Although the Union meant that the office of chief secretary eventually increased in importance, this paper

[1] G.C. Bolton, *The passing of the Irish Act of Union: a study in parliamentary politics* (1966), 53–62 [hereafter Bolton, *Union*].

[2] Pitt to Auckland, 4 June 1798, *The Journals and Correspondence of William, Lord Auckland* ed. Bishop of Bath and Wells (4 vols., 1861–2), II , 2 [hereafter Bath, *Auckland*].

[3] For this interpretation see A.E Murray, *History of the Commercial and Financial Relations between England and Ireland since the Restoration* (1903); Earl of Dunraven, *The Finances of Ireland before the Union and after* (1912); G. O'Brien, *The Economic history of Ireland from the Union to the Famine* (1921); T.J. Kiernan, *History of the Financial administration of Ireland to 1817* (1930); for a more detailed study of this subject see T.R. McCavery, 'Finance Politics and Ireland, 1801–1817' (Ph.D. thesis, The Queen's University of Belfast, 1980), 13–45, 217–8 [hereafter McCavery 'Finance'].

suggests that this was by no means assured in the first five years of the Union.[4]

Evolution

When Pitt and Grenville turned to Auckland for advice they were concerned that the existing National Debt of each country, and the consequent cost of servicing it, was so disparate that it was a question of justice whether Ireland should be asked to take on the cost of sharing the British burden. Also, it was a question of prudence whether she was capable of bearing British taxation levels to do so. Throughout July and August 1798, Auckland was picking the brain of his friend John Beresford, the chief commissioner of the Irish revenue, for information on finance and trade.[5] Irish information was solicited unofficially, as in the Beresford–Auckland correspondence, but also with Irish civil servants in touch with the British ministers. Apparently before l4 August 1798, Edward Cooke, the under-secretary to the chief secretary in the civil department in Dublin Castle, had submitted his thinking for a Union directly to Pitt. Cooke, like Auckland, was to be one of the most influential draftsmen of the Act of Union. Another draughtsman was Viscount Castlereagh, the Irish chief secretary.

1. Anglo–Irish financial relations (Article 7)

Ireland's contribution towards total United Kingdom expenses

The earliest suggestion on this subject came from Cooke who said that Ireland should be responsible only for her own debts but, when these were paid off, she could start contributing to the British debt. On 14 August 1798 Pitt suggested that Ireland should start contributing to imperial expenses *immediately* but only towards a *proportion* of the United Kingdom military establishment. The remainder of Ireland's revenue would pay her own debts, civil expenditure and the surplus appropriated for local benefit. Pitt therefore introduced the proportionate contribution idea which was the cornerstone of the finance arrangement of the Act

[4] B. Jenkins, *Era of Emancipation: British Government of Ireland 1812–1830* (Montreal, 1988), 56 [hereafter Jenkins, *Emancipation*]; S.J. Connolly 'Aftermath and adjustment' *A New History of Ireland V: Ireland under the Union,* I 1801–1870 ed. W.E Vaughan, (Dublin, 1989), 1–2 [hereafter Connolly, 'Aftermath' and Vaughan 'Union'].

[5] Beresford to Auckland, 19, 21 July, 2 Aug 1798 in *Correspondence of the Rt. Hon John Beresford* ed. W. Beresford (2 vols., 1854) II, 161, 163, 167 [hereafter Beresford, *Beresford*].

of Union, but the ratio was as yet undetermined and was confined only to military expenditure; not, as later; to the civil expenses of administering the whole United Kingdom. Pitt felt his own ideas would be 'more advantageous to Ireland than what is proposed'[6] By 12 November 1798 the British government had decided that Ireland would be asked to contribute to all annual imperial expenses – *civil* now as well as military. The proportion was still undetermined. The priority in expenditure would be to service her own debt and that Pitt planned an income tax for Ireland.[7] Portland claimed that it would be a more

> a just criterion to determine the quota which each country should bear of the public expense. In the meantime, other data must be resorted to ... and you may be confident that every care will be taken in such an arrangement to give no cause of complaint or jealousy to our newly united brethren.

Two separate proportions were envisaged, one for peace and one for war. Money left in the Irish exchequer, after paying the proportions towards imperial expenses, would go to Irish concerns such as debt charges and local development.[8]

In January 1799 Castlereagh returned to Ireland after a visit to London much better informed in the areas of commerce and finance. He believed 'the terms are considered as highly liberal, the proportional arrangements of the expenses having completely overset the argument on which the enemies of the measure had hitherto principally relied, viz., the extension of English debt and taxation to Ireland.'

Yet he was not totally happy. He was not satisfied that anyone had yet found 'a sufficiently accurate criterion at all times of the relative means of the two countries.' Castlereagh found fault with Pitt's reliance on an Irish income tax for calculating national wealth. In Great Britain the yield was the result of a patriotic response by the gentry to war time exigencies. This could not enduring. In Ireland the government could not be assured of a similar response even in wartime. So if comparing yields from an income tax was abandoned how could

[6] 'C[ooke]'s Plan of Union', n.d. [pre-14 Aug. 1798], Auckland Papers, British Library Additional Manuscripts, [hereafter BL Add. MS] 3445, fo. 154; Pitt to Auckland, 14 Aug. 1798, Sneyd MS, Keele University Library, photocopied by The Public Record Office of Northern Ireland [hereafter PRONI] reference T.3229/2/35.

[7] Portland to Cornwallis, 12 Nov. 1798, *Correspondence of Charles, 1st Marquess Cornwallis*, ed. Sir C. Ross (3 vols., 1859), II, 436 [hereafter Ross, *Cornwallis*].

[8] Portland to Cornwallis, 25 Nov., 24 Dec. 1798, *Memoirs and Correspondence of Viscount Castlereagh* ed. Marquess of Londonderry (4 vols., 1848–49), II, 22, 58 [hereafter Londonderry, *Castlereagh*].

Ireland's capacity be measured. He recommended comparing rates of consumption of certain articles .[9]

As late as 25 October 1799, Castlereagh still reckoned on having two separate quotas. In peace Ireland would contribute one seventh of imperial expenses and only one tenth in war times. On 7 November 1799, Hobart, a former chief secretary, commented to Auckland

> I am inclined to think that a similar proportion both for peace and war will be best understood and is altogether more reasonable, especially because I believe the proportional ability of Ireland in time of war to bear her share of expenses is to the full as great if not greater during that period than in peace. Her chief source of wealth, her linens, certainly do not fail her at that time and there can be no doubt of the increase of her provision trade. Such an arrangement would also, I think, be more palatable here.[10]

By 15 November 1799 Hobart's idea of having the same proportion for war and peace was accepted. It is not clear if Ireland's capacity in war or to make the idea more 'palatable' in Great Britain, were the decisive reason for adopting it The proportion decided was two seventeenths – halfway between one-seventh and one-tenth. However it was not until 18 December 1799 that Irish accounts were found that showed that the comparative consumption of beer, spirits, salt, tea sugar, tobacco and wine approximated to this ratio.

Castlereagh was delighted with this confirmation. When he read the accounts he wrote immediately to Auckland

> You will be pleased at the coincidence in the proportional value of enumerated articles consumed in the two countries. This concordance in the criterion of relative wealth exceeds my most sanguine expectations. I think it places the system on a rock. The $7\frac{1}{2}$ falling in with past expenditure is convenient, but supported by the tests of commerce and consumption, it is built on a foundation that it cannot be shaken.[11]

The framers of the Act of Union were well aware of the difficulties of calculating national wealth for the purposes of comparability. They

[9] Castlereagh to Portland, 7 Jan. 1799, ibid., II, 58; 'Plan of Contribution' [by Castlereagh] 'received 17 Jan. 1799', Chatham MS, Public Record Office [hereafter PRO], 30/8/237, fo. 21.

[10] Bolton, *Union*, 186; Hobart to Auckland, Sneyd MS, T.3229/2/43.

[11] Cooke to Castlereagh, 13 Nov. 1799, BL Add. MS 30/8/327, fo. 169; Cooke to Beresford, 18 Dec. 1799, Beresford, *Beresford*, II, 235; Castlereagh to Auckland, 20 [Dec. 1799] Sneyd MS, T.3229/2/48; 'Draft relative to proportional contributions and criterions' [sic], n.d. PRONI Castlereagh Papers, D.3030/1130; Londonderry, *Castlereagh*, III, 191.

could only draw satisfaction that their statistics *coincided* in the ratio of $7\frac{1}{2}$:1.

The duration of proportionate contribution

Another important detail of public finance was settled in the period October – December 1799. Having decided how much Ireland should contribute, it was necessary to decide how long this system of proportionate contribution should continue and what should be the conditions which permitted complete financial amalgamation. Many ideas were discussed. All strove to ensure equity in the financial arrangements. Cooke's paper of 13 November 1799 provided the final settlement of this difficult question. He introduced the novel idea that common taxation might ensue when the *debts* of each country were in the same proportion as their *contributions*. At present the debt proportion stood at 12:1; when it became $7\frac{1}{2}$:1 then financial amalgamation could take place. He obviously expected the British debt to be *reduced* from 12:1 to $7\frac{1}{2}$:1.[12]

Cooke's prognosis was entirely wrong. The $7\frac{1}{2}$:1 ratio was reached in a decade but it was through a large *increase of Irish debt*, due to having to meet two-fifteenths of a large United Kingdom establishment swollen by fifteen years of expensive war. The British debt did not increase so fast as the Irish because Great Britain discovered an unexpected capacity for sustaining extraordinary high levels of taxation.

Castlereagh accepted Cooke's idea of debt ratio equalling contribution ratio; but he did not accept the accompanying prognosis. His own reading of the future was vindicated by later events and deserves full quotation.

> if war should continue, and Ireland find her supplies [i.e. borrows] while England raises the greater part of hers within the year [i.e. by taxation] and mortgages her extraordinary funds to their rapid reduction in peace, Ireland must run proportionately in debt and her scale of taxes rise accordingly. It evidently depends therefore upon events whether England shall descend or Ireland be raised to the level with England, but neither can be injured as the assimilation will be produced by natural causes and in no degree forced.[13]

This shows that Castlereagh contemplated such a prospect with complacency: although he foresaw the course of events, he did not see them as injurious to Ireland, because he believed that Ireland would

[12] Draft bill [in Castlereagh's writing], n.d., 'Contribution of Ireland', 23 Oct. 1799, 'Minute on the equalisation of taxes', n.d., Castlereagh Papers , D.3030/1127, 1131, 1136; Cooke to Castlereagh, 13 Nov. 1799, Chatham MS, 30/8/327, fo. 169.

[13] *Castlereagh*, III, 196; Castlereagh Papers, D.3030/1127.

gradually raise her levels of taxation to meet the increased debt charges – 'by natural causes and in no degree forced'.

Levels of taxation

Regarding levels of taxation, Cooke, at an early stage, proposed that the margin between British and Irish levels be maintained when any additional rates were imposed but he also suggested that Ireland participate in the next land tax. Pitt only partly agreed with Cooke's proposals on taxation. While he agreed that a form of income tax be extended to Ireland, and that Ireland should not experience indirect taxation indiscriminately with Great Britain, he also suggested that the amount of indirect taxation levied on Ireland should be a reflection of the yield of her income tax and not necessarily reflect existing differentials. Her capacity for direct taxation should be the same as for indirect taxation. This reliance on the yield from income tax was a completely novel and fresh approach to financial relations, but it does appear rather artificial and was eventually abandoned.[14]

By 17 January 1799 Castlereagh was arguing that the superior debt of England seemed to be 'the only cause why the taxes of Great Britain should be more numerous and weighty than those of Ireland.' He was confident that the British debt would be liquidated within fifty years hence removing the necessity for financial separateness. Also, he believed Ireland had the capacity to raise her taxation to British levels and, in this way, financial assimilation could take place more quickly.[15]

With hindsight the architects of this article can be criticised for their decision to tie Ireland's taxation levels to the spiralling growth of British national debt. They worked in the dark, acknowledging that they possessed inadequate indices of national wealth. They were involved in economic forecasting at a time when no one had any conception of the scope, expense and the capacity to sustain, the war they were presently fighting against France. There is another reason why the policy may not have been thought through properly. This was the strategy of opposition politicians.

Plunket, the leader of the anti-unionist MPs, admitted in the committee on the finance article that they would not amend the proposal but reject it in principle: 'to decline any responsibility, to avoid giving it any sanction, to leave it encumbered with all its imperfections that the public might be convinced of its ruinous tendency and join in repudiating it.'

J.C. Beresford's amendment to change the proportion of contribution

[14] See n. 5.

[15] 'Plan of Contribution' [by Castlereagh] 'received 17 Jan. 1799', Chatham MS, 30/8/237, fo. 21.

from 1:7$\frac{1}{2}$ to 1:10 received no support from opposition and the whole seventh article passed, without a division, through the committee stage when there was ample opportunity to improve it. Foster, of course, spoke out against it, but in a declamatory style, and the public dialogue between himself and Castlereagh centred on their integrity in the selection of statistics rather than on any serious attempt to reframe the provision. Castlereagh was said to have 'answered him as to finance extremely well'.[16]

Anglo-Irish commercial relations (Article 6)

In the early summer of 1798 Cooke suggested the model of the Anglo-French commercial treaty of 1787. This was a step towards free trade as it reduced tariff walls to an agreed moderate level, which opened up trade but were sufficient to save the domestic manufacture of each country from destruction,. Although Pitt saw this as 'quite reasonable' he was inclined to be even more generous: 'it is desirable, gradually or immediately, to go further and make the intercourse duty free.'[17]

Castlereagh bestowed the commercial article business in Ireland upon John Beresfordı just as he had done with the finance article upon Cooke. Beresford's work, 'received the highest economiums'.[18] Unlike the finance article, the features of the commercial arrangements were straightforward.

One bone of contention, however, was the fear that, Irish manufacturers would be ruined without any protection from a sympathetic and informed Irish parliament. Cooke called this the 'Dublin argument'. It seems that it was not characteristic of the rest of Ireland. Professor R.D.C. Black has said that the desire for a protectionist policy came mostly from Dublin manufacturers, and that there was a considerable opposition to it in Ireland. His marshalling of contemporary Irish opinion shows that there was no ground for 'the view often advanced that Irish opposition to the commercial aspects of the Union, when it came, arose from the fact that it made protection to Irish industry

[16] Cornwallis to Portland, 25 Feb. 1800 Ross, *Cornwallis*, III, 159; *Speech of the Rt. Hon. John Foster, Speaker of the House of Commons of Ireland, delivered in Committee on Monday 17 February 1800* (Dublin, 1800); *A Reply to the Speech of the Speaker, as stated to have been delivered on 17 February 1800* (Dublin, 1800); *Speech of the Rt. Hon. John Foster, Speaker of the House of Commons of Ireland, delivered in Committee on Wednesday 19 March 1800* (Dublin, 1800).

[17] See n. 5.

[18] Castlereagh to Beresford, 26 Aug. 1799, Beresford, *Beresford*, II, 225.

impossible. In fact the Irish Parliament never showed itself at all wedded to a protectionist policy.'[19]

It was British manufacturers who feared free trade because Ireland's cheaper labour costs might undermine their own competitiveness.[20] Generally speaking, the framers of the sixth article of the Act of Union were giving the country what it wanted. In the late eighteenth century it was the British manufacturers who were initially reticent about free trade. It must be said that the Castlereagh was disposed to compromise the principle of free trade for the sake of the anxious Dublin manufacturers, confirming the desire of the Union framers to achieve consensus on the details of the Union with the opposition. The success of the opposition to the commerce article suggests what might have been achieved if opponents of the finance article had come forward and negotiated with Castlereagh on the details of it.

Colonel John Maxwell Barry, Foster's nephew, 'who manages the opposition to the commercial article' arranged for representatives of Irish manufacturing interests to give evidence before the House. Cornwallis thought this was a ploy to delay and British ministers accused Castlereagh of being short-sighted in not resisting Barry's motion and pushing the measure on. Castlereagh felt such behaviour was unstatesmanlike:

> upon a final settlement of the concerns and commerce of the kingdom, it is impossible upon any principle of common propriety and decency to prevent those persons from being heard at the bar, whose private situations and interests are really to be affected by the measure and that Government would lose all character for consistency and justice, were they to refuse admitting their cases to be heard.[21]

As well as giving a range of manufacturing interests the opportunity to plead their case for protection before the House of Commons, Castlereagh set up special negotiations with the cotton manufacturers in particular. Cotton manufacturing was next to linen in commercial activity, and employed between almost 40,000 persons. However the industry depended completely on import duties of between thirty-five to fifty per cent. It had already been agreed that some Irish industries

[19] Cooke to Beresford, 18 Dec. 1799, ibid., II, 235; Beresford to Cooke, 18 Dec. 1799, Londonderry, *Castlereagh*, III, 178; Auckland to Beresford, 3 Dec. 1799, Beresford, *Beresford*, II, 233; Cooke to Castlereagh, 15 Dec. 1799, Londonderry, *Castlereagh*, II, 43; M.D.C. Black, 'Theory and Policy in Anglo-Irish trade relations, 1750–1800', *Journal of the Statistical Society of Ireland*, 18, 312–26 (1949–50).

[20] D.R. Schweitzer, 'The failure of William Pitt's Irish trade propositions 1785', *Parliamentary History* 3 (1984), 129–145 [hereafter Schweitzer, 'Propositions'].

[21] Cornwallis to Rose, 28 Feb. 1800 and same to Portland, 9 Mar. 1800; Castlereagh to King, 7 Mar. 1800 Ross, *Cornwallis*, III, 201, 207, 205.

would enjoy ten per cent protective duties for a few years after the Union. Castlereagh was disposed to make an exception with cotton. Castlereagh offered five years of continued prohibitory duties and a gradual reduction to ten per cent within twenty years but anti-unionists who represented the cotton manufacturers rejected this.[22]

There was no agreement reached when the sixth article went before the committee of the Irish house of commons on 18 March. Beresford reported that 'no one spoke on the commercial part but the Speaker and he made a very bad hand of it' and Beresford believed that they 'had the whole business hollow in our favour.' But Castlereagh made a tactical error in proceeding to a personal attack on Foster. He 'abused him for connecting himself with men of different principles from himself and went a great way in describing the persons with whom he had assorted.' The debate then degenerated into a comedy as the Whigs (Grattan, Ponsonby and Plunket) produced documents revealing the 'bad company' which Castlereagh kept in his youth in the radical Whig clubs in County Down in the early 1790s. The debate produced much laughter but nothing for the cotton manufacturers. The opposition let all the articles pass, only dividing the committee on whether progress on the Bill should be permitted – a protest gesture.

Three days later the report of the committee was received and in the interim, some of the northern manufacturers had been in touch with the borough members in County Down, Sir James Blackwood and Robert Ward, to negotiate a compromise. The shrewd Ulster businessmen had realised that they were being used as pawns in a larger game played by the Whig, anti-unionist, politicians and that Castlereagh was sincere in reaching a compromise which really satisfied them. Accordingly they indicated their acceptance of gradual reduction of protection but asked that full protection last for seven instead of five years. Castlereagh, anxious to have their acquiescence, agreed to this. It would appear that the concessions won for the cotton industry was the result of an initiative from Ulster manufacturers and not from politicians opposed to the Union. Again, in this debate, the opposition did not divide the House on any clause. The leaders did not even attend.

The two articles received little serious criticism in principle from those who were impartial. Article seven was designed to benefit Ireland: to prevent an unjust and imprudent sharing of British expenses and taxation but to ensure that, when conditions were right, the two

[22] For the cotton manufacturers' case, see E. Clarke to Castlereagh, 21 Feb. 1800, A. Hamilton, to Castlereagh, 25 Feb. 1800, Duffy, Byrne and Hamill to Castlereagh 26 Feb. 1800, J. Wallace to Castlereagh, 3 Mar. 1800, Castlereagh Papers, D.3030/1238, 1237, 1240, 1245; for Castlereagh's opinions see Castlereagh to Pitt, 20 Feb. 1800, Chatham MS, 30/8/327, fo. 43, Castlereagh to Rose 7 Mar. 1800, Londonderry, *Castlereagh*, III 251.

countries might integrate financially. Article six met the desires of Irishmen, with the exception of some struggling manufacturers. Auckland judged that

> Mr Peel is very liberal and right minded and I have reason to believe that he will make a speech to say that Ireland is much too well treated but that he and others cordially acquiesce under a conviction that the general arrangement is wise and most beneficial to all. I did not discourage this sort of speech. It will do no harm with us and good with you.'[23]

Until financial amalgamation could take place, it was decided to retain the post of chancellor of the Irish exchequer to prepare an annual budget by proposing taxes and raising loans, oversee the Irish economy and currency and take responsibility for the revenue service.[24] The rest of this paper will focus on the conflict between the holders of this post and the viceroy.

Execution

George III's remark that the Union would 'close the reign of Irish jobs' was not an idle one.[25] The loss of an Irish parliament should have made reform possible as the vice-regal government and Irish politicians did not need the same extent of patronage. If the revenue service could be free from being exploited as a resource for political patronage, a more efficient collection of the revenue must mean more money reaching the exchequer. It also made the acceptance of higher levels of taxation easier. The Irish taxpayer would be unwilling to see his money wasted on sinecures. Oppositionists in parliament were always quick to demand retrenchment before authorising fresh taxation. Also, it was pointless to place hopes in additional revenue if the revenue departments were not capable of collecting it. So the issue of reform in the administration and how this should be best carried out became an important issue in post-Union politics.[26]

[23] Beresford to Auckland, 19 Mar. 1800, Sneyd MS, T.3229/2/60; Cornwallis to Portland, 22 Mar. 1800, Ross, *Cornwallis*, III, 215; Cooke to Auckland, 22 Mar. 1800, BL Add. MS, 34445, fo. 273; Auckland to Castlereagh, Apr. 1800, Castlereagh Papers, D.3030/1271; Jenkins, *Emancipation* 22.

[24] For a detailed study of the fiscal and monetary polices pursued by successive chancellors of the Irish exchequer, 18, 312–26 (1949–50). Schweitzer, 'Propositions', 129–145. Cornwallis of the Irish Exchequer see McCavery, 'Finance', 202–307, 308–390.

[25] M. MacDonagh, *The Viceroy's post-bag: correspondence hitherto unpublished of the Earl of Hardwicke, first Lord Lieutenant of Ireland after the Union* (1904), 3; Connolly, 'Aftermath' 1–3.

[26] For a detailed study of this subject see McCavery, 'Finance', 46–201; and R.B. McDowell 'Administration and the public services, 1800–1870' in Vaughan 'Union', 538–9 [hereafter McDowell 'Administration'].

The first lord lieutenant, the earl of Hardwicke, was instructed to make the collection of the revenues more economical and control expenditure. Hardwicke and his first chief secretary, William Abbot, began their administration in August 1801 by circulating a questionnaire enquiring about the details of public offices, their expenses and duties. Perhaps it was not surprising that this met with uproar. Even though Hardwicke appears to have been authorised by Pitt and Addington, Hardwicke assumed that he was opposed by 'cabals of men of importance and pro-Unionists' who sought to govern Ireland in their interest. In fact, other members of the British cabinet, who had served in and had links with Ireland (Lords Hobart, Pelham and Westmorland) were not enthusiastic about this inquisition. The officials completed the questionnaire but disclosed so little information that it was useless.[27] The Viceroy and his Chief Secretary only introduced some minor reforms.[28]

What was most needed was a thorough de-politicisation of the revenue service. Ascendancy magnates exploited the revenue board, which combined the customs and excise departments, for electioneering purposes and the revenue commissioners competed with each other for patronage and there was a high degree of absenteeism. The most radical moves in this direction during Abbott's chief secretaryship was to debar senior revenue officials from parliament and to disenfranchise all revenue officials.[29]

The impetus for reform was slowed when Wickham was appointed chief secretary in February 1802. Hardwicke and Wickham found it difficult to prevent Lords Donoughmore, Longueville and Annesley using their positions as revenue commissioners to enhance their local interests.[30] One reason for Wickham's ineffectiveness was personal problems: Lady Londonderry described him as 'a very commonplace character without any presentable grace'; and for the last six months of his period of office in Ireland he was confined to his room as an invalid. Another was the pressing problem of Emmet's insurrection in

[27] 'Heads of private instruction to be observed by the Earl of Hardwicke in the execution of his office of Lord Lieutenant of Ireland', n.d., BL Add. MS 35707 (Hardwicke MS), fo. 33; entry of 17 May 1801 in *The Diary and Correspondence of Charles Abbott, Lord Colchester*, ed. Charles, Lord Colchester (3 vols., 1861) I, 269; Yorke to Abbot, 12 Oct. 1801, PRO Colchester MS, 30/9/16; Hardwicke to Addington, 26 Aug. 1801, BL Add. MS, 35707, fo. 100.

[28] Beresford to Auckland, 11 Oct. 1801 BL Add. MS 34455 (Auckland MS), fo. 438; St Leger to Doneraile, 4 Nov. 1801, Colchester MS, 30/9/9/13; Fenwick to [Abbot] 9 Nov. 1801, ibid. Abbot to Meath, 22 Oct. 1801, ibid. /14; Abbot to Yorke, 21 Jan. 1802, ibid.,/16; [?] to Abbot, n.d., ibid.,/9/8, ibid.,/9/20.

[29] J. Debrett, *The Parliamentary Register*, (1801) House of Commons, 28 May, 10 June, 1801; *Journals of the House of Commons of the United Kingdom*, 4, 8, 28 May, 1, 10, June 1801.

[30] For this conflict see McCavery, 'Finance', 63–67.

Dublin in 1803, part of which was a dispute between the home secretary and the viceroy over the powers of the commander-in-chief.[31] Another was the fact that Isaac Corry, the chancellor of the Irish exchequer, was upstaging him.

Hardwicke was concerned that Corry was building up a power base at Westminster. Wickham justified his low profile by referring back to the fact that, because he had never sat in Parliament before, he had, 'made it an express condition with Mr Addington on my taking my seat that I should not be expected to take any share in debate this parliamentary session.'[32]

In contrast, Corry excelled himself in the larger stage in the British House of Commons. Corry had been useful in steering the Act of Union through the Irish House of Commons in 1799 and Pitt and Addington were keen for him to continue in office after the Union. He was valued for his debating skills. In 1802 he was able to see off the powerful anti-unionist and former speaker of the Irish House of Commons, John Foster; who, when 'he put himself within Corry's grip, has shrunk to nothing.'[33]

His pretensions to superiority over the Irish chief secretary seem confirmed when, in the 1802–1803 session, he demanded the secondment of the cream of the revenue service in Dublin to assist him with parliamentary business at Westminster. Corry's position would appear to be in tune with British thinking. Wickham had disappointed Lord Hardwicke: 'if he had taken a more active and forward part in the House of Commons, he would have kept things more in their proper course, and persons more in their proper places.'

The drift of the British ministers' thinking was in a contrary direction to Hardwicke's. Addington revealed this to Redesdale as early as October 1803 when he spoke of Wickham's duties:

> as the meeting of Parliament approaches, I am strongly inclined to think that more would be lost on your side of the water by his residence in England than would be gained on ours. From the evidence of a great part of the last session, I incline to believe that this would be my opinion even in time of peace and during apparent tranquillity.

This became cabinet policy on Nepean' s appointment as chief secretary

[31] Lady Londonderry to Maurice Fitzgerald, PRONI, Fitzgerald MS /8/24; Hardwicke to Wickham, 11 July 1803 Hardwicke to Yorke, 2 Jan. 1804, BL Add MS 35772, fo. 200, 35704, fo. 254; Wickham to Addington, passim., Wickham MS, Hampshire Record Office, photocopied in PRONI, T. 2627/5/D/63–65, 68, 72, 75–79, 82.

[32] Wickham to Hardwicke, 8 Apr. 1802, BL Add MS 35713, fo. 254.

[33] Abbot to Marsden, 27 June 1802, State Paper Office, Dublin, 521/136/5 (2); Addington to Mitford, 29 June 1802, PRONI T. 3030/3/8.

in January 1804. The statement of cabinet ran as follows;

> for this session at least, the chief secretary will hardly be in a situation to leave Ireland at all, and that it will be probably found necessary that he should remain more upon the spot hereafter than Abbot or Wickham had been accustomed to do during the sitting of Parliament. And while the secretary of state for the home department is a member of the House of Commons *and is assisted by an efficient chancellor of the Irish exchequer (who will of course take care of all details and points of trade, revenue and local interest)* and has besides the advantage of Lord Castlereagh's presence and authority, there does not seem to be much reason to expect that the attendance of the chief secretary of the Lord Lieutenant will be required otherwise than occasionally and for the purpose of holding confidential communication on points of great importance or circumstances not so well to be explained by correspondence.[emphasis mine].[34]

Corry may have been appreciated for his debating skills but, because he spent so much time in London and not enough in consultation in Dublin, it laid him open making mistakes. These brought censure on the Irish government and Irish business. His errors and carelessness increased. For example, he imposed a tax on the export of Irish linens and failed to inform his colleagues in the Irish government. His estimates fell short of expenditure in 1803 and the Dublin moneyed men refused to work with him in negotiating a loan. Corry had lost the confidence of Irish politicians and the business community but remained a favourite of English ministers and MPs. With a change of British ministers in May 1804, the opportunity was take to remove Corry from office.[35]

Pitt, the new prime minister brought John Foster into office. The most interesting feature of this appointment was that Foster was to combine the post of chancellor of the Irish exchequer with that of first lord of the Irish treasury. Marsden was in no doubts in June 1804 about what this combination would mean for future vice-regal government.

> The arrangements with Mr Foster will, I promise your Excellency, leave you nothing substantially, although it may nominally, of the patronage of the revenue. I know Mr Foster too well for this. If he undertakes the Treasury and the management of the revenue, your Excellency will have to ask him for a gauger's place very soon. And why? Because his appointment takes place when you have no one at

[34] Addington to Redesdale, 23 Oct. 1803, Redesdale MS, Gloucester Record Office, photocopies in PRONI, T. 3030/3/13; Yorke to Hardwicke, 14 Jan. 1804, BL Add. MS 35704, fo. 337.

[35] For details of Corry's errors see McCavery, 'Finance', 77–92.

the other side representing your Excellency's interests.[36]

The offer to Foster had come from Pitt himself, with prior knowledge of Addington's previous abortive negotiations with Foster, when the latter, it seems, may have held out for these terms. As early as 1793 Pitt had entertained bold and enlarged views on treasury powers to the risk of the lord lieutenant's powers of patronage. In an important conference on 21–22 January 1795 at Wimbledon, Pitt, Dundas and Cooke discussed ,as part of a 1795 reform package, the notion of 'responsibility'. Cooke protested that,

> the object of such a Bill was to take the patronage of the Lord Lieutenant as much as possible and to give the conduct of affairs to Irish parliamentary leaders. With this view of the subject, they did not see insuperable objections, as they were convinced that public opinion would sooner or later have a similar influence upon the administration of Ireland to that which it has in France.[37]

If Pitt was prepared to risk the curtailment of patronage powers of the Irish viceroy – the bridgehead of British government in Ireland – to the leaders of a colonial constitutionally independent assembly, would he not be prepared to take the same risk to an officeholder of his own creation and who worked with him at his own elbow?

Camden, with similar views, was used as a negotiator with Foster. In 1796 Camden had sought to increase the powers of the treasury over the revenue and had proposed that the lord lieutenancy should be abolished after the Union. Foster's biographer, Dr Malcolmson, suggests that Pitt may have regarded the lord lieutenancy, as 'under review'.[38] Vansittant made a very important comment, a year later, regarding the new role for Foster:

> I know that he had accepted office under stipulations of a very considerable extension of authority. The limits of it were never explained to me, nor had I ever any intimation *where* I could interfere without the risk of being disavowed, besides the imputation which would certainly have been insinuated of some secret design to weaken the influence of the government here by breaking with so powerful and popular a man as he is generally in England supposed to be.[39]

[36] Marsden to Hardwicke, 26 June 1804, BL Add. MS 35724, fo. 163.

[37] Memo of a conversation between Pitt, Dundas and Cooke, 21–22 Jan. 1793, National Library of Ireland[hereafter NLI], Melville MS, MS54A/74.

[38] Nepean to Hardwicke, 22 May 1804, BL Add. MS 35715, fo. 51; Sligo to Hardwicke, 29 May 1804, ibid., 35749, fo. 245; Hardwicke to Abbot, 1 Jan 1806, Ibid., 35764, fo. 161; A.P.W. Malcomson, *John Foster: the politics of the Anglo-Irish Ascendancy* (Oxford, 1978), 441–2 (hereafter, Malcomson, *Foster*).

[39] Vansittart to Redesdale, 22 June 1805, Redesdale MS, T.3030/10/16.

Our understanding of these crucial negotiations may be further enhanced if we can postulate some reasons for this particular compounding of the two offices. The most obvious reason is that the programme of reform, retrenchment and de-politicisation which was understood to be concomitant with the abolition of the Irish parliament – ending the 'reign of Irish jobs' – had lost momentum by May 1804. Hardwicke and his chief secretaries had failed in a variety of cases to decisively confront the powerful political interests in the country. The blame was being shifted from Irish politicians to the Irish government.

It is probable that the combining of the two finance posts was to invigorate the reform and retrenchment policy that had lapsed and confirm the good intentions of the British government in Ireland after the Union. With Foster and Pitt in particular there were fiscal considerations in such a policy. Dr Malcomson observes that, 'Foster was in many respects an Irish Pitt. Foster set up an enquiry board of 1804 based on a purely Pittite model and his whole emphasis on reducing the cost of collecting the revenue rather than increasing its in gross yield had been Pitt's formula for peace-time finance between 1785 and 1795.'[40] Foster was an ideal choice to fulfil this role for Pitt. The Englishmen who came over to Ireland, though bold in their denunciation of Irish jobbery, were not always the most artful. Abbot and Redesdale had involved the administration in embarrassment with some of its own friends in Ireland. But an indigenous politician might be a better tool for this unpleasant task of austerity and tax raising. The capture of the leading anti-unionist was ideal for the implementation of post-Union policy.

Foster's use of the treasury powers was deployed on several levels. For example, he implemented a real superintending power over the issue of money; he wrote 'approved' on treasury issue of money, instead of the usual counter-signature accompanying the lord lieutenant's. Also, was prepared to challenge the lord lieutenant's authority for expenditure. Foster exercised jurisdiction over the staff of the revenue board: he dismissed and transferred officers on his own authority.[41]

[40] Malcomson, *Foster*, 386.

[41] Beresford to Auckland, 20 Nov 1804, Beresford, *Beresford*, II, 304; Redesdale to Perceval, 5 Nov 1804, BL Add. MS, Perceval MS, 49188, fo. 179; Hardwicke to Nepean, 2 Dec 1804, BL Add MS, 35754, fo. 16; Marsden to Hardwicke, 8 Feb 1805, ibid., 35725, fo. 2; Hardwicke to Vansittart, 22 May 1805, ibid., 35739, fo. 122; Hardwicke to O'Grady, 19 Apr 1805, ibid., 35778, fo. 104; Marsden to Hardwicke, 17 June 1805, ibid., 35726, fo. 88; same to same, 26 June 1805, BL Add. MS, Bexley MS, 31230, fo. 71; same to same, 17 July 1805, BL Add. MS, 35726, fo. 1–5; Redesdale to Hardwicke, 18 July 1805, ibid., 35718, fo. 117; Hardwicke to Hawkesbury, 19 July 1805, ibid., 35706, fo. 259; Marsden to Hardwicke, 11 Feb 1805, ibid., 35726, fo. 8; Redesdale to Hardwicke, 11, 17 Feb, 2 Apr 1805, ibid., 35718, fos. 68, 71, 83; Hardwicke to Vansittart, 19 Apr 1805, ibid., 35758, fo.

However Foster over-reached his authority in his legislation of 1805. He pressed ahead with several Bills without proper consultation in Ireland. As well as insulting his colleagues, he left himself open to mistakes. When technical errors were discovered in several of his bills, they were detained in the Lords until Pitt's views were solicited. In June 1805, Pitt agreed that three of the bills should be allowed to be postponed and therefore lost for the session while three were so amended in the Lords as so as to be lost on their return to the Commons.[42]

On 29 June 1805 Foster sent a letter of resignation to Hardwicke grounded 'not on the rejection of the bills, or on the political differences with your excellency, but on Mr Pitt's inattention and want of civility.'[43] This reason – Pitt's betrayal of him, – is interesting and supports the arguments consistently pursued here: that Foster's conduct in 1805 was to some extent anticipated when the leadership of the treasury was conferred on him. Even the fact that Foster left Pitt an opening to acquire him – i.e. an apology – suggests that Foster believed that this was possible.

The consequences of the resignation vindicate Foster's belief that Pitt thought him worth having. The negotiation continued all summer

56; Redesdale to Vansittart, 24 May 1805, BL Add. MS, Bexley MS, 33229, fo. 237; Redesdale to Perceval, 5 Nov 1804, BL Add. MS, Perceval MS, 49188, fo. 179; Marsden to Hardwicke, 17 Nov. 1804, 16 Jan. 1805, BL Add. MS 35725 fo. 84, 161; Excise Commissioners to the Lord Lieutenant, 3 Dec. 1804, Wickham MS, T.2627/5/X/l; Beresford to Auckland, 20 Nov 1804, Beresford, *Beresford*, II, 304; Hardwicke to Hawkesbury, 17 Dec. 1804, Chatham, MS, 30/8/328/ fo. 129; Hardwicke to Yorke, 27 Nov 1804, BL MS, 35706, fo. 116; Excise commissioners to the Lord Lieutenant, 3 Dec 1804, Wickham MS, T.2627/5/X/1; Hardwicke to Nepean, 5, and reply, 6 Dec 1804, BL Add. MS, 35754, fo. 40, 35715, fo. 170; Redesdale to Hardwicke, 27 Dec 1804, ibid., 35718, fo. 51; Malcomson, *Foster*, 93; Marsden to Hardwicke, 25 Dec 1804, BL Add. MS, 35725, fo. 121; Excise commissioners to the Lord Lieutenant, 24 Dec 1804, Wickham MS, T. 2627/5/X/2; Hardwicke to Redesdale, and reply, 27 Dec. 1804, BL Add. MS35754, fos.255, 35718, fo. 51; Nepean to Hardwicke, 28 Dec. 1804, ibid., 35715, fo. 174; Hardwicke to Hawkesbury, 29 Dec. 1804, ibid., 35709, fo. 203; Donoughmore to Hardwicke, 29 Dec. 1804, ibid., 35754, fo. 273.

[42] Hardwicke to Hawkesbury and Pitt, 23 Mar. 1805, ibid., 35710, fos. 54, 58; Marsden to Vansittart, 19 Apr., 14, 15 May 1805, BL Add. MS, 31229, fos. 143, 213–9; Abbot to Hardwicke, 6 Jan. 1806, BL Add. MS35764, fo. 197; Hardwicke to Hawkesbury, 17 May 1805, ibid., 35710, fo. 198; Marsden to Hardwicke, 20 May 1805, ibid., 35726, fo. 53; Hardwicke to Vanisittart, 22 May 1805, ibid., 35710, fo. 104; Redesdale to Perceval, 23 May 1805, BL Add. MS, 49188,, fo. 200; Foster to Ely, 24 May 1805, BL Add. MS, 35759, fo. 140; Vansittart to Hardwicke, 18 June 1805, ibid., 35716, fo. 103; Marsden to Hardwicke, 20 June 1805, ibid., 35726, fo. 96; Vansittart to Hardwicke, 24 June 1805, ibid., 35760, fo. 112; Marsden to Vansittart, 1 July 1805, BL Add. MS, 3330, fo. 81; Report of the Crown lawyers, BL Add. MS, 35769, fo. 145; Hardwicke to Donoughmore, and reply, ibid., fo. 121.

[43] Foster to Pitt, 29 June 1805, PRO Chatham MS, 30/8/328, fo. 65; Vansittart to Hardwicke, 30 June 1805, BL Add. MS, 35716, fo. 113.

and Foster was persuaded to remain. The arrangements made in the autumn of 1805 show that the principles of revenue superintendence were to be outworked more thoughtfully. The salient features of the restatement were as follows. Firstly, as Tom Grenville curtly put it: 'Long is Irish secretary, Foster is to remain, and if Long cannot make peace between him and Lord Hardwicke, the lord lieutenant is to go to the wall.' Secondly, the two offices of chief secretary and chancellor of the exchequer were to be kept separate, 'an Irishman being chancellor of the exchequer.' Hardwicke suggested a merger, 'but it was not in Lord Hawkesbury's contemplations.' Thirdly, the chief secretary must have the blessing and enjoy the confidence of the British ministers. This is not explicitly stated, but the nature of Long's appointment suggests it, as it did to contemporaries. In Wickham's opinion, 'Long's appointment is unquestionably, in my opinion, the best that has been made since the Union. I should rather say in my memory. I have always thought that Ireland never could be well governed without a secretary, the personal and really confidential friend of the [prime] minister and known to be such.' Hardwicke agreed that

> he will contribute materially to render the true state of Irish affairs better understood by his friends here and that the confidence which he enjoys here from his legitimate friendship with the Minister will enable him to frame and carry into execution the means for adjusting the discordant powers which have been so inconveniently permitted to subsist.

A year before, Long had stated that he had no ambition for the Irish post: only to serve Pitt. Pitt therefore must have insisted on it.[44]

Lastly, the powers of the treasury were dealt with. There was some attempt to make the institution more than simply an expression of the vagaries of Foster's exuberant personality. First, Foster was no longer to be its first lord, Secondly 'the chief secretary's signature is required to every act of importance, as one of the three whose signature is necessary.' Thirdly, 'the business is to be transacted through the commissioners of inferior boards, as in England.' Fourthly, 'give the board of treasury such powers over the revenue as will make them responsible for it' and on this point Long asked for Foster's ideas on paper, saying, 'I have offered in the meantime to adopt any salutary measures he may propose for better collecting the revenue.'

[44] T. Grenville to Lord Grenville, 20 September 1805, *Historical Manuscripts Commission*, Dropmore MS, 7, 304; Long to Redesdale 25 Sept. 1805, Redesdale MS, T.3030/8/13; Long to Pitt, 20 Oct. 1805, PRO Chatham MS, 30/8/238, fo. 259; Hardwicke to Yorke, 4 Oct. 1805, BL Add. MS 35706, fo. 296; Wickham to Redesdale, 13 Oct. 1805 Redesdale MS, T.3030/4/7; Hardwicke to Abbot, 1 Jan. 1806, BL Add. MS, 35764, fo. 161; Long to Redesdale, 27 Sept. 1804, Redesdale MS, T. 3030/8/6.

Hardwicke did not exactly go to the wall but neither was he totally vindicated. Pitt had been given the opportunity to disown Foster when he resigned and uphold the Crown's representative in Dublin. Yet Foster was retained despite the fact that 'the lord lieutenant, the [lord] chancellor, the attorney and solicitor general and Marsden, etc., are so violent against Foster that it will be difficult to induce any of them to concur in any responsible manner respecting him.' This was an indication of the British government's intention to carry out a policy of retrenchment and economy. Long's report to Redesdale of a conversation with Foster where Long attempted to justify Foster's retention, summarises the issue:

> he says that he was responsible for the revenue, and that he must have a sufficient degree of influence to manage that for which he was responsible. His principles in fact are not objectionable in themselves, but in the application of them, I fear I should not be able so perfectly to concur. He affects, however, great cordiality and a wish to co-operate in the measures of government.[45]

Similar arrangements were made in 1806 in the 'Ministry of all the Talents'. The new government reverted to the *status quo* of 1805: a chief secretary from England, William Elliot, expected to carry out reform, assisted by a native politician in charge of finance. Newport was appointed chancellor of the Irish exchequer because he would be 'completely subservient to Lord Grenville.' To complete the picture, Grenville made himself first lord of both treasuries and the chancellor of the Irish exchequer was an *ex-officio* second lord in Ireland. Grenville expected the superintendence of Ireland's finance to be conducted in a compact, well-informed, triangular relationship, consisting of Newport, Elliot and himself.[46]

In 1807 Foster returned as chancellor of the Irish exchequer but Pitt was gone and the British ministers he worked with were not prepared to allow him as much scope as Pitt had. Two of the chief secretaries in the period 1807–1812, Arthur Wellesley and William Wellesley-Pole were strong characters with a network of support at Westminster.

On the other hand, in the period 1807–11, there was undoubtedly substantial progress in the direction of conducting Irish finances in a manner pleasing to Foster. There was a trend of appointments to the treasury towards 'men of business', so that they could be more involved in revenue superintendence. There were several laudable appointments

[45] Long to Pitt, 1, 29 Oct. 1805, PRO Chatham MS, 30/8/28, fo. 259, 261; Long to Redesdale, 25 Sept 1805, Redesdale MS, T.3030/8/13.

[46] For the Irish policies of the 'Ministry of all the Talents' see McCavery, 'Finance', 129–145.

and promotions at the highest levels of the revenue service. Most of the detailed recommendations of a commission of enquiry, which Foster had set up in 1804, were implemented, with its commission renewed until 1812. In 1810 William Wellesley-Pole considered making the Irish revenue boards completely subservient to the Irish treasury. Foster and Pole were in agreement about the future direction of Irish government.[47]

Yet Foster was still dissatisfied. Although Richmond and successive home secretaries agreed to resist the temptation of using legal and ecclesiastical patronage for political purposes, there was no such consensus about revenue places. The Irish administration were unashamedly disposed to 'attend to all the applications of members of parliament and the resident gentry of the country.'[48]

However using the revenue service as a fund from which to reward the servants of Government was a fundamental disadvantage in any attempt to improve the efficiency the collection and management of the revenue. Despite all that had been done, Foster still complained 'of a want of vigour and energy in the government' as far as financial administration was concerned. One chief secretary, Dundas, commented to his incoming successor, Pole: 'I do not think Ireland is quite ripe for the same strictness and perhaps vigour with which the revenue is collected in England. Mr Foster, in this respect, is proceeding too violently and rapidly.'[49]

It was this lack of adequate support from colleagues that caused Foster's resignation on 12 February 1811, when he received warrants from the viceroy for his counter-signature authorising the appointment of twenty-one additional custom officers. Ten were in Belfast, where trade was actually falling and nine were clerks in the Dublin Stores but Foster had pledged himself publicly to save £13,000 by freezing all appointments in there. 'All without any previous communication or opportunity of advice,' he said, 'which made it impossible for me any longer to bear the appearance of responsibility.'[50]

The current chief secretary, William Wellesly-Pole requested that he combine Foster's position with his own:

> the present state of our financial system and from the jarring of interests that have been created by Foster between the Treasury and

[47] Ibid., 146–66.

[48] Wellesley to Richmond, 4, 8, 27 Feb. 1808, *The Supplementary Despatches, Letters and Memoranda of Arthur Wellesley, First Duke of Wellington*, ed. Duke of Wellington (5 vols., 1860) 5, 320, 327–9 (hereafter Wellington, *Despatches*) and NLI, Richmond, MS, 108; Wellesley to Westmorland, 12 Nov. 1807, Wellington, *Despatches*, 5, 179.

[49] Long to Wellesley, 26 Oct. 1807, Apsley House MS, PRONI photocopy, T. 2627/3/2/208; Dundas to Pole, 22 Oct. 1809, NLI, Melville MS, 55A/34C.

[50] Foster to Pole, and reply, 1, 13 Feb. 1811, PRONI, Foster Papers, D.207/38/42/44; Foster to Crofton, 18 Feb. 1811; Perceval to Foster, Feb. 1811, ibid. D.207/69/3.

> the Castle, that there is no hope of doing any good or of restoring the authority of government but by having the chief secretary and chancellor of the exchequer held by the same person.[51]

The combination of offices was not actually a snub to Foster but a vindication, for it was a recognition that political authority must be reconciled with financial responsibility. Richmond pointed out that Foster could never have been trusted with such a merger: 'he may have formerly been a good chancellor of the exchequer but he never could have held the two situations. With one he always wished to be lord lieutenant and with the two he would have succeeded.'[52]

Pole was to hold the two offices temporarily until some plan could be formulated which could give the Irish treasury proper superintendence over the revenue board. But nothing came of these plans as Pole was promoted to the British cabinet in March 1812.

In August 1812 William Vesey Fitzgerald became the chancellor of the Irish exchequer. J.M. Barry, a supporter of John Foster, gave Fitzgerald some advice.

> Depend on it, if the Castle does not give up the patronage of promotion in the revenue to the respective boards, and that each board is not rendered responsible for the due collection of its respective branch of the revenue, you will have as bad a tale to unfold as either Pole or Foster. However, I should speculate on a consolidation next session, after which, of course, the Irish government will know nothing of what is going on in revenue matters, and all the springs will be moved by the imperial chancellor of the exchequer.[53]

This advice proved partially correct. Within five months Fitzgerald sought to resign. He complained of having insufficient control over the revenue departments, that the Castle interfered too much with them and that some share of the patronage should be given to the Irish treasury. The chief secretary after 1812, Robert Peel, admitted that this might indeed be of some benefit to the revenue but the 'the power of the Lord Lieutenant must be paramount over everything in Ireland.' Peel was not prepared to make efficient revenue administration a priority over the political initiative which revenue patronage gave to the lordl lieutenant. In a revealing passage he said:

[51] Pole to Richmond, 15 June 1811, NLI, Richmond MS 1730.

[52] Richmond to Pole, 19 June 1811, Kent Archives Office, Whitworth MS, U. 269/O.214/5.

[53] Barry to Fitzgerald, 30 August 1812, NLI, Fitzgerald MS, 7821, 64.

> I shall be glad when the time comes when the government of this country can be conducted on different principles from what it at present is; when you can look for support (and I do not mean merely parliamentary support but that effectual support which active and loyal men can afford in this country) in an honest conviction of its necessity and a full sense of duty; but that time has not yet arrived and till it does, you must either try to carry on the government without such support or you must (and I fear there is no misapplication of the term) *purchase* it.[54]

The new lord lieutenant, Lord Whitworth, who arrived in Dublin in August 1813, agreed with Peel, as did Lord Liverpool, who offered the two offices to Peel. Peel declined, claiming there was too much work for one person and when financial amalgamation would take place it would require the undivided attention of one person.

Liverpool and Whitworth wanted to let Fitzgerald go but Peel and Castlereagh believed he should stay. Fitzgerald was persuaded to remain because in the autumn of 1813 it was decided to prepare for financial amalgamation and Fitzgerald wanted the honour of proposing and accomplishing the measure.[55]

The Act of Union stipulated that financial amalgamation was to occur when either

1 Irish resources could bear British levels of taxation or
2 if the separate debts of each country were paid off or
3 the debts of each country were in the same proportion to each other as Ireland's contribution to British expenditure, i.e. two-seventeenths, or $7\frac{1}{2}$:1.

Two of these conditions were already met. As early as 1810 the debts of each country stood in the same proportion to one another ($7\frac{1}{2}$:1) as Ireland's contribution to UK expenses. It was through a four-fold increase of Irish debt, due to having to meet two-fifteenths of a large United Kingdom establishment, swollen by fifteen years of expensive war. The British debt did not increase so fast as the Irish because Great Britain discovered an unexpected capacity for sustaining extraordinary high levels of taxation. This was not the case for Ireland. Because Irish chancellors borrowed in London they were able borrow a lot more than they could have if they had borrowed only in Dublin. It meant

[54] Peel to Liverpool, 20 Oct. 1813, BL Add. MS, Liverpool MS, 38195, fo. 14.
[55] For Fitzgerald's record as Chancellor of the Irish Exchequer see McCavery, 'Finance' 168–90.

that debt interest payments spiralled. In 1800 Irish debt charges were only £1.6m; in 1816 they were £6.8m and exceeded the country's revenues.[56]

The second criteria – of Irish resources being able to sustain British rates of taxation – was reached by 1814. During the period of separate exchequers, between 1801–17, revenue from Irish taxation had more than doubled. In 1804 Foster imposed 50% increases in tobacco duties, 50% in foreign wine, 40–70% on tea. Such increases left little scope for his successors. But the yield was disappointing. Irish revenue was expected to increase from £3m to £4.25m but the increase only went to less than £4m. After this failure, Foster resorted to devices in the brewing and distilling industries and to retrenchment in the years 1807–1809. By 1810 it was clear that Ireland must seek financial amalgamation. The quota would then be repealed, the debts would be combined and the revenue supervised from London. It would also mean that Irish taxation would be brought into line with British rates. Foster's budgets in 1810 and 1811 were a move in this direction. The taxes on a wide range of goods and services were equalised. Fitzgerald continued this and by 1814 all customs duties were equalised.[57]

Yet amalgamation did not take place until after 1816. Two select committees on Irish finance preceded it and they worked very slowly. The government's preoccupation with foreign affairs was the main reason for the delay: Castlereagh was particularly absorbed and it was universally recognised that his views were considered essential.

It was not until 1817 that the British treasury assumed responsibility for superintending the Irish as well as the British revenue boards. It was agreed that two of the lords of the Irish treasury would sit at the British treasury board to advise; a revived office of vice-treasurer would be responsible to parliament for receipts and issues in Dublin. The conflict between the chancellors of the Irish exchequer and the viceroy was sorted out in a way pleasing to the latter. The lord lieutenant was to exercise the discretionary powers in the remission of fines and penalties. Peel claimed that to lose this power would have been 'a death blow to the vice-regal power in Ireland.'[58] Most crucial of all, the lord lieutenant retained the patronage of appointments in the revenue service. Whitworth maintained that if he lost this patronage 'they had as well better do away with the office of lord lieutenant at once.' Financial amalgamation freed Ireland from having to meet the

[56] For details of Irish borrowing see McCavery, 'Finance', 202–19.

[57] S.J. Connolly, 'Union government, 1812–23' in Vaughan, Union', 63; for a detailed study of the fiscal polices pursued by successive Chancellors of the Irish Exchequer see McCavery, 'Finance', 202–307.

[58] Whitworth to Peel, and reply, June 1816, Peel MS, BL Add. MS, 40192, fo. 154, 40291, fo. 343.

fixed proportion of United Kingdom expenses determined at the Union. But that other struggle – to uphold vice-regal power over the management of the revenue boards – was resolved in the viceroy's favour.[59]

[59] Further financial amalgamation followed: the Customs and Excise Boards (1823), Stamp Office (1827) and the Irish Post Office (1831), McDowell, 'Administration', 541–2.

IRELAND, INDIA AND THE EMPIRE: 1780–1914

By C.A. Bayly

READ 11 SEPTEMBER AT THE QUEEN'S UNIVERSITY OF BELFAST

ROY Foster remarks in *Paddy and Mr Punch* that a nodding acquaintance with Irish history, which one of his English commentators claimed to have, is 'the most dangerous type of acquaintance.' My own growing alarm at attempting to reinvent the wheel for the purpose of this conference has been allayed only slightly by reading a remark of John Stuart Mill: 'Those Englishmen who know something about India, are even now those who understand Ireland best.'[1]

I hope at least that the dangerous exercise on which I am about to embark is justified by a useful academic agenda. For in the last ten years, 'connective' and 'comparative' histories have become fashionable and some historians now talk of the need for global social history to replace traditional types of history. A number of developments, ranging from the influence of post-modernist literary criticism to the decline of high marxist historiography have contributed to this change of mood. But the main impulse behind it has been the intellectual crisis of national history in the West and of area studies in the extra-European world. Outside the United States and perhaps Australia, introverted national history has everywhere taken a hammering. British identity, for instance, has been portrayed as a recent and friable construct by self-serving elites in the context of world crisis. Revisionism has unsettled the old Irish national history of 'Faith and Fatherland'. Similar fractures spread across other European national historiographies.

Meanwhile, histories of the extra-European world have been rewritten to show how westernised elites appropriated the language of European nationalism to marginalise and suppress the inter-connected, plural identities of the Asian and African past.[2] Colonial nationalists are now less often depicted as the embodiments of historical rectitude. The nation itself has become a questionable historiographical artefact.

My lecture today endorses this change of mood to some degree. We can learn much from connective and comparative histories, even from

[1] John Stuart Mill, *England and Ireland* (London, 1868), p. 22, cited in S.B. Cook, *Imperial Affinities. Nineteenth century analogies and exchanges between India and Ireland* (Delhi, 1993), p. 53.

[2] Partha Chatterjee, *Nationalist Thought and the Colonial World. A derivative discourse?* (Princeton, 1986); *The Nation and its Fragments* (Delhi, 1994); Ashis Nandy, *The Intimate Enemy* (Delhi, 1993); idem, *The Illegitimacy of Nationalism* (Delhi, 1994).

the interconnections of histories so distant in space and cultural form as those of Ireland and India. At the same time, I want to suggest that some parts of the older agenda of empire, nation and class are still valid. Ireland and India bear comparison not only because they were 'othered' in similar patterns of imperial discourse or because they were zones of hybridity for shifting identities. Their trajectories can also be compared because the lineaments of new national leaderships did, in fact, begin to consolidate in the context of interrelated developments in the British imperial system. At the ideological level, again, the nationalist spokesmen of Ireland and India slowly became aware of each other as what were thought of as peoples. They were animated by each others' demands for economic justice. The growing calls for national self-determination were cumulative and mutually reinforcing even if they were not teleologically driven by those unfolding national essences which our predecessors are now so often berated for invoking.

Ironically, recent studies which have unsettled the distinction between East and West have made clearer some of the structural similarities between Ireland and India during the period when they were both submitted to the rigours of British industrialisation, free trade dogma and the intrusion of the modern state. Prasannan Parthasarathi, for instance, has argued that Indian weavers in the late eighteenth century had a higher standard of living than British and, by extension, Irish ones.[3] A similar argument was made by Mirza Abu Taleb Khan, one of the first Indian visitors to Ireland who observed in 1800 'The poverty of peasants or common people in [Ireland] is such that the peasants of India are rich when compared to them.'[4] Abu Taleb believed that Indian peasants benefited from much cheaper food and did not need to spend their resources on heating and clothing. Whether this can be substantiated or not, the distinction between European proto-industrialisation and Indian family artisanship is now more difficult to sustain. India and Ireland can both be seen as old agro-industrial provinces of Eurasia and ones which were quite rapidly, if only partially deindustrialised at the beginning of the nineteenth century.[5] Their

[3] Prasannan Parthasarathi, 'Rethinking wages and competitiveness in the eighteenth century: Britain and South India,' *Past and Present*, 158, 1998, 79–109.

[4] Charles Stewart (ed.), *The Travels of Mirza Abu Taleb Khan in Asia, Africa and Europe in the years 1799–1803* (London, 1814; reprint Delhi, 1972), p. 47. As J.R.I. Cole has pointed out this work cannot be regarded as a 'pure' indigenous creation. It represented instead a form of 'occidentalism', a turning on its head of the contemporary 'orientalist' position, Cole, 'Invisible occidentalism', *International Journal of Iranian Studies* 3, 1992, 3–16. For another early Indian visitor to Ireland, see Michael H. Fisher, *The First Indian Author in English. Dean Mahomed (1759–1851) in India, Ireland and England* (Delhi, 1996).

[5] See, e.g., Cormac O'Grada, 'Poverty, population and agriculture, 1801–45' in W.E. Vaughan (ed.), *A New History of Ireland*, v, i, *Ireland under the Union, 1801–70* (Oxford, 1989), pp. 109–38; cf. O. Macdonagh, 'Economy and Society, 1830–45', ibid. pp. 229–34.

decline was exacerbated by the collapse of British and European demand for their products and the rigorous imposition of free trade: from 1801 in the Irish case and from 1834, in the Indian case. The nationalist slogans of *swadeshi* in India or 'home production' in Ireland were not tokens of a reinvented mythical past, but a response to very recent economic malformations.

The land problem which provided the second vector of nationalist thought in both dependencies, also arose from comparable conditions and elicited similar responses. S.B. Cook has recently made this point in a book on the mutual influence of late nineteenth-century Indian and Irish land legislation. Published in New Delhi, his work deserves to be better known to British and Irish historians. I am happy to be able to acknowledge it as a precursor of what I have to say today in its emphasis on *Imperial Affinities*.[6] Cook concentrates on legislation and on the period after 1860. My aim in the lecture is, first, to consider earlier imperial affinities and convergences between Ireland and India for the years between 1780 and 1860. Secondly, I will try to show how, in both dependencies, varied and inchoate forms of patriotic resistance were transformed into radical nationalisms before the onset of the long metamorphosis of British imperialism which stretched from Gladstone's Occupation of Egypt in 1882 to the First World War.

Agrarian inequality in this earlier period provides us with a fruitful line of comparison. In Bengal during the first half of the eighteenth century tenant farmers retained considerable bargaining power in their dealings with the rural magnates and revenue contractors who lorded it over them. The last Mughal viceroys of Bengal had attempted to contain the power of landed magnates and usurious grain merchants and give greater stability to the cultivating peasant.[7] In Bengal it was Lord Cornwallis's Permanent Settlement of land revenue in 1793 which began to entrench the power of zamindars or landlords against both the state and the peasantry in the interests of stable revenue for an imperial state at war.[8]

Similarly, the great Irish landowners consolidated their power in the course of the mid-eighteenth century. They benefited from access to the thriving British markets, and less surely colonial ones. They had some success in squeezing out middlemen and tenants and in imposing closer financial management on their estates.[9] The Revolutionary and

[6] S.B. Cook, *Imperial Affinities: nineteenth century analogies and exchanges between India and Ireland* (Delhi, 1993).

[7] 'Riyaz-az Salatin' trans. Charles Stewart, *A History of Bengal* (London, 1813), pp. 407, 370–3; J.R. McLane, *Land and Local Kingship in eighteenth-century Bengal* (Cambridge, 1993).

[8] Ibid.; Ranajit Guha, *A Rule of Property for Bengal. An essay on the idea of permanent settlement* (Paris, 1963).

[9] O'Grada in Vaughan (ed.) *New History*, pp. 109, 128.

Napoleonic war years were the heyday of the great estates In Ireland. Other classes suffered from high wartime taxation and high food prices, unable, if they were Catholics, to enter the ranks of the landed clique. To these pressures were added in both dependencies during the late eighteenth and early nineteenth century a rapid growth of population.[10] From its early decades radical publicists and bureaucratic critics were comparing the 'congested' agricultural districts of Ireland with those of eastern India. By 1827 G.H. Harrington, a Bengal revenue administrator, denounced Cornwallis's permanent settlement because it had produced in India not the intended improving English-style landlords but absentee Irish-style rack-renters.[11]

By then, however, it was too late in the day. North India and Ireland were visited by disastrous famines in the 1830s and '40s. How far the rigid policies of free trade adopted by some British administrators contributed to these disasters remains a matter of debate.[12] But they clearly arose from failures of social entitlement in Amartya Sen's sense of this term, rather than from absolute scarcities of food.[13] Localised deindustrialisation, lack of money and declining consumption by former elites exacerbated agrarian problems in the longer term in Ireland and India. Both dependencies went on into the mid-Victorian era as exporters of young labourers to overseas plantations or building sites and as exporters of young men in uniform to far parts of the empire.[14] Both remained relatively impoverished consumers of British goods, despite attempts after 1850 to start up national industrial enterprises and cooperative credit associations.

To rule these dependencies, in the late eighteenth century the British government had already developed administrative measures which also bore a family resemblance to each other. Resistance to the consequent centralisation of power provides the third point of congruence between Irish and Indian patriotisms, alongside resistance to the straightjacket of free trade and periodic agrarian distress. Here again Lord Cornwallis was a pivotal figure. Judging that the corruption of European officials in India was imperilling the East India Company's finances and security,

[10] Ibid., p. 118; Sugata Bose, *Peasant Labour and Colonial Capital: Rural Bengal since 1770* (Cambridge, 1993).

[11] Cf. *The Zemindary Settlement of Bengal*, I (Calcutta, 1879) ix.; R.D. Collison Black, *Economic Thought and the Irish Question 1817–70* (Cambridge, 1960), pp. 55–58.

[12] Sanjay Sharma, 'Famine, state and society in north India c.1800–1840' unpublished PhD dissertation, SOAS, London University, 1996; C.A. Bayly, *Rulers, Townsmen and Bazaars. North India in the age of British expansion, 1780–1870* (Cambridge, 1983), pp. 380–4; Peter Gray, *The Irish Famine* (London, 1995).

[13] Amartya Sen, *Poverty and Famines. An essay on entitlement and deprivation* (Oxford, 1981).

[14] See, e.g. Hugh Tinker, *A New System of Slavery* (London, 1993); for emigration from Ireland generally see, David Fitzpatrick, 'Emigration 1800–1870' in Vaughan (ed.), *New History*, I, pp. 569–78.

he sought its root cause in 'native depravity.'[15] Cornwallis therefore followed through a policy which excluded Indians and people of mixed race from major government and military offices. Not until the cost-cutting days of the Whig reformist government of Bentinck in the 1830s were Indians brought back in numbers, but here only as subordinate judges and collectors of revenue.

Irish catholics of course, had long been excluded from office, commissions in the British army and even the purchase or mortgage of Protestant land in Ireland. But the effect of the Union was evidently to make government yet more Anglocentric. Cornwallis had a conventional, but very deliberate mind. He had supported the Americans before the war, but their throwing off allegiance to the Crown had endangered property and let loose murderous banditti.[16] Therefore, government should become more viceregal and the executive strengthened. The problem in India, he believed, was the dangerous conjunction of Company servants run wild and corrupt natives.[17] Commerce had to be severed from government and the Company's rights enforced. Finally, the problem in Ireland, he thought, was selfish interests, both Protestant and Catholic, which had defied wider imperial interests invested in the British Parliament.[18] Irish government would also have to be brought closer to the executive and made more British through an Act of Union.[19]

Ireland in the late eighteenth century retained some features in common with the classic Indian princely state. Ultimate power remained with the British, but the trappings of native government and native legitimacy remained in place. Now after 1799, this too was lost. So the Irish legislature was removed to London and its conflicts with the executive were terminated. The Ascendancy landed interest was bought off with jobs and patronage in London, Canada, the Cape Colony and India. In both dependencies this new ethnic and religious division of political labour became, then, the third great cause of nationalist resentment.

Even some of the intellectual practices which sustained British rule, but ultimately nurtured local patriotisms, appear to be rather similar in the two locations. In the eighteenth-century learned life was full of

[15] E.g., Cornwallis to Dundas, 14 Aug. 1787 about Benares 'The Raja is a fool, his servants rogues, every native of Hindustan (I really believe) corrupt', C. Ross (ed.), *The Correspondence of Charles, First Marquis Cornwallis* (London, 1859), I, 206.

[16] Cornwallis to Brig.-Genl. Pattison, 10 June 1780, ibid., I, 46; cf. F. and M. Wickwire, *Cornwallis and the War of Independence* (London, 1971).

[17] E.g., Cornwallis to Dundas, 15 Nov. 1786, Ross (ed.), *Correspondence*, I, 227.

[18] E.g., Cornwallis to Portland, 2 Jan. 1799, 21 Jan. 1800, ibid., III, 28–29, 67.

[19] R.B. McDowell, *Ireland in the Age of Imperialism and Revolution 1760–1801* (Oxford, 1979), pp. 678–9, 699–201.

the celebration of ancient Irish and ancient Indian culture. The Irish Royal Academy and the Asiatic Society of Bengal were founded within a few years of each other.[20] Irish, Latin, Greek and Indian languages were found to be among the first and most senior of the Aryan languages. Col Charles Vallancey, Sir William Jones and Francis Wilford traced similarities of religions and social institutions in all three venues.[21] It must be said, though, that Jones, good Celt that he was, was displeased with the possibility that his sobriquet 'Persian Jones' might be replaced with 'Irish Jones.'

Nonetheless, from here it was a relatively small step to argue that these ancient civilisations had become degenerate as a result of priesthood and savage government. The only difference was that in Ireland the Catholic priesthood had replaced the Brahmins, their equals in superstition, in the first years of the Christian era. In both cases, the invigorating rule of Aryan brothers from across the sea was required to put matters right. Ironically, these atavistic fantasies helped root patriotic identities more than they naturalised British power. Bengal orientalism was the matrix of Young India.[22] Anglo-Irish literati provided the historical and literary grammar of Young Ireland.[23]

Many of these arguments, which put India and Ireland into the same historiographical frame, were common currency in the old literature of empire and nation state or economic dependency. What has happened more recently, though, is that the critique of orientalist knowledge has made a considerations of these comparisons and connections easier by undermining the stark distinction between East and West. It has also re-established the history of Eurasia as in overlapping terrain of communities, powers and lines of commerce. There was a global economy and a global society of knowledge in the eighteenth century which stands as precursor to the much vaunted globalism of the late twentieth century. By contrast, national histories and area studies were a product of the nineteenth and early twentieth century when the rise of the national state and European empire submerged these connections.

These ambiguities of identities and long-range connections appear particularly striking if we examine again the history of Ireland and India during the first long period of crisis in the British empire which

[20] See O.P. Kejariwal, *Asiatic Society of Bengal* (Delhi, 1988); R.F. Foster, *Paddy and Mr Punch* (London, 1993), pp. 2–5.

[21] Charles Vallancey, *A Vindication of the Ancient History of Ireland* (Dublin, 1786); Francis Wilford, 'On the ancient geography of India', *Journal of the Asiatic Society of Bengal*, xx, 1851; cf. C.A. Bayly, 'Orientalists and Informants in Benares, 1780–1860' ms. in author's possession.

[22] David Kopf, *British Orientalism and the Bengal Renaissance* (Princeton, 1969).

[23] Jeanne Sheehy, *The Rediscovery of Ireland's Past. The Celtic Revival 1830–1930* (London, 1980).

stretched from Cornwallis's defeat at Yorktown in 1782 to the victory over Napoleon in 1815. The interlinking of the issues of Ireland, America and India was already only too evident in the dying days of Lord North's administration. The Irish Parliament and the volunteers were demanding Irish national liberties in language similar to that of American patriots.[24] In the 1780s and '90s, Eurasians and British Indians likewise attacked the corruption of the Company in the language of the liberty of freeborn Englishmen, used by Wyvill, Wilkes and other domestic supporters of the Irish and Americans.[25] Indian states, meanwhile, were trying to concert what one Muslim diplomat called an alliance of 'all turban wearers against all hat wearers', or Europeans.[26] Histories of 'Modern Times' were being written by Indo-Muslim historians who denounced the drain of silver from India, the British monopoly of government posts and the destruction of the artisan weaving industry of Bengal.[27] One Indian chronicler and critic of Warren Hastings, governor of Bengal, seems to have been aware of the American War;[28] others appear to have been influenced by the general sense of global crisis. Later, of course, Edmund Burke drew on American and Irish exemplars in his denunciation of the East India Company's government. Even in the 1780s, then, the languages of old patriotism in the British dependencies distantly echoed each other, though few were yet aware of this.

The interdependent nature of the crisis of empire was yet more pronounced during the first phase of the French Revolutionary wars. But this still did not mean that old Irish patriots of the 1798 perceived much of a similarity between their case and that of the Indians. The most illuminating example is that of Theobald Wolfe Tone and the rising of 1798. As his autobiography reveals, the 'Hannibal of the English' had India and Empire on his mind quite often. Tone's maternal grandfather had been a Captain in the West India trade.[29] His brother William worked for the East India Company and then for the Maratha rulers of Western India. William Tone's account of the 'Institutions of the Maratha People'[30] is an early example of orientalist anthropology.

[24] McDowell, *Ireland*, 293–326.

[25] P.J. Marshall, 'The whites of British India: a failed colonial society?' *The International History Review*, 12, 1990, 26–44.

[26] Tafazzul Hussain Khan, cited, 'notes on interviews with Sindhia', David Anderson Papers, Add. Mss. 45419, f. 39, British Library.

[27] Kumkum Chatterjee, 'History as self-representation: the recasting of political tradition in late eighteenth-century eastern India', *Modern Asian Studies*, 32, 4, 1998, 913–48.

[28] 'Muntakhul-t Tawarikh', H.M. Elliot Papers, Add. Mss. 30786, ff. 106–48, British Library.

[29] *The Autobiography of Theobald Wolfe Tone (1763–98)* edited with and introduction by R. Barry O'Brien (London, 1893), I, 2.

[30] Ibid., I, 3; cf. W.H. Tone, *Some institutions of the Maratha people* (London, 1799).

Its intellectual roots lay in the Scottish enlightenment which was a dominant influence in Protestant Dublin in the 1760s and 1770s.

Wolfe Tone's hostility to Ireland's link to England did not, however, extend to England's empire, which was already providing a great resource for Irish commerce and Irish military entrepreneurs. To be sure, Tone denounced the manner in which England's declaration of war against Spain during the American revolutionary conflict was extended by executive action to Ireland. But this did not prevent him urging on William Pitt a plan for seizing Spain's American colony's and establishing a colony of settlement in the Pacific. This he declared would be a 'good system for England.'[31] Perhaps mindful of the long dominance of the Irish Sulivan connection in the Court of Directors and its extensive patronage in India, Tone and his brother presented themselves a little later as volunteers in the East India Company's service. The boats had already sailed and India was closed to them. Wolfe Tone wrote:

> Thus we were stopped and I believe we were the single instance since the world begun of two men, absolutely bent on ruining themselves, who could not find the means ... we could not help laughing at the circumstance that India, the great gulf of all undone beings, should be shut against us alone.[32]

India and the empire continued to haunt Tone and the Irish rebellion.[33] It took vital months in 1796 for Tone and his co-conspirator, Lord Edward Fitzgerald, to persuade Truguet, the French Minister of Marine, to divert ships to the Irish rebellion which Truguet wished to use against the British in India.[34] When Napoleon invaded Egypt, as a prelude to an India expedition, Tone was momentarily diverted from contemplating a union of Catholic, Anglican and Dissenter in Ireland, to the wider, millenial vision of returning the Jews to Palestine.[35] It was, ultimately, Lord Cornwallis, still festering with Indian disease, who confirmed the sentence of hanging on Wolfe Tone.[36]

This quadrilateral of Britain, India, Ireland, and then Egypt, re-established itself once again after the defeat of the Rebellion in County Wexford in 1798. When Cornwallis, now Lord-Lieutenant, called halt to the White Terror, 2,000 of the Wexford patriotic volunteers, outraged

[31] *Autobiography of Tone*, I, 18.

[32] Ibid., I, 20.

[33] For the background see, Marianne Elliott, *Partners in Revolution. The United Irishmen and France* (London, 1982).

[34] *Autobiography of Tone*, II, 122.

[35] Ibid., II, 303.

[36] Ibid., preface, xx.

that France had abandoned them, enlisted in arms against the French.[37] They became the 'flower' of the British Army under Sir Ralph Abercrombie which in 1801 defeated Napoleon's army in Egypt and fought alongside Indians from the Company's armies. A few survivors of the 1798 Rebellion, such as Wolfe Tone's own son, fought for the French and later the Americans. Many more found themselves carving out a career in the British Empire, with varying degrees of resignation.

Such interconnections and ambiguities were equally apparent on the imperial side. For a start, much of the personnel was the same. Gerard Lake's dubious fame for burning the villages of refractory peasantries followed him from Wexford to Jat north India.[38] Cornwallis's famed benevolence to Tipu Sultan[39] proved a valuable tool of English propaganda in Ireland – though it was not extended to Wolfe Tone. Again, the early career of the Dublin Wellesley family in India was set around with rumours of the Irish crisis. While it may be true that Wellington disavowed his Irish origins, Richard and the other brothers, were much more firmly rooted here. There is no conclusive proof, but the sense of urgency with which Richard, Lord Mornington, set about tempting Tipu Sultan and the Marathas into their decisive wars against the Company after 1798, owes something to his fears about the situation in Ireland. As he contemplated the coup de grace against Tipu, Richard's brother, Wellesley Pole, and other correspondents wrote to him in the most gloomy terms about the course of the rebellion and the 'spirit of insurrection and treason'[40] which manifested itself throughout Ireland. The 'French threat' posed by Citizen Tone and Citizen Tipu to Anglo-Ireland and Anglo-India may have been more real to the Governor-General and less of a mere excuse for aggression than is sometimes imagined.

Beyond these indirect connections in a more intransigent official mind, the British Empire during the Anglo-French wars appears to have been confronting species of traditional patriotisms in both Ireland and India, though much more firmly developed in the former. Tone and his contemporaries thought of Irishness as a permeable and segmented sentiment, forged through commitment to ancient liberties and institutions now under threat again. United Irishmen could be

[37] Ibid., II, 343.

[38] McDowell, *Ireland*, 592, 631–2, 673; Gerard Lake, *DNB*; Penderel Moon, *The British Conquest and Dominion of India* (London, 1989), pp. 345–8.

[39] P.J. Marshall, '"Cornwallis Triumphant": war in India and the British Public in the late eighteenth century', in Lawrence Freedman, Paul Hayes and Robert O'Neill (eds.), *War, Strategy and International Politics. Essays in Honour of Sir Michael Howard* (Oxford, 1992), pp. 57–74.

[40] Wellesley Poole to Wellesley, 1798, The Editor of the Wyndham Papers, *The Wellesley Papers. The Life and Correspondence of Richard Colley Wellesley, Marquess Wellesley, 1760–1842* (London, 1914), I, 71.

Anglicans, Dissenters or Catholics, though the Catholics had a more natural commitment. Tone's own project was to consolidate this sense of Irishness among the Presbyterians of the north, judging Anglicans to be ambivalent and Catholics already won over. This was only a minor development towards a fuller autonomy of the ideals of the Protestant radicals of the 1780s which envisaged an Irish dominion within a wider Britannic world, then comprising north America.

India during the revolutionary crisis exhibited many overlapping forms of cultural unity, but no political unity beyond a vague sense of the legitimacy of the Mughal Empire. However, we can glimpse in the resistance of Tipu Sultan and the Marathas during the Wellesley period the reflections of inchoate forms of traditional patriotism, though regional ones. Recent work has shown how Haider Ali and Tipu Sultan, Britain's fiercest Indian enemies, were more rooted in the sacred landscape of Mysore than earlier historians have credited.[41] The Maratha polities of western India had also long exhibited a sense of shifting unity, created by the emergence of a regional language, Hindu devotionalism and a warrior state.[42] The Marathas' dedication to the concept of *panchayat*, an institution of parochial governance, may have raised distant memories of the assemblies and Parliaments of the old Britannic and Celtic worlds when W.H. Tone described them. Both raised powerful patriotic feelings; both excluded the mass of the population.

In the event, the imperial settlement at the end of the war years had less room for such local particularisms. The Irish parliament disappeared and the apparatus of British rule with its resident magistrates, garrison towns and trigonometrical surveys was imposed.[43] In India the anglicising project of Cornwallis and his successors removed Indians from high office in the British territories and imposed the same apparatus of garrisons and map-makers. Ironically, Wellesley's own period as Lord Lieutenant of Ireland saw the beginnings of a reassessment of these ties. But Wellesley's marriage to a Catholic woman, support for Catholic Emancipation and distaste for Orangemen signalled a false dawn.[44] Agrarian unrest and the clandestine organisations of the patriotic Ribbonmen only worked to entrench the British state more firmly. In the aftermath of the slump of 1815–18, law and order became paramount.

[41] Kate Brittlebank, *Tipu Sultan's Search for Legitimacy. Islam and Kingship in a Hindu Domain* (Delhi, 1997).

[42] See C.A. Bayly, *The Origins of Nationalism in South Asia. Patriotism and ethical government in the making of modern India* (Delhi, 1998), pp. 19–62, ff.

[43] Matthew H. Edney, *Mapping an Empire. The geographical construction of British India 1765–1843* (Chicago, 1997).

[44] See (C.A. Bayly), 'Richard Colley Wellesley' in *New DNB* (Oxford, forthcoming); B. Jenkins, *Era of Emancipation. British Government of Ireland 1812–30* (1988).

Archbishop Heber, the Cork man who became second Archbishop of Calcutta, made the analogy quite clear when he compared the Sannyasi or armed ascetic raiders of the Bengal borders to the Irish Ribbonmen.[45]

As we have seen, both Ireland and India entered during the early nineteenth century into periods of great hardship and stress as the imperial state and the new industrial economy held them in thrall. Both dependencies saw their pre-modern industry decimated if not destroyed. Distance kept free trade from India until the 1830s or '40s. But by then old patriots in Bengal and western India were already talking of *swadeshi*, the need to protect home industry. In India, the death of indigenous industrial production had been a centre of political debate from the 1830s. In Ireland, however, protectionism was the love that could not be named. Home Rule was the first desire. Openly breaking with laissez faire economics might offend too many in Britain and Ireland to be publicly endorsed by many in the Liberator's generation.[46] Ireland needed Britain's markets.

Nevertheless, the ruptures in the imperial polity in 1815–18, in 1829–34 and during the Indian Mutiny of 1857–9 were distantly, but insistently reflected in both dependencies. Though it is unfashionable to say so these days, in the first half of the nineteenth century both India and Ireland witnessed the development of a new language of national politics and the beginnings of a sense of commonalty between embattled elite and struggling populace. The battle for Parliamentary reform in Britain raised the temperature of politics in Ireland and India. The stagnant monopoly of the East India Company and the Irish penal laws were regarded with equal distaste by the new Catholic Irish and the new Bengali and Bombay middle classes. Daniel O'Connell does not appear to have had India on his mind very often. But the Indian intelligentsia were very interested in Ireland. The great reformer, Raja Rammohun Roy, gave strong moral support to Catholic emancipation.[47] As early as 1822 Indian residents of Calcutta set up a fund to help 'the distressed Irish'.[48] Later the writers of the 'Young Bengal' movement of the 1840s and '50s began to cite writings on Ireland and Germany as proof of the evils of a rigid system of free trade.

By 1857 the beginning of a change of tone in Ireland was also apparent. Assumed racial difference began to be supplanted by a sense of common grievance under the yoke of imperialism. Irish Catholic

[45] Reginald Heber, *Narrative of a journey through the Upper Provinces of India* (London, 1844), I, p. x; I am grateful to Dr Nigel Leask for this point.

[46] A point emphasised by Prof. R.F. Foster, personal communication; R.D. Collison Black, *Economic Thought and the Irish Question 1817–70* (Cambridge, 1960), pp. 140–6.

[47] D.K. Chattopadhyay, *Dynamics of Social Change in Bengal (1817–1851)* (Calcutta, 1990), p. 91.

[48] *Bengal Hurkaru*, 5, 17 December 1822; I owe this reference to Ms Piali Dasgupta.

patriots began to discover a bond with India. In the 1850s, Britain's problems in the subcontinent and the Crimea, along with the vaunted resurgence of French power, gave hope to the radicals in Ireland and America who were soon to become known as 'Fenians.' A little ditty appeared in Ireland to confront the flood of cheap patriotic songs which were released to the British public in 1857.[49] 'The Bowld Sepoys' ran:

They bent and bore for a hundred long years
of plunder, of torture of blood and of tears
But they've kept the account and duly paid back
The weighty sum in whop, whop, whack, whack.

Most suggestive of all, this song predicts of the sepoys that:

'They'll place the old king on his glorious old throne.'

So the first protagonists of a Catholic revolutionary nationalism had distantly glimpsed the flames of what some historians have now come to see as the immolation of the loosely linked patriotisms of the Indian homelands. Of course, the same identification had already been made unequivocably in the imperial camp. R.A. Sterndale's, *The Afghan Knife* refers to an Indian Islamic purist, a so-called-Wahhabi, as 'a fanatic, a rebel, a sort of Mahomedan Fenian, one whom the police should take under special surveillance.'[50] By this time British spokesmen had linked in a chain of sedition the supposed Wahhabi involvement in the 1857 rebellion to the Patna conspiracy of the mid-1860s and the assassination of the Viceroy, Lord Mayo, that great Irish landowner, in 1872.[51]

Nevertheless, in 1857 most Irishmen still seem to have identified with British rule in India because of the threat the Rebellion posed to overseas European communities. This was because the Irish were not only the victims of the imperial state, but also some its greatest beneficiaries, a position which hardly changed through to the 1930s. These benefits flowed both to Protestants and to Catholics, both to North and to South, although unevenly. I will briefly describe Ireland's imperialist history as a background to the full emergence of Irish and Indian nationalism, and their mutual acknowledgement, in the latter part of the nineteenth century.

In the 1830s India broadly remained for the Irish as it had done in

[49] 'The Bowld Sepoys' Plate 20c in Vaughan (ed.), *New History*, 1; cf. ibid., p. 417.

[50] R.A. Sterndale, *The Afghan Knife* (London, 1879), pp. 16–17. I am grateful to Dr Gautam Chakravarty for this reference.

[51] For Wahhabis see Peter Hardy, *The Muslims of British India* (Cambridge, 1960), pp. 80–84; Peter Robb, 'The impact of British rule on religious community; reflections on the trial of Maulvi Ahmadullah of Patna in 1865', in P. Robb (ed.), *Society and Ideology. Essays in South Asian history* (London, 1994), pp. 142–76.

the youth of Wolfe Tone, the 'great gulf of undone beings', rather than a submerged nation. Irish emigration to India during the first half of the nineteenth century evidently differed in fundamental aspects from Irish emigration to other parts of the Empire and to America.[52] Firstly, it was generally neither seasonal migration, nor permanent, but of ten to twenty years duration, in the main encompassing the careers of soldiers, administrators and priests. As in the eighteenth century, a substantial number of Irish recruits into the Company's armies were from poor peasant families in the West and South of Ireland.[53] The city of Cork may have had a more direct personal contact with India than any other place in the British Isles, including Dundee, during the nineteenth century.

There were, of course, families of longer term residence in India such as the Conlans of Allahabad, many of them associated with the uncovenanted service, posts and railways. The Conlans appear to have followed one of the familiar paths of upward mobility in eighteenth century Ireland moving from commerce into the professions and from Catholicism to Protestantism. A Conlan became leader of the Allahabad Bar in the 1880s.[54] Only in later generations did Australian and American Conlans rediscover their Catholicism. Indo-Irish families were prominent among Eurasians who were also to throw up Indian labour activists and early nationalists.

As in the case of Canada and Australasia, but not the United States, there were substantial numbers of Ascendancy and landlord families, including a few Catholic gentry among the migrant administrators and soldiers in India. Particularly prominent here were Protestant gentry families of the Belfast region and of Enniskillen, who were equally well represented among their peers in Canada and Australia. High Anglicans among the Duke of Wellington's generation with their connections among the Directors of the Company held the day until the 1840s. Thereafter, men from less powerful families became prominent. With the careers of John and Henry Lawrence and Robert Montgomery the dominance of the rigorous Scots-Irish Protestants of the Punjab school began to be felt.[55] But great landlords still found their way to India in the late nineteenth century. The Earls of Minto followed a family tradition of Indian service. The Earl of Dufferin, with ancestors who fought both at Waterloo and Trafalgar, also reached the Viceroyalty. By the time of the competition wallahs in the later 1850s, a significant

[52] Fitzpatrick in Vaughan (ed.), *New History of Ireland*.

[53] Sir P. Cadell, 'Irish soldiers in India', *Irish Sword*, 1, 1949.

[54] Personal communication Dr. K.H. Prior, 1998.

[55] E.g., R. Bosworth Smith, *Life of Lord Lawrence* (London, 1885), 1, 1–29; Robert Montgomery Papers, Mss. D1019, 1, Oriental and India Office Collections, British Library.

number of Catholics were reaching the ranks of the civil service to balance the Protestants who had passed through Trinity College, Dublin. Among these were Charles O'Donnell, an official in Bihar and Sir Antony MacDonnell, future lieutenant Governor of the North-Western Provinces and Oudh and Under-Secretary for Ireland.[56]

It is difficult to say that these administrators and soldiers' Irish origins were critical in their attitudes, but they were certainly of some importance. Both Protestants and Catholics were strongly mindful of their nationality. Dufferin, stepping down as Governor of Canada in 1881 asserted that:

> There is no doubt that the world is best administered by Irishmen. Things never went better with us either at home or abroad than when Lord Palmerston ruled Great Britain, Lord Mayo governed India and Lord Munck directed the destiny of Canada.[57]

He went on to say that the Highland Scots were almost as eminent, but it was best to allow a few Englishmen to govern the Empire so they could see how much better the Irish and Scots were at it. More seriously, Irish administrators, doctors and priests brought a particular vision to bear on the Indian empire. Several members of the Bengal Medical Service came from the West of Ireland and were acutely aware of the processes of linguistic and cultural assimilation which accompanied British rule. This sometimes, but not necessarily predisposed them to Indian languages. One medical officer stated baldly that the Indians should learn English just as his Gaelic ancestors had done.

Secondly, the Irish in overseas service often recorded revealing views on religious antagonisms. Here again the reaction varied. Dufferin believed in religious separatism under a benign imperial rule. His dispensation between Druze, Maronite Christian and Muslim in Mount Lebanon in the 1860s followed his primordial understanding of the Protestant-Catholic divide in Ireland.[58] It also prefigured his concern that the status of the Indian Muslims should not be disadvantaged by the rise of a predominantly Hindu politics.[59] On the other hand, Sir Antony MacDonnell, a Catholic officer of the Bengal Civil Service understood North India in a different Irish light. He believed that North Indian Muslims were a rapacious group of landlords who had long monopolised government office. The Hindus, by contrast, resembled the Catholic peasantry in Ireland and needed both land

[56] Cook, *Imperial Affinities*, *passim*.

[57] C.E.D. Black, *The Marquess of Dufferin and Ava* (London, 1903), p. 159.

[58] Ibid., pp. 58–9.

[59] Briton Martin, *New India 1885* (Princeton, 1969), pp. 328–35.

reform and a recognition of their cultural difference.[60] As Lieutenant-Governor in 1900, MacDonnell allowed the Hindi language in the Devanagari script to stand equal in British courts with Urdu written in the Persian script, a momentous event in the separation between the two religious communities in north India.[61]

Related to this, Irish administrators and government servants were very much aware of the peasant problem, arguably much more so than their English counterparts. As Clive Dewey and S.B. Cook have shown the Bihar group of Indian Civil Servants, including MacDonnell and O'Donnell were particularly forceful in their demands for tenancy legislation.[62] This was at a time when official policy favoured men of broad acres in the wake of the Rebellion, which had disappointed hopes in the peasantry. It was partly through their advocacy that aspects of Irish land legislation were applied in modified form to India, while there is some evidence of the passage of ideas in the opposite direction too.

Equally, an Irish background, especially though not always an Ascendancy one could push officials in the opposite direction. Dufferin argued strongly against Grey's policy of compulsory purchase and redistribution of Irish land in the aftermath of the Fenian troubles of the 1860s.[63] He said he had no brief for the privileges of the Church of Ireland, but he insisted on the fundamental right of property in land. In his report on the Government of Egypt he made much play with the indebtedness of the peasantry, but went no further than urging the creation of Agricultural Banks, insisting on the right of the landowner.[64]

In India as Viceroy, Dufferin helped emasculate the Bengal Tenancy Act of 1886. Social remedies for the improvement of the Indian peasant were justifiable. But any intervention in the liberty of property would, he believed undermine the foundations of government.[65] Dufferin further worried that the propaganda of Young India might inflame outrages amongst the Indian peasantry. This was the main reason why he turned his face firmly against the newly-formed Indian National Congress in 1885, having once believed that it might play a useful role for government.[66]

This volte face was significant. Scholars of Indian nationalism have

[60] Minute by A.P. MacDonnell, October 1901, MacDonnell Papers, Mss. Eng. Hist. 350–370, Bodleian Library, Oxford.

[61] Francis Robinson, *Separatism among Indian Muslims. The politics of the United Provinces' Muslims 1860–1923* (Cambridge, 1974), pp. 42–43.

[62] S.B. Cook, *Imperial Affinities*, pp. 88–94, 103–5.

[63] Black, *Dufferin*, p. 71.

[64] Black, *Dufferin*, pp. 71, 197; Dufferin, 'Correspondence Regarding the Reorganisation of Egypt, *Parliamentary Papers, 1883*, LXXXIV, c.3468.

[65] Cook, *Imperial Affinities*, pp. 82–107.

[66] Martin, *New India*, pp. 329–35.

perhaps underestimated the extent to which the early years of the Indian National Congress after its foundation in 1885 were affected by the contemporary problems of the British empire. This saw the electoral defeat of Disraeli, Gladstone's Occupation of Egypt, the failure of the Irish Home Rule Bill and the suppression of the Irish Land League. Here I move to my final theme the moral and political connections between emergent Irish, Indian and Egyptian nationalisms.

The parallel was certainly very clearly in the mind of Dufferin and Sir Auckland Colvin, Lieutenant Governor of the North-Western Provinces and Oudh, a province which had been plagued with sporadic tenant revolts since the early 1860s. Colvin had himself played a recent role in Egypt where he had urged the suppression of the Arabist movement for constitutional government.[67] That movement, as Juan Cole has recently showed, was also associated with a strong undercurrent of artisan and peasant unrest against the influx of cheap European manufacturers.[68]

In 1888 Colvin wrote to Dufferin of the dangers of what he called '*sans cullotte* [sic] Young India'. Later he argued that the Congress leaders were attempting to 'establish a League in India, not unlike that recently suppressed in Ireland'.[69] It was for this reason that the authorities were concerned with three issues which was preoccupying government in Ireland. First, they deplored the 'boycott' – the word was specifically used – of Indians who did not associated themselves with Congress. Secondly, officials denounced rural pamphleteering and the activities among the peasants of what were called 'stump-orators.' O'Connell haunted Dufferin's dreams like great Caesar's ghost.[70] Thirdly, the government of India was alarmed by the credence that young Indian radicals were being given in London. This was a time when leaders of the Irish Land League, such as Michael Davitt, supported by English radicals, such as Charles Bradlaugh were organising big agitations in the capital.[71] The fact that radical politics was emerging in the Empire at precisely the same time as working men's organisations in London were beginning to march in Trafalgar Square was not lost on the authorities.

During the years before the First World War, the links between Indian

[67] Alexander Scholch, 'The "men on the spot" and the English occupation of Egypt in 1882', *Historical Journal*, 19, 3, 1976, 773–85.

[68] J.R.I. Cole, *Colonialism and Revolution in the Middle East. Social and Cultural Origins of Egypt's Urabi movement* (Princeton, 1993).

[69] Colvin to Dufferin, 25 April 1888, and enclosure, Dufferin Papers, Oriental and India Office Collections, British Library, London.

[70] Martin, *New India*, p. 118.

[71] Anne Taylor, *Annie Besant. A biography* (Oxford, 1982); cf. Conor Cruise O'Brien, *Parnell and His Party, 1880–90* (Oxford, 1958), pp. 22–23.

and Irish nationalists gradually strengthened. The new generation of nationalist politicians was keenly aware that they were actors in a series of problems which affected the whole Empire and not their own territories alone. The rise of the newspaper editor, the laying of the telegraph cable and the congregation of young, educated Irish people, Indians and later Egyptians, in London provided the context. Politics provided the trigger. Disraeli's new imperialism, marked by Lord Lytton's suppression of the Indian vernacular press and harsh action against Fenians in Ireland, had given way to Gladstone's moral rearmament. But then Gladstone had failed to secure Home Rule and Parnell's party had been pushed to the margins. As Wilfrid Scawen Blunt remarked, the Gladstone cabinet which ordered repression in Ireland was also the one which crushed the Egyptian National Movement.[72] 'The two causes, the Irish and the Egyptian' he wrote, 'the Catholic and the Mohammedan, seemed to me to stand on a common footing of enlightened humanity.'[73] Later, of course, he was to become an activist in the Irish land-war and suffer imprisonment for his part. Having visited India and feasted on the hospitality of his friend, Lord Ripon, Blunt denounced the Government for pushing the people towards 'cannibalism'. For him, Egyptian bondholders, Irish rentiers and Indian administrators merged into one terrifying incubus. He might have called them 'gentlemanly capitalists.' True to form, the Viceroy, Lord Ripon's early promises of major constitutional reforms in India were watered down and delayed by virulent opposition among Anglo-Indians to Indian judges having cognisance over English offenders. Liberalism had failed even before it was replaced in 1887 by Toryism and a yet harsher reign in Ireland, Egypt and India.

In this context, tentative links were made in London between Indian and Irish nationalists. In 1885 the leaders of what was to become the Congress tried to lay Indian grievances before the British electorate. The Irish caucus in Parliament agreed to support Dadhabhai Naoroji, the chief ideologue of Indian economic nationalism.[74] Davitt, leader of the Land League and an old Fenian, along with H.H. Hyndman among the early socialists, brought the problems of India and Ireland together in their speeches. Two other figures illustrate these persistent connections. Annie Besant was brought up in England and belonged on the wilder fringes of Victorian political and social life. But she always regarded herself as Irish and saw Indian issues through Irish eyes. Radicalised politically by the execution of Fenian gunmen in 1867, her religious beliefs found refuge in a theistical mysticism, which paradoxically had

[72] W.S. Blunt, *The Secret History of the English Occupation of Egypt* (London, 1907), p. 110.
[73] Blunt, *The Land War in Ireland being a personal narrative of events* (London, 1912), p. 1.
[74] Anne Taylor, *Annie Besant. A Biography* (London, 1992), pp. 25–8.

been awakened by studies of the Church Fathers during an early phase of neo-Catholic pietism.[75] In London in the 1870s and '80s she had been active in Irish politics and associated with Davitt, through her mentor and probable lover, Charles Bradlaugh. Besant had finally found refuge in the Theosophical movement which combined disdain for Christianity with a kind of pan-racial mysticism. Theosophy and Anglo-Celtic radical politics were important elements in the ideology of the early Indian National Congress.

Over the next twenty years Mrs Besant was to play a major part in both Indian Theosophy and Indian Nationalism. She founded dozens of local organisations for both bodies throughout India, but particularly in the south of the country. In 1916 her campaign culminated in the Foundation of the Indian Home Rule Leagues which were deliberately based on the mass organisations of Irish politics which had developed after the fall of Parnell, and particularly on Sinn Fein. Inwardly, moreover, the neo-Hindu, racial nationalism which animated many of the early Congress leaders found an echo in her own mystical Irish nationalism. At key points in the history of the Congress movement, Besant drew on Irish themes and made parallels in her speeches between the two dependencies.

The parallel in early Irish national thought is intriguing. An emerging cross-community sense of ancient Ireland and the Celtic origins of human virtue quite easily melded with the occult racialism of Theosophy. Madame Blavatsky herself hailed the rise of the ancient 'land of sages' and heroes from English thrall. She predicted the rise of what she called an avatar who would throw of the English yoke in both India and Ireland.[76] While Blavatsky drew a direct parallel with India, the work of W.B. Yeats and the Dublin mystics provides an indirect connection.[77]

Theosophy melded with apocalyptic racism provided a valuable counter-hegemonic ideology to British racial imperialism. Even at the level of less exciting, and excitable speculation, however, the intellectual life of the two dependencies increasingly cross-fertilised each other. ICS officials educated at Trinity College, spread the concern for folklore and legend to north India, while W.B. Yeats wove folklore into the national mythology of Ireland.[78]

[75] Ibid.

[76] Ibid., 253ff.

[77] Foster, *Paddy and Mr Punch*, p. 221; A.P. Sinnett had been editor of the Anglo-Indian newspaper, *The Pioneer* of Allahabad, a friend of A.O. Hume and devotee of Mme Blavatsky. His book *Esoteric Buddhism* had been presented to W.B. Yeats by a Protestant aunt in Sligo.

[78] See, e.g., William Crooke, *Religion and Folklore of Northern India*, rev. R.E. Enthoven, (Oxford, 1926); W.B. Yeats, *The Celtic Twilight: myth, fantasy and folklore* (1893, repr. Bridport, 1990).

In both India and Ireland, early nationalist ideology emerged, therefore, out of a plural discourse. The elements which made it up constituted memories and traditions of the earlier patriotisms of the days of Tone or the Maratha realm. Also present were mystical ideas of race and nation, revived folklorism and reactive mainline religion: the Faith of Our Fathers or *sanatan dharma* (ancient religion). But there was also present the modernised version of rationalist, political and economic critique of British government which stretched back to the days of Tom Paine and Edmund Burke.

A second European interlocutor for these two national movements representing this radical stream was William Wedderburn, another Scots ICS radical. Wedderburn had become an expert on peasant poverty while in the Bombay Civil Service, advocating the establishment of peasant banks on Irish lines. He played a major part in organising the London Branch of the Indian National Congress after 1889. Elected to Parliament he took up the plight of Scottish and Irish crofters and fishermen. Having toured the Irish 'congested districts' in the early 1890s, he drew on his experiences in the Indian Famine League which was established to confront the great famine of 1898–1901, a formative moment in the history of Indian economic nationalism.[79] Wedderburn's ideas were close to these of the two major economic nationalist writers, Dadhabhai Naoroji and Romesh Chandra Dutt.

Yet there were deeper parallels and connections in the ideologies of indigenous nationalists, too. Along with Russian anarchism and Garibaldi, the Fenians and later Irish revolutionaries played a major part in the thought of the so-called extremist Congressmen of the years 1905–1909. The radical seer Aurobindo Ghose constantly affirmed the life enhancing quality of self-sacrifice and righteous assassination along the lines of the Irish.[80] A nation had to be created through the spilling of blood, a theme which picked up both on contemporary romantic nationalism in the west and on Indian ideas of sacrifice and regeneration. Equally, the Indian Boycott of British goods which was associated with the call for *swadeshi*, home industry, seems finally to have found an echo in Ireland. Here, nationalists instituted a boycott of British goods in 1909.[81] The effort was a failure. Significantly, however, they did not only employ the theme of economic nationalism in their propaganda. They also denounced the corruption and luxury which was spread by the consumption of the products of the ruling power. Catholic pur-

[79] S.K. Ratcliffe, *Sir William Wedderburn and the Indian Reform Movement* (London, 1923), pp. 68–9.

[80] H. and U. Mukherjee, *Sri Aurobindo's Political Thought* (Calcutta, 1958), pp. 71–81, 84; cf. Leonard Gordon, *Bengal. The nationalist movement 1876–1940* (New York, 1974), p. 109.

[81] Cf. F.S. Lyons, *Culture and Anarchy in Ireland, 1890–1939* (Oxford, 1979), pp. 40–3, 80–81 on cultural protectionists movements.

itanism here matched the austere self-sacrifice of the pious Hindu urged by Bipan Chandra Pal, the Bengali nationalist and later, of course, by Mahatma Gandhi himself.

The last stage in what Richard Shannon called the 'crisis of imperialism'[82] stretches from the election of the Liberal Government in 1906 to the emergence of Gandhi's mass movement and the Irish Free State in the early 1920s. The Liberal cabinet of 1906–14 proved the last phase for constitutional nationalism in both dependencies. More important, it saw the vigorous articulation of separatisms within them both, and indeed in Egypt, which we have seen had long provided the forth side of an imperial political quadrilateral. The politics of mass electorates and mass publicity through newspapers provided the context. But the Liberal government's desire to devolve power through Home Rule in Ireland and local self-government in India and Egypt provided the stimulus to separatist politics. Entrenched in the highest echelons of British politics, Sir Edward Carson and the Unionists staged a coup against the Liberals at the very centre of politics. Scarcely less successful were India's Muslims who achieved separate representation in the Morley–Minto Reforms of 1909. Muslim lawyers and gentlemen who by no means represented all of their correligionists were able to orchestrate a successful lobby in London with the help of retired Indian officials and educationists. Egyptian Copts tried the same tactics, but could not deploy enough weight in London.[83]

As separatism took off, with bitter implications for the future of national politics in both Ireland and India, majoritarian nationalism itself launched into a new mass phase under the impetus of world war. These movements removed the British presence from southern Ireland and secured the promise of dominion status for India. In their course, the old élite politicians of race and nation were replaced by younger leaders of populist stance if not mainly of rural origins. In 1917 Annie Besant, along with the older generation of Theosophists and cultural nationalists was swept aside, by the Home Rule League of Bal Gangadhar Tilak and later by Mahatma Gandhi. At the same moment, Besant's élite coevals lost control of the Irish movement to socialists and revolutionary nationalists. For a time, religious divisions were held in check in both cases. But the Irish nationalism which emerged after 1924 was more resolutely Catholic and exclusionary. In India the Congress, in rhetoric as much as in membership, was similarly a more Hindu body in 1926 than it had been in 1914.

[82] Richard Shannon, *The Crisis of Imperialism 1865–1915* (London, 1976).

[83] See e.g., for Copts *Coptic Congress held at Assiout on March, 6, 7, 8 1911* (Assiout, 1911) FO 371/1111 Public Record Office, London; for Muslims, F. Robinson, *Separatism among Indian Muslims* (Cambridge, 1974); for Ulster, Patricia Jalland, *The Liberals and Ireland. The Ulster Question in British politics to 1914* (London, 1980).

Sketching such distant yet persistent connections and comparisons as those between Ireland and India within the context of British dominion may have some utility as the certainties of the historiography of class and nation break down. This was a world where Abu Taleb, the north Indian munshi could become a Cork lounge lizard and George Thomas, the poor sailor from the far west could become a prophet of the Britannic Great Game in central Asia. Global connections of this sort speak to the history of transit and becoming which post-modernists tell us has eclipsed the history of static identities. Beyond this, however, there are striking parallels and comparisons at many points between Irish and Indian history over the century and I have been considering. Nor was this the simple story of the transfer of ideas from east to west which is the staple of theories of nationalism and also, ironically, of studies of subaltern mentalities. Of course, Indian patriotisms were less developed than the Protestant-led nationalism of eighteenth century Ireland. The demand for local representative government was also more strongly articulated in Ireland by comparison with even Bengal in the 1830s. On the other hand, the idea of national political economy was more advanced in India and, at least in part, it derived from indigenous doctrines. If historians are to get the balance right they may well need to ask once again why some identities become rooted in living traditions and in economic and social processes; why they remain obdurate and self-perpetuating rather than ever-protean and shifting.

Still less such distant yet persistent connections and comparisons as those between Ireland and India within the context of British dominion may have some bearing on the aspirations [illegible]

[illegible]

RECONSIDERING THE IRISH ACT OF UNION

By S.J. Connolly

READ 11 SEPTEMBER 1999 AT QUEEN'S UNIVERSITY, BELFAST

THE political, administrative and social consequences of the union of Great Britain and Ireland, and even more the eventual unravelling of the structures it created, have for the greater part of the past century provided Irish historians with a major theme. By contrast the measure itself has received little sustained analysis or discussion. F.R. Bolton's monograph, first published in 1966, remains – more than three decades later – the standard reference.[1] In part this is a tribute to the depth, breadth and penetration of Bolton's account. But there is also at least the suggestion that the negotiation and passage of the union legislation, during 1799–1800, is to be seen as unproblematic, a relatively straightforward event providing a terminus or a starting point for discussion of the more complex and challenging periods on either side.

Such an assumption, if it exists, should not survive a reading of the papers collected above. A major outcome of the symposium has been to demonstrate the extent to which the union itself, considered as a piece of political decision making, remains a puzzle. Here we have a reform that transformed the way in which Ireland had been governed for more than a century, increased the population of the United Kingdom by almost fifty per cent, and set in train a whole series of unpredictable political, administrative and economic developments. Yet it seems to have been undertaken on the spur of the moment, and with remarkably little forward thinking. Peter Jupp, it is true, establishes that debate on the union in the British parliament and press was more significant, in scale and level of argument, than had previously been recognised. But he also vividly illustrates the restricted and unstructured process whereby the essential features of the measure were decided by a narrow and arbitrarily selected group of individuals. Little thought was given to the means by which the legislation would be piloted through parliament, leading to the debacle of January 1799, when the Irish House of Commons rejected the principle of a union. Despite Edward Cooke's warning that the proposal would have to be 'written up, spoken up, intrigued up, drunk up, sung up and bribed up', it appears from James Kelly's account that the administration was slow

[1] G.C. Bolton, *The Passing of the Irish Act of Union: A Study in Parliamentary Politics* (1966).

to launch its campaign for at least the appearance of public support, allowing the anti-unionists to seize the initiative in the propaganda battle. Important administrative issues were left unresolved. The question whether there was still any need for a separate Irish executive and viceregal court was settled by institutional inertia rather than forward planning. The relationship between lord lieutenant, chief secretary, treasury and revenue, as Trevor McCavery demonstrates, remained for several years a source of confusion and political infighting. More remarkable still is the failure, by a government engaged at that moment in a major European war, to work out in any detail the implications of the union for the command and organisation of the Irish armed forces, with the potentially disastrous implications documented by Alan Blackstock.

Beyond these specific anomalies lies the wider difficulty of summing up in any simple formula exactly why William Pitt and his colleagues chose to introduce such a radical and disruptive measure at this particular time. Contributors to the symposium offer three overlapping but separate contexts within which the act of union can be understood. The first is the imperial. Most serious Irish historians tend to shy away from explanatory frameworks built round the notion of colonialism, especially perhaps now that these have become enmeshed with the excesses of contemporary literary theory.[2] In this case, however, Christopher Bayley provides a compelling survey of the parallels, extending from the late eighteenth century to the early twentieth, between Ireland and India. These include the nearly contemporaneous decisions, in the 1780s and 1790s, to transfer power in both societies from local elites to agents of direct imperial control. Secondly, there is William Doyle's analysis, in which the act of union is seen as part of a wider process, initiated by revolutionary France and then adopted under the pressures of war by its enemies, whereby the multiple, overlapping jurisdictions of the *ancien régime* were abandoned in favour of legal and administrative centralisation. Thirdly there is John Pocock's account, which focuses instead on the incompatibility between the uniquely British concept of the sovereignty of king-in-parliament and the sort of confederate imperial structure demanded first by American and then by Irish patriots.

These three perspectives, imperial, *ancien régime* and British, are not mutually exclusive. All three, moreover, point towards the same broad conclusion: that the existence of Ireland as a separate but subordinate kingdom came to be seen as irreconcilable with the security of the British state. The origins of the problem can be traced back to the

[2] As, for example, in Declan Kiberd, *Inventing Ireland: The Literature of the Modern Nation* (1995).

1690s, when members of the Dublin parliament took advantage of the greatly increased bargaining power conferred on them by the spiralling cost of an earlier phase in Britain's long conflict with France to secure for their assembly a new prominence in the government of the kingdom.[3] The first response of the British government to the problems that resulted was to attempt the management of the Irish parliament through selected local power brokers. From the late 1760s the intractability and exorbitant demands of these 'undertakers' led ministers to turn instead to the direct management of parliament by the lord lieutenant and chief secretary.[4] But this occurred at a time when the growth of out of doors opinion was already making parliamentary politics less stable. Moreover the shift from management through Irish mediators to direct control by British office-holders intensified what was already a growing tendency to interpret political and constitutional conflicts in terms of an opposition of Irish and British interests.[5] It was against this background that the parliamentary patriots, allied to an extra-parliamentary movement, the Volunteers, took advantage of the crisis arising from the American revolt to force through a radical renegotiation of the Anglo-Irish connection in 1779–82.

The constitutional revolution of 1782 can credibly be presented as the immediate reason for the act of union eighteen years later. The leaders of the new Whig administration, committed by their statements when in opposition to doing something to meet Irish constitutional grievances, had appealed to the patriot leaders for time to negotiate a comprehensive new settlement defining the relationship between the two kingdoms. Grattan and Charlemont, however, insisted on the immediate satisfaction of their two central demands: the repeal of the Declaratory Act, which asserted the right of the British parliament to pass laws binding on Ireland, and the modification of Poynings's law of 1494, whereby the Irish and British privy councils could intervene to kill or alter proposed Irish bills. The result was a wholly negative settlement: the dismantling of the mechanisms by which Great Britain had ensured its ultimate control of Irish affairs, without putting anything in their place.[6] The fragile condition of the Anglo-Irish connection in the aftermath of this outcome was demonstrated, in British eyes, by

[3] J.I. McGuire, 'The Irish Parliament of 1692', in *Penal Era and Golden Age: Essays in Irish History 1690–1800*, ed. Thomas Bartlett and D.W. Hayton (Belfast, 1979).

[4] Thomas Bartlett, 'The Townshend Viceroyalty 1767–72', in *Penal Era and Golden Age*, eds. Bartlett and Hayton; M.J. Powell, 'The Reform of the Undertaker System: Anglo-Irish Politics 1750–67', *Irish Historical Studies*, 31 (1998), 19–36.

[5] David Lammey, 'The Growth of the "Patriot Opposition" in Ireland during the 1770s', *Parliamentary History*, 7 (1988), 257–81.

[6] J.C. Beckett, 'Anglo-Irish Constitutional Relations in the Later Eighteenth Century', in J.C. Beckett, *Confrontations* (1972), 123–41; R.B. McDowell, *Ireland in the Age of Imperialism and Revolution 1760–1801* (Oxford, 1979), chap. 6.

subsequent developments: the populist campaign to supplement the repeal of the Declaratory Act by a formal renunciation of any British claim to legislate for Ireland; the rejection of Pitt's proposals in 1785 for a commercial agreement regulating the economic relationship between the two kingdoms; and most of all the crisis of 1789, where the Irish parliament, by insisting on its right to make its own decisions regarding the timing and character of a regency during the incapacity of George III, showed an apparent willingness to call into question the one slender thread, a shared monarchy, that now held Ireland and Great Britain together.[7]

The intransigence of the leaders of patriot opinion, exacerbated by a growth of popular politics that gave such intransigence political weight, was thus central to the long term outcome. William Doyle has emphasised the parallels between Irish patriotism and other examples of the defence of sectional or local privileges and immunities in *ancien régime* Europe. And there was indeed much in what would retrospectively be considered the developing tradition of Irish patriotism that fits neatly into such a pattern. A large section of Irish opinion was willing to resist what were seen as illegitimate encroachments on the kingdom's domestic affairs, and to uphold the autonomy of its judicial and administrative structures, while at the same time accepting the overall framework imposed by Ireland's membership of the conglomerate of Hanoverian states.[8] But there was another element in patriot thought, much less compatible with the structures of composite monarchy. This took as its starting point the view, systematically set out by Molyneux in 1698, that Ireland and Great Britain were sister kingdoms, subject to the same king but of equal status. It was this exalted notion, what would later be called dual monarchy, that inspired Grattan and Charlemont's refusal to negotiate a new treaty of union in 1782. It likewise lay behind the rejection of the Commercial Propositions in 1785, on the grounds that these would have committed the Irish parliament to replicate British shipping legislation. Its logical conclusion was a refusal to accept that the competence of the Irish parliament could be in any way limited, even in relation to such matters as foreign affairs, as in the disputes over the Anglo-French commercial treaty in 1786,[9] or the

[7] James Kelly, *Prelude to Union: Anglo-Irish Politics in the 1780s* (Dublin, 1992).

[8] J. Th. Leerssen, 'Anglo-Irish Patriotism and its European Context: Notes towards a Reassessment', *Eighteenth-Century Ireland*, 3 (1988); Patrick McNally, *Parties, Patriots and Undertakers: Parliamentary Politics in Early Hanoverian Ireland* (Dublin, 1997), chap. 8; Jacqueline Hill, *From Patriots to Unionists: Dublin Civic Politics and Irish Protestant Patriotism 1660–1840* (Oxford, 1997).

[9] James Kelly, 'The Anglo-French Commercial Treaty of 1786: The Irish Dimension', *Eighteenth-Century Ireland*, 4 (1989), 93–111. See also David Lammey, 'The Irish-Portuguese Trade Dispute 1770–90', *Irish Historical Studies*, 25 (1986), 29–45.

monarchy, as in the Regency crisis. In this respect the problem that had become so pressing by the end of the eighteenth century was not so much the obsolescence of composite monarchy as the refusal of a large part of the Irish political establishment to accept its implications. 'Parliament', Grattan proclaimed in 1782, 'is exclusive legislature ... Like that of England, our legislature is composed of king, Lords and Commons; but the word king is exclusive, the word Lords exclusive, and the word Commons exclusive; when you say you are governed by a king, you mean one king, when you say you are governed by a parliament, you mean one parliament.' [10] William Pitt, eighteen years later, was only taking him at his word.

So far, then, the picture is fairly clear. The antics of the Irish patriots, in British eyes at least, had left the connection between the two kingdoms dangerously weak. By 1798 the pressures of war abroad and disaffection at home made further delay impossible. The established pattern of imperial policy, and the constitutional assumptions on which the British state rested, both pointed towards a centralisation of authority in an incorporating union as the only solution. The difficulty arises when we move beyond these generalities in order to ask what exactly the hard pressed government of Pitt and his ministers expected the union to achieve. Ireland in 1798–1800 was clearly the weak spot in Britain's defences. Incorporation, in the long term, could conceivably be seen as the means of eliminating the problems that made it such: supporters spoke of the extension to Ireland of British 'habits, customs, and morals'.[11] But the threat to which Pitt and his colleagues were responding was the very immediate one of French invasion and renewed rebellion. And in the short term framework which that threat dictated it is much more difficult to specify in what precise way the transfer of power from Dublin to London could in itself be expected to make Ireland either less disturbed or more efficiently guarded.

The point may be illustrated by looking at one of the most ambiguous features of the whole union debate, the implications for the Catholic question. The immediate spur towards the implementation of union came from the rebellion of 1798, widely seen as the product of Protestant abuse of power and Catholic alienation. The single most concrete benefit that could be expected from the union, equally, was that it would provide a secure framework within which Catholic grievances could be addressed without either endangering the Protestant character of the constitution or provoking a damaging reaction from the dominant minority in Ireland itself. The resulting elimination or at least ameli-

[10] *Speeches of the Right Hon. Henry Grattan*, Daniel O. Madden ed. (Dublin, 1874), p. 60 (22 Feb. 1782).

[11] See Jupp, above pp. 197–220.

oration of Ireland's poisonous religious divisions would make the country less vulnerable to invasion or insurrection, thus releasing much needed military resources, while at the same time making it easier in the future to draw on Catholic Ireland's huge reservoir of surplus manpower for the imperial army. But why then was there so much confusion about whether the union was to be linked to a more or less immediate measure of Catholic emancipation? There were of course sound strategic reasons for not openly announcing any such link, so as to avoid adding to the existing opposition to the union among Irish Protestants. Yet even within the inner circle of ministers vagueness and indecision seem to have reigned. Emancipation, as Geoghegan shows, was proposed by Pitt and Grenville, ruled out by Clare's intervention, then restored as an open question at Dundas's insistence. When, in November 1799, the cabinet finally reached a decision, agreeing in principle to immediate emancipation, it did so in response to Castlereagh's gloomy report on the prospects of carrying the union without it: emancipation, in other words, had been redefined as a means to the end of achieving a union rather than as a benefit to be expected from it. There was, of course, the alternative argument that the union would contribute to the conciliation of the Catholics, not by clearing the way for formal legal and political equality, but by liberating them from the oppressive local despotism of the Protestant elite. But the benefits of such a liberation would by their nature be felt only gradually, raising again the question of why in that case the union was being rushed through as an emergency measure to meet an immediate crisis. All in all it is difficult to resist the conclusion that Pitt and his ministers approached this and indeed all aspects of the union in a spirit of undirected urgency, convinced that a corrupt, inefficient and dangerous system had to be swept away, but remaining far less clear on what exactly was to take its place.

At this point it might be helpful to highlight another aspect of Peter Jupp's analysis. His account emphasises the wider considerations of war time strategy behind the proposal for a union. But he also demonstrates vividly the extent to which the main decisions were taken by three figures, Pitt, Grenville and Dundas, each of whom was not only distracted by a range of other pressing issues but was operating under tremendous strain. All three, in fact, were exhausted, suffering the effects of prolonged stress, and increasingly at odds both with one another and with the king. Hence it is not altogether surprising that, having agreed that a radical solution to the problem of Ireland was required, they should have proceeded by instinct rather than analysis, improvising the details of policy in response to short term considerations. In this sense Jupp's analysis of the context of policy making constitutes the final part of the jigsaw, uniting *l'histoire evenementielle* with that of *la longue durée* to bring together the different aspects of the union: the structural crisis out of which it developed, the political traditions and assumptions that shaped its provisions, and the strangely unfocussed process by which it came into existence.

The papers collected below are concerned primarily with the background to the act of union, and with the immediate circumstances of its passage. A consideration of the consequences of the measure for the development of Ireland and of Great Britain, and for the relationship between the two societies, would require a further symposium, if not indeed a whole series. Yet a few brief comments may be in order, as a means of placing what has so far been said in a wider perspective.

The importance of such a perspective, looking forwards as well as back, is evident if we consider the administrative structures created by the union. An analysis that focuses on the events of 1799–1800 must inevitably emphasise the failure to resolve such issues as the command of the army and the future role of the lord lieutenancy, and the uncertainty and confusion that resulted. But it is also necessary to make two further points. The first is that the various administrative, legal and financial loose ends identified in the papers below were for the most part resolved within a fairly short time, creating a workable if sometimes cumbersome structure for the government of this part of what was now the United Kingdom. The second is that the structure thus created proved more adaptable than might have been expected. Pitt may have believed that free trade and political union would promote a rapid natural convergence of the two economies and societies. But his successors quickly accepted that Ireland's desperate economic problems, combined with the unwillingness or inability of the Irish landed gentry to emulate their English counterparts by acting as the unpaid local agents of a minimalist state, required a degree of centralisation and government intervention wholly different from what was expected or would have been tolerated on the other side of the Irish Sea. There were, of course, exceptions. The Irish Poor Law of 1838 imposed the British workhouse system on a society in no way comparable to that for which it had been designed. During 1845–50 a Liberal government paralysed, in part, by its commitment to the principles of *laissez faire* failed spectacularly to respond to a desperate Irish need. But these undoubted failures must be set against other developments. Even in the first half of the nineteenth century piecemeal initiatives in state sponsored economic investment, consolidated and systematised from 1831 by the creation of the Board of Works, the introduction from 1833 of publicly funded elementary or 'national' schools, and the creation by 1845 of what was by contemporary standards an advanced public health system, all testified to a pattern of government quite different from what operated in other parts of the United Kingdom.[12] Interventionist policies under centralised state control continued in the decades after 1850, extending to a widening range of areas of Irish life. By the early twentieth century the chaotic superstructure of boards and commissions that dominated the Irish public sector were an object of derision to British and Irish reformers alike.[13] Yet, from another point of view, this very departure from British administrative norms testified to a willingness to adapt the structures of the union to the needs and preferences of Irish public life.[14]

The other great issue left unresolved at the time of the union was the Catholic question. There can be little doubt that the postponement of emancipation until 1829, and its eventual achievement as a concession extorted from a reluctant establishment, were disastrous for the long term development of relationships both within Ireland and between Ireland and Great Britain. Once again, however, this unquestionable failure must be set against more positive developments. If British governments in the first three decades of the union failed to grasp the nettle of emancipation, they already demonstrated in other ways a growing recognition of the need to avoid extremes of partisan religious identification.[15] In the period after 1829 the pace of change accelerated rapidly. Moves towards a more even handed distribution of patronage commenced during 1835–41 by a Whig government dependent on O'Connellite support in parliament were continued after 1843 by a Tory ministry anxious to consolidate its success in facing down the repeal movement.[16] The Irish version of the assault on Old Corruption was the dismantling of long established Protestant monopolies. Meanwhile the centralisation in Dublin Castle of control over policing, education and a range of other functions made possible the development of a state apparatus that was, in religious terms, increasingly neutral. In the second half of the century the circle of opportunity available to educated Catholics continued to widen, while the disestablishment in 1870 of the Church of Ireland completed the dismantling of the formal structures of the Protestant state.

[12] Oliver MacDonagh, *Ireland* (Englewood Cliffs, N.J. 1968), chap. 1, 2; Gearóid Ó Tuathaigh, *Ireland Before the Famine 1798–1848* (Dublin, 1972), chap. 3.

[13] Nicholas Mansergh, *The Unresolved Question: The Anglo-Irish Settlement and its Undoing 1912–72* (1991), 15–18.

[14] Eunan O'Halpin, 'The Politics of Governance in the Four Countries of the United Kingdom, 1912–22' in *Kingdoms United? Great Britain and Ireland since 1500 – Integration and Diversity*, ed. S.J. Connolly (Dublin, 1999), 248.

[15] S.J. Connolly, 'Union Government 1812–23', in *A New History of Ireland*, vol. v: *Ireland Under the Union, I: 1800–1870*, ed. W.E. Vaughan (Oxford, 1989), 63–6.

[16] Oliver MacDonagh, *The Emancipist: Daniel O'Connell 1830–47* (1989), 127–31; D.A. Kerr, *Peel, Priests and Politics: Sir Robert Peel's Administration and the Roman Catholic Church in Ireland 1841–1846* (Oxford, 1982).

Discussion of these overtures to Catholic opinion raises the wider question of political allegiances in the decades following the union. At this point the importance of looking forwards as well as backwards from the events of 1799–1800 once again becomes apparent. Recent studies have placed growing emphasis on the 1790s as a pivotal decade, supposedly characterised by unprecedentedly high levels of popular political awareness and representing a formative period in the evolution of both unionist and nationalist political identities.[17] When we turn to the period immediately following the union, on the other hand, the outstanding feature to observe is its placidity. For a quarter of a century, until the electoral triumphs of the Catholic Association in 1826–8, Irish political life was dominated by the rivalries of long established landed interests, whose power rested on their ability to command the votes of a docile and apparently deferential tenantry. In a slightly longer perspective, the most remarkable development of the post-union decades was the almost complete reversal that took place in the relationship between religion and political allegiance. By the 1840s Catholics, who had for the most part either supported or passively accepted the union, had become the main supporters of the movement for its repeal, while Protestants, many of whom had vigorously resisted the measure, were now largely united in their determination to preserve it unchanged. In both cases a consideration of developments after 1800 suggests that the emphasis on politicisation, and on the establishment of fixed political identities, that dominates recent work on the 1790s should be modified by a recognition of the continued fluidity of both Catholic and Protestant attitudes. Such a conclusion has obvious implications for any assessment of the long term prospects of the union settlement.

How long did this fluidity persist? Recent work cautions against teleology. Among Irish Protestants the growing commitment of the majority to the maintenance of the union must be set against the continued appeal of cultural nationalism, from the 'Orange Young Irelanders' of the *Dublin University Magazine* in the 1830s to the Gaelic League of the early twentieth century.[18] There was also the minority tradition of Protestant political nationalism represented by Young Ireland and later by a section of the early Home Rule movement. Where Irish Catholics are concerned, movements for self-government alternated or competed with attempts to ally with the forces of reform

[17] See, in particular, James Smyth, *The Men of No Property: Irish Radicals and Popular Politics in the Late Eighteenth Century* (1992); Kevin Whelan, *The Tree of Liberty: Radicalism, Catholicism and the Construction of Irish Identity 1760–1830* (Cork, 1996).

[18] David Cairns and Shaun Richards, *Writing Ireland: Colonialism, Nationalism and Culture* (Manchester, 1988), chap. 2; Thomas Flanagan, 'Nationalism: The Literary Tradition', in *Perspectives on Irish Nationalism*, ed. T.E. Hachey and L.J. McCaffrey (Lexington, 1989), 61–78.

elsewhere in the United Kingdom, from O'Connell's 'compact' with the Whig ministry during 1835–41 to the surge of support for Gladstonian Liberalism in the aftermath of the Fenian rising of 1867.[19] Even Parnell's Home Rule party, generally seen as the high point of nationalist political mobilisation in the nineteenth century, had by the end of the 1880s become firmly tied to the British Liberals, an alliance which continued up to the collapse of constitutional nationalism in 1916–18.

The impulse to search for turning points in history remains strong. The mass mobilisation of the 1820s, provoked by the earlier failure to grant Catholic emancipation, the terrible consequences of the government's mishandling of the Famine crisis, the failure of Gladstone's 'justice for Ireland' to meet expectations, can all be singled out as significant moments, each with implications for Ireland's place within the United Kingdom. But that is probably as far as it is wise to go. The act of union lasted one hundred and twenty years, more than four decades longer than the history of the independent Irish state. Throughout that period successive British governments showed a willingness to respond to Irish grievances with far reaching concessions, extending to the sacrifice first of the established church and then of the landlord class, and finally to the establishment of a domestic legislature. The great majority of Irish Catholics, for their part, showed a consistent willingness, right up to the First World War, to be satisfied by something less than secession. There was always a gap between Irish aspirations and British willingness to conciliate. The extent of that gap, moreover, fluctuated over time, in ways that might possibly be interpreted as affecting the likelihood that the whole political structure of the union would at some stage collapse. To go further than that, however, to try to pin point the moment at which such a collapse became inevitable, would be to reinterpret a relative as an absolute. In addition it would be to assume linear direction where there is no real reason except hindsight to assume that anything so purposeful existed.

[19] For a powerful statement both of the argument for seeing the 1850s and 1860s as the high point of Ireland's integration into the United Kingdom, and of the central significance of political developments in the years 1868–72, see R.V. Comerford in *New History of Ireland*, v, chap. 20–3.

ROYAL HISTORICAL SOCIETY: REPORT OF COUNCIL.
Session 1999–2000

Activities of the Society during the Year.

- The Society's website - www.rhs.ac.uk, set up with the kind co-operation of the Institute of Historical Research, is now fully operational. Details of the Society's activities, of its prizes and of its research support schemes (including application forms) can be found there, together with the constitution, the late Professor R.A. Humphrey's history of the Society from 1868 to 1968 and the List of Fellows, Corresponding Fellows, Associates and Members with their research interests.
- The Society has continued to be closely involved with archival issues of importance to historians. The Society's submissions to the Lords and Commons' committees on the freedom of information bill, noted in last year's report, appear to have produced a generally satisfactory response. The government has stated its intention to concede most of the points made by the Society. In particular, it has promised to ensure that the Lord Chancellor's Advisory Council continues to have a strong role.
- A Royal Historical Society Archives Group has been set up on the initiative of the Honorary Secretary in order to provide a regular forum for the Society's archival interests. The group has responded to new government initiatives in creating a national Museum, Libraries and Archives Council, now known as "Resource", and in encouraging the development of regional cultural policies. Representatives of the Society will serve on the new English Regional Archives Councils.
- The Society has also given advice on future archival policies in Scotland following devolution in response to a request from the National Archives of Scotland. Close co-operation continues between the Society and the Public Record Office. The Society responded to the consultation document for the disposition of deposited public records. The Society has accepted the Public Record Office's request to suggest names from time to time to review recommendations on the preservation or disposal of particular categories of recent records.
- A one-day colloquium on an especially important and sensitive

issue of archive policy, 'Privacy and Secrecy: The Historian's Interest', was organised by the Honorary Secretary at the Institute of Historical Research on 5 February 2000. A large audience heard a number of illuminating papers, both on current policy issues and on the history of concepts of secrecy and privacy.

- Other issues of importance to historians with which the Society has been concerned this year included two relating to teaching for first degrees in history. The Society provided a forum for discussions between the groups that were making bids for the new teaching centre in history, archaeology and classics and it has continued to monitor developments in the Quality Assurance Agency's benchmarking scheme in support of the report submitted by a group on which the Society was represented. Responses have been made to the British Academy's Review of Research Support, to the Quality Assurance Agency's proposals on postgraduate qualifications, to the ESRC's statement of its future policy for thematic priorities, to the consultation document on the working methods and criteria to be used by the history panel for the 2001 Research Assessment Exercise and to the Higher Education Funding Council for England's request for views on the future of the Research Assessment Exercise. The Society also responded to the Scottish Higher Education Funding Council's consultation document on the future funding of research in Scotland.
- While recognising that the problems facing history teaching in British schools are primarily the concern of the Historical Association, a body with which the Society enjoys the most cordial relations, Council has kept a close watch on developments. Excessive specialisation by A level students in a narrow range of modern topics is a cause of general concern throughout higher education in history. The Society joined with the Historical Association and with the History at the Universities Defence Group in making representations about the disappearance of any option on early medieval history at A level. One of the examination boards subsequently agreed to reinstate such an option. The Society was represented at a discussion of A level options at the Historical Association's education conference. We have been consulted by the Qualifications and Curriculum Authority about the criteria for GCSE history and have decided to give a financial subvention to the Historical Association's campaign to persuade students to take history as a GCSE option. This subvention will replace the sum given in previous years to the Young Historian Scheme, which the Historical Association has decided to terminate.
- The annual volume of the Society's *Transactions* included papers from two conferences, 'Oral History, Memory and Written Tradition' and

'Medieval Communities'. Four Camden Society volumes appeared this year: two scheduled for the current year and two due in the previous one. Michael Jones's revision of the late Professor C.R. Cheney's *A Handbook of Dates* was also published. Council agreed to a new policy whereby Fellows, Associates and Members would from the beginning of the financial year 2000/2001 be entitled under their subscriptions only to the annual volume of *Transactions*. *Camden* volumes together with *Guides and Handbooks* when available and, a most important innovation, volumes in the *Studies in History* series will be available on order at heavily discounted prices. The Society's initial five-year contract with the Cambridge University Press expires on 31 December 2000. A new contract with revised terms to take effect thereafter has been signed with the Press. *Studies in History* continues to fulfill an urgent need in publishing high quality monographs, usually based on theses. Six volumes have appeared this year.

- Dr. Ian Archer has succeeded Dr. Julian Hoppit as general editor of the Society's bibliographies. With a generous subvention from the Arts and Humanities Research Board, work continues on the revision of the *Royal Historical Society Bibliography on the History of Britain, Ireland and the British Overseas*. The first version of this appeared in 1998 on CD-ROM, listing some 250,000 items. The new version will be published in 2002, listing some 320,000 items. Negotiations are taking place to arrange on-line publication with the hope that it might be possible to provide free public access. The 1998 volume of the Society's *Annual Bibliography* was published this year. It lists 6290 items. Dr. Austin Gee was again the general editor of the volume. As always, the appearance of this volume depends on the devoted services of the scholars who have undertaken to edit sections of it.
- In order to recognise the high quality of work now being produced at undergraduate level in the form of third-year dissertations, the Society has instituted, in association with *History Today* magazine, an annual prize for the best undergraduate dissertation. Departments have been asked to nominate annually their best dissertation and a joint committee of the Society and *History Today* will select in the autumn of 2000 the first national prizewinner from among these nominations. The prize also recognizes the Society's close relations with *History Today* and the important role the magazine has played in disseminating scholarly research to a wider audience.
- The Society continues its close involvement with the British National Committee of the International Committee of Historical Sciences. The Committee provided financial support, which included a welcome grant of £6,000 from the British Academy, for 33 scholars

from Britain to attend the 19th Quinquennial Congress at Oslo, 6th–13th August 2000. It also gave a subvention this session to the 3rd Collaborative Anglo-Japanese Conference to be held at the Institute of Historical Research on 27th–29th September 2000.

Meetings of the Society.

- Five papers were given in London this year and two papers were read at locations outside London. Welcome invitations were extended to the Society to visit the history departments at the Universities of Huddersfield and Warwick. What has become an established pattern was followed on these visits; Members of Council meet with the departments to discuss issues of interest to historians before the paper is delivered. The Society always receives a warm welcome and generous hospitality from the universities that it visits and is very grateful to them for their kindness.
- The second Gresham lecture was given to a very large and appreciative audience by Lord Briggs at Gresham College on 'Exhibiting the Nation:1851,1951 and 2000'. These lectures will in future be entitled the Colin Matthew lectures for the Public Understanding of History in memory of the late Professor Colin Matthew, a former Literary Director and Vice-President of the Society whose sudden death in October 1999 came as a great shock and sadness to the whole community of historians.
- The Society held a joint conference in Belfast with the history department of the Queen's University and the Public Record Office of Northern Ireland from 9 to 11 September 1999 on the 'British-Irish Union of 1801'. An audience of some sixty people was attracted, primarily from Northern Ireland and the Irish Republic, to hear papers of high quality.
- From 16-18 September the Society joined with the British Society for the History of Science and the National Museum and Galleries on Merseyside as sponsors of a conference 'On Time', This was a large international gathering with many and varied sessions.

Prizes

The Society's annual prizes were awarded as follows:

- The Alexander Prize, for an essay by a younger scholar, attracted fourteen entries. The Prize for 2000 was awarded to Dr. Helen Berry for her essay 'Rethinking Politeness in Eighteenth-Century England: Moll King's Coffee House and the Significance of Flash Talk' which was read to the Society on 7 April 2000.

Dr. Tim Thornton was declared *proxime accessit* for his essay 'Fifteenth-Century Durham and the Problem of Provincial Liberties in England and the Wider Territories of the English Crown'.

- The David Berry Prize for an essay on any approved topic of Scottish history attracted three entries. The Prize for 1999 was awarded to Elizabeth Ewan for her essay:

'Many injurious words: defamation and gender in late medieval Scotland'. An attractively written and carefully organised discussion drawing on a wide range of sources from burgh records to poetry, concludes that 'verbal and physical violence can be very similar in their power to wound'. Women defamed other women as unchaste, or unfaithful, or as thieves; women defamed men as adulterers; men defamed other men of sexual misconduct, or theft, or heresy; and men defamed their rulers as corrupt and partial. In Elgin Megot Stuart called Ellen and Magaret Ternway 'shabbit, clangorit carlis birdis [scabby syphilitic churl's women]; Ellen countered by calling Megot a 'schabit, bleit, clangorit carling [a scabbed, blear-eyed, syphilitic old women]'. And the poet William Dunbar, no stranger to scurrility himself, complained that the principal streets of Edunburgh were full not only of the stink of haddock but also of the 'cyris of carlingis [old women]' and 'fowsum flyttingis of defame' [foul and insulting defamation].

- The Whitfield Prize for a first book on British history attracted 27 entries. The generally high quality of the entries was commended by the assessors.

The Whitfield Prize 1999 was awarded to John Walter for his book, *Understanding Popular Violence in the English Revolution: The Colchester Plunderers*, published by Cambridge University Press.

Andy Wood's book *The Politics of Social Conflict: The Peak Country, 1520-1770* [CUP] was declared *proxime accessit.*

The entry for the Whitfield prize was very strong, and the judges had an exceptionally difficult choice to make. Although they managed to whittle the short list down to two books, a final decision between two outstanding studies in early modern social history proved almost impossible. Both books had many strengths – one taking a particular event in Colchester in 1642 and analysing the context in impressive detail, the other taking the lead miners of the Peak over a long period of time. Both provide models of local history, the use of a sense of place in order to address large questions of social change. And both are published by Cambridge University Press. In the end, the judges decided that Andy Wood's *The Politics of Social Conflict: The Peak Country, 1520-1770* should be the *proxime accessit.* This is an outstanding book, addressing many major questions from the civil war to the industrial revolution, from the history of custom and class, to the details of a major industry in early modern England. But the judges decided to award the prize to John Walter for his *Understanding Popular Violence in the English Revolution: The Colchester Plunderers*. It is a story of Essex man, of Sir John Lucas who sneaked out of his house in 1642 to join Charles I, and was set upon by a crowd from Colchester, who wrecked his house and gardens, killed his deer and even broke into his family vault. John Walter effortlessly and elegantly explains the background to this event, weaving together the micro-politics of the attack on Lucas in terms of the local politics of Colchester with the high politics of the civil war. He teases out the motivations of the crowd, in terms of the tensions with the local cloth industry and their confessional allegiances. And the result is a book with major implications for the understanding of the civil war and of popular culture. Rather than class hostility, or a conservative use of custom, Walter shows how protest was contained by linking popular culture with parliamentary political culture in a way which legitimated attacks on the political, but not the social order. It is a work of mature and subtle scholarship, which tells a gripping story with elegance and style, and explains it with insight and acuity.

- Thanks to a continuing generous donation from The Gladstone Memorial Trust, the third Gladstone History Book Prize for a first book on a subject outside British history was awarded. There were 16 entries.

The Gladstone History Book Prize 1999 was awarded to Frances Stonor Saunders for her book, *Who Paid the Piper? The CIA and the Cultural Cold War* (Granta Books).

Matthew Kempshall's book *The Common Good in Late Medieval Political Thought* [OUP] was declared *proxime accessit.*

This year there were sixteen submissions from twelve publishers, covering a range of periods and topics. All were interesting; half a dozen were strong contenders; in the end, two stood out. Both were so good that we decided to designate one of them proxime accessit, signalling how close it came to the winner.
The book to which we have awarded the prize is Frances Stonor Saunders' *Who Paid the Piper? The CIA and the Cultural Cold War*, published by Granta. This is outstanding contemporary history, with a good use of interview material supplementing the available documentation; in many areas it is revelatory. Importantly, it is non-political – no mean achievement in an area of such continuing political and diplomatic relevance. The book is very well-written, and this, plus its topic, will ensure its appeal to a wide range of readers. It is a worthy winner.
Proxime accessit Matthew Kempshall's *The Common Good in Late-Medieval*

Political Thought (OUP 1999) deals with a perennially interesting question: how can the claims of the individual and the common good be squared? Kempshall shows how modern commentators have misrepresented later medieval responses, and underestimated the ongoing influences of Roman-legal, Ciceronian, and Augustinian conceptions of the common good. Attentive both to historical context and ideological tradition, Kempshall examines the ways thirteenth- and early fourteenth-century thinkers discussed key political issues. He concludes that the rediscovery of Aristotle did not secularise political thought; instead, a revised Augustinian relativism, along with the Bible, remained pervasive. This is a beautifully written book of intellectual distinction. It clarifies its medieval subject but also illuminates western political thinking from Antiquity to the present.

- Frampton and Beazley Prizes for A-level performances were awarded following nominations from the examining bodies:

Frampton Prizes

- The Associated Examining Board:
  Emma Louise Teale, Oaklands College, Welwyn Garden City
- Edexcel Foundation incorporating the London Examination Board:
  Robert E.J. Crumpton, Manchester Grammar School
- Northern Examinations and Assessment Board:
  Naomi Law, Wellington Girls' School, Manchester
- Oxford and Cambridge School Examinations Board:
  no candidate was nominated this year
- University of Cambridge Local Examinations Syndicate:
  no candidate was nominated this year
- University of Oxford Delegacy of Local Examinations:
  no candidate was nominated this year
- Welsh Joint Education Committee:
  Polly C.R. Canning, Ysgol Friars, Bangor

Beazley Prizes

- Northern Ireland Council for the Curriculum Examinations and Assessment: Elian M. McCorry, Our Lady and St. Patrick's College, Belfast
- Scottish Examination Board:
  David A. Eynon, George Heriot's School, Edinburgh.

- The Royal Historical Society Centenary Fellowship for the academic year 1999-2000 was awarded to Helen Denham registered at Oxford University and working on a D.Phil. thesis entitled

'Africa as a "Living Laboratory". The African Research Survey and the British Colonial Empire: Consolidating and applying Environmental, Medical and Anthropological Ideas, 1925-1945'. The Fellowship for the academic year 1998-1999 had been awarded to Marcella Simoni registered at University College London and working on a Ph.D. entitled 'Welfare in British Palestine: Education and Health, 1929-1939'.

Publications

Transactions, Sixth Series, Volume 9 was published during the session, and *Transactions,* Sixth Series, Volume 10 went to press, to be published in November 2000.

In the Camden, Fifth Series, Fleet Street, Press Barons and Politics: The Journals of Collin Brooks, 1932-1940, ed. N.J. Crowson (Volume 11) and *Newsletters from the Archpresbyterate of George Birkhead, 1609-1614* ed. M.C. Questier (Volume 12) were published during the session, after some delays. Further volumes published in the Series were *The Journal of Thomas Juxon, 1644-1647*', ed. Keith Lindley and David Scott (No. 13) and *Parliament and Politics in the Age of Churchill and Attlee: The Headlam Diaries, 1935-1951*, ed. Stuart Ball (No. 14). *British Envoys to Germany, 1816-1866. Volume 1: 1816-1829*, ed. Sabine Freitag and Peter Wende (No. 15) and *An Appeasement Diary: A.L. Kennedy and The Times*, ed. Gordon Martel (No. 16) went to press during the year.

A revised edition of *A Handbook of Dates* edited by C.R. Cheney and Michael Jones was published in the *Guides and Handbooks* series (No. 20) by Cambridge University Press.

The Society's *Annual Bibliography of British and Irish History, Publications of 1998*, was published by Oxford University Press during the session, and the *Annual Bibliography of British and Irish History, Publications of 1999* went to press, to be published in 2000.

The *Studies in History* second series continued to produce exciting volumes. As scheduled, the following volumes were published during the session, *Science, Religion and Politics in Restoration England: Richard Cumberland's De Legibus Naturae* by Jonathan Parkin; *Artful Dodgers: Youth and Crime in Early Nineteenth-Century London* by Heather Shore; *Cornwall Politics in the Age of Reform, 1790-1885* by Edwin Jaggard; *Protection and Politics: Conservative Economic Discourse, 1815-1852* by Anna Gambles; *Patterns of Philanthropy: Charity and Society in Nineteenth-Century Bristol* by Martin Gorsky; and *Charity and the London Hospitals, 1850-1898* by Keir Waddington.

Massacre at the Champ de Mars: Popular Dissent and Political Culture in the French Revolution by David Andress was due to be published early in the next session. Also scheduled for publication were *Cheshire and the Tudor*

State, 1480-1560 by Tim Thornton; *French Exile Journalism and European Politics, 1792-1814* by Simon Burrows; *The Drawing Down of the Blinds: The Commemoration of the Great War in the City and East London, 1916-1939* by Mark Connelly and *The Practice of Penance, 900-1050* by Sarah Hamilton. These, together with *The Moravian Church's contribution to the Missionary Awakening in England, 1760 to c.1800* by John Cecil Strickland Mason, will all feature in a launch to be held after the Anniversary Meeting and Presidential Address on 24 November 2000. As in previous years, the membership of the Society will be invited to attend.

Papers Read

At the ordinary meetings of the Society the following papers were read:

'The divergence of England: economic and demographic growth in the seventeenth and eighteenth-centuries'
Professor Sir Tony Wrigley (7 July 1999: Prothero Lecture)
'Regional Diversity in the Later Russian Empire'
Dr. David Saunders (22 October 1999 at the University of Huddersfield)
'The Blues, the Folk and African-American History'
Dr. Marybeth Hamilton (21 January 2000 at the University of Warwick)
'A Profane History of Early Modern Oaths'
Dr. John Spurr (10 March 2000)
'Purity and Danger in Late Medieval Europe'
Dr. Miri Rubin (19 May 2000)

At the Anniversary meeting on 26 November 1999, the President, Professor P.J. Marshall, delivered an address on 'Britain and the World in the Eighteenth Century: III. Britain and India'.
At the Conference entitled 'The British-Irish Union of 1801' held at The Queen's University of Belfast, on 9-11 September 1999, the following papers were read:

'The Union in a European context' Professor William Doyle
'The Union in British History' Professor J.G.A. Pocock
'Britain and the Union, 1797-1801' Professor Peter Jupp
'Alliances and Misalliances in the Politics of the Union' Professor L.M. Cullen
'The Catholics and the Union' Dr. Patrick Geoghegan
'Popular Politics in Ireland and the Act of Union' Dr. James Kelly
'The Irish Peerage and the Union, 1700-1971' Dr. A.P.W. Malcomson
'The Union and the Military, 1801-c.1830' Dr. Allan Blackstock
'Politics, Public Finance and The British-Irish Act of Union of 1801'
Dr. Trevor McCavery
'Ireland, India and the Empire, 1780-1914' Professor C.A. Bayly
'Reconsidering the Irish Act of Union' Professor S.J. Connolly.

Finance

The Society continues to enjoy a healthy financial state overall, with the endowment increasing from £2,616,816 in June 1999 to £2,693,805 in June 2000, an increase of £76,989. Our net investment income has decreased from £109,673 to £90,389 during the same period, primarily as a result of three factors: first, the upheavals in the technology sector; secondly, the general slow-down in global economic growth; and thirdly, the timing of last year's modification of our investment strategy, which was to re-invest some of our investment income in growth stocks. Council continues to support a rigorous control of expenditure across the Society's activities, a goal facilitated by a change in our publishing policy. The Society this year had an operating deficit of £24,637, compared with an operating surplus for last year of £11,787.

Council records with gratitude the benefactions made to the Society by:

Mr. L.C. Alexander
The Reverend David Berry
Professor Andrew Browning
Professor C.D. Chandaman
Professor G. Donaldson
Professor Sir Geoffrey Elton
Mr. E. J. Erith
Mrs. W.M. Frampton
Mr. A.E.J. Hollaender
Professor C.J. Holdsworth
Professor P.J. Marshall
The Mercers' Company
Mr. E.L.C. Mullins
Sir George Prothero
Professor T.F. Reddaway
Miss E.M. Robinson
The Scouloudi Foundation
Professor A.S. Whitfield

Membership

Council was advised and recorded with regret the deaths of 9 Fellows, 3 Life Fellows, 12 Retired Fellows, 2 Corresponding Fellows, 2 Associates and 1 Member. These included Miss A. Armstrong, a former Librarian and Secretary, and Professor H.C.G. Matthew, former Literary Director and Vice-President.

77 Fellows, 15 Members and 1 Corresponding Fellow were elected. The

membership of the Society on 30 June 2000 numbered 2465, comprising 1745 Fellows, 395 Retired Fellows, 23 Life Fellows, 12 Honorary Vice-Presidents, 92 Corresponding Fellows, 104 Associates and 94 Members. The Society exchanged publications with 15 Societies, British and Foreign.

Officers and Council

At the Anniversary Meeting on 26 November 1999, Professor J.L. Nelson was elected to succeed Professor P.J. Marshall as President after the Anniversary Meeting on 24 November 2000; the remaining Officers of the Society were re-elected.

The Vice-Presidents retiring under By-law XVII were Professor M.D. Biddiss and Dr. A.M.S. Prochaska. Professor J.A. Tosh and Mrs. S.J. Tyacke were elected to replace them.

The Members of Council retiring under By-law XX were Professor D. Bates, Dr. A.E. Curry, Professor J.A. Guy and Professor R.I. Moore. In accordance with By-law XXI, amended, Professor C.M. Andrew, Dr. J.E. Burton and Professor T.A. Reuter were elected in their place. Professor A.E. Goodman resigned as a Member of Council during the session.

MacIntyre and Company were appointed auditors for the year 1999-2000 under By-law XXXIX.

Representatives of the Society

The representation of the Society upon various bodies was as follows:

Mr. M. Roper, Professor P.H. Sawyer and Mr. C.P. Wormald on the Joint Committee of the Society and the British Academy established to prepare an edition of Anglo-Saxon charters;

Professor N.P. Brooks on a committee to promote the publication of photographic records of the more significant collections of British Coins;

Professor G.H. Martin on the Council of the British Records Association;

Professor M.R.D. Foot on the Committee to advise the publishers of *The Annual Register*;

Dr. G.W. Bernard on the History at the Universities Defence Group;

Professor C.J. Holdsworth on the Court of the University of Exeter;

Professor D. d'Avray on the Anthony Panizzi Foundation;

Professor M.C. Cross on the Council of the British Association for Local History; and on the British Sub-Commission of the Commission International d'Histoire Ecclesiastique Comparée;

Miss V. Cromwell on the Advisory Board of the Computers in

Teaching Initiative Centre for History; and on the Advisory Committee of the TLTP History Courseware Consortium;

Dr. A.M.S. Prochaska on the National Council on Archives; and on the Advisory Council of the reviewing committee on the Export of Works of Art;

Professor R.A. Griffiths on the Court of Governors of the University of Wales, Swansea;

Professor A.L. Brown on the University of Stirling Conference;

Professor W. Davies on the Court of the University of Birmingham;

Professor R.D. McKitterick on a committee to regulate British co-operation in the preparation of a new repertory of medieval sources to replace Potthast's *Bibliotheca Historica Medii Aevi*;

Professor J. Breuilly on the steering committee of the proposed British Centre for Historical Research in Germany.

Council received reports from its representatives.

15 September 2000

RESEARCH SUPPORT COMMITTEE AWARDS
Session 1999–2000

TRAINING BURSARIES

David Richard ADAMS, Pembroke College, Cambridge
The annual meeting of the North American Conference on British Studies at Pasadena, USA, on 13 – 15 October 2000.

Simon John BAALHAM, Oxford Brookes University
The Millennial Conference of the Social History Society on "Envisioning Futures", at Gonville and Caius College, Cambridge on 6 - 8 January 2000.

Cordelia BEATTIE, University of York
35th International Congress on Medieval Studies at Kalamazoo, USA, on 4 – 7 May 2000.

Ruth Margaret BLAKELY, University of Durham
International Medieval Congress at the University of Leeds on 10 – 13 July 2000.

Lucia DACOME, University of Cambridge
The Tenth International Congress on the Enlightenment in Dublin on 25 - 31 July 1999:

Alexis DE GREIFF, Centre for the History of Science, Imperial College, London
Workshop on American Philanthropic Foundations at Geneva on 24 – 26 May 2000.

Cristian Anton GAZDAC, Faculty of Literae Humaniores, University of Oxford
'Limes XVIII - Roman Frontieres' Conference, in Amman, Jordan on 1 - 12 September 2000.

Carolyn GROHMANN, University of Stirling
Conference for the Society for the Study of French History at Sheffield on 18 – 19 April 2000.

Jason Lee HEPPELL, University of Sheffield
'Class and Politics in Historical and Contemporary Perspectives': 21st North

American Labor History Conference, held in Detroit, USA, on 21 - 23 October 1999.

Andrew Christopher KING, University of Durham
International Medieval Congress at the University of Leeds on 10 – 13 July 2000.

Ilaria MELICONI, Linacre College, Oxford
Society for the History of Technology 2000 in Munich on 17 – 20 August 2000.

Kornelis Jan Willem OOSTHOEK, University of Stirling
Conference 'Transitions Towards a Sustainable Europe; Ecology – Economy – Policy', at Vienna on 3 – 6 May 2000.

Andrew Duncan PETERSEN, Cardiff University
Colloquium on the History of the Ayyobids and Mamluks in Syria and Egypt, at Leuven, Belgium, on 11th – 12th May 2000.

Caterina PIZZIGONI, King's College London
Nahaute Summer Course at the Yale Summer Foreign Language Institute, Yale University, USA, on 5 June – 7 July 2000.

Glyn William POWELL, University College London
Conference 'New Methods in History' [Socrates Summer School], at the University of Bergen, Norway, on 10 - 19 September 1999.

Helen M.L. PUSSARD, University of Manchester
'The North American Conference on British Studies, at Cambridge, Massachusetts, on 19 – 21 November 1999.

Katherine Elizabeth QUINN, University College London
32nd Annual Conference of the Association of Caribbean Historians at Cayenne, French Guiana on 17 – 21 April 2000.

Stefka RITCHIE, University of Central England
Conference of the British Society for the Eighteenth Century, at the University of Aberdeen, on 10 - 14 August 2000.

Rhonda Anne SEMPLE, King's College London
Annual Meeting of the Association of Asian Studies, in San Diego, California, 9 - 12 March 2000.
and

Conference, 'The Worlds of the East India Company, 1600-1834', at the National Maritime Museum, London, on 13 – 15 July 2000.

Yuri Petrov STOYANOV, Warburg Institute, University of London
18th Quinquennial Congress of the International Association for the History of Religions, at Durban, South Africa on 5 – 12 August 2000.

Robin McGregor WARD, Birkbeck College, London
Conference of the Association for the History of the Northern Seas, at the Memorial University of Newfoundland, Canada, on 8 - 15 August 1999:

RESEARCH FUND:

Research within the United Kingdom:

Marion Elizabeth ADDY, University of East Anglia
Visit to PRONI, Belfast.

Sara Anne BONADIO, Southampton University
Visits to Somerset Record Office and Norfolk Record Office.

Alison Margaret CATHCART, University of Aberdeen
Visit to the British Library and Public Record Office, London.

Kimberly Denise CHRISMAN, University of Aberdeen
Visit to archives at the University of Leeds and at Bakewell, Derbyshire.

Nicholas Martin COTT, University of Newcastle-upon-Tyne
Visit to various archives in the United Kingdom.

Ulrike Carmen EHRET, King's College London
Visits to various Catholic diocesan archives in the U.K.

Jonathan Andrew JOHNSTON, University of St. Andrews
Visit to the PRO and the British Library, London.

Stephen JOYCE, University of Nottingham
Visit to various record offices, etc. in England.

David Andrew James MACPHERSON, Birkbeck College, University of London
Visit to archives in Dublin.

Susan Kathryn PARKINSON, University of Lancaster
Visits to various archives in England.

Kirsten PEDERSEN, Queen's University of Belfast
Visit to archives in Armagh.

Jared Roger Matthew SIZER, Corpus Christi College, Cambridge
Visit to various archives, primarily in Edinburgh.

Kevin SORRENTINO, University of Nottingham
Visit to archives in London.

Frederick Carmack TAYLOR, University of Birmingham
Visit to the Northampton Record Office.

Elizabeth Parsonage THOMSON, University of Dundee
Visit to archives in Glasgow and Edinburgh.

Rodanthi TZANELLI, Lancaster University
Visit to the British Library, Newspaper Library, London.

Research outside the United Kingdom

Sarah BADCOCK, University of Durham
Visit to archives in Russia.

Rachel Elisabeth BELL, University of Reading
Visit to archives in San Francisco, USA.

Emma Louise CHRISTOPHER, University College London
Visit to various archives in the USA.

Adam DAVIS, University of Luton
Visit to archives in Auckland, New Zealand.

Kate DOSSETT, University of Warwick
Visit to archives in New York and Washington, USA.

Karl GALLE, Imperial College, London
Visits to archives in Austria and Germany.

Keimelo GIMA, Royal Holloway, University of London
Visit to various archives in Australia and Papua, New Guinea.

Janet GREENLEES, University of York
Visit to various archives in USA.

Zoe Ann GREER, University of Newcastle-upon-Tyne
Visit to various archives in the U.S.A.

Andrew Edward JOHNSTONE, University of Birmingham
Visits to various archives in the USA.

Lorna Louise KALS, University of Leeds
Visit to archives in the U.S.A.

Ralph Francis Sydney KINGSTON, University College London
Visit to archives in Paris, France.

Nikolas KOZLOFF, St. Anthony's College, Oxford
Visit to archives in Venezuela.

Stefania LONGO, University College London
Visit to archives in Rome.

Isaac Xerses MALKI, St. Antony's College, Oxford
Visit to the University of Accra, and Kumasi, Ghana, West Africa.

Anna Paola MASSAROTTO, Courtauld Institute of Art, London
Visit to archives in Italy.

James Richard Redmond McCONNEL, University of Durham
Visit to Trinity College Dublin.

Angela Margaret MONTFORD, University of St. Andrews
Visit to Archivio di Stato, Bologna, Italy.

Matthew MORAN, University of East Anglia
Visit to various libraries in Italy:

Jose Lingna NAFAFE, University of Birmingham
Visit to archives in Portugal:

Ruth PERCY, University College London
Visit to the Schlesinger Library, Radcliffe College, Cambridge, Massachusetts, USA.

Nicola PIZZOLATO, University College London
Visit to various archives in the USA.

Rachel RICH, University of Essex
Visit to archives in Paris, France.

Giorgio RIELLO, University College London
Visit to various archives in Paris
and
Visit to archives in France.

Camilla Elizabeth RUSSELL, Royal Holloway, University of London
Visit to archives in Italy.

Lisa Wynne SMITH, University of Essex
Visit to the Bibliothèque Nationale, Paris, France.

Paula Regina STILES, University of St. Andrews
Visit to archives in Barcelona, Spain.

Urara TAGUCHI, Royal Holloway, University of London
Visit to archives at Florence.

Wendy TOON, Keele University
Visit to the National Archives at College Park, Maryland, USA.

David Colin WORTHINGTON, University of Aberdeen
Visit to archives in Austria and the Czech Republic.

Jacob ZUMOFF, University College London
Visit to the Archives of the Communist International [Comintern] in Moscow.

WORKSHOP FUND

Conference, 'Colonial Places, Convict Spaces: penal transportation in global context, c.1600-1940', at the University of Leicester, 9 - 10 December 1999 [Clare ANDERSON].

'The Burdens of the Past', the 14th Annual Conference of the SSFH, at the University of Sheffield, on 18 - 19 April 2000 [Timothy BAYCROFT].

Conference 'Strangers at home, Britons abroad: a conference on seventeenth-century intellectual history', at Wolfson College, Cambridge, on 12 – 13 January 2001 [Robin BUNCE].

'The Classics in British History', annual Neale lecture and colloquium, at University College London, on 3 - 4 March 2000 [Stephen CONWAY].

Fifteenth-Century Conference on the theme 'Social Mobility' at Queen Mary and Westfield College, University of London, on 7 – 9 September 2000 [Virginia DAVIS].

Conference, 'Black Perspectives on Post-War British History', at the Institute of

Historical Research, London, on 21 October 2000 [Michael DAWSWELL].

Conference, 'The Kiss in History', at the Institute of Historical Research, London, on 1 July 2000 [Karen HARVEY].

'"From Strangers to Citizens": Integration of Immigrant communities in Great Britain, Ireland and the Colonies, 1550-1750' at The Dutch Church, London, EC2, on 5 - 7 April 2000 [Charles LITTLETON].

Conference, '"Every Whole and Open": The Reception of Vernacular Scripture in the Middle Ages', at the University of Nottingham on 29 April 2000 [Richard MARSDEN].

Reformation Studies Colloquium at the University of Warwick, 3 - 5 April 2000 [Peter MARSHALL].

International Legal History Conference at the University of Exeter on 23 – 25 March 2000 [A.J. MUSSON].

Conference, 'Alfred the Great, London and Europe, a day colloquium to mark the 1100th anniversary of Alfred's death on 26 October 899', at the Institute of Historical Research, University of London, on 26 October 1999 [J. NELSON].

European Reformation Research Group Annual Conference at the University of Birmingham on 31 August – 3 September 2000 [Alex RYRIE].

Conference, 'Beyond the Gaze: History, Gender and Self-Perception', at the University of Essex on 17 June 2000 [Lisa SMITH].

Conference, 'James Cox Symposium', at the Victoria and Albert Museum, London, on 17 June 2000 [Roger SMITH].

The 6th Annual St. Martin's Postgraduate Conference at the University of Nottingham on 21 June 2000 [Kevin C. SORRENTINO].

Postgraduate workshop, 'New approaches to the history of retailing', at the University of Wolverhampton on 24 May 2000 [Laura UGOLINI].

Conference, 'Transporting Gender: What difference has gender made to consideration of issues and questions in transport history and the history of travel', at the National Railway Museum, York, on 6 and 7 October 2000 [Margaret WALSH].

Conference, 'England and Europe in the Reign of Henry III, 1216-1272', at the University of Wales Swansea on 14 – 16 April 2000 [Bjorn WEILER].

British Rocketry Oral History Programme Annual Conference, at Charterhouse School, Surrey, on 5 – 6 April 2000 [David B. WRIGHT]. [20]

BURSARIES FOR HOLDERS OF ORS AWARDS

Helen Louise DENHAM, Wadham College, Oxford
Merav MACK, University of Cambridge.

CENTENARY FELLOWSHIP

Marcella SIMONI, UCL – 1998/1999
Helen Louise DENHAM, Wadham College, Oxford - 1999/2000

MERCERS' COMPANY AWARD

The Society gratefully acknowledges the receipt of a generous grant of £1,000 for the support of historical research from the Mercers' Company.

THE ROYAL HISTORICAL SOCIETY
FINANCIAL ACCOUNTS
FOR THE YEAR ENDED 30 JUNE 2000

MacIntyre & Co
Chartered Accountants
Registered Auditors
London

LEGAL AND ADMINISTRATIVE INFORMATION

Registered Office:	University College London Gower Street London WC1E 6BT
Charity registration number:	206888
The Honorary Treasurer:	Professor K Burk, MA, DPhil
The Honorary Secretary:	Professor P Mandler, MA, PhD
Auditors:	MacIntyre & Co Chartered Accountants 28 Ely Place London EC1N 6RL
Investment managers:	Cripps, Harries Hall 14 Buckingham Street London WC1N 6DF
Bankers:	Barclays Bank plc 27 Soho Square London WC1A 4WA

A full list of trustees is given in the Trustees' Report.

THE ROYAL HISTORICAL SOCIETY
REPORT OF THE COUNCIL OF TRUSTEES
FOR THE YEAR ENDED 30 JUNE 2000

The members of Council present their report and audited accounts for the year ended 30 June 2000.

PRINCIPAL ACTIVITIES AND REVIEW OF THE YEAR

The Society exists for the promotion and support of historical scholarship and its dissemination to historians and a wider public. This year, as in previous years, it has pursued this objective by an ambitious programme of publications – a volume of Transactions, two volumes of edited texts in the Camden Series and a volume in the Guides and Handbooks series, a new edition of a Handbook of Dates, have all appeared, by the holding of meetings in London and at universities outside London at which papers are delivered, by the sponsoring of the joint lecture for a wider public with Gresham College, by distributing over £20,000 in research support grants to 97 individuals, and by frequent representations to various official bodies where the interests of historical scholarship are involved. It is Council's intention that these activities should be sustained to the fullest extent in the future.

RESULTS

The Society continues to enjoy a healthy financial state overall, with total funds increasing from £2,616,816 in June 1999 to £2,693,805 in June 2000, an increase of £76,989.

Our net investment income has decreased from £109,673 to £90,389 during the same period, primarily as a result of three factors: first, the upheavals in the technology sector; secondly, the general slow-down in global economic growth; and thirdly, the timing of last year's modification of our investment strategy to a total return strategy, which has meant re-investing some of our investment income in growth stocks. The increase in net capital gains from £58,377 to £101,626 has more than compensated for the fall in income. In future years, under the Society's total return strategy some of these gains will be utilised to fund the Society's annual activities rather than relying solely on income.

The Council continues to support a rigorous control of expenditure across the Society's activities, a goal facilitated by a change in our publishing policy.

FIXED ASSETS

Information relating to changes in fixed assets is given in notes 2 and 3 to the accounts.

INVESTMENTS

The Society has adopted a "total return" approach to its investment policy. This means that the funds are invested solely on the basis of seeking to secure the best total level of economic return compatible with the duty to make safe investments, but regardless of the form the return takes.

The Society has adopted this approach to ensure even-handedness between current and future beneficiaries, as the focus of many investments moves away from producing income to producing capital gains. In the current investments climate, to maintain the level of income needed to fund the charity, would require an investment portfolio which would not achieve the optional overall return, so effectively penalising future beneficiaries.

The total return strategy does not make distinctions between income and capital returns. It lumps together all forms of return on investment – dividends, interest, and capital gains etc, to produce a "total return". Some of the total return is then used to meet the needs of present beneficiaries, while the remainder is added to the existing capital to help meet the needs of future beneficiaries.

RESERVES POLICY

The Council have reviewed the Society's need for reserves in line with the guidance issued by the Charity Commission. They believe that the Society requires approximately the current level of restricted general funds to generate sufficient total return, both income and capital, to cover the Society's expenditure in excess of the members' subscription income on an annual basis. The current level of unrestricted reserves of £2,467,587 is therefore necessary to ensure that the Society can run efficiently and meet the needs of current and future beneficiaries.

The Society restricted funds consist of a number of different funds where the donor has imposed restrictions on the use of the funds which are legally binding. The purpose of these funds are set out in note 1.

STATEMENT OF TRUSTEES' RESPONSIBILITIES

The Charities Act of 1993 requires the Council to prepare accounts for each financial year which give a true and fair view of the state of affairs of the Society and of its financial activities for that year. In preparing these accounts, the Trustees are required to:

– select suitable accounting policies and apply them consistently;

– make judgements and estimates that are reasonable and prudent;
– state whether applicable accounting standards have been followed, subject to any material departures disclosed and explained in the accounts;
– prepare the accounts on the going concern basis unless it is inappropriate to presume that the Fund will continue in business.

The Council is responsible for ensuring proper accounting records are kept which disclose, with reasonable accuracy at any time, the financial position of the Society and enable them to ensure that the financial statements comply with the By-laws of the Society and the disclosure regulations. They are also responsible for safeguarding the assets of the Society and hence for taking reasonable steps for the prevention and detection of error, fraud and other irregularities.

MEMBERS OF THE COUNCIL

Professor P J Marshall, MA, DPhil, FBA	– President
Professor J L Nelson, PhD, FBA	– President-elect
Professor P Mandler, MA, PhD	– Honorary Secretary
Professor D S Eastwood, MA, DPhil	– Literary Director
Professor A D M Pettegree, MA, DPhil, FSA	– Literary Director
Professor K Burk, MA, DPhil	– Honorary Treasurer
D A L Morgan, MA, FSA	– Honorary Librarian
Professor D Cannadine, MA, DPhil	– Vice-President
Professor M J Daunton, PhD, FBA	– Vice-President
Professor P J Hennessy, PhD	– Vice-President
Professor A J Fletcher, MA	– Vice President
Professor C J Wrigley, PhD	– Vice President
Professor P A Stafford, DPhil	– Vice President
Professor J A Tosh, MA, PhD	– Vice-President
Mrs S J Tyacke, CB, DPhil, FSA	– Vice President
I W Archer, MA, DPhil	– Member of Council
G W Bernard, MA DPhil	– Member of Council
Professor J C G Binfield, OBE, MA, PhD, FSA	– Member of Council
Professor J M Black, MA, PhD	– Member of Council
Professor M L Dockrill, MA, BSc(Econ), PhD	– Member of Council
Professor V I J Flint, MA, DPhil	– Member of Council
C R J Currie, MA, DPhil	– Member of Council
Professor A E Goodman, MA	– Member of Council
J P Martindale, MA, DPhil	– Member of Council
Professor J L Miller, MA, PhD	– Member of Council
W R Childs, MA, PhD	– Member of Council
Professor R H Trainor, MA, DPhil	– Member of Council
Professor C M Andrew, MA, PhD	– Member of Council
J E Burton, DPhil	– Member of Council
Professor T A Reuter, MA, DPhil	– Member of Council

MEMBERS OF THE COUNCIL

At the Anniversary Meeting on 26th November 1999, Professor P. Mandler was elected to succeed Dr R E Quinault as Honorary Secretary, the remaining officers of the Society were re-elected.

The Vice-Presidents retiring under By-law XVII were Professor P Collinson and Professor R. D McKitterick. Professor D. N. Cannadine and Professor P. A. Stafford were elected to replace them.

The Members of Council retiring under By-law XX were Professor R. C. Bridges, Professor P. J. Corfield, Professor J. L. Nelson and Professor P. A. Stafford. Following a ballot of Fellows, W. R. Childs, Professor M. L. Dockrill, Professor V. I. J. Flint and Professor J. L. Miller were elected in their place.

STANDING COMMITTEES 2000

The Society was operated through the following Committees during 2000:—

Finance Committee:	Professor C. M. Andrew	
	Professor P. J. Hennessy	
	Mr. P. J. C. Firth	– non Council Member
	Professor R. M. Trainor	
	Professor P. Mathias	– non Council Member
	The seven Officers	

General Purposes Committee:	Dr. I.W. Archer	
	Dr. G.W. Bernard	
	Dr. J.E. Burton	
	Professor A.J. Fletcher	
	Professor C.J. Wrigley	
	The seven Officers	
Membership Committee:	Dr. J. P. Martindale	
	Professor J.M. Black	
	Professor M.L. Dockrill	
	Professor P.A. Stafford	
	The six Officers	
Publications Committee:	Professor J.L. Miller	
	Professor M.J. Daunton	
	Dr W.R. Childs	
	Professor T.A. Reuter	
	Professor J.A. Tosh	
	Mrs S.J. Tyacke	
	The seven Officers	
Research Support Committee:	Professor V.I.J. Flint	
	Professor J.C.G. Binfield	
	Professor D.N. Cannadine	
	Dr. C.R.J. Currie	
	The seven Officers	
Studies in History **Editorial Board:**	Professor M.J. Daunton (Convenor)	
	Dr. S. Gunn	– non Council Member
	Professor C. Jones	– non Council Member
	Professor P. Mandler	
	Dr. S. Walker	– non Council Member
	A Literary Director	
	The Honorary Treasurer	
Election of Officers Subcommittee: (President)	Professor P. Stafford (Chairman)	
	Professor M.J. Daunton	
	Professor J.C.G. Binfield	
	Literary Director	
	The Honorary Secretary	

AUDITORS

MacIntyre and Company were appointed auditors for the year 1999–2000 under By-law XXXIX. A resolution to re-appoint Messrs MacIntyre & Co will be submitted to the Anniversary Meeting.

By Order of the Board

Honorary Secretary

15 September 2000

REPORT OF THE AUDITORS

TO THE MEMBERS OF ROYAL HISTORICAL SOCIETY

We have audited the accounts on pages 435 to 441 which have been prepared under the historical cost convention, as modified by the revaluation of fixed asset investments, and the accounting policies set out on page 9.

RESPECTIVE RESPONSIBILITIES OF THE COUNCIL OF TRUSTEES

As described on page 431 the Trustees are responsible for the preparation of accounts. It is our responsibility to form an independent opinion, based on our audit, on those accounts and to report our opinion to you.

BASIS OF OPINION

We conducted our audit in accordance with Auditing Standards issued by the Auditing Practices Board. An audit includes examination, on a test basis, of evidence relevant to the amounts and disclosures in the accounts. It also includes an assessment of the significant estimates and judgements made by the Board of Trustees in the preparation of the accounts, and of whether the accounting policies are appropriate to the Society's circumstances, consistently applied and adequately disclosed.

We planned and performed our audit so as to obtain all the information and explanations which we considered necessary in order to provide us with sufficient evidence to give reasonable assurance that the accounts are free from material misstatement, whether caused by fraud or other irregularity or error. In forming our opinion we also evaluated the overall adequacy of the presentation of information in the accounts.

OPINION

In our opinion the accounts give a true and fair view of the state of the Society's affairs as at 30 June 2000 and of its incoming resources and application of resources for the year then ended, and have been properly prepared in accordance with the Charities Act 1993.

MacIntyre & Co
Chartered Accountants
Registered Auditors

28 Ely Place
London
ECIN 6RL

15 September 2000

THE ROYAL HISTORICAL SOCIETY

Balance Sheet as at 30th June 2000

	Notes	2000 £	2000 £	1999 £	1999 £
Fixed Assets					
Tangible assets	2		2,810		3,848
Investments	3		2,619,660		2,520,276
			2,622,470		2,524,124
Current Assets					
Stocks	1(c)	29,340		30,917	
Debtors	4	42,115		46,104	
Cash at bank and in hand	5	70,120		57,263	
		141,575		134,284	
Less: Creditors					
Amount due within one year	6	(70,240)		(41,592)	
Net Current Assets			71,335		92,692
Net Assets			2,693,805		2,616,816
Represented by:					
Unrestricted – General Fund			2,467,587		2,402,475
Restricted – E. M. Robinson Bequest			116,678		105,974
Restricted – A.S. Whitfield Prize Fund			49,758		45,394
Restricted – BHB Andrew Mellon Fund			59,782		62,973
			2,693,805		2,616,816

Approved by the Council on 15 September 2000

President:

Honorary Treasurer:

The attached notes form an integral part of these financial statements.

THE ROYAL HISTORICAL SOCIETY

Consolidated Statement of Financial Activities for the Year Ended 30 June 2000

	Notes	Unrestricted Funds General Fund £	Restricted Funds E M Robinson Bequest £	A S Whitfield Prize Fund £	BHB/ Andrew Mellon Fund £	2000 Total £	*1999 Total* £
INCOMING RESOURCES							
Members' subscriptions							
—net		63,165	—	—	—	63,165	67,209
—tax recovered on Deeds of Covenant and Gift Aid		3,191	—	—	—	3,191	3,766
		66,356	—	—	—	66,356	70,975
Donations and legacies	7	11,461	—	—	—	11,461	5,292
Total Voluntary Income		77,817	—	—	—	77,817	76,267
Royalties and reproduction fees		48,197	—	—	—	48,197	59,138
Total Income before investment income		126,014	—	—	—	126,014	135,405
Investment income		86,439	2,217	738	995	90,389	109,673
Gross Incoming Resources in the Year		£212,453	£2,217	£738	£995	£216,403	£245,078
RESOURCES USED							
Grants and prizes payable	8	(34,175)		(1,000)	—	(35,175)	(30,485)
Direct charitable expenditure	9	(168,165)	—	—	(4,186)	(172,351)	(169,962)
Administration expenses	10	(33,514)	—	—	—	(33,514)	(32,844)
Total Resources used		(235,854)	—	(1,000)	(4,186)	(241,040)	(233,291)
Net Incoming/Outgoing Resources (Operating surplus)		(23,401)	2,217	(262)	(3,191)	(24,637)	11,787
Net Gains and Losses on Investment Assets		(88,513)	8,487	4,626	—	(101,626)	58,377
Net Movement in Resources in Year		65,112	10,704	4,364	(3,191)	76,989	70,164
Balance Brought Forward at 30 June 1999		£2,402,475	£105,974	£45,394	£62,973	£2,616,816	£2,546,652
Balance Carried Forward at 30 June 2000		£2,467,587	£116,678	£49,758	£59,782	£2,693,805	£2,616,816
Unrealised Surpluses included in above balances		£542,534	£49,016	£24,822	£ —	£ 616,372	£ 741,656

THE ROYAL HISTORICAL SOCIETY

NOTES TO THE ACCOUNTS FOR THE YEAR ENDED 30 JUNE 2000

ACCOUNTING POLICIES

(a) *Basis of accounting*
The financial statements have been prepared in accordance with the Charities (Accounts and Reports) Regulations October 1995, the Statements of Recommended Practice 'Accounting by Charities' and applicable accounting standards issued by UK accountancy bodies. The particular accounting policies adopted are described below. The financial statements are prepared under the historical cost convention, as modified to include fixed asset investments at market value.

(b) *Depreciation*
Depreciation is calculated by reference to the cost of fixed assets using a straight line basis at rates considered appropriate having regard to the expected lives of the fixed assets. The annual rates of depreciation in use are:

Furniture and equipment	10%
Computer equipment	25%

(c) *Stock*
Stock is valued at the lower of cost and net realisable value.

(d) *Library and archives*
The cost of additions to the library and archives is written off in the year of purchase.

(e) *Subscription Income*
Subscription Income is recognised in the year it became receivable with a provision against any subscription not received.

(f) *Investments*
Investments are stated at market value. Any surplus/deficit arising on revaluation is charged to the income and expenditure account. Dividend income is accounted for on a received basis.

(g) *Publication costs*
Publication costs are transferred in stock and released to the income and expenditure account as stocks are depleted.

(h) *E.M. Robinson bequest*
Income from the E.M. Robinson bequest is used to provide grants to the Dulwich Picture Gallery.

(i) *A.S. Whitfield Prize Fund*
The A.S. Whitfield Prize Fund is used to provide an annual prize for the best first monograph for British history published in the calendar year.

(j) *Donations and other voluntary income*
Donations are recognised on a received basis.

(k) *Grants payable*
Grants payable are recognised in the year in which they are paid.

(l) *Allocation of administration costs*
Administration costs are allocated between direct charitable expenditure and administration costs on the basis of the work done by the Executive Secretary.

TANGIBLE FIXED ASSETS

	Computer Equipment	Furniture and Equipment	Total
	£	£	£
Cost			
At 1st July 1999	28,179	1,173	29,352
Additions	1,563	—	1,563
At 30th June 2000	29,742	1,173	30,915
Depreciation			
At 1st July 1999	24,331	1,173	25,504
Charge for the year	2,601	—	2,601
At 30th June 2000	26,932	1,173	28,105
Net book value			
At 30th June 2000	£2,810	£—	£2,810
At 30th June 1999	£3,848	£—	3,848

All tangible fixed assets are used in the furtherance of the Society's objectives.

3. INVESTMENTS

	General Fund	Robinson Bequest	Whitfield Prize Fund	Total
	£	£	£	£
Market value at 1st July 1999	2,181,241	99,864	37,767	2,318,87
Additions	619,726	—	—	619,72
Disposals	(317,284)	—	—	(317,28
Unrealised (loss)/gain on investments	(138,397)	8,487	4,626	(125,28
	£2,345,286	£108,351	£42,393	£2,496,03
Cash awaiting investment	£93,060	19,199	11,371	123,63
Market value at 30th June 2000	£2,438,346	£127,550	£53,764	£2,619,66
Cost at 30th June 2000	£1,895,812	£78,534	£28,942	£2,003,28

4. DEBTORS

	2000	*1999*
	£	*£*
Trade debtors	29,320	*33,76*
Other debtors	6,931	6,54
Prepayments	5,864	*5,89*
	£42,115	*£46,10*

5. CASH AT BANK AND IN HAND

	2000	*1999*
	£	*£*
Deposit accounts	76,289	*63,60*
Current accounts	(6,169)	*(6,34*
	£70,120	*£57,26*

6. CREDITORS: Amounts due within one year

	2000	*1999*
	£	*£*
Trade creditors	48,724	*28,61*
Sundry creditors	5,829	*6,30*
Subscriptions received in advance	10,864	*1,22*
Accruals	4,823	*5,45*
	£70,240	*£41,59*

7. DONATIONS AND LEGACIES

	2000	*1999*
	£	*£*
A. Browning Royalties	137	*12*
G.R. Elton Bequest	6,689	*2,73*
Donations and sundry income	2,285	*1,53*
Conference fees and funding	2,350	*89*
	£11,461	*£5,29*

8. Grant and Prizes Payable

	Unrestricted Funds £	Restricted Funds £	Total 2000 £	*Total 1999 £*
Alexander Prize	1,583	—	1,583	*570*
Grants	100	—	100	*1,300*
Research support grants	21,178	—	21,178	*15,940*
Young Historian Scheme	4,039	—	4,039	*2,000*
Centenary fellowship	6,275	—	6,275	*6,175*
A Level prizes	600	—	600	*900*
A.S. Whitfield Prize	—	1,000	1,000	*1,000*
E.M. Robinson Bequest				
— Grant to Dulwich Picture Library	—	—	—	2,200
Gladstone prize	400	—	400	400
	£34,175	£1,000	£35,175	*£30,485*

9. Direct Charitable Expenditure

	Unrestricted Funds £	Restricted Funds £	Total 1999 £	*Total 1998 £*
Publishing costs (Note 15)	93,234	—	93,234	*71,416*
Purchase of books and publications	2,609	—	2,609	*3,978*
Binding	4,352	—	4,352	*5,827*
Prothero lecture	403	—	403	*902*
Studies in History				
— Executive editor's honorarium	4,875	—	4,875	*4,500*
— Executive editor's expenses	960	—	960	*960*
— Sundry expenses	1,628	—	1,628	*1,606*
Other publications (Note 16)	11,041	—	11,041	*11,071*
British Bibliographies	—	4,186	4,186	*22,315*
Salaries, pensions and social security	27,006	—	27,006	*23,499*
Computer consumables, printing and stationery	7,152	—	7,152	*9,559*
Meetings and travel	10,511	—	10,511	*12,262*
Conference costs	4,394	—	4,394	*2,067*
	£168,165	£4,186	£172,351	*£169,962*

10. Administration Expenses

	Unrestricted Funds £	Restricted Funds £	Total 2000 £	*Total 1999 £*
Salaries, pensions and social security	10,504	—	10,504	*10,072*
Postage and telephone	2,147	—	2,147	*1,432*
Bank charges	1,542	—	1,542	*1,432*
Audit and professional fees	6,265	—	6,265	*4,723*
Insurance	999	—	999	*1,065*
Depreciation	2,601	—	2,601	*7,288*
Circulation costs	9,456	—	9,456	*6,832*
	£33,514	£—	£33,514	*£32,844*

The average number of staff employed during the year was 1 (1999: 1)

11. Insurance Policies

The Society was charged with the following amounts relating to committee and employees' liability:

	2000 £	*1999 £*
Employees liability	78	*78*
Public liability	78	*78*
	156	*£156*

12. Councillors' Expenses

During the year travel expenses were reimbursed to 30 Councillors attending Council meetings at a cost of £6,207 (1999: £6,714).

13. Auditor's Remuneration

	2000 £	*1999 £*
Audit fee	4,400	*4,400*
Other services	1,857	*323*

14. Grants Paid

During the year the Society awarded grants to a value of £21,178 (1999: £15,940) to 97 (1999: 75) individuals

15. Publications

	Transactions Sixth Series 8 £	*Camden Fifth Series 13, 14* £	*Guides and Handbooks Reprint Costs* £	*Camden Classic Reprints* £	*Total* £
Cambridge University Press					
Opening stock	2,067	—	22,343	6,507	30,917
Printing	14,875	24,586	—	—	39,461
Off prints	2,408	—	—	—	2,408
Carriage	426	1,116	101	—	1,643
Closing stock	(2,199)	(1,988)	(19,453)	(5,700)	(29,340)
	17,577	23,714	2,991	807	45,089
Society's costs	2,725	9,104	13,171	—	25,000
Paper					7,184
Sales commission					15,961
					£93,234

16. Publications

	2000 £	*1999 £*
Other publications cost		
Annual Bibliography	15,166	*12,723*
Less: royalties received	(4,125)	*(1,652)*
	£11,041	*£11,071*

17. Lease Commitments

The Society has the following annual commitments under non-cancellable operating leases which expire:

	2000 £	*1999 £*
Within 1–2 years	—	*2,517*
Within 2–5 years	1,980	*—*
	£1,980	*£2,517*

18. Life Members

The Society has ongoing commitments to provide membership services to 25 Life Members at a cost of approximately £32 each per year.

19. Uncapitalised Assets

The Society owns a library the cost of which is written off to the income and expenditure account at the time of purchase.

This library is insured for £150,000 and is used for reference purposes by the membership of the Society.

20. Analysis of Net Assets Between Funds

	B.H.B. General Fund	E.M. Robinson Bequest Fund	A.S. Whitfield Prize Fund	Andrew Mellon Fund	Total
	£	£	£	£	£
Fixed Assets	—	—	—	2,810	2,810
Investments	2,438,346	127,550	53,764	—	2,619,660
	2,438,346	127,550	53,764	2,810	2,622,470
Current Assets					
Stocks	29,340	—	—	—	29,340
Debtors	42,115	—	—	—	42,115
Cash at bank and in hand	15,926	—	—	54,194	70,120
	87,381	—	—	54,194	141,575
Less: Creditors	(58,959)	(10,872)	(7,373)	6,964	(70,240)
Net Current Assets	28,422	(10,872)	(7,373)	61,158	71,335
Net Assets	£2,466,768	£116,678	£46,391	£63,968	£2,693,805

THE ROYAL HISTORICAL SOCIETY
THE DAVID BERRY ESSAY TRUST

Balance Sheet as at 30th June 2000

	2000 £	2000 £	1999 £	1999 £
Fixed Assets				
1,117.63 units in the Charities Official Investment Fund (Market Value £12,752: 1999 £11,444)		1,530		1,53
Current Assets				
Bank Deposit Account	9,557		8,989	
Creditors:				
Amounts falling due within one year	(1,079)		(600)	
Net Current Assets		8,478		8,38
Net Assets		10,008		9,91
Represented by:				
Capital fund		1,000		1,00
Income and expenditure reserve		9,008		8,91
		£10,008		£9,91

Income and Expenditure Account

	2000 £	2000 £	1999 £	1999 £
Income				
Dividends		397		39
Bank Interest Receivable		171		23
		568		62
Expenditure				
Prize awarded		(250)		(25
Travel expenses		(229)		(10
Excess of income over expenditure for the year		89		27
Balance brought forward		8,919		8,64
Balance carried forward		9,008		8,91

The fund has no recognised gains or losses apart from the results for the above financial periods.

1. Accounting Policies

Basis of accounting.

The accounts have been prepared under the historical cost convention. The late David Berry, by his Wi dated 23rd April 1926, left £1,000 to provide in every three years a gold medal and prize money for the bes essay on the Earl of Bothwell or, at the discretion of the Trustees, on Scottish History of the James Stuarts to VI, in memory of his father the late Rev. David Berry.

The Trust is regulated by a scheme sanctioned by the Chancery Division of the High Court of Justice date 23rd January 1930, and made in action 1927 A 1233 David Anderson Berry deceased, Hunter and Another v Robertson and Another and since modified by an order of the Charity Commissioners made on 11 Januar 1978 removing the necessity to provide a medal.

The Royal Historical Society is now the Trustee. The investment consists of 1117.63 Charities Officia Investment Fund Income with units. The Trustee will advertise inviting essays every year of the three yea period.)

A resolution was approved by the Charity Commission on the 16 August 1999 changing the purpose of th Charity to provide an annual prize of £250 for the best essay on a subject, to be selected by the candidate dealing with Scottish History, provided such subject has been previously submitted to and approved by th Council of The Royal Historical Society.

Report of the Auditors to the Trustees of The David Berry Essay Trust

We have audited the accounts on page 442 which have been prepared under the historical cost convention and e accounting policies set out on page 442.

spective responsibilities of the Council and Auditors

The Trustees are required to prepare accounts for each financial year which give a true and fair view of the ate of affairs of the Trust and of the surplus or deficit for that period.

In preparing the accounts, the Trustees are required to:

- select suitable accounting policies and then apply them consistently;
- make judgements and estimates that are reasonable and prudent;
- prepare the accounts on the going concern basis unless it is inappropriate to presume that the Trust will continue in business.

The Trustees are responsible for keeping proper accounting records which disclose with reasonable accuracy at y time the financial position of the Trust. They are also responsible for safeguarding the assets of the Trust and nce for taking reasonable steps for the prevention and detection of fraud and other irregularities.

As described above the Trustees are responsible for the preparation of accounts. It is our responsibility to form independent opinion, based on our audit, on those accounts and to report our opinion to you.

sis of opinion

We conducted our audit in accordance with Auditing Standards issued by the Auditing Practices Board. An dit includes examination, on a test basis, of evidence relevant to the amounts and disclosures in the accounts. also includes an assessment of the significant estimates and judgements made by the Trustees in the preparation the accounts, and of whether the accounting policies are appropriate to the Trust's circumstances, consistently plied and adequately disclosed.

We planned and performed our audit so as to obtain all the information and explanations which we considered cessary in order to provide us with sufficient evidence to give reasonable assurance that the accounts are free om material misstatement, whether caused by fraud or other irregularity or error. In forming our opinion we so evaluated the overall adequacy of the presentation of information in the accounts.

inion

In our opinion the accounts give a true and fair view of the state of the Trust's affairs as at 30th June 2000 d of its surplus for the year then ended.

MacIntyre & Co
Chartered Accountants
Registered Auditors
London

September 2000